The American Pageant

Fifth Edition/Volume II

A History of the Republic

THOMAS A. BAILEY

Stanford University

D. C. HEATH AND COMPANY
Lexington, Massachusetts Toronto London

Preface to the Fifth Edition

In preparing this edition I have retained the essential features of the book that was accorded a friendly reception when first published some twenty years ago. I gather from scores of letters addressed to me by students that they especially like the interest-sustaining features which have enabled them to read and remember with some degree of satisfaction, even enjoyment. To this end I have incorporated the essential basic information while shunning encyclopaedic detail. I have interwoven within a broad chronological framework the threads of political, diplomatic, military, economic, social, and cultural developments. I have stressed the leading actors, as well as the acted upon, regardless of sex, color, or creed. I have avoided excessively involved sentence structure and pedantic words. I have subordinated philosophical abstractions to concrete imagery. Finally, I have tried to lighten and brighten the narrative by injecting from time to time colorful anecdotal bits, pointed short quotations, and other touches that make history come alive. My experience in more than forty years of teaching has been that we remember best that which engages our attention.

Specifically, a new chapter on the Nixon years has been added, and the last chapter on social crosscurrents has been updated and expanded. A total of about 100 new illustrations, including many likenessess of famous women and representatives of various minorities, now appear in the margins. In most cases there is accompanying commentary, not only for the new pictures but also for the old. To provide a kind of supplementary book of source readings, the marginal areas now contain more than 300 pithy and pungent quotations. The bibliographies have been updated, and some earlier statements have been modified to square with the most recent scholarship.

For critical readings of the recent new material I am indebted to friends and colleagues in the profession: Stephen M. Dobbs, David M. Kennedy, Hugh Ross, and Paul B. Ryan.

Dr. Hugh Ross has made the necessary changes and additions in *The American Pageant Guidebook,* as well as in *The American Pageant Quizbook,* which contains the answer keys to both supplementary manuals.

THOMAS A. BAILEY
Department of History
Stanford University
Stanford, California

Contents

Maps

Charts and Tables

Sail, sail thy best, ship of Democracy,
Of value is thy freight, 'tis not the Present only,
The Past is also stored in thee,
Thou holdest not the venture of thyself alone, not of
  the Western continent alone,
Earth's résumé entire floats on thy keel, O ship, is
  steadied by thy spars,
With thee Time voyages in trust, the antecedent na-
  tions sink or swim with thee,
With all their ancient struggles, martyrs, heroes, epics,
  wars, thou bear'st the other continents,
Theirs, theirs as much as thine, the destination-port
  triumphant. . . .

WALT WHITMAN
Thou Mother With Thy Equal Brood, 1872

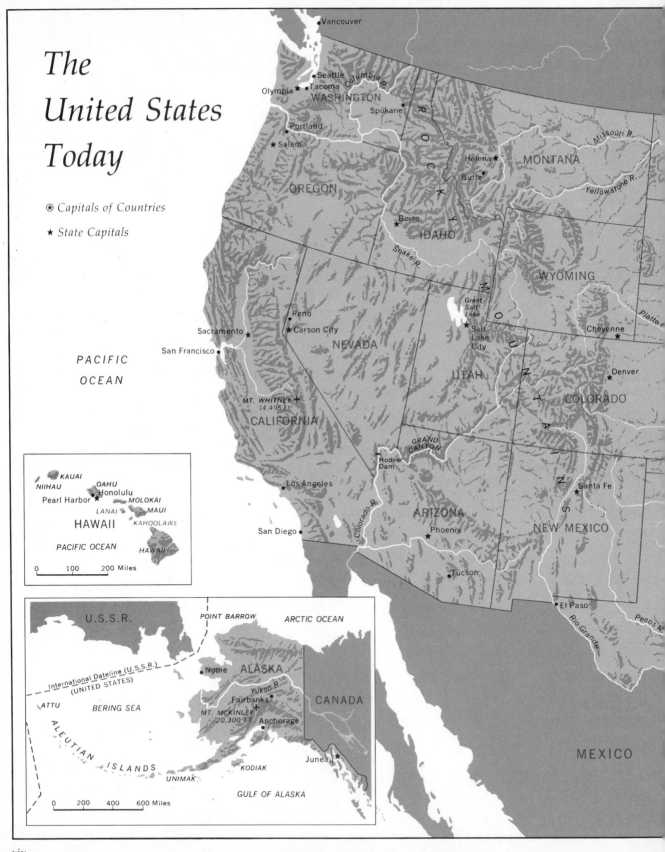

The United States Today

⊛ *Capitals of Countries*

★ *State Capitals*

Vancouver

Seattle
Olympia ★ Tacoma
WASHINGTON
Spokane
Portland
★ Salem

OREGON

Columbia R.

Helena ★
Butte
MONTANA

Missouri R.

Yellowstone R.

Boise
IDAHO

Snake R.

WYOMING

Reno
Sacramento ★ ★ Carson City

San Francisco

NEVADA

Great
Salt
Lake

Salt
Lake
City ★

UTAH

Cheyenne ★

Platte R.

Denver ★

COLORADO

PACIFIC

OCEAN

MT. WHITNEY +
14,495 Ft.

CALIFORNIA

GRAND
CANYON

Hoover
Dam

Colorado R.

Los Angeles

San Diego

ARIZONA

Phoenix ★

Tucson

Santa Fe ★

NEW MEXICO

El Paso

Rio Grande

Pecos R.

Hawaii inset

KAUAI
NIIHAU
OAHU
Honolulu
Pearl Harbor ★
LANAI MOLOKAI
MAUI
KAHOOLAWE
HAWAII

PACIFIC OCEAN

HAWAII

0   100   200 Miles

Alaska inset

U.S.S.R.

POINT BARROW

ARCTIC OCEAN

International Dateline (U.S.S.R.)
(UNITED STATES)

Nome
ALASKA

ATTU

BERING SEA

Yukon R.
Fairbanks
MT. MCKINLEY
20,300 FT.
Anchorage

CANADA

ALEUTIAN ISLANDS

UNIMAK

KODIAK

Juneau ★

GULF OF ALASKA

MEXICO

The Ordeal of Reconstruction

With malice toward none, with charity for all, with firmness in the
right as God gives us to see the right, let us strive on to finish the
work we are in, to bind up the nation's wounds, to care for him who
shall have borne the battle and for his widow and orphan, to do all
which may achieve and cherish a just and lasting peace among our-
selves and with all nations.

Abraham Lincoln, Second Inaugural, March 4, 1865

The Problems of Peace

Staggering tasks confronted the American people, North and
South, when the guns grew cold. About a million and a half
warriors in blue and gray had to be demobilized, readjusted to
civilian life, and reabsorbed by the war-deranged economy. Civil
government likewise had to be put back on a peacetime basis, and
purged of encroachments by the military men.

The desperate plight of the South has eclipsed the fact that reconstruction had to be undertaken also in the North, though less
spectacularly. War-inflated industries had to be deflated to a peace
footing; factories had to be retooled for civilian needs.

Financial problems also loomed large in the North, now that
the piper had to be paid. The national debt had shot up from a
modest $65,000,000 in 1860 to nearly $3,000,000,000 in 1865—a

President Andrew Johnson (1808–1875), an "accidental President," was the first Chief Executive to be impeached by the House, though narrowly acquitted by the Senate. A former U.S. Senator from Tennessee, he was reelected in 1875 to the Senate that had tried him seven years earlier. Library of Congress.

Many red-blooded Americans resented the French intrusion in Mexico. H. L. Higginson wrote to his sister: ". . . I mean to go to Mexico and fight the French after this war is done. It . . . would certainly be good fun to cut off those little red-legged sinners, who have been swelling about their fighting and victory."

colossal sum for those days but one that a prudent government could pay. At the same time, war taxes had to be reduced to less burdensome levels.

Physical devastation inflicted by invading armies, chiefly in the South and Border States, had to be repaired. This herculean task was ultimately completed, but with discouraging slowness. Moral devastation, most evident in greed and loose living, took longer to mend because it was deeper-rooted and harder to see.

Other weighty questions clamored for answers. What was to be done with approximately 4,000,000 Negro slaves suddenly being plunged into the cold bath of freedom? Were the seceded states to be brought back into the Union on the old basis, and if so, with or without punishment?

What of the captured Confederate ringleaders, all of whom were liable to charges of treason? During the war a popular song had been "Hang Jeff Davis to a Sour Apple Tree," and even innocent children had lisped it. Davis was temporarily clapped into irons during the early days of his two-year imprisonment. But he and his fellow "conspirators" were finally released, partly because the odds were that no Virginia jury would convict them. All "rebel" leaders were finally pardoned by President Johnson as a Christmas present in 1868.

Potential Foreign Foes: France and Britain

Disputes in the diplomatic arena likewise pressed for attention. Most immediately ominous was the presence of a strong French army in Mexico. There, behind the din of the Civil War, Napoleon III had enthroned an Austrian tool, the "Archduke" Maximilian, on the ruins of a crushed republic—all in flagrant violation of the Monroe Doctrine.

The North, so long as it was convulsed by war, pursued a walk-on-eggs policy toward France. But when the shooting stopped, Secretary of State Seward, speaking with the authority of nearly a million bayonets, turned on the heat. By 1867 Napoleon realized that his costly gamble was doomed. He reluctantly took French leave of his ill-starred puppet, who crumpled ingloriously before a Mexican firing squad. With his death the Monroe Doctrine took on new life.

Embittered relations with England were less easily handled. Northerners nursed vengeful memories of British sympathy for the Confederates, as highlighted by the *Alabama* and other British-built "pirates." American anger was also directed at Canada where, despite the vigilance of British authorities, Southern agents had actively plotted to burn Northern cities. In one Confederate raid into Vermont, three banks were plundered and one American citizen was killed.

Hatred of England was especially virulent among the Irish-Americans, many of them Civil War veterans, who sought to help the cause of "ould Oireland" by striking north. They raised several tiny "armies," each consisting of a few hundred green-shirted men, and launched invasions of Canada, notably in 1866 and 1870. The Canadians condemned the Washington government for permitting such unneutrality. But the administration was hampered by the prevalence of too much anti-British venom, and by the presence of too many Irish-American voters.

As fate would have it, two great nations emerged from the fiery furnace of the American Civil War. One was a reunited United States; the other was a united Canada. The act establishing the Dominion of Canada was passed by the British Parliament in 1867, two years after Lee had surrendered. It was partly designed to bolster the Canadians, both politically and spiritually, against the prospective vengeance of the United States.

The Prostrate South

Dismal indeed was the picture presented by the war-racked South when the rattle of musketry died. Not only had an age perished but a civilization had collapsed, in both its economic and its social structure. The moonlight-and-magnolia Old South of ante-bellum days had gone with the wind.

Handsome cities of yesteryear, like Charleston and Richmond, were gutted and weed-choked. An Atlantan returned to his once-fair home town and remarked, "Hell has laid her egg, and right here it hatched."

War had everywhere left its searing mark on social institutions. Churches were battered and dilapidated. The educational system was disrupted, with countless schools destroyed, many teachers killed in battle, and endowments wiped out. Sherman's Yankee invaders had reputedly stabled their horses in the dormitories of the University of South Carolina.

A "Jeff Davis Necktie." (Twisted Iron Rail).

Economic life had creaked to a halt. Banks and business houses had locked their doors, ruined by runaway inflation. Factories were smokeless, silent, dismantled. The transportation system had broken down almost completely. Before the war, five different railroad lines had converged on Columbia, South Carolina; now the nearest connected track was twenty-nine miles away. Efforts to untwist the rails corkscrewed by Sherman's soldiers were bumpily unsatisfactory.

Agriculture—the economic lifeblood of the South—was almost hopelessly crippled. Once-white cotton fields now yielded a lush harvest of green weeds. Seed was scarce, livestock had been driven off by the plundering Yankees, and the footloose black labor supply had taken to the highways and byways. Heartrending instances were reported of white men hitching themselves to plows, while women or children gripped the handles. Not until 1870 did the seceded states produce as large a cotton crop as that of the fateful year 1860.

A Dethroned but Defiant Aristocracy

The planter aristocrats were virtually ruined by the war. Reduced to proud poverty, they were confronted with damaged or burned mansions, lost investments, and semi-worthless land. In addition, their slaves, once worth about $2,000,000,000, had been freed in one of the costliest confiscations of history. Some whites were assisted by the pitiful savings of their former slaves; a few peddled pies or took in washings. Women and children, some reared in luxury, were found begging from door to door.

Several thousand of the former "cotton lords" were unable to face up to their overpowering burdens. They departed for the Far West, or for Mexico and Brazil, where their children gradually became Mexicanized or Brazilianized. A few desperate Southerners sought escape in suicide, including the distinguished Virginia soil expert, Edmund Ruffin, who ironically had fired one of the first shots at Fort Sumter.

"The Re-United States."
This English cartoon reflects typical sympathy for the South. *Punch*, 1865.

But most of the impoverished planters labored courageously to restore the glory that had once been the South. General Robert E. Lee, for example, accepted the presidency of Washington College in Virginia—later Washington and Lee—and became a respected educator.

In teeter-totter fashion, the loss of the aristocrats was in some degree the gain of the common folk. The poorest of the poor whites, not possessing much to begin with, stood to gain from change—and some of them did. As the once-rich abandoned their broad ancestral estates, a number of small farms became available. A kind of curious economic leveling took place, with the rich leveled down and some of the poor leveled up. But many dreary years were to pass before the economic health of the South equaled that of 1860.

High-spirited Southerners, including many women, were unwilling to acknowledge defeat. Having fought gallantly, they felt that they had not been beaten but had worn themselves out beating the North, like an arm-weary pugilist. Many of them, mourning the triumph of brute strength over righteousness, believed that they had won a moral victory. To them the struggle, though a "Lost Cause," was still a just war. They were conscious of no crime, and still believed that their view of secession was correct. A song sung in the South during the postwar years revealed no love for the Union:

I'm glad I fought agin her, I only wish we'd won,
And I ain't axed any pardon for anything I've done.

Continued defiance by Southerners was disquieting. It revealed itself in references to "damyankees" and to "your government" instead of "our government." A bishop in one Southern diocese even refused to pray for President Andrew Johnson, though the latter was in sore need of divine guidance. The Southerners would have avoided much misery if they had only realized that no great rebellion has ever

ended with the victors sitting down to a love feast with the vanquished.

Unfettered Freedmen

The ordinary ex-slave, freed by the war and the 13th Amendment,
was understandably bewildered. Life under the lash had inevitably
left him immature or warped—socially, politically, emotionally. To
turn him loose upon the cold world was like opening the door of an
orphanage and telling the children they were free to go where they
liked and do as they wished. One of the cruelest misfortunes ever
to be visited upon the much-abused black was to jerk him overnight
from bondage to freedom, without intermediate preparation, safeguards, or benefits.

Most of the Negroes were understandably unsettled by their new
status. A goodly number of the more faithful remained on the old
plantation, still addressing their former owner as "massa." But tens
of thousands naturally took off to enjoy their newly found freedom;
and common expressions were "free as a bird" and "free as a fool."
Many freedmen no doubt were spurred on by the understandable
fear that they might be re-enslaved, as indeed large numbers in
effect were.

The inexperience of the ex-slaves unfortunately left them exposed
to the schemes of greedy whites. A "grapevine" rumor had spread
among the blacks that on a given day the Washington government
would present each family with "forty acres and a mule." White
swindlers would sell for five dollars a set of red, white, and blue pegs,
with which the trusting Negro had only to stake out his acreage.
Quickly disillusioned, he was left with few acres and no mule.

Ex-slaves were undoubtedly a problem, especially in those areas
where they outnumbered the whites two to one or even ten to one.
They stole food in their hunger, and got drunk on pilfered liquor, as
did shiftless whites. Other stalwart Negroes, many of whom had
served in the Union armies, would jostle the whites off the sidewalks
into the gutter, as whites had done to them in the days of slavery.

No doubt the luckless Negro was also in some ways a menace to
himself. Once a slave to the white man, he was now a slave to hunger
and cold and disease, even in cities like Washington, D. C. Countless
tens of thousands of friendless and rootless souls perished, especially
children. The heartrending sequel suggests that the abolitionists, in
clamoring for overnight emancipation without adequate guidance
and financial support, had conferred a dubious boon on the bonds-
men.

Carl Schurz described a Fourth of
July affair in Savannah, Georgia in
1865. "The colored firemen of this city
desired to parade their engine on the
anniversary of our independence. . . .
In the principal street of the city the
procession was attacked with clubs and
stones by a mob . . . and by a crowd
of boys swearing at the d——d niggers.
The colored firemen were knocked
down, some of them severely injured,
their engine was taken away from
them, and the peaceable procession
dispersed."

"Black Codes" in the "Black Belt"

The Freedmen's Bureau, as organized in 1865 by the War Department, was designed primarily to help the Negroes over the rough places.* Its primary functions were to feed, adjust, and educate the ex-slaves. Many blacks had a passion for learning, partly because they wanted to close the gap between themselves and the whites, and partly because they longed to read the Word of God. In three years the Freedmen's Bureau taught an estimated 200,000 black folk the elements of reading. In one elementary class in North Carolina sat four generations of the same family, ranging from a six-year-old tot to the seventy-five-year-old grandmother.

Unhappily the Freedmen's Bureau, though doing much commendable work in its early career, proved to be a feeble prop indeed. It gradually became the tool of the ultra-partisan Republicans in the North, and hence fell into deep disfavor among Southern whites.

Readjusting the Negro also meant inducing him to work as a wage laborer. He was inclined, in many cases, to regard freedom from bondage as freedom from work. The crushed Cotton Kingdom could not rise from its weeds until the fields were once more put under the plow and hoe. This goal could not be attained without a dependable labor supply, which the restless Negro was not providing. He was inclined to work a few days for wages, and then run off to spend his newly acquired "fortune." (Slavery had not bred thrift.) There was serious talk in the South of using large numbers of Chinese coolies, and several hundred were actually imported.

"Black Codes" were the answer of the white legislatures in the South to the problem of a stable laboring force. Pre-Civil War laws governing enslaved Negroes were no longer binding, and substitute statutes seemed necessary. The new codes were naturally more liberal than the old ones, but they were not liberal enough in the eyes of Northern anti-slaveryites and forward-looking Southerners.

Some of the "Black Codes" were undeniably too severe. They provided that if the Negro "jumped" his labor contract, he would forfeit his back wages. Other codes stipulated that if he ran off, mileage costs would be paid the white Negro-catchers who dragged him back. In Mississippi the captured Negro could be fined and then hired out to pay off his fine—an arrangement that resembled slavery itself.

An even broader purpose lay behind the "Black Codes." They were designed to protect the Negro from his own immaturity, and to protect the whites from the Negroes. It is significant that the codes were generally harshest where the "black belt" was blackest—that is, where the ex-slaves outnumbered their ex-masters most heavily.

Yet any whitewashing of the "Black Codes" could not conceal one ugly fact. The sponsors of at least some of them had in view restoring, as nearly as possible, the old slave system in a different guise. This

Early in 1866 one Congressman quoted from a Georgian: "The blacks eat, sleep, move, live, only by the tolerance of the whites, who hate them. The blacks own absolutely nothing but their bodies; their former masters own everything, and will sell them nothing. If a black man draws even a bucket of water from a well, he must first get the permission of a white man, his enemy. . . . If he asks for work to earn his living, he must ask it of a white man; and the whites are determined to give him no work, except on such terms as will make him a serf and impair his liberty."

---

* The official title was Bureau of Refugees, Freedmen and Abandoned Lands. Much of the abandoned land was sterile, and most of it was ultimately returned to the whites.

objective was partially achieved as thousands of impoverished Ne-groes slipped into the status of share-crop farmers, as did many of the former landowning whites. The whole luckless group gradually sank into a debtor's morass of virtual peonage, and remained there for generations. Once slaves to masters, countless blacks became slaves to the soil and their creditors.

"Black Codes" naturally left a painful impression in the North. This was notably true of former anti-slavery centers, where the Southern restrictions were painted in especially lurid hues. If the Negroes were being re-enslaved, men asked one another, had not the Boys in Blue spilled their blood in vain? Had the North really won the war?

Johnson: the Tailor President

Few Presidents have ever been faced with a more perplexing sea of troubles than that confronting Andrew Johnson. What manner of man was this medium-built, black-eyed, black-haired Tennessean, now Chief Executive by virtue of the bullet that killed Lincoln?

No citizen, not even Lincoln, has ever reached the White House from humbler beginnings. Born to impoverished parents in North Carolina, and early orphaned, Johnson never attended school but was apprenticed to a tailor at age ten. Ambitious to get ahead, he taught himself to read, and later his wife taught him to write and do simple arithmetic. A self-made man, he was inclined to overpraise his maker.

Johnson early became identified with politics in Tennessee, to which he had moved when seventeen years old. He shone as an im-passioned champion of the poor whites against the planter aristo-crats, although he himself owned a few slaves. He excelled as a two-fisted stump speaker before angry and heckling crowds, among whom on occasion he could hear a pistol being cocked. Elected to Congress, he attracted much favorable attention in the North (but not the South) when he refused to secede with his own state. After Tennessee was partially "redeemed" by Union armies, he was ap-pointed war governor, and served courageously in an atmosphere of danger.

Johnson's Tailor Shop. Library of Congress.

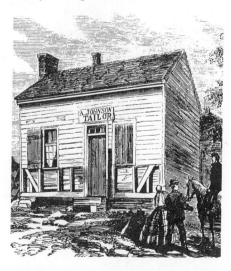

The finger of destiny now pointed to Johnson for the Vice-Pres-idency. Lincoln's Union Party in 1864 needed to attract support from the War Democrats and other pro-Southern elements, and Johnson, a Democrat, seemed to be the ideal man. Unfortunately, he appeared at the vice-presidential inaugural ceremonies the following March in a scandalous condition. He had recently been afflicted with typhoid fever, and although not known as a heavy drinker, he was urged by his friends to take a stiff bracer of whiskey. This he did—with dis-graceful results.

"Old Andy" Johnson was no doubt a man of parts—unpolished

parts. He was intelligent, able, forceful, and gifted with homespun honesty. Steadfastly devoted to duty and to the people, he was a dogmatic champion of states' rights and the Constitution. He would often present a copy of the document to visitors, and he was buried with one as a pillow.

Yet the man who had raised himself from the tailor's bench to the President's chair was a misfit. A Southerner who did not understand the North, a Tennessean who had won the distrust of the South, a Democrat who had never been accepted by the Republicans, a President who had never been elected President, he was not at home in a Republican White House. Hotheaded, contentious, and stubborn, he was a diamond in the rough. A reconstruction policy devised by the angels might well have failed in his tactless hands.

Lenient Johnsonian Justice

Johnson got off on the right foot as far as vengeful Northerners were concerned. Upon Lincoln's death, his hatred of the "stuck-up" planter aristocrats again flared forth, and he threatened to reconstruct the South with fire and hemp.

Applause burst from Republicans, especially the Radical or dominant wing of the party. These were the extremists who had condemned Lincoln's go-slow abolition policy, and they were determined to reconstruct the South radically—that is, with a rod of iron. Many Radicals wanted to safeguard the rights of the Negro; others were corrupted by a lust for power and punishment. Some of them were secretly pleased when the assassin's bullet removed Lincoln, for the martyred President had shown tenderness toward the South. Spiteful "Andy" Johnson would presumably be a pliant tool in their hands.

Johnson as a Parrot.
Harper's Weekly.

But time and responsibility sobered Johnson, and within a few weeks he veered toward Lincoln's "rosewater" ten-percent plan. Lincoln had decreed in 1863 that, as a first step, a group of voters equal to one-tenth of the voting population of any Southern state in 1860 must take the oath of allegiance to the United States. The next step would be the erection of a new state government under a constitution which accepted the abolition of slavery. Lincoln would then recognize the purified new regime.

Several conquered Southern states, taking advantage of Lincoln's lenient ten-percent plan, had reorganized their governments by 1864. But Congress flatly refused to seat their duly elected representatives. The Radical Republicans, though by no means all Republicans, were determined that the South should suffer more severely for its sins.

The plan adopted by Johnson in 1865 rather resembled Lincoln's lenient ten-percent plan; in some respects it was even more generous. It disfranchised certain leading Confederates, including those with taxable property worth more than $20,000, but it permitted the other whites to reorganize their own state governments. Special state conventions were to be summoned. These would be required to repeal the ordinances of secession, repudiate all Confederate debts, and ratify the slave-freeing 13th Amendment.

Republican Radicals in the Saddle

In the second half of 1865, the new Southern state governments were rapidly organized under the "soft" Lincoln-Johnson plan. Elections were duly held for Senators and Representatives in Congress. When that body convened in December 1865, scores of distinguished Southerners were on hand to claim their seats.

The appearance of these ex-rebels was a natural but costly blunder. Voters of the South, seeking able representatives, had turned instinctively to their experienced statesmen. But most of the Southern leaders were "tainted" by active association with the "Lost Cause." Among the delegations elected to Congress were four former Confederate generals, five colonels, and various members of the Richmond cabinet and Congress. Worst of all, there was the ninety-pound but brainy Alexander Stephens, former Vice-President of the Confederacy, still under indictment for treason.

Inevitably, the presence of these "whitewashed rebels" infuriated the Radical Republicans in Congress. The war had been fought to restore the Union, but the Radicals now saw that they could promote their own ends by postponing restoration. During the conflict the Republicans in Congress had enjoyed a relatively free hand after the South had seceded, and they were eager to retain this advantage. On December 4, 1865, the first day of the session, they banged shut the door in the faces of the newly elected Southern delegations.

Looking to the future, the Republicans were alarmed to note that a restored South would be stronger than ever in Congress. Before the war a Negro had counted as three-fifths of a man in apportioning Congressional representation. Now he was five-fifths of a man. Eleven Southern states had seceded; they had lost the war; and now they were entitled to twelve more votes in Congress than they had previously enjoyed. Thirty of their votes were based on blacks who as yet could not cast a ballot. The old slogan was evidently being reversed to read, "To the *vanquished* belong the spoils." Again the question was raised in the North: Who won the war?

Radicals had good reason to fear that ultimately they would be shoved aside. Southerners might join hands with ex-Copperheads and discontented farmers of the North and West, and then win control of Congress. If this happened, they could destroy the industrial and financial foundations of the Republican Party, which had entrenched itself deeply behind the smoke screen of the Civil War. Specifically, the Southerners might lower the high war tariffs, over-

Before President Johnson softened his Southern policy, his views were Radical. Speaking in April 21, 1865, he declared: "It is not promulgating anything that I have not heretofore said to say that traitors must be made odious, that treason must be made odious, that traitors must be punished and impoverished. They must not only be punished, but their social power must be destroyed. If not, they will still maintain an ascendancy, and may again become numerous and powerful; for, in the words of a former Senator of the United States, 'When traitors become numerous enough, treason becomes respectable.' "

throw monopoly, repeal the free-farm Homestead Act, and curtail the lavish grants of land to the railroads. The ex-Confederates might even go so far as to repudiate the national debt and re-enslave the Negro. These last two possibilities, though remote, alarmed Republican bondholders and ex-abolitionists alike.

Radical Republicans, seeking to avert such reverses, had a potent ace in the hole—the Negro vote. If they could give the ballot to the ex-slave and induce him to do their bidding, they would hold a powerful hand. They probably could offset the efforts of the Southerners to unite with the numerous Northern agrarians to destroy Republican dominance in Washington.

Republican agitation for Negro suffrage—that is, more democracy—was prompted by both idealistic and selfish motives. Idealists like Senator Charles Sumner were striving not only for Negro freedom but for racial equality. They believed that the ex-bondsman should have the ballot for protection against the whites, and for the development of civic responsibility as well. But less idealistic Radical Republicans—how numerous one cannot say—were plainly more interested in the welfare of the party than in that of the Negro. They would "Republicanize" the South by making the freedman their tool; they would rule or ruin—and eventually they did both, temporarily.

Johnson Clashes with Congress

On what terms should the seceded states now be readmitted? Lincoln had argued—and Johnson agreed—that the Southern states had never legally withdrawn from the Union. Their formal restoration would therefore be relatively simple. But the Radical Republicans insisted that the seceders had forfeited all their rights—had committed "suicide"—and could be readmitted only as "conquered provinces" on such conditions as Congress should decree.

Most powerful of the Radical Republicans was crusty Representative Thaddeus Stevens of Pennsylvania, then seventy-four years old. He was a curious figure, with a protruding lower lip, a heavy black wig on a bald head, and a deformed foot. A devoted friend of the Negro, he had defended runaway slaves without fee and had insisted on burial in a Negro cemetery. His hatred of the South, already violent, was intensified when Confederate cavalry raiders pillaged and burned his Pennsylvania ironworks. He even talked wildly at times of exterminating the ex-Confederates, and of handing their estates over to the Negroes as compensation for unpaid sweat.

When Congress convened for its fateful session in December, 1865, the Radical Republicans were prepared to call the tune. Led by the zealous Stevens, a masterly parliamentarian with a razor-sharp mind and withering sarcasm, they not only denied the Southern members seats, but promptly set up the Joint (House-Senate) Com-

This Republican cartoon shows Johnson knocking Negroes out of the Freedman's Bureau by his veto. Thomas Nast in *Harper's Weekly*, 1866.

mittee on Reconstruction. The clubfooted Pennsylvanian, as chairman of the House contingent, was the most influential member of this committee of fifteen. Cracking the whip relentlessly from his driver's seat, he became, as much as any one man, virtual ruler of the nation for more than a year.

A clash between the high-riding Radicals and the strong-willed Johnson was inevitable. It came in February, 1866, when the President vetoed a bill (later repassed) to extend the life of the Freedmen's Bureau. He stubbornly regarded the measure as an unconstitutional invasion of the rights of the Southern states.

Aroused, the Radicals quickly struck back. In March, 1866, they passed the Civil Rights Bill, which conferred on the Negroes the boon of American citizenship and also struck at the "Black Codes." Johnson resolutely vetoed this objectionable measure on constitutional grounds, but in April the Radicals in Congress steam-rollered it over his veto—something that they repeatedly did henceforth. The helpless President, dubbed "Sir Veto" and "Andy Veto," was reduced to a partial figurehead as Congress assumed the dominant role in running the government. One critic called Johnson "the dead dog of the White House."

The Radicals now undertook to rivet the principles of the Civil Rights Bill into the Constitution as the 14th Amendment. They feared that the Southerners might one day win control of Congress and repeal the hated law. The proposed amendment, as approved by Congress and sent to the states in June, 1866, was sweeping. It (1) conferred civil rights (but not the vote) on the Negro; (2) reduced proportionately the representation of a state in Congress and in the Electoral College if it denied the Negro the ballot; (3) disqualified from federal and state office ex-Confederates who as federal officeholders had once taken an oath "to support the Constitution of the United States"; and (4) guaranteed the federal debt, while repudiating all Confederate debts. (See text of 14th Amendment in Appendix.)

Thaddeus Stevens (1792–1868), who regarded the seceded states as "conquered provinces," promoted much of the severe Reconstruction legislation, including the Fourteenth (civil rights) amendment. Among the foremost in the impeachment of President Johnson, he was extremely bitter over the outcome. Library of Congress.

Principal Reconstruction Plans

1864–1865	1865–1866	1866–1867	1867–1877
Lincoln's ten-percent plan	*Johnson's version of Lincoln's plan*	*Congressional plan: ten-percent plan with 14th Amendment*	*Congressional plan of military reconstruction: 14th Amendment plus Negro suffrage, later established nationwide by 15th Amendment*

Thus the scheme of the Radicals was roughly the broad 14th Amendment superimposed upon the lenient Lincoln-Johnson plan.

These terms were not intolerably severe, though highly objectionable to the still defiant Southerners. Negro suffrage was not yet forced on them, but they would be shorn of considerable political power if they did not adopt it voluntarily.

Swinging 'Round the Circle with Johnson

As 1866 lengthened, the battle was squarely joined between the Radical Congress and the President. The burning issue was whether reconstruction was to be carried out with the drastic 14th Amendment or without it.

The crucial Congressional elections of 1866—more crucial than some presidential elections—were fast approaching. President Johnson was naturally eager to escape from the clutch of the Radical Congress by securing a majority favorable to his soft-on-the-South policy. Invited to dedicate a Chicago monument to Stephen A. Douglas, he undertook to speak at various cities en route in support of his views.

Johnson's famous "Swing around the Circle," beginning in the late summer of 1866, was an oratorical serio-comedy of errors. The President delivered a series of "give 'em hell" speeches, in which he accused the Radicals in Congress of having planned large-scale anti-Negro riots and murder in the South. As he spoke, hecklers hurled insults at him. Reverting to his stump speaking days in Tennessee,

"The Reconstruction Dose." This Republican cartoon shows Johnson as a bad boy urging the South to reject the medicine with which Dr. Congress, backed up by Mrs. Columbia, is trying to restore her health. *Frank Leslie's Illustrated Newspaper*, 1867.

he shouted back angry retorts, amid cries of "You be damned" and "Don't get mad, Andy." The dignity of his high office sank to a new low, as the old charges of drunkenness were revived.

As a vote-getter, Johnson was highly successful—for the opposition. His inept speechmaking heightened the cry, "Stand by Congress" against the "Tailor of the Potomac." When the ballots were counted, the Radicals had rolled up more than a two-thirds majority in both Houses of Congress. Yet the outcome did not necessarily mean that the country favored Radical reconstruction. In many Congressional districts the voters had a devil's choice between an ex-Copperhead and a Radical, and they held their noses and chose the latter.

The setback at the polls merely widened the gap between the ruthless Radicals and the stiff-necked Southerners. If Johnson had been farsighted, he would have urged the Southern states to accept the 14th Amendment as the best possible terms they could get. But he encouraged them to resist. They probably needed no prompting, for all of the "sinful eleven," except Tennessee, defiantly spurned the 14th Amendment. Their spirit was reflected in a Southern song:

And I don't want no pardon for what I was or am,
I won't be reconstructed and I don't give a damn.

Johnson Swings Around the Circle

Reconstruction by the Sword

Radicals in Congress now felt fully justified in imposing on the South the drastic Military Reconstruction Act of March 2, 1867, supplemented by three other measures. The controversial legislation swept away the lily-white Southern state governments, which had been reorganized under Johnson's auspices. It set up five military districts, each commanded by a Union general and policed by blue-clad soldiers, about 20,000 all told. More than that, the Radical restrictions, reinforced by requirements forced into the new state constitutions, disfranchised additional tens of thousands of Southern white leaders.

Congress additionally laid down stringent conditions for the readmission of the seceded states. The wayward sisters were required to ratify the 14th Amendment, thus giving the ex-slave his rights as a citizen. But the bitterest pill of all to white Southerners was the stipulation that they guarantee in their state constitutions full suffrage for their former slaves. One result was the election of more than a dozen black Congressmen, including two Senators, who as a group did creditable work.

Radical Republicans were so intent on Negro suffrage that they left nothing to chance. The danger loomed that once the unrepentant states were readmitted, they would amend their constitutions so as to withdraw the ballot from the blacks. The only ironclad safeguard was to incorporate Negro suffrage in the federal Constitution. This

MILITARY RECONSTRUCTION, 1867
(five districts and commanding generals)

goal was finally achieved, three years after the Military Reconstruction Act of 1867, by the 15th Amendment. Passed by Congress in
1869, it was ratified by the required number of states in 1870. (For
text, see Appendix.)

Military reconstruction of the South, as launched in 1867, was
probably unconstitutional. Congress not only usurped certain functions of the President as commander-in-chief, but they set up a questionable martial regime. The Supreme Court had already ruled, in the
case of *Ex parte Milligan* (1866), that military tribunals could not
properly try civilians, even during wartime, in areas where the civil
courts were open. Peacetime military rule, which involved an arbitrary suppression of newspapers, was obviously contrary to the spirit
of the Constitution.

After shackling the President, the Radicals even succeeded in
browbeating the Supreme Court. The learned justices, no doubt
fearing that their own powers were in jeopardy, avoided giving
serious offense to the Radical Congress. They even refused, on tech-
nicalities, to assert themselves when they might have intervened.
But public sentiment in the North gradually turned against the Radicals. The Supreme Court took heart from this changing atmosphere,
and beginning in 1876 it stamped the brand of unconstitutionality on
a number of the Congressional reconstruction laws. But by this time
—nine years after the first Military Reconstruction Act—the eggs had
been scrambled.

Beginning with 1867, and under the stern eye of Union soldiers,
new state governments had been set up in the South. They promptly
fell under the control of the much-maligned "scalawags" and "carpetbaggers," who in turn used the Negroes as political henchmen.
The "scalawags" were Southerners, sometimes able Southern Unionists and ex-Whigs, who were regarded as traitors by the ex-Confed-

Senator Hiram R. Revels (1822–
1901), the first black U.S. Senator,
was elected in 1870 to the seat
that had been occupied by
Jefferson Davis when the South
seceded. Library of Congress.

erates and who collaborated in creating the new regime. The "carpet-baggers" were mainly Northern adventurers and fortune seekers ("vultures"), who supposedly packed all their worldly goods into a single carpetbag. Though many of these "damn Yankees" were offensive to the South, a kinder feeling was shown toward carpet-baggers who came down with some capital, a willingness to work, and a capacity to "mind their own business"—that is, not "meddle" with Negroes.

Prodded into line by federal officials, the Southern states got on with the distasteful task of constitution making. By 1870 all of them had reorganized their governments and had been accorded full rights. The hated "Blue Bellies" were withdrawn from police work only when the new Radical regimes seemed to be firmly entrenched. Finally, in 1877, ten years after the long ordeal of military reconstruction had begun, the last federal bayonets were removed from state politics.

Southern Reconstruction by State

State	Readmitted to representation in Congress	Home rule (Democratic regime) re-established	Comments
Tenn.	July 24, 1866		Ratified 14th Amendment in 1866, and hence avoided Military Reconstruction.*
Ark.	June 22, 1868	1874	
N.C.	June 25, 1868	1870	
Ala.	June 25, 1868	1874	
Fla.	June 25, 1868	1877	
La.	June 25, 1868	1877	Federal troops restationed in 1877, as result of Hayes-Tilden electoral bargain.
S.C.	June 25, 1868	1877	Ditto
Va.	Jan. 26, 1870	1869	
Miss.	Feb. 23, 1870	1876	
Texas	Mar. 30, 1870	1874	
Ga.	[June 25, 1868] July 15, 1870	1872	Readmitted June 25, 1868, but returned to military control after expulsion of Negroes from legislature.

* Tennessee is the only state of the secession to observe Lincoln's birthday as a legal holiday. Of the eleven states of the Confederacy, all officially observe Robert E. Lee's birthday (Jan. 19) and seven officially observe Jefferson Davis' birthday (June 3): Alabama, Florida, Georgia, Mississippi, South Carolina, Tennessee, and Texas.

"We Accept the Situation."
An expression of Republican rejoicing over prospective Negro suffrage and the disfranchisement of ex-confederates. Thomas Nast in *Harper's Weekly*, 1867.

Enfranchised Freedmen

A sudden thrusting of the ballot into the hands of the ex-slaves, between 1867 and 1870, set the stage for stark tragedy. Wholesale liberation was probably unavoidable, given the feverish conditions created by war. But wholesale suffrage was avoidable, except insofar as the Radicals found it necessary for their own ends, both selfish and idealistic.

Bewildered, the blacks were poorly prepared for their new responsibilities as citizens and voters. Democracy is a delicate mechanism, which requires education and information. Yet about nine-tenths of the 700,000 adult Negro males, usually denied learning by state law, were illiterate. When registering, many did not know their ages: boys of sixteen signed the rolls. Some of these voters could not even give their last names, if indeed they had any, and many took any surname that popped into their heads. On the voting lists of Charleston, South Carolina, there were forty-six George Washingtons and sixty-three Abraham Lincolns.

Thousands of the ablest Southern whites were meanwhile being denied the vote, either by act of Congress or by the new state constitutions. At one dinner in South Carolina, the company consisted of a distinguished group of ex-governors, ex-Congressmen, and ex-judges. The only voter in the room was the Negro who served the meal. In some localities, about half the eligible white voters were temporarily disfranchised, and at one time the black voters in five Southern states outnumbered the white voters, many of whom were also illiterate.

By glaring contrast most of the Northern states, before the ratification of the 15th Amendment in 1870, withheld the ballot from their tiny black minority. Southerners naturally concluded that the Radicals were hypocritical in insisting that the Negro in the South be allowed to vote. One prominent North Carolinian jibed:

To every Southern river shall Negro suffrage come,
But not to fair New England, for that's too close to hum.

Gradual suffrage for qualified Negroes would have been far better for all concerned than hasty, wholesale suffrage. Presidents Lincoln and Johnson had both advised such a course. They would have given the ballot only to those ex-slaves who—through education, property ownership, or soldier-service—had indicated that they could assume the responsibilities of a voting citizen. The Radicals countered by saying that one learned to vote by voting, just as one learned to swim by getting into the water.

In retrospect, the Republicans made haste too fast. The South might have accepted some kind of gradual Negro suffrage with some degree of grace. But the Radicals, seeking continued power, brushed aside the long-range welfare of the freedman. He could well have prayed for deliverance from his so-called friends. The outcome was bad for the ex-slaves, bad for the white Southerners, and bad for the Republicans. Large-scale Negro voting in the South was jeopardized, once the federal troops had withdrawn support, and within another generation the black voter had virtually disappeared.

Representative Thaddeus Stevens, in a Congressional speech, January 3, 1867, urged the ballot for blacks out of concern for them and out of bitterness against the whites: "... I am for Negro suffrage in every rebel state. If it be just, it should not be denied; if it be necessary, it should be adopted; if it be a punishment to traitors, they deserve it."

Black-and-Tan Legislatures in the South

Some of the new Southern legislatures created in 1867–1870, not unlike some Northern legislatures, presented unseemly scenes. They were dominated by newly arrived carpetbaggers, despised scalawags, and docile Negroes. Some of the ex-bondsmen were remarkably well educated, but others were illiterate. In most of the states, the black legislators constituted a minority, often a strong minority. In only one—proud South Carolina—did they command an over-all majority by virtue of controlling the lower house. (The whites had boycotted the polls.) Ex-slaves there held offices ranging from speaker to doorkeeper. Negroes who had been raising cotton under the lash of the overseer were now raising points of order under the gavel of the speaker.

Greatly to their credit, these black-and-white legislatures passed much desirable legislation and introduced many overdue reforms. In some states a better tax system was created, charities were established, public works were launched, property rights were guaranteed to women, and free public schools were encouraged—for Negroes as well as whites. Some of these reforms were so welcome that they were retained, along with the more enlightened state constitutions, when the Southern whites finally regained control.

But the good legislation was too often obscured by a carnival of corruption and misrule. Graft and theft ran wild, especially in states like South Carolina and Louisiana, where designing whites used Negroes as catspaws. The worst black-and-tan legislatures purchased, under "legislative supplies," such items as hams, perfumes, suspenders, bonnets, corsets, champagne, and a coffin. One "thrifty" carpetbag governor in a single year "saved" $100,000 from a salary of $8000.

Public debt in the Southern states doubled and trebled, as irresponsible carpetbag legislatures voted appropriations and bond issues with lighthearted abandon. Burdensome taxes were passed in Mississippi, where some 6,000,000 acres were sold for delinquent taxes. The disfranchised and propertied whites had to stagger along under a tax burden that sometimes rose ten or fifteenfold. (This was but another glaring instance of taxation without representation.) When the whites at length regained control of these governments, they repudiated over $100,000,000 of the indebtedness that they regarded as improperly incurred. But before the war many of the Southern states were undertaxed, judged by Northern standards, and the slaves, now citizens, required education and other expensive social services in a war-damaged area.

During this hectic era, corruption was also rampant in the North, among Republicans as well as Democrats. The notorious Tweed Ring of New York City probably stole more millions, though with greater sophistication, than the worst of the carpetbag legislatures combined. And when the Southern whites regained the whip hand, graft by no means disappeared under Democratic auspices. It was bipartisan, biracial, bisectional, and bicameral.

Knights of the White Sheet

A Victim of the Ku Klux Klan. From an anonymous pamphlet of 1872.

Deeply embittered, otherwise decent Southern whites resorted to savage measures against Negro-carpetbag control. A number of secret organizations blossomed forth, the most notorious of which was the Ku Klux Klan, founded in Tennessee in 1866. Besheeted night riders, their horses' hoofs muffled, would hammer on the cabin door of a politically ambitious Negro. In ghoulish tones one thirsty horseman would demand a bucket of water. Then, under pretense of drinking, he would pour it into a rubber attachment concealed beneath his mask and gown, smack his lips, and declare that this was the first water he had tasted since he was killed at the battle of Shiloh. If fright did not produce the desired effect, force was employed.

Such tomfoolery and terror proved partially effective. Many Negroes and white carpetbaggers, quick to take a hint, shunned the polls. But those stubborn souls who persisted in their forward ways were flogged, mutilated, or even murdered. In one Louisiana parish in 1868, the whites in two days killed or wounded two hundred victims; a pile of twenty-five bodies was found half-buried in the woods. By such atrocious practices was the Negro "kept in his place"—that is, down. The Klan, whose original purposes were partly subverted, unfortunately became a refuge for numerous bandits and cutthroats. Any scoundrel could don a sheet.

Radicals in Congress, outraged by this night-riding lawlessness, passed the harsh Force Acts of 1870 and 1871. Federal troops were able to stamp out much of the "lash law," but by this time the "Invisible Empire" had already done its work of intimidation. Many of the outlawed groups continued their tactics in the guise of "dancing clubs," "missionary societies," and "rifle clubs," though the net effect of all the hooded terrorists has probably been exaggerated. Economic reprisals were often more effective, especially when causing the Negro to lose his job.

Shortsighted attempts by the Radicals to exploit the ex-slave as a voter backfired badly. The white South, for many decades, openly flouted the 14th and 15th Amendments. Wholesale disfranchisement of the Negro, starting conspicuously about 1890, was achieved by intimidation, fraud, and trickery. Among various underhanded schemes were the literacy tests, unfairly administered by whites to the advantage of illiterate whites. In the eyes of otherwise honorable Southerners, the goal of White Supremacy fully justified dishonorable devices.

Johnson Walks the Impeachment Plank

Radicals meanwhile had been sharpening their hatchets for President Johnson. Annoyed by the opposition of the "drunken tailor" in the White House, they falsely accused him of maintaining there a harem of "dissolute women." Not content with curbing his authority, they decided to remove him altogether by constitutional processes.* Under existing law the president pro tempore of the Senate, the unscrupulous and rabidly Radical "Bluff Ben" Wade of Ohio, would then become President.

Ticket for the Impeachment Trial

As an initial step, the Radicals in 1867 passed the Tenure of Office Act—as usual over Johnson's veto. Contrary to precedent, the new law required the President to secure the consent of the Senate before he could remove his appointees, once they had been approved by that body. One purpose of the Radicals was to freeze into the Cabinet the Secretary of War, Edwin M. Stanton, a holdover from the Lincoln administration. Though outwardly loyal to Johnson, he was secretly serving as a spy and informer for the Radicals. Another purpose was to goad Johnson into breaking the law, and thus establish grounds for his impeachment.

* For impeachment, see Art. I, Sec. II, para. 5; Art. I, Sec. III, paras. 6, 7; Art. II, Sec. IV, in Appendix.

The Tenure of Office Act ran counter to the ABC's of sound government. The President is responsible to the country for the conduct of his administration; and if his appointees turn out to be inefficient, disloyal, or corrupt, he should not be saddled with them for political purposes by his foes in the Senate. Johnson, believing the Tenure of Office Act to be unconstitutional, was eager to get a test case before the Supreme Court. (That eminent tribunal finally ruled indirectly in his favor fifty-eight years later.) Expecting reasonable judicial speed, Johnson summarily dismissed the two-faced Stanton early in 1868. The President did not believe that the law applied to Lincoln's holdovers, even though the Radicals insisted otherwise.

A Radical-influenced House of Representatives struck back swiftly. By a count of 126 to 47, it voted to impeach Johnson for "high crimes and misdemeanors," as called for by the Constitution. Most of the specific accusations grew out of the President's so-called violation of the ("unconstitutional") Tenure of Office Act.

A Not-Guilty Verdict for Johnson

With evident zeal, the Radical-led Senate now sat as a court to try Johnson on the trumped-up impeachment charges. The House conducted the prosecution. The trial aroused intense public interest and, with a thousand tickets printed, proved to be the biggest show of 1868. Johnson fortunately kept his dignity and sobriety, and maintained a discreet silence. His battery of attorneys was extremely able, while the House prosecutors, including oily-tongued Benjamin F. Butler and embittered Thaddeus Stevens, bungled their flimsy case.

Extreme pressure was put on Senator Ross of Kansas to find President Johnson guilty. He received a telegram from "D. R. Anthony and 1000 others" which read: "Kansas has heard the evidence, and demands the conviction of the President." Ross replied, "I do not recognize your right to demand that I shall vote either for or against conviction. I have taken an oath to do impartial justice . . . and I trust I shall have the courage and honesty to vote according to the dictates of my judgment and for the highest good of my country." An angry Anthony shot back, "Kansas repudiates you as she does all perjurers and skunks."

On May 16, 1868, the day for the first voting in the Senate, the tension was electric, and heavy breathing could be heard in the galleries. By a margin of only one vote, the Radicals failed to muster the two-thirds majority for Johnson's removal. Seven independent-minded Republican Senators, courageously putting country above party, voted "not guilty." (Not one of the seven "renegades" was re-elected to the Senate, though this fact was not clearly related to Republican vengefulness.)

The Radicals were infuriated. "The country is going to the Devil!" cried the crippled Stevens as he was carried from the hall. President-to-be Wade had even sketched out his Cabinet, with the unscrupulous Benjamin F. Butler as Secretary of State. But the nation, though violently aroused, accepted the verdict with a good temper that did credit to its political maturity. In a less stable republic, an armed uprising might have erupted against the President.

Unquestionably the outcome of the trial was a triumph for good government. If a hostile two-thirds majority in Congress can remove the President at will, then there is a breakdown of the traditional separation of powers between the legislative and executive branches. The Radicals were evidently determined to handcuff the Presidency, and possibly also the Supreme Court. Had they done so, they might have established a kind of Congressional dictatorship. They over-reached themselves but their plans miscarried by a shockingly narrow margin.

Justice finally prevailed. Johnson was no doubt guilty of bad speeches, bad judgment, and bad temper. But he was hardly guilty of high crimes and misdemeanors, as envisioned by the framers of the Constitution. His only real crime was to stand stalwartly in the path of the Radicals.

The Purchase of "Walrussia"

Johnson's administration, though largely reduced to a figurehead, achieved its most enduring success in the field of foreign relations.

The Russians by 1867 were in a mood to sell the vast and chilly expanse now known as Alaska. They had already overextended themselves in North America, and they saw that in the likely event of another war with England they probably would lose their defenseless province to the sea-dominant British. Alaska, moreover, had been ruthlessly "furred out" and was a growing economic liability. The Russians were therefore eager to unload their "frozen asset" on the Americans, and they put out seductive feelers in Washington. They preferred the United States to any other purchaser, primarily because they wanted to strengthen further the Republic as a barrier against their ancient enemy, Britain.

ALASKA AND THE CONTIGUOUS U.S. (a comparison)

In 1867 Secretary of State Seward, an ardent expansionist, signed a treaty with Russia which transferred Alaska to the United States for the bargain price of $7,200,000. But Seward's enthusiasm for these frigid wastes was not shared by his countrymen. The American people, still preoccupied with reconstruction and other internal vexations, were economy-minded and anti-expansionist.

Then why did Congress and the American public sanction the purchase? For one thing Russia, alone among the powers, had been conspicuously friendly to the North during the recent Civil War. Americans did not feel that they could offend their great and good friend, the Czar, by hurling his walrus-covered icebergs back into his face. Besides, the territory was rumored to be teeming with furs, fish, and gold, and it might yet "pan out" profitably—as it later did. So Congress and the country accepted "Seward's Polar Bear Garden," somewhat wry-facedly and derisively but nevertheless hopefully. The speculative nature of the transaction not only appealed to Yankee love of a bargain, but did something to dispel the gloom of the re-construction era.

The Harvest of Hate from Reconstruction

Reconstruction ranks as one of America's most tragic failures. The

Columbia Urges a Vote for Crippled
Black Veteran. Thomas Nast,
Harper's Weekly, 1865.

Republic fumbled away a splendid opportunity to close the bloody
chasm between North and South. Yet such were the war-born hatreds that much of this unreason was perhaps inevitable. The nation
passed through one of the most disgraceful decades of its history, as
"reconstruction" took on some of the aspects of "redestruction."

The Civil War was fought openly—and on the whole honorably.
When it was over, there were no wholesale blood purges. No one was

executed for a purely political offense, though the foreign-born head of one Confederate prison was hanged, as were the surviving conspirators in the Lincoln assassination. Probably no large-scale and unsuccessful revolt has ever ended with so little head-rolling.

But if the Yankee victor chopped off no heads, he ground the face of his fallen foe into the dust. If the fighting was conducted cleanly, the same could not be said of the reconstructing. The noble Northern ideals of national unity and human freedom were suffocated in an orgy of hate and corruption. To many Southerners, reconstructing was a more grievous wound than the fighting itself; it left "The Angry Scar."

The Republican Party, with its luckless Negro recruits, was indelibly besmirched with the brush of reconstruction. Southern believers in White Supremacy were driven into the ranks of the Democratic Party, and the Solid South solidified—the Democratic South.

Ill-prepared black voters, duped by Radicals, had allegedly done so poorly that the South found further justification for denying them the ballot. Negroes were technically free, but only partially free, while the Negro-white problem was far from solved.

In the light of hindsight, the Radical reconstruction program was much too narrowly conceived. It could well have embraced the social and economic rehabilitation of the South, including the Negro. At a time when weed-choked Southern lands were going begging, hundreds of thousands of acres could have been made available to the ex-slave at low cost, or no cost, as Thaddeus Stevens and others had urged. But indifference and ingrained American resistance to radical change, especially regarding property rights, proved too strong.

The Age of Hate—as Reconstruction has been called—stirred up a vast amount of racial antagonism and sectional bitterness. Conquered Southerners, outraged by the black-carpetbag-scalawag legislatures, were more determined than ever to "keep the Negro in his place," and wasted much energy in keeping him there. The woes of war were tragic enough, but to them were added the passions of Radical reconstruction. From them came a horrible harvest from which the nation was long in recovering—if it has ever fully recovered.

SELECT READINGS

Recent scholarship is embodied in J. G. RANDALL and DAVID DONALD, *The Civil War and Reconstruction* (rev. ed., 1969), in K. M. STAMPP, *The Era of Reconstruction, 1865–1877* (1965),* in R. W. PATRICK, *The Reconstruction of the Nation* (1967), and in AVERY CRAVEN, *Reconstruction: The Ending of the Civil War* (1969). A popularized survey is HODDING CARTER, *The Angry Scar: The Story of Reconstruction* (1959). The plight of the Negro is stressed in J. H.

FRANKLIN, *Reconstruction: After the Civil War* (1961).* For the recent tendency to be harsh on Johnson see E. L. MCKITRICK, *Andrew Johnson and Reconstruction* (1960)*; W. R. BROCK, *An American Crisis: Congress and Reconstruction, 1865–1867* (1963)*; and LA WANDA and J. H. COX, *Politics, Principle, and Prejudice, 1865–1866* (1963). A still-useful older study is H. K. BEALE, *The Critical Year* [1866] (1930). Radiating pro-Southern indignation are C. G. BOWERS, *The Tragic Era* (1929)* and G. F. MILTON, *The Age of Hate* (1930). See also E. M. COULTER, *The South During Reconstruction, 1865–1877* (1947) and F. B. SIMKINS, *The South, Old and New* (1947). P. H. BUCK's Pulitzer-prize *The Road to Reunion, 1865–1900* (1937)* is comprehensive. Special studies of value are W. B. HESSELTINE, *Lincoln's Plan of Reconstruction* (1960); G. R. BENTLEY, *A History of the Freedmen's Bureau* (1955); F. W. KLINGBERG, *The Southern Claims Commission* (1955); H. L. TREFOUSSE, *The Radical Republicans* (1969); and J. B. JAMES, *The Framing of the Fourteenth Amendment* (1956),* which further challenges the theory of a big-business conspiracy. See also R. P. SHARKEY, *Money, Class and Party: An Economic Study of Civil War and Reconstruction* (1959).* The Negro receives attention in J. M. MCPHERSON, *The Struggle for Equality: Abolitionists and the Negro in the Civil War and Reconstruction* (1964)* and C. V. WOODWARD, *The Strange Career of Jim Crow* (2nd rev. ed., 1966),* which reveals rigid Negro segregation as a late 19th-Century development. See also the succinct treatment by ROBERT CRUDEN, *The Negro in Reconstruction* (1969).* Useful biographies are FAWN M. BRODIE, *Thaddeus Stevens: Scourge of the South* (1959)* and B. P. THOMAS and H. M. HYMAN, *Stanton: The Life and Times of Lincoln's Secretary of War* (1962). Also *Harvard Guide,** Pt. V.

RECENT REFERENCES

ROBERT CRUDEN, *The Negro in Reconstruction* (1969); DAVID DONALD, *Charles Sumner and the Rights of Man* (1970); M. L. BENEDICT, *The Impeachment and Trial of Andrew Johnson* (1973).

* Available in paperback.

25

Grantism and Republican Rule, 1869–1880

It was my fortune, or misfortune, to be called to the office of Chief Executive without any previous political training. . . . Mistakes have been made, as all can see and I admit, but it seems to me oftener in the selections made of the assistants appointed. . . . Failures have been errors in judgment, not intent.

Grant's "Farewell Apology," 1876

Grant: Warrior Turned Politician

A firm-mouthed and stubbily bearded General U. S. Grant, with his slightly stooped body measuring a shade over five feet eight, did not cut an impressive figure. Yet he was by far the most popular Northern hero to emerge from the Civil War. Grateful citizens of Philadelphia, Washington, and his home town (Galena, Illinois) passed the hat around, and in each place presented him with a house. New Yorkers tendered him a check for $105,000. The general, silently puffing his cigar, accepted all these gifts with open arms, as if the Republic owed them to him for having rescued the Union.

Grant probably could have received the presidential nomination in 1868 from either the Democrats or the Republicans. He had not actively identified himself with any political party; his one presidential vote had been cast for the Democratic ticket in 1856. The simplehearted soldier, totally without experience in non-military

Grant Unhorses Seymour.
Harper's Weekly, 1868.

office, was a better judge of horseflesh than of political associates. But having skyrocketed from obscurity, he was a living example of the American success story. His political naïveté was actually a point in his favor. The people were weary of all the wrangling in Washington between Congress and Johnson; and the notion still prevailed that a good general was bound to make a good President. Success in civil war seemed to guarantee success in civil office.

The Republicans, now freed from the Union Party coalition of war days, were in fine fettle. Meeting in Chicago in 1868, they enthusiastically nominated Grant for the Presidency. Their anti-slavery goal, which had originally brought the Republican Party into being, had been attained. But their leaders, having tasted the fleshpots of power, could find other reasons for keeping themselves in office. The Republican platform sounded a clarion call for continued reconstruction of the South with bayonets, and for honest repayment of Civil War borrowings.

Grant, always a man of few words, struck a highly popular note in his letter of acceptance when he said, "Let us have peace." This noble sentiment became a leading slogan of the campaign, and was later engraved on his Hudson River tomb.

Democrats, especially those in the South, had strong feelings against the conquering Grant, whom they called "Grant the Drunkard" and "Grant the Butcher." One soldier claimed, "If the people desire military rule, Grant should be elected, for from my knowledge of the man I will stake my reputation on the prediction that if he is elected he will proclaim himself dictator within twelve months after he is sworn into office."

The "Bloody Shirt" Elects Grant

Expectant Democrats, meeting in New York City later in 1868, were torn by factions. Many of the Middle Western delegates, representing an unprosperous section, were agitated by the "money question." During the war thrifty citizens had bought federal bonds with depreciated paper greenbacks. These investors, most of them well-to-do Easterners, were now clamoring to be paid back in gold. But the poorer agrarian Democrats, insisting on "the same currency for the bondholder and the plowholder," forced a "repudiation" plank into the platform. It baldly proclaimed "the Ohio Idea"—that is, government obligations should be paid in greenbacks, unless otherwise stipulated. The Democrats also denounced military reconstruction of the South by the Radical Republicans.

The Middle Western Democrats got the "repudiation" platform, but the Eastern Democrats got the candidate. Deadlocked over various aspirants, they finally stampeded to the chairman of the convention, the able but reluctant Horatio Seymour. Two-time governor of New York, he had become badly tarred with alleged Copperheadism during "the late unpleasantness."

The ensuing campaign, with its parades and waving torches, was spirited. Republicans whipped up enthusiasm for Grant, "The Man Who Saved the Nation." "Waving the Bloody Shirt"—that is, reviving unpleasant memories of the Civil War—became for the first time a prominent feature of a presidential campaign.* It found expression in such slogans as "The Party that Saved the Union Must Rule It," "Vote As You Shot," and "Scratch a Democrat and You

---

* The expression is said to have derived from a speech by Representative Benjamin F. Butler, who waved before the House the bloodstained nightshirt of a Klan-flogged carpetbagger.

Will Find a Rebel." The Republicans also blasted the "rag money" (greenback) proposal of the Democrats when they shouted, "Repudiate the Repudiators."

Grant won with relative ease. He bagged 214 votes in the Electoral College to 80 for Seymour, and 3,012,833 popular votes to 2,703,249. Yet the Republicans could not take their future control "for Granted," as the expression went. Even with his enormous personal popularity, the quiet warrior triumphed because of the many enfranchised Negroes and the many disfranchised Southerners. A majority of all whites who voted appear to have supported Seymour, and three unreconstructed Southern states would almost certainly have gone for him in a completely free election.

No one could now deny the importance of the black voter. The simple arithmetic was that while Grant won by a majority of only 300,000 votes, an estimated 500,000 ex-slaves cast their ballots for him. This alarming evidence that the Negro vote could swing an election hardened the Radicals in their determination to continue their drastic military reconstruction. Whatever the cost, the ballot must be kept in the hands of the compliant Negroes.

The Era of Good Stealings

The population of the Republic continued to increase by giant leaps, despite the awful bloodletting of the Civil War. By 1870, the year after Grant's inauguration, the census revealed over 38,000,000 souls, a gain of 22.6% over the previous decade. The United States was now the third largest white nation, ranking behind Russia and France.

But the moral stature of the Republic regrettably fell far short of matching its physical stature. The war, like most wars, had bred waste, extravagance, speculation, and graft. Where so much money is thrown about with wild abandon, a great deal sticks to the wrong fingers. A calloused public showed an appalling indifference toward dishonest practices. Nothing could better illustrate the truism that a people have no better government than they deserve.

Corruption was commonplace. A scandalous number of judges and lawyers, though by no means all of them, were purchasable or otherwise untrustworthy. Foreign investors were cheated out of their savings by railroad promoters, who in one instance left the bond-buyers with only "two streaks of rust and a right of way." Unscrupulous stock-market manipulators were a cinder in the public eye. Yet in certain circles they even commanded admiration for their buccaneering tactics, which sometimes involved the hiring of armed thugs to fight pitched battles for them.

Notorious in the financial world were two millionaires, "Jubilee Jim" Fisk and Jay Gould. The corpulent Fisk—bold, impudent, un-

Jay Gould (1836–1892), a cold, calculating, unscrupulous and undersized financial buccaneer, was widely disliked for his ruthlessly acquisitive financial practices, especially in combining railroads.

principled—was often seen in public with "cuddlesome women" behind a span of fast horses. He succeeded in plundering the Erie Railroad of millions. If Fisk provided the "brass," the undersized and cunning Jay Gould provided the brains of the combination. (He died leaving an estate worth $72,000,000.) One dishonest New York legislator took $75,000 from Gould's rival, and then accepted an additional $100,000 from Gould, double-crossing the low bidder. In that era a cynical but apt definition of an honest politician was one who, when bought, would stay bought.

A few skunks can pollute a large area. Although the great majority of businessmen and government officials were decent and law-abiding, the whole atmosphere was fetid. The Man in the Moon, it was said, had to hold his nose when passing over the earth. With the air so badly contaminated, the gullible Grant could hardly have been expected to scent some of the worst evil-doing in public life.

A West Pointer in the White House

U. S. Grant had less training and aptitude for civilian office than perhaps any of his predecessors. A first-rate professional soldier, he turned out to be a third-rate President. Mighty economic and social changes were sweeping the country, but the newly arrived politician was blissfully unaware of their deeper currents. As a military man, he expected heel-clicking obedience to his orders. Four of his secretaries were generals; and for a time even the White House butler was a former mess sergeant.

As a good general, Grant chose his Cabinet with all the secrecy of a night assault on Richmond, not even sharing his inner thoughts with Mrs. Grant. When the choices were revealed, the experts were dumbfounded. The Cabinet was a hodgepodge scraped together without regard for the usual political and geographical niceties. It embraced personal acquaintances, incompetents, and money-getters, to all of whom Grant was tenaciously loyal. Having failed repeatedly in business, he was unduly impressed by those who had succeeded.

In naming the Cabinet, the guiding rules seem to have been three. Were you behind a house-for-Grant movement? Or a check-for-Grant movement? Or had you stood loyally by him when he was down at the heel? Several able and high-minded men, by sheer luck, managed to land in the Cabinet, but they were soon squeezed out. The one noteworthy exception was Secretary of State Hamilton Fish, a wealthy New Yorker at whose home Grant had been wined and dined. Fish lasted almost the entire eight years and proved, by happy accident, to be one of the ablest secretaries of state.

At the outset, Grant was mildly favorable to civil service reform. But the politicians quickly changed his feeble convictions, after plying him with expensive cigars, choice wines, and even fast horses.

James Fisk (1834–1872), a flashy speculator-capitalist, was one of the most notorious figures of the Grant Era. Although married for seventeen years, he kept numerous mistresses, including a famous actress. He was fatally shot by a jealous male rival in New York's Grand Central Hotel.

A congenial crowd of hangers-on frequented the White House, and these political vultures soon convinced the general that the way to virtue was through partisan Republican politics. Grant's election was a godsend to his in-laws of the Dent family, several dozen of whom ultimately attached themselves to the public payroll. A weak Civil Service Commission was authorized by Congress in 1871, but the easygoing Grant showed little enthusiasm for backing it, and Congress ceased to vote it funds.

The soldier-President at first favored leniency toward the South, in the spirit of his generous terms at Appomattox. But the Radicals flocked around him; and he who had been magnanimous in war became vindictive in peace. His famous "Let us have peace" was forgotten, and the cruelest days of reconstruction ground forward under his direction.

A National Carnival of Corruption

Debased ethics during the Grant era are well illustrated by a fantastic scheme of Jim Fisk and Jay Gould. This crafty pair conceived the plot, in 1869, of "cornering" the gold on the New York market and netting additional millions. Their cunning game could succeed only if the Federal Treasury would hold back its funds. The conspirators worked on Grant directly, and also through his brother-in-law, who received $25,000 for his complicity. On "Black Friday" (September 24) Fisk and Gould madly bid the price of gold skyward, while scores of honest businessmen were driven to the wall. The bubble broke when the Treasury, contrary to Grant's earlier assurances, was compelled to release gold. A Congressional probe proved that the President had been stupid and indiscreet—but not crooked. Himself relatively honest, he served as a front for dishonesty.

The Sumner-Grant row over Santo Domingo generated fury. In private the Senator would condemn Grant as "a colossus of ignorance," while Grant, when told that Sumner did not believe in the Bible, snapped, "No, he did not write it." Grant even shook his fist as he passed Sumner's house and hinted that if he were not President there would be a challenge to a duel.

Grant likewise swallowed a scheme to annex the Caribbean republic of Santo Domingo, in which American speculators were actively involved. Sincerely believing that the island would serve useful strategic purposes, he arranged in 1869 for a treaty of annexation to be submitted to the Senate. The chairman of the Senate Committee on Foreign Relations, outspoken Charles Sumner, denounced the plot as fraudulent and engineered its defeat. Grant, deeply angered, got sweet revenge when he had the Senator deposed from his chairmanship.

The notorious Tweed Ring in New York City, though unrelated to Grant, mirrored his times. Burly "Boss" Tweed, 240 pounds of rascality, employed bribery, graft, and fraudulent elections to milk the metropolis of an estimated $50,000,000 to $200,000,000. He adopted the cynical rule: "Addition, division, and silence." The books recorded, for example, a payment of $138,000 to a plasterer for two days of labor. Honest citizens were cowed into silence. If they protested, their tax assessments were raised.

Boss Tweed Manipulates Ballots.
Thomas Nast in *Harper's Weekly,* 1871.

Tweed's luck finally ran out. The New York *Times* secured damning evidence in 1871 and courageously published it, though offered $5,000,000 not to do so. A gifted cartoonist, Thomas Nast, pilloried Tweed mercilessly, after spurning a heavy bribe to desist. The portly thief complained that his illiterate following could not help seeing "them damn pictures." A New York attorney, Samuel J. Tilden, headed the prosecution and gained fame which later paved the path to a presidential nomination. After various delays and escapes, Tweed was finally put behind bars.

Grant himself was tarred by the Crédit Mobilier scandal, even though it had done its dirtiest work in 1867–1868, before he took office. The Crédit Mobilier was a railroad construction company, formed by the insiders of the transcontinental Union Pacific Railway. They craftily hired themselves to build the line, paying themselves, for example, $50,000 a mile for construction that cost $30,000 a mile. In one year the Crédit Mobilier paid dividends of 348%. Fearing that Congress might call a halt, the company furtively distributed some shares of its valuable stock to certain key Congressmen.

The scandal was finally exposed by a New York newspaper in 1872, and some of the worst charges were confirmed by a Congressional investigation. Two members of Congress were formally censured, and the Vice-President of the United States was shown to have accepted twenty shares of stock and some dividends. Congressman

James A. Garfield, later President, was cleared after damaging but inconclusive evidence had been presented. The whole deplorable episode further highlighted the low moral tone of private and public life in the Reconstruction Era.

Embroilments Abroad with Spain and Britain

The exploited masses of Cuba rose against Spain in 1868, and did battle for ten smoke-filled years. Grant prematurely and blunderingly issued a proclamation recognizing their belligerency. But Secretary Fish, striving to avoid a clash with Spain, discreetly pigeonholed the document.

Serious trouble with Spain developed anyhow. In 1873 the Spaniards seized the *Virginius*, a steamer carrying arms to the rebels and flying the Stars and Stripes with dubious legality. Although the capture took place on the high seas, the Spanish officials in Cuba forthwith executed as "pirates" fifty-three of the passengers and crew, including several American citizens. A wave of anger swept the United States. Hostilities with Spain seemed unavoidable, even though the Civil War navy was decayed and worm-eaten. But Spain was finally persuaded to pay damages to the families of those executed, and war was averted for twenty-five years.

Friction with Britain was basically much more alarming than that with Spain, for long-standing grievances against the British continued to rankle. Nothing caused American blood pressure to mount more alarmingly than the unsettled accounts left by the *Alabama* and her sister raiders.

The Johnson administration had attempted to grapple with the prickly *Alabama* problem. In 1869 the State Department negotiated a treaty with Britain which adjusted outstanding controversies, but did so in a manner too soft-handed for American tempers. Senator Charles Sumner, by a typically violent speech, helped defeat the pact in the Senate. He not only claimed $15,000,000 in *direct* damages for the depredations of the *Alabamas*, but intemperately added $2,110,000,000 for certain *indirect* damages and for prolonging the war for two years—at $1,000,000,000 a year. As England would not pay this enormous sum, the plain implication was that she ought to turn Canada over to the United States.

Britishers were outraged by the introduction of these indirect claims, especially in such preposterous amounts. Their mood was now such that no settlement whatever was possible for more than two years.

England Arbitrates the Alabama Claims

With the passage of time, the British felt increasingly troubled by their sorry role in the *Alabama* business. Fair-minded Englishmen

Aroused by the *Virginius* affair, the Governor of Indiana sent a telegram to a New York mass meeting: "Spain cannot be permitted to maintain her authority in Cuba by means which civilized nations regard as atrocious, and, in the cause of humanity and good government, the United States should now extend their sympathy and power over that island."

Senator Charles Sumner (1811–1874), substantially recovered from the Brooks beating on his head, continued to make intemperate speeches during the Civil War and after. A leading exponent of radical reconstruction, he nevertheless had a large hand (with Secretary Seward) in the purchase of Alaska. National Archives.

had long been uneasy, and now even those with less tender consciences were perceiving that they had created a bad precedent. Suppose that rebellion should again erupt in Ireland. What was to prevent the rebels, with generous gifts from Irish-Americans, from building a half-dozen *Alabamas* in American ports, and then wiping British shipping from the seas?

After protracted negotiations, the repentant British signed the Treaty of Washington in 1871. They not only agreed to submit the *Alabama* dispute to arbitration, but they even consented to terms that would virtually forfeit their case. Five arbitrators met in Geneva, Switzerland, and assessed Britain $15,500,000 for damages caused by the commerce raiders.

The Geneva Award of 1872 was a landmark in international arbitration. As such, it set a wholesome precedent. It also healed a festering sore in Anglo-American relations, which for some years thereafter continued on a happier plane. The British were particularly pleased to wipe out the dangerous precedent created by the *Alabama*. On a wall of the Foreign Office in London they hung the canceled draft for $15,500,000, as a warning to future ministries to be more careful.

Britain and America Settle Differences, to discomfiture of Irishman. Thomas Nast, *Harper's Weekly*, 1871.

Both the Treaty of Washington and the Geneva Award, largely the handiwork of patient Secretary Fish, were praiseworthy accomplishments. They were an oasis of achievement in a desert of scandal, and they were used as persuasive arguments for Grant when he ran for a second term.

The Liberal Republican Revolt of 1872

By 1872 a powerful reformist wave was beginning to build up throughout the nation. Decent citizens were distressed by the stench of "Grantism" and by the severity of reconstruction in the South. They noted in alarm that Grant was eager to run a second time, and that the Republican spoilsmen were eager to run him again. Reform-minded citizens gradually banded together to organize the Liberal Republican Party. Voicing the slogan "Turn the Rascals Out," the reformers urged purification of the Washington administration and amnesty for the South.

The Liberal Republicans, though presented with a priceless opportunity to win with a top-flight candidate, muffed their chance. Their Cincinnati nominating convention, heavily studded with starry-eyed reformers, fell into the hands of amateurish newspapermen and scheming politicians. This "conclave of cranks" astounded the country by nominating the querulous and brilliantly erratic Horace Greeley as their likeliest candidate.

Greeley was ill-equipped for the Presidency, despite his household reputation as editor of the New York *Tribune*. Though a fearless moral force, he was dogmatic, emotional, petulant, and notoriously unsound in his political judgments. He did not even look like a President. With a cherubic face and innocent blue eyes peering through steel-rimmed spectacles, he would amble along in a white coat and hat, clutching a green umbrella—like a character stepping from the pages of Charles Dickens.

The office-hungry Democrats, grasping at "anything to beat Grant," wryly endorsed Greeley. In doing so they "ate crow" in large gulps, for the eccentric editor had long assailed them as traitors, slave whippers, saloonkeepers, horse thieves, and idiots. Yet Greeley pleased the Democrats, North and South, when he pleaded for a clasping of hands across "the bloody chasm."

As expected, the regular Republicans renominated Grant on a platform that made a polite bow to civil service reform. Seldom has the voter been confronted with such a devil's choice. Both candidates had made their reputations in fields other than politics, and each was eminently unqualified, by temperament and lifelong training, for high political office.

The campaign of 1872 was mud-splattered in the extreme. The Republicans, desperately waving the Bloody Shirt, demanded to know if the cause won on the battlefield should be lost at the polls. Greeley was denounced as an atheist, a communist, a free-lover, a vegetarian, a brown-bread eater, an idiot, and a co-signer of Jefferson Davis' bail bond. "Grant beat Davis—Greeley bailed him," ran the slogan. When it was all over, "Honest Old Horace," who had waged a surprisingly good campaign on the stump, wondered if he had been running for the Presidency or the penitentiary. Grant in turn was

Greeley and the Democrats "Swallow" Each Other. A Republican jibe at the forced alliance between these former foes. Thomas Nast in *Harper's Weekly*, 1872.

denounced as a dictator, a loafer, a swindler, an ignoramus, a drunkard, and an "utterly depraved horse jockey."

Grant's still-great personal popularity pulled him through, as the regular Republicans shouted, "Grant us another term." He was further aided by distrust of Greeley, by nationwide prosperity, by the Bloody Shirt, and by the Negro vote in the South. Greeley was so badly beaten that Grant mistakenly regarded the result as a thumping endorsement of his administration—wrongdoing and all. The count in the electoral column was 286 to 66, in the popular column 3,597,132 to 2,834,125.

For Greeley, the end was tragic. Within a month he lost his wife, the election, his job, his mind, and his life.

The Liberal Republican movement, though outwardly a failure, left enduring footprints. It frightened the Republicans into cleaning their own house before they were thrown out of it. Three weeks after Greeley's nomination in 1872, the Republican Congress passed a general amnesty act, which removed political disabilities from all except some five hundred ex-Confederate leaders. Many of the Liberal Republicans (though not Greeley) advocated tariff reduction, and five weeks after his nomination Congress materially reduced the high Civil War duties. The Liberal Republican clamor for civil service reform likewise helped persuade the Republicans to fumigate the Grant administration—at least partially.

American third parties have traditionally perished because their more desirable reforms have been stolen by the regular parties: they succeeded by failing. This was the epitaph engraved on the tombstone of the Liberal Republicans.

Depression Doldrums in the Seventies

The evil repute of the scandal-scarred Grant years was worsened by the paralyzing panic that broke in 1873, the first since 1857. Basic causes seem to have been overspeculation and overexpansion, chiefly in mining, manufacturing, railroading, and grain farming. The crash was finally precipitated in 1873 by a financial crisis in Vienna. This overseas flurry set off a disastrous chain reaction, which resulted in the panicky recalling of loans made by Europeans to borrowers in the United States.

America's economic house of cards collapsed with frightening rapidity. The first severe shock came with the failure of the New York banking firm of Jay Cooke & Company, headed by the fabulously rich Jay Cooke, financier of the Civil War. Boom times became gloom times as more than five thousand businesses went bankrupt; and in New York City an army of unemployed riotously battled the police.

Even before the panic descended, the greenback issue had again popped up. Strong pressure was developing in the business world to redeem in gold—"sound money"—the depreciated paper currency

General W. T. Sherman wrote from Paris to his brother: "I feel amazed to see the turn things have taken. Grant who never was a Republican is your candidate; and Greeley who never was a Democrat, but quite the reverse, is the Democratic candidate."

issued during the Civil War. On the other hand, the agrarian and debtor groups—the "cheap money" men—demanded a generous printing of more greenbacks. They argued that a sharp rise in the prices of their depressed farm products would follow more issuance of the "battle-born currency." At the same time, the debtors would be able to pay off their debts more easily, for dollars would in theory become cheaper and easier to acquire.

The inflationists died hard. They forced a bill through Congress in 1874 designed to expand the paper currency from $382,000,000 to a maximum of $400,000,000 in greenbacks. The "hard money" or "gold standard" advocates clamored for Grant to wield his veto; the "soft money" men insisted that he honor the will of the people as expressed in Congress. After much painful indecision, Grant vetoed the inflationary measure, thereby winning the plaudits of the gold-moneyites.

In the light of subsequent misfortunes, a moderate inflation of the currency would have been a boon to the country. There simply was not enough to go around. From 1870 to 1880 the per capita circulation of money had actually *decreased* from $19.42 to $19.37, even though American business, on the eve of the new industrial revolution, was beginning to require a sharp increase in the money supply. (See chart, p. 619.)

"Sound money" men also redoubled their demands for "resumption." By this they meant resuming the practice, abandoned early in the Civil War, of having the Treasury redeem its paper currency on demand with metallic money. In 1875 a Republican Congress finally passed a hotly debated resumption law, effective in 1879. Grant's name continued to be associated with sound money, though not with sound government.

Republican prospects in the Congressional elections of 1874 were not roseate. The twin burdens of persisting panic and mounting scandal proved overpowering. The electorate, in a tidal wave of resentment, swept a Democratic majority into the House of Representatives—the first since 1858.

The End of Grantism

The breath of scandal in Washington now reeked of alcohol. In 1875 the public learned that a gigantic Whiskey Ring had been robbing the Treasury of millions in revenue. "Let no guilty man escape," insisted Grant. But when he discovered his private secretary among the culprits, his views speedily changed. He volunteered a written statement for the jury, with all the weight of his exalted office behind it, and the thief escaped.

Rottenness in the Grant administration was further laid bare by a half-dozen or so other sickening scandals. In 1876 the news broke

Chief Justice Chase put the issue in a nutshell in a private letter (1866), "The way to resumption is to resume." On Resumption Day (1879) the orator Robert G. Ingersoll, speaking from the sub-Treasury steps in Wall Street, proclaimed (with Biblical overtones), "I am thankful I have lived to see the day when the greenback can raise its right hand and declare 'I know that my Redeemer liveth.'"

"All Smoke." Thomas Nast Dismisses
Grant Scandals, *Harper's Weekly*, 1872.

that Secretary of War Belknap, married to two successively extravagant wives, had pocketed (or they had) some $24,000 by selling the privilege of disbursing supplies—often shoddy—to the Indians. The House unanimously voted to impeach him. But Belknap went scot-free when the Senate failed to muster enough votes for conviction, largely because he had resigned and doubts arose as to senatorial jurisdiction. Grant, ever loyal to his crooked friends, saved Belknap's skin by not only accepting his resignation but doing so "with great regret."

Yet Grant's "eight long years of scandal" were not all bad. The agony of reconstruction was nearing an end, and the "bloody chasm" was being closed by amnesty. Substantial achievements were recorded in foreign affairs; the nation was expanding westward with marvelous rapidity; and industry was on the verge of a phenomenal boom. The young Republic was so big and powerful that while scandals might shame it, they could not lame it. America was like a rhinoceros bulldozing its way through a jungle, annoyed but not hampered by ticks and lice.

It is a curious fact that the gullible Grant, who put dishonest men into office, was an unconscious father of civil service reform. The scandals of his two terms goaded many citizens into action, and added to the popularity of what spoilsmen sneeringly dubbed "snivel service" reform.

The Blaine Bubble Bursts

Hangers-on around Grant, like fleas urging their dog to live, begged the "Old Man" to try for a third term in 1876. The General, blind to his ineptitudes, showed a disquieting willingness. But the House of Representatives, by a lop-sided bipartisan vote of 233 to 18, spiked the third-term boom. It passed a resolution which sternly reminded the country—and Grant—of the anti-dictator implications of the two-term tradition.

Conspicuous among the Republican hopefuls was James G. Blaine, a radiantly personable Congressman from Maine. Among other gifts, the "Magnetic Statesman" had a photographic memory for faces and names. With fine presence, flashing eyes, and a pleasing voice, he was a thrilling speaker. Strongly inclined to demagoguery, he would twist the British Lion's tail for Irish votes, and wave the Bloody Shirt for veteran votes. The fact that he himself had not heard the whine of Confederate bullets led to the jibe "Invisible in war, invincible in peace."

Blaine's candidacy was sweeping along under full sail when suddenly, in the spring of 1876, it struck a reef. The news leaked out that Blaine, as Speaker of the House in 1869, had used his influence to secure a land grant for a Southern railroad, and that he had later sought and received financial favors from the same company. Blaine theatrically tried to clear his skirts before the House by reading carefully selected parts of the incriminating letters. But since he would not reveal the unread portions, even at the risk of losing the Presidency, the conclusion seemed justified that he had been prostituting his high public office for private gain. Other damaging revelations, which exposed an elastic conscience, came out in later years and raised further doubts as to how he had acquired his obvious wealth. The postscript, "Burn this letter," hurt his cause.

Few voters could doubt Blaine's energy and ability, but many did doubt his honesty and integrity. The best that can be said for him is that he had merely done what scores of other men in public life had been doing. But moral standards were now rising—and he got caught with his hand too near the cookie jar.

One of Blaine's rivals for the presidential nomination was the handsome and imperious Roscoe ("Lord Roscoe") Conkling, United States Senator from New York. He had tangled with Blaine in a Congressional debate in 1866, and Blaine had withered him into silence by referring to his "turkey gobbler strut." Cartoonists thereafter por-

President Rutherford B. Hayes (1822–1893), nineteenth President of the United States. Library of Congress.

trayed Conkling as a turkey gobbler, with the curl that he affected in the middle of his forehead. But the statuesque New Yorker ultimately got sweet revenge by helping to keep Blaine out of the Presidency.

Blaine's chances for the nomination seemed excellent, despite these drawbacks, when the Republicans met in Cincinnati. The convention was swept off its feet by the orator Robert G. Ingersoll, who nominated Blaine as "the Plumed Knight." But the delegates adjourned amid rumors that it was unsafe to turn on the gas lights, and when they met the next day they were in a more sober mood. A compromise candidate was indicated.

The man finally chosen was bearded Rutherford B. Hayes, a man obscure enough to be dubbed "the Great Unknown." Of medium height and weight, he was distinguished by a high-domed forehead above a heavy reddish beard. Though not brilliant, he possessed common sense and uncommon ability. As a "Grade B" war hero, he appealed to the Civil War veterans; wounded several times, he had risen to the rank of major general. Thrice governor of the doubtful and electorally potent state of Ohio,* he had proved himself to be a courageous and honest administrator. To the delight of reformers, he had come out foursquare for cleansing the civil service. His platform promised reform, sound money, and "permanent pacification" of the South.

"President" Tilden's Temporary Triumph

Samuel J. Tilden, the bachelor governor of New York, received the enthusiastic nomination of the Democrats in St. Louis. Although he had made a national reputation by helping to smash the Tweed Ring, Tilden was unimpressive in appearance. Boyish-faced and smooth-shaven, he was slightly built, sickly (an eyelid drooped), nervous and weak-voiced ("Whispering Sammy"). His leadership was intellectual rather than oratorical. The Democratic platform bitterly condemned the long years of Republican scandal, and held out a glowing promise of civil service reform.

Lack of confidence in Republican honesty was offset by a keen recollection of Democratic Copperheadism during the late "rebellion." Alarmed Republicans again unfurled the frayed Bloody Shirt and shouted, "Avoid Rebel Rule," "Vote As You Shot," and "The Boys in Blue Will See It Through." They pointed with pride to Hayes' spotless record, and proclaimed, "Hurrah! For Hayes and Honest Ways!" The Democrats countered with "Turn the Rascals Out" and "Tilden and Reform."

Samuel J. Tilden, President-reject

---

* Partly because of its large number of electoral votes, Ohio has become "the modern mother of Presidents," supplanting Virginia. A political saying of the 1870's went:
Some are born great,
Some achieve greatness,
And some are born in Ohio.

Hayes—Republican

Tilden—Democratic

Disputed

HAYES-TILDEN DISPUTED ELECTION OF 1876 (with electoral vote by state)

"I DON'T KNOW."

1900!

A Kuklux Notice posted up in Mississippi during the Election of 1876.

A Brutal Warning to Negro Voters

Secretive Samuel Tilden, though hailed as a reformer, had vulnerable joints in his armor. "Slippery Sam" had formed unsavory connections with corrupt Tammany Hall; "Thrifty Sam" had allegedly dodged much of his income tax in 1863. In addition, he had made a fortune—he died worth $6,000,000—by working hand in glove as an attorney with Jim Fisk and other "robber barons." Yet all these accusations against Tilden were weakened by the corruption and depression of the Grant era.

As the returns poured in, Tilden apparently had swept the country. He quickly amassed 184 electoral votes of the needed 185, with twenty votes in four states doubtful because of irregular returns.* Surely Tilden could glean at least one of these, especially in view of the fact that he had polled 264,292 more popular votes than Hayes, 4,036,298 to 4,300,590.

Republican leaders, though at first disposed to concede defeat, quickly rallied. They cleverly sent "visiting statesmen" to the three doubtful Southern states of Louisiana, South Carolina, and Florida, presumably "to steal the election." The Democrats, no less zealous, likewise dispatched "visiting statesmen." With such skilled persuaders at work, all three of the disputed Southern states submitted two sets of returns, one Democratic and one Republican. The brutal truth is that both parties in these states had been guilty in some degree of irregularity, which included bribery, forgery, ballot-box stuffing, intimidation, and violence.

* Nineteen of these comprised the total electoral vote of Louisiana, South Carolina, and Florida. The twentieth was one of Oregon's three votes. Hayes carried Oregon, but one of its electors turned out to be ineligible because he was a federal officeholder (a postmaster), contrary to the Constitution (see Art. II, Sec. I, para. 2, Appendix).

Dishonors Equal between Republicans and Democrats

As the weeks drifted by, the deadlock tightened. The Constitution merely stipulates that the electoral returns from the states shall be sent to Congress, and in the presence of the House and Senate they shall be *opened* by the president of the Senate (see Art. XII). But who should *count* them? On this point the Constitution was silent. If counted by the president of the Senate (a Republican), the Republican returns would be selected. If counted by the Speaker of the House (a Democrat), the Democratic returns would be chosen.

Compromise or clash seemed inevitable. The danger loomed that there would be no President on March 4, 1877; and this uncertainty slowed the wheels of business. ''On to Washington!'' and ''Tilden or blood!'' cried Democratic hotheads, and some of their armed ''Minute Men'' began to drill with a view to seating their ''victorious'' leader. Behind the scenes, the statesmen were laboring frantically, and an agreement was gradually hammered out in the Henry Clay tradition —the much-underrated Compromise of 1877.

Thomas Nast Favors a Truce. *Harper's Weekly,* 1877.

The election deadlock itself was to be broken by the Electoral Count Act, which passed Congress early in 1877. It set up an electoral commission consisting of fifteen men selected from the Senate, the House, and the Supreme Court. The fifteenth member of the commission, according to Democratic schemes, was to have been the giant-sized Justice David Davis, an independent—with Democratic leanings. But at the last moment he resigned from the Bench to go to the Senate, and the only remaining members of the Supreme Court were Republicans. A Republican rhymester chortled at the Democrats:

They digged a pit, they digged it deep,
They digged it for their brother;
But through their sin they did fall in
The pit they digged for t'other.

Composition of the Electoral Commission, 1877

	Republicans	Democrats
Senate (Republican majority)	3	2
House (Democratic majority)	2	3
Supreme Court	3	2
Total	8	7

In February, 1877, about a month before inauguration day, the Senate and House met together in an electric atmosphere to settle the dispute. The roll of the states was tolled off alphabetically. When Florida was reached—the first of the three Southern states with two sets of returns—the disputed documents were referred to the electoral commission, which sat in a nearby chamber. After prolonged discussion the members agreed, by the partisan vote of eight Republicans to seven Democrats, to accept the Republican returns. Outraged Democrats in Congress, tasting defeat, undertook to launch a filibuster "until hell froze over."

Renewed deadlock was avoided by the rest of the complex Compromise of 1877, already partially concluded behind closed doors. The Democrats reluctantly agreed, in part, that Hayes might take office in return for his withdrawing intimidating federal troops from the two states in which they remained, Louisiana and South Carolina. The Republicans also promised the Democrats a substantial share of federal offices, and long-overdue federal support for internal improvements, chiefly railroads, in the impoverished South. Not all of these promises were kept in later years. But the Democrats permitted Hayes to receive the remainder of the disputed returns—all by the partisan vote of eight to seven. So close was the margin of safety that the explosive issue was settled only three days before the new President was officially sworn in.

The outcome was a triumph for democratic government—a victory for neither candidate but for the American people. Many long-exiled Democrats had been aroused almost to the point of renewed civil war. But the lethargic Tilden, though regarding himself as honestly elected, acquiesced in the "steal" in order to avert an internal upheaval. Four more years of Republicanism seemed better than four more years of rebellion.

The ugly truth is that neither party came into court with clean hands. Republicans probably threw out enough ballots by fraud in the disputed states to rob Tilden of the election. Southern Democrats, for their part, probably "bulldozed" enough Negroes away from the polls to deprive Hayes of the popular majority. In a sense the Democrats "stole" the election, but the Republicans "stole" it back.

Cold-water Integrity on the Potomac

Aching Bayonet Tooth Removed. Contemporary cartoon.

Rutherford ("Rutherfraud") B. Hayes was the only President, except possibly J. Q. Adams, to take office with a cloud on his title. He was pilloried in the press as "Old 8 to 7" and "His Fraudulency," and was cartooned with "Fraud" on his honest brow. All this cut him deeply. A man of unsullied honor and high ideals—a "Queen Victoria in breeches"—he believed himself rightfully elected. Lucy Webb Hayes, his wife and childhood sweetheart, was a kindred spirit. Family prayers were offered daily; and since both the President and Mrs. Hayes were temperance advocates, "Lemonade Lucy" served no alcohol. "The cold water administration" swept the fetid, smoke-laden atmosphere out of the wineless White House.

Hayes began vigorously and impressively. He selected a top-flight Cabinet, and in fulfillment of his pre-election bargain, included an ex-Confederate general (D. M. Key) as Postmaster General. Several weeks after taking office, Hayes boldly withdrew the last federal troops that were supporting carpetbag governments, also in accord with the behind-the-scenes Compromise of 1877. This was an act of real courage. The President was denounced by vindictive Republicans, and especially by the carpetbaggers who craved "four more years of good stealing."

The removal of these remaining army units was epochal. It marked not only the "redemption" of the South, but the official end of political and military reconstruction. The bayonet-supported dominance of the Republicans in Louisiana and South Carolina collapsed when the last blue-clad soldiers withdrew, and the Solid Democratic South speedily solidified.* If Hayes, a Union general and a Republican, could be viciously condemned for withdrawing the troops, Tilden, a non-veteran and a Democrat, probably would not have dared to take the same action.

Hayes—the idealist, reformer, and political purist—parted company with the spoilsmongers. He believed that public office should not be a private preserve, and that strict business principles should prevail in governmental affairs. His inaugural address contained the refreshing declaration, "He serves his party best who serves his country best." But to his acute distress, he was unable to carry out all his noble principles. Persistent pressures finally forced him to reward with political plums a number of corrupt Southern carpetbaggers, conspicuously those who by irregular means had procured his election. He was upbraided by the reformers for having placed corruptionists in high office, and by the party hacks for not having ladled out the political gravy more generously.

Hayes enjoyed greater success in cleaning out the New York Customs House. This key agency was a hotbed of politics and a vital cog in Senator Conkling's political machine. It employed some 1300 persons who, together with blood relatives and in-laws, wielded a formidable bloc of votes. The Collector of the Port, Chester A. Arthur—later President of the United States—had become deeply involved in objectionable political activity as a henchman of Senator Conkling.

Hayes was determined to curb the spoils system in New York, while slapping at the Conkling-Grant faction. He summarily removed both Arthur and a subordinate, and forthwith nominated two replacements without consulting Conkling. The "Peacock Senator," fearing that he would lose control of the New York political machine, fought the confirmation of Hayes' nominees tooth and nail. But after a prolonged struggle, the President triumphed and was able to install his own men.

Hayes' diary entry for March 24, 1877 read: "The number of applications for office made to Mrs. Hayes and other members of the family is so great that a rule has been adopted that such applications will not be considered. No person connected with me by blood or marriage will be appointed to office."

Unhappy political spoilsmen were heard to remark that Hayes "was the type of man who, if Pope, would have felt called upon to appoint a few Protestant cardinals."

* Federal troops have routinely been stationed in the South since early days, for defense of the coast and protection against Indians. Thousands of soldiers were there before and after the "withdrawal"; Hayes merely restationed them so as not physically to support the two carpetbag regimes.

By this time Hayes was a man without a party. Denounced as "Granny" Hayes and a "Goody Two-Shoes" reformer, he was openly repudiated by the old-line politicians. He had earlier declared himself to be a single-termer, and this decision proved to be a face-saver because he probably could not have won renomination in any event.

The Distress of the Debtor

Hayes' years were ones of alarming unrest and turbulence. The explosive atmosphere was largely a by-product of the long years of depression and deflation following the Panic of 1873. Labor disorders, flaring forth into uncontrolled violence, convulsed a number of the major Eastern cities in 1877. The paralyzing railroad strikes of that year, which verged on civil war in places like Baltimore and Pittsburgh, forced Hayes to call out the federal troops. Order was not restored until scores of rioters had been killed or injured. Neither the President nor anyone else in authority seems to have had a real appreciation of the deeper significance of changing economic currents. The new industrial age was bringing monopoly to business, injustice to labor, and depression to the farmer.

Numerous debtor groups, desperately seeking relief, grasped at the silver will-o'-the-wisp. Ably abetted by the pro-silver Congressmen, they were dropping their demand for more greenbacks in favor of the unlimited coinage of silver in the value-ratio of sixteen ounces of silver to one of gold.

The "sacred white metal," according to its sponsors, had received a raw deal. In the early 1870's it had not been presented to the federal mints in quantity, because it commanded a higher price in the open market than the 16-to-1 ratio of the Treasury. Congress therefore had formally dropped the coinage of silver dollars in 1873. Fate played a grim joke later in the 1870's when Western silver "strikes" shot production up and forced the price down. Westerners and debtors then belatedly began to assail the "Crime of '73," and demand a return to the "Dollar of Our Daddies," instead of the hated "rag money."

As pressure mounted, the clash over currency grew more intense. "Soft money" or "dishonest money" men indignantly demanded the free and unlimited coinage of all silver mined at the ratio of 16 to 1. "Hard money" or "sound money" advocates, for their part, scornfully demanded the coinage of none at all. A compromise was finally reached by Congress in the Bland-Allison Act of 1878, originally sponsored by Representative Richard P. ("Silver Dick") Bland of Missouri. The law provided that the Treasury, instead of coining all silver presented, would purchase from two to four million dollars' worth of bullion a month and coin it into dollars then worth only 93 cents intrinsically. Hayes, a "sound money" man, vetoed the bill. But the silverite inflationists triumphantly repassed it.

"Substance and Shadow." Metallic (specie) dollar the substance; the depreciated paper greenback the shadow. *Harper's Weekly*, 1875

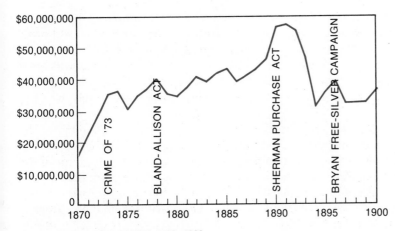

U.S. SILVER PRODUCTION, 1870–1900

Resumption was the other pressing financial issue of the era. The redemption of paper currency by the Treasury with metallic money was resumed on January 1, 1879, as authorized by act of Congress four years earlier. This step was finally taken despite the efforts of the "soft money" advocates to engineer a repeal. But when greenback holders found that they could get gold on demand, they kept the lighter and more convenient folding money. The credit of the government, as expected, rose sharply with this honoring of its outstanding obligations.

Hayes and Foreign Friction

Economic unrest swept to California and included docile Chinese among its victims. By 1880 the Golden State could count 75,000 of these Oriental newcomers, or 9% of its entire population. In San Francisco, workingmen known as Kearneyites were violently aroused against the competition of cheap Chinese labor. Led by Denis Kearney, an Irish-born demagogue who numbered among his followers many immigrants from Erin's Isle, they cried, "Immeriky fur Immerikans, bejabers." Scores of harmless Orientals were abused in various ways, including the forcible cutting off of precious pigtails. Others were murdered outright.

Even law-abiding citizens on the Pacific Coast viewed the low-wage Chinese with alarm. In a catch-as-catch-can economic contest, the beef eater had no chance against the rice eater, who allegedly considered dead rats a delicacy. The present tens of thousands of coolies were regarded as a menace, the prospective millions as a calamity.

Congress finally responded to all this uproar in 1879, when it passed a bill severely restricting the influx of Chinese laborers. But

Hayes, ever the man of honor, vetoed this discriminatory measure on the grounds that it violated the existing treaty with China. Although "Missey" Hayes was burned in effigy by outraged Californians, there was no alternative but to negotiate a new pact. This was done in 1880, and two years later Congress slammed the door on Chinese coolies for a period of ten years. Subsequent laws barred the door completely.

Another hot spot developed over the prospective piercing of the isthmus connecting the two Americas. Under the dynamic leadership of the seventy-four-year-old Ferdinand de Lesseps, conqueror of the Isthmus of Suez, a French company was organized to dig the Panama Canal. Many Americans feared that the gigantic enterprise was but an entering wedge for the French government to violate the Monroe Doctrine. President Hayes, in a message to Congress in 1880, sternly warned that any future canal would be "virtually a part of the coastline of the United States."

Undaunted, the French promoters began to make the dirt fly at Panama in 1883. But the audacious undertaking was crippled by various obstacles, especially yellow fever, which swept away thousands of workers and caused de Lesseps to be dubbed "the Great Undertaker." Bankruptcy finally overwhelmed the company in 1889, amid shattering financial scandals, and jungle vines rapidly smothered its rusting machinery. What Hayes could not prevent, nature did.

President Hayes, though not a great statesman, has been undeservedly belittled. Opposed by his party leaders and thwarted by Democratic majorities in Congress, he was able to secure little ex-

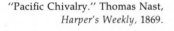

"Pacific Chivalry." Thomas Nast, *Harper's Weekly,* 1869.

cept routine legislation. But he brought to his exalted office a high degree of patriotism, conscientiousness, and devotion to duty. He helped to make reform respectable. His signal contribution was to show that a Republican could be inflexibly honest—and also resistant to designing "friends." He not only revived faith in the integrity of his party, but restored faith—badly needed faith—in the integrity of the national government.

SELECT READINGS

The scandal-rocked Grant era is treated with brevity in J. G. RANDALL and DAVID DONALD, *The Civil War and Reconstruction* (rev. ed., 1969) and in BRUCE CATTON, *U. S. Grant and the American Military Tradition* (1954).* The best full-length life of Grant is W. B. HESSELTINE, *Ulysses S. Grant* (1935); see also ALLAN NEVINS' Pulitzer-prize *Hamilton Fish: The Inner History of the Grant Administration* (1936); L. D. WHITE, *The Republican Era, 1869–1901* (1958)* [Pulitzer prize]; HENRY ADAMS' doleful classic *The Education of Henry Adams* (1918)*; and H. W. MORGAN, ed., *The Gilded Age* (1963).* Impressive is IRWIN UNGER's Pulitzer-prize *The Greenback Era: A Social and Political History of American Finance, 1865–1879* (1964).* New light on the election of 1876 appears in C. V. WOODWARD, *Reunion and Reaction* (rev. ed., 1956).* Consult also HARRY BARNARD, *Rutherford B. Hayes and His America* (1954) and S. P. HIRSHON, *Farewell to the Bloody Shirt, 1877–1893* (1962).* The great strikes are described in R. V. BRUCE, *1877: Year of Violence* (1959). Also *Harvard Guide,* * Pt. V.

RECENT REFERENCES

DAVID DONALD, *Charles Sumner and the Rights of Man* (1970).

* Available in paperback.

26

Personalities, Politics, and Reform 1880–1889

When more of the people's sustenance is exacted through the form of [tariff] taxation than is necessary to meet the just obligations of Government . . . such exaction becomes ruthless extortion and a violation of the fundamental principles of a free Government.

President Grover Cleveland, Message to Congress, December 6, 1886

General Garfield vs. General Hancock

As the presidential campaign of 1880 neared, Grant's stock once more rose sharply. Republican spoilsmen, long frustrated by Hayes, pined for "four more good years of stealing." The third-term tradition, they argued, applied only to three *consecutive* terms. The "Old Man" himself had embarked upon a globe-girdling tour in 1877, during which he was royally acclaimed. But his return, wildly cheered at San Francisco in September, 1879, was prematurely timed. Enthusiasm for him had definitely waned before the Republican convention met in its star-spangled hall.

The stage was set for fireworks when the Republicans gathered at Chicago. General Grant, quite willing to run again, was nominated by Senator Roscoe Conkling of New York. The speaker's thrilling oration began:

And if asked what state he hails from,
  This our sole reply shall be,
"From near Appomattox Court-house,
  With its famous apple-tree."

On the first thirty-five ballots Grant led his chief rival, the magnetic Blaine of Maine. Hopelessly deadlocked over the two aspirants, the convention finally stampeded to a dark horse, James A. Garfield of Ohio. The victor—a tall (six feet), heavily bearded, and broad-shouldered Congressman—had commended himself to the delegates by an eloquent speech nominating for the Presidency a fellow Ohioan, John Sherman.

Garfield enjoyed numerous assets. Born in politically potent Ohio, and in a log cabin, he had worked his way up from poverty by driving mules on the towpaths of the Ohio Canal. Later he had served brilliantly as a volunteer officer in the Civil War, and had finally risen to the rank of major general.

Crestfallen Grant spoilsmen received some slight consolation. The delegates chose for the Vice Presidency Senator Conkling's close political henchman, Chester A. Arthur of New York. The platform, generously draped in the folds of the Bloody Shirt, declared emphatically for the protective tariff, and somewhat feebly for civil service reform. One Republican delegate from Texas blurted out, "What are we here for, except the offices?"

Frustrated Democrats, still wrathful over having been robbed of the Presidency in 1876, declared in their Chicago platform that the "great fraud" overshadowed all other issues. But decrepit "Old Sammy" Tilden, four years older and sicker than in 1876, declined to run again.

Cheering Democratic delegates then turned to tall and handsome General Winfield S. Hancock—"Hancock the Superb." Their nominee was a West Pointer who had served brilliantly in the Civil War, especially at Gettysburg, where he was wounded. His nomination refuted the common charge that only Republican officers had fought for the North; and he was popular in the South, where he had fair-mindedly headed one of the military reconstruction districts. The Democratic platform declared for civil service reform and a "tariff for revenue only."

Harassed by office-seekers and others, Garfield burst out, shortly before his assassination, "My God! What is there in this place that a man should ever want to get into it."

The Republican Victory of 1880

Old issues were expiring and new ones were shunned like leprosy by the politicians, who were reluctant to alienate votes. The Republicans deliberately turned their backs on deepening economic and social injustices, and strove desperately to wring another President from the Bloody Shirt by refighting the Civil War and reemancipating the Negro. Eugene Field sneered at would-be Democratic reformers:

Out on reformers such as these;
  By Freedom's sacred powers,
We'll run the country as we please;
  We saved it, and it's ours.

Actually, the Southern issue was a relatively minor one for the first time since the Tippecanoe campaign of 1840.

Hancock proved to be an upstanding and outspoken candidate. His character and military record were spotless, though he was absurdly accused of cowardice in battle. When asked for his views on the tariff, he candidly replied, "The tariff question is a local question." The jubilant Republicans, seizing upon this apparent stupidity, almost literally jeered Hancock out of the Presidency by proclaiming that he was "a good man, weighing 250 pounds." But the truth is that any general tariff bill is the product of pressures by many local-interest groups, which may range from Pennsylvania iron smelters to California lemon growers.

Garfield, though joyously hailed as "the Canal Boy," ran into troubled waters. He had been tainted by the Crédit Mobilier scandal, allegedly in the sum of $329, and energetic Democrats now chalked these telltale figures on buildings, walls, and fences. Undaunted, the Republicans raised a lush campaign fund by assessing officeholders a percentage of their salaries (as job insurance), and by "frying the fat" out of huge corporations (as tariff insurance). Indiana was "drenched" with Republican money ("soap"), which helped to ease it into the Garfield column.

"Boatman Jim" Garfield barely scraped across the electoral reefs. He polled only 9464 more votes than Hancock—4,454,416 to 4,444,952—but his margin in the Electoral College was the comfortable one of 214 to 155. Garfield's victory was essentially an endorsement of the status quo, including prosperity and tariffs. It was also an expression of persisting distaste for the rebellion-bedaubed Democrats.

The Martyrdom of Garfield

James A. Garfield, sworn in on March 4, 1881, ranked well above the average President in ability, education, and experience. A graduate of Williams College, he had served for a time as president of what came to be Hiram College in Ohio. As one of the ablest orators in Congress, he was in wide demand as a speaker; and as a devout member of the Church of Christ, he was active as a lay preacher. He was a kindly, generous, warm-hearted Christian gentleman, and a devoted son who turned and kissed his mother after taking the inaugural oath. But he had one serious weakness: he hated to hurt people's feelings by saying "no."

Dividing the spoils, which ultimately divided the party, brought Garfield no peace. For every appointment there were seemingly twenty disappointments. The overwhelming inrush of office-hungry Republicans finally wrung from Garfield the exclamation, "My God! What is there in this place that a man should ever want to get into it?" At the outset, he awarded the prize plum of the Secretaryship of State to his close friend and the uncrowned king of the party, James G. Blaine. The "Plumed Knight" accepted the post as a kind of consolation prize, and with the expectation of being the "premier" of the Cabinet. Confidently planning to pursue a "spirited" foreign policy for eight years, Blaine bought an imposing house, which his ambitious wife intended to make a social center of Washington.

Conkling and Blaine Struggle for Power Behind Throne. Thomas Nast, *Harper's Weekly*, 1881

Trouble was meanwhile brewing with the pro-Grant Senator Conkling of New York, a colossus of conceit. As a member of the spoilsman or "Stalwart" faction of the Republican Party, he was angered by the nomination of Garfield, who belonged to Blaine's "Half-Breed" faction—half Stalwart and half reformist. Conkling was further enraged when his bitterest enemy, Blaine, was tendered the key position in the new administration. The two Half-Breeds, Blaine and Garfield, were apparently scheming to parcel out the loaves and fishes of office to the disadvantage of the Conklingites. An inevitable explosion came when Garfield, apparently hand in glove with Blaine, appointed an archrival of Conkling to the coveted office of Collector of the Port of New York.

Conkling fought senatorial confirmation of the new appointment with all the weapons at his command. But when he discovered that he was not gaining ground, he spectacularly resigned and returned to Albany, where he expected to be reelected by the legislature. The junior Senator from New York followed the lead of his senior colleague in resigning, and was thereafter dubbed "Me Too" Platt. Vice-President Arthur also journeyed to Albany, there to buttonhole legislators in behalf of his former political chief (Conkling), so as to discredit his current political chief (Garfield). Conkling's scheme finally backfired when the New York legislature failed to re-elect him and "Me Too" Platt. Both men were thereupon retired to private life—Platt temporarily—without irreparable loss to public life.

Conkling and Platt as Spoiled Children. Thomas Nast, *Harper's Weekly*, 1881

While "the Battle of Albany" was thus raging, tragedy struck. A disappointed and mentally deranged office seeker, Charles J. Guiteau, shot President Garfield in a railroad station in Washington. The victim, after lingering in agony for eleven weeks, died on September 19, 1881. Guiteau, when seized, reportedly cried, "I am a Stalwart. Arthur is now President of the United States." The implication was that now the Conklingites would all get good jobs. At his trial, Guiteau went so far as to ask all those who had benefited politically by the assassination to contribute to his defense fund. He was found guilty of murder and hanged.

Statesmen are dead politicians, the saying goes, and Garfield's "martyrdom" undoubtedly enhanced his reputation. His half-year term was too short to permit a fair estimate, but he showed considerable indecision and took no vigorous steps toward civil service reform. His tragic death tended to draw the veil of charity over his shortcomings. Brutal though the thought is, Garfield's greatest single service to his country probably was to die when he did and as he did. An unwitting martyr to the evils of spoils-seeking, he departed this life in such a way as to shock the nation into taking action to correct flagrant abuses. The government had indeed come to a pretty pass when it was a case of "an office—or your life."

The Office Dignifies President Arthur

Garfield's death was rendered all the more shocking by the low repute of his successor. "My God! 'Chet' Arthur President of the United States!" was a frequently heard exclamation. A graduate of Union College, with Phi Beta Kappa honors, Arthur was a wealthy, handsome, and dignified widower who enjoyed a well-stocked wine cellar, an extensive library, and a wardrobe that included eighty pairs of trousers. He could wear his clothes to advantage, for he was tall (6 feet 2) and well-proportioned, and affected a mustache with full sideburns. Formerly a machine politician at the New York Customs House, he had been dismissed for purely political reasons from the only important post he had ever held before becoming Vice-President.

Arthur Takes Presidential Oath. *Harper's Weekly*, 1881

But the shock of new responsibilities caused "Prince" Arthur to rise to unexpected heights. He actually turned out to be a far better President than the country deserved for having elected a Vice-President of his spoils-system antecedents. Pushing aside political ambition, he did not pull wires unduly in an attempt to secure the presidential nomination in 1884. Proving to be an able administrator, he prosecuted certain post office frauds with commendable vigor, and reorganized his administration with a number of excellent appointments.

Conklingite Stalwarts, eagerly seeking to take advantage of their old crony, met a frosty reception. People soon perceived that Arthur intended to make no clean sweep of the Half-Breeds in favor of the Stalwarts, though some officeholders were dropped. Members of the Conkling clique were so deeply disgusted that they almost regretted Garfield's death. Anxious citizens, many of whom had feared that the White House would become a loafing place for the old "custom-house crowd," were agreeably surprised.

Unhappily, the bullet that killed Garfield also killed Blaine's hopes. The ambitious Half-Breed, unable to get along with the Stalwart Arthur, left the Cabinet. Yet his brief term as Secretary of State had been marked by vigor and vision. "Jingo Jim" Blaine had made a somewhat bullying attempt, without success, to induce the British to give up their joint rights to a future Isthmian canal at Nicaragua or Panama, as guaranteed by the Clayton-Bulwer Treaty of 1850 (See p. 412.). Far more praiseworthy and significant was Blaine's dream of Pan-Americanism. Moving boldly, he had issued a call in 1881 to the Latin American nations for the first Pan-American Conference in Washington, but his timid successor rather rudely recalled the invitations.

Civil Service Reform and Naval Reform

Agitation for cleansing the civil service meanwhile had become irresistible. Garfield's murder, combined with noxious political scandals, increased the pressure, and Arthur commendably threw his influence behind the movement.

The Republican Party itself began to reveal unexpected enthusiasm for reform, partly because it had lost control of the House in the midterm elections of 1882. Lame-duck Republican legislators were fearful that their opponents would win the Presidency in 1884 and appoint only Democrats to office. To forestall such a disaster, they suddenly showed the zeal of death-bed penitents for a civil service law. Democrats, who had clamored for reform when there was little chance of their cutting the political pie, now cooled off; they had no desire to "freeze" Republican incumbents in their jobs. Ironically, the civil service bill as finally passed was sired by the Republicans and damned by the Democrats.

The Pendleton Act of 1883—the so-called Magna Carta of civil service reform—instituted several desirable changes. It prohibited, at least on paper, financial assessments on jobholders, including lowly scrubwomen. It established a merit system—that is, appointment to office on the basis of aptitude rather than "pull." It set up a Civil Service Commission, which was to administer open competitive examinations to applicants for posts in the *classified service*. But offices not "classified" by the President were still the footballs of politics.

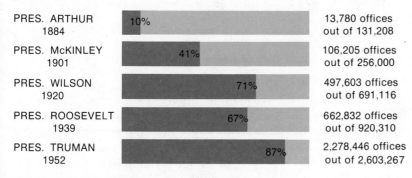

PRES. ARTHUR 1884	10%	13,780 offices out of 131,208
PRES. McKINLEY 1901	41%	106,205 offices out of 256,000
PRES. WILSON 1920	71%	497,603 offices out of 691,116
PRES. ROOSEVELT 1939	67%	662,832 offices out of 920,310
PRES. TRUMAN 1952	87%	2,278,446 offices out of 2,603,267

GROWTH OF CLASSIFIED CIVIL SERVICE
(Subject to Competitive Requirements)

U.S. Salutes Foreign Ships with Peashooters. *Harper's Weekly,* 1881

Ironically, the success of the new anti-spoilsmen law depended largely on the cooperation of a seasoned ex-spoilsman, President Arthur. Fortunately, he cooperated with vigor. By 1884 he had classified nearly 14,000 federal offices, or about 10% of the total. Succeeding Presidents added substantially to the classified group, especially after their party had been defeated and their appointees were in danger of being swept out. This practice of snatching the plums of office from the mouths of the victors led to a cynical reversal of an old slogan: "To the *vanquished* belong the spoils."

Though widely acclaimed, the Pendleton Act fell far short of achieving a thorough reform of the civil service. But it did establish the principle of merit, and it did halt the tide of spoilsmongering that had been rising since Jackson's day. More than that, it reversed the tide slightly, and later overwhelmingly. By the middle of the next century about 90% of the federal offices were classified or "blanketed" under civil service.

America's worm-eaten navy, which still carried on its rolls the pre-1812 wooden *Constitution*, was likewise in urgent need of modernization. The Civil War fleet, a collection of "floating washtubs," had been allowed to rust and rot away as the nation concentrated on internal expansion. With only two iron ships, the navy was far inferior to the iron-and-steel navies of the major European powers, and in certain categories even to that of Chile. American indifference to possible danger was almost unbelievable.

After prolonged debate, Congress in 1883 reluctantly appropriated money for four new ships—the nucleus of a modern steel navy. This was a modest beginning, but a noteworthy one. Succeeding administrations added more and stronger warships. By the time the Spanish-American War broke out in 1898, the navy ranked about fifth among world navies, and was able to give an impressive account of itself.

One good term deserves another. The achievements of Arthur were such that he fully merited a nomination "in his own right." But having angered both the Conklingites and the Blaineites, he was turned out to pasture in 1885, and the next year died of a cerebral hemorrhage.

The Blaine-Cleveland Mudslingers of 1884

Blaine's nomination in 1884, despite rumblings of opposition, was inescapable. The sparkling Maineite, blessed with almost every political asset except a reputation for honesty, was the clear choice of the Republican convention in Chicago. Reformers within the party had threatened to desert if the "Plumed Knight" were chosen, and thousands of them opposed the ticket or supported it only halfheartedly. They were sneeringly dubbed "Mugwumps"—a word of Indian derivation apparently meaning "holier than thou."

Victory-starved Democrats, encouraged by the nomination of a tainted Republican, believed that they could win with an outstanding reformer. At Chicago they turned enthusiastically to Grover Cleveland, a burly bachelor with a drooping mustache and a taste for chewing tobacco. A solid rather than a brilliant lawyer of forty-seven, he had rocketed from the mayoralty of Buffalo to the governorship of New York and the presidential nomination in three short years. The orator who placed his name before the convention lauded his courageous record as "reform governor," and added that the younger men also loved him "for the enemies he has made." Strong men make strong enemies; and Cleveland, "the unowned candidate," had made many enemies of the right kind, including the unsavory political bosses of Tammany Hall.

In high spirits the Democrats extolled their spotlessly honest candidate, "Grover the Good." At the same time they assailed the spotted Blaine, whom they represented as the "tattooed man"—tattooed with countless political dishonesties. They gleefully headlined newly unearthed letters that Blaine had penned, some of which ended with the furtive admonition "Burn this letter."

Resolute Republicans, eager to retaliate, delved deeply into the past of bachelor Cleveland. At the outset the worst they could do was to brand him a drunkard, because as a young man he had allegedly guzzled much beer. But further probing uncovered the report that he had been involved in an affair with a Buffalo widow, to whom an illegitimate son had been born, now eight years old. Although several other men had been attentive to her at the same time, Cleveland had forthrightly assumed full responsibility and had made financial provision for the unwelcome offspring.

Faithful Democrats, who had launched the campaign on such a high moral plane, were demoralized. They hurried to Cleveland and urged him to lie like a gentleman, but their ruggedly honest candidate insisted, "Tell the truth." Thereupon the Democrats, without Cleveland's sanction, desperately attempted to make something of Blaine's premarital relations with his wife. The devoted husband explained away these nasty charges with considerable plausibility.

The story circulated that Cleveland, when handed some papers reflecting on Blaine's morality, had them burned, remarking, "The other side can have a monopoly of all the dirt in this campaign."

The campaign of 1884 sank to perhaps the lowest level in American experience, as the two parties grunted and shoved for the hog trough of office. Few fundamental differences actually separated them. Even the Bloody Shirt had faded to a pale pink.* The tariff received considerable attention, as the Democrats contended for reduction and the Republicans tried to tar them with the brush of free trade. But personalities rather than principles claimed the headlines.

---

* Neither Blaine nor Cleveland had served in the Civil War. Cleveland had hired a substitute to go in his stead while he supported his widowed mother and two sisters. Blaine was the only candidate nominated by the Republicans from Grant through McKinley (1868 to 1900) who had not been a Civil War officer.

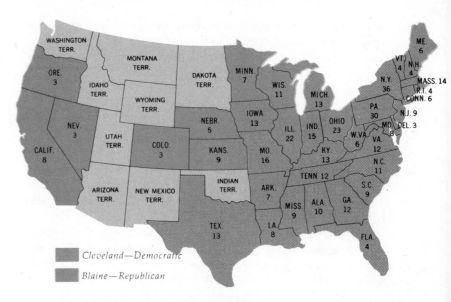

PRESIDENTIAL ELECTION OF 1884 (with electoral vote by state)

"I Want My Pa!"
Malicious anti-Cleveland
cartoon from *Puck*.

The air resounded with slogans. In the great cities enormous crowds of Democrats surged through the streets, chanting—to the rhythm of left, left, left, right, left—such froth as: "Burn, burn, burn this letter!" The Republicans replied with "No, no, no free trade" and (tauntingly) "Ma, ma, where's my pa?" From the Democrats came the defiant answer, "Gone to the White House, ha, ha, ha!"

Cleveland, who swept the Solid South, squeaked through with 219 to 182 electoral votes, and 4,874,986 to 4,851,981 popular votes. The contest hinged on the state of New York, which Blaine lost by the paper-thin plurality of 1149 votes out of 1,167,169 cast. Basically, the issue narrowed down to a choice between public dishonesty and private immorality. Blaine's shady record, which alienated the Mugwumps, was apparently the deciding factor, plus a business depression, which always handicaps the party in power.

As the campaign entered its final stench, a half-dozen or so mishaps had weakened Blaine in the pivotal state of New York. Noteworthy was the blunder of an obscure Republican clergyman, who publicly proclaimed that the Democrats were the party of "Rum, Romanism, and Rebellion"—an accusation that was especially offensive to Roman Catholic Irishmen. Blaine, who was present at the time, did not have enough presence of mind to repudiate the statement at once. Silence seemed to give consent, and the wavering Irishmen who were driven into the Cleveland camp were probably numerous enough to cost Blaine the election.

The Confederates "Capture" Washington under Cleveland

As bull-necked Cleveland solemnly took the inaugural oath in

1885—the first Democrat to do so since Buchanan twenty-eight years before—a huge question mark hung over his portly frame (5 feet 11, 270 pounds). Could the party of disunion be trusted to govern the Union? A favorite Republican allegation of these years was that although not all Democrats had been rebels, all rebels had been Democrats. In fact, the Democratic Party was widely regarded in the North as "the left wing of the new Confederate army." The Republicans professed to fear economic chaos, repudiation of the Civil War debt, assumption of the defunct Confederate debts, and the awarding of federal pensions to ex-Confederates. Finally, the Republicans suspected the Democrats of conspiring to repeal the war-born amendments—the 13th, 14th, and 15th—and to push the Negro back into bondage. One freedman came to his former owner and said that since he was going to be re-enslaved, he wanted his kind old master back.

Grave responsibilities of leadership were laid on Cleveland's broad shoulders. One of his most pressing obligations was to show that not only Democrats could be trusted but Southern Democrats as well. In fact the South, for the first time in a quarter of a century, was to enjoy a real share in the national government. Cleveland's task was made the more difficult because his practical experience had

Cleveland Holds Helm in Gale.
Thomas Nast, *Harper's Weekly,* 1885

been limited to New York politics: inflexible and ingrown, he had no broad comprehension of the political and economic forces then convulsing the country.

The Democratic Party, furthermore, was as difficult to manage as a spirited colt. It consisted of frustrated Southerners and disgruntled Northerners, liberally besprinkled with relatively recent immigrants. And Cleveland was not a suave or skillful political leader. Inclined to put his foot down rather than slide it down, he could not work well in party harness. As tactless as a mirror and as direct as a bulldozer, he was outspoken, unbending, and profanely hot-tempered.

Cleveland's Cabinet consisted mostly of obscure or unknown men: the Democrats, who had been out of office since 1861, had not made the headlines. Cleveland further narrowed the North-South chasm by appointing to his Cabinet two ex-Confederates. One of them was a general, whose elevation provoked an outraged protest from the Grand Army of the Republic (G.A.R.)—a politically potent fraternal organization of several hundred thousand Civil War veterans, predominantly Republicans. The initials G.A.R. were humorously interpreted to mean "Generally All Republicans."

As for the civil service, Cleveland was a moderate reformer who had faith in the merit system. He believed that "public officials are trustees of the people"—an expression which was shortened to read, "A public office is a public trust." Yet the federal offices were packed with long-lived Republicans, and the dislodging of some of them could hardly be avoided.

Pressures from office seekers at length became overwhelming. The Democrats, who were ravenously hungry after their twenty-four years of exile, believed that the true path to reform was to turn out Republican "rascals" and put in their own people. They even recommended ex-convicts to Cleveland who, decrying the "damned everlasting clatter for offices," retorted that "a Democratic thief is as bad as a Republican one." In the interests of party harmony, he finally turned over the task of decapitating Republicans to the First Assistant Postmaster General, tactful Adlai E. Stevenson.* "Adlai's ax" chopped off the heads of about 40,000 incumbent postmasters.

But "Old Grover" won few friends by his grudging concessions. The Mugwumps complained because he did not push reform far enough; the starving Democrats condemned his stinginess. Some of the latter even made a determined attempt to repeal the Pendleton Civil Service Act.

The President Resists Pension Panhandlers

Cleveland, ever rigidly honest, believed that the pension roll should be an honor roll. The list should contain the names of men

Cleveland Calls a Halt to Logrolling. Thomas Nast, *Harper's Weekly,* 1886

---

* Grandfather of the Democratic presidential nominee in 1952 and 1956.

who had been crippled in the service of their country, not scheming malingerers and "bloodsuckers." Cleveland's position was made especially difficult because he was a Democrat and a non-veteran, and because the Grand Army of the Republic was remobilizing for new raids on the Treasury.

Existing pension legislation contained glaring loopholes. The original law, passed in 1862 during the Civil War, made provision for the veteran and his family in the event of disability or death. But many ex-soldiers, through neglect or ignorance, failed to file their claims for service-connected disabilities until much later. The Arrears of Pensions Act of 1879, passed under President Hayes, attempted to deal fairly with these worthy ex-soldiers by granting them arrears payments from the time of their discharge to the time of filing their claims.

Back pension payments, usually involving hundreds of dollars in lump sums, attracted grafters as honey attracts flies. Dishonest pension attorneys sprang forward to ferret out able-bodied veterans and induce them to file fraudulent claims. If the hardheaded Pensions Bureau rejected such an application, the claimant might appeal to his Congressman who, mindful of the powerful G.A.R., would often introduce a special bill.

Hundreds of private pension bills were thus logrolled through Congress, and then sent to the White House. Handouts were granted to deserters, to bounty jumpers, to men who had never served, and to ex-soldiers who in later years had incurred disabilities in no way connected with war service. Cleveland, a slave to his conscience, read these bills carefully, vetoed several hundred of them, and then laboriously penned individual veto messages for Congress. On occasion he would wax sarcastic, as when referring to one man's "terrific encounter with the measles."

Despite his conscientious use of the veto, Cleveland signed hundreds of private pension bills. But he received little credit for trying to separate the needy from the greedy. His critics, predominantly of the G.A.R., accused him of having fallen victim to the "tyranny of the trivial." Pointing to the overflowing treasury, they insisted that this was no time for penny pinching at the expense of veterans—even those who claimed that their eyes had been weakened by Civil War diarrhea.

A lavish Congress attempted to add several hundred thousand new pensioners to the rolls when, in 1887, it passed the Dependent Pension Bill. This overgenerous law awarded a pension to any veteran who had served ninety days and who was now unable to earn his living. Cleveland courageously vetoed the bill; he feared that it would encourage fraud and put worthy veterans in an undesirable class. It stayed vetoed.

Cleveland heaped insult on injury when, also in 1887, he ordered

Early in his first administration Cleveland wrote to friends, "All this time, like a nightmare, this dreadful, damnable office-seeking hangs over me and surrounds me. . . . The d——d everlasting clatter for offices continues . . . and makes me feel like resigning and hell is to pay generally."

certain captured Confederate flags to be returned to the South. This conciliatory gesture was greeted with a roar of "Treason!" from Republican ex-soldiers; and the National Commander of the G.A.R. cried, "May God palsy the hand that wrote that order!" Cleveland was forced to back down when he discovered that only Congress could authorize a return of the flags. Eighteen years later, under a Republican Congress, this step was quietly taken. The passions of war had cooled, and what had once seemed disgraceful was then graceful.

Cleveland Battles for a Lower Tariff

During the Civil War the tariff schedules had been jacked up to new high levels, partly to raise revenue for the insatiable military machine. American industry, which was preponderantly Republican, had profited from this protection, and was loath to see the sheltering benefits reduced in peacetime. But the high duties continued to pile up revenue at the customhouses, and by 1881 the Treasury's annual income in excess of expenditures had mounted to an embarrassing $145,000,000. Most of the government's revenue, in those pre-income tax days, came from the tariff.

The Republican Congress in 1883 had, somewhat halfheartedly, attempted to reduce the tariff schedules. But the results of this first general revision since the Civil War were disappointing. The so-called "Mongrel Tariff," thanks to energetic lobbyists for industry, provided no real reduction and actually increased certain rates.

Grover Cleveland, the rustic Buffalo attorney, had known little about the tariff before entering the White House. But as he read up on the subject, he was much impressed by arguments for lowered barriers. Since tariffs are normally shouldered off onto the consumers by the manufacturers in the form of increased prices, Cleveland concluded that a high tariff taxed the many for the benefit of the few. He likewise perceived that a moderate tariff would lower prices to the consumer, principally by permitting more competition from foreign goods. As for protection, he concluded that perhaps the public needed protection from the giant corporations as much as the giant corporations—once "infant" industries—needed protection from low-wage foreigners.

In his determination to reduce the mounting surplus by lowering the tariff, Cleveland bluntly told Congress (December, 1887), "Our progress toward a wise conclusion will not be improved by dwelling upon the theories of protection and free trade. This savors too much of bandying epithets. It is a *condition* which confronts us, not a theory."

Swelling surpluses were clearly an evil. They withdrew money from circulation at a time when a multiplying population and an expanding industry needed more currency rather than less. Surpluses were also a standing temptation to grafters and bureaucratic vultures. The federal government is not a profit-making institution, and it should not take more money from people's pockets than necessary for legitimate expenditures. Since a tariff is an indirect tax, Cleveland

Cleveland Files Rough Edges from
Tariff. *Harper's Weekly,* 1888

believed, along with the Democratic platform, that "unnecessary
taxation is unjust taxation."

Congress could reduce the vexatious surplus in two ways. One
was to squander it on pensions and "pork-barrel bills," and thus
curry favor with veterans and other self-seeking groups. The other
was to lower the tariff—something that the big industrialists vehemently opposed.

Cleveland, who did not regard the Treasury as a grab bag, believed that the more honest course was to reduce customs duties. He
repeatedly tried to prod Congress in this direction, but he encountered only Democratic apathy and Republican hostility. His irritation

mounting, he decided to force a dramatic showdown on the tariff. He would bring the issue sensationally to the attention of the country by an appeal over the heads of the members of Congress.

In alarm, the Democratic politicians begged Cleveland not to stir up the hornet's nest of the tariff. The nation was prosperous, and if the President would only mark time, he was almost certain to be re-elected, with the other Democrats riding into office on his flowing coattails. But Cleveland spurned the flabby course. "What is the use," he insisted, "of being elected or re-elected unless you stand for something?"

An anti-Cleveland Republican newspaper, the Philadelphia *Press*, reacted violently to the President's tariff message: "A thousand thanks to President Cleveland for the bold, manly, and unequivocal avowal of his extreme free-trade purposes! And a thousand rebukes and defeats for the false, dangerous, and destructive policy which he thus frankly and unreservedly proclaims!"

Like a bombshell, Cleveland's low-tariff appeal burst upon Congress late in 1887. The annual message of the President had always been devoted to a review of the year's events, but Cleveland concentrated his fire solely on the tariff. Despite Republican charges, he did not advocate free trade at all—merely a reduction of the tariff to more manageable levels.

Cleveland succeeded admirably in forcing the issue out into the open. Democrats everywhere were profoundly depressed; Republicans were jubilant over the so-called "Free Trade Manifesto." Blaine gloated, "There's one more President for us in [tariff] protection." The British were pleased, for they had long been on a free-trade basis and they were hampered by America's high protective walls. But British approval was no asset in an anti-British United States.

Harrison Ousts "Old Grover" in 1888

Grover Cleveland was renominated at St. Louis in 1888 by the dismayed Democrats. They had no other outstanding leader; and even Cleveland's critics conceded that their best chance for victory lay with him.

The Republican convention at Chicago was less cut-and-dried. Blaine still had enthusiastic followers, many of whom shouted, "Blaine or Bust." But the aging and ailing "Plumed Knight" bowed out when he saw that he could not get a near-unanimous nomination, and that he would again be dragged in the gutter. He urged as a compromise choice Benjamin Harrison of Indiana, whom the convention finally nominated.

Harrison, with his stumpy legs, short neck, and long blond beard, was not an impressive figure (five feet six) or a commanding leader. A graceful orator, an honest Presbyterian elder, and a prosperous corporation lawyer, he had served one term in the United States Senate. He hailed from the doubtful and electorally potent state of Indiana; he had risen to the rank of brigadier general in the Civil War on the strength of meritorious combat service; and he sprang from one of the most distinguished families in American history. His grandfather was President ("Old Tippecanoe") Harrison. The grandson, "Little Ben," was joyously hailed as "Young Tippecanoe," and was pictured as wearing his grandfather's military hat. Democrats maliciously cartooned him as rattling around in the oversize martial headgear.

The campaign of 1888 was waged on a fairly high level, quite in contrast with the Blaine-Cleveland brawl four years earlier. There was some feeble flapping of the Bloody Shirt, and some slight attention to the private life of Cleveland. The "Beast of Buffalo," who had married his beautiful twenty-one-year-old ward (27 years his junior) during his second year in the White House, was now absurdly accused of beating his wife during drunken fits. But the tariff was the prime issue. Republican and Democratic propagandists flooded the country with some ten million pamphlets on the subject.

Yet the two parties shadow-boxed rather than tangled on the tariff. The Democrats advocated a tariff for needed revenue only, while their opponents extravagantly denounced "free trade." Shouting "Tippecanoe and tariff, too!" the Republicans insisted that a high tariff was needed to protect American labor, with its high wage, from the competition of "pauper Europe." They also argued with much force that "a surplus is easier to handle than a deficit."

Politicians in both camps energetically twisted the British Lion's tail. A quarrel had recently come to a head over the Canadian fisheries, and the Irish-American vote seemingly had to be cultivated by stirring up passions against England. Out in California a man claiming English birth wrote to the British minister in Washington, Sir Lionel Sackville-West, for advice on how to vote. The stupid diplomat replied, in effect, that a vote for Cleveland was a vote for England. Republicans jubilantly seized upon the indiscreet Sackville-West letter and made it a front-page sensation. The crucial Irish vote in New York, normally Democratic, began to slip away; and Cleveland was forced to bundle the "damned Englishman" off home—one of the few wobbly acts of his entire career. Crowds of gleeful Republicans surged through the streets of New York chanting:

West, West, Sackville-West,
He didn't want to go home,
But Cleveland thought it best.

Accusations that the administration favored both England and free trade proved highly embarrassing. They doubtless alienated enough Irish and other anti-English voters to damage the Democrats seriously. One Republican song hailed Cleveland as "England's favorite candidate."

The specter of a lowered tariff spurred the Republicans to frantic action. They raised a war chest of some three million dollars—the lushest yet—largely by "frying the fat" out of frightened industrialists. The money was widely used to line up corrupt "voting cattle"

President Benjamin Harrison (1833–1901), a staunch charter member of the Republican Party, was a distinguished but colorless corporation lawyer who hailed from his grandfather's town of North Bend, Ohio.

known as "repeaters" and "floaters." In Indiana, a crucial state, votes were shamefully bought for as high as $20 each.

On election day, Harrison nosed out Cleveland, 233 to 168 electoral votes. A change of 6502 votes in New York would have reversed the outcome. The popular count was 5,439,853 for Harrison to 5,540,309 for Cleveland who, though defeated, polled 100,456 more votes than the winner. Such are the curiosities of the Electoral College. Cleveland may or may not have lost the Presidency by boldly arousing the sleeping dog of the tariff issue. But the election statistics indicate that if he had raised the question six months or so earlier, and had allowed time for the campaign of education to sink in, he might have won handily.

Cleveland: Man of Granite Principle

On the night before the inauguration of Harrison, a crowd of jubilant Republicans tauntingly serenaded the darkened White House with a popular campaign ditty directed at Grover Cleveland:
Down in the cornfield
Hear that mournful sound;
All the Democrats are weeping—
Grover's in the cold, cold ground!
But Grover was to rise again and serve as President for four more years.

The first Cleveland administration on the whole was a success, even with the dragging anchor of a Republican Senate. The President displayed a rare degree of courage, honesty, and concern for the public welfare. Among other laudable achievements, he retrieved for the government some 81,000,000 acres of the public domain in the West —land that in many cases had been improperly acquired by the "cattle barons" or the railroad "octopus."

Cleveland's accomplishments did not end here. He pushed the construction of the new steel navy even more energetically than his predecessor had. His administration, as will be noted, could claim two legislative landmarks in 1887: the Dawes Act, designed to control the Indians, and the Interstate Commerce Act, designed to curb the railroads.

Some men grow in office; others swell. Cleveland grew, although it must be admitted that with his countrified background he had much room for growth. Under pressure to show that the treason-stained Democrats could be trusted to govern in the interests of the nation as a whole, he measured up to his high responsibility.

Cleveland remarked, shortly after his defeat, that he would rather have his name attached to his tactless tariff message than be President. "Perhaps I made a mistake from the party standpoint," he said, "but damn it, it was right." He demonstrated anew that doing the honest thing often wins more applause from the voters, especially in the long run, than kowtowing for votes. "Politics be damned" can be the most effective politics—and Cleveland would be heard from again.

SELECT READINGS

Politics and administration are surveyed in H. W. MORGAN, *From Hayes to McKinley: National Party Politics* (1969) and in L. D. WHITE, *The Republican Era, 1869–1901* (1958).* See also MATTHEW JOSEPH-

SON's critical *The Politicos, 1865–1896* (1938).* Grover Cleveland is sketched in H. S. MERRILL, *Bourbon Leader* (1957)* and sympathetically revealed in ALLAN NEVINS' Pulitzer-prize *Grover Cleveland* (1932). The best one-volume lives are R. G. CALDWELL, *James A. Garfield* (1931) and G. F. HOWE, *Chester A. Arthur* (1934). See also D. S. MUZZEY, *James G. Blaine* (1934). Special studies of significance are ARI HOOGENBOOM, *Outlawing the Spoils: A History of the Civil Service Reform Movement, 1865–1883* (1961)* and D. M. PLETCHER, *The Awkward Years: American Foreign Relations under Garfield and Arthur* (1962). The fullest treatment is H. J. CLANCY, *The Presidential Election of 1880* (1958). See also GLENN TUCKER, *Hancock the Superb* (1960). Also *Harvard Guide,** Pt. V.

RECENT REFERENCES

H. WAYNE MORGAN, *From Hayes to McKinley: National Party Politics, 1877–1896* (1969).

* Available in paperback.

27

Transportation, Industry, and Labor, 1865–1900

The railroads are not run for the benefit of the dear public. That cry is all nonsense. They are built for men who invest their money and expect to get a fair percentage on the same.

William H. Vanderbilt, 1882

The Iron Colt Becomes an Iron Horse

The feverish years after the Civil War witnessed an unparalleled outburst of railroad construction. When Lincoln was shot in 1865, there were only 35,000 miles of steam railways in the United States, mostly east of the Mississippi. By 1900 the figure had spurted up to 192,556, or more than that for all Europe combined.

Transcontinental railroad building was so costly and risky as to require governmental subsidies. The extension of rails into thinly peopled regions was unprofitable until the areas could be built up; and private promoters were unwilling to suffer initial losses. Congress, impressed by arguments supporting military and postal needs, began to advance liberal money loans to two favored cross-continent companies in 1862, and added enormous donations of acreage paralleling the tracks. All told, Washington rewarded the railroads with 155,504,994 acres, while the western states contributed 49,000,000 more—a total area larger than Texas.

Ordinary maps, showing in solid black ribbons the huge areas handed to the railroads, are misleading. The federal grants of land along the tracks were awarded, checkerboard fashion, in alternate sections. Furthermore, about one-sixth of the total acreage thus given away was taken back by the government because the recipients had violated the original agreements.

Loud criticisms, especially in later years, were leveled at the lavish disposal of so valuable a birthright to greedy corporations. But critics were prone to overlook the fact that the land was virtually worthless until the railroads could open it up to people and industry. Besides, the government itself received certain valuable services from the subsidized lines, including preferential rates for military purposes.

Frontier villages touched by the magic wand of the iron rail became flourishing cities; those that were bypassed often withered away as "ghost towns." Little wonder that communities fought one another for the privilege of playing host to the railroads. Ambitious towns customarily held out monetary and other attractions to the builders, who sometimes blackmailed them into contributing more generously.

Spanning the Continent with Rails

Deadlock in the 1850's over the proposed transcontinental railroad was broken when the South seceded, leaving the field to the North. In 1862, the year after the guns first spoke at Fort Sumter, Congress made provision for starting the much-talked-about line. One weighty argument for action was the urgency of bolstering the Union, already disrupted, by binding the Pacific Coast more securely to the rest of the Republic.

FEDERAL LAND GRANTS TO RAILROADS

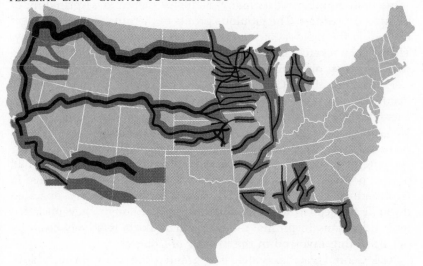

The color portions, often misleadingly shown as wide black strips, indicate areas within which the railroads *might* be given some land. The heavy black lines are in proportion to the land finally granted to the railroads (the actual checkerboard arrangement cannot be represented in so small a map). See R. S. Henry, "The Railroad Land Grant Legend in American History Texts," *Mississippi Valley Historical Review,* xxxii (1945), 180.

The *Union* Pacific Railroad—note the word "Union"—was thus commissioned by Congress to thrust westward from Omaha, Nebraska. For each mile of track constructed, the company was granted twenty square miles of land, alternating in 640-acre sections on either side of the track. For each mile the builders were also to receive a generous federal loan, ranging from $16,000 on the flat prairie land to $48,000 for mountainous country. The laying of rails began in earnest after the Civil War ended in 1865; and with juicy loans and land grants available, the "groundhog" promoters made all possible haste.

Sweaty construction gangs, containing many Irish "Paddies" (Patricks) who had fought in the Union armies, worked at a frantic pace. On one record-breaking day, a sledge-and-shovel army of some 5000 men laid ten miles of track. A favorite song was:

Then drill, my Paddies, drill;
  Drill, my heroes, drill;
Drill all day,
  No sugar in your tay,
Workin' on the U. P. Railway.

Leland Stanford (1824–1893), multi-millionaire railroad builder and director, a California governor and U.S. Senator, he founded and endowed Stanford University as a memorial to his only son, who died as a youth. Stanford University.

When hostile Indians attacked, the laborers would drop their picks and seize their rifles. Scores of men lost their lives as they built the line with one hand and fended off the whooping red men with the other. Relaxation and conviviality were provided by the tented towns, known as "hells on wheels," which sprang up at rail's end, sometimes numbering as many as 10,000 men and a sprinkling of painted prostitutes. The fabulous profits of the huge enterprise were reaped by the insiders of the Crédit Mobilier construction company. They slyly pocketed $73,000,000 for some $50,000,000 worth of breakneck construction, while bribing Congressmen to look the other way.

Rail laying at the California end was undertaken by the Central Pacific Railroad. This line pushed boldly eastward from boom-town Sacramento, over and through the towering, snow-clogged Sierra Nevada. Four farseeing men—the so-called Big Four—were the chief financial backers of the enterprise. The quartet included the heavy-set, enterprising ex-Governor Leland Stanford of California, who had useful political connections, and the burly, energetic Collis P. Huntington, an adept lobbyist. The Big Four cleverly operated through two construction companies, and although they pocketed tens of millions in profits, they kept their skirts relatively clean by not becoming involved in the bribery of Congressmen.

The Central Pacific, which was granted the same princely subsidies as the Union Pacific, had the same incentive to haste. Some 10,000 pig-tailed Chinese coolies, with picturesque basket hats and flapping pantaloons, proved to be cheap, efficient, docile, and expendable (many lost their lives in premature explosions). The rocky Sierra Nevada presented a formidable barrier; and the nerves of the

Big Four were strained when the coolies could chip only a few feet a day through rocky tunnels, while the Union Pacific was galloping westward across the plains.

A "wedding of the rails" was finally consummated near Ogden, Utah, in 1869, as two locomotives kissed cowcatchers. The colorful ceremony included the breaking of champagne bottles and the driving of a last ceremonial (golden) spike, with Governor Stanford clumsily wielding a silver sledgehammer.* In all, the Union Pacific built 1086 miles; the Central Pacific, 689.

Completion of the transcontinental line—a magnificent engineering feat for that day—was one of America's most impressive peacetime undertakings. It spiked the West Coast more firmly to the Union, and foreshadowed a flourishing trade with the Orient. It penetrated the arid barrier of the deserts, while paving the way for the phenomenal growth of the Great West. Men compared this electrifying achievement with the Declaration of Independence and the emancipation of the slaves; jubilant Philadelphians again rang the cracked bell of Independence Hall.

Binding the Country with Railroad Ties

With the westward trail now blazed, four other transcontinental lines were completed before the century's end. None of them secured monetary loans from the federal government, as did the Union Pacific and the Central Pacific. But all of them, except the Great Northern, received generous grants of land.

* The spike was promptly removed and is now exhibited at the Stanford University Museum. There were two other gold ceremonial spikes.

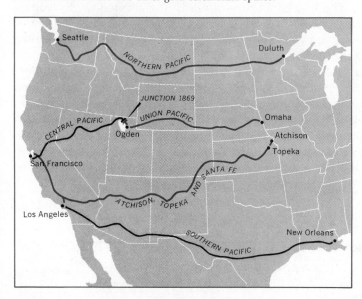

EARLY PACIFIC RAILWAY LINES

The Northern Pacific Railroad, stretching from Lake Superior to Puget Sound, reached its terminus in 1883. On this gala occasion, builder Henry Villard, the German-born journalist-railroad man, dispatched over it his "Gold Spike Special," loaded with notables.

Two other lines paralleled to some extent in New Mexico and California. One—the Atchison, Topeka, and Santa Fe—stretching through the Southwestern deserts to California, was completed in 1884. The other, the Southern Pacific, ribboned from New Orleans to San Francisco, and was consolidated in the same year. Two of the Big Four of Central Pacific fame—Huntington and Stanford—had a large hand in the construction and exploitation of the new line (with which the Central Pacific was later merged). The South finally won its direct route to the West Coast.

The last spike of the last of the five transcontinental railroads of the 19th Century was hammered home in 1893. The Great Northern, which ran from Duluth to Seattle north of the Northern Pacific, was the creation of a far-visioned Canadian-American, James J. Hill, a bear-like man who was probably the greatest railroad builder of all. Endowed with a high sense of public duty, he perceived that the prosperity of his railroad depended on the prosperity of the area that it served. He ran agricultural demonstration trains through the "Hill Country," and imported from England blooded bulls, which he distributed to the farmers. His enterprise was so soundly organized that it rode through later financial storms with flying colors.

Yet the romance of the rails was not without its sordid side. Much of the early construction was dangerously hasty and flimsy. A main object of subsidy chasers seemed to be to throw down any kind of line so as to get the lavish federal bounties, and then go back and rebuild later. The breathless pace of rail laying also led to extravagant costs. One result was overcapitalization or "stock watering"—that is, the marketing of two or three times more stock than was represented by the physical value of the railroad.*

In 1892, General Weaver, nominee of the Populists, wrote regarding the railroad magnates: "In their delirium of greed the managers of our transportation systems disregard both private right and the public welfare. Today they will combine and bankrupt their weak rivals, and by the expenditure of a trifling sum possess themselves of properties which cost the outlay of millions. Tomorrow they will capitalize their booty for five times the cost, issue their bonds, and proceed to levy tariffs upon the people to pay dividends upon the fraud."

Pioneer builders were often guilty of gross overoptimism. Avidly seeking land bounties, and pushing into areas that lacked enough potential population to support a railroad, they sometimes laid down rails that led "from nowhere to nothing." When prosperity failed to smile upon their coming, they went into bankruptcy, carrying down with them the savings of trusting investors. Many of the large railroads in the post-Civil War decades passed through bankruptcies, mergers, or reorganizations.

Railroad Consolidation and Mechanization

The success of the Western lines was facilitated by welding to-

---

* "Stock watering" originally referred to the practice of making cattle thirsty by feeding them salt, and then having them bloat themselves with water before they were weighed in for sale.

gether and expanding the older Eastern networks, notably the New York Central. The moving genius in this enterprise was "Commodore" Cornelius Vanderbilt—burly, boisterous, white-whiskered. Having made his millions in steamboating, he daringly turned, in his late sixties, to a new career in railroading. Though ill-educated, ungrammatical, coarse, and ruthless, he was clear-visioned. Offering superior service at lower rates, he amassed a fortune of $100,000,000. His name is perhaps best remembered through his contribution of $1,000,000 to the founding of Vanderbilt University in Tennessee.

Two significant new improvements proved a boon to the railroads. One was the steel rail, which Vanderbilt helped popularize when he replaced the old iron tracks of the New York Central with the tougher metal. Steel was safer and more economical because it could bear a heavier load. A standard gauge of track width likewise came into wide use during the post-war years, thus eliminating the expense and inconvenience of numerous changes from one line to another.

Other refinements played a vital role in railroading. The Westinghouse air brake, widely adopted in the 1870's, was a marvelous contribution to efficiency and safety. The Pullman Palace Cars, advertised as "gorgeous traveling hotels," were introduced on a considerable scale in the 1860's. Alarmists condemned them as "wheeled torture chambers" and potential funeral pyres, for the wooden cars were equipped with swaying kerosene lamps. Appalling accidents continued to be an almost daily tragedy, despite safety devices like the telegraph, double-tracking, and (later) the block signal.

Cornelius Vanderbilt (1794–1877) established a shipping-land transit line across Nicaragua, in response to the California gold rush. In 1873 he was the first to connect New York and Chicago by rail.

Revolution by Railways

Metallic fingers of the railroads touched intimately countless phases of American life. For the first time a sprawling nation became united in a physical sense, bound together with ribs of iron and steel.

More than any other single agency, the railroad network spurred the amazing industrialization of the post-Civil War years. Puffing locomotives opened fresh markets for manufactured goods, and sped raw materials to the factory. The forging of the rails themselves provided the largest single backlog for the adolescent steel industry.

The screeching Iron Horse likewise stimulated mining and agriculture, especially in the West. It took the farmer out to his land, carried the fruits of his toil to market, and brought him his manufactured necessities. Clusters of farm settlements paralleled the railroads, just as they earlier had the rivers.

Railways boomed the cities, and played a leading role in the great cityward movement of the last decades of the century. The iron monsters could feed enormous concentrations of people, and at the same time insure them a livelihood by providing raw materials and markets.

Railroad companies also stimulated the mighty stream of immigration. Seeking settlers to whom their land grants might be sold at a profit, they advertised seductively in Europe, and sometimes offered to transport the newcomers free to their farms.

Finally, the railroad, more than any other single factor, was the maker of millionaires. A raw new aristocracy, consisting of "lords of the rail," replaced the old Southern "lords of the lash." The multi-webbed lines became the playthings of Wall Street; and colossal wealth was amassed by stock speculators and railroad wreckers like "Jubilee Jim" Fisk and the pious rascal "Uncle Daniel" Drew. As the Benéts have said,

He toiled not, neither did he spin,
*But how he raked the dollars in!**

Mightier millions were made less sensationally by the Vanderbilts, the Hills, and other empire builders.

Wrongdoing in Railroading

Corruption lurks nearby when fabulous fortunes can be amassed overnight. The generous loans and bounties, whether granted by federal or local authorities, led inevitably to the bribery of legislators and to other evil practices, most notoriously in the case of the Crédit Mobilier.

Some of the arrogant "railroad barons" felt no obligation whatever to the public. Regarding their railroads as purely private preserves, they resented outside interference. "Can't I do what I want with my own?" was a common query. A heady sense of power replaced a sobering sense of responsibility. Crusty old Cornelius Vanderbilt of the New York Central, when told that the law stood in his way, reportedly burst out: "Law! What do I care about the law? Hain't I got the power?"† His son, William H. Vanderbilt, when asked in 1883 about the discontinuance of a fast mail train, is said to have snorted, "The public be damned!"

Some of the railroad kings were virtually industrial monarchs. As manipulators of an unprecedented natural monopoly, they exercised more direct control over the lives of more people than did the President of the United States—and their term was not limited to four years. Yet giants like Vanderbilt and Hill did serve a useful function by bringing order out of chaos, and by otherwise improving transportation service.

As the decade of the 1880's lengthened, the long-suffering public

A Rich and Arrogant William H. Vanderbilt. New York *Daily Graphic*

* Rosemary and Stephen Vincent Benét, *A Book of Americans* (Rinehart and Company, copyright 1933), p. 95. Reprinted by permission.

† "I won't sue you," Vanderbilt reportedly wrote some associates, "for the law is too slow. I'll ruin you."

began to rebel against railroad "robber-baronism." Many of the money-hungry railway kings would put their heads together and resort to the practice of pooling—that is, raising rates in a given area by secret agreement, and then pooling or sharing the profits. Other rail barons granted secret rebates or "kickbacks" to powerful shippers. Some lines would discriminate in rates and services against their enemies. Others would slash their rates on competing lines, and make up their losses on non-competing lines, where they might charge more for a "short haul" than for a long one.

Railroad moguls, moreover, were adept in protecting their privileged position. They would issue free passes to journalists, legislators, and other public men. They would bribe judges and legislatures, maintain powerful lobbies, and elect their own "creatures" to high office. They would also contribute freely to the campaign funds of "friendly" politicians, who in turn would support the "railroad rascals."

Extortionate rates were the chief complaint against the railroads. Charging "all that the traffic would bear," the companies had the farmer at their mercy, especially where rivers and canals did not offer alternate routes. A difference of only a few cents a bushel in production costs might spell the difference between relative prosperity and crushing indebtedness. In some communities a man did not even dare to go into private business without the "permission" of the railroad. The railway magnates, in their turn, argued that they had to pay dividends on their stock—often heavily "watered"—and hence had to charge high rates.

Charles F. Adams, a high-minded railroad man, testified in 1885: "The pass system is an outrage. There is no reason whatever why anyone should be carried free over a railroad any more than why he should be boarded and lodged free at a hotel, drive free in public carriages, or order goods without paying for them in shops. Yet, and especially in the West, things are getting to such a pass that no man who has money, or official position, or influence . . . thinks he ought to pay anything for riding on a railroad."

Government Bridles the Iron Horse

It was not healthy that so many should be at the mercy of so few. Impoverished farmers, especially in the Middle West, began to wonder if the nation had not escaped from the slavery power only to fall into the hands of the money power, as represented by the railroad plutocracy.

But the American people, though quick to respond to political injustice, were slow to combat economic injustice. Dedicated to free enterprise and to the principle that competition is the soul of trade, they cherished a traditionally keen pride in progress. They remembered that Jefferson's ideals were hostile to governmental interference with business. Above all, there shimmered the "American dream": the hope that in a catch-as-catch-can economic system anyone might become a millionaire.

The depression that followed the Panic of 1873 goaded the embattled farmers into organized protest. Their efforts were especially vigorous in the Middle West where, as will be noted, they launched the Granger movement (Patrons of Husbandry). In response to such pressures the various state legislatures attempted to regulate the railroad monopoly, and in Illinois the legislators achieved considerable initial success. The feeling was growing that either the state had to control the railroads or the railroads would one day control the state.

State railway restrictions suffered a severe setback in 1886, in the famed Wabash case. The Supreme Court in Washington decreed that the individual state, while free to control commerce solely within its borders, could not regulate railroad traffic moving in interstate commerce. Under the Constitution such action was reserved solely for Congress (see Art. I, Sec. VIII, para. 3). Foes of railroad monopoly had long been urging federal control, and the whole explosive issue was now tossed into the legislative mill in Washington.

After heated debate, Congress passed the epochal Interstate Commerce Act of 1887. It specifically prohibited such vicious practices as rebates and the pooling of profits. It required the railroad company to publish its rates. It decreed that there should not be a higher charge for a short haul than for a long haul, and forbade unfair discrimination against shipments or shippers. Finally, it set up the Interstate Commerce Commission (I.C.C.) to enforce and administer the new legislation.

Results were disappointing. The law designed to corral the mechanical monsters did not greatly alarm many operators, and was even welcomed by those eager to end cutthroat tactics. Some railroad stocks actually rose after the passage of the act. Moreover, the law displayed only toothless gums, as is so often true of "first" legislation. The courts further weakened possible control by ruling that the Interstate Commerce Commission had no power to fix rates and make other regulations. All this lay in the lap of the future.

Uncle Sam's Wild West Show. The new Interstate Commerce Commission cautiously sets about lassoing refractory railroads under Uncle Sam's watchful eye. *Harper's Weekly,* 1887

But the Interstate Commerce Act of 1887, though undeniably flabby and extravagantly overpraised, ranks as a red-letter law. It was the first large-scale attempt by Washington to regulate any kind of private business in the interests of society at large. It was the curtain raiser for more effective railroad legislation later, in that it inscribed on the statute books the principle of federal control. It foreshadowed the doom of completely rugged individualism in industry, in that it served full notice that America was no longer to be the happy hunting ground of the privileged few, at the expense of the underprivileged many.

Miracles of Mechanization

Post-war industrial expansion, partly a child of the railroad network, rapidly began to assume gigantic proportions. When Lincoln was elected in 1860, the Republic ranked only fourth among the manufacturing nations of the world. By 1894 it had spurted into first place; and it has never relinquished that leadership. Why the sudden upsurge?

Liquid capital, previously scarce, was now becoming abundant. The word "millionaire" had not been coined until the 1840's, and in 1861 only a handful of men were in this class. But the Civil War, partly through profiteering, created immense fortunes; and these accumulations could now be combined with the customary borrowings from foreign capitalists.

The amazing natural resources of the nation were now about to be fully exploited, including coal, oil, and iron. For example, the Minnesota–Lake Superior region, which had yielded some iron ore by the 1850's, contributed the incredibly rich Mesabi range by the 1890's. This priceless bonanza, where mountains of red-rusted ore could be scooped up by steam shovels, ultimately became a cornerstone of a vast steel empire.

Unskilled labor, both home-grown and imported, was now cheap and plentiful. Steel, the keystone industry, came to be based largely on the sweat of low-priced immigrant labor, working in two twelve-hour shifts, seven days a week.

American ingenuity at the same time played a vital role in the Second American Industrial Revolution. Techniques of mass production, pioneered by Eli Whitney, were being perfected by the Captains of Industry. American inventiveness flowered luxuriantly in the postwar years: between 1860 and 1890 some 440,000 patents were issued. Business operations were facilitated by the cash register, the stock ticker, and Christopher Sholes' typewriter ("literary piano"), which brought home-confined women into industry. Urbanization was speeded by the refrigerator car, the electric dynamo, and F. J.

Regarding the exploitation of immigrant labor, Ralph W. Emerson wrote in 1860: "The German and Irish millions, like the Negro, have a great deal of guano in their destiny. They are ferried over the Atlantic, and carted over America, to ditch and to drudge, to make corn cheap, and then to lie down prematurely to make a spot of green grass on the prairie."

Sprague's electric railway, which displaced animal-drawn cars. A New Orleans mass meeting proclaimed:

Lincoln Set the Negroes Free!
Sprague Has Set the Mule Free!
The Long-Eared Mule No More Shall Adorn Our Streets.

One of the most ingenious inventions was the telephone, introduced by Alexander Graham Bell in 1876. A teacher of the deaf who was given a dead man's ear to experiment with, he remarked that if he could make the dumb talk, he could make iron speak. America was speedily turned into a nation of "telephoniacs," as a gigantic system was erected on his invention. The social impact of this instrument was further revealed when an additional army of "number please" ladies was attracted from the home into industry. Telephone boys were at first employed at switchboards but their profanity shocked patrons.

The most versatile inventor of all was Thomas A. Edison, who as a youth had been considered so dull-witted that he was taken out of school. This "Wizard of the Wires" ran a veritable invention factory in New Jersey. He is perhaps best known for his perfection in 1879 of the electric light, which he unveiled after trying some six thousand filaments. So deaf that he was not easily distracted, he displayed sleepless energy and a flair for practical money-making schemes rather than pure science. He invented, perfected, or did useful exploratory work on the phonograph, the mimeograph, the dictaphone, and the moving picture. "Genius," he said, "is one percent inspiration and ninety-nine percent perspiration."

Mr. Edison has perfected the Phonograph

This is the Instrument

THE EDISON "CONCERT" PHONOGRAPH

Advertisement of the new Edison phonograph from *Harper's Weekly.*

The Trust Titan Emerges

Expanding markets and daring leadership further stimulated industrialization. The rapid growth of population created millions of new consumers, as industrial giants stepped forward to exploit them. Men like Andrew Carnegie, the steel king, J. Pierpont Morgan, the Bankers' Banker, and John D. Rockefeller, the oil baron, to name only three, were sensationally successful in developing important new techniques.

A breath-taking expansion of industry after the Civil War was partly sparked by the perfecting of the trust. This innocent-appearing device was designed to control a large share of the market for some one commodity—for example, petroleum. The stockholders in various smaller oil companies would assign their stock to the board of directors of the *trust*. This board, acting as *trustees* for the stockholders, would pay them dividends from the profits of the consolidated enterprise. "Let us prey" was said to be the unwritten motto.

The monopolistic trust enjoyed immense advantages. These were especially striking when compared with the earlier types of business, all of which had been individually owned or operated as small partnerships or corporations. Like ordinary corporations, the trust was not only permanent but it limited the financial liability of its stockholders. In addition, its great size enabled it to enjoy the money-saving techniques of mass production, and hence to market cheaply, if it chose, a high-quality product. It could limit production, fix prices, and extort favorable railroad rates. So effective was the new colossus that it was often able to drive weaker competitors to the wall and achieve monopoly or near-monopoly. Yet the trust, despite its ruthlessness, played a crucial role in the emergence of the industrialized new America.

The Supremacy of Steel

"Steel is king!" might well have been the exultant war cry of the new industrialized generation. The mighty metal ultimately held together the new steel civilization, from skyscrapers to coal scuttles, while providing it with food, shelter, and transportation.

Now taken for granted, steel was a scarce commodity in the wood-and-brick America of Abraham Lincoln. Considerable iron went into railroad rails and bridges, but steel was expensive and was used largely for products like cutlery. The early Iron Horse snorted exclusively over iron rails; and when in the 1870's "Commodore" Vanderbilt of the New York Central began to use steel rails, he was forced to import them from England.

Yet within an amazing twenty years the United States had outdistanced all foreign competitors, and was pouring out more than one-third of the world's supply of steel. By 1900 the Americans were pouring as much as England and Germany combined. The nation's emergence as an industrial power was hardly less spectacular than its later emergence as a major political and military power.

Bessemer Steel Converter. Courtesy of Bethlehem Steel Co.

What wrought the transformation? Chiefly the invention in the 1850's of a method of making cheap steel—the Bessemer process. It was named after a derided British inventor, although an American had stumbled on it a few years earlier. William Kelly, a Kentucky manufacturer of iron kettles, discovered that cold air blown on red-hot iron caused the metal to become white-hot by igniting the carbon and thus eliminating impurities. He tried to apply the new "air boiling" technique to his own product, but his customers decried "Kelly's fool steel" and his business declined. Gradually the Bessemer-Kelly process won acceptance, and these two "crazy men" ultimately made possible the present steel civilization.

A revolutionary steel-fabricating process was not the whole story. America was one of the few places in the world where one could find relatively close together abundant coal for fuel, rich iron ore for smelting, and other essential ingredients for making steel. The nation also boasted an abundant labor supply, guided by industrial know-how of a high order. The stage was set for miracles of production.

Carnegie and Other Men of Steel

Kingpin among steelmasters was Andrew Carnegie, an under-sized, charming Scotsman. As a tow-headed lad, he was brought to America by his impoverished parents in 1848, and got a job as a bobbin boy at $1.20 a week. Mounting the ladder of success so fast that he almost scorched the rungs, he forged ahead by working hard, doing the extra chore, cheerfully assuming responsibility, and smoothly cultivating influential people.

After accumulating some capital, Carnegie entered the steel business in the Pittsburgh area. A gifted organizer and administrator, he achieved success by picking high-class associates and by eliminating many of the middlemen. Although inclined to be tough-fisted in business, he was not a monopolist and disliked monopolistic trusts. His remarkable organization was a partnership which involved, at its maximum, about forty "Pittsburgh millionaires." By 1900 Carnegie was producing one-fourth of the nation's Bessemer steel, and the partners were dividing profits of $40,000,000 a year, with the "Napo-

Carnegie Presents the Trust as a "Trustworthy" Beast. *Harper's Weekly.*

leon of the Smokestacks" himself receiving a cool $25,000,000. These were the pre-income-tax days, when millionaires were really rich and profits represented take-home pay.

Into the picture now stepped the financial giant of the age, J. Pierpont Morgan. "Jupiter" Morgan had made a legendary reputation for himself and his Wall Street banking house by financing the reorganization of railroads, insurance companies, and banks. An impressive figure of a man, with massive shoulders, shaggy brows, piercing eyes, and a bulbous, acne-cursed red nose, he had established an enviable reputation for integrity. He did not believe that "money power" was dangerous, except when in dangerous hands—and he did not regard his hands as dangerous.

The force of circumstances brought Morgan and Carnegie into collision. By 1900 the canny little Scotsman, weary of turning steel into gold, was eager to sell his holdings. Morgan had meanwhile plunged heavily into the manufacture of steel pipe tubing. Carnegie, cleverly threatening to invade the same business, was ready to ruin his rival if he did not receive his price. The steelmaster's agents haggled with the imperious Morgan for eight agonizing hours, and the financier finally agreed to buy out Carnegie for over $400,000,000. Fearing that he would die "disgraced" with so much money, Carnegie dedicated the remaining years of his life to giving it away for public libraries, pensions for professors, and other philanthropic purposes—in all disposing of about $350,000,000.

Morgan moved rapidly to expand his new industrial empire. He took the Carnegie holdings, added others, "watered" the stock liberally, and in 1901 launched the enlarged United States Steel Corporation. Capitalized at $1,400,000,000, it was America's first billion-dollar corporation—a larger sum than the total estimated wealth of the nation in 1800. The Industrial Revolution, with its hot Bessemer breath, had at last come into its own.

Carnegie wrote in 1889: "The man who dies leaving behind him millions of available wealth, which was his to administer during life, will pass away 'unwept, unhonored, and unsung,' no matter to what uses he leaves the dross which he cannot take with him. Of such as these the public verdict will then be: 'The man who dies thus rich dies disgraced.'"

Rockefeller Grows an American Beauty Rose

A sudden emergence of the oil industry was one of the most striking developments of the years during and after the Civil War. Traces of oil found on streams had earlier been bottled for back-rub and other patent medicines, but not until 1859 did the first well in Pennsylvania—"Drake's Folly"—pour out its liquid "black gold." Almost overnight an industry was born which was to take more wealth from the earth—and more useful wealth at that—than all of the gold extracted by the Forty-Niners and their Western successors. The soaring popularity of kerosene as an illuminant for lamps struck a crippling blow at the old whale-oil business.

John D. Rockefeller—lanky, shrewd, ambitious, abstemious (he neither drank, smoked, nor swore)—came to dominate the oil industry. Born to a family of precarious income, he became a success-

Rockefeller Nips Competing Buds.
Literary Digest, 1905

ful businessman at age nineteen. One upward stride led to another, and in 1870 he organized the Standard Oil Company of Ohio, nucleus of the great trust formed in 1882. Locating his refineries in Cleveland, he sought to eliminate the middleman and squeeze out competitors.

Pious and parsimonious, Rockefeller flourished in an era of completely free enterprise. So-called piratical practices were employed by "corsairs of finance," and business ethics were distressingly low. Rockefeller, operating "just to the windward of the law," pursued a policy of rule or ruin. "Sell all the oil that is sold in your district" was the hard-boiled order that went out to his local agents.

Rockefeller—"Reckafellow," Carnegie once called him—was not inclined to mercy. He ironhandedly ruined competitors by cutting prices until his victim went bankrupt or sold out, whereupon higher prices would be likely to return. Rockefeller's son later said that the giant American Beauty rose could be produced "only by sacrificing the early buds that grow up around it." His father pinched off the small buds with complete ruthlessness. Employing spies and extorting secret rebates from the railroads, he even forced the lines to pay him rebates on the freight bills of his competitors! Nelson Rockefeller later remarked that his grandfather broke no laws but "a lot of laws were passed because of him."

The Standard Oil Company was undeniably heartless, but its rivals were no less so in this age of dog-eat-dog competition. A kind of socioeconomic savagery prevailed in the jungle world of big business where, in certain areas, only the fittest survived. By 1877 Rockefeller controlled 95% of all the oil refineries in the country, and could raise or lower prices at will. His profits were enormous: in 1891 Standard Oil paid 12% dividends.

On the other side of the ledger, Rockefeller's oil monopoly did turn out a superior product at a relatively cheap price. It achieved important economies, both at home and abroad, by its large-scale methods of production and distribution. This, in truth, was the tale of the other trusts as well. The efficient use of expensive machinery called for bigness, and consolidation proved more profitable than ruinous price wars.

Other trusts blossomed along with the American Beauty of oil. These included the Sugar Trust, the Tobacco Trust, the Leather Trust, and the Harvester Trust, which amalgamated some two hundred competitors. The meat industry arose on the backs of bawling Western herds, and Meat Kings like Gustavus F. Swift and Philip Armour took their place among the new royalty. Wealth was coming to dominate commonwealth.

Government Tackles the Trust Evil

Monstrous trusts, with their thirst for power, had neither souls nor social consciences. Rockefeller, who believed in the Divine Right of Monopoly, wielded more influence over more people than many kings. "God gave it to me," he is said to have remarked of his princely fortune. Many an industrial tycoon, defying state control, became a kind of private state within a public state. The ideal of "social stewardship" was still a stranger.

Plutocracy, like the earlier slavocracy, took its stand firmly on the Constitution. The clause which gave Congress sole jurisdiction over interstate commerce was a godsend to the monopolists; their high-priced lawyers used it time and again to thwart controls by the state legislatures. Giant trusts likewise sought refuge behind the 14th Amendment, which had been originally designed to protect the rights of the ex-slaves as persons. The courts ingeniously interpreted a corporation to be a legal "person," and decreed that as such it could not be deprived of its property by a state without "due process of law" (see Art. XIV, para. 1). There is some highly questionable evidence that clever corporation lawyers, when the 14th Amendment was being fashioned in 1866, deliberately inserted this loophole.

Great industrialists likewise sought to incorporate in "easy states," like New Jersey, where the restrictions on Big Business were mild or nonexistent. For example, the Southern Pacific Railroad, with much of its trackage in California, was incorporated in Kentucky.

The growing concentration of capital, through trusts and other combines, was astounding. By 1890 the value of all property in the United States was estimated at $65,000,000,000, of which $25,000,000,000 represented the assets of corporations. Cynics sneered that U.S.A. meant United Syndicates of America.

At long last, the masses of the people began to mobilize against monopoly. They first tried to control the trusts through state legislation, as they had earlier attempted to curb the railroads. Failing here, as before, they were forced to appeal to Congress. After prolonged pulling and hauling, the Sherman Anti-Trust Law of 1890 was finally signed into law.

The Sherman Act flatly forbade combinations in restraint of trade, without any distinction between "good" trusts and "bad" trusts. Bigness, not badness, was the sin. The law proved ineffective, largely because it had only baby teeth or no teeth at all, and because it contained legal loopholes through which clever corporation lawyers could wriggle. But the new act was unexpectedly effective in one respect. Contrary to its original intent, it was used to curb labor unions or labor combinations which were deemed to be restraining trade.

Early prosecutions of the trusts by the Justice Department under the Sherman Act of 1890, as it turned out, were neither vigorous nor successful. The decisions in seven of the first eight cases presented by the Attorney General were adverse to the government. More new trusts were formed in the 1890's under President McKinley than dur-

Industrial millionaires were condemned in the Populist Platform of 1892: "The fruits of the toil of millions are boldly stolen to build up colossal fortunes for a few . . . and the possessors of these, in turn despise the Republic and endanger liberty. From the same prolific womb of governmental injustice we breed the two great classes—tramps and millionaires."

ing any other like period. Not until 1914 were the paper jaws of the Sherman Act fitted with reasonably sharp teeth. Until then, there was some question whether the government would control the trusts or the trusts the government.

But the iron grip of monopolistic corporations was being threatened. A revolutionary new principle had been written into the law books by the Sherman Anti-Trust Act of 1890, as well as by the Interstate Commerce Act of 1887. Private greed must henceforth be subordinated to public need.

The New Birth of the New (Industrial) South

Agriculture in the post-war South was meanwhile gradually struggling back to its maimed feet. Much of the cotton was grown by Negro and white sharecroppers, who farmed land, often with one mule, for a share of the crop. Many of these unfortunate creatures, slipping into debt, rapidly became enchained to the soil as virtual peons. The cotton industry as a whole received a welcome uplift when the by-products of cotton, notably cottonseed oil, were first marketed profitably on a wholesale basis.

Successful machine production of cigarettes, beginning in the 1880's, is associated with the colorful figure of James Buchanan Duke. Famous for his "Duke's Mixture," he operated from Durham, North Carolina, the home of roll-your-own Bull Durham, and later of Chesterfields. Such distinguished literary figures as Tennyson, Carlyle, and Lowell were all Bull Durham addicts. Duke became president of the monopolistic American Tobacco Company, and many of his millions went eventually for the endowment of Duke University, near Durham.

Henry Grady, the Atlanta editor, urged the New South to industrialize. In a Boston speech in 1889 he described the burial in Georgia of a Confederate veteran: "The South didn't furnish a thing on earth for that funeral but the corpse and the hole in the ground. . . . They buried him in a New York coat and a Boston pair of shoes and a pair of breeches from Chicago and a shirt from Cincinnati, leaving him nothing to carry into the next world with him to remind him of the country in which he lived, and for which he fought for four years, but the chill of blood in his veins and the marrow in his bones."

Cotton manufacturing in the South, earlier established on a small-ish scale, shot ahead in the 1880's. Southerners had long resented having to ship their fiber to New England, and their cry was "Bring the mills to the cotton." The South had the raw product, water power, cheap land, cheap labor, a mild climate, low taxes, seaports, and railroads. The two chief drawbacks were the scarcity of capital and the lack of know-how.

Smokestacks in increasing numbers began to prick the Southern skyline. As capital was amassed—much of it from the North—new textile mills were erected, and many of the older New England factories closed up shop and moved closer to the cotton. The iron industry also secured a firm footing, particularly in besmogged Birmingham, "the Pittsburgh of the South," which enjoyed close proximity to both coal and iron ore.

Diversification of industry was no doubt a boon to the South. Poor whites who were drawn into the sordid villages near the factories lived in no bed of roses, but most of them were probably better off

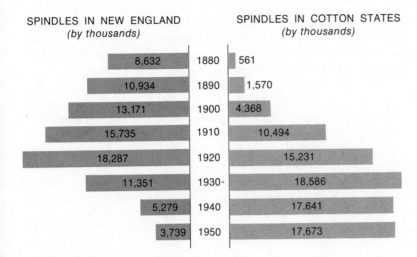

SPINDLES IN NEW ENGLAND (by thousands)		SPINDLES IN COTTON STATES (by thousands)
8,632	1880	561
10,934	1890	1,570
13,171	1900	4,368
15,735	1910	10,494
18,287	1920	15,231
11,351	1930	18,586
5,279	1940	17,641
3,739	1950	17,673

COTTON MANUFACTURING MOVES SOUTH

than when they had eked out an existence in shacks on hookworm-ridden plots. For weal or woe, the vibration of the loom, the screech of the saw, the roar of the furnace, and the thunder of the locomotive proclaimed that the New South—the Industrialized South—had arrived.

The Impact of the New Industrial Revolution on America

Economic miracles wrought during the decades after the Civil War enormously increased the wealth of the Republic. The standard of living rose sharply, and the well-fed American worker enjoyed more physical comforts than his co-workers in any other powerful nation. Urban centers mushroomed as the insatiable factories demanded more American labor, and as immigrants poured into the vacuums created by new jobs.

Early Jeffersonian ideals were withering before the smudgy blasts from the smokestacks. As agriculture declined in relation to manufacturing, America could no longer aspire to be a nation of small freehold farms. Jefferson's concepts of free enterprise, with neither help nor hindrance from Washington, were being thrown out the factory window. Tariffs had already provided assistance, and the long arm of federal authority was now committed to decades of corporation curbing and "trust busting."

Probably no single group was more profoundly affected by the new Industrial Age than women. Sucked into industry by recent inventions, chiefly the typewriter and the telephone switchboard, millions of stenographers and "hello girls" achieved a new economic and social independence. Female careers also meant delayed marriages and smaller families.

The clattering Machine Age likewise accentuated class divisions.

Cartoonist Thomas Nast hails the new industrialized South as "The Queen of Industry," in *Harper's Weekly*, 1882.

"Industrial buccaneers" flaunted bloated fortunes, while their rags-to-riches spouses displayed glittering diamonds. Such extravagances evoked bitter criticism. Some of it was envious but much of it rose from the small and increasingly vocal group of socialists and other radicals, many of whom were recent European immigrants. The existence of an oligarchy of money was amply demonstrated by the fact that by 1900 about one-tenth of the people owned and controlled nine-tenths of the nation's wealth.

Finally, strong pressures for foreign trade developed as the tireless machine threatened to flood the domestic market. American products radiated out all over the world—notably the five-gallon kerosene can of the Standard Oil Company. The flag follows trade, and empire tends to follow the flag—a harsh lesson that America was soon to learn.

In Unions There Is Strength

Sweat of the laborer lubricated the vast new industrial machine. Yet the wageworker did not share proportionately with either the employers or society the benefits of the Age of Big Business.

The workingman, suggestive of the Roman galley slave, was becoming a lever-puller in a giant mechanism. His originality and creativeness were being stifled, and less value than ever before was being placed on manual skills. Before the Civil War he might have toiled in a small plant, whose owner hailed him in the morning by his first name and inquired after his wife's gallstones. But now the factory hand was employed by a corporation—depersonalized, bodiless, soulless, and often conscienceless. The directors knew him not; and in fairness to their stockholders they did not feel that they could engage in large-scale private philanthropy.

As new machines were invented, many of the regular employees were thrown out of work. In the long run more jobs were created than destroyed, but in the short run the manual worker was often hard hit. Labor is the most perishable of all commodities. A pair of shoes unsold today may be sold tomorrow, but a day's labor not sold today is lost forever.

A glutted labor market, moreover, severely handicapped the wage earners. The vast new railroad network could shuttle unemployed workers, including Negroes and immigrants, into areas where wages were high, and thus beat standards down. The inpouring Europeans further worsened conditions. During the 1880's and 1890's and later, the labor market had to absorb several hundred thousand unskilled workers a year.

Individual laborers were powerless to battle singlehandedly against giant industry. Forced to organize and fight for basic rights, they found the dice heavily loaded against them. The corporation could dispense with the individual worker much more easily than the worker could dispense with the corporation. The employer could pool vast wealth through thousands of stockholders, retain high-priced lawyers, buy up the local press, and put pressure on the politicians. He could import strikebreakers ("scabs") and employ thugs to beat up labor organizers. In 1886 Jay Gould reputedly boasted, "I can hire one-half of the working class to kill the other half."

Corporations had still other weapons in their arsenals. They could call upon the federal courts—presided over by well-fed and conservative judges—to issue injunctions ordering the strikers to cease striking. If defiance and disorders ensued, the company could request the state and federal authorities to bring in troops. An employer could lock his doors against rebellious workers—a process called the "lockout"—and then starve them into submission. He could compel them to sign "ironclad oaths" or "yellow dog contracts," both of which were solemn agreements not to join a labor union. He could put the names of agitators on a "black list" and circulate it among fellow employers. A corporation might even own the "company town," with its high-priced grocery stores and "easy" credit. Oftentimes the worker sank into perpetual debt—a status that strongly resembled serfdom.

The public, annoyed by recurrent strikes, was often deaf to the outcry of the worker. American wages were perhaps the highest in the world, although a dollar a day for pick-and-shovel labor does not seem excessive. Carnegie and Rockefeller had battled their way to the top, and the view was common that the laborer could do likewise. Somehow the strike seemed like a foreign importation—socialistic and hence unpatriotic. Big Business might combine into trusts to raise prices, but the worker must not combine into unions to raise wages. Unemployment seemed to be an act of God, who somehow would take care of the laborer.

"The Root of the Matter." Foreign-appearing labor agitator urges a work stoppage on a reluctant artisan. Thomas Nast in *Harper's Weekly,* May 8, 1886.

Labor Limps Along

Labor unions, which had been few and disorganized in 1861, were given a strong boost by the Civil War. This bloody conflict, with its drain on manpower, put more of a premium on labor; and the mounting cost of living provided an urgent incentive to unionization. By 1872 there were several hundred thousand organized workers and thirty-two national unions, including such crafts as bricklayers, type-setters, and shoemakers.

The National Labor Union, organized in 1866, represented a giant-boot stride by the workingmen. It lasted six years and attracted the impressive total of some 600,000 members, including the skilled, unskilled, and farmers. Its keynote was social reform, although it agitated for such specific goals as the eight-hour day and the arbitration

Henry George, the tax reformer, observed, in 1879, "The methods by which a trade union can alone act are necessarily destructive; its organization is necessarily tyrannical."

of industrial disputes. It finally succeeded in winning an eight-hour day for government workers, but the devastating depression of the 1870's dealt it a knockout blow. Labor was generally rocked back on its heels during these hectic years. Wage reductions in 1877 touched off a series of strikes on the railroads which were so violent as to verge on civil war.

A new organization—the Knights of Labor—seized the torch dropped by the defunct National Labor Union. Officially known as The Noble Order of the Knights of Labor, it began inauspiciously in 1869 as a secret society, with a private ritual, passwords, and a grip. Secrecy, which continued until 1881, would forestall possible reprisals by employers.

The Knights of Labor, like the National Labor Union, sought to include all workers in "one big union." Their slogan was: "An injury to one is the concern of all." A welcome mat was rolled out for the skilled and unskilled, for men and women, for whites and underprivileged Negroes, some 90,000 of whom joined. The Knights excluded only liquor dealers, professional gamblers, lawyers, bankers, and stockbrokers.

Setting up broad goals, the embattled Knights refused to thrust their lance into politics. Instead, they campaigned for economic and social reform, including producers' cooperatives and codes for safety and health. Voicing the war cry, "Labor is the only creator of values and capital," they frowned upon industrial warfare while fostering industrial arbitration. The ordinary work day was then ten hours or more, and the Knights waged a determined campaign for the eight-hour stint. A favorite song of these years ran:

Hurrah, hurrah, for labor, it is mustering all its powers,
And shall march along to victory with the banner of eight hours.

Under the eloquent leadership of Terence V. Powderly, an Irish-American of nimble wit and fluent tongue, the Knights won a number of strikes for the eight-hour day. By 1886, though their claim of a million members was evidently exaggerated, they were clearly a force to be reckoned with.

Unhorsing the Knights of Labor

Despite their outward success, the Knights were riding for a fall. They became involved in a number of May Day strikes in 1886, about half of which failed. A focal point was Chicago, which contained about 80,000 Knights. The city was also honeycombed with a few hundred anarchists, many of them foreign-born, who were advocating a violent overthrow of the American government.

Tensions rapidly built up to the bloody Haymarket Square episode. Labor disorders had broken out, and on May 4, 1886, the

Knights of Labor at Odds with Skilled Craft Unions. Capital looks on happily. Thomas Nast, *Harper's Weekly,* 1886

Chicago police advanced on a meeting called to protest alleged brutalities by the authorities. Suddenly a dynamite bomb was thrown which killed or injured several dozen persons, including policemen.

Hysteria swept the Windy City. Eight anarchists were rounded up, although nobody proved that they had anything to do directly with the bomb. But the judge and jury held that since they had preached incendiary doctrines, they could be charged with conspiracy. Five were sentenced to death, one of whom committed suicide, and the other three were given stiff prison terms.

Agitation for clemency mounted. In 1892, some six years later, John P. Altgeld, a German-born Democrat of strong liberal tendencies, was elected governor of Illinois. After studying the Haymarket case exhaustively, he pardoned the three survivors. Violent abuse was showered on him by the conservatives; unstinted praise by those who thought the men innocent. He was defeated for re-election, and died a few years later in relative obscurity. Whatever the merits of the case, Altgeld displayed courage in opposing what he regarded as a gross injustice.

The Haymarket Square bomb helped blow the props from under the Knights of Labor. They were associated in the public mind, though mistakenly, with the anarchists. The eight-hour movement suffered correspondingly, and subsequent strikes by the Knights met with scant success.

Another fatal handicap of the Knights was their inclusion of both skilled and unskilled workers. Unskilled labor could be easily replaced by strikebreaking "scabs." High-class craft unionists, who enjoyed a semi-monopoly of skills, could not readily be supplanted, and hence enjoyed a superior bargaining position. They finally wearied of sacrificing this advantage in order to pull the chestnuts of the unskilled out of the fire. By 1890 the Knights had melted away to 100,000 members, and these gradually fused with other protest groups of the 1890's.

The A. F. of L. to the Fore

Samuel Gompers (1850–1924).
National Archives.

In later years Samuel Gompers declared, "Show me the country in which there are no strikes and I'll show you that country in which there is no liberty."

The powerful American Federation of Labor, which next stole the spotlight, was largely a creation of squat, square-jawed Samuel Gompers. This colorful Jewish cigar maker, born in a London tenement and removed from school at age ten, was brought to America when thirteen. Taking his turn at reading informative literature to fellow cigar makers in New York, he was pressed into overtime service because of his strong voice. Rising spectacularly in labor ranks, he was elected president of the American Federation of Labor every year from 1886 to 1924, except one.

Significantly, the American *Federation* of Labor was just what it called itself—a federation. It consisted of an association of self-governing national unions, each of which retained its independence, with the A. F. of L. unifying over-all strategy. No individual laborer as such could join the central body.

Gompers adopted a down-to-earth approach, soft-pedaling attempts to engineer sweeping social reform. A bitter foe of socialism, he kept the Federation squarely on the well-worn path of conservatism. He had no quarrel with capitalism as such, but he wanted labor to win its fair share. All he wanted, he said simply, was "More." His objectives were better wages and hours, as well as other improved conditions for the worker. Another major goal of Gompers was the "trade agreement" authorizing the "closed shop"—or all-union labor. His chief weapons were the walkout and the boycott, enforced by "We don't patronize" signs. The stronger craft unions of the Federation, by pooling funds, were able to amass a war chest that would enable them to ride out prolonged strikes.

The A. F. of L. thus established itself on solid foundations. Although attempting to speak for all workers, it fell far short of being representative of them. Composed of skilled crafts, like the carpenters and the bricklayers, it was willing to let unskilled laborers, especially Negroes, shift for themselves. Though hard pressed by big industry, the Federation was basically non-political. But it did attempt to persuade members to reward friends and punish foes at the polls. The A. F. of L. weathered the Panic of 1893 reasonably well, and by 1900 it could boast a membership of 500,000. Critics referred to it, with questionable accuracy, as "the Labor Trust."

Labor disorders continued throughout the years from 1881 to 1900, during which there was an alarming total of over 23,000 strikes. These disturbances involved 6,610,000 workers, with a total loss to both employers and employees of $450,000,000. The strikers lost about half their strikes, and won or compromised the remainder. Perhaps the gravest weakness of organized labor was that it still embraced only a small minority of all workingmen.

But attitudes toward labor had begun to change perceptibly by 1900. The public was beginning to concede the right of workingmen

Advertisement in a 1904 Issue of the *American Federationist* (official magazine of the A.F. of L.).

to organize, to bargain collectively, and to strike. As a sign of the times, Labor Day was made a legal holiday by act of Congress in 1894. A few enlightened industrialists had come to perceive the wisdom of avoiding costly economic warfare by bargaining with the unions and signing agreements. But the vast majority of employers continued to fight organized labor, which achieved its grudging gains only after recurrent strikes and frequent reverses. Nothing was handed to it on a silver platter. Management still held the whip hand, and several trouble-fraught decades were to pass before labor was to gain a position of relative equality with capital. If the Age of Big Business had dawned, the Age of Big Labor was still some distance from the horizon.

SELECT READINGS

A penetrating survey is s. p. HAYS, *The Response to Industrialism, 1885–1914* (1957).* More detailed are IDA M. TARBELL, *The Nationalizing of Business, 1878–1898* (1936) and L. M. HACKER, *The World of Andrew Carnegie, 1865–1901* (1968). See also E. C. KIRKLAND, *The Coming of the Industrial Age* (1960), his *Industry Comes of Age: Business, Labor, and Public Policy, 1860–1897* (1961),* and his *Dream and Thought in the Business Community, 1860–1900* (1956).* RAY GINGER, *The Age of Excess: The United States from 1877 to 1914* (1965)* handles colorfully both industrial and social development, as does J. A. GARRATY, *The New Commonwealth, 1877–1890* (1968).* MATTHEW JOSEPHSON assails the business tycoons in *The Robber Barons* (1934).* On the railroads see R. E. RIEGEL, *The Story of the Western Railroads* (1926),* and OSCAR LEWIS' popularly written *The Big Four* (1938). Also popularized are s. H. HOLBROOK, *The Story of American Railroads* (1947) and *The Age of the Moguls* (1953).* More recent studies are G. R. TAYLOR and I. D. NEU, *The American Railroad Network, 1861–1890* (1956); R. W. FOGEL, *The Union Pacific Railroad: A Case in Premature Enterprise* (1960) and *Railroads and American Economic Growth* (1964); W. S. GRISWOLD, *A Work of Giants: Building the First Transcontinental Railroad* (1962); and JAMES MCCAGUE, *Moguls and Iron Men* (1964), also the story of the first transcontinental railroad. ALLAN NEVINS is favorably disposed in his *Study in Power: John D. Rockefeller* (2 vols., 1953); see also H. F. WILLIAMSON and A. R. DAUM, *The American Petroleum Industry: The Age of Illumination, 1859–1899* (1959). On steel, consult DAVID BRODY, *Steelworkers in America* (1960). C. V. WOODWARD, *Origins of the New South, 1877–1913* (1951)* is an admirable analysis. Organized labor is treated in PHILIP TAFT, *The A.F. of L. in the Time of Gompers* (1957) and *The A.F. of L. from the Death of Gompers to the Merger* (1959). Also useful are J. O. MORRIS, *Conflict within the AFL: A Study of Craft versus Industrial Unionism, 1901–1938* (1958); G. N. GROB, *Workers and Utopia: A Study of Ideological Conflict in the American Labor Movement, 1865–1900* (1961)*; and BERNARD MANDEL, *Samuel Gompers* (1963). See also S. R. SPENCER, *Booker T. Washington and the Negro's Place in American Life* (1955).* Also *Harvard Guide*,* Pt. V.

RECENT REFERENCES

JOSEPH F. WALL, *Andrew Carnegie* (1970).

* Available in paperback.

28

New Social and Cultural Horizons, 1865–1900

*We heartily approve all legitimate efforts to prevent the United
States from being used as the dumping ground for the known criminals and professional paupers of Europe.*

Democratic National Platform, 1892

Aliens within the Gates

The nation's upsurging population foreshadowed momentous
social and cultural changes—changes hardly less spectacular than
those occurring in industry. The census of 1870 enrolled 39,818,449
souls; that of 1900 almost doubled the earlier figure with a remarkable 75,994,575. Urban centers were booming marvelously, owing
largely to expanding industry and multiplying railroads. By 1890,
three out of ten Americans were city dwellers, in striking contrast
to the overwhelmingly rural population of stagecoach days.

Despite the jostling of movement and change, a sturdy and
honest middle class continued to provide stability. Proud possessors of homes and farms, these solid, industrious folk formed the
nation's backbone. Gaudy new millionaires of the Gilded Age,
who were struggling to rise from the cash register to the social
register, merely provided the froth.

The brightly colored stream of immigration from Europe continued to widen. In every decade from the 1850's through the

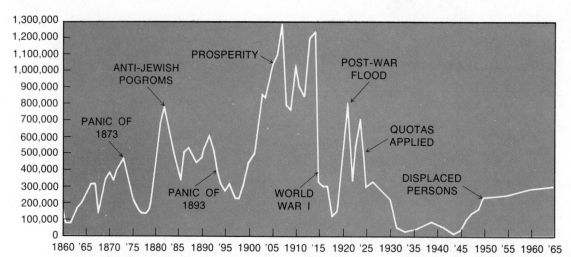

ANNUAL IMMIGRATION, 1860–1965

1870's, more than 2,000,000 aliens had stepped upon America's shores. By the 1880's the stream had become a rushing torrent, for in that decade a record-breaking total of more than 5,000,000 poured in. A new high for a single year was reached in 1882, when 788,992 arrived—or over 2100 a day. This figure was not exceeded until 1903.

Until the 1880's, the bulk of these immigrants were easy to assimilate. Most of them had come from the British Isles and Western Europe, chiefly Germany and Scandinavia. They were generally fair-skinned Anglo-Saxon and Teutonic types; and they were usually Protestants, except for the Catholic Irish and some Catholic Germans. They boasted a comparatively high degree of literacy, and were accustomed to some kind of constitutional government. Their native institutions were such that their Americanization was usually speedy, especially when they took up farms.

But in the 1880's a new element appeared, commonly known as the New Immigration. For the first time in American experience, a substantial proportion of the new arrivals came from Southern and Eastern Europe. Among them could be found swarthy and black-bearded Italians, Croats, Slovaks, Magyars, Greeks, and Poles. In the 1880's these picturesque new types totaled 19% of the inpouring immigrants; by the first decade of the next century they constituted an astonishing 66% of the total inflow. "Old-line" Americans asked if the nation had become a melting pot, a stew kettle, or a dumping ground.

South Europe Uprooted

Why were these bright-shawled and quaint-jacketed strangers hammering on the gates? An unfortunate few were paupers, feeble-minded, or criminals, whose home governments were eager to assist them out of the fatherland. Some were fleeing compulsory military service. But the vast majority emigrated because America was painted as the Land of Opportunity; and they sought to escape the poverty and squalor of their native soil. Unfortunately, many of them merely exchanged one slum for another; their children, rather than they, profited from the transplanting.

"America fever" proved highly contagious in Europe. The New World "paradise" was often described in glowing colors by the "America letters" of those already here—letters that were soiled by the hands of many readers. "We eat here every day," wrote one jubilant Pole, "what we get only for Easter in our [native] country." The Land of the Free was also blessed with high wages, free homesteads for the settler, religious freedom, unusual civil liberties, and the absence of a ruling caste.

Profit-seeking Americans trumpeted throughout Europe the attractions of the new Promised Land. Industrialists wanted cheap labor, railroads wanted buyers for their land grants, states wanted more population, and steamship lines wanted more human cargo for their holds. In fact, the ease and cheapness of emigrating greatly accelerated the transoceanic flood. Travel in steerage was an ordeal; but it was not the nightmare of colonial days, and it was soon over.

As the century lengthened, savage persecution of minorities in Europe drove many shattered souls to American shores. In the 1880's the Russians turned violently upon their own Jews, chiefly in the Polish areas. Tens of thousands of these nerve-racked refugees, fleeing their burning homes, arrived in the seaboard cities of the Atlantic Coast, notably New York. Too poor to move farther, they huddled together in the already stinking slums, and there they found Americanization unusually difficult.

Anti-foreignism or "nativism," earlier touched off by the Irish and Germans in the 1840's and 1850's, once more flared forth. The hordes from Eastern and Southern Europe were especially hard to digest. They were non-Teutonic and preponderantly Roman Catholic; they had been accustomed to cringe before despotism; they were generally illiterate; they were poverty-stricken; and they tended to hive together in the jam-packed cities rather than move out to farms. The "Little Italys" and "Little Polands" of New York and Chicago were soon to claim more inhabitants than many of the largest cities of the Old Country.

These newcomers, who threatened to drown the earlier comers in a foreign sea, aroused widespread alarm. They were not only numerous but they had a high birth rate, as is common among people with a low standard of living and enough youth and vigor to pull up stakes. Old-line Americans protested that the original Anglo-Saxon Puritan stock would soon be outbred and outvoted. Still more hor-

Regarding immigration, the Democratic platform of 1892 announced, "We heartily approve all legitimate efforts to prevent the United States from being used as the dumping ground for the known criminals and professional paupers of Europe."

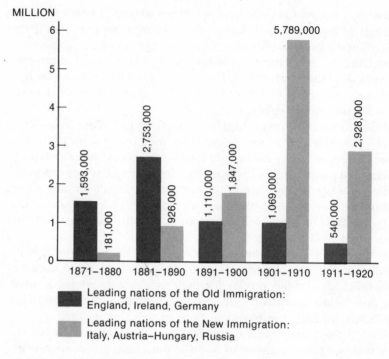

OLD AND NEW IMMIGRATION (by decade)

rifying was the prospect that it would be mongrelized by a mixture of "inferior" South European blood, and that the Anglo-Saxon types would disappear in a darker blend. T. B. Aldrich, a son of New England, cried out in anguish:

O Liberty, white Goddess! is it well
To leave the gates unguarded?

"Native" Americans voiced additional complaints. They objected to the creation of new rabbit-hutch slums, and condemned what they branded as the pauperism and bad morals of "smelly" Europeans. The alien arrivals were also assailed for a willingness to work for "starvation" wages, and for importing in their intellectual baggage such dangerous "isms" as socialism, communism, and anarchism. Many Big Business leaders, who welcomed the flood of cheap manual labor, began to fear that they had embraced a Frankenstein's monster.

Narrowing the Welcome Mat

Anti-foreign organizations, common in the 1840's and 1850's, were now revived in a different guise. Notorious among them was the American Protective Association (A.P.A.), which was created in 1887 and which soon claimed a million militant members. In seeking its "nativist" goals, the A.P.A. urged voting against Roman Catholic candidates for office, and sponsored the publication of lustful fantasies about runaway nuns.

Organized labor was quick to throw its weight behind the move to choke off the rising tide of foreigners. The newly arrived Europeans, frequently used as strikebreakers, were hard to unionize because of the language barrier, the strangeness of their new surroundings, and the relatively high wages. Labor leaders argued, not illogically, that if American industry was entitled to protection from foreign goods, the American workingman was entitled to protection from foreign laborers.

Regulation of immigration had, from earliest days, been entrusted to the states. Those with favored ports of entry—such as New York, Boston, and Philadelphia—grappled with the problem as best they could. But there was always the loophole of the "easy states," as well as the possibility of smuggling in foreigners, often diseased or deranged "scum," by way of Canada and Mexico. The task of regulating immigration, like that of regulating the railroads and the trusts, ultimately became so burdensome that it had to be dumped into the lap of the Washington government.

Congress finally erected partial bars against the inpouring immigrants. The first restrictive law—that of 1882—banged the gate in the faces of paupers, criminals, and convicts, all of whom had to be returned at the expense of the careless or greedy shipper. Congress further responded to pained outcries from organized labor when, in 1885, it prohibited the importation of workmen under contract—usually for sub-standard wages. In later years, other federal laws lengthened the list of undesirables by adding such categories as the insane, polygamists, prostitutes, alcoholics, anarchists, and persons afflicted with contagious diseases. A proposed literacy test, long a goal of the "nativists" because it would favor the Old Immigration over the New, met vigorous opposition. It was not enacted until 1917, after three Presidents had vetoed it on the grounds that literacy was more a test of opportunity than of intelligence.

The year 1882, in addition to the first federal restrictions against certain undesirables, brought forth a law to bar completely one racial group—the Chinese (see p. 532). Hitherto America had gathered to her mighty breast the oppressed and underprivileged of all races and climes. Hereafter the gates would be padlocked against defective undesirables—plus Chinese. Four years later, in 1886, the Statue of Liberty was erected in New York harbor as a gift from the people of France. But the words of Emma Lazarus that were inscribed on the base rang a bit hollow:

. . . Give me your tired, your poor,
Your huddled masses yearning to breathe free,
The wretched refuse of your teeming shore.

President Cleveland declared in 1897: "It is said . . . that the quality of recent immigration is undesirable. The time is quite within recent memory when the same thing was said of immigrants who, with their descendants, are now numbered among our best citizens."

Advocates of more rigid restriction specifically accused the New Immigrants of exploiting America. This charge was partially true of those who came with the intention of going back to the Old Country when they had "made their pile." Of the approximately 20,000,000 newcomers who arrived from 1820 to 1900, about 5,000,000 "birds of passage" returned. But most of the aliens who came were exploited to some extent by dollar-conscious Americans, whether in verminous city slums or sooty mining slums. These displaced Europeans, unlike "nativists" cradled in America, became American citizens with their clothes on. They stepped off the ship, many of them full-grown and well muscled, ready to put their shoulders to the nation's industrial wheels. The Republic owes much to these later comers—to their brawn, their brains, their courage, and their reforming zeal.

New Frontiers in the Cities

A vast cityward movement was gathering momentum in the 1880's and 1890's, not only in the United States but elsewhere in the world. In 1860 no American city could boast a million inhabitants; by 1890, New York, Chicago, and Philadelphia had spurted past the million mark. By 1900 New York, with some 3,500,000, was the second largest city in the world, outranked only by London. It was dubbed "a nightmare in stone."

This spectacular drift to the city is not hard to explain. It was speeded by machine-made jobs, by seductively high wages, and by the growing monotony of the farm, where there were too many cows to milk and hogs to feed. Urban centers were becoming more attractive, with their network of telephones and their bright lights, especially after the flickering gaslight era gave way to electricity. Noteworthy also were improvements in central heating, public water systems, indoor plumbing, sewage disposal, asphalt pave-

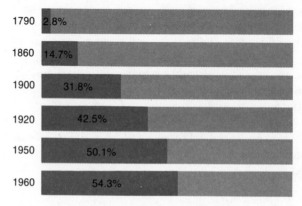

1790 2.8%
1860 14.7%
1900 31.8%
1920 42.5%
1950 50.1%
1960 54.3%

Percent of total population living in cities of 10,000 or more

THE SHIFT TO THE CITY

ments, and transportation. The giant Brooklyn Bridge, dedicated in 1883, blazed the way for bigger and better spans. Electric-powered elevated cars and subways were introduced near the end of the century, inspiring the quip "The public be jammed." Congestion in the cities was markedly relieved by the cloud-brushing skyscraper in 1885; the Americans were apparently becoming modern cliff dwellers.

But the jagged skyline of America's perpendicular civilization could not conceal the ugliness of a feverish growth. Some of the showier cities, like skyscrapered New York, resembled beautiful women with dirty necks and out-at-the-toes shoes. Human pigsties, known as slums, became more crowded, more dirty, more rat infested, more unhealthful. Thousands of families were trapped in ill-ventilated and foul-smelling shacks and cellars, without plumbing. In these wretched tenements, conspicuously in New York's infamous "Lung Block," hundreds of immigrants coughed away their lives. "Flophouses" abounded where the half-starved and unemployed might sleep for a few cents on verminous mattresses. Democracy found difficult rootage in the garbage-strewn alleyways. Yet, marvelous to relate, the vast majority of these underprivileged souls grew up to be decent and law-abiding citizens.

Crime and corruption, like lice, flourished in the teeming cities. Criminals ranged from burly thugs with blackjacks to "city slickers" palming off "gold bricks" on "hayseeds" from the country. Crookedness in city government was most luridly exemplified by New York's notorious Tweed Ring. The boss and the machine made willing tools of the befuddled and purchasable immigrants. America's governmental system, nurtured in wide-open spaces, was least successful in the cement forests and asphalt jungles of the great cities.

Challenges to the Church

Bells tolling every Sunday morning in countless belfries sounded deceptive tones. Worshipers had vastly increased in numbers, but they had decreased in the intensity of their religious convictions. In the age-old struggle between God and the Devil, the Wicked One had registered dismaying gains. The mounting emphasis was on materialism; distressing numbers of devotees worshiped "the bitch goddess success." Money was the accepted measure of achievement, and the new Gospel of Wealth proclaimed that God prospered the righteous.

The traditional faith of the fathers received additional blows from new trends, including a booming sale of books on comparative religion and on historical criticism as applied to the Bible. Most unsettling of all was *On the Origin of Species,* a highly controversial volume published in 1859, on the eve of the Civil War, by the English naturalist Charles Darwin. He set forth in lucid form the sensational theory that man had slowly evolved from lower forms of life—a

Darwin wrote in 1871, "Man is descended from a hairy, tailed quadruped, probably arboreal in its habits. . . . For my part I would as soon be descended from a baboon . . . as from a savage who delights to torture his enemies . . . treats his wives like slaves . . . and is haunted by the grossest superstitions."

Two Irishmen Doubt Darwinian Evolution. *Harper's Weekly,* 1883

theory that was soon summarized to mean "the survival of the fittest." In American minds the struggle for the survival of the Union eclipsed for a time that for the survival of the fittest, and the real impact of Darwinism was delayed until the postwar years.

Evolution cast serious doubt on a literal interpretation of the Bible, which relates how God created the heaven and the earth in six days. Conservatives, or "Fundamentalists," stood firmly on the Scripture as the inspired and infallible word of God, and they condemned the "bestial hypothesis" of the Darwinians. "Modernists" parted company with the "Fundamentalists," and flatly refused to accept the Bible in its entirety as either history or science.

This furious battle over Darwinism created rifts in the churches and colleges of the post-Civil War era. "Modernist" clergymen were removed from their pulpits; teachers of biology who embraced evolution were dismissed from their chairs. But as time wore on, an increasing number of liberal thinkers were able to reconcile Darwinism with Christianity. They heralded the revolutionary theory as a newer and grander revelation of the ways of the Almighty. As W. H. Carruth observed:

Some call it Evolution,
And others call it God.

But Darwinism undoubtedly did much to loosen religious moorings and to promote unbelief among the gospel-glutted. The most bitterly denounced skeptic of the era was a golden-tongued orator, Colonel Robert G. Ingersoll, who lectured widely on "Some Mistakes of Moses" and "Why I Am an Agnostic." He might have gone far in public life if he had stuck to politics and refrained from attacking orthodox religion by "giving hell hell," as he put it.

Denominational Gains and Losses

Protestant churches, in particular, suffered heavily from the weakening of religious ties. The larger houses of worship, with their stained-glass windows and thundering pipe organs, were tending to become a kind of sacred diversion or amusement. Growing complacent with wealth, the churches were distressingly slow to raise their voices against social and economic abuses. John D. Rockefeller was a pillar of the Baptist Church; J. Pierpont Morgan, of the Episcopal Church. Trinity Episcopal Church in New York actually owned some of the city's worst slum property. Critics charged that theology was drowning out true religion.

The Roman Catholic and Jewish faiths gained enormous strength from the New Immigration. By 1900 the Roman Catholics had increased their lead as the largest single denomination, numbering nearly 9,000,000 communicants. Roman Catholic and Jewish groups kept the common touch better than many of the leading Protestant churches. Cardinal Gibbons (1834–1921), an urbane Catholic leader devoted to American unity, was immensely popular with Roman Catholics and Protestants alike. Acquainted with every President from Johnson to Harding, he employed his liberal sympathies to assist the American labor movement.

By 1890 the variety-loving American could choose from one hundred and fifty religious denominations, two of them newcomers. One was the band-playing Salvation Army, which invaded America from England in 1879 and established a beachhead on the street corners. Appealing frankly to the down-and-outers, the so-called "Starvation Army" did much practical good, especially with free soup.

The other important new faith was the Church of Christ, Scientist (Christian Science), founded by Mrs. Mary Baker Eddy in 1879, after she had suffered much ill-health. Preaching that the true practice of Christianity heals sickness, she set forth her views in a book entitled

Mrs. Mary Baker Eddy (1821–1910). Used with permission © 1929, renewed 1957 The Christian Science Publishing Society. All Rights Reserved

Mrs. Eddy's *Science and Health* declared, "We classify disease as error, which nothing but Truth or Mind can heal, and this Mind must be divine, not human."

Science and Health with Key to the Scriptures (1875), which sold an amazing 400,000 copies before her death. A fertile field for converts was found in America's hurried, nerve-racked, and urbanized civilization, to which Mrs. Eddy held out the hope of relief from discords and diseases through prayer as taught by Christian Science. When she passed on in 1910, she had founded an influential church which embraced several hundred thousand devoted worshipers.

Learning for Young and Old

Public education continued its upward climb. The ideal of tax-supported elementary schools, adopted on a nationwide basis before the Civil War, was still gathering strength. Americans were accepting the truism that a free government cannot function successfully if the people are shackled by ignorance. Beginning about 1870, more and more states were making at least a grade-school education compulsory, and this gain, incidentally, helped check the frightful abuses of child labor. In compulsory education the war-torn South lagged behind its sister states.

Spectacular indeed was the spread of the high schools, especially by the 1880's and 1890's. Before the Civil War, private academies at the secondary level were common, and tax-supported high schools were rare, numbering only several hundred. But the concept was now gaining impressive support that a high-school education, as well as a grade-school education, was the birthright of every citizen. By 1900 there were some six thousand high schools. In addition, free textbooks were being provided in increasing quantities by the taxpayers of the states during the last two decades of the century.

Other trends were noteworthy. Teacher-training schools, then called "normal schools," experienced a striking expansion after the Civil War. In 1860 there were only twelve of them; in 1910, over three hundred. Kindergartens, earlier borrowed from Germany, also began to gain strong support. The New Immigration in the 1880's and 1890's brought vast new strength to the private Catholic parochial schools, which were fast becoming a major pillar of the nation's educational structure. One important result was a decreased dominance by nonreligious public education.

America's educational system, though showering benefits on children, passed by millions of adults. This deficiency was partially remedied by the Chautauqua movement, a successor to the lyceums, which was launched in 1874 on the shores of Lake Chautauqua, in New York. The organizers achieved gratifying success through nationwide public lectures, often held in tents and featuring well-known speakers, including the incomparable Mark Twain. In addition, there were extensive Chautauqua courses of home study, for which 100,000 persons enrolled in 1892 alone.

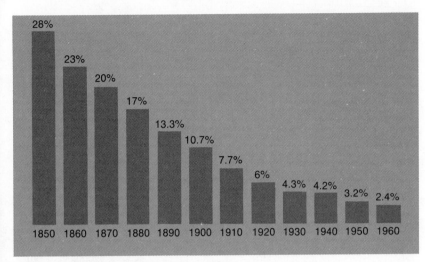

THE DECLINE OF ILLITERACY
In Persons Over 10 Years Old
(Percentage of Population Illiterate)

Crowded cities, despite their cancers, generally provided better educational facilities than the old one-room, one-teacher red schoolhouse. The success of the public schools is attested by the falling of the illiteracy rate from 20% in 1870 to 10.7% in 1900. Americans were developing a profound faith in education, often misplaced, as the sovereign remedy for their ills.

Booker Washington and Negro Education

The neglected Negro was not getting his fair share of the educational harvest. A notable leader emerged in the person of a slave-born mulatto, Booker T. Washington, who had slept under a board sidewalk in order to save pennies for his education. Called in 1881 to head a new Negro normal and industrial school at Tuskegee, Alabama, he began with forty students in a tumble-down shanty. Undaunted by adversity, he undertook to teach the Negroes useful trades so that they could gain self-respect and merit a position of economic equality, but not social equality, with the whites. His policies were assailed as "Uncle Tomism" by certain Negro intellectuals who feared that their race was being condemned to manual labor and perpetual inferiority. But Washington, "the white man's black," stuck to his guns, and through his gifts as a speaker and organizer did much to improve Negro education and race relations until his death in 1915.

A stellar member of the Tuskegee faculty, beginning in 1896, was slave-born George Washington Carver, who as an infant in Missouri was kidnapped and ransomed for a horse worth $300. He became an

Booker T. Washington (1856–1915). Tuskegee Institute.

internationally known agricultural chemist who helped the economy of the South by discovering hundreds of new uses for the lowly peanut (shampoo, axle grease), sweet potato (vinegar), and soy bean (paints).

Foremost among the challengers of Booker Washington's leadership at Tuskegee at the turn of the century was Dr. W. E. B. Du Bois, a Massachusetts-born mixture of Negro, French, Dutch, and Indian blood ("Thank God, no Anglo-Saxon," he would add). A graduate of Harvard, he was the first black to receive the Ph.D. at that prestigious institution. Contending (unlike Booker Washington) for complete equality, he became a founding father of the National Association for the Advancement of Colored People in 1910, and a leading Negro intellectual acclaimed for his contributions to history, sociology, and poetry. He died in 1963, in his 95th year, after having moved to Africa in the hope of finding greater equality.

The Hallowed Halls of Ivy

Colleges and universities also shot up like lusty young saplings in the decades after the Civil War. Parents in multiplying numbers were eager to make sacrifices so that their children might secure a college education—something that now seemed indispensable in the scramble for the golden apple of success. The educational battle for women, only partially won before the war, now turned into a rout of the masculine diehards. Women's colleges, like Vassar, were gaining ground; and universities open to both sexes were blossoming forth, notably in the Middle West.

Dr. David Starr Jordan, First President of Stanford University. Burton Crandall Collection, Hoover Institution, Stanford University.

The almost phenomenal growth of higher education owed much to the Morrill Act of 1862. This enlightened law, passed after the South had seceded, provided a generous grant of the public lands to the states for support of education. "Land-grant colleges," most of which became state universities, in turn bound themselves to provide certain services, such as military training. The Hatch Act of 1887, supplementing the Morrill Act, provided federal funds for the establishment of agricultural experiment stations in connection with the land-grant colleges.

Private philanthropy richly supplemented federal grants to higher education. Many of the new industrial millionaires, developing tender social consciences, donated immense fortunes to educational enterprises. A "philanthropist" was cynically described as "one who steals privately and gives publicly." In the twenty years from 1878 to 1898 these money barons gave away about $150,000,000. Noteworthy among the new private universities of high quality to open their doors were Cornell (1865) and Leland Stanford Junior (1891), the latter founded in memory of the deceased fifteen-year-old only child of a builder of the Central Pacific Railroad. The University of Chicago, opened in 1892, speedily forged into a front-rank position, owing largely to the lubricant of Rockefeller's oil millions. A Chicago newspaper was prompted to proclaim:

Let us then be up and doing,
  All becoming money kings;
Some day we may be endowing
  Universities and things.

Rockefeller died at 97, after having given some $550 million for philanthropic purposes.

High-School and College Graduates, 1870–1968

Year	Number Graduating from High School	Number Graduating from College	Interim Population Increase
1870	16,000	9,371	
1880	23,634	10,353	26.0%
1890	43,731	15,539	25.5%
1900	94,883	27,410	20.7%
1910	156,429	37,199	21.0%
1920	311,266	48,622	14.9%
1930	666,904	122,484	16.1%
1940	1,221,475	186,500	7.2%
1950	1,199,700	432,058	14.5%
1960	1,864,000	392,440	18.4%
1970	c.3,015,000	c.746,000	

Significant also was the sharp increase in professional and technical schools, where modern laboratories were replacing the solo experiment performed by the instructor before his class. Towering among the specialized institutions was the Johns Hopkins University, opened in 1876, which maintained the nation's first high-grade graduate school. Several generations of American scholars, repelled by snobbish English cousins and attracted by painstaking Continental methods, had attended German universities. Johns Hopkins ably carried on the Germanic tradition of profusely footnoted tomes. Reputable scholars no longer had to go abroad for a gilt-edged graduate degree; and Dr. Woodrow Wilson, among others, received his Ph.D. at Johns Hopkins.

The March of the Mind

Cut-and-dried, the old classical curriculum in the colleges was on the way out, as the new industrialization brought insistent demands for "practical" courses and specialized training in the sciences. The elective system, which permitted students to choose more courses in

During Eliot's presidency these inscriptions appeared on the 1890 Gate to the Harvard Yard: ENTER TO GROW IN WISDOM. DEPART BETTER TO SERVE THY COUNTRY AND MANKIND.

Edison in his laboratory. In 1878 he declared, "I speak without exaggeration when I say that I have constructed three thousand different theories in connection with the electric light . . . Yet in only two cases did my experiments prove the truth of my theory."

cafeteria fashion, was gaining popularity. It received a powerful boost in the 1870's, when Dr. Charles W. Eliot, a vigorous young chemist, became president of Harvard College and embarked upon a lengthy career of educational statesmanship. During the closing decades of the century, summer school courses and university extension work were securing a promising foothold.

Winds of "dangerous doctrines" threatened to shipwreck freedom of teaching in the colleges. Disagreeable incidents involved the dismissal of professors who taught evolution or expressed hostility to high tariffs. For many years, some of the Big Business alumni of Yale vainly sought the bald scalp of the low-tariff economist and sociologist William Graham Sumner.

Medical schools and medical science after the Civil War were prospering. Despite the enormous sale of patent medicines and Indian remedies—"good for man or beast"—the new scientific gains were reflected in improved public health. Revolutionary discoveries abroad, such as those of the French scientist Louis Pasteur and the English physician Joseph Lister, left their imprint on America. The popularity of heavy whiskers waned as the century ended; such hairy adornments were now coming to be regarded as germ traps. As a result of new health-giving precautions, including campaigns against public spitting, life expectancy at birth was measurably increased.

Many capable scientists and thinkers adorned university faculties, but few enjoyed international reputations. American genius shone best in applying scientific knowledge to practical problems, as was notably true of the wizardly Thomas A. Edison. One of the most brilliant philosophers thus far produced in America, the slight and sickly William James (1842–1910), served for thirty-five years on the Harvard faculty. Through his numerous writings he gave wide currency to the philosophical concept known as pragmatism, which emphasized the practical side of thinking. Truth was to be tested, above all, by the practical consequences of belief, by action rather than theories. This kind of reasoning chimed in with the mood of a materialistic, cash-value America, which was already hotly in pursuit of the dollar.

The Appeal of the Press

Books continued to be a major source of edification and enjoyment, for both juveniles and adults. Best sellers of the 1880's were generally old favorites like *David Copperfield* and *Ivanhoe*.

American authors, many with unpublished manuscripts on their hands, were greatly encouraged by new copyright arrangements. In 1891, after a half-century or so of debate, Congress enacted a law making possible an international copyright. Foreign writers could henceforth secure royalties from America, and American writers could hope to reap rewards from abroad. (Longfellow had been "honored" by some twenty unauthorized publishers in England.) Aspiring young American authors no longer had to fear the competition of cheap, royaltyless foreign reprints.

Well-stocked public libraries—the poor man's university—were making encouraging progress, especially in Boston and New York. The magnificent Library of Congress building, which opened its doors in 1897, provided thirteen acres of floor space in the largest and costliest edifice of its kind in the world. A new era was inaugurated by the generous gifts of Andrew Carnegie. This open-handed Scotsman, book-starved in his youth, contributed $60,000,000 for the construction of public libraries all over the country. By 1900 there were about nine thousand free circulating libraries in America, each with at least three hundred books.

Roaring newspaper presses, spurred by the invention of the linotype in 1885, more than kept pace with the demands of a word-hungry public. But the heavy investment in machinery and plant was accompanied by a growing fear of offending advertisers and subscribers. Bare-knuckle editorials were, to an increasing degree, being supplanted by feature articles and non-controversial syndicated material. The day of slashing journalistic giants like Horace Greeley was passing.

Sensationalism, at the same time, was beginning to debase the public taste. The semi-literate immigrants, combined with straphanging urban commuters, created a profitable market for news that was simply and punchily written. Sex, scandal, and other human-interest stories were blatantly headlined, as a vulgarization of the press accompanied the growth of circulation. Critics complained in vain of "presstitutes."

Two new journalistic tycoons emerged. Joseph Pulitzer, Hungarian-born and near-blind, was a leader in the techniques of sensationalism in St. Louis and especially with the New York *World*. His use of the colored comic supplements, featuring the "Yellow Kid," gave the name of Yellow Journalism to his lurid sheets. A close and ruthless competitor was youthful William Randolph Hearst, who had been expelled from Harvard College for a crude prank. Able to draw on his California father's mining millions, he ultimately built up a powerful chain of newspapers, beginning with the San Francisco *Examiner* in 1887.

Unfortunately, the over-all influence of Pulitzer and Hearst was not altogether wholesome. Although both championed many worthy causes, both prostituted the press in their struggle for increased circulation; both "stooped, snooped, and scooped to conquer." Their flair for scandal and sensational rumor was happily somewhat offset by the introduction of syndicated material and by the strengthening

Scotsman Carnegie Besieged by Money Seekers. Minneapolis *Tribune*, 1899

of the news-gathering Associated Press, which had been founded in the 1840's.

Apostles of Reform

Cover of Bellamy's Book Published in Finland, 1907. Workers reach toward rising sun.

Magazines partially satisfied the public appetite for good reading, notably old standbys like *Harper's*, the *Atlantic Monthly*, and *Scribner's Monthly*. Possibly the most influential journal of all was the liberal and highly intellectual New York *Nation*, which was read largely by professors, preachers, and publicists as "the weekly Day of Judgment." Launched in 1865 by the Irish-born Edwin L. Godkin, a merciless critic, it crusaded militantly for civil service reform, honesty in government, and a moderate tariff. The *Nation* attained only a modest circulation—about ten thousand in the 19th Century—but Godkin believed that if he could reach the right ten thousand leaders, his ideas through them might reach the ten millions.

Another journalist-author, Henry George, was an original thinker who left an enduring mark. Poor in formal schooling, he was rich in idealism and in the milk of human kindness. After seeing poverty at its worst in India, and land grabbing at its greediest in California, he took pen in hand. His classic treatise, *Progress and Poverty,* undertook to solve "the great enigma of our times"—"the association of progress with poverty." Arguing that poverty is attributable to rent, he concluded that a single tax on land was the remedy for many social and economic ills.

George soon became one of the most controversial figures of his age. His single-tax ideas were so horrifying to propertied men that his manuscript was rejected by numerous publishers. Finally brought out in 1879, the book gradually broke into the best-seller lists and ultimately sold some three million copies. George also lectured widely in America, where he influenced thinking about the maldistribution of wealth, and in Britain, where he left an indelible mark on English Fabian socialism.

Edward Bellamy, a quiet Massachusetts Yankee, was another journalist-reformer of remarkable power. In 1888 he published a socialistic novel, *Looking Backward*, in which the hero, falling into a hypnotic sleep, awakens in the year 2000. He "looks backward" and finds that the social and economic injustices of 1887 have melted away under an idyllic government. To a nation already alarmed by the trust evil, the book had a magnetic appeal and sold over a million copies. Scores of Bellamy Clubs sprang up to discuss this mild Utopian socialism, and they definitely influenced American reform movements near the end of the century.

Literary Landmarks

American post-war literature, unhappily, did not live up to its pre-war promise. Perhaps too many future authors, North and South, had fallen on the battlefield; perhaps the money-grubbing goals of the new industrial era were unfavorable to artistic achievement. Perhaps New England was becoming too narrow, smug, and in-grown, as the brilliant Boston school of writers gradually burned it-self out. The romantic sentimentality of a youthful era was giving way to a rugged realism that reflected more faithfully the materialism of an industrialized age.

In an era of poetical decline, Walt Whitman was one of the few luminaries of yesteryear who remained active. Although shattered in health by service as a Civil War nurse, he brought out successive— and purified—revisions of his hardy perennial, *Leaves of Grass.* The assassination of Lincoln inspired him to write two of the most moving poems in American literature, "O Captain! My Captain!" and "When Lilacs Last in the Dooryard Bloom'd."

The curious figure of Emily Dickinson, one of America's most gifted lyric poets, did not emerge until 1886, when she died and her poems were discovered. A Massachusetts spinster and recluse, dis-appointed in love, she wrote over a thousand short lyrics on odd scraps of paper. Only two were published during her lifetime, and those without her consent. As she wrote:

How dreary to be somebody!
How public, like a frog
To tell your name the livelong day
To an admiring bog!

Among the lesser poetical lights was a tragic Southerner, Sidney Lanier (1842–1881). Oppressed by poverty and ill-health, he was torn between flute playing and poetry. Dying young of tuberculosis, he wrote some of his finest poems while afflicted with a temperature of 104°. He is perhaps best known for his "The Marshes of Glynn," a poem of faith inspired by the current clash between Darwinism and orthodox religion.

No other Southern poet came as close as Lanier to the first rank in the postwar years of the 19th Century. Undistinguished for literature before the Civil War, Dixieland had even less reason for distinction after it. An obscure poet, J. G. Coogler, wrote in 1897:

Alas for the South: her books have grown fewer—
She never was much given to literature.

In novel writing, William Dean Howells (1837–1920), an Ohioan, achieved genuine distinction in his mastery of realism and his per-fection of form. Perhaps the best-known of his numerous books is *The Rise of Silas Lapham* (1885), an absorbing tale of the newly rich class in America. Although he had never attended high school, he was offered professorships of literature at Harvard, Yale, and Johns

Hopkins, to say nothing of honorary degrees from six universities, including Oxford.

Another distinguished novelist and master of realism was Henry James (1843–1916), a brother of the Harvard philosopher, William James. A New Yorker who turned from the law to literature, he found his favorite theme in the contrast between Americans and Europeans of the leisure class, especially Englishmen. He finally took up residence in England, as did some of his disillusioned literary brethren, and died a naturalized British subject.

Stephen Crane, the fourteenth child of a Methodist minister, published at age twenty-four *The Red Badge of Courage* (1895). This stirring novel of a young Civil War recruit under fire was a triumph of realism, though the author had never seen a battle and wrote solely from the printed records. He died of tuberculosis in 1900, when only twenty-nine.

Literature for the Masses

General Lewis Wallace—lawyer-soldier-author—was a colorful figure. Having fought with distinction in the Civil War, he sought to combat the prevailing wave of Darwinian skepticism with his novel *Ben Hur: A Tale of the Christ* (1880). A phenomenal success, the book sold an estimated two million copies in many languages, including Arabic and Chinese, and later appeared on stage and screen. It was the *Uncle Tom's Cabin* of the anti-Darwinists, who found in it support for the Holy Scriptures.

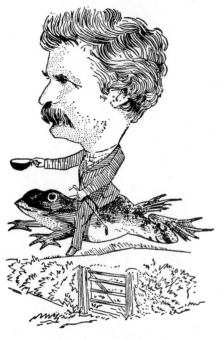

Mark Twain on his Celebrated Jumping Frog From a poster advertising one of his public lectures.

Two other writers, Bret Harte and Mark Twain, rode out of the West. Harte (1836–1902), a foppishly dressed New Yorker, had moved to California, where he found fame and temporary fortune by striking it rich with gold-rush stories. He is best known for his realistic "The Luck of Roaring Camp" and "The Outcasts of Poker Flat," and for the popular poem "Plain Language from Truthful James." It advertised a common California prejudice:

That for ways that are dark
  And for tricks that are vain,
The heathen Chinee is peculiar. . . .

Mark Twain, christened Samuel L. Clemens (1835–1910), was one of the few literary giants yet produced by America. Poorly schooled in frontier Missouri, the footloose "Prince of Humorists" received much of his education in the great University of Experience. For a time he served as a pilot on the Mississippi River, and later took his pen name, Mark Twain, from the boatman's cry meaning "two fathoms." Moving to California, he attracted some attention with his *The Celebrated Jumping Frog of Calaveras County and Other Sketches* (1867), and particularly with his *The Innocents Abroad* (1869), an almost instantaneous success.

Many other books flowed from Twain's busy pen. His *The Adventures of Tom Sawyer* (1876) and *The Adventures of Huckleberry Finn* (1884) rank among American masterpieces, though initially regarded in snobbish New England circles as "trash." His later years were soured by bankruptcy growing out of unwise investments, and he was forced to take to the lecture platform and amuse what he called "the damned human race." A great tribute was paid to his self-tutored genius—and to American letters—when England's Oxford University awarded him an honorary degree in 1907. Journalist, humorist, satirist, and foe of social injustice, he made his most enduring contribution in recapturing frontier realism and humor in the authentic American dialect.

A far less talented writer was Horatio ("Holy Horatio") Alger, a Puritan-reared New Englander, who in 1866 forsook the pulpit for the pen. Deeply interested in New York newsboys, he wrote more than a hundred volumes of juvenile fiction that sold over one hundred million copies. His stock formula was that virtue, honesty, and industry are rewarded by success, wealth, and honor—a kind of survival of the purest, especially non-smokers, non-drinkers, non-swearers, and non-liars. Although Alger's own bachelor life was criticized, he implanted morality and the conviction that there is always room at the top (especially if one is lucky enough to save the life of the boss' daughter and marry her).

Cheaper and more sensational were the millions of "dime novels." Paint-bedaubed Indians and quick-triggered gunmen like "Deadwood Dick" shot off vast quantities of powder, as virtue invariably triumphed. These lurid "paperbacks" were frowned upon by parents, but goggle-eyed youths read them in haylofts or in schools behind the broad covers of geography books. The king of dime novelists was Harlan F. Halsey, who made a fortune by dashing off about 650 novels, sometimes one in a day.

Critics condemned Mark Twain's writings on both moral and grammatical grounds. In Chapter One of *Huckleberry Finn* the famous author relates, "You don't known about me without you have read a book by the name of *The Adventures of Tom Sawyer;* but that ain't no matter. That book was made by Mr. Mark Twain, and he told the truth, mainly. There was things which he stretched, but mainly he told the truth."

Women in Arms

Once the shackles were stricken from the slave, American reforming zeal turned to other goals, including woman's rights. Fiery females increased their cry for the ballot, particularly after it had been forced into the hands of illiterate Negroes. An austere fighting Quakeress, Susan B. Anthony (1820–1906), continued as a militant leader, despite showers of rotten eggs and decayed vegetables. Many critics insisted that women were made for loving, not voting.

This persistent crusade for female suffrage—"Ballots for Both"—registered encouraging gains before the end of the century. Growing numbers of women were being permitted to vote in local elections, particularly on issues relating to the schools. Wyoming Territory—later called "the Equality State"—reflected the high regard of the West for the scarcer sex when it granted unrestricted suffrage to women in 1869. This important breach in the dike once made, many states followed Wyoming's example. Paralleling these triumphs, most of the states by 1890 had passed laws to permit wives to own or control their property after marriage.

The "softer" sex was becoming more independent, though American females had long enjoyed a degree of freedom unknown in Europe. Industrialization and urbanization were luring tens of thousands of women into business. A career was now an attractive alternative to early matrimony; hence marriages were being delayed and parents were having fewer children. Smaller families were also a result of crowded conditions in the cities, higher living standards, and the spread of birth control.

Marriages and Divorces, 1890–1968

Year	Marriages	Divorces	Ratio of Divorces to Marriages
1890	570,000	33,461	1–17
1900	709,000	55,751	1–12
1910	948,166	83,045	1–11
1920	1,274,476	170,505	1–7
1930	1,126,856	195,961	1–5
1940	1,595,879	264,000	1–6
1950	1,667,231	385,144	1–4.3
1960	1,523,381	393,000	1–3.8
1968	2,059,000	582,000	1–3.5

Mrs. Nation advertised as a lecturer. Courtesy Kansas Historical Society.

A gradual emancipation of females was reflected in a disquieting increase in the divorce rate. A partial explanation was that womenfolk no longer would tolerate abuse at the hands of their lords and masters. Uniformity in divorce laws, owing to the chaotic states'-rights tradition, was lamentably lacking, and "easy states," like Nevada and Wyoming, did a bustling business in dissolving marital ties.

Prohibition of Alcohol and Social Progress

Alarming gains by Demon Rum spurred the temperance reformers to redoubled zeal. Especially obnoxious to them was the shutter-doored corner saloon, misleadingly called "the poor man's club." It helped keep both him and his family poor. Liquor consumption had increased during the nerve-racking days of the Civil War; and immigrant groups, accustomed to alcohol in the Old Country, were hostile to restraints. Whiskey-loving foreigners in Boston would rudely hiss temperance lecturers.

The National Prohibition Party, organized in 1869, polled a sprinkling of votes in some of the ensuing presidential elections. Among the favorite songs of these sober souls were "I'll Marry No Man If He Drinks," "Vote Down the Vile Traffic," and "The Drunkard's Doom." Typical was:

Now, all young men, a warning take,
And shun the poisoned bowl;
'Twill lead you down to hell's dark gate,
And ruin your own soul.

Militant ladies entered the alcoholic arena, notably when the Woman's Christian Temperance Union (W.C.T.U.) was organized in 1874. The white ribbon was its symbol of purity; the saintly Frances E. Willard—also a champion of planned parenthood—was its leading spirit. Less saintly was a muscular and mentally deranged "Kansas Cyclone," Mrs. Carry A. Nation, whose first husband had died of alcoholism. With her hatchet she boldly smashed saloon bottles and bars, and her "hatchetations" brought considerable disrepute to the prohibition movement by the violence of her one-woman crusade.

But rum was now on the run. The potent Anti-Saloon League was formed in 1893, with its members singing, "The Saloon Must Go"

Putting the Burden Where it Belongs
The cartoonist argues that the costs of crime and pauperism, the offspring of alcohol, should be borne by the dealers in alcohol. *Harper's Weekly,* 1883

and "Vote for Cold Water, Boys." State-wide prohibition, which had registered surprising gains in Maine and elsewhere before the Civil War, was sweeping new states into the "dry" column. The great triumph—but only a temporary one—came in 1919, when the national prohibition amendment (18th) was attached to the Constitution.

Banners of other social crusaders were aloft. The American Society for the Prevention of Cruelty to Animals was created by Henry Bergh in 1866, after he had witnessed brutality to horses in Russia. The American Red Cross was launched in 1881, with the dynamic five-foot Clara Barton, an "angel" of Civil War battlefields, as a leading spirit. Organized philanthropy, a forerunner of the Community Chest, was becoming popular, beginning with Buffalo in the 1870's, and was replacing the old haphazard methods of giving. More money went into salaries and other collection costs, but the recipients of charity also got more, despite a poet's protest against

The organized charity, scrimped and iced,
In the name of a cautious, statistical Christ.

Artistic Triumphs

America still lacked artists to match her magnificent mountains. Art had been of sickly growth in the rustic years of the Republic, largely because of an absence of leisure and wealth. The nation now had both, but the results were unspectacular. Perhaps the roar of the industrialized civilization repelled the delicate muses; perhaps art itself was becoming mechanized. Roll-film cameras, popularized by George Eastman in the 1880's, enabled every man to be his own artist.

Yet several portrait painters of distinction emerged, notably James Whistler (1834–1903). This eccentric and quarrelsome Massachusetts Yankee had earlier been dropped from West Point after failing in chemistry. "Had silicon been a gas," he later jested, "I would have been a major general." Moving to Europe, he did much of his work in England, including the celebrated portrait of his mother. Another gifted portrait painter, likewise self-exiled in England, was John Singer Sargent (1856–1925). His flattering but somewhat superficial likenesses of the British nobility were highly prized.

Other brush wielders, no less talented, brightened the artistic horizon. Self-taught George Inness (1825–1894) looked like a fanatic with his long hair and piercing gaze, but he became America's leading landscapist. Thomas Eakins (1844–1916) attained a high degree of realism in his paintings, a quality not appreciated by portrait sitters who wanted their moles overlooked. Boston-born Winslow Homer (1836–1910), who as a youth had secretly drawn sketches in school, was perhaps the greatest painter of the group. Earthily American and largely resistant to foreign influences, he revealed rugged realism

Clara Barton (1821–1912), a shy Massachusetts school teacher, was afflicted with attacks of nervous prostration during the first half of her life. (She lived to be 91.) Following her work with the Civil War wounded, she went to Europe and became interested in the International Red Cross, which the U.S. had refused to join because of the traditional fear of foreign entanglements. Returning, she established the American National Red Cross, which she headed from 1881 to 1904. She wrote extensively on the subject, and directed efforts to peacetime disasters as well as to those of war.

and boldness of conception. His canvases of the sea and of fisherfolk were masterly, and probably no American artist has excelled him in portraying the awesome power of the ocean.

Probably the most gifted sculptor yet produced by America was Augustus Saint-Gaudens (1848–1907). Born in Ireland of an Irish mother and a French father, he became an adopted American. Although he sculptured many noble statues, his most striking work is the "Adams Monument," a shrouded and enigmatic female figure representing grief or a kindred emotion. It was erected in a Washington cemetery by the historian Henry Adams in memory of his beloved wife, who had committed suicide.

Music too was gaining popularity. America of the 1880's and 1890's was assembling high-quality symphony orchestras, notably in Boston and Chicago. The famed Metropolitan Opera House of New York was erected in 1883. In its fabled "Diamond Horseshoe" the newly rich, often under the pretense of enjoying the imported singers, would flaunt their jewels, gowns, and furs. A marvelous discovery was the reproduction of music by mechanical means. The phonograph, though a squeakily imperfect instrument when invented by the deaf Edison, had by 1900 reached over 150,000 homes. Americans were rapidly being dosed with "canned music."

The most original architects of the era sought to escape the hodge-podge borrowings from Europe by stressing usefulness of design—realism in building. The most noteworthy contribution of this sort was the steel-skeleton skyscraper. Coming first as a ten-story building in Chicago in 1884, it was made practicable by the perfecting of the elevator. An opinionated Chicagoan, Louis H. Sullivan (1856–1924), added much to the skyscraper by his guiding principle, "Form follows function."

A revival of classical architectural forms—and a setback for realism —came with the great Columbian Exposition. Held in Chicago in 1893, it honored the four hundredth anniversary of Columbus' first voyage. This so-called "dream of loveliness," which was visited by 27,000,000 people, did much to raise American artistic standards and promote city planning, although many of the spectators were attracted primarily by the torsal contortions of a hootchy-kootchy dancer, "Little Egypt."

"New York a Few Years from Now." A curiously prophetic cartoon by Thomas Nast in 1881, three years before the Chicago skyscraper was completed. *Harper's Weekly,* August 27, 1881.

Hamlin Garland, the well-known novelist and writer of short stories, was immensely impressed by the cultural value of the Chicago Colombian Exposition. He wrote to his aged parents on their Dakota farm, "Sell the cook stove if necessary and come. You *must* see this fair."

The Business of Amusement

Fun and frolic were not neglected by the workaday American. The pursuit of happiness, heralded in the Declaration of Independence, had by century's end become a frenzied scramble. People sought their pleasures fiercely, as they had overrun their continent fiercely. And now they had more time to play.

Varied diversions beckoned. As a nation of "joiners" contemptuous of royalty, Americans inconsistently sought to escape from democratic equality in the aristocratic hierarchies of lodges. The legitimate stage still flourished, as appreciative audiences responded to the lure of the footlights. Vaudeville, with its coarse jokes and graceful acrobats, continued to be immensely popular during the 1880's and 1890's.

The circus—high-tented and multi-ringed—finally emerged full-blown. Phineas T. Barnum, the master showman who had early discovered that "the public likes to be humbugged," joined hands with James A. Bailey in 1881 to stage the "Greatest Show on Earth."*

Colorful "Wild West" shows, first performed in 1883, were even more distinctively American. Headed by the knightly, goateed and free-drinking William F. ("Buffalo Bill") Cody, the troupe included war-whooping Indians, live buffalo, and deadeye marksmen. Among them was the girlish Annie Oakley. Rifle in hand, at thirty paces she could perforate a tossed-up card half a dozen times before it fluttered to the ground. (Hence the term "Annie Oakley" for a punched ticket, later for a free pass.)

Baseball, already widely played before the Civil War, was clearly emerging as the national pastime, if not a national mania. A league of professional players was formed in the 1870's, and in 1888 an all-star baseball team toured the world, using the pyramids as a backstop while in Egypt.

A gladiatorial trend toward spectators' sports, rather than participants' sports, was well exemplified by football. This rugged game, with its dangerous flying wedge, had become popular well before 1889, when Yaleman Walter C. Camp chose his first "All American" team. The Yale-Princeton game of 1893 drew fifty thousand excited spectators, while foreigners complained that the nation was getting sports "on the brain."

Even pugilism, with its long background of bare-knuckle brutality, gained a new and gloved respectability in 1892. Agile "Gentleman Jim" Corbett, a scientific boxer, wrested the world championship from the aging and alcoholic John L. Sullivan, the fabulous "Boston Strong Boy."

Two crazes swept the country in the closing decades of the century. Croquet became enormously popular, though condemned by moralists of the "naughty nineties" because it exposed feminine ankles and promoted flirtation. The low-framed "safety" bicycle came to replace the high-seated model. By 1893 a million bicycles were in use, and thousands of young ladies, jokesters remarked, were turning to this new "spinning wheel."

Basketball was invented in 1891 by James Naismith, a Y.M.C.A. instructor in Springfield, Massachusetts. Designed as an active indoor

Out-Curve. From a manual on how to pitch a baseball, 1885

---

* Now Ringling Bros. and Barnum and Bailey Combined Shows, Inc.

sport that could be played during the winter months, it spread rapidly and enjoyed enormous popularity in the next century.

The land of the skyscraper was plainly becoming more standardized, owing largely to the new industrialization. To an increasing degree, Americans were falling into the ways of lock-step living—playing, reading, thinking, and talking alike. They were eating the same canned food, wearing the same ready-made clothes. But what they had lost in variety, they were gaining in efficiency. They were still inseparably wedded to the ideal of unlimited human progress, and they still glimpsed, with invincible optimism, the unexplored vistas that stretched into the future.

SELECT READINGS

See previous chapter for titles by Hays, Tarbell, Ginger, and Spencer. Colorful social histories are J. A. GARRATY, *The New Commonwealth, 1877–1890* (1968),* ALLAN NEVINS, *The Emergence of Modern America, 1865–1878* (1927) and A. M. SCHLESINGER, *The Rise of the City, 1878–1898* (1933). On the role of immigration, see OSCAR HANDLIN's Pulitzer-prize *The Uprooted* (1951)* and JOHN HIGHAM, *Strangers in the Land* (1955).* Useful also is BLAKE MC KELVEY, *The Urbanization of America, 1860–1915* (1963). The church for the era is treated in F. P. WEISENBURGER, *Ordeal of Faith* (1959) and *Triumph of Faith* (1964). For intellectual currents see H. S. COMMAGER, *The American Mind* (1950)*; RICHARD HOFSTADTER, *Social Darwinism in American Thought* (rev. ed., 1955)*; J. E. GOULD, *The Chautauqua Movement* (1961)*; AUGUST MEIER, *Negro Thought in America, 1880–1915* (1963)*; and S. R. SPENCER, *Booker T. Washington and the Negro's Place in American Life* (1955).* On reform, consult C. A. BARKER, *Henry George* (1955) and S. E. BOWMAN, *The Year 2000* (Bellamy) (1958); on literature, VAN WYCK BROOKS, *The Confident Years* (1952) and *Howells* (1959); on architecture, SHERMAN PAUL, *Louis Sullivan* (1962)*; on sport, F. R. DULLES, *America Learns to Play* (1940). Also *Harvard Guide,** Pt. V.

* Available in paperback.

29

The Great West and the Agricultural Revolution, 1865–1890

Up to our own day American history has been in a large degree the history of the colonization of the Great West. The existence of an area of free land, its continuous recession, and the advance of American settlement westward, explain American development.

Frederick Jackson Turner, 1893

The Indian Barrier to the West

When the Civil War crashed to a close, the frontier line was still wavering westward. A long fringe of settlement, bulging outward here and there, ran roughly north through central Texas and onward to the Canadian border. Between this jagged line and the settled areas on the Pacific slope, there were virtually no white men. The only exceptions worth mentioning were the islands of Mormons in Utah, occasional trading posts and gold camps, and a few scattered Spanish-Mexican settlements in the Southwest.

Sprawling in expanse, the Great West was a rough square which measured about one thousand miles on each side. Embracing mountains, plateaus, deserts, and plains, it was the habitat of the Indian, the buffalo, the wild horse, the prairie dog, and the coyote. Twenty-five years later—that is, by 1890—the entire domain had been carved into states, except for four territories. Men flung themselves greedily on this enormous prize, as if to ravish it. Never before in human experience, probably, had so huge an area been reduced so rapidly to a semblance of civilization.

The Indians, to their misfortune, stood in the path of the white man. Like the blades of mighty scissors, two lines of onward moving pioneers were closing in simultaneously—one from the Pacific Coast, the other from the trans-Mississippi West. A clash was inevitable between an acquisitive civilization and a static culture, for the march of progress crushed under its feet the hunting grounds and hence the food supply of the red man.

Tens of thousands of half-naked Indians roamed the spacious Western plains in 1860. Some of them had surrendered immense portions of their ancestral lands, but not until they had received solemn promises from the Great White Father in Washington that they would be left alone and would receive annual gifts of food, clothing, and other supplies. Regrettably, the federal agents were often corrupt, and palmed off moth-eaten blankets, spoiled beef, and other defective provisions on the friendless redskins. One of these cheating officials, on a salary of $1500 a year, returned home after four years with an estimated $50,000.

Grasping "palefaces" were guilty of many additional provocations. They flagrantly disregarded treaty promises, openly seized the land of the Indians, wantonly slaughtered their game, and occasion-

One disheartened Indian complained to the white Sioux Commission created by Congress, "Tell your people that since the Great Father promised that we should never be removed we have been moved five times. . . . I think you had better put the Indians on wheels and you can run them about wherever you wish."

STATES OF THE GREAT WEST (with dates of admission)

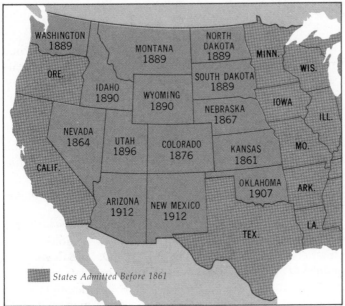

For exact order of admission, see table in Appendix.

ally debauched their squaws. During the Civil War the Sioux of Minnesota, facing starvation and taking advantage of the white man's quarrel, went on the warpath and murdered several hundred settlers. The uprising was finally crushed by federal troops, and nearly forty of the culprits, after a trial, were hanged at a well-attended mass execution.

From 1868 to about 1890, almost incessant warfare raged in various parts of the West between Indians and whites. A printed list of the names of the engagements alone covers over one hundred pages. The fighting was fierce and harrowing, especially the winter campaigning in sub-zero weather. Many of the regular troops were veterans of the Civil War, and their ranks embraced four crack Negro units, including the famous 10th Cavalry. All told, about one fifth of all troops assigned to the frontier during these years were black. Generals Sherman, Sheridan ("the only good Indian is a dead Indian"), and Custer, all of whom had won their spurs in the Civil War, gathered further laurels in the West. They were matched against formidable adversaries, for the Indians of the plains, unlike those first encountered by the American colonists, rode swift ponies and enjoyed baffling mobility. To the disgust of the American soldiers, "the hostiles" were often better armed than the federal troops sent against them with clumsy muzzle-loaders. The War Department was perhaps not so much to blame as conscienceless white fur traders, who would provide the Indians with the most modern repeating rifles.

Receding Red Men

A young lieutenant told Colonel Chivington that to attack the Indians would be a violation of pledges. "His reply was, bringing his fist down close to my face, 'Damn any man who sympathizes with Indians.' I told him what pledges were given the Indians. He replied, 'That he had come to kill Indians, and believed it to be honorable to kill Indians under any and all circumstances. . . .'"

Savagery was not all on the side of the Indians. Where fighting is protracted and uncivilized, the ethics of combat are ordinarily pulled down to a more primitive level. Whites were often the immediate aggressors, and they sometimes shot peaceful red men on sight, just to make sure they would give no trouble. At Sand Creek, Colorado, in 1864, Colonel J. M. Chivington's militia massacred in cold blood some 400 Indians who apparently thought they had been promised immunity. Squaws were shot praying for mercy, children had their brains dashed out, and braves were tortured, scalped, and unspeakably mutilated. On several notorious occasions, innocent Indians were killed for outrages committed by their fellow tribesmen; sometimes they were shot just for "sport."

Unquestionably, the most spectacular of these clashes was the Sioux War of 1876–1877, touched off when a horde of gold-greedy white men rushed into the Black Hills of South Dakota during the stampede of 1875. The proud and warlike Sioux, their lands invaded despite treaty guarantees, took to the warpath. Conspicuous among their leaders was heavy-set Sitting Bull, a medicine man as wily as he was influential.

Sioux braves were hotly pursued by impetuous George A. Custer, the buckskin-clad "boy general," now demoted to lieutenant-colonel. Attacking what turned out to be a superior force of some 2500 well-armed warriors near the Little Big Horn River in present Montana, the "White Chief with Yellow Hair" and his 264 officers and men were wiped out in 1876 when two supporting columns failed to come to their rescue.* (Sitting Bull sat out this battle, safely "making medicine" in his tent.) But white reinforcements later arrived, and Sitting Bull and the remnants of his band were finally driven to Canada, whence hunger forced them to return and surrender.

The Nez Percé Indians of Idaho were likewise goaded into warfare in 1877, when gold-crazed white miners trespassed upon their beaver streams. Chief Joseph, a noble and unusually humane leader, established himself as a remarkable strategist when he undertook a retreat of fifteen hundred miles to Canada, only to be cornered thirty miles from safety.

Fierce Apache tribes of Arizona and New Mexico were perhaps the most difficult to subdue. Led by Geronimo, whose eyes blazed hatred of the whites, they were pursued into Mexico by federal troops using the sun-flashing heliograph, a communication device, which impressed the Indians as "big medicine." Scattered remnants of the braves were persuaded to surrender after their squaws had been exiled to Florida. The Apaches ultimately became successful farmers in Oklahoma, where they raised stock instead of lifting scalps.

This relentless fire-and-sword policy of the whites at last shattered the spirit of the Indians. The vanquished redskins were finally ghettoized in "human zoos," known as reservations, there to eke out a sullen existence as wards of the government. Their white masters had at last discovered that the red men were much cheaper to feed than to fight.

The taming of the Indians was engineered by a number of factors. Of cardinal importance was the railroad, which shot an iron arrow through the heart of the West. Locomotives ("bad medicine wagons") could bring out unlimited numbers of troops, farmers, cattlemen, sheepherders, and settlers. The luckless Indians were also ravaged by the white man's diseases, to which they showed little resistance, and by his firewater, to which they showed almost no resistance. Finally, the virtual extermination of the buffalo resulted in the near-extermination of the plains Indians.

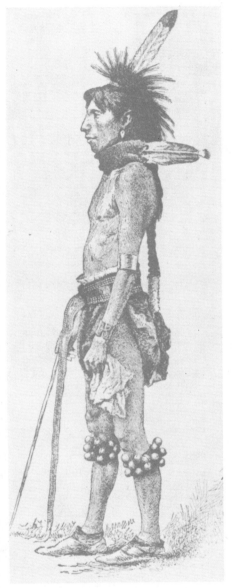

An Aboriginal Sioux Warrior

Bellowing Herds of Bison

Millions of buffalo—described by early Spaniards as "hunchback

---

*When the whites wiped out redskins, the engagement (in white history books) was usually a "battle"; when the Indians wiped out whites, it was a "massacre." Strategy, when practiced by red men, was "treachery."

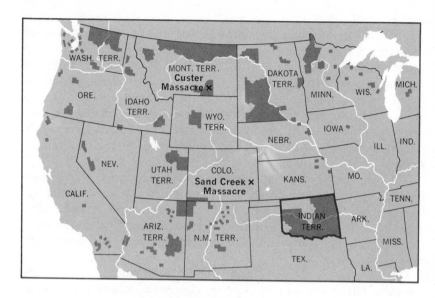

INDIAN RESERVATIONS, 1883

For two famous paintings of Indians hunting buffalo see the color portfolio following pages 366 and 814.

cows"—blackened the Western prairies when the Americans first arrived. These shaggy, lumbering animals were the staff of life for the Indian. Their flesh provided food; their dried dung provided fuel ("buffalo chips"); their hides provided clothing, lariats, bowstrings, and harness.

When the Civil War closed, there were still some fifteen million of these meaty beasts grazing on the Western plains. In 1868 one of the Kansas Pacific locomotives had to wait eight hours for a herd to amble across the tracks; experience had shown that trying to smash through would produce only mangled flesh and derailment. Much of the food supply of the railroad construction gangs came from buffalo steaks. "Buffalo Bill" Cody—sinewy, telescopic-eyed, and a crack shot—killed over four thousand in eighteen months while employed by the Kansas Pacific.

With the building of the railroad, the massacre of the herds began in dead earnest. Most of the stupid creatures were slain for their hides and in response to the insatiable demand for buffalo robes, then highly fashionable. Others were felled merely for their tongues or a few other choice cuts, while the rest of the carcass was left to be picked by the vultures. Countless buffalo were shot for sheer amusement with repeating rifles. "Sportsmen" on lurching railroad trains would lean out the windows and blaze away at the brutes to satisfy their lust for slaughter or excitement.

Such wholesale butchery could have only one end. By 1885 fewer than a thousand buffalo were left, and the once-numerous quadrupeds were in danger of complete extermination. Somewhat like the Indians, a few thousand of the beefy animals have been kept

About 1875, when the buffalo were still numerous, a popular cowboy song emerged:

Oh, bury me not on the lone prairie,
Where the wild coyotes will howl over me,
Where the buffalo roams and the wind roars free;
Oh, bury me not on the lone prairie!

alive, largely as living museum pieces. The whole story is a shocking example of the greed and waste that accompanied the conquest of the continent.

"Lo, the Poor Indian!"

By 1890 the Indian was an administrative problem rather than a military menace, even though occasional bands of alcoholically aroused braves would "go off the reservation." The principal tasks of the whites were to police the red men and adjust them to a more restricted life. The national conscience, already a bit uneasy, had been pricked in 1881 when a sentimental poet-novelist, Helen Hunt Jackson, published her devastating *A Century of Dishonor*. This book was a historical account of governmental injustice in treating and cheating the Indian. Even more disquieting in many ways was her supplementary novel, *Ramona* (1884), a love story of injustice to the California aborigines. This romantic tale ultimately sold some 600,000 copies.

Patience Until the Indian is Civilized
The white victim of Indian raids gets cold comfort from Secretary of the Interior Carl Schurz, the German-American reformer. Thomas Nast, *Harper's Weekly,* 1878

An aroused public sentiment now demanded that something be done for the shabbily treated red men. A most significant response came in 1887, when Congress passed the Dawes Act—the first serious attempt on a national scale to civilize the Indians. Tribes hitherto had been regarded as domestic nations within the American nation, and until 1871 hundreds of treaties had been made with them as with foreign governments. The Dawes Act provided for dissolving many of the tribes as legal entities, and for wiping out tribal ownership of property. Land was now granted to individual Indians, with 160 acres going to the head of a family, double that amount if grazing areas were involved. But lest designing whites be tempted to get the Indians drunk and trick them into signing away their birthright for a song, the holdings were made inalienable for twenty-five years. In the end the red man came out with less land and more liabilities.

Further changes in Indian policy occurred in succeeding decades. In 1906 the Burke Act extended the probationary period of Uncle Sam's stepchildren before granting full citizenship. The goal was also adopted of preserving the cultural heritage of the Indians, instead of forcing them to travel completely the "white man's road." Full citizenship was granted in 1924.

Under the new federal policies, defective though they were, the Indian population started to mount slowly. The total number had been reduced by 1887 to about 243,000—the result of bullets, bottles, and bacteria—but the census of 1960 counted 524,000. Possibly more Indians dwell in the United States today than were here when Columbus came, even though their blood is much diluted with that of their conquerors.

The "noble red man" was partly a creation of literary imagination, especially that of novelist James Fenimore Cooper. Rapacious and

The Indian fought back because the white man encroached upon his land, and the white man fought back because the Indian fought back. In 1867 Mark Twain wrote for a San Francisco newspaper, "The Cooper Indians [the idealized Indians of novelist James Fenimore Cooper] are dead—died with their creator. The kind that are left are of altogether a different breed, and cannot be successfully fought with poetry, and sentiment, and soft soap, and magnanimity."

unfriendly whites, overlooking the same defects in their own kind, have referred to the Indians as dirty, lousy, cruel, treacherous, polygamous, lazy, and thieving. The truth is that the redskins were children of a more primitive culture, and one cannot fairly judge them by other standards. Yet many of them, notably the Cherokees who were resettled in Oklahoma, have shown noteworthy adaptability to the economic ways of the whites.

Despite many bloody clashes, the American people owe a genuine debt to the Indian. He traded the furs which kept many of the early colonies on their economic feet. He provided corn, potatoes, tobacco, tomatoes, maple sugar, beans, squash, and other foods, while demonstrating how they could be produced. He showed the white men how to make birch canoes, snowshoes, and toboggans, and taught the value of many medicinal plants and herbs. He added immeasurably to pioneering difficulties, but above all he helped make the Americans a tough and resourceful people. A substantial part of the nation's history can be written in terms of a relentless, three-hundred-year campaign against the Indians—one of the decisive campaigns of world history.

Mining: From Dishpan to Ore-Breaker

Beyond doubt the conquest of the Indians and the coming of the railroad were life-giving boons to the mining frontier. The golden gravel of California continued to yield "pay dirt," and in 1858 an electrifying discovery convulsed Colorado. Avid "Fifty-Niners" or "Pike's Peakers" rushed west to rip at the ramparts of the Rockies. But there were more miners than minerals; and many a gold-grubber, with "Pike's Peak or Bust" inscribed on the canvas of his covered wagon, creaked wearily back with the added inscription, "Busted, by Gosh." Yet countless bearded fortune seekers stayed on, some to strip away the silver deposits, others to extract nonmetallic wealth from the earth in the form of golden grain.

"Fifty-Niners" also poured feverishly into Nevada in 1859, after the fabulous Comstock Lode had been uncovered. A fantastic amount of gold and silver, worth more than $340,000,000, was mined by the "Kings of the Comstock" from 1860 to 1890. The scantily populated state of Nevada, "child of the Comstock Lode," was prematurely railroaded into the Union in 1864, partly to provide three electoral votes for President Lincoln.

Smaller "lucky strikes" drew frantic gold-and-silver seekers into Montana, Idaho, and other Western states. Boom towns, known as "Helldorados," sprouted from the desert sands like magic. Every third cabin was a saloon, where sweat-stained miners drank bad liquor ("rotgut") in the company of bad women. Lynch law and hempen vigilante justice, as in early California, preserved some semblance of order. And when the "diggings" petered out, the gold-seekers decamped, leaving picturesque "ghost towns" silhouetted in the desert, like Virginia City, Nevada.

Once the loose surface gold was gobbled up, ore-breaking machinery had to be imported to smash the gold-bearing quartz. This operation was so expensive that it could ordinarily be undertaken only by corporations pooling the wealth of stockholders. Gradually the Age of Big Business came to the mining industry. Dusty, bewhiskered miners, dishpans in hand, were replaced by the impersonal and beardless corporations, with their costly machinery and trained engineers. The once-picturesque gold-washer became just another day laborer, for it took gold to get gold.

Yet the mining frontier had played a vital role in subduing the continent. Magnet-like, it attracted population and wealth, while advertising the wonders of the wild West. The amassing of precious metals helped finance the Civil War, facilitated the building of railroads, and forced a partial solution of the Indian problem. The outpouring of silver and gold enabled the Treasury to resume specie payments in 1879, and precipitated the silver issue into American politics. "Silver Senators," representing the thinly peopled "acreage states" of the West, used their disproportionate influence to promote the interests of the silver men. Finally, the mining frontier added to American folklore and literature, as the writings of Bret Harte and Mark Twain so colorfully attest.

Beef Bonanzas and the Long Drive

When the Civil War ended, the grassy plains of Texas supported several million tough, long-horned cattle. These scrawny beasts, whose horn spread sometimes reached eight feet, were killed primarily for their hides. There was no way of getting their meat profitably to market.

The problem of marketing was neatly solved when the transcontinental railroads thrust their iron fingers into the West. Cattle could now be shipped bodily to the stockyards and, under "beef barons" like the Swifts and Armours, the highly industrialized meatpacking industry sprang into existence as a main pillar of the economy. Drawing upon the gigantic stockyards at Kansas City and Chicago, the packers could ship their fresh products to the East Coast in the newly perfected refrigerator cars.

A spectacular feeder of the new slaughterhouses was the "Long Drive." Texas cattle raisers, with herds numbering from one thousand to ten thousand head, would drive their animals slowly over the unfenced and unpeopled plains until they reached a railroad terminal. The bawling beasts grazed en route on the free government grass. Favorite terminal points were fly-specked "cow towns" like Dodge

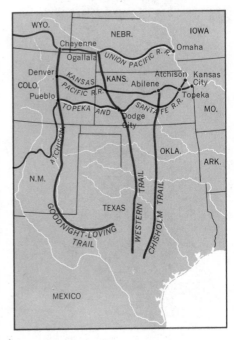

CATTLE TRAILS

City—"the Bibulous Babylon of the Frontier"—and Abilene (Kansas), Ogallala (Nebraska), and Cheyenne (Wyoming). At Abilene, order was maintained by "Judge Colt" in the person of Marshal James B. ("Wild Bill") Hickok, a fabulous gunman who reputedly killed only in self-defense or in line of duty, and who was finally shot in the back while playing poker.*

As long as lush grass was available, the Long Drive proved profitable—that is, to the luckier cattlemen who escaped the Indians, stampedes, cattle fever, and other hazards. From 1866 to 1888 bellowing herds, totaling over 4,000,000 steers, were driven northward from the beef bowl of Texas. In peak years the profits to some cattlemen would soar as high as 40%. The steer was king in a Cattle Kingdom richly carpeted with grass.

What the Lord giveth, the Lord also taketh away. The railroad made the Long Drive; the railroad also unmade the Long Drive, primarily because the locomotives ran both ways. The same rails that bore the cattle from the open range to the kitchen range brought out the homesteader and the sheepherder. Both of these intruders, amid flying bullets, built barbed-wire fences that were too numerous to be cut down by the cowboys. Furthermore the terrible winter of 1886–87, with blinding blizzards that reached 68° below zero, left thousands of dazed cattle starving and freezing. Overexpansion and overgrazing likewise took their toll, as the cowboys slowly gave way to ploughboys.

The only escape for the stockman was to make cattle raising a big business and avoid the perils of overproduction. Breeders learned to fence their ranches, lay in winter feed, import blooded bulls, and produce fewer and meatier animals. They also learned to organize. The Wyoming Stock-Growers' Association, especially in the 1880's, virtually controlled the state and its legislature. Many high-handed and illegal practices went on, but such was the over-rapid taming of the "Wild West."

These were the days when cowboyhood was in flower. The equipment of the lone cowhand—from "shooting irons" and ten-gallon hat to chaps and high-heeled boots—served a useful, not an ornamental, function. A "genuwine" gun-toting cowpuncher, riding where men were men and smelled like horses, could boast:

I'm wild and woolly
And full of fleas;
Ain't never been curried
Below the knees.

Old-Time Texas Cowman. By Frederick Remington, 1888.

* Frontier marshals like Hickok, Wyatt Earp, and "Bat" Masterson have been highly romanticized: some were little better than criminals who shot men from behind curtains. They were less "fast on the draw" and less accurate with their "sixguns" than commonly portrayed.

These bronzed and bowlegged Knights of the Saddle, with colorful trappings and cattle-lulling songs, became an authentic part of American folklore. A surprising number of them were Negroes, who especially enjoyed the freedom of the open range.

Free Land for Free Men

A new day dawned for Western farmers with the Homestead Act of 1862—an epochal measure vigorously opposed by the South before secession. The law provided that a settler could acquire as much as 160 acres of land (a quarter section) by living on it five years, improving it, and paying a nominal fee of ten dollars. Pre-emption, or first choice, was still possible for certain squatters at $1.25 an acre.

The Homestead Act marked a drastic departure from previous policy. Hitherto public land had been sold primarily for revenue; now it was to be given away to encourage a rapid filling of empty spaces and to provide a stimulus to the family farm—"the backbone of democracy." The act was a godsend to a host of farmers who could not afford to buy large holdings; and during the forty years after its passage about half a million families carved out new homes in the vast open stretches.

But the Homestead Act often turned out to be a cruel hoax. The standard 160 acres, quite adequate in the well-watered Mississippi basin, frequently proved quite inadequate on the rain-scarce Great Plains. Thousands of homesteaders were forced to give up the one-sided struggle. Uncle Sam, it was said, bet 160 acres against ten dollars that the settler could not live on his homestead for five years. One of these unsuccessful gambles in Greer County, western Oklahoma, inspired a folk song:

Hurrah for Greer County! The land of the free,
The land of the bedbug, grasshopper, and flea;
I'll sing of its praises, I'll tell of its fame,
While starving to death on my government claim.

Naked fraud was spawned by the Homestead Act and sister laws. Perhaps ten times more of the public domain wound up in the clutches of land-grabbing promoters than in the hands of bona fide farmers. Unscrupulous corporations would use "dummy" homesteaders—often aliens bribed with cash or a bottle of beer—to grab off the best properties containing timber, minerals, and oil. Settlers would later swear that they had "improved" the property by erecting a "twelve by fourteen" dwelling, which turned out to measure twelve by fourteen *inches*. In later years the Washington officials were only partially successful in unraveling the tangled skein of deceit. So functioned the government's first big "giveaway" program.

Taming Western Deserts

The life-giving railways also played a major role in developing the agricultural West, primarily through the profitable marketing of crops. In addition, the railroad officials induced Americans and European immigrants to buy the cheap lands earlier granted to the companies by the government. A leader in such "induced colonization" was the Northern Pacific Railroad, which at one time had nearly a thousand paid agents in Europe distributing roseate leaflets in various languages.

A shattering of the myth of the Great American Desert further opened the gateways to the agricultural West. The wind-swept prairies were for the most part treeless, and the tough sod had been pounded solid by millions of buffalo hoofs. Pioneer explorers and trappers had assumed that the soil must be sterile, simply because it was not heavily watered and did not support immense forests. But once the prairie sod was broken—and this was done in Kansas with special plows pulled by four powerful yoke of oxen—the earth proved to be astonishingly fruitful.

This boom in Western farming was aided by additional stimulants. Improved irrigation techniques—"the miracle of water"—caused deserts to bloom, notably in Mormon Utah. Tough strains of wheat that were resistant to cold and drought were imported from Russia, and they blossomed into billowing yellow carpets. New flour-milling processes, which brought John S. Pillsbury of Minneapolis both fame and fortune, increased the demand for grain.

AVERAGE ANNUAL PRECIPITATION

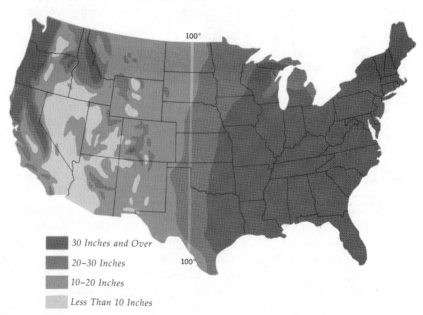

100°

100°

■ 30 Inches and Over

■ 20–30 Inches

■ 10–20 Inches

Less Than 10 Inches

Wheat growers were lured out onto the poorer marginal lands, owing to the high prices in the 1870's resulting from crop failures in other parts of the world. Farmers rashly pushed beyond the 100th meridian as far west as the semi-arid regions of eastern Colorado and Montana, where they developed the special techniques of "dry" farming. To their dismay, they were to discover in the next decade that dry farming succeeds best in wet years, and that dusty farms produce dust bowls.

Barbed wire, hardly less than the railroad, bound together the Great West. Fences were necessary to contain livestock, as well as to enclose water holes. Wood was too scarce on the treeless prairies, and ordinary wire would not hold a rampaging steer. In 1874 Joseph F. Glidden invented a superior type of barbed wire, and in 1883 the company using his patent was turning out 600 miles of the new product each day. Among other contributions, barbed wire gave the farmer greater protection against trespassing cattle, although spelling the doom of the Long Drive.

The Far West Comes of Age

The Great West experienced a fantastic growth of population from the 1870's to the 1890's. A current quip was that one could not tell the truth about the West without lying. Confederate and Union veterans alike moved into the sunset with their families, as did tens of thousands of inpouring immigrants.

A parade of new Western states proudly joined their Eastern sisters. Boom-town Colorado, offspring of the Pike's Peak gold rush, was greeted in 1876 as "the Centennial State." In 1889–1890 a Republican Congress, eagerly seeking more Republican electoral and Congressional votes, admitted in a wholesale lot six new states: North Dakota, South Dakota, Montana, Washington, Idaho, and Wyoming. The Mormon Church formally and belatedly banned polygamy in 1890, but not until 1896 was Utah deemed worthy of admission. Only Oklahoma, New Mexico, and Arizona remained to be erected into states from contiguous territory on the mainland of North America.

In a last gaudy fling, the Washington government made available to settlers vast stretches of fertile plains formerly occupied by the Indians in the district of Oklahoma ("the Beautiful Land"). Scores of overeager and well-armed "sooners," illegally jumping the gun, had entered Oklahoma territory. They had to be evicted repeatedly by federal troops, who on occasion would shoot the horses of intruders. On April 22, 1889, all was in readiness for the legal opening, and some 50,000 "boomers" were poised expectantly on the boundary line. At high noon the bugle shrilled, and a horde of "Eighty-Niners" poured in on lathered horses or careening vehicles. That night a lonely spot on the prairie had mushroomed into the tented city of

One prod toward abolishing polygamy in Utah came in the Republican platform of 1888, "The political power of the Mormon Church . . . is a menace to free institutions, a danger no longer to be suffered. Therefore we pledge the Republican party to . . . place upon the statute books legislation stringent enough to divorce the political from the ecclesiastical power, and thus stamp out the attendant wickedness of polygamy."

Sooners and Boomers in Oklahoma

Guthrie, with over 10,000 souls. By the end of the year Oklahoma boasted 60,000 inhabitants, and Congress erected into a territory the domain that in 1907 was to be "the Sooner State."

The mad haste of the "boomers" underscored the fact that fertile free land was no longer abundant. In 1890—a watershed date—the Superintendent of the Census announced that for the first time in America's experience a frontier line was no longer discernible. All the unsettled areas were now broken into by isolated bodies of settlement.

This momentous announcement has somehow led to a pair of misconceptions. One is that the year 1890 marked a sharp break with the past; the other is that thereafter little or no land was taken up under the Homestead Act of 1862.

Actually, few Americans in 1890 realized that the fading frontier line had disappeared. The Homestead Act remained on the books—and still does—and more millions of acres were taken up after 1890 than between 1862 and 1890. But in general the new lands were less desirable, and many sterile or parched farms, though well watered with sweat, had to be abandoned. To this day the federal government, which owns nearly one-fourth of all American soil, has many millions of acres which may be homesteaded. But they are mostly grazing lands and other marginal areas incapable of sustaining a decent standard of living. From time to time, considerable acreage is rendered attractive for homesteading by the completion of irrigation or reclamation projects. In these ways the frontier survived its "death" by several decades.

As the 19th Century neared its sunset, the westward-tramping American people were disturbed to find that their fabled free land was going or had gone. The Secretary of War had prophesied in 1827 that it would take five hundred years to fill the West. But when the nation learned that its land was not inexhaustible, the seeds were planted in the public mind for the belated conservation movement of later decades.

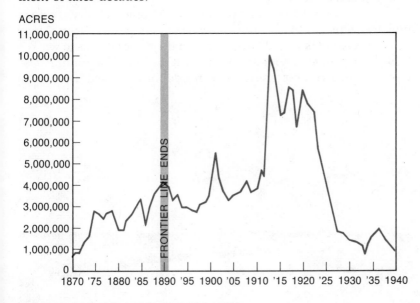

HOMESTEADS FROM THE PUBLIC LANDS
Acreage Covered by Perfected Entries

The Folding Frontier

The frontier was more than a place: it was also a state of mind and a symbol of opportunity. Its passing ended a romantic phase of the nation's internal development, and created new economic and psychological problems.

Traditionally footloose, the American has been notorious for his mobility; the automobile trailer is a typically American vehicle. The nation's farmers, unlike the European peasant, have seldom remained rooted to their soil. The sale of land for a profit, as settlement closed in, was often the settler's most profitable crop.

Much has been said about the frontier as a "safety valve." The theory is that when hard times came, the unemployed who cluttered the city pavements merely moved west, took up farms, and prospered.

In truth relatively few city dwellers, at least in the populous Eastern centers, emigrated to the frontier during depressions. Most of them did not know how to farm; few of them could raise enough money to transport themselves west and then pay for livestock and expensive machinery. The initial outlay for equipment had become so heavy by the 1880's and 1890's that the West was decreasingly a land of opportunity for farmers, though it might be for ranchers, miners, and day laborers. A large proportion of the settlers who moved west came from farms on the older frontier, which was within striking distance of the new frontier.

But the "safety-valve" theory does have some validity. For one thing, free acreage lured westward a host of immigrant farmers. Many of these newcomers would have stayed in the Eastern cities to worsen problems of unemployment and slum-festering. The frontier also drew off some restless spirits, and no doubt exercised a powerful

The Long Drive.
Harper's Weekly, 1874

psychological influence. Even though the Easterner seldom pulled up stakes and moved west, in theory he could always flee to the frontier. This prospect often gave a lift to his drooping spirit—and perhaps also a lift to the wages paid by his employer.

Once the fertile and well-watered free lands were gone, farmers could no longer move west in significant numbers. They had to stand and fight, and consequently they voiced their grievances more and fled from them less. Some farmers actually turned their backs upon the West and moved east. In fact, the vast cityward movement near the end of the century partially replaced the old Westward Movement.

American history cannot be properly understood unless it is viewed in the light of this westward-moving experience—an experience that was centuries-long and soul-searing. Though raucous and raw, the frontier was the cradle of youthful and robust Americanism, and it left an enduring imprint on the older settlements. The Wild West, with its pistol-popping days, was about to disappear. But much of its distinctive flavor remained with the American people, among whom lingered its incurable optimism, its resilient toughness, its handy-man resourcefulness, its zestful eagerness for social and economic reform. Its spirit still endures in the cowboy-worship of the ever-popular Western fiction and movies, which recapture the spirit of the sagebrush saga, when men were men and women were scarce and highly prized.

The Farm Becomes a Factory

The role of the American farmer, who had once been a jack-of-all trades, was rapidly changing. In colonial days he had lived on a kind of Robinson Crusoe's island; he had raised his own food, and his womenfolk had woven the clothing. But diversification of crops declined with the passing decades; and after the Civil War, if not earlier, the immense grain-producing areas of the Mississippi Valley found themselves in the throes of an agricultural revolution. Prices were so favorable that the farmer was concentrating on a single money-crop, such as wheat or corn. He could use his profits to buy his foodstuffs at the country store, instead of raising them himself. He could secure his manufactured goods in town or by mail order, perhaps from the Chicago firm of Aaron Montgomery Ward, established in 1872, with its first catalog a single sheet.

A large-scale farmer was now both a specialist and a businessman. As a cog in the vast industrial machine, he was intimately tied in with banking, railroading, and manufacturing. He had to buy expensive machinery to plant and to harvest his crops. A powerful steam engine could drag behind it simultaneously the plow, seeder, and harrow. The speed of harvesting wheat was immensely increased in the 1870's by John F. Appleby's twin binder, and then in the 1880's

In 1884, P. A. Kropotkin, an exiled Russian revolutionist, then imprisoned in France, unwittingly described the plight of the American farmers while focusing on those in Europe: "The Golden Age of the small farmer is over. He can barely get along. He is in debt to the cattle-dealer, the land speculator, the usurer. Mortgages ruin whole communities, even more than taxes."

Marsh Harvester and Appleby Binder

by the "combine"—the combined reaper-thresher, which was drawn by twenty to forty horses, and which both reaped and bagged the grain. Widespread use of such costly equipment naturally called for first-class management. But the farmer, often unskilled as a business-man, was inclined to blame the banks and railroads, rather than his own shortcomings, for his losses.

This amazing mechanization of agriculture in the post-war years was almost as striking as the mechanization of industry. America was rapidly becoming the world's bread basket and butcher shop. The farm was attaining the status of a factory—an outdoor grain factory. Bonanza wheat farms of the Minnesota–North Dakota area, for ex-ample, were enormous. By 1890 there were at least a half-dozen of them larger than 15,000 acres, with communication by telephone from one part to another. King Wheat was achieving an increasingly prominent position in the galaxy of agricultural potentates.

Deflation Dooms the Debtor

Once the farmer became chained to a one-crop economy—wheat or corn—he was in the same leaky boat with the cotton grower of the South. As long as prices stayed high, all went well. But when they skidded in the 1880's, bankruptcy fell like a blight upon the farm belts.

The grain farmer was no longer the master of his own destiny. He was engaged in one of the most fiercely competitive of busi-nesses, for the price of his product was determined in a world market by the world output. If the wheat fields of Argentina, Russia, and other foreign countries smiled, the price of his grain would fall and he would face ruin, as he did in the 1880's and 1890's.

Low prices and a deflated currency were the chief worries of the frustrated farmer—North, South, and West. If he had borrowed $1000 in 1885, when wheat was worth about a dollar a bushel, he expected to pay back the equivalent of 1000 bushels, plus interest, when his mortgage fell due. But if he let his debt run to 1890, when wheat had fallen to about fifty cents a bushel, he would have to pay back the price of 2000 bushels for the $1000 he had borrowed, plus interest. This unexpected burden struck him as unjust, though his steely-eyed creditor often branded the complaining farmer a slippery and dishonest rascal.

The deflationary pinch on the debtor flowed partly from the static money supply. There were simply not enough dollars to go around, and as a result prices were forced down. In 1870, the currency in circulation for each person was $19.42; in 1890 it was only $22.67. Yet during these twenty years business and industrial activity, increasing manyfold, had intensified the scramble for available currency.

The forgotten farmer was caught on a treadmill. Despite unremitting toil, he operated year after year at a loss, and lived off his fat as best he could. In a vicious circle, his farm machinery increased his output of grain, lowered the price, and drove him even deeper into debt. Mortgages engulfed homesteads at an alarming rate; by 1890 Nebraska alone reported more than 100,000 farms blanketed with mortgages. The repeated crash of the sheriff-auctioneer's hammer kept announcing to the world that another sturdy American husbandman had become landless in a landed nation.

Ruinous rates of interest, running from 8% to 40%, were charged on mortgages, largely by agents of Eastern loan companies. The

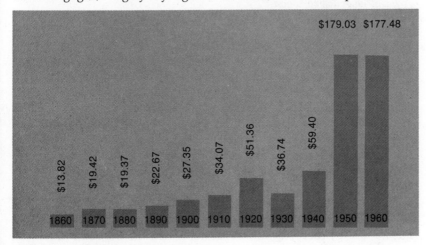

PER CAPITA MONEY IN CIRCULATION

A contemporary farm protest song, "The Kansas Fool," ran:

The bankers followed us out west;
And did in mortgages invest;
They looked ahead and shrewdly planned,
And soon they'll have our Kansas land.

windburned sons of the sod, who felt that they deserved praise for developing the country, cried out in despair against the loan sharks and the Wall Street octopus. Laws against excessive interest charges brought little relief.

Farm tenancy rather than farm ownership was spreading like stinkweed. The trend was especially marked in the share-cropping South, where cotton prices also sank dismayingly. By 1880 one-fourth of all American farms were operated by tenants. The United States was ready to feed the world, but under the new industrial feudalism the farmers were about to sink into a status suggesting Old World serfdom.

Unhappy Husbandmen

Even Dame Nature ceased smiling, as her powerful forces conspired against agriculture. Mile-wide clouds of grasshoppers, leaving "nothing but the mortgage," periodically ravaged prairie farms. The terrible cotton-boll weevil was also wreaking havoc by the early 1890's.

The good earth was going sour. Floods added to the waste of erosion, which had already washed the topsoil off millions of once-lush Southern acres. Expensive fertilizers were urgently needed. A long succession of droughts seared the trans-Mississippi West, beginning in the summer of 1887. Whole towns were abandoned. "Going home to the wife's folks" and "In God we trusted, in Kansas we busted" were typical laments of many impoverished farmers, as they fled their weather-beaten shacks and sun-baked sod houses. One irate "poet" proclaimed:

Fifty miles to water,
A hundred miles to wood,
To hell with this damned country,
I'm going home for good.

To add to his miseries, the soil-tiller was gouged by his government—local, state, and national. His land was overassessed and he paid painful local taxes, while wealthy Easterners concealed their stocks and bonds in safe-deposit boxes. Protective tariffs of these years, while pouring profits into the pockets of the manufacturer, imposed heavy burdens on agriculture, especially in the South. Cotton producers or grain growers had to sell their low-priced, unprotected product in a fiercely competitive world market, while buying their high-priced, manufactured goods in a protected home market.

The farmer was also "farmed" by the corporations and processors. He was at the mercy of the Harvester Trust, the Barbed Wire Trust, and the Fertilizer Trust, all of which could control output and raise

Western Ghost Town.
Harper's Weekly, 1874

prices to extortionate levels. Middlemen took a juicy "cut" from the selling price of the goods that he bought, while storage rates for his grain at the warehouses and elevators were pushed up by the operators.

In addition, the railroad octopus had the grain growers in its grip. Freight rates could be so high that the farmer sometimes lost less if he burned his corn for fuel than if he shipped it. If he raised his voice in protest, the ruthless railroad operators might let his grain spoil in damp places, or refuse to provide him with cars when needed.

By 1890 the farmers comprised nearly one-half of the population, but they were hopelessly disorganized. The manufacturers and railroads, which were well organized, employed persuasive lobbyists. But the farmers were by nature independent and individualistic—dead set against consolidation or regimentation. They never did organize successfully to restrict production until forced to do so by Washington nearly half a century later, in Roosevelt's New Deal days. Meanwhile they were slowly being goaded into a large-scale political uprising.

The Farmers Take Their Stand

Agrarian unrest had flared forth earlier in the Greenback movement shortly after the Civil War. Prices sagged in 1868, and a host of farmers unsuccessfully sought relief from low prices and high indebtedness by demanding an inflation of the currency with paper money.

The National Grange of the Patrons of Husbandry—better known as the Grange—was organized in 1867. Its leading spirit was Oliver H. Kelley, a shrewd and energetic Minnesota farmer then working as a clerk in Washington. A primary objective at first was to stimulate the minds of the farm folk by social, educational, and fraternal activities.

With picnics, music, and lecturers, the Grange had much colorful appeal. Kelley, a Mason, introduced a mumbo-jumbo of passwords and secrecy, as well as a four-ply hierarchy, ranging (for men) from Laborer to Husbandman, and (for women) from Maid to Matron. The movement was a godsend to the sun-bonneted and bony-handed womenfolk, who were cursed with loneliness in widely separated farmhouses. The Grange spread like an old-time prairie fire, and by 1875 claimed 800,000 members, chiefly in the Middle West and South. Buzzing with gossip, these ginghamed and gallused folk often met in red schoolhouses around pot-bellied stoves.

The Grangers gradually raised their goals from self-improvement to improvement of the farmers' plight. In a determined effort to escape the clutches of the trusts, they established cooperatives for both consumers and producers. Their most ambitious experiment was an

The Grange Awakening the Sleepers The farmer tries to arouse the apathetic public to the dangers of the onrushing railroad monopoly. Culver Service.

attempt to manufacture harvesting machinery, but this venture, partly as a result of mismanagement, ended in financial disaster.

Embattled Grangers also went into politics, enjoying their most gratifying success in the grain-growing regions of the upper Mississippi Valley, chiefly in Illinois, Wisconsin, Iowa, and Minnesota. There, through state legislation, they strove to regulate railway rates and the storage rates charged by railroads and by the operators of warehouses and grain elevators. Many of the state courts, notably in Illinois, were disposed to recognize the principle of public control of private business for the general welfare. But a number of the so-called Granger Laws were badly drawn, and they were bitterly fought through the high courts by the well-paid lawyers of the "interests." Following judicial reverses, most severely at the hands of the Supreme Court in the famous Wabash Railroad decision of 1886 (see p. 560), the Grangers faded rapidly in influence. But their organization has lived on as a vocal champion of farm interests, while brightening rural life with social activities.

Farmers' grievances likewise found a vent in the Greenback Labor Party, which combined the inflationary appeal of the earlier Greenbackers with a program for improving the lot of labor. In 1878, the high-water mark of the movement, the Greenback-Laborites polled over a million votes and elected fourteen members of Congress. In the presidential election of 1880 the Greenbackers ran General James B. Weaver, an old Granger who was a favorite of the Civil War veterans and who possessed a remarkable voice and bearing. He spoke to perhaps a half-million citizens in a hundred or so speeches, but polled only 3% of the total popular vote.

The Passionate Populist Crusade

A striking manifestation of rural discontent, cresting in the late 1880's, came through the Farmers' Alliances, North and South, white and Negro. Like the Grangers, these groups sponsored picnics and other social gatherings; they bestirred themselves in politics; they organized cooperatives of various kinds; and they sought to break the strangling grip of the railroads and manufacturers. By about 1890 the members of the Farmers' Alliances probably numbered about 1,000,000 hard-bitten souls, many of whom sang, "Toilers Unite" and "Where Will the Farmer Be?"

A new grouping—the People's Party—began to emerge spectacularly in the early 1890's. Better known as the Populists, and cynically dubbed the "Popocrats," these zealous folk attracted countless recruits from the Farmers' Alliances. The higher the foreclosure rate on mortgages, the deeper the anger of the farmers. Numerous whiskered prophets—not to say "crackpots"—sprang forward to lead the Populists. Among these assorted characters loomed an eloquent red-

Conservatives branded the Populists "Calamity Shouters," "Calamity Prophets," and "Calamity Howlers." In 1892 the Chicago *Tribune* much underestimated the appeal of the Populists when it sneered, "The calamity platform adopted by the Populists at Omaha might invite a limited measure of support in a droughty season or a grasshopper year."

Mary E. Lease (1853–1933).
Courtesy of the Kansas
Historical Society.

haired "spellbinder," Ignatius Donnelly of Minnesota, who was three times elected to Congress.

The queen of the "calamity howlers" was undeniably Mary Elizabeth ("Mary Yellin'") Lease, a tall, mannish woman who was called "the Kansas Pythoness." In 1890 she made an estimated 160 speeches. Upbraiding the moneyed aristocracy, and denouncing the government "of Wall Street, by Wall Street, and for Wall Street," she reportedly cried that the Kansans should raise "less corn and more hell." They did. The big-city New York *Evening Post* snarled, "We don't want any more states until we can civilize Kansas." To many Easterners, complaint, not corn, was the chief crop of the Westerners.

Yet the Populists, despite their peculiarities, were not to be laughed aside. In deadly earnest, they were leading an impassioned crusade to relieve the misfortunes of the farmer. Smiles faded from Republican and Democratic faces alike as countless thousands of Populists sang, "Good-bye, My Party, Good-bye." Yawning Eastern plutocrats would have done well to heed these Western "hayseeds," for at long last the calloused and sun-baked sons of the prairies were marshaling their vast political strength.

SELECT READINGS

Vivacious chapters appear in R. A. BILLINGTON, *Westward Expansion* (3d ed., 1967). W. P. WEBB's provocative *The Great Plains* (1931)* is a landmark. The Indians are discussed in R. K. ANDRIST, *The Long Death* (1964)* and W. H. LECKIE, *The Military Conquest of the Southern Plains* (1963). On mining see RODMAN PAUL, *Mining Frontiers of the Far West, 1848–1880* (1963)* and W. S. GREEVER, *The Bonanza West* (1963). For beef, see E. S. OSGOOD, *The Day of the Cattleman* (1929)*; LEWIS ATHERTON, *The Cattle Kings* (1961); and P. DURHAM and E. L. JONES, *The Negro Cowboys* (1965). EVERETT DICK has a picturesque story in *The Sod-House Frontier* (1937). Indispensable is J. D. HICKS, *The Populist Revolt* (1931)*; more sweeping is F. A. SHANNON, *The Farmers' Last Frontier: Agriculture, 1860–1897* (1945)* and G. C. FITE, *The Farmers' Frontier, 1865–1900* (1966). An older work is S. J. BUCK, *The Granger Movement* (1913).* See also MARTIN RIDGE, *Ignatius Donnelly* (1962); NORMAN POLLACK, *The Populist Response to Industrial America* (1962)*; W. T. K. NUGENT, *The Tolerant Populists: Kansas Populism and Nativism* (1963). Also *Harvard Guide,** Pt. V.

* Available in paperback.

30

The Revolt of the Debtor, 1889–1900

You come to us and tell us that the great cities are in favor of the gold standard. We reply that the great cities rest upon our broad and fertile prairies. Burn down your cities and leave our farms, and your cities will spring up again as if by magic. But destroy our farms, and the grass will grow in the streets of every city in the country.

William J. Bryan, "Cross of Gold Speech," 1896

The Return of the Republicans under Harrison

Benjamin Harrison—stocky, heavily bearded, and dignified—was inaugurated President under weeping heavens on March 4, 1889. The outgoing Grover Cleveland obligingly held an umbrella over him. The incoming President was an honest and earnest party man, but unhappily he was brusque and abrupt. He could charm a crowd of ten thousand people with his oratory, but he would chill them individually with a clammy handshake. He came to be known, rather unfairly, as "the White House Ice Chest."

James G. Blaine, uncrowned king of the party, received the coveted Secretaryship of State as a consolation prize. Still burning with ambition, the "Plumed Knight" did not get along well with his chief. Harrison, admittedly a lesser figure, rather resented his headstrong subordinate.

During the recent presidential campaign, Harrison had made his polite bow to civil service reform. But the Republicans, after their four-year fast, clamored hungrily for the fleshpots of federal office. Harrison followed the strict letter of the civil service law, but beheaded many Democrats. To his credit, he appointed to the Civil Service Commission a bespectacled and violently energetic New Yorker, Theodore Roosevelt. This eager-beaver young politician got his position as a reward for his oratory in the recent campaign, but ironically his new job was to prevent crass spoilsmanship.

Republicans in the House of Representatives could hardly expect smooth sailing; they had only three votes more than the necessary quorum of 163 members. If the Democrats continued their practice of refusing to answer roll calls, the Republicans could muster a quorum only with difficulty. The Democrats were also prepared to make numerous delaying motions. These included time-consuming demands for a roll call to determine the presence of a quorum, even though one was obviously present.

Into this explosive cockpit stepped the new Republican Speaker of the House, Thomas B. Reed of Maine. A hulking figure who towered six feet three inches, he had already made his mark as a masterful debater. Cool and collected, he spoke with a harsh nasal drawl, and wielded a verbal harpoon of sarcasm. One Congressman who had declaimed that he would "rather be right than President," like Henry Clay, was silenced by Reed's rasping sneer that he would "never be either." Strong men cringed at "the crack of his quip."

Early in 1890 the redoubtable Reed undertook singlehandedly to change the House rules. He believed that the majority should legislate, in accord with democratic practices, and not be crippled by a filibustering minority. He therefore ignored Democratic speakers who sprang to their feet and sought to suggest the absence of a quorum. In piecing out quorums, he counted as present certain Democrats in the chamber who had not answered the roll and who, rule book in hand, furiously denied that they were legally present. For three days pandemonium rocked the House, while Reed held his ground, reputedly counting as present Congressmen who were in the barber shop or on trains headed for home.

The gavel rule of "Czar" Reed finally prevailed. The Fifty-first or "Billion Dollar" Congress—the first in peacetime to appropriate approximately this sum—gave birth to a bumper crop of legislative babies. When the Democrats won control of the House two years later, they paid Reed the compliment of adopting some of his reforms for speedier action.

Speaker Thomas B. Reed (Czar Reed), 1839–1902. Although from the politically unimportant state of Maine, he was regarded at his peak as presidential timber. Bitterly opposing the war with Spain and the acquisition of the Philippines, he retired from Congress in 1899 to practice law. It was said of him that he would rather let go with a cutting remark and lose a friend than hold his tongue and retain one.

Political Gravy for All

President Harrison, himself a Civil War general, was disposed to deal generously with his old comrades-in-arms. He appointed as Commissioner of Pensions James Tanner, who had lost both legs at

Bull Run. A notorious pension lobbyist, Corporal Tanner promised to drive a six-mule team through the Treasury, and to wring "from the hearts of some the prayer, 'God help the surplus'." His extravagance and ineptitude cost him his job in less than a year, but he cut a wide swath while there.

The "Billion Dollar Congress" cooperated by opening wide the federal purse in the Pension Act of 1890. It showered pensions on all Civil War veterans who had served for ninety days and who were now unable to do manual labor. Between 1891 and 1895 the host of pensioners was thus raised from 676,000 to 970,000, and by the time Harrison left office in 1893 the annual bill had shot up from $81,000,000 to $135,000,000.

This policy of liberality toward old soldiers had special attractions for Republican politicians. It helped to solve the problem of the Treasury surplus—a problem that had bedeviled President Cleveland. It helped to save the protective tariff by making plausible, even necessary, the continuance of high customs duties. It helped to secure Republican votes, for the aging veterans of the G.A.R. (Grand Army of the Republic) were grateful to the G.O.P. (Grand Old Party) for its handouts.

"Czar" Reed's gavel, pounding imperiously, drove through Congress additional bills, conspicuous among which was the Sherman Anti-Trust Act of 1890. This pioneering law, though a feeble bludgeon, did something to quiet the mounting uproar against bloated corporations.

Noteworthy also was the Sherman Silver Purchase Act of 1890. The Western miners were acutely unhappy over the limited silver-purchase program under the Bland-Allison Law of 1878, and many of the silverites were demanding unrestricted government buying of the "beloved white metal." At the same time, many debt-burdened Western and Southern farmers were clamoring for the unlimited coinage of silver. They were convinced that the addition of an immense amount of metallic money would inflate the currency, and thus make for higher prices and easier debt payments. The "Gold Bug" East looked with conservative horror on any such tampering with the money supply, but hungered for the profits that might be reaped from a boost in the tariff schedules.

Thus the stage was set for a huge logrolling operation. Western silver agitators agreed to support a protective tariff, which they detested; Eastern protectionists agreed to support a silver bill, which they distrusted. As a part of the resulting Sherman Silver Purchase Act of 1890, the Treasury was to buy a total of 4,500,000 ounces monthly—about all that was being mined—and pay for it in notes redeemable in either silver or gold. This new law, while boosting the price for the miners, would approximately double the minimum amount of silver that could be acquired under the old Bland-Allison law.

BILLION-DOLLARISM ↑ HOLE

President Harrison
Disposes of Surplus.
Puck, 1892

McKinley's Tariff Bill

High-protection Republicans, mistakenly claiming a mandate from the voters in the presidential election of 1888, prepared to push the tariff schedules higher. A bill was sponsored in the House by William McKinley of Ohio, who was soon to be dubbed "the high priest of high protection." Rates were boosted to the highest peacetime level yet—an average of 48.4% on dutiable goods. A bothersome surplus was disposed of by putting raw sugar on the free list and giving a bounty of 2 cents a pound to American sugar producers.

The McKinley Bill, by raising slightly the tariff duties on certain agricultural products, made a feeble attempt to quiet the outcries of the farmers. But the concession was a hollow one indeed. Few foreign growers of farm produce—wheat, corn, barley, potatoes—could hope to compete with the soil-rich Americans on their own ground.

These new duties on manufactured goods, as ill luck would have it, actually brought new woes to the farmer. Some Eastern manufacturers raised their prices even before the law went into effect. Tin peddlers—a number of them reportedly in the pay of the Democrats—went systematically from house to house in the Middle West, displaying their wares to the housewife. They would cleverly but dishonestly say that yesterday a pie pan sold for ten cents, but today for twenty-five cents—all because of the wicked new Republican tariff.

Sweeping tariff revisions, like the McKinley Act, have usually boomeranged against the party in power. Mounting discontent against the McKinley Bill, combined with other grievances, caused the voters to rise in their wrath, especially in the Middle Western farm belt. The Congressional landslide of 1890 reduced the Republican membership of the House from 166 to a scant 88 members, as compared with 235 Democrats. Farmers' Alliance men were notably successful in the Southern and Western states, and the new Congress was to contain nine of their spokesmen. Even the highly publicized McKinley was swept out of office, partly because of a Democratic gerrymander* of his district. But he was elected governor of Ohio the next year, and remained in the limelight.

* To "gerrymander" is to rearrange electoral districts in such a way as to submerge the voting strength of the opposition. In Massachusetts in 1812 one grotesquely shaped district resembled a salamander; hence the term "*gerry*mander," after Gov. Gerry.

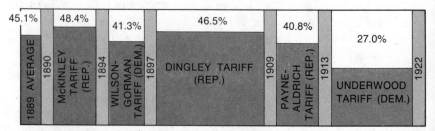

AVERAGE PERCENTAGE RATES ON DUTIABLE GOODS, 1890–1922
(See p. 279 for earlier figures; p. 849 for later figures.)

The Presidential Hopefuls of 1892

Malcontents among laborers and farmers, aroused to new fury by the McKinley Bill, were about to fuse into the Populist Party early in 1892. Many of them were members of the old Farmers' Alliance. In the spirit of a camp-meeting revival they sang:

Bring out the good old ballot, boys,
We'll right *our every* wrong.

In July, 1892, the Populists formally met at Omaha in their presidential nominating convention, which turned out to be a "mass meeting of maniacs." They uproariously nominated for the Presidency the personable and eloquent old Greenbacker, General James B. Weaver.

The Populist platform, which received a forty-minute ovation, was a scorching summation of grievances. It horrified the Eastern conservatives by proclaiming that "tramps and millionaires" come from "the same prolific womb of governmental injustice." It demanded the free and unlimited coinage of silver at the ratio of 16 to 1, as a means of increasing the currency in circulation. It urged a graduated income tax. It insisted on government ownership of the telephone and telegraph, and particularly of the railroad. The time had come, the Populists declaimed, "when the railroad corporations will either own the people or the people must own the railroads. . . ."

Several weeks earlier, in June, 1892, the Republicans had gathered in Minneapolis. Renomination of the frigid Harrison was unavoidable, even though he was cordially disliked by the party bosses. Three days before the convention met, Secretary Blaine dramatically resigned from the Cabinet, as if to focus attention on himself. But the aging and ailing "Plumed Knight's" plume was drooping badly, and Harrison was easily renominated on a platform that vigorously upheld the protective tariff.

The Democratic Man of Destiny was the portly but energetic ex-President, Grover Cleveland. He had built up a profitable law practice in New York City, and after hobnobbing with a wealthy clientele, had become increasingly conservative in outlook. Yet such was his reputation that he was nominated at Chicago on the first ballot.

Unhorsing President Harrison

On the whole the presidential campaign of 1892 was clean, quiet, and creditable. Republicans cried, "Grover, Grover, all is over," while the Democrats came back with the chant:

Grover! Grover!
Four years more of Grover,
Out they go, in we go,
Then we'll be in clover.

A few faint appeals were made to the fast-fading Bloody Shirt. Among suggestive Republican songs were "When [General] Harrison Heard the Bugle's Call" and "How Will the Soldier Vote?" But the tariff, as in the preceding campaign, was the overshadowing issue. High-tariff Republicans chorused, "Hail Protection" and "Good-bye, Free Traders, Good-bye." Low-tariff Democrats countered with "Drive the High-Tariff Tinkers to the Wall" and "Free Wool to Make Our Breeches."

An epidemic of strikes then sweeping the country proved damaging to Harrison's cause: they eloquently refuted the shopworn Republican argument that high protection meant high wages. The most notorious outburst flared forth at Carnegie's Homestead plant near Pittsburgh, following a pay slash for the steelworkers. Company officials called in three hundred armed Pinkerton detectives. Defiant strikers, armed with rifles and dynamite, forced their assailants to surrender after a pitched battle in which ten persons were killed and some sixty wounded. Troops were eventually summoned, and both the strike and the union were broken. But this unsavory episode—lead instead of bread—doubtless cost the Republicans thousands of votes.

With this unexpected boost from the Pinkerton Agency, Cleveland unhorsed Harrison. "Old Grover" polled 277 electoral votes to his opponent's 145, and 5,556,918 popular votes to 5,176,108. Cleveland,

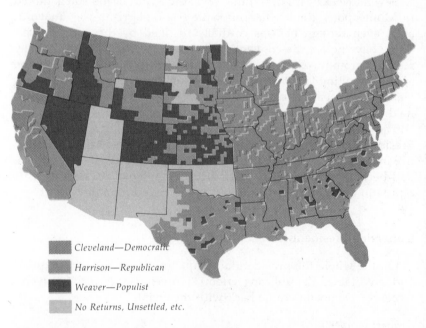

Cleveland—Democratic

Harrison—Republican

Weaver—Populist

No Returns, Unsettled, etc.

PRESIDENTIAL ELECTION OF 1892 (showing vote by county)

Note the concentration of Populist strength in the semi-arid farming regions of the western half of the country. (Compare with annual precipitation map on p. 612.)

like Andrew Jackson, received a popular plurality three times, though he took office only twice.

The Populists made a remarkable showing. Singing "Good-bye, Party Bosses," they rolled up 1,041,028 popular votes and 22 electoral votes for General Weaver. They thus became one of the few third parties in American history to break into the electoral column. But their electoral votes came only from six Middle Western and Western states, four of which (Kansas, Colorado, Idaho, and Nevada) fell completely into the Populist basket. The new party failed to gain valuable allies when the indebted farmers of the Solid South, though sorely tempted, refused to desert the Democratic camp in large numbers.

The Southern Negroes, tens of thousands of them attracted by Populist reforms, were heavy losers. When the white ruling class discovered that their vote could not be controlled, all remaining Negro suffrage in the South was virtually eliminated. More than a half century was to pass before the blacks could again vote in considerable numbers. Accompanying this disfranchisement were more severe Jim Crow laws, backed up by atrocious lynchings and designed primarily to keep the Negro segregated in public places.

"Old Grover" Cleveland Again

Grover Cleveland took office once again in 1893, the only President ever re-elected after defeat. He was the same old bull-necked and bull-headed Cleveland, with a little more weight, polish, conservatism, and self-assertiveness. He was still inclined to put his foot down rather than slide it down, to demand a whole loaf or none, to go his own resolute way rather than hold his nose and play ball with the politicians. But if it was the same old Grover Cleveland, it was not the same old country: the debtors were up in arms, and the advanced shadows of panic were falling.

Cleveland's Attorney General, Richard Olney, was a stocky and conservative Yankee, cut from the same piece of cloth as his stubborn and pugnacious chief. As a wealthy corporation lawyer associated with the railroads, he had no stomach for a vigorous prosecution of big business under the Interstate Commerce Act and the Sherman Anti-Trust Act. His record was generally one of weakness and deliberate failure, for he was not a man to "betray a trust." He joyfully lost his cases.

Hardly had Cleveland seated himself in the presidential chair when the devastating Panic of 1893 burst about his burly frame. Lasting for about four years, it was in some respects the worst of the century. Contributing causes were no doubt the splurge of over-speculation, labor disorders, and the current agricultural depression. Free-silver agitation had also damaged American credit abroad, and the usual pinch on American finances had come when European

A popular protest song of the 1890's among Western farmers was entitled "The Hayseed." One stanza ran:

> I once was a tool of oppression,
> And as green as a sucker could be,
> And monopolies banded together
> To beat a poor hayseed like me.

banking houses, after earlier failures, began to call in loans from the United States.

Distress was acute and widespread. About eight thousand American business houses collapsed in six months, and dozens of railroad lines went into the hands of receivers. Business executives "died like flies under the strain," wrote Henry Adams. Soup kitchens were set up for the unemployed, while gangs of hoboes ("tramps") wandered aimlessly about the country. Local charities did their feeble best, but the federal government, bound by the let-nature-take-its-course philosophy of the century, was unable to relieve the suffering masses.

Cleveland, who had earlier been bothered by a surplus, was now burdened with a deficit. Under the Sherman Silver Purchase Act, the Treasury was required to issue legal tender notes for the silver bullion that it bought. Owners of the paper currency would then present it for gold, and by law the notes had to be reissued. New holders would repeat the process, thus draining away gold in an "endless chain" operation.

In his special message to Congress (1893) Cleveland said: "Unless Government bonds are to be constantly issued and sold to replenish our exhausted gold, only to be again exhausted, it is apparent that the operation of the silver-purchase law now in force leads in the direction of the entire substitution of silver for the gold in the Government Treasury, and that this must be followed by the payment of all Government obligations in depreciated silver."

Alarmingly, the gold reserve in the Treasury dropped below $100,000,000, which was popularly regarded as the safe minimum for supporting about $350,000,000 in outstanding greenbacks. Cleveland saw no alternative but to halt the bleeding away of gold by engineering a repeal of the Sherman Silver Purchase Act of 1890. For this purpose he summoned Congress into an extra session in the summer of 1893.

Unknown to the country, complications threatened from another quarter. A malignant growth had developed on the roof of Cleveland's mouth, and it had to be removed on a private yacht with extreme secrecy. If the President had died under the knife, his place would have been taken by the "soft money" Vice-President, Adlai E. Stevenson—an eventuality that would have deepened the crisis.

In Congress the debate over the repeal of the silver act was meanwhile running its heated course. An eloquent young Congressman from Nebraska, the thirty-three-year-old William Jennings Bryan, held the galleries spellbound for three hours as he championed the cause of free silver. The friends of silver announced that "hell would freeze over" before Congress passed the repeal measure. But an angered Cleveland used his office-giving power to break the filibuster in the Senate. He thus alienated the Democratic silverites and disrupted his party at the very outset of his administration.

Gold Shortages and Job Shortages

The hemorrhaging of gold from the Treasury was only partially stopped by the repeal of the Sherman Silver Purchase Act. Other currency was still being presented for redemption, and in February,

1894, the gold reserve sank to a dismaying $41,000,000. The nation was in grave danger of going off the gold standard.

Again Cleveland was forced to act vigorously. As a champion of sound money, he could see no alternative but to sell government bonds for gold and deposit the proceeds in the Treasury. Two bond issues were floated in 1894, totaling over $100,000,000, but the "endless chain" operations continued relentlessly.

Early in 1895, Cleveland turned in desperation to J. P. Morgan and a Wall Street syndicate. After tense negotiations at the White House, the bankers agreed to lend the government $65,000,000 in gold. They were obviously in business for profit, so they charged a commission amounting to about $7,000,000. But they did make a significant concession when they agreed to obtain one-half of the gold abroad and take the necessary steps to dam it up in the leaky Treasury. The loan, at least temporarily, helped restore confidence in the nation's finances. Following one more public bond sale and a business upswing, the crisis was surmounted.

But the bond deal stirred up a storm. The Wall Street ogre, especially in the eyes of the silverites and other debtors, was a symbol of all that was wicked and grasping. Cleveland's secretive dealings with mighty "Jupiter" Morgan were savagely condemned as a "sellout" of the national government. But Cleveland was certain that he had done no wrong. Sarcastically denying that he was "Morgan's errand boy," he asserted: "Without shame and without repentance I confess my share of the guilt."

Ragged armies of the unemployed, victims of the depression, were meanwhile staging demonstrations. The most famous of these marches was that of "General" Jacob S. Coxey, a wealthy Ohio quarry owner, who started for Washington in 1894 with several score of men, accompanied by a score or so of newspaper reporters. His platform included a demand that the government relieve unemploy-

West and South Feed the Country
While Wall Street Milks It
A cartoon of the 1890's highly popular
with Democrats and Populists.

ment by an inflationary public works program, supported by some $500,000,000 in legal tender notes to be issued by the Treasury. Coxey himself rode in a carriage with his wife and infant son, appropriately named Legal Tender Coxey, while his tiny "army" tramped along behind, singing:

We're coming, Grover Cleveland, 500,000 strong,
We're marching on to Washington to right the nation's wrong.

The "Commonweal Army" of Coxeyites finally straggled into the nation's capital. But the "invasion" took on the aspects of a comic opera when "General" Coxey and his "lieutenants" were arrested for walking on the grass. Other armies—"petitions in boots"—were less well behaved, and accounted for considerable disorder and pillage.

Cleveland Crushes the Pullman Strike

Violent flare-ups accompanied labor protests, notably in Chicago. Most frightening was the crippling Pullman strike of 1894. Eugene V. Debs, an impetuous but personally lovable labor leader, had helped organize the American Railway Union of about 150,000 members. The Pullman Palace Car Company, which maintained a model town near Chicago for its employees, was hit hard by the depression and cut wages about one-third. But it did not reduce rent for the company houses. The workers finally struck—in some places overturning Pullman cars—and paralyzed railway traffic from Chicago to the Pacific Coast.

This terrorism in Chicago was serious but not completely out of hand. At least this was the judgment of Governor Altgeld of Illinois, a friend of the downtrodden who had pardoned the Haymarket Square anarchists the year before (see p. 573). But Attorney General Olney, an archconservative and an ex-railroad attorney, urged the dispatch of federal troops. His legal grounds were that the strikers were interfering with the transit of the United States mail. Cleveland supported Olney with the ringing declaration, "If it takes the entire army and navy to deliver a postal card in Chicago, that card will be delivered."

After the Pullman strike collapsed, Debs said, "No strike has ever been lost." In 1897 he declared, "The issue is Socialism versus Capitalism. I am for Socialism because I am for humanity."

To the delight of conservatives, the Pullman strike was crushed by bayonet-supported intervention from Washington. Debs and his leading associates, who had defied a federal court injunction to cease striking, were sentenced to six months' imprisonment for contempt of court. Ironically, the lean labor agitator spent much of his enforced leisure reading radical literature, which had much to do with his later leadership of the Socialist movement in America.

Embittered cries of "government by injunction" now burst from organized labor. This was the first time that such a weapon had been used conspicuously by Washington to break a strike, and it was all the more distasteful because defiant laborites who were held in con-

"King" Debs Blocks Railroads.
Harper's Weekly, 1894

tempt could be imprisoned without jury trial. Signs multiplied that employers were striving to smash labor unions by court action. Non-labor elements of the country, including the Populists and other debtors, were likewise incensed. They saw in the brutal Pullman epi-sode further proof of an unholy alliance between Big Business and the courts.

Democratic Tariff Tinkering

The McKinley Tariff of 1890 had been designed to keep protection high and the surplus low. It succeeded admirably in achieving both goals. By 1894 the Treasury was faced with an alarming deficit of $61,000,000.

In Congress the Democrats undertook to frame a tariff that would provide adequate revenue with moderate protection, as they had promised in the Cleveland-Harrison campaign of 1892. A bill aimed at securing these objectives was introduced in the House. As a con-cession to the Populists and other foes of "plutocracy," the measure included a tax of 2% on incomes over $4000. Joseph H. Choate, a wealthy lawyer, growled, "Communistic, socialistic."

When the new tariff bill reached the Senate, it ran afoul of a swarm of lobbyists in the pay of Big Industry. After much button-holing and vote trading, the Wilson-Gorman Bill was drastically revamped by the addition of over 630 amendments. The Sugar Trust stirred up a scandal when it inserted benefits to itself worth a sweet $20,000,000 a year. As a result of such backstairs pressures, the Wilson-Gorman law of 1894 fell scandalously short of establishing a low tariff, even though it did reduce the existing McKinley rates from 48.4% to 41.3% on dutiable goods. (See chart, p. 628.)

Cleveland was outraged by what he regarded as a gross betrayal of Democratic campaign pledges. In an angry outburst he denounced the bill as "party perfidy and party dishonor"—to the glee of the Republicans. But to veto the patchwork affair would leave the even higher McKinley Tariff on the books, so Cleveland grudgingly let the bill become law without his signature. The Wilson-Gorman hodgepodge at least had the redeeming feature of the income tax, which was highly popular among the masses.

But the income tax lasted less than a year. In 1895 the Supreme Court, by a five-to-four decision, struck down this part of the Wilson-Gorman Act.* The only popular feature of the unpopular tariff law thus perished under the judicial tomahawk. A chorus of denunciation rose from the Populists and other impoverished groups, who found further proof that the courts were only the tools of the plutocrats.

Democratic political fortunes naturally suffered. The tariff dynamite which had blasted the Republicans out of the House in 1890 now dislodged the Democrats, with a strong helping hand from the depression. Revitalized Republicans, singing "The Soup House" and "Times Are Mighty Hard," won the Congressional elections of 1894 in a landslide, and now had 244 votes to 105 for the Democrats. The prospects of the Republicans for 1896 seemed roseate. They were openly boasting that they had only to nominate a "rag baby" or a "yaller dog," and they could put it in the White House. Such optimism misread the signs of the times.

Discontented debtors, especially the Populists, were turning in throngs to free silver as a cure-all. An enormously popular pamphlet, entitled Coin's Financial School (1894), was being distributed by the hundreds of thousands of copies. Written by William Hope Harvey, it was illustrated by clever woodcuts, one of which depicted the gold ogre beheading the beautiful silver maiden. In fiction parading as fact, the booklet showed how the "little professor"—"Coin" Harvey—overwhelmed the bankers and professors of economics with his brilliant sallies in behalf of free silver. The belief was gaining momentum among silverites and debtors that there was a foul conspiracy on foot, both nationally and internationally, to elevate gold above silver.

The pamphlet Coin's Financial School had the fictional boy wizard, named Coin, give a speech in Chicago. It was in part directed at hated England, upholder of the gold standard: "A war with England would be the most popular ever waged on the face of the earth. [Applause.] If it is true that she can dictate the money of the world, and thereby create world-wide misery, it would be the most just war ever waged by man. [Applause.]"

Illustration from Silverite Booklet. 1894
(*Coin's Financial School*)

McKinley: Hanna's Fair-Haired Boy

The leading candidate for the Republican presidential nomination in 1896 was ex-Congressman McKinley of Ohio, sponsor of the ill-starred tariff bill of 1890. He had established a creditable Civil War record, having risen to the rank of major; he hailed from the electorally potent state of Ohio; and he could point to long years of honorable service in Congress, where he had made many friends by his kindly and conciliatory manner. Rather small in stature (five feet seven), and with a high forehead and a prominent chin, he added to his inches by his dignity and by his resemblance to Napoleon I—a characteristic seized upon by the cartoonists. He was widely hailed as "the Napoleon of Protection" and "the Advance Agent of Prosperity."

As a presidential candidate, McKinley was peculiarly the creation

---

* It violated the "direct tax" clause. See Art. I, Sec. IX, para. 4, Appendix. The 16th Amendment to the Constitution, adopted in 1913, permitted an income tax.

Hanna Raises "Honest" Money in Wall Street. New York *Journal,* 1896

of a fellow Ohioan, Marcus Alonzo Hanna. The latter had made his fortune in the iron business, and he now coveted the role of President-maker. He was personally attracted to McKinley; "I love McKinley," he once said. When the overgenerous Ohio Congressman faced bankruptcy after unwisely endorsing a friend's notes for about $100,000, Hanna and his wealthy associates paid off the obligation.

Hanna, as a wholehearted Hamiltonian, believed that a prime function of government was to aid business. Honest, earnest, rough, and direct, he became the personification of Big Industry in politics. He was often cartooned, quite unfairly, as a bloated bully in a loud checkered suit with a dollar sign on each checker. As a conservative in business, he was a confirmed "standpatter," content not to rock the boat. He believed that in some measure prosperity "trickled down" to the laborer, whose dinner pail was full when business flourished. He trusted in trusts.

A hard-fisted Hanna, although something of a novice in politics, organized his pre-convention campaign for McKinley with consummate skill and with a liberal outpouring of his own money. "Czar" Reed was a leading challenger. But his sarcastic tongue had made too many enemies, and he was too rigidly opposed to silver. The convention steam roller, well lubricated with Hanna's dollars, nominated McKinley on the first ballot at St. Louis in June, 1896.

The Republican platform cleverly straddled the monetary question. It declared for the gold standard, even though McKinley's voting record in Congress had been embarrassingly friendly to silver. But the platform made a gesture toward the silverites when it came out for international bimetallism, or a world-wide gold-silver standard. The joker was that all the leading nations of the world would have had to agree to such a scheme, and this obviously they would not do. Additionally the platform condemned hard times and Democratic incapacity, while pouring praise on the protective tariff.

Bryan: Silverite Messiah

Dissension riddled the Democratic camp. Cleveland no longer led his party; dubbed "the Stuffed Prophet," he was undeniably the most unpopular man in the country. Labor-debtor groups remembered too vividly the silver-purchase repeal, the Pullman strike, the back-stairs Morgan bond deal. Ultraconservative in finance, Cleveland was now more a Republican than a Democrat on the silver issue.

Rudderless, the Democratic convention met in Chicago in July, 1896, with the silverites in command. Shouting insults at the absent Cleveland, they refused, by a vote of 564 to 357, to endorse their own administration. They had the enthusiasm and the numbers; all they lacked was a leader.

A new Moses suddenly appeared in the person of William Jennings Bryan of Nebraska. Then only thirty-six years of age and known as "the Boy Orator of the Platte,"* he stepped confidently onto the platform before 15,000 people. His masterful presence was set off by handsome features, a smooth-shaven jaw, and raven-black hair. He radiated honesty, sincerity, and energy. He had a good mind but not a brilliant one; he was less a student of books than of human nature; and he possessed broad human sympathies. His was a great heart rather than a great head; a great voice rather than a great brain.

In Chicago the setting was made to order for a magnificent oratorical effort. Bryan could be sure of a sympathetic hearing, for as a Congressman and a nationwide lecturer he had already emerged as one of the leading champions of free silver. A hush fell over the convention as he stood before it. With an organ-like voice that rolled into the outer corners of the huge hall, he delivered a fervent plea for silver. Rising to supreme heights of eloquence, he thundered, "We will answer their demands for a gold standard by saying to them: 'You shall not press down upon the brow of labor this crown of thorns, you shall not crucify mankind upon a cross of gold.'"

The Cross of Gold speech was a sensation. Swept off its feet in a tumultuous scene, the convention nominated Bryan the next day on the fifth ballot. The platform declared for the unlimited coinage of silver at the ratio of sixteen ounces of silver to one of gold, though the market ratio was about thirty-two to one.

Democratic "Gold Bugs," unable to swallow Bryan, bolted their party over the silver issue. Conservative Senator Hill of New York, when asked if he was a Democrat still, reportedly replied, "Yes, I am a Democrat still—*very* still." The Democratic minority, including Cleveland, charged that the Populist-silverites had stolen both the name and the clothing of their party. They nominated a lost-cause ticket of their own, and many of them, including Cleveland, hoped for a McKinley victory.

Populists were left out in the cold, for the Democratic majority had appropriated their main plank—"sixteen to one." The bulk of the confused "Popocrats," rather than submit to a hard-money McKinley victory, endorsed Bryan in their convention. Singing "The Jolly Silver Dollar of the Dads," they became in effect the "Demo-Pop" party. But many of the original Populists refused to support Bryan, and went down with their colors nailed to the mast.

Hanna Leads the "Gold Bugs"

Mark Hanna smugly assumed that he could make the tariff the focus of the campaign. But Bryan, a dynamo of energy, forced the

"Miss Democracy" in a Quandary on Eve of 1896 Convention. *New York Advertiser*

---

* One contemporary commented brutally that the Platte River was "six inches deep and six miles wide at the mouth."

A Republican view of Bryan. A variant of this satire was "In Go(l)d We Trust." New York *Press*, 1896.

free-trade issue into a back seat when he took to the stump in behalf of free silver. Sweeping through twenty-seven states and traveling 18,000 miles, he made between five and six hundred speeches—thirty-six in one day—and even invaded the East, "the enemy's country." Vachel Lindsay caught the spirit of his oratorical orgy:

Prairie avenger, mountain lion,
Bryan, Bryan, Bryan, Bryan,
Gigantic troubadour, speaking like a siege gun,
*Smashing Plymouth Rock with his boulders from the West.**

Free silver became almost as much a religious as a financial issue. Hordes of fanatical free-silverites hailed Bryan as the Messiah to lead them out of the wilderness of debt. They sang, "We'll All Have Our Pockets Lined with Silver" and "No Crown of Thorns, No Cross of Gold."

Bryan created panic among Eastern conservatives with his threat of converting their holdings overnight into fifty-cent dollars. The "Gold Bugs" vented their alarm in abusive epithets, which ranged all the way from "fanatic" and "madman" to "traitor" and "murderer." "In God We Trust, with Bryan We Bust," the Republicans sneered, while one Eastern clergyman cried, "That platform was made in Hell."

Widespread fear of Bryan and the "silver lunacy" enabled "Dollar Mark" Hanna, now chairman of the Republican National Committee, to shine as a money raiser. He "shook down" the trusts and plutocrats, and piled up an enormous "slush fund" for a "campaign of education"—or of propaganda, depending on one's point of view. The Republicans amassed the most formidable political campaign chest thus far in American history. At all levels—national, state, and local—it amounted to about $16,000,000, as contrasted with about $1,000,000 for the poorer Democrats—roughly "sixteen to one." With some justification, the Bryanites accused Hanna of "buying" the election, and of floating McKinley into the White House on a tidal wave of greenbacks. The Republicans definitely had the edge in money and mud.

Appealing to The Pocketbook Vote

With gold gushing into his coffers, Hanna waged a high-pressure campaign against silver. He distributed tens of millions of pamphlets, tracts, leaflets, and posters, many of them in the native languages of immigrant groups. He sent out hundreds of "spellbinders" onto the stump, where they engaged in the free and unlimited coinage of speeches. There was a maximum of shouting and a minimum

* Vachel Lindsay, *Collected Poems* (The Macmillan Company, copyright 1925), p. 99 ("Bryan, Bryan, Bryan, Bryan").

of thinking, primarily because only a few trained economists were able to grasp fully the implications of silver-and-gold bimetallism—and even they disagreed. "The whole currency question," wrote the humorist "Mr. Dooley" (F. P. Dunne), "is a matter of lungs."

Republicans harped constantly on their promise of prosperity. Reminding the voters of Cleveland's "Democratic panic," they appealed to the "belly vote" with their prize slogan: "McKinley and the Full Dinner Pail." McKinley, though an effective orator, was no match for Bryan in the rough-and-tumble of stump speaking. He remained at his Ohio home, conducting a quiet and dignified "front porch" campaign. Stressing prosperity, he read calm and confident little speeches to delegations of visiting Republicans.

Bryan's cyclonic campaign, launched with irresistible enthusiasm, began to lose steam as the weeks passed. If the election had been held in August, instead of November, the golden-voiced "Peerless Leader" might well have won. But Hanna's splendid organization and far-flung campaign of "education" gradually began to tip the scales. Also, during the weeks just before the election, the price of wheat rose sharply, owing largely to crop failures abroad. Hostility to the Republican Party in the vast wheat belt began to wane, even though agriculture generally remained depressed.

Fear probably was the strongest ally of Hanna, the worst enemy of Bryan, who allegedly had "silver on the brain." Republican businessmen placed contracts with manufacturers, contingent on the election of McKinley. A few factory owners, with thinly veiled intimidation, paid off their workers and told them not to come to work on Wednesday morning if Bryan won. Such were some of the refinements of the "Stop Bryan, Save America" crusade.

Class Conflict: Plowholders vs. Bondholders

Hanna's campaign methods paid off, for on election day McKinley triumphed decisively. The vote was 271 to 176 in the Electoral College, and 7,104,779 to 6,502,925 in the popular column. Responding to fear, hope, and excitement, an unprecedented outpouring of voters flocked to the polls. McKinley ran strongly in the populous East, where he carried every county of New England, and in the upper Mississippi Valley. Bryan's states, concentrated in the debt-burdened South and the trans-Mississippi West, involved more acreage than McKinley's but less population—only the South and the desert, cynics said.

The free-silver election of 1896—the most significant since Lincoln's victories in 1860 and 1864—highlighted serious sectional cleavages. One basic reason for Bryan's defeat, despite his strength in the South and West, was his lack of appeal to the solvent farmer and the urban laborer. Many an Eastern wage earner voted for his

In gold-standard England there was much relief over McKinley's victory. **The London** *Standard* **commented, "The hopelessly ignorant and savagely covetous waifs and strays of American civilization voted for Bryan, but the bulk of the solid sense, business integrity, and social stability sided with McKinley. The nation is to be heartily congratulated."**

PRESIDENTIAL ELECTION OF 1896 (with electoral vote by state)

job and his full dinner pail, threatened as they were by free silver, free trade, and closed factories.

Unhappily the Bryan-McKinley battle likewise produced an ugly class conflict, probably the most serious since the election of Jefferson in 1800. Debtors, hard-pinched farmers, poorer folk, and other malcontents were for the most part pitted against the more prosperous pillars of society. It was the age-old story of the underprivileged many against the privileged few, of the indebted back country against the wealthier seaboard, of the country against the city, of the agrarians against the industrialists, of Main Street against Wall Street, of the nobodies against the somebodies.

As a matter of simple humanitarianism, the mortgage-crushed farmers deserved some relief from social and economic ills not of their own making. They did not regard themselves as "dishonest," especially when they cried out against having to pay back dearer dollars than those they had borrowed. Silver was a symbol—a misleading symbol—of their plight. Bryan himself believed that the basic issue was not free silver but free people—a free people seeking escape from the clutches of plutocracy.

The outcome was a smashing victory for Big Business; Alexander Hamilton again triumphed from the grave. McKinley's election no doubt upheld the nation's financial honor and averted serious economic strains. But these dangers were grossly exaggerated by Hanna's propaganda mill, with its unwritten slogan, "In Gold We Trust."

Republican Standpattism Enthroned

An eminently "safe" McKinley took the inaugural oath in 1897.

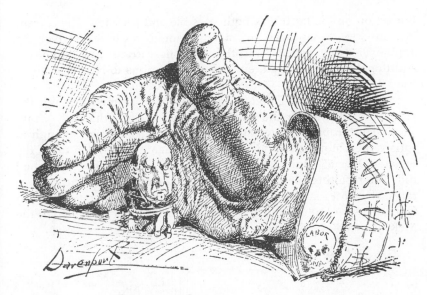

McKinley in the Palm of Hanna's Hand.
New York *Journal,* 1896

Though a man of considerable ability, he was an ear-to-the-ground politician who seldom got far out of line with majority opinion. His cautious, conservative nature caused him to shy away from the flaming banner of reform—or even of progressivism. Business was given a free rein, and the trusts, which had trusted him in 1896, were allowed to develop mighty muscles without serious restraints.

McKinley, unlike Cleveland, worked smoothly in party harness. With impeccable white vest, he seemed never to perspire, even in cruelly muggy Washington. Able to get along well with Congress—he had served there for many years—he shone best at reconciling conflicting interests. Conciliatory and warm-handed, he would send an angry-faced man away beaming, sometimes wearing a carnation from the presidential desk. He continued to maintain intimate relations with Hanna but he was by no means under the thumb of his mentor, despite Vachel Lindsay's cruel query:

Where is McKinley, Mark Hanna's McKinley,
His slave, his echo, his suit of clothes?

Not surprisingly, the new "standpat" Cabinet was both conservative and aged. The venerable Senator John Sherman of Ohio, now seventy-four years old and suffering from a serious loss of memory, was "kicked upstairs" into the post of Secretary of State. Hanna coveted his Senate seat, and Sherman was induced to resign so that the governor of Ohio could reward McKinley's benefactor with the vacated place.

The tariff issue, which had played second fiddle to silver in the "Battle of '96," quickly forced itself to the fore. Cautious Republicans were reluctant to tackle legislation that would firmly establish the gold standard; there were still too many silverites left in Congress.

But action on the tariff was both possible and pressing. The current Wilson-Gorman law was not raising enough revenue to cover the annual Treasury deficits, and the Republican trusts had purchased additional protection by their lush contributions to Hanna's "slush fund."

In due course the Dingley Tariff Bill was jammed through the House in 1897, under the pounding gavel of the rethroned "Czar" Reed. The proposed new rates were high, but not high enough to satisfy the paunchy lobbyists, who once again descended upon the Senate. Over 850 amendments were tacked onto the overburdened bill. The resulting piece of patchwork finally established the average rates at 46.5%, substantially higher than the Democratic Wilson-Gorman Act of 1894, and in some categories even higher than the McKinley Act of 1890. (See chart, p. 628.)

Speaker "Czar" Reed Ignores Financial Gunpowder, *Harper's Weekly*, 1895

Inflation without Silver

Prosperity, long lurking around the corner, began to return with a rush in 1897, the first year of McKinley. The depression of 1893 had run its course, and farm prices rose. Paint-thirsty Middle Western barns blossomed out in new colors, and the wheels of industry increased their hum. Republican politicians, like crowing roosters causing the sun to rise, claimed credit for bringing in the sunlight of prosperity.

The Gold Standard Act, loudly demanded by hard-moneyites who had voted for McKinley, was not passed by the Republicans until 1900, when many silverites had left Congress. It provided that the paper currency was to be redeemed freely in gold. Last-ditch silverites fought the bill with bitterness but without success. The cries of the inflationists, further choked by returning prosperity, gradually died away. Thus ended some twenty years of paternalistic attempts to "do something" for the debtor.

In retrospect, a controlled expansion of American currency in the 1880's and 1890's was clearly desirable. Prices were depressed, money was tight, and the volume of currency in circulation lagged far behind the increasing volume of business. (See chart, p. 619.) Agrarian debtors had a good cause: relief from social and economic hardship through an inflation of the dollar supply. But free silver, which aroused exaggerated fears, was a poor sword. By brandishing this tinseled weapon, Bryan actually defeated his own ends. The free-silver fixation not only discredited the case for needed currency expansion, but seriously set back the movement for agrarian reform.

Nature and science gradually provided an inflation that the "Gold Bug" East had fought so frantically to prevent. Electrifying discoveries of new gold deposits in Canada (Klondike), Alaska, South Africa, and Australia eased the pressure, as did the perfecting of the cheap cyanide process for extracting gold from low-grade ore. Moderate inflation thus took care of the currency needs of an explosively expanding nation. The tide of "silver heresy" rapidly receded, and the "popocratic" fish were left gasping high and dry on a golden-sanded beach.

SELECT READINGS

Consult the books by Hicks and Shannon cited for the previous chapter. A comprehensive survey is H. U. FAULKNER, *Politics, Reform, and Expansion, 1890–1900* (1959).* On Cleveland, see ALLAN NEVINS' Pulitzer-prize *Grover Cleveland* (1932) and J. R. HOLLINGSWORTH, *The Whirligig of Politics* (1963). Harrison is fully portrayed in H. J. SIEVERS, *Benjamin Harrison, Hoosier Statesman: From the Civil War to the White House, 1865–1888* (vol. II, 1959) and *Benjamin Harrison: Hoosier President* (vol. III, 1968). The most recent scholarly treatment is P. E. COLETTA, *William Jennings Bryan: Political Evangelist, 1860–1908* (1964). On the 1896 campaign consult S. L. JONES, *The Presidential Election of 1896* (1964); R. F. DURDEN, *The Climax of Populism: The Election of 1896* (1965)*; and P. W. GLAD, *The Trumpet Soundeth: William Jennings Bryan and His Democracy, 1896–1912* (1960)* and *McKinley, Bryan, and the People* (1964).* Consult also P. E. COLETTA, *William Jennings Bryan: Political Evangelist, 1860–1908* (1964) and THEODORE SALOUTOS, *Farmer Movements in the South, 1865–1933* (1960).* McKinley is belatedly done justice in MARGARET LEECH's Pulitzer-prize *In the Days of McKinley* (1959) and in H. W. MORGAN, *William McKinley and His America* (1963). Also *Harvard Guide,** Pt. V.

* Available in paperback.

31

The Path of Empire

We assert that no nation can.long endure half republic and half empire, and we warn the American people that imperialism abroad will lead quickly and inevitably to despotism at home.

Democratic National Platform, 1900

Faint Stirrings of Imperialism

A momentous shift in American foreign policy occurred in the sunset decades of the 19th Century. It roughly paralleled the far-reaching changes which were taking place in manufacturing, agriculture, and the social structure.

Before the Civil War, the United States had adopted two basic foreign policies regarding Europe. One was the isolationist creed of non-involvement and non-entanglement in foreign broils. It meant in brief, "We'll keep out." The other was the Monroe Doctrine, which meant basically, "You keep out." The Republic had warned the non-American powers to stay away, partly because it valued its freedom from European despots, and partly because it wanted to continue its expansive Manifest Destiny without hindrance. In addition to these two basic policies, the nation had made some halting progress toward the arbitration of international disputes, especially those with powerful European nations which could not be profitably fought.

The Civil War, with its violent dislocations, naturally affected foreign policy. A spirit of isolation continued with full vigor, while the Monroe Doctrine emerged with new laurels after the ejection of the French intruders from Mexico in 1867. But the once-potent impulse of Manifest Destiny was dead. Too much blood and treasure had gone down the sewer of Civil War; too much energy and enterprise were being poured into Reconstruction, Indian fighting, railroad building, and other outlets. From the end of the Civil War to the 1880's, the indifference of most Americans to the outside world was almost unbelievable.

In 1881 James G. Blaine, the "spirited" Secretary of State, brought a refreshing new outlook to American foreign policy. He had visions of expanding the nation's economic and diplomatic interests into the Far East, the Pacific, and especially Latin America. As a warm admirer of the pioneer Pan-Americanist Henry Clay, he issued invitations to the Latin American republics for the first great Pan-American conclave, to be held at Washington. But the bullet that killed President Garfield blasted Blaine's plans, and his stodgy successor in the State Department rather abruptly cancelled the project.

Blaine's burning interest in Latin America also extended to the proposed Isthmian canal. But here loomed one insurmountable legal obstacle. By the terms of the yellowing Clayton-Bulwer Treaty of 1850, the United States had agreed with Britain on joint control and protection of the prospective waterway. In a resolute attempt to shake off this shackle, Blaine dispatched a series of blustering notes to London. Even though the British Lion stood annoyingly firm, the "Plumed Knight's" resounding phrases stirred American sensitivity and pride.

As far as a Pan-American conference was concerned, Blaine had cast his seeds on fertile ground. One of his successors in the State

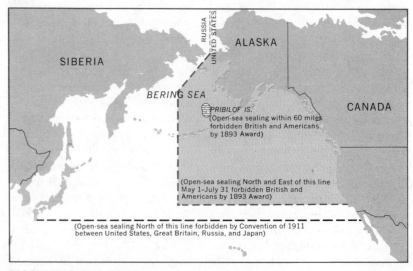

PROTECTING THE SEALS

Department gradually began to see the light regarding the "Big Sister" policy. The United States again issued invitations for the first general meeting of its kind, and eighteen American republics sent delegates to Washington in 1889. By a curious turn of the wheel, Blaine returned as Secretary of State under Harrison, just in time to shine in the role of host.

If achievement could be measured by flowery words, the First Pan-American Conference was a sensational success. But the concrete results were meager. The frock-coated delegates did little more than open a crack in the door for economic cooperation through reciprocal tariff reduction. They also set up a clearinghouse for information, ultimately known as the Pan-American Union, and later housed in a Carnegie-given marble palace in Washington. But the Washington Conference itself was a trail-blazing beginning—the first of a long and increasingly important series of inter-American assemblages.

Blaine's Chip-on-the-Shoulder Diplomacy

The rising new spirit in America manifested itself in a series of diplomatic crises or near-wars in the late 1880's and early 1890's

Seals were the bone of contention with Britain. The United States had acquired with Alaska the two tiny Pribilof Islands, the breeding place of some four million fur seals. Sealskin coats were then fashionable, and Canadian seal poachers found it profitable to range off America's islands outside the three-mile limit. There they reddened the water with the indiscriminate slaughter of the sleek mammals.

Drastic action was needed to save the seals from going the way of the buffalo. In the late 1880's, American revenue vessels boldly seized several Canadian sealing craft on the high seas. The Canadians and British reacted angrily against this violation of freedom of the seas—ironically, a time-honored American principle.

Secretary Blaine, who inherited the quarrel, had a good ethical case but a poor legal one. Yet he strove energetically to persuade London that since the United States owned the breeding ground of the seals, it had some jurisdiction over the furry creatures outside the three-mile line. The unrestrained slaughter, he argued, was contrary to good public morals.

This dispute over seals was finally referred to an arbitral tribunal sitting at Paris in 1893. After due deliberation, the arbitrators decided every major legal point against the United States. But to safeguard the seals they set up a closed zone (which happened to be too small) and a closed season (which happened to be the wrong time of the year). The result was a resounding defeat for both the Americans and their seals, but something of a victory for international arbitration. The salvation of the disappearing herd was to come in 1911 by a different type of international agreement (p. 720).

In the quarrel with Britain over seals that were allegedly American, Secretary James G. ("Jingo Jim") Blaine used undiplomatic language in his formal protests. One finds such pronouncements as, "The law of the sea is not lawlessness" and "One step beyond that which Her Majesty's Government has taken in this controversy and piracy finds its justification."

Other diplomatic controversies quickened the patriotic pulse. The United States skirted close to the brink of bloodshed with Germany in 1889, over the palm-shaded islands of Samoa. The Republic almost clashed with Italy in 1891, when eleven Italians were lynched in New Orleans, following a series of murders that pointed to the stiletto of the Sicilian Blackhanders. Diplomatic relations were severed; war impended. Ominously, the Italian navy, on paper at least, was much the stronger. But hostilities were happily averted when the United States, as a friendly gesture, agreed to pay $25,000 to Italy.

An even uglier clash in 1892 involved Chile. That string-bean shaped republic had recently been convulsed by civil war, and the Washington government was accused of showing undue sympathy toward the faction that eventually lost. In an atmosphere of hostility, a party of sailors from an American warship, the *Baltimore*, was allowed shore leave at Valparaiso. A fight broke out in the True Blue saloon, and when order was restored, two American sailors were dead and nearly a score of others were injured. President Harrison, the aroused ex-soldier, made stern demands on Chile, and hostilities seemed inevitable. Alarm spread to the Pacific Coast of the United States, for Chile, as a Pacific naval power, boasted some formidable modern warships.

So enormous was the power of the United States, actual and potential, that Chile was finally forced to knuckle under and pay an indemnity of $75,000. The Chileans have never completely forgotten what to them was undue severity—using a sledgehammer to crush a butterfly. Although the ordinarily aggressive Blaine in this instance tried to restrain the anger of his chief, much of the good will he had so laboriously created at the recent Pan-American Conference went down the drain.

Monroe's Doctrine and the Venezuelan Squall

America's anti-British animus, which periodically came to a head, flared forth ominously in 1895–1896 over Venezuela. For more than a half-century the jungle boundary between British Guiana and Venezuela had been in dispute. The Venezuelans, whose claims on the whole were extravagant, had repeatedly urged arbitration. But the prospect of a peaceful settlement faded when gold was discovered in the disputed area.

President Cleveland, a champion of righteousness and no lover of Britain, at length decided upon a strong protest. His no less pugnacious Secretary of State Olney was authorized to present to London a smashing note, which Cleveland later dubbed a "twenty-inch gun" blast. Olney declared in effect that the British, by attempting to dominate Venezuela in this quarrel and acquire more territory, were flouting the Monroe Doctrine. London should therefore submit the

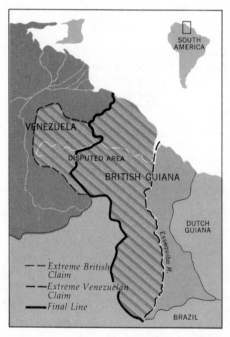

THE VENEZUELA–BRITISH GUIANA
BOUNDARY DISPUTE

The Real British Lion
A widespread American concept in the 1890's.
New York *Evening World,* 1895

dispute to arbitration. Not content to stop here, Olney haughtily informed the number-one naval power that the United States was now calling the tune in the Western Hemisphere.

British officials, unimpressed, took four months to prepare their reply. Preoccupied elsewhere, they were inclined to shrug off Olney's lengthy blast as just another twist of the Lion's tail designed to elicit cheers from Irish-American voters. When London's answer finally came, it flatly denied the relevance of the Monroe Doctrine, while no less emphatically spurning arbitration. In short, the affair was none of America's business.

President Cleveland—"mad clear through," as he put it—sent a bristling special message to Congress. He urged an appropriation for a commission of experts, who would run the line where it ought to go. Then, he implied, if the British would not accept this rightful boundary, the United States would fight for it.

The entire country, irrespective of political party, was swept off its feet in an outburst of hysteria. War seemed inevitable, even though Britain had thirty-two warships of the battleship class to only five for America.

Fortunately, sober second thoughts prevailed on both sides of the Atlantic. The British, though vastly annoyed by their upstart cousins, had no real urge to fight. Canada was vulnerable to American armies, and Britain's rich merchant marine was vulnerable to American commerce raiders. The European atmosphere was menacing, for Britain's traditional policy of "splendid isolation" was bringing dangerous isolation. Russia and France were unfriendly; and Germany, under the saber-rattling Kaiser Wilhelm II, was about to challenge British naval supremacy.

"The World's Plunderers." Thomas
Nast, *Harper's Weekly*, 1885

The Venezuelan crisis had evidently passed its peak when the
German Kaiser, blunderingly and unwittingly, increased chances of
a peaceful solution. An unauthorized British raiding party of six
hundred armed men was captured by the Dutch-descended Boers in
South Africa, and the Kaiser forthwith cabled his congratulations to
the victors. Overnight, British anger against America was largely deflected to Germany. After further negotiations, London consented to
arbitrate the Venezuelan dispute. The final decision, ironically,
awarded the British the bulk of what they had claimed from the beginning.

America had skated close to the thin ice of a terrible war, but the
results on the whole were favorable. The prestige of the Monroe
Doctrine was immensely enhanced. Europe was irked by Cleveland's
claim to domination in this hemisphere, and both Latin America and
Canada were somewhat alarmed. But he had made his claim stick.
Many Latin American republics were pleased by the determination
of the United States to protect them, and when Cleveland died in
1908, some of them lowered their flags to half-mast.

The chastened British, their eyes fully opened to the European peril, were now determined to cultivate Yankee friendship. They inaugurated an era of "patting the Eagle's head," which replaced a century or so of America's "twisting the Lion's tail." Growing numbers of Englishmen were willing to heed Tennyson's earlier injunction:

Be proud of those strong sons of thine
Who wrench'd their rights from thee!

Inspiring the New Manifest Destiny

A heady new spirit of Manifest Destiny had begun to surge through American veins by the early 1890's. A reconstructed South was rising again; and the closing of the frontier indicated that old energies would have to be diverted into different channels. America was bursting with a sense of power generated by the vast increase in her population, wealth, and industrial productiveness. "Expand or explode" was accepted as an elemental law, and many manufacturers were seeking new overseas markets for the contents of their bulging warehouses.

Other forces were stimulating international-mindedness. The lurid yellow press of Pulitzer and Hearst was whetting the popular taste for excitement. The missionary-conscious churches were on the lookout for new overseas vineyards to till. Outward-looking advocates of a "large policy" were interpreting Darwinism to mean that the earth belonged to the energetic, the strong, the fit—that is, to the virile Americans. Jingoes, including the fight-thirsty young Theodore Roosevelt and the scholarly Congressman Henry Cabot Lodge, were whooping it up for expansion and, if need be, war.

A new steel navy was being pushed with vigor. It found a potent ally in the pen of Captain Alfred T. Mahan, who in 1890 published *The Influence of Sea Power upon History, 1660–1783.* His basic theme was that the twin prizes of victory and world dominion went to those nations that won and retained control of the sea—findings that were avidly read by Englishmen, Germans, and Japanese. Mahan thus unwittingly stimulated the fateful naval race that gained momentum at the turn of the century.

In the United States, the gospel according to Mahan eventually shaped the thinking of many large-minded Americans. They came to believe that naval power and world power were Siamese twins. Red-blooded citizens redoubled their agitation for a mightier navy, while demanding an American-built Isthmian canal that would shuttle the nation's warships from the Atlantic to the Pacific and back.

New great-power alignments were jelling. Germany was emerging as the colossus of Europe, and as a latecomer in the colonial scramble was scooping up leavings from the banquet table of earlier diners.

In 1897, the year before the Spanish-American War, Captain Mahan wrote in *The Interest of America in Sea Power,* "Whether they will or no, Americans must begin to look outward."

Japan's debut as a world power came when she gave anemic China a bad beating during 1894–1895, thereby exposing the weakness of the Chinese Empire to a predatory world. In 1898 the Germans, responding to the world-wide spirit of grab, extorted a valuable leasehold from China at Shantung; and in the same year the Russians followed suit at Port Arthur.

A dangerous spirit of bellicosity suffused America by 1898. People craved new sensations, for many were bored with threadbare issues like the tariff and free silver. The nation had not fought a rousing war for over thirty years, and a restless younger generation was envious of the Civil War veterans, with their idealized tales of "tenting on the old camp ground."

War scares with Germany, Italy, Chile, and Britain had whetted the national appetite, while leaving it frustrated. If America was going to show the world that she was "some pumpkins," she might have to fight somebody. If she was going to "keep up with the Joneses," she would have to acquire overseas real estate, as the other powers were doing. The upsurge of the new Manifest Destiny became as irresistible as that of the old Manifest Destiny in the 1840's and 1850's.

Three-Power Schemings in Samoa

The broad-bosomed Pacific Ocean witnessed some of the first manifestations of the new Manifest Destiny. As early as 1878, the United States had secured rights to a naval base in Samoa, at the

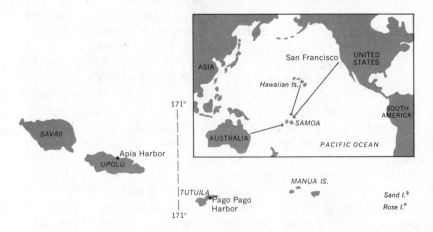

GERMAN SAMOA, 1899   AMERICAN SAMOA, 1899

harbor of Pago Pago, where American sailors and whalers had found refreshment of various kinds. Britain and Germany also became covetously interested in this idyllic archipelago, and Britons, Germans, and Americans frantically intrigued with the natives for commercial and strategic control. Robert Louis Stevenson, who had gone to Samoa in an attempt to shake off tuberculosis, has left us a graphic picture of the rivalries in his book *A Footnote to History* (1892).

Tension mounted to the breaking point between the Germans and Americans. On a memorable day in 1889, the crews of three German and three American men-of-war were glowering at each other over loaded guns. Hostilities might well have started then and there, had not a frightful hurricane wrecked all six warships in Apia harbor.

Stiffly bowing diplomats meanwhile had gathered at the Berlin Conference, meeting in the spring of 1889. Discussions went forward under the direction of the imperious Prince Bismarck, with the no less imperious Secretary Blaine cabling instructions from Washington to the American delegates. The solution finally adopted was a clumsy three-way protectorate, operated jointly by the Americans, Germans, and British. This awkward arrangement drew wide criticism in America as a reckless departure from the non-entanglement warnings of the Founding Fathers.

The Samoan sequel was the familiar story of too many cooks overheating the broth. In 1899, ten years later, the islands were divided outright between Germany and America, with Britain granted compensation elsewhere. A new mood was evidently coming over the American people when they were prepared to risk entanglement—even war—for these faraway island flyspecks.

Spurning the Hawaiian Pear

Paradisiacal Hawaii had early attracted the attention of Americans. In the morning years of the 19th Century, the breeze-brushed islands were a way station and provisioning point for Yankee shippers, sailors, and whalers. In 1820 came the first New England missionaries, who preached the twin blessings of Protestant Christianity and protective calico. They came to do good—and did well; their sons did even better. In some respects Honolulu took on the earmarks of a typical New England town.

Americans gradually came to regard the Hawaiian Islands as a virtual extension of their own coastline. The State Department, beginning with the 1840's, sternly warned other powers to keep their hands off. America's grip was further tightened in 1875 by a commercial reciprocity agreement, and in 1887 by a treaty with the native government guaranteeing priceless naval-base rights at spacious Pearl Harbor.

But trouble, both economic and political, was brewing in the lan-

THE HAWAIIAN ISLANDS

Queen Liliuokalani (1838–1917), the last reigning Queen of Hawaii, whose opposition to reforms led to her dethronement, aided and abetted by Americans. She unsuccessfully sought $450,000 in compensation from the U.S. government, but the territorial legislature granted her considerable financial support. She wrote many songs, the most famous of which was *Aloha Oe* or *Farewell to Thee,* played countless times by Hawaiian bands for departing tourists. Hawaii Public Archives.

guid insular paradise. Sugar culture, which had become immensely profitable, was dealt a crushing blow in 1890 when the McKinley Tariff erected barriers against the Hawaiian product. White planters, mostly Americans, were further alarmed by the increasingly autocratic tendencies of dusky Queen Liliuokalani, who insisted that native Hawaiians should control Hawaii. Desperate whites, though only a tiny minority, organized a successful revolt early in 1893. It was openly assisted by American troops, who landed under the unauthorized orders of the expansionist American minister in Honolulu. "The Hawaiian pear is now fully ripe," he wrote exultantly to his superiors in Washington, "and this is the golden hour for the United States to pluck it."

Hawaii, like Texas of earlier years, seemed ready for annexation—at least in the eyes of the ruling American whites. An appropriate treaty was rushed to Washington. But before it could be railroaded through the Senate, the Republican President Harrison went out and the Democratic President Cleveland came in. Cleveland, who set great store by "national honesty," suspected that his powerful nation had gravely wronged the deposed Queen Liliuokalani.

Cleveland abruptly withdrew the treaty from the Senate, and then sent a special investigator to Hawaii. The subsequent probe revealed the damning fact that a majority of the Hawaiian natives did not favor annexation at all. But the white revolutionists were firmly in the saddle, and Cleveland could not unhorse them without using armed force—a step which American public opinion would never have tolerated. Although the Queen could not be reinstated, the sugar-coated move for annexation had to be abandoned temporarily.

The question of annexing Hawaii touched off the first full-fledged imperialistic debate in American experience. Cleveland was savagely criticized for trying to stem the New Manifest Destiny, and a popular jingle ran:

. . . Liliuokalani,
Give us your little brown hannie.

But Cleveland's motives, in a day of international land grabbing, were honorable both to himself and to his country.

Revolt in the Cuban Pesthouse

Cuba's masses, frightfully misgoverned, again rose against their Spanish oppressor in 1895. The roots of their revolt were partly economic. Sugar production—backbone of the island's prosperity—was crippled when the American tariff of 1894 restored high duties on the toothsome product.

Driven to desperation, the insurgents adopted a scorched-earth policy. They reasoned that if they did enough damage, Spain might be willing to move out. Or the United States might move in, and help the Cubans win their independence. In pursuance of this destructive strategy, the *insurrectos* put the torch to cane fields and sugar mills; they even dynamited passenger trains.

American sympathies, ever on the side of patriots fighting for freedom, went out to the Cuban underdogs. Aside from pure sentiment, the United States had an investment stake of about $50,000,000 in Cuba, and an annual trade stake of about $100,000,000. Moreover, Spanish misrule in Cuba menaced the shipping routes of the West Indies and the Gulf, and less directly the future Isthmian canal.

Fuel was added to the Cuban conflagration in 1896 with the coming of General ("Butcher") Weyler. He undertook to crush the rebellion by herding many civilians into barbed-wire concentration camps, where they could not give assistance to the armed *insurrectos*. Lacking proper sanitation, these enclosures turned into deadly pestholes, in which the victims died like flies.

An outraged American public demanded action. Congress in 1896 overwhelmingly passed a resolution which called upon President Cleveland to recognize the belligerency of the revolted Cubans. But as the government of the insurgents consisted of hardly more than a few fugitive leaders under palm trees, Cleveland—an anti-jingoist and anti-imperialist—refused to budge. He defiantly remarked that if Congress declared war he would not, as Commander-in-Chief, issue the necessary order to mobilize the army.

The Mystery of the Maine Explosion

Atrocities in Cuba were made to order for the sensational new "yellow journalism." William R. Hearst and Joseph Pulitzer, then engaged in a titanic duel for circulation, attempted to outdo each other with screeching headlines and hair-raising "scoops." Lesser competitors zestfully followed suit.

Where atrocity stories did not exist, they were invented. Hearst sent the gifted artist Frederic Remington to Cuba to draw sketches, and when the latter reported that conditions were not bad enough to warrant hostilities, Hearst is alleged to have replied, "You furnish the pictures and I'll furnish the war." Among other outrages, Remington depicted Spanish customs officials brutally disrobing and searching an American woman. Most readers of Hearst's *Journal*, their indignation soaring, had no way of knowing that such tasks were performed by female attendants.

"Butcher" Weyler was removed in 1897, yet conditions steadily worsened. There was some talk in Spain of granting the restive island a type of self-government, but such a surrender was so bitterly opposed by many Spaniards in Cuba that they engaged in furious riots. Early in 1898 Washington sent the battleship *Maine* to Cuba, osten-

Remington's Disrobing Propaganda. New York *Journal*, 1897

The Spanish Brute. From *Judge*.

sibly for a "friendly visit" but actually to protect and evacuate Americans if a dangerous flare-up should again occur.

This already explosive situation suddenly grew acute, on February 9, 1898, when Hearst sensationally headlined a private letter written by the Spanish minister in Washington, Dupuy de Lôme. The indiscreet epistle, which had been stolen from the mails, described President McKinley as an ear-to-the-ground politician who lacked good faith. The resulting uproar was so violent that De Lôme was forced to resign.

A tragic climax came a few days later, on February 15, 1898, when the *Maine* mysteriously blew up in Havana harbor, with a loss of 260 officers and men. Two investigations of the iron coffin were undertaken, one by United States naval officers, the other by Spanish officials, whom the Americans would not trust near the wreck. The Spanish commission announced that the explosion had been internal and presumably accidental; the American commission reported that the blast had been caused by a submarine mine. Washington, not unmindful of popular indignation, spurned Spanish proposals of arbitration.

The riddle of how the *Maine* was blown up, and by whom, has never been solved. Internal accidental explosions had occurred in warships with distressing frequency. Cuban insurgents may have sunk the vessel to force America into the war on their side; irresponsible and unauthorized Spanish officials may have done so. Spanish authorities in Cuba, acting under orders from home, were suspected. But this is the least plausible theory of all, for the Madrid government was actually doing everything it honorably could to avert hostilities.

Red-blooded Americans, now war-mad, blindly accepted the least likely explanation. Lashed to fury by the yellow press, they leaped to the conclusion that the Spanish government had been guilty of intolerable treachery. The battle cry of the hour became:

Remember the Maine!
To hell with Spain!

Nothing would do but to hurl the "dirty" Bourbon flag from the hemisphere.

McKinley Unleashes the Dogs of War

A popular belief that professional diplomats cause wars is not borne out by the events of 1898. American negotiators, by patient persuasion, had induced the Madrid authorities to yield to the first two of Washington's basic demands, namely a revocation of reconcentration and an armistice in Cuba with the rebels.

But the American public was on fire for war. The cautious Chief

Executive was condemned by jingoes as "Wobbly Willie" McKinley, while fight-hungry Theodore Roosevelt reportedly snarled that the "white-livered" occupant of the White House did not have "the backbone of a chocolate éclair." The President, whose shaken nerves required sleeping pills, was even being hanged in effigy.

McKinley's private desires clashed sharply with the public demands of the people. He did not want hostilities, for he had seen enough bloodshed as a major in the Civil War. Mark Hanna and Wall Street did not want war, for business might be unsettled. But a frenzied public, prodded by the yellow press, clamored for war to free the abused Cubans. The President, recognizing the inevitable, finally yielded and gave the people what they wanted.

But public pressures did not fully explain McKinley's course. He had no faith in Spain's promises regarding Cuba; she had made them and broken them before. He was certain that there would have to be a showdown sooner or later. He believed in the democratic principle that the people should rule, and he was loath to deny the American masses what they demanded—even if it was not good for them. He also perceived that if he stood out against war, the Democrats would make political capital out of his stubbornness. Bryan might sweep into the Presidency two years later under a banner inscribed, "Free Cuba and Free Silver." The gold-standard McKinley was a staunch party man, and to him it seemed better to break up the remnants of Spain's once-glorious empire than to break up the Grand Old Party—especially since war seemed inevitable.

On April 11, 1898, McKinley sent his war message to Congress, urging armed intervention to free the oppressed Cubans. The legislators responded uproariously with what was essentially a declaration of war. In a burst of self-righteousness, they likewise adopted the Teller Amendment. This proviso proclaimed to the world that when America had overthrown Spanish misrule, she would give the Cubans their freedom—a declaration that caused imperialistic Europeans to smile skeptically.

Dewey's May Day Victory at Manila

The American people plunged into the war lightheartedly, like school boys off to a picnic. Bands blared incessantly "There'll Be a Hot Time in the Old Town Tonight" and "Hail, Hail, the Gang's All Here."

But such jubilation seemed premature to European observers. The regular army, commanded by corpulent Civil War oldsters, was unprepared for a war under tropical skies. It numbered only 2100 officers and 28,000 men, as compared with some 200,000 Spanish troops in Cuba. The American navy, at least to transatlantic experts, seemed slightly less powerful than Spain's. European powers, moreover,

President William McKinley (1843–1901) was traditionally regarded as a pliant tool of Mark Hanna and Republican big business. He is now rated by historians as a reasonably able President who was his own man, despite a proper concern for public opinion. Tender-hearted as regards Spanish atrocities in Cuba, he was notably considerate toward his long-ailing wife, who suffered embarrassing seizures in public.

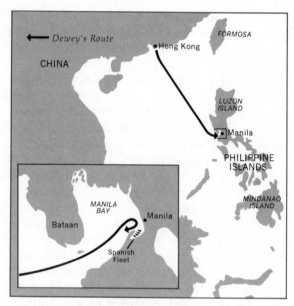

DEWEY IN THE PHILIPPINES, 1898

were generally friendly to their Old World associate. The only conspicuous exception was the ally-seeking British, who were ardently wooing their giant daughter in the west.

Yet in one important respect Spain's apparent superiority was illusory. Her navy, though formidable on paper, was in wretched condition. It labored under the added handicap of having to operate thousands of miles from its home base. But the new American steel navy, now fifteen years old and ranking about fifth among the fleets of the world, was in fairly good trim, though the war was to lay bare serious defects.

The readiness of the navy owed much to two men: the easygoing Secretary Long and his bellicose subordinate Assistant Secretary Theodore Roosevelt. The Secretary hardly dared leave his desk for fear that his overzealous underling would stir up a hornets' nest. On February 25, 1898, while Long was away for a weekend, Roosevelt had cabled Commodore George Dewey, commanding the American Asiatic Squadron at Hong Kong, to descend upon Spain's Philippines in the event of war. McKinley subsequently confirmed these instructions, even though an attack in the faraway Far East seemed like a strange way to free nearby Cuba.

Dewey carried out his orders magnificently on May 1, 1898. Sailing boldly with his six warships at night into the fortified harbor of Manila, he trained his guns the next morning on the ten-ship Spanish fleet, one of whose craft was only a moored hulk without functioning engines. The entire collection of antiquated and overmatched vessels was quickly destroyed, with a loss of nearly four hundred Spaniards killed and wounded, and without the loss of a single life in Dewey's fleet. An American consul who was there wrote that all the American sailors needed was cough drops for throats made raw by cheers of victory.

Unexpected Imperialistic Plums

George Dewey, quiet and taciturn, became a national hero overnight. He was promptly promoted to the rank of admiral, as the price of flags rose sharply. An amateur poet blossomed forth with:

Oh, dewy was the morning
Upon the first of May,
And Dewey was the Admiral,
Down in Manila Bay.
And dewy were the Spaniards' eyes,
Them orbs of black and blue;
And dew we feel discouraged?
I dew not think we dew!

Yet Dewey was in a perilous position. He had destroyed the enemy fleet, but he could not storm the forts of Manila with his sailors. His nerves frayed, he was forced to wait in the steaming-hot bay while troop reinforcements were slowly assembled in America.

Foreign warships meanwhile had begun to gather in the harbor, ostensibly to safeguard their nationals in Manila. The Germans sent five vessels—a naval force more powerful than Dewey's—and their haughty admiral defied the American blockade regulations. After several disagreeable incidents, Dewey lost his temper and threatened the arrogant German with war. Happily, the storm blew over. The British commander, by contrast, was conspicuously successful in carrying out London's new policy of friendliness. A false tale consequently spread that the British dramatically interposed their ships to prevent the Germans from blowing the Americans out of the water.

Long-awaited American troops, finally arriving in force, captured Manila on August 13, 1898. They collaborated with the Filipino insurgents, commanded by their well-educated, part-Chinese leader, Emilio Aguinaldo. Dewey, to his later regret, had brought this shrewd' and magnetic revolutionist from exile in Asia, so that he might weaken Spanish resistance.

These thrilling events in the Philippines had meanwhile focused attention on Hawaii. An impression spread that America needed the archipelago as a coaling and provisioning way station, in order to send supplies and reinforcements to Dewey. The truth is that the United States could have used the islands without annexing them, so eager was the white-dominated Honolulu government to compro-

Emilio Aguinaldo (*c.* 1869–1964), leader of the Philippine insurrection against American rule, never became completely reconciled. Charged with collaborating with the Japanese invaders in World War II, he was taken into custody in 1945 but not tried. After all his brushes with death, he died in Manila in 1964 in his ninety-fifth year.

mise itself. But an appreciative American public would not leave Dewey in the lurch. A joint resolution of annexation was rushed through Congress and approved by McKinley on July 7, 1898.

The residents of Hawaii, granted American citizenship with annexation, received full territorial status in 1900. These events in the idyllic islands, though seemingly sudden, were but the culmination of nearly a century of Americanization by sailors, whalers, traders, and missionaries.

The Confused Invasion of Cuba

Shortly after the outbreak of war, the Spanish government ordered a fleet of warships to Cuba. It was commanded by Admiral Cervera, who protested that his wretchedly prepared craft would court suicide. Four armored cruisers finally set forth (one without its main battery), accompanied by six torpedo boats, three of which had to be abandoned en route.

Panic seized the Eastern seaboard of the United States, even though Cervera would obviously have to stop at a West Indian port to replenish his coal supply. American vacationers abandoned their seashore cottages, while nervous investors moved their securities to inland depositories. Demands for protection poured in on Washington from nervous citizens, and the Navy Department was forced to detach some useless old Civil War ships to useless places for morale purposes. (The power of a panicky and ignorant public opinion is a fearsome thing, and if Spain had been stronger the results could have been disastrous.) Cervera finally found refuge in bottle-shaped Santiago harbor, Cuba, where he was blockaded by the much more powerful American fleet.

Sound strategy seemed to dictate that an American army be sent in from the rear to drive out Cervera. Command of the invading force was entrusted to three-hundred-pound General William R. Shafter, a leader so blubbery and gout-stricken that he had to be carried about on a door. The ill-prepared American conquerors were unequipped for war in the tropics, though amply provided with heavy woolen underwear and uniforms designed for sub-zero operations against the Indians.

The "Rough Riders," a part of the invading army, now charged onto the stage of history. This colorful regiment of volunteers, short on discipline but long on dash, consisted largely of Western cowboys and other hardy characters, with a sprinkling of ex-polo players and ex-convicts. Commanded by Colonel Leonard Wood, the group was organized principally by the glory-hungry Roosevelt, who had resigned from the Navy Department to serve as lieutenant colonel. Though totally without military experience, he used his strong political "pull" to secure his commission and to by-pass physical stan-

With a mixture of modesty and inmodesty Colonel Roosevelt wrote privately in 1903 of his Rough Riders: "In my regiment nine-tenths of the men were better horsemen than I was, and probably two-thirds of them better shots than I was, while on the average they were certainly hardier and more enduring. Yet after I had had them a very short while they all knew, and I knew too, that nobody else could command them as I could."

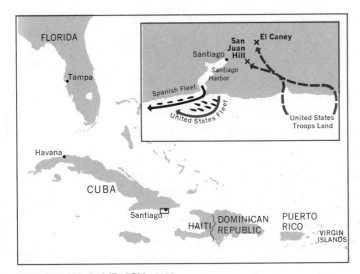

THE CUBAN CAMPAIGN, 1898

dards. He was so nearsighted that as a safeguard he took along a dozen pair of spectacles, cached in handy spots.

About the middle of June a bewildered American army of 17,000 men finally embarked at congested Tampa, Florida, amid scenes of indescribable confusion. The "Rough Riders," fearing that they would be robbed of glory, rushed one of the transports, and courageously held their place for almost a week in the broiling sun. About half of them finally got to Cuba without most of their horses, and the bowlegged regiment then came to be known as "Wood's Weary Walkers."

Shafter's landing near Santiago, Cuba, was made without serious opposition. Defending Spaniards, even more disorganized than the Americans, were unable to muster at this spot more than two thousand men. Brisk fighting broke out on July 1 at El Caney and San Juan Hill, up which Colonel Roosevelt and his horseless "Rough Riders" charged, with strong support from two crack Negro regiments. They suffered heavy casualties, but the colorful colonel, having the time of his life, shot a Spaniard with his revolver, and rejoiced to see his victim double up like a jack rabbit. He later wrote a book on his exploits which, "Mr. Dooley" remarked, ought to have been entitled *Alone in Cubia* [*sic*].

Curtains for Spain in America

The American army, fast closing in on Santiago, spelled doom for the Spanish fleet. Admiral Cervera, again protesting against suicide, was flatly ordered to fight for the honor of the flag. The odds against him were heavy: the guns of the U.S.S. *Oregon* alone threw more metal than his four armored cruisers combined. After a running chase, on July 3, the foul-bottomed Spanish fleet was entirely destroyed, as the wooden decks caught fire and the blazing infernos were beached. About five hundred Spaniards were killed, as compared with one for the Americans. "Don't cheer, men," admonished Captain Philip of the *Texas;* "the poor devils are dying." Shortly thereafter Santiago surrendered.

Hasty preparations were now made for a descent upon Puerto Rico before the war should end. The American army, commanded by Indian-fighter General Nelson A. Miles, met little resistance, as most of the population greeted the invaders as conquering heroes. "Mr. Dooley" was led to refer to "Gin'ral Miles' Gran' Picnic an' Moonlight Excursion." By this time Spain had satisfied her honor and, on August 12, 1898, she signed an armistice.

The "Round Robin" that Colonel Roosevelt and seven fellow officers signed read in part: "We . . . are of the unanimous opinion . . . that the army is disabled by malarial fever to the extent that its efficiency is destroyed, and that it is in a condition to be practically entirely destroyed by an epidemic of yellow fever. . . . The army must be moved at once, or perish. As the army can be safely moved now, the persons responsible for preventing such a move will be responsible for the unnecessary loss of many thousands of lives."

If the Spaniards had held out a few months longer in Cuba, the American army might have melted away. The inroads of malaria, typhoid, dysentery, and yellow fever became so severe that hundreds were incapacitated—"an army of convalescents." Others suffered from odorous canned meat known as "embalmed beef." Fiery and insubordinate Colonel Roosevelt, who had no regular military career to jeopardize, was a ringleader in making demands on Washington that the army be moved before it perished. About 25,000 men, 80% of them ill, were transferred to chilly Long Island, where the light summer clothing finally arrived.

One of the worst scandals of the war was the high death rate from sickness, especially typhoid fever. This disease was rampant in the unsanitary training camps located in the United States. All told, nearly 400 men lost their lives to bullets; over 5000 to bacteria and other causes.

A "goat" had to be found, even though the American people themselves were basically to blame for the ineptitudes and blunders. They had insisted on plunging into war without adequate preparations. The victim of their wrath proved to be Secretary of War Alger, a wealthy lumberman, whom McKinley was finally forced to dismiss. He might have ranked as a competent Secretary of War—if there had been no war.

McKinley Heeds Duty, Destiny, and Dollars

Late in 1898 the Spanish and American negotiators met in Paris, there to begin heated discussions. McKinley had sent five commissioners, including three Senators, who would have a final vote on their own handiwork. War-racked Cuba, as expected, was freed from her Spanish overlords. The Americans had little difficulty in securing the Pacific island of Guam, which they had captured early in the conflict from Spaniards who had not known that a war was on. They also picked up Puerto Rico, the last crumb of Spain's once magnificent American empire.

Knottiest of all was the problem of the Philippines, a veritable apple of discord. These lush islands not only embraced an area larger than the British Isles but contained a completely alien population of some seven million souls. McKinley was confronted with a devil's dilemma. He did not feel that America could honorably give them back to Spanish misrule, especially after she had fought a war to free Cuba. And she would be turning her back upon her responsibilities in a cowardly fashion, he believed, if she simply pulled up anchor and sailed away.

Other alternatives for the Philippines were trouble-fraught. The ill-prepared native Filipinos, if left to govern themselves, might fall into anarchy. One of the major powers might then try to seize them, possibly aggressive Germany, and a world war might be touched off into which the United States would be sucked. Seemingly the least of the evils consistent with national honor and safety was to acquire all the Philippines, and then perhaps give them their freedom later.

President McKinley, ever sensitive to public opinion, kept a carefully attuned ear to the ground. The rumble that he heard seemed to call for the entire group of islands. Zealous Protestant missionaries were eager for new converts; and the invalid Mrs. McKinley, to whom her husband was devoted, expressed deep concern about the half-naked natives. Wall Street had generally opposed the war; but awakened by the booming of Dewey's guns, it was clamoring for profits in the Philippines. "If this be commercialism," cried Mark Hanna, then "for God's sake let us have commercialism."

A tormented McKinley, so he was later reported as saying, finally went down on his knees seeking divine guidance. An inner voice seemed to tell him to take all the Philippines and Christianize and civilize them. This solution apparently coincided with the demands of the American people as well as with the McKinley-Hanna outlook. The mixture of things spiritual and material in McKinley's reasoning was later slyly summarized by an historian: "God directs us—perhaps it will pay." Profits thus joined hands with piety.

Fresh disputes broke out with the Spanish negotiators in Paris, once McKinley had reached the thorny decision to keep the Philippines. Manila had been captured the day *after* the armistice was signed, and the islands could not properly be listed among the spoils of war. The deadlock was broken when the Americans at length agreed to pay Spain $20,000,000 for this Philippine liability—one of the best bargains the Spaniards ever drove and their last great haul from the New World. Ex-Speaker "Czar" Reed sneered at America's having acquired millions of Malays, at three dollars a head, "in the bush."

Uncle Sam's White Elephant. New York *Herald,* 1898

America's Course (Curse?) of Empire

The signing of the pact of Paris—a trouble-fraught document—touched off one of the most impassioned debates of American history. Except for glacial Alaska and coral-reefed Hawaii, the Republic had hitherto acquired only contiguous territory on the continent. All previous acquisitions had been thinly peopled and capable of ultimate statehood. But in the Philippines the nation had on its hands a distant tropical area, thickly populated by Asiatics of alien race, tongue, religion, and governmental institutions.

Foes of annexation—anti-imperialists—had other arrows in their quiver. The Filipinos panted for freedom; and to annex them would violate the "consent of the governed" philosophy in the Declaration of Independence. Despotism abroad might well beget despotism at home. Finally, annexation would propel the United States into the political and military cauldron of the Far East.

Yet the expansionists or imperialists could sing a seductive song. They appealed to patriotism and to the glory of annexation—"don't dishonor the flag by hauling it down." Stressing the opportunities for exploiting the islands, they played up possible trade profits. Manila, in fact, might become the Hong Kong of the Far East. The richer the natural resources of the islands appeared to be, the less capable of self-government the Filipinos seemed to be. Rudyard Kipling, the British poet laureate of imperialism, urged America down the slippery path:

Take up the White Man's burden—
Ye dare not stoop to less—
Nor call too loud on Freedom
To cloak your weariness.

The Expansion Rooster. *San Francisco Chronicle,* 1900

In short, the wealthy Americans must help to uplift (and exploit) the underprivileged, underfed, and underclad of the world.

In the Senate the Spanish treaty ran into such heated opposition that it seemed doomed to defeat. But at this juncture the silverite Bryan unexpectedly sallied forth as its champion. As a Democratic volunteer colonel whom the Republicans had carefully kept out of Cuba, he apparently had no reason to help the McKinley administration out of a hole. But free silver was dead as a political issue. Bryan's foes assumed that he was preparing to fasten the stigma of imperialism on the Republicans, and then to sweep into the Presidency in 1900 under the flaming banner of anti-imperialism.

Bryan could support the treaty on plausible grounds. He argued that the war would not officially end until America had ratified the pact. She already had the islands on her hands, and the sooner she accepted the document, the sooner she could give the Filipinos their independence. After Bryan had used his personal influence with certain Democratic Senators, the treaty was approved, on February 6,

1899, with only one vote to spare. But the responsibility, as Bryan had foreseen, rested primarily on the Republicans.

Perplexities in Puerto Rico and Cuba

Puerto Rico was a poverty-stricken island, the fertility of whose million inhabitants, including many Negroes, outran that of their soil. By the Foraker Act of 1900 Congress accorded the Puerto Ricans a limited degree of popular government, and in 1917 granted them United States citizenship. Although the American regime worked wonders in education, sanitation, good roads, and other physical improvements, many of the inhabitants continued to clamor for independence.

A complex legal problem was posed by the question: Did the Constitution follow the flag? Did American laws, including tariff laws, apply with full force to the newly acquired possessions, chiefly the Philippines and Puerto Rico? Beginning in 1901 with the Insular Cases, a badly divided Supreme Court decreed in effect that the flag outran the Constitution, and that the outdistanced document did not necessarily extend with full force to the new windfalls. Congress was thus left with a free hand to determine the degree of applicability. The Court had apparently modified its views somewhat under the pressure of public opinion as expressed in the presidential election of 1900. This shift led "Mr. Dooley" to quip that whether the Constitution followed the flag or not, the Supreme Court followed the "iliction returns."

Cuba, scorched and chaotic, presented another headache. An American military government, set up under the administrative genius of General Leonard Wood, wrought miracles in government,

Uncle Sam: "By gum, I rather like your looks." *Rocky Mountain News* (Denver), 1900

General Wood Cleans Up Cuba.
Minneapolis *Tribune,* 1899

finance, education, agriculture, and public health. Under his leadership a frontal attack was launched on yellow fever. Spectacular experiments were performed by Dr. Walter Reed and others upon American soldiers, who volunteered as human guinea pigs; and the stegomyia mosquito was proved to be the lethal carrier. A cleanup of breeding places for mosquitoes wiped out yellow fever in Havana, while removing the recurrent fear of epidemics in cities of the South and the Atlantic seaboard.

The United States, honoring its self-denying Teller Amendment of 1898, withdrew from Cuba in 1902. Old World imperialists could scarcely believe their eyes. But the Washington government could not turn this rich and strategic island completely loose on the international sea; a grasping power like Germany might secure dangerous lodgment near America's soft underbelly. The Cubans were therefore forced to write into their constitution of 1901 the so-called Platt Amendment.

The hated amendment placed a severe hobble on the Cubans. They bound themselves not to impair their independence by treaty, or by contracting a debt beyond their resources. They further agreed that the United States might intervene with troops to restore order and to provide mutual protection. Finally, they promised to sell or lease needed coaling or naval stations, ultimately two and then one (Guantánamo), to their powerful "benefactor."

New Horizons in Two Hemispheres

In essence the Spanish-American War was a kind of gigantic coming-out party. Despite a common misconception, the conflict did not cause the United States to become a great power. Dewey's thundering guns merely advertised the fact that the nation was already a great power.

The war itself was short (113 days), spectacular, low in casualties, and uninterruptedly successful—despite the bungling. American prestige rose sharply, and European powers grudgingly accorded the Republic more respect. In Germany, Prince Bismarck reportedly growled that there was a special Providence which looked after drunkards, fools, and the United States of America. At times it seemed as though not only Providence but the Spaniards were fighting on the side of the Yankees. So great in fact was America's good fortune that rejoicing citizens found in the victories further support— misleading support—for their aversion to adequate preparedness.

An exhilarating new spirit thrilled America. National pride was touched and cockiness was increased by what John Hay called a "splendid little war."* Enthusiasm over these triumphs made easier

---

* Anti-imperialist William James called it "our squalid war with Spain. . . ."

the rush down the thorny path of empire. America did not start the war with imperialistic motives, but after falling through the cellar door of imperialism in a drunken fit of idealism, she wound up with imperialistic and colonial fruits in her grasp. The much-criticized British imperialists were pleased, partly because of the new-found friendship, partly because misery loves company. But America's German rival was envious, and Latin American neighbors were deeply suspicious of Yankee greed.

By taking on the Philippine liability, the United States became a full-fledged Far Eastern power. Hereafter these distant islands were to be a "heel of Achilles"—a kind of indefensible hostage given to Japan. With singular shortsightedness, the Americans assumed dangerous commitments that they were later unwilling to defend by proper naval and military outlays.

But the lessons of unpreparedness were not altogether lost. Captain Mahan's big navyism seemed vindicated, and pride in the exploits of the navy brought popular support for more and better battleships. The inept Secretary Alger was succeeded in the War Department by a masterly organizer, Elihu Root, who established a general staff and founded the War College in Washington. His genius later paid dividends when the United States found itself involved in the World War of 1914–1918.

One of the happiest results of the conflict was the further closing of the "bloody chasm" between North and South. Thousands of patriotic Southerners had flocked to the Stars and Stripes, and the gray-bearded General Joseph ("Fighting Joe") Wheeler—a Confederate cavalry hero of about a thousand Civil War skirmishes and battles—was given a command in Cuba. He allegedly cried, in the heat of battle, "To hell with the Yankees! Dammit, I mean the Spaniards."

A no less gratifying result was the victory over disease. Without the conquest of yellow fever, which had helped ruin the French project in Panama, there might have been no Isthmian canal. The splendid pioneering work of Dr. Jesse W. Lazear, who lost his life, and Dr. James Carroll, who suffered a severe heart ailment, deserve unstinted praise. These unsung heroes of the test tube merit no less acclaim than war heroes like Admiral George Dewey and Colonel Theodore Roosevelt.

Three years after the Spanish-American War ended a foreign diplomat in Washington remarked, "I have seen two Americas, the America before the Spanish American War and the America since."

SELECT READINGS

Refer to Leech and Morgan (on McKinley) and Nevins (on Cleveland) for the previous chapter. Main outlines are sketched in F. R. DULLES, *America's Rise to World Power, 1898–1954* (1955)* and in H. W. MORGAN, *America's Road to Empire* (1965).* See also E. R. MAY, *Imperial Democracy* (1961); WALTER LAFEBER, *The New Empire*

(1963)*; J. W. PRATT, *Expansionists of 1898* (1936)*; and W. A. RUSS, *The Hawaiian Revolution* (1959) and *The Hawaiian Republic* (1961). W. A. SWANBERG, *Citizen Hearst* (1961)* is colorful. On the war itself see FRANK FREIDEL, *The Splendid Little War* (1958)* and WALTER MILLIS, *The Martial Spirit* (1931). A helpful biographical study is R. L. BEISNER, *Twelve Against Empire: The Anti-Imperialists, 1898–1900* (1968). Also *Harvard Guide,** Pt. V.

RECENT REFERENCES

E. BERKELEY TOMPKINS, *Anti-Imperialism in the United States: The Great Debate, 1890–1920* (1970).

---

* Available in paperback.

32

America on the World Stage, 1899–1909

. . . I never take a step in foreign policy unless I am assured that I shall be able eventually to carry out my will by force.

Theodore Roosevelt, 1905

Little Brown Brothers in The Philippines

Regrettably, the liberty-loving Filipinos were tragically misled. They had assumed that they, like the Cubans, would be granted their freedom after the war. A clear-cut pledge by Congress to this effect probably would have averted the sorry sequel, but the Senate by the narrowest of margins refused to pass such a resolution. Bitterness toward the American troops continued to mount, and finally erupted into open insurrection on February 4, 1899, under Emilio Aguinaldo.

The war with the Filipinos, unlike the "splendid" little set-to with Spain, was sordid and prolonged. It involved more savage fighting, more soldiers killed in action, and far more scandal. Anti-imperialists redoubled their protests. In their view the United States, having plunged into war with Spain to free Cuba, was now fighting ten thousand miles away to rivet shackles on a people who asked for nothing but liberty.

As the ill-equipped Filipino armies were defeated, they melted into the jungle to wage a vicious guerrilla warfare. Many of the primitive natives used barbarous methods, and inevitably the infuriated American troops sank to their level. A brutal soldier song betrayed inner feelings:

Damn, damn, damn the Filipinos!
Cross-eyed kakiak ladrones!
  Underneath the starry flag
  Civilize 'em with a Krag [rifle],
And return us to our own beloved homes.

Atrocity tales shocked and rocked the United States, for such methods did not reflect America's better self. Uncle Sam's soldiers were goaded to such extremes as the painful "water cure"—that is, forcing water down the victim's throat until he yielded information or died. Reconcentration camps were even established which strongly suggested those of "Butcher" Weyler in Cuba. America, having begun the Spanish war with noble ideals, now dirtied her hands. One New York newspaper published a reply to Rudyard Kipling's famous poem:

We've taken up the white man's burden
  Of ebony and brown;
Now will you kindly tell us, Rudyard,
  How we may put it down?

The backbone of the Filipino insurrection was finally broken in 1901, when Aguinaldo was captured by a clever if unsporting ruse. But sporadic fighting dragged on for many dreary months.*

The problem of a government for the conquered islanders worried President McKinley who, in 1899, appointed a Philippine Commission to make appropriate recommendations. In its second year this body was headed by the future President, William H. Taft, an able and amiable lawyer-judge from Ohio who weighed about 350 pounds. Forming a strong attachment for the Filipinos, he called them his "little brown brothers" and danced light-footedly with their tiny women. But among the American soldiers, sweatily combing the jungles, a different view of the insurgent prevailed:

He may be a brother of Big Bill Taft,
But he ain't no brother of mine.

"Benevolent assimilation" of the Philippines proceeded with painful slowness. Millions of American dollars were poured into the islands to improve roads, sanitation, and public health. Important economic ties, including trade in sugar, developed between the two peoples. American teachers—"pioneers of the blackboard"—set up an unusually good school system and helped make English a second language. But all this vast expenditure, which profited America

---

* Two decades after collaborating with the Japanese invaders in World War II, Aguinaldo died in 1964, in his 94th year.

Liberty Halts American Butchery in the Philippines. *Life,* 1899

little, was ill appreciated. The Filipinos, who hated compulsory civilization, preferred less sanitation and more liberty. Like caged hawks, they beat against their gilded bars until they finally got their full freedom, on the Fourth of July, 1946.

John Hay Defends China (and U.S. Interests)

Uncle Sam waded deeper into the chill international waters in 1899, when American delegates attended the world disarmament conference at The Hague, in the Netherlands. Summoned at the invitation of the Russian Czar, the parley disappointed high hopes of reducing arms. But it did succeed in further codifying international law. It also set up the Permanent Court of Arbitration at The Hague, housed in the magnificent "Temple of Peace" donated by steelman Andrew Carnegie.

Exciting events had meanwhile been brewing in faraway and enfeebled China. Following her defeat by Japan in 1894–1895, the imperialistic European powers, notably Russia and Germany, moved in. Like vultures descending upon a stranded whale, they began to tear away valuable leaseholds and economic spheres of influence from the Manchu government.

A growing group of Americans viewed the vivisection of China with alarm. Churches were worried about their missionary vineyards; manufacturers and exporters feared that Chinese markets would be monopolized by Europeans. An alarmed American public, openly prodded by the press and unofficially prodded by certain free-trade Britons, demanded that Washington do something. Secretary of State John Hay, a quiet but witty poet-novelist-diplomat with a flair for capturing the popular imagination, finally decided upon a dramatic move.

In the summer of 1899 Hay dispatched to all the great powers a communication soon known as the Open Door note. He urged them to announce that in their leaseholds or spheres of influence they would respect certain Chinese rights and the ideal of fair competition. In short, in their dealings with foreign traders the intruding powers would observe the Open Door. The principle was not new, for America had tried repeatedly to make it the basis of her commercial dealings with China in the 19th Century. But the phrase "Open Door" quickly caught the public fancy and gained wide acceptance.

The commercial interests of both Britain and America were imperiled by the power grabs in China, and a close understanding between the two powers would have helped both. Yet as Secretary Hay wrote privately in in June, 1900, " . . . Every Senator I see says, 'For God's sake, don't let it appear we have any understanding with England.' How can I make bricks without straw? That we should be compelled to refuse the assistance of the greatest power in the world [Britain], *in carrying out our own policy*, because all Irishmen are Democrats and some [American] Germans are fools—is enough to drive a man mad."

Hay's proposal of this self-denying policy caused much squirming in the leading capitals of the world. It was like asking all men who do not have thieving designs to stand up and be counted. Italy alone accepted the Open Door unconditionally; she was the only major power that had no leasehold or sphere of influence in China. Britain, Germany, France, and Japan all accepted, but subject to the condition that the others acquiesce unconditionally. Russia, with covetous designs on China's Manchuria, in effect politely declined. But John Hay, rather than run the risk of a flat rejection, cleverly interpreted the Russian refusal as an acceptance, and proclaimed that the Open Door was in effect. Under such dubious midwifery was the infant born, and no one should have been surprised when the child proved to be sickly and relatively short-lived.

Hinging the Open Door in China

Open Door or not, patriotic Chinese were angered by being used as a mat by the Europeans. In 1900 a super-nationalistic group known as the Boxers broke loose with the cry "Kill Foreign Devils." Over two hundred missionaries and other luckless whites were murdered, and a number of foreign diplomats were besieged in the capital, Peking.

A rescue force of some 18,000 soldiers, hastily assembled, arrived in the nick of time. This multi-nation contingent consisted of Japanese, Russian, British, French, German, and American troops, with the American contribution some 2500 men. Such participation in a joint military operation, especially in Asia, was plainly contrary to the nation's time-honored principles of non-entanglement and non-involvement. But America had not been a Far Eastern power in the days of the Founding Fathers.

The victorious allied invaders acted angrily and vindictively. They assessed prostrate China an excessive indemnity of $333,000,000, of which America's share was to be $24,500,000. When Washington discovered that this sum was much more than enough to pay damages and expenses, it remitted about $18,000,000. The Peking government, appreciating this gesture of goodwill, set aside the money to educate a selected group of Chinese students in the United States. These bright young men later played a significant role in the Westernization of the Orient.

Secretary Hay now let fly another paper broadside, for he feared that the triumphant powers might use the Boxer outrages as a pretext for carving up China outright. His new circular note to the powers in 1900 announced that henceforth the Open Door would embrace the territorial integrity of China, in addition to her commercial integrity. Hay remembered his previous rebuff; this time he did not ask for formal acceptances.

Defenseless China was spared partition during these troubled years. But her salvation was probably not due to Hay's fine phrases, which the American people were loath to back up with fighting men. China owed her preservation far more to the strength of the competing powers; none of them could trust the others to gain an advantage.

John Hay (1838–1905), a gifted writer, poet, novelist, historian, and wit, first attained some prominence as assistant private secretary to President Lincoln, whom he affectionately called "The Tycoon" and "A Backwoods Jupiter." Graduating from the diplomatic service (including the ambassadorship to London), he became a headline-catching Secretary of State under President McKinley, notably with the "Open Door." President Roosevelt pushed him into the back seat and ungraciously referred to him as a "fine figurehead."

Kicking "Teddy" Roosevelt Upstairs

President McKinley's renomination by the Republicans in 1900 was a foregone conclusion. He had piloted the country through a victorious war; he had acquired rich, though onerous, real estate; he had established the gold standard; and he had brought the promised prosperity of the full dinner pail. "We'll stand pat!" was the poker-playing counsel of Mark Hanna. McKinley was renominated at Philadelphia on a platform that smugly endorsed prosperity, the gold standard, and overseas expansion.

An irresistible vice-presidential boom had developed for "Teddy" Roosevelt (T.R.), the cowboy-hero of San Juan Hill. Capitalizing on his war-born popularity, he had been elected governor of New York, where Thomas C. ("Easy Boss") Platt had found him headstrong and difficult to manage. Platt and his cronies therefore devised a scheme to kick the colorful colonel upstairs into the Vice-Presidency.

This plot to railroad Roosevelt worked beautifully. Gesticulating wildly, he attended the nominating convention, where his Western-style cowboy hat made him stand out like a white crow. He had no desire to die of slow rot in the vice-presidential burying ground, but he was eager to prove that he could get the nomination if he wanted it. He finally gave in when, to the accompaniment of cries of "We

Two Views of the Rough Rider as Vice-President. *Left,* Washington *Times; right,* Washington *Post*

Want Teddy," he received a unanimous vote, except for his own. A frantic Hanna reportedly moaned that there would be only one heartbeat between that wild-eyed "madman"—"that damned cowboy"—and the Presidency of the United States.

William Jennings Bryan, now a colonel also, was the odds-on choice of the Democrats, meeting at Kansas City. He was not a shooting-war hero, but he had run the risks of typhoid fever and "embalmed beef" in army camps. The free-silver issue was now defunct, but Bryan, a slave to consistency, forced a silver plank down the throats of his protesting associates. He thus helped crucify himself on a cross of silver. The Democratic platform proclaimed, as did Bryan, that the "paramount" issue was Republican overseas imperialism.

Imperialism or Bryanism in 1900?

Campaign history partially repeated itself in 1900. McKinley, the soul of dignity, sat safely on his front porch, as before. Bryan, also as before, took to the stump in a cyclonic campaign, assailing both imperialism and Republican-fostered trusts.

The super-energetic, second-fiddle Roosevelt out-Bryaned Bryan. He toured the country with revolver-shooting cowboys, and his popularity cut heavily into Bryan's support in the Middle West. Flashing his magnificent teeth and pounding his fist fiercely into his palm, Roosevelt denounced all dastards who would haul down Old Glory.

Bryanites loudly trumpeted their "paramount" issue of imperialism. Lincoln, they charged, had abolished slavery for 3,500,000 Africans; McKinley had re-established it for 7,000,000 Malayans. But the question of imperialism was actually stale; it had been agitating the novelty-loving American people for more than two years. The Republic had the Philippines on its hands anyhow, and the real question was not "Should it keep them?" but "What should it do with them in the future?"

Republicans responded by charging that "Bryanism," not imperialism, was the paramount issue. By this accusation they meant that Bryan would rock the boat of prosperity, once he got into office with his free-silver lunacy and other dangerous ideas. The voters were much less concerned about imperialism than about "Four Years More of the Full Dinner Pail" and "Let Well Enough Alone." Prosperity at home seemed more important than freedom abroad. When the smoke cleared off, McKinley had triumphed by a much wider margin than in 1896: 7,207,923 to 6,358,133 popular votes, and 292 to 155 electoral votes.

Victory for the Republicans was not a mandate for or against imperialism, legend to the contrary. The confused voters were not asked to decide this issue but, basically, to select either McKinley or Bryan. Many citizens who favored Bryan's anti-imperialism feared his free silver; many who favored McKinley's "sound money" hated his imperialism. If there was any mandate at all it was for the two "P's": prosperity and protection. Content with good times, the country anticipated four more years of a full dinner pail crammed with fried chicken. And "Boss" Platt of New York gleefully looked forward to inauguration day, when he would see Roosevelt "take the veil" as Vice President.

"Four More Years of Full Dinner Pails." Contemporary cartoon.

The dilemma presented to many voters by the choice between Bryan and McKinley in 1900 is well exemplified in a letter that one citizen wrote to ex-President Cleveland: "It is a choice between evils, and I am going to shut my eyes, hold my nose, vote, go home and disinfect myself."

T.R.: Brandisher of the Big Stick

Kindly William McKinley had scarcely served another six months when, in September, 1901, he was murdered by a deranged anarchist. Roosevelt became President at age forty-two, the youngest thus far in American history. Knowing that he had a reputation for impulsiveness and radicalism, he sought to reassure the country by proclaiming that he would carry out the policies of his predecessor. Cynics sneered that he would indeed carry them out—to the garbage heap.

What manner of man was Theodore Roosevelt, the red-blooded blue-blood? Born into a wealthy and distinguished New York family, he had fiercely built up his spindly, asthmatic body by a stern and self-imposed routine of exercise. Graduating from Harvard with Phi Beta Kappa honors, he published at the age of twenty-four the first of some thirty volumes of muscular prose. Then came busy years, which involved duties as a ranch owner and bespectacled cowboy in the Dakotas, followed by various political posts. When fully developed, he was a barrel-chested five feet ten, with prominent teeth, squinty eyes, droopy mustache, and piercing voice.

The Rough Rider's high-voltage energy was electrifying. Believing that it was better to wear out than to rust out, he would shake the hands of some 6000 persons at one stretch, or ride horseback a hundred miles in a day as an example for portly cavalry officers. Not surprisingly, he gathered about him a group of athletic, tennis-playing cronies, who were popularly dubbed "the Tennis Cabinet."

Incurably boyish and bellicose, Roosevelt loved a fight—"an elegant row." He never ceased to preach the virile virtues and to denounce civilized softness, with its pacifists and other "flubdubs" and "mollycoddles." An ardent champion of military and naval preparedness, he adopted as his pet proverb, "Speak softly and carry a big stick, [and] you will go far." If a statesman had the Big Stick, he could work his will among foreign nations without shouting; if he lacked it, shouting would do no good. T.R. had both a big stick and a shrill voice.

Teddy and the Big Stick.
New York *Globe*

Wherever Roosevelt went, there was a great stir. Shockingly unconventional, he loved to break hoary precedents—the hoarier the better. He was a colossal egoist, and his self-confidence merged with self-righteousness. So sure was he of the correctness of his convictions that he impetuously branded people liars who disagreed with him. As a true cosmopolite, he loved people and mingled with all ranks of men, from Catholic cardinals to professional prize fighters, one of whom blinded a Rooseveltian eye in a White House bout.

An outspoken moralizer and reformer, Roosevelt preached righteousness from the White House pulpit. John Morley, a British author, found him an interesting combination of St. Paul and St. Vitus. Yet he was an opportunist who would compromise rather than butt his head against a stone wall. He was, in reality, much less radical than his blustery actions would indicate. A middle-of-the-roader, he stood just a little left of center, and bared his mule-like molars at liberals and reactionaries alike.

Roosevelt rapidly developed into a master politician with an idolatrous personal following. T.R.—as he was called—had an enormous popular appeal, partly because the common man saw in him a fiery champion. A magnificent showman, he was always front-page copy; and his cowboyism, his bear shooting, his outsize teeth, and his pince-nez glasses were ever the delight of the cartoonist. Though a staunch party man, he detested many of the dirty-handed bosses; but he learned, as Cleveland never did, to hold his nose and work with them.

Above all, Roosevelt was a direct-actionist. He believed that the President should lead; and although he made mistakes, he kept things noisily moving—generally forward. Never a lawyer, he condemned the law and the courts as too slow. He had no real respect for the delicate checks and balances among the three branches of the government. Finding the Constitution too rigid, he would on occasion ignore it; finding the Senate too windy, he would often circumvent it; finding Congress too rebellious, he tried a mixture of coercion and compromise on it.

T.R. finally developed his extraordinary "stewardship theory," which must have made Jefferson and others writhe in their graves. The President, so he felt, may take any action in the general interest that is not specifically forbidden by the laws and the Constitution. Wallace Irwin noted:

The Constitution rides behind
  And the Big Stick rides before,
(Which is the rule of precedent
  In the reign of Theodore.)*

Colombia Blocks the Canal

Foreign affairs absorbed much of Roosevelt's bullish energy. Having traveled extensively in Europe, he enjoyed a far more intimate knowledge of the outside world than most of his predecessors.

The Spanish-American War had emphasized the need of constructing the long-talked-about canal, through which only printer's ink had ever flowed. Anxious Americans had learned a dramatic object lesson when the battleship *Oregon,* stationed on the Pacific Coast at the outbreak of hostilities, made a full-speed dash around South America to join the fleet in Cuban waters. Alarmists speculated on what might have happened if she had not arrived in time for the battle of Santiago, and if the Spanish fleet had been stronger. An Isthmian canal would plainly augment the strength of the navy by increasing its mobility. Such a waterway would also make easier the defense of such recent acquisitions as Puerto Rico, the Philippines, and Hawaii, while facilitating the operations of the American merchant marine.

The Battleship *Oregon.* Naval Photographic Center.

Initial obstacles in the path of the canal builders were legal rather than geographical. By the terms of the ancient Clayton-Bulwer Treaty, concluded with Britain in 1850, the United States could not secure exclusive control over such a route. But by 1901 America's British cousins were willing to yield ground. Confronted with an unfriendly Europe and bogged down in the South African Boer War, they conceded the Hay-Pauncefote Treaty in 1901. It not only gave the United States a free hand to build the canal, but conceded the right to fortify it as well.

* From "The Ballad of Grizzly Gulch," in *At the Sign of the Dollar* (1903). Reprinted by permission of the author.

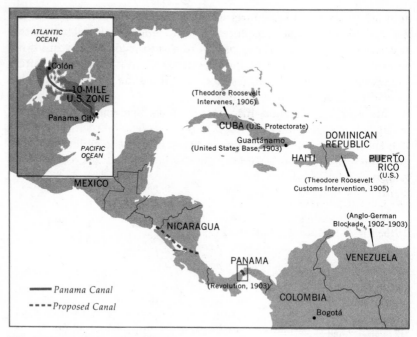

BIG STICK IN THE CARIBBEAN

Legal barriers now removed, the next question was: Where should the canal be dug? Many American experts favored the Nicaraguan route, but the agents of the old French Canal Company were eager to salvage something from the costly failure at S-shaped Panama. Represented by a young, energetic, and unscrupulous engineer, Philippe Bunau-Varilla, the New Panama Canal Company suddenly dropped the price of its holdings from $109,000,000 to the fire-sale price of $40,000,000.

The Nicaragua-versus-Panama issue was hotly debated in Congress, where a serious objection to Nicaragua was its volcanic activity. Providentially for Bunau-Varilla, Mount Pelée, on the West Indian island of Martinique, blew its top in May, 1902, and wiped out some thirty thousand souls. The clever Frenchman hastily secured ninety Nicaraguan postage stamps, each bearing a picture of the country's most fearsome volcano, and sent one to each Senator. Hanna delivered a persuasive Senate speech, in which he stressed the engineering advantages of the Panama route. In June, 1902, Congress finally accepted his views.

The scene now shifted to Colombia, of which Panama was an unwilling part. A treaty highly favorable to the United States was negotiated in Washington with the agent of the Colombian government in Bogotá. It granted the lease of a six-mile-wide zone in perpetuity, in return for $10,000,000 and an annual payment of $250,000. But when the pact was submitted to the Bogotá Senate, it was unanimously rejected. The Isthmian strip was regarded as one of

Colombia's most valuable natural assets, and many Colombians felt that they were not getting enough money. Evidence later unearthed indicates that if Washington had been willing to pay an additional $15,000,000, the pact would have been approved.

Roosevelt was infuriated by his setback at the hands of what he called those "dagoes." Frantically eager to be elected President "in his own right" in 1904, he was anxious to "make the dirt fly" to impress the voters. "Damn the law," he reportedly cried in private, "I want the canal built!" He assailed "the blackmailers of Bogotá" who, like armed bandits, were blocking the onward march of civilization. He failed to point out that the Senate of the United States also rejects treaties.

Uncle Sam Creates Puppet Panama

Impatient Panamanians, who had rebelled numerous times, were ripe for another revolt. They had counted on a wave of prosperity to follow construction of the canal, and they feared that the United States would now turn to the Nicaraguan route. Bunau-Varilla was no less disturbed by the prospect of losing the company's $40,000,000. Working hand in glove with the Panama revolutionists, he raised a tiny "patriot" army consisting largely of members of the Panamanian fire department, plus five hundred "bought" Colombian troops—price reportedly $100,000.

The Panama revolution occurred on November 3, 1903, with the incidental killing of a Chinese bystander and a donkey. Colombian troops were gathered to crush the uprising, but American naval forces would not let them cross the isthmus. Roosevelt justified this highly questionable interference by a strained interpretation of the treaty of 1846 with Colombia. (This pact obligated Washington to maintain the "perfect neutrality" of the Isthmus, obviously against outsiders.)

Roosevelt moved rapidly to make steamy Panama a virtual outpost of the United States. Three days after the uprising, he hastily extended the right hand of recognition. Fifteen days later, Bunau-Varilla, who was now the Panamanian minister despite his French citizenship, signed the Hay–Bunau-Varilla treaty in Washington. The price of the canal strip was left the same, but the zone was widened from six to ten miles. And the French company gladly pocketed its $40,000,000 from the United States Treasury.

Roosevelt, it seems clear, did not actively plot to tear Panama from the side of Colombia. But the conspirators knew of his angrily expressed views, and they counted on his using the Big Stick to prevent Colombia from intervening. Yet the Rough Rider became so indiscreetly involved in the affair as to create the impression that he had been a secret party to the intrigue.

Unhappily the United States suffered a black eye as a result of

T.R. Intervenes in Panama.
New York *Globe*

Roosevelt's "cowboy diplomacy." European imperialists, who were old hands at this sort of thing, could now raise their eyebrows sneeringly at America's superior moral pretensions—and they did.

Completing the Canal and Appeasing Colombia

The so-called rape of Panama marks an ugly downward lurch in Uncle Sam's relations with Latin America. Much fear had already been aroused by the recent seizure of Puerto Rico and by the Yankee stranglehold on Cuba. The fate of Colombia, when she dared defy the Colossus of the North, indicated that her weak sister republics were not safe. The era of the bullying "Big Brother" policy was definitely launched.

In 1911 Roosevelt made a costly boast in a speech in Berkeley, California: "I am interested in the Panama Canal because I started it. If I had followed traditional, conservative methods I would have presented a dignified state paper . . . to Congress and the debates on it would have been going on yet; but I took the Canal Zone and let Congress debate; and while the debate goes on the Canal does also."

Roosevelt heatedly defended himself against all charges of evildoing. He claimed that he had received a "mandate from civilization" to start the canal, and that Colombia had wronged the United States by not permitting herself to be benefited. To deal with these "blackmailers," he insisted, was like "nailing currant jelly to the wall."

But T.R. was not completely candid. He failed to point out that the Nicaragua route was about as feasible, and that it was available without a revolution. Yet this alternative would have involved some delay, and the presidential election of 1904 was fast approaching.

Active work was begun on "making the dirt fly" in 1904, but grave difficulties were encountered, ranging from labor troubles to landslides. The organization was finally perfected under an energetic but autocratic West Point engineer, Colonel George Washington Goethals. At the outset, sanitation proved to be more important than excavation. Colonel William C. Gorgas, the quiet and determined exterminator of yellow fever in Havana, ultimately made the Canal Zone "as safe as a health resort."

Americans finally succeeded where Frenchmen had failed. In 1914 the colossal canal project was completed at an initial cost of about $400,000,000, just as World War I was breaking out. The whole enterprise, in the words of the English writer James Bryce, was "the greatest liberty Man has ever taken with Nature."

Roosevelt as ex-President continued to exult over this geographical surgery. He was at pains to point out that even though the debate went on over his "rape'" of Panama, ships went through the canal. Colombia had offered to arbitrate her grievance, but the United States, though often preaching arbitration, declined to risk a decision at the hands of foreigners. Subsequent Democratic Congresses, willing to do penance for the Republican sins of Roosevelt, attempted to apologize to Colombia and to indemnify her for her loss. But the still-violent Rough Rider cried that this would be done over his dead body, and his friends in the Senate defeated the proposed treaty.

Oil provided an unexpected lubricant. Gushers of liquid "black

Roosevelt Makes the Dirt Fly at Panama. New York *Herald,* 1903; reprinted by permission of the New York *Sun,* Inc.

gold" were discovered in Colombia, and would-be exploiters from Yankeeland were getting the cold shoulder. Roosevelt had died in 1919, and in 1921 the United States Senate acted. Suddenly troubled by a tender conscience, it approved a heart-balm treaty, which granted Colombia $25,000,000 without an apology. But such a sum is in itself an apology. The tragedy is that in 1903 about half this so-called "canalimony," in addition to the original $10,000,000, would probably have averted the scandal.

Roosevelt and Venezuelan Vexations

Tropical Venezuela lay in the iron grip of dictator Cipriano Castro, whom Roosevelt branded "an unspeakably villainous little monkey." Castro had defaulted on his nation's indebtedness to certain European powers, and late in 1902 Britain took the lead in inducing Germany to join in collecting the debts. Roosevelt had no serious objections: he believed that misbehaving republics might properly be "spanked."

Spanking proved effective. The Germans sank two Venezuelan gunboats, and with unnecessary ruthlessness bombarded a town early in 1903. Dictator Castro hastened to accept an arbitration proposal that he had earlier spurned, and Washington was glad to transmit his acceptance to the European powers.

Opinion in the United States, less acquiescent, was now angrily aroused against this iron-fisted intervention. The British ringleaders, fearful of ruining the newly won American friendship, pulled in their horns, leaving Germany to bear the full brunt of Yankee disapproval. The European powers finally accepted arbitration of their monetary claims in 1903, and the unhappy affair was patched up.

Roosevelt released the "inside" story a dozen or so years later, when he was aroused against a Germany that had brutally invaded Belgium. Describing a threatening ten-day ultimatum which he had presented to the Kaiser, he indicated that he had big-sticked the Germans out of Venezuela. Although historians have cast serious doubt on his tale, he may have exerted some behind-the-scenes influence on the German Emperor. Among other pressures, Admiral Dewey was stationed menacingly in the Caribbean with a powerful naval force.

Monroe Doctrine, A Live Wire. New York *Herald,* by permission of the New York *Sun,* Inc.

The Monroe Doctrine no doubt gained muscle as a result of the Venezuela episode, whatever question may exist as to Roosevelt's dramatic tale. A resentful American public had served warning that it would frown upon European powers which, with mailed fist, set out to "spank" its weak Latin American neighbors.

T.R.'s Perversion of Monroe's Doctrine

Defaulted debts also concerned the revolution-rent Dominican Republic, whose "chronic wrongdoing" Roosevelt deplored. He feared that the Germans or other Europeans might come as bill collectors. If they came, they might stay; if they stayed, they would violate the Monroe Doctrine; if they violated the Monroe Doctrine, the United States might have to fight them.

T.R. therefore evolved a devious policy of "preventive intervention," better known as the Roosevelt corollary of the Monroe Doctrine. Under it Americans would intervene themselves, take over the customhouses, pay off the debts, and keep the troublesome powers on the other side of the Atlantic. The United States had a moral obligation to do so, Roosevelt argued, because it would not permit the European nations themselves to intervene in the bankrupt banana republics. In short, no outsiders could push the Latin nations around except Uncle Sam, Policeman of the Caribbean.

This new brandishing of the Big Stick in the Caribbean became effective in 1905. It was formalized by a Dominican treaty two years later, after Roosevelt had engaged in a "glorious" quarrel with the Senate. Dominican officials, who had raked in much juicy graft, were not happy over such interference, and they acquiesced only after some judicious arm-twisting from Washington. But from a debt-collecting point of view, the customhouse intervention was a success.

Roosevelt's corollary, though tacked onto the Monroe Doctrine, bore only a strained relation to the original dictum of 1823. Monroe had in effect said to the European powers, "Thou shalt not intervene." T.R. changed this warning to mean, "We shall intervene to prevent you from intervening." The Roosevelt doctrine was actually so radical as to be a completely new policy, but it gained readier acceptance by being associated with the honored name of Monroe. Yet in its own right the corollary had considerable merit as a defensive stroke.

Roosevelt's rewriting of Monroe's doctrine had its dark side. It probably did more than any other one step to promote the "Bad Neighbor" policy begun in these years. As time wore on, the new corollary was used to justify wholesale interventions and repeated landings of the Marines, all of which helped turn the Caribbean into a "Yankee lake." Latin Americans mistakenly cursed the unoffending Monroe, when they should have cursed the offending Roosevelt. To them it seemed as though the Monroe Doctrine, far from providing a shield, was a cloak behind which the United States sought to strangle them. Wallace Irwin slyly criticized the new interventionism:

Here's a bumper to the doctrine of Monroe, roe, roe,
*   And the neighbors whom we cannot let alone;*
Through the thirst for diagnosis we're inserting our proboscis
*   Into everybody's business but our own.**

The shadow of the Big Stick likewise fell on Cuba in 1906. Revolutionary disorders brought an appeal from the Cuban president and, "necessity being the mother of intervention," United States Marines

Roosevelt wrote to a correspondent in February, 1904, "I have been hoping and praying for three months that the Santo Domingans would behave so that I would not have to act in any way. I want to do nothing but what a policeman has to do. . . . As for annexing the island, I have about the same desire to annex it as a gorged boa-constrictor might have to swallow a porcupine wrong-end-to."

* From "Monroe Doctrinings," in *Random Rhymes and Odd Numbers* (The Macmillan Company, copyright 1906). Reprinted by permission of the publisher.

were landed. These police forces were withdrawn temporarily in 1909, but in Latin American eyes the episode was but another example of the creeping power of the Colossus of the North.

The Big Stick in Two Hemispheres

Booted and spurred, Roosevelt had meanwhile been charging into the Canada-Alaska boundary controversy. America's vast northern neighbor had, for several years, seriously disputed the line between herself and the Alaska panhandle. Washington contended that under the original Russo-American treaty of 1824, the boundary should follow the snake-like windings of the coast. The Canadians argued that the line should be run straighter, leaving the heads of the deeper inlets in their hands. Finally in 1903 a treaty was concluded between London and Washington. It referred the controversy to six "impartial justices of repute," three Americans appointed by President Roosevelt and three British subjects—two Canadians and one Briton—named by their King.

The so-called Alaska boundary arbitration actually created disputes. Roosevelt, cocksure as usual, convinced himself that the Canadian claims were "an outrage pure and simple." Behind the scenes, he displayed his Big Stick, threatening that if America lost he would seize what was properly hers with troops. The key British arbitrator, faced with the awful responsibility of starting a war, may have been unduly swayed. At length the tribunal voted four to two—

THE ALASKAN BOUNDARY SETTLEMENT, 1903

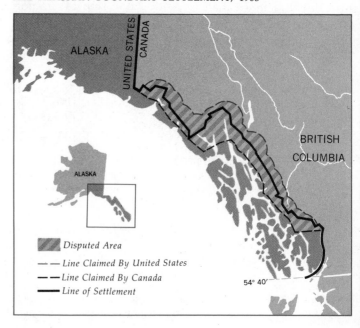

the two being Canadians—in favor of the basic American contention, although narrowing somewhat the coastal strip. The Canadians were deeply angered, perhaps more so by the British, who had betrayed them, than by Roosevelt, who had browbeaten them.

A bigger storm had meanwhile been brewing in North Africa over French-protected Morocco, at which the imperial-minded Germans were casting covetous eyes. In 1905 the Kaiser landed there and made a saber-rattling speech. Overnight an international storm blew up, involving France and Britain as the chief adversaries of Germany. At the prompting of the Kaiser, Roosevelt consented to help arrange for an international conference at Algeciras, Spain, in 1906.

Two American delegates were sent to the parley on Morocco, despite the non-entanglement warnings of the Founding Fathers. Roosevelt privately took the side of France, partly because he distrusted the Kaiser, whom he dubbed "that autocratic zigzag." When deadlock developed at Algeciras, the President flourished his Big Stick at the erratic German ruler and, in his own words, gently "stood him on his head." As the German army was not ready to march, the Kaiser backed down and suffered something of a diplomatic defeat.

T.R. Upholds the World.
New York *World*

But why should America be embroiling herself in Morocco? Her trade and investment stake—the Open Door—was negligible. Roosevelt in effect was developing a further new interpretation of the Monroe Doctrine. He evidently believed that he was justified in intervening in overseas crises that might touch off globe-girdling hostilities, because such a conflagration probably would suck his nation in. His timely intervention may possibly have prevented world-wide war from breaking out in 1906 rather than in 1914.

The Second Hague Disarmament Conference met in 1907. Although officially called by the Czar, as before, it was actually initiated by Roosevelt, who responded to the proddings of American public opinion. Nothing was accomplished in the area of arms reduction, owing largely to the opposition of militaristic Germany to disarmament and arbitration. But the Conference did adopt some useful regulations on such subjects as international debt collection, humane warfare, and the rights and obligations of neutrals. Although the United States was represented at The Hague—another step away from isolation—the war-loving Roosevelt, deep in the Japanese crisis, was rather indifferent to the sessions.

Underdog Sympathy in the Russo-Japanese War

The Russian bear, having lumbered across Asia, was seeking to bathe his frostbitten paws in the ice-free ports of China's Manchuria, particularly Port Arthur. To Japan, Manchuria and Korea in Czarist hands were pistols pointed at her strategic heart. Russian troops had invaded Manchuria during the Boxer outburst of 1900, and despite solemn promises were not withdrawing. The Czar was obviously stalling until his trans-Siberian railroad could be finished, as it would be in a few months. With the clock ticking against them, the Japanese suddenly triggered war in 1904 by a devastating sneak attack on the Russian fleet at Port Arthur.

On paper, American sympathies should have gone out to Russia, for she was a traditional friend of long standing. During the 19th Century the United States had managed to get along unusually well with her, primarily because of a common bitterness against Britain, and also because Americans had little to do with the Russians. But by the sunset of the century the ancient grudge against Mother England was evaporating, and the Yankees were coming into direct contact with Russia as she menaced their Open Door interests in China. The American people were also repelled by her naked imperialism, and especially by Czarist despotism, as highlighted by shocking descriptions of Siberian prison camps in American magazines of the 1880's and 1890's. Worst of all were the terrible massacres of Russian Jews, which broke out anew with frightful fury at the time of the Russo-Japanese War.

Tiny Japan had a sentimental claim to American sympathy, for she was peculiarly the protégé of the United States. The Americans had forced open her gates to Western civilization, and they had taken great pride in the speed with which she had acquired a veneer of Occidental culture. As between Russia and Japan, Russia seemed to be the big bully and Japan the underdog—and American hearts went out to the Japanese. The Russians resentfully reminded America how they had stood by her during the dark days of her Civil War—though for selfish reasons, as is now known.

FAR EAST, 1904–1905

Roosevelt Engineers the Peace of Portsmouth

Undersized but efficient, the Japanese administered a humiliating series of beatings to the inept Russians in Manchuria and on the sea. But as the war dragged on, Japan began to run short of men and yen—a weakness she did not want to betray to the enemy. The Tokyo officials therefore approached Roosevelt in the deepest secrecy, and asked him to take steps that would bring the peace negotiators together.

Although Roosevelt did not relish the thankless role of umpire, he felt that a speedy end of the war was to America's interests. Either Japan or Russia might collapse, thus upsetting the balance of power in the Far East. The surviving combatant would then become dominant, to the jeopardy of America's commercial, missionary, and other interests.

Under Roosevelt's vigorous shepherding, the Japanese and Russian delegates gathered near Portsmouth, New Hampshire, in 1905.

The politely bowing Orientals, on the basis of their victories, presented stern demands. They asked for a huge indemnity and for all of the island of Sakhalin, which commands the Amur River—the Mississippi of Siberia.

Agreement at Portsmouth was difficult. Roosevelt encountered stubbornness in both the Japanese and Russians; in disgust he branded the Czar "a preposterous little creature." After he had blustered behind the scenes, the Japanese grudgingly gave ground. They abandoned their claims for an indemnity, and agreed to accept half of Sakhalin. But they strengthened their pre-eminent position in Korea, and displaced Russia as the dominant foreign power in Manchuria.

Brickbats rained upon the President, "the honest broker," from both sides. The Russians, accusing him of being a Jewish "Rosenfelt," insisted that they could have whipped their foe. The Japanese, whose expectations had been raised, felt robbed of their indemnity. Throughout Japan, Roosevelt's portrait was turned to the wall. But he found some solace in the Nobel Peace Prize of 1906, which he probably deserved, despite his glorification of war.

Two historic friendships withered on the windswept plains of Manchuria. That between Russia and America, already strained, fell upon more evil days. That between Japan and America entered upon a more troubled phase. The United States had emerged in 1898 as a great power, with crucial interests in the Far East. During 1904–1905 Japan likewise emerged as a great power, with conflicting ambitions. Uncle Sam could no longer pat his bright little protégé on the head and show him off. Japan and America were now rivals; and feelings of suspicion, fear, and jealousy were bound to supplant the one-time happy relationship. To many Americans, the Nipponese were getting too big for their kimonos.

There is a curious modernity about what Roosevelt wrote to a British friend in May, 1905: "I like the Russian people, but abhor the Russian system of government and I cannot trust the word of those at the head."

Japanese Coolies in California

The population of America's Pacific Coast was directly affected by the Russo-Japanese War. A new restlessness came to the rice paddies of Japan, largely as a result of the dislocations and tax burdens caused by the recent conflict. Numerous Japanese laborers, with their wives and swarming offspring, began to pour into the spacious valleys of California. By 1906 there were approximately 70,000 Japanese on the Pacific Coast.

Nervous Californians, confronted by another "yellow peril," were fearful of being drowned in an Oriental sea. Seizing upon a new variant of the old anti-Chinese slogan, they cried, "The Japanese must go." The eastern part of the United States, indifferent to the prolific Japanese, did not share the alarm of the Pacific Coast.

A showdown on the Japanese influx came in 1906. Following the frightful earthquake and fire of that year in San Francisco, the local school authorities, pressed for space, decreed that Oriental children should attend a special school. This edict, though aimed at overage Japanese "boys," was designed basically to advertise to the rest of the nation the alarm of California over the inflow of cheap coolie labor.

Instantly, the Japanese school incident brewed an international crisis. The people of Japan, highly sensitive on questions of race, regarded this discrimination as an insult to them and their beloved children. On both sides of the Pacific, irresponsible war talk sizzled in the yellow press—the real "yellow peril." Roosevelt, who as a Rough Rider had welcomed shooting, was less happy over the prospect of California's stirring up a war which all the other states would have to fight. He therefore invited the entire San Francisco Board of Education, headed by a bassoon-playing mayor under indictment for graft, to come to the White House.

T.R. finally broke the deadlock, but not until he had waved his Big Stick and bared his big teeth. The Californians were induced to repeal the offensive school order and to accept what came to be known as "the Gentlemen's Agreement." This secret understanding was worked out, during 1907–1908, by an exchange of diplomatic notes between Washington and Tokyo. The Japanese, for their part, agreed to stop the flow of coolies to the American mainland by withholding passports. Californians, their fears allayed, henceforth slept easier.

"Isn't it a Daisy?" Uncle Sam Admires his Battleship Fleet. Philadelphia *Record*

The World Cruise of the Great White Fleet

Roosevelt, who loved grand flourishes, dreamed up a fantastic one, partially for the benefit of Japan. Though not a coward, he was afraid that the Japanese thought him afraid. He suspected that his intercession between California and Japan was being interpreted in Tokyo as prompted by fear of the Nipponese. The American navy was then second among the navies of the world, thanks to his zeal for preparedness, and that of Japan was fifth. Partly to impress the Japanese with the potency of the Big Stick, he decided to send the entire battleship fleet out to the Pacific Coast, and subsequently from there all the rest of the way around the world.

Pained protests arose from American critics. They charged that the mad scheme would provoke war; that the fleet would break down or be sunk; and that the Eastern seaboard would be stripped of its defenders. But Roosevelt stood firm, and later in 1907 the sixteen smoke-belching battleships started from Virginia waters. Their commander pointedly declared that he was ready for "a feast, a frolic, or a fight."

The Great White Fleet—to the accompaniment of cannonading champagne corks—received a series of tumultuous outpourings. At

South American ports the Yankee warships were greeted with heart-warming rejoicing, for to many they were the effective teeth of the Monroe Doctrine against European invasion. The flotilla finally reached the Pacific Coast in safety, and then steamed on to Hawaii, New Zealand, and Australia. After the customary cheers, the ships headed for Japanese waters, where alarmists claimed that secret mines were planted.

An overwhelming reception in Japan was the high point of the trip. Tens of thousands of kimonoed school children had been trained to wave tiny American flags and sing "The Star-Spangled Banner"—in English. In the happy diplomatic atmosphere created by the visit of the fleet, the Root-Takahira agreement of 1908 was reached with Japan. Both powers solemnly pledged themselves to respect each other's territorial possessions in the Pacific, and to uphold the Open Door in China. The once fight-thirsty Roosevelt, who thus went out of his way to avoid a fight with Japan, regarded the battleship cruise as his most important contribution to peace.

After visiting the Mediterranean, the fleet steamed into home waters early in 1909, just in time to usher out the Roosevelt regime in a blaze of glory. Unquestionably the spectacular voyage—the Big Stick in action—popularized and accelerated American naval preparedness, while probably stimulating worldwide navalism. The Monroe Doctrine was correspondingly strengthened against European intervention. Finally, this breath-taking demonstration wrote another chapter in America's emergence as a great power, and in the development of international-mindedness in her people.

SELECT READINGS

Broad outlines appear in F. R. DULLES, *America's Rise to World Power* (1955).* More detailed is H. K. BEALE, *Theodore Roosevelt and the Rise of America to World Power* (1956).* Standard lives of Theodore Roosevelt are H. F. PRINGLE's barbed, Pulitzer-prize *Theodore Roosevelt* (1931)* and W. H. HARBAUGH, *Power and Responsibility* (1961). On the Open Door see TYLER DENNETT's Pulitzer-prize *John Hay* (1933) and A. W. GRISWOLD, *The Far Eastern Policy of the United States* (1938).* On the Japanese problem consult RAYMOND ESTHUS, *Theodore Roosevelt and Japan* (1966), C. E. NEU, *An Uncertain Friendship: Theodore Roosevelt and Japan, 1906–1909* (1967), ROGER DANIELS, *The Politics of Prejudice* (1962), and W. R. BRAISTED, *The United States Navy in the Pacific, 1897–1909* (1958). Also *Harvard Guide,* Pt. VI.

* Available in paperback.

33

Theodore Roosevelt and the Square Deal

When I say I believe in a square deal I do not mean . . . to give every man the best hand. If the cards do not come to any man, or if they do come, and he has not got the power to play them, that is his affair. All I mean is that there shall be no crookedness in the dealing.

President Theodore Roosevelt, 1905

T.R.'s Square Deal for Labor

Theodore Roosevelt, though something of an imperialistic busybody abroad, was a liberal at home. His sportsman's instincts prompted him to demand a "square deal" for capital, labor, and society at large. He was especially concerned about the public, caught in the middle.

The "square deal" for labor received its acid test in 1902, when a crippling strike broke out in the anthracite coal mines of Pennsylvania. Some 140,000 besooted workers, many of them illiterate immigrants, had long been frightfully exploited and accident-riddled. They demanded, among other improvements, a 20% increase in pay and a reduction of the working day from ten to nine hours.

Unsympathetic mine owners, confident that a chilled public would react against the miners, refused to arbitrate or even negotiate. One of their spokesmen, the multimillionaire George F. Baer, reflected the high-and-mighty attitude of certain ungenerous employers. Workers, he wrote, would be cared for "not by the labor agitators, but by the Christian men to whom God in His infinite wisdom has given the control of the property interests of this country. . . ." Closed minds meant closed mines.

As coal supplies dwindled, factories and schools were forced to shut down, and even hospitals felt the icy grip of winter. Desperately seeking a solution, Roosevelt summoned representatives of the striking miners and the mine owners to the White House. He was vastly annoyed by the "extraordinary stupidity and bad temper" of the "wooden-headed gentry" who operated the mines. As he later confessed, if it had not been for the dignity of his high office, he would have taken one of them "by the seat of the breeches" and "chucked him out of the window."

Roosevelt finally resorted to his trusty Big Stick when he threatened to seize the mines and operate them with federal troops. Even though coal cannot be mined with bayonets, the owners grudgingly consented to arbitration. A compromise decision ultimately gave the miners a 10% pay boost and a working day of nine hours. But their union was not officially recognized as a bargaining agent.

Keenly aware of the mounting antagonisms between capital and labor, Roosevelt urged Congress to create a new Department of Commerce and Labor. This goal was achieved in 1903. (Ten years later the agency was split into two.) An important arm of the newly born Department of Commerce and Labor was the Bureau of Corporations, which was authorized to probe businesses engaged in interstate commerce. The Bureau was highly useful in helping to break the stranglehold of monopoly, and in clearing the road for the era of "trust busting."

New Railroad Restrictions

Americans love bigness but hate monopoly, and Roosevelt shared their prejudices. The bite of the much-ballyhooed Sherman Anti-Trust Act of 1890 had proved almost completely toothless, and "trustification" was spreading at an alarming rate. The President, who habitually hurled harsh words at the "predatory rich," was distressed by the sinister power and wealth of the trusts. To him free enterprise did not mean freedom for the wealthy to exploit the poor.

"Trusts" rapidly came to be a fighting word. Roosevelt believed that these gigantic organizations, with their efficient tools of production, were here to stay. In his eyes, bigness did not necessarily spell badness. He concluded that there were "good" trusts, with public consciences, and "bad" trusts, with unbridled greed and lust for power. Yet the less discriminating public began to cry with increasing vigor, "Smash the trusts." Thrown on the defensive, the monop-

In a public address in 1902 on trusts Roosevelt said, "Those men who advocate wild and foolish remedies which would be worse than the disease are doing all in their power to perpetuate the evils against which they nominally war. . . . As sensible men, we must decide that it is a great deal better that some people should prosper too much than that no one should prosper enough. So that the man who advocates destroying the trusts by measures which would paralyze the industries of the country is at least a quack, and at worst an enemy to the Republic."

The Sherman Anti-Trust Law Returns from the Dead. Bartholomew in the Minneapolis *Journal*

olists countered by insisting that success in business was not a crime, and that prosecution under anti-trust laws was often persecution. But there was clearly a crying need for judicious regulation—for policing rather than punishing.

Similarly the many-webbed railroads, grown arrogant like the trusts, were sorely in need of restraint. The Interstate Commerce Act of 1887, tossed as a feeble sop to the public, had proved almost completely illusory. Railroad barons could endlessly appeal all decisions on rates to the federal courts—a process that might take ten years.

Under the spurs of the ex-cowboy, Congress passed effective railroad legislation, beginning with the Elkins Act of 1903. This curb was aimed primarily at the rebate evil, which had now become so rampant that some operators actually welcomed regulation. Heavy fines could henceforth be imposed, not only on the railroads that gave rebates but also on the shippers who accepted them. Within a few years a number of railroads and manufacturers were convicted under the new law and suffered painful penalties. A spectacular case hit the headlines in 1907, when Judge Kenesaw Mountain Landis found the Standard Oil Company guilty on 1462 counts of accepting rebates. He thereupon fined the offending corporation an unprecedented $29,240,000. But a higher court set aside his judgment, which seemed more like vengeance than justice.

Much more effective than the Elkins Act in restraining the railroads was the Hepburn Act of 1906. Free passes, with their hint of bribery, were severely restricted. The once-infantile Interstate Commerce Commission was expanded, and its reach was extended to include express companies, sleeping-car companies, and pipelines. For the first time the Commission was given real molars when it was authorized, on complaint of shippers, to nullify existing rates and establish maximum rates.

Though backed by an exasperated public, the Hepburn Act lost some of its proposed teeth in the Congressional machinery. The House passed it by the overwhelming margin of 346 to 7, but in the more conservative Senate the railroad lobby rallied for a last-ditch stand. The lobbyists finally secured a compromise proviso to the effect that rate decisions might be appealed to the federal courts. But the burden of initiating action rested squarely on the railroads and other carriers.

T.R.: Trust Buster with a Padded Stick

Roosevelt, as a trust buster, first burst into the headlines in 1902 with an attack on certain railroads. In a spectacular move he authorized his Attorney General to file suit under the Sherman Anti-Trust Act against the Northern Securities Company. This gigantic corporation was a holding company, of which J. P. Morgan was the chief financier, and "Empire Builder" James J. Hill the leading organizational genius. These Napoleonic planners sought to achieve a virtual monopoly of the railroads of the Northwest, and potentially of an even vaster area.

The railway promoters appealed to the highest tribunal. Early in 1904, by a five-to-four decision, the Supreme Court held that the Northern Securities Company violated the Sherman Anti-Trust Act and must be dissolved. This decision jolted the financial world and angered Big Business, but greatly enhanced T.R.'s reputation as a trust smasher.

Roosevelt's Big Stick crashed down on other giant monopolies, as he initiated over forty legal proceedings against them. The Supreme Court in 1905 declared the Beef Trust illegal, and the heavy hand of justice fell upon monopolists handling sugar, fertilizer, harvesters, and other key commodities.

But the dissolution of a trust did not necessarily mean its destruction. Many of the so-called victories for the public were sensational rather than substantial. The biggest trusts were too brawny and too deeply entrenched; and after setbacks in the courts they would cleverly assume, quicksilver-like, other and sometimes more monopolistic forms. Shortly after the sensational dissolution of the Standard Oil Company in 1911, the stock of the much-condemned corporation doubled in value and the price of gasoline and kerosene rose.

Roosevelt did not swing his Big Stick with maximum force, despite his exaggerated prestige as a trust crusher. Unwilling to throw overboard completely the time-honored traditions of free enterprise,

In 1912, some three years after leaving the White House, Roosevelt wrote, "When I came into office that law [Sherman Anti-Trust Act] was dead; I took it up and for the first time had it enforced. We gained this much by the enforcement: we gained the establishment of the principle that the government was supreme over the great corporations; but that is almost the end of the good that came through our lawsuits."

he felt that the solution of the trust problem lay in regulation rather than in strangulation. "Mr. Dooley" thus summarized T.R.'s views: "On wan hand I wud stamp thim undher fut; on th' other hand not so fast."

In truth more trusts were formed under Roosevelt than under the combined administrations of his predecessor (McKinley) and his successor (Taft). To be sure, the Rough Rider could point with pride to the Bureau of Corporations and to new regulatory railway legislation. But he is best known for having reactivated the Sherman Anti-Trust Act rather than for having secured sweeping anti-trust laws. The huge industrial combines were actually mightier when Roosevelt left the White House than they had been when he entered it. His allegedly wishy-washy successor, William Howard Taft, "busted" more trusts than he did. But some of these prosecutions had been launched under Roosevelt, and certainly the task of succeeding Presidents would have been more difficult if he had not flourished his Big Stick at bloated monopoly.

Earth Control

In his annual message to Congress (1907), Roosevelt declared prophetically, "We are prone to speak of the resources of this country as inexhaustible; this is not so. The mineral wealth of the country, the coal, iron, oil, gas, and the like, does not reproduce itself, and therefore is certain to be exhausted ultimately; and wastefulness in dealing with it to-day means that our descendants will feel the exhaustion a generation or two before they otherwise would."

Pushful Americans, assuming that their natural resources were inexhaustible, had ravaged their vast domain with unparalleled speed and greed. The West was eager to accelerate the process, for it believed that rapid expansion "built up the country" and increased prosperity by pushing up land values. As for being worried about the future, common frontier queries were, "Why preserve the wilderness when we've been fighting it for years?" and "What has posterity ever done for us?" But long before the end of the 19th Century, far-visioned men could see that such a squandering of the nation's birthright would have to be halted or America would sink into the poverty of backward European areas.

A feeble step in the right direction had come under President Hayes in 1877, when Congress passed the Desert Land Act. The federal government agreed to sell up to 640 acres at $1.25 an acre, provided that the purchaser would reclaim the thirsty soil in three years. This pioneering law led to some irrigation and much fraud. Witnesses would swear that they had seen the land being irrigated—which often meant that a bucket of water had been poured on it.

An aroused Congress, faced with the end of the frontier, had finally made a major move toward conservation. In the law of 1891 it authorized the President to set aside public forest lands for national reserves. Under Presidents Harrison, Cleveland, and McKinley some 46,000,000 acres of magnificent trees were rescued from the lumberman's saw and preserved for a grateful posterity.

Congress had further grappled with the reclamation problem in 1894, when it approved the Carey Act. Arid federal lands in the West would be ceded to individual states, provided that the state in each instance would cause the land to be irrigated and settled upon. This forward-looking measure, through the happy marriage of desert and water, led to the cultivation of about a million barren acres.

A new day in the history of conservation dawned with the advent of Roosevelt. He looked upon the crusade, though still in the creeping stage, as one phase of the fight against predatory corporations. Huntsman, naturalist, rancher, lover of the great out-of-doors, he was appalled by the pillaging of timber and mineral resources. By 1900 only about a quarter of the virgin forests remained erect, three-fourths of them in private hands. Roosevelt proceeded to set aside in federal reserves some 125,000,000 acres, or almost three times the acreage saved in the same way by his three predecessors. He similarly earmarked millions of acres of coal deposits, as well as water resources useful for irrigation and power. To set a good example, in 1902 he banned Christmas trees from the White House.

But the dynamic President's concept of conservation went far beyond these immediate goals. In his mind the whole question was tied up with the destruction of wildlife, with forest fires, and with dust storms in treeless areas. He was deeply concerned about floods caused by the indiscriminate cutting of timber, and about the erosion of gutted lands that seemingly cried aloud for fertilizers. He was eager to do something about the silting up of rivers by turbulent floods, and about improving the navigation of streams, lakes, and canals through a long-range program of flood control. He repeatedly made vigorous recommendations to Congress designed to improve these conditions, although remedial action in some areas was like locking the barn door after the horse was stolen.

THE EXTENT OF EROSION, 1934

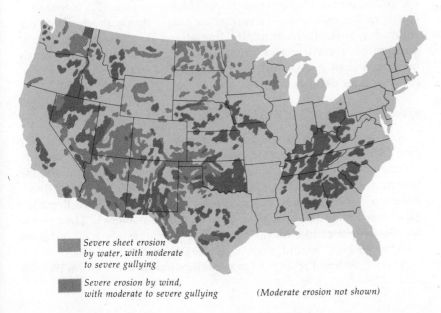

Severe sheet erosion by water, with moderate to severe gullying

Severe erosion by wind, with moderate to severe gullying

(Moderate erosion not shown)

Roosevelt as "*A Practical Forester.*" From St. Paul *Pioneer Press*.

Campaigning in Kansas in 1910, ex-President Roosevelt said, "Of all the questions which can come before this nation, short of its existence in a great war, there is none which compares in importance with the great central task of leaving this land even a better land for our descendants than it is for us, and training them into a better race to inhabit the land and pass it on. Conservation is a great moral issue, for it involves the patriotic duty of insuring the safety and continuance of the nation."

Roosevelt Champions Conservation

Roosevelt, though by far the noisiest, was not the first conservationist. Other zealots before him had broken important ground, notably Gifford Pinchot, head of the federal Division of Forestry and a red-blooded member of T.R.'s "Tennis Cabinet." But Roosevelt seized the banner of leadership, and charged into the fray with all the weight of his prestige, his energy, his firsthand knowledge, and his slashing invective.

The thirst of the desert still unslaked, Congress responded to the whip of the Rough Rider by passing the Newlands Act of 1902. Washington was authorized to collect money from the sale of public lands in the sun-baked Western states, and then use these funds for the development of irrigation projects. Settlers repaid the cost of reclamation from their now-productive soil, and the money was put into a revolving fund to finance more such enterprises. The giant Roosevelt Dam, constructed in Arizona on the Salt River, was appropriately dedicated by ex-President Roosevelt in 1911.

Roosevelt's most dramatic single move toward conservation came in 1908, when he summoned the Conference of Governors to Washington. The group consisted of prominent governors, justices of the Supreme Court, selected members of Congress, and celebrities like Bryan, Cleveland, and Carnegie. One encouraging result was to inspire the governors to carry on the good work at home. Eighteen months later, forty-one states had set up active conservation commissions.

Conservation, including reclamation, was probably Roosevelt's most enduring tangible achievement. The Isthmian canal would have been dug sooner or later, but lands that are eroded and resources that are gutted do not readily come back. The super-active President took conservation out of the conversation stage, threw the force of his colorful personality behind it, dramatized it, and aroused public opinion to a constructive crusade. Conservation under Roosevelt became almost a religion; its more truly scientific stages were to come in later decades.

Elected President "In His Own Right"

Roosevelt looked forward to the election of 1904 with keen concern. Resenting the sneering title "His Accidency," he was eager to secure popular endorsement by election under his own colors. He was undeniably the idol of the masses—the children's "Teddy Bear" honored his bear-shooting exploits—but the conservative Republican bosses regarded him as an unmanageable maverick. They pined for a standpatter like Mark Hanna, his only possible rival, who, as "Roosevelt luck" would have it, died early in 1904.

The "Cowboy President" was nominated at Chicago in 1904 by

acclamation. As an antidote to his presumed radicalism, the delegates chose for Vice-President a frigid standpatter from Indiana, Charles W. Fairbanks—dubbed "Icebanks." The platform likewise offset Roosevelt's wild tendencies by upholding tariff protection and the gold standard, while letting the trusts off with a verbal slap on the wrist.

Radical Bryan Democrats, twice led down to defeat by the "Peerless Leader," were unhorsed at the St. Louis convention. The hard-bitten conservative wing, now back in the saddle, loudly demanded a "safe and sane" candidate. Eastern "safe-and-saners" managed to nominate the colorless Judge Alton B. Parker, an impeccably respectable New York lawyer of high character. As a vote getter of considerable power in his home state, "Parker the Silent" was actually more liberal than his reactionary followers represented him to be.

Anti-T.R. Election Cartoon. New York *World*, 1904

The Democratic platform reflected the unhappiness of the party over Roosevelt's usurpations of legislative and judicial functions. It flayed his administration as "spasmodic, erratic, sensational, spectacular, and arbitrary." No reference was made to the silver issue, though Parker angered the Bryanites by sending a telegram to the convention in which he came out bluntly for the gold standard.

The ensuing canvass proved tame. Judge Parker, hitting at Rough Riderism, demanded a "government of law, not of men." He finally injected some fireworks when he accused the Republicans of collecting campaign funds from corporations which expected favors in return. Roosevelt promptly cried "liar," but a subsequent Congressional investigation proved that the charge had considerable validity. The Standard Oil Company contributed a lubricant of $125,000.

Full dinner pails added luster to the Republican cause, but the overshadowing issue was T.R.'s Big Stick personality—"Theodore Roosevelt, one and indivisible." His popularity was not dimmed by loose charges that while in Cuba he had shot a Spaniard in the back; and his worshipful following sang lustily, "Three Cheers for the Rough Rider" and "We Want Teddy for Four Years More."

The colorful cowboy romped home in a canter, and proved to be the first "accidental" President to succeed himself. The electoral count was 336 to 140; the popular count, 7,623,486 to 5,077,911. Roosevelt's avalanche even swept down into the border state of Missouri. The painfully pedestrian Parker proved to be the worst-beaten major candidate since Horace Greeley was snowed under in 1872. Many pro-silver Bryanites, protesting Parker's stand for gold, boycotted the polls.

This victory was a glorious personal triumph for the strenuous President and "my policies." The voters clearly preferred Roosevelt, the impetuous candidate of the conservative party, to Parker, the conservative candidate of the impetuous party. In his hour of elation the "dee-lighted" winner announced that he regarded his partial first term of three and one-half years as a full term, and that under no circumstances would he be a candidate for a third term. This was a tactical blunder, for the power of the king wanes when the people know that he will be dead in four years.

The "Roosevelt Panic" of 1907

Prosperity suffered a sharp setback in 1907, when a short but devastating panic descended. It was partly a reaction to world-wide economic trends, partly the result of the billions of dollars in corporation stock that had glutted the market. Centering heavily in Wall Street, the financial flurry was known as "the Rich Man's Panic," and was featured by frightened "runs" on banks. Suicides and criminal indictments were common.

The financial world hastened to blame Roosevelt for the panic. It cried that this "quack," "demagogue," and "crazy man" had unsettled industry by his boat-rocking tactics. Conservatives damned him as "Theodore the Meddler," and branded the current distress "the Roosevelt Panic." The hot-tempered President lashed back at his critics when he accused "certain malefactors of great wealth" of having deliberately engineered the monetary crisis to force the government to relax its assaults on trusts.

Fortunately, the Panic of 1907 paved the way for long-overdue fiscal reforms. Precipitating a currency shortage, the flurry laid bare the need for a more elastic medium of exchange. In a crisis of this sort, the hard-pressed banks were unable to increase the volume of their money, and those with ample reserves were reluctant to lend to their less fortunate sisters. Congress in 1908 responded to existing pressures by passing the Aldrich-Vreeland Act, which authorized National Banks to issue emergency currency backed by various kinds of collateral. The path was thus smoothed for the epochal Federal Reserve Act of 1913.

"You Dirty Boy" (T.R. Cleans High Finance). *Puck,* 1907

Roots of Reformism

Hardly had the 20th Century dawned when the nation was convulsed by a reform movement, the like of which had not been seen since the 1840's. Roosevelt's name is connected with this feature of his presidential years, and hasty observers have assumed that he was one of the mainsprings behind it. The truth is that he was not so much a reformer as the beneficiary of a riptide of reform.

The ground swell of the new reformist wave went far back—to the Greenback Labor Party of the 1870's, the Farmers' Alliance of the 1880's, and the Populists of the 1890's. As the turn of the century approached, critics of political, economic, and social evils became steadily more numerous and more noisy. The gist of their complaints was that the problems of government had become too complex for the machinery of government. An outworn philosophy of hands-off individualism seemed increasingly out of place in the new machine age. America, so angry reformers charged, now had a government of, by, and for the crooked corporations. The nation was admittedly better off than many foreign lands, but not nearly so well off as its natural resources should have made it. The Promise of American Life had plainly not been fulfilled.

Well before 1900 individual crusaders had made noteworthy contributions to the literature of reform. They included Henry George, with his single-tax treatise *Progress and Poverty* (1879), and Edward Bellamy, with his *Looking Backward* (1888), the most famous of the Utopian novels.* The keen-eyed and keen-nosed Danish immigrant Jacob A. Riis, a reporter for the New York *Sun,* published in 1890 *How the Other Half Lives.* His account was a damning indictment of the dirt, disease, vice, and misery of the rat-gnawed human rookeries known as New York slums. Riis deeply influenced Theodore Roosevelt, who later headed the New York Police Commission.

"Bloated trusts" and "dirty-handed millionaires" had already come under fire from Bryan, Altgeld, and the Populist leaders. Gifted knights of the pen also entered the fray. In 1894 Henry Demarest Lloyd charged headlong into the Standard Oil Company with his book entitled *Wealth versus Commonwealth.* Embittered and lonely Dr. Thorstein Veblen published in 1899 *The Theory of the Leisure Class,* a violent assault on such evils as "predatory wealth," the idle rich, and absentee landlordism. A brilliant young novelist-reformer, Frank Norris, portrayed the deadly grip of the California railroads on the wheat farmers in *The Octopus* (1901); and in its sequel, *The Pit* (1903), he mercilessly exposed Chicago wheat speculators.

Socialists, now swelling in numbers, must take high rank among the caustic critics of existing injustices. Many of them were European immigrants who decried "bloody capitalism," and they began to register appreciable strength at the ballot boxes as the century turned. They received much of their inspiration from abroad, where countries like Germany were launching daring experiments in state socialism. In faraway Australia and New Zealand, too, socialist reforms were being undertaken which attracted much notice in America.

The Socialists found a gifted ally in young Jack (John Griffith) London, the illegitimate-born, ill-educated "oyster pirate" of San Francisco Bay, who became a prolific writer of novels. Steeped in Darwin and in Marx and other German thinkers, London was deeply concerned with the class struggle and with the clash between the civilized brain and primitive force. His stirring tales, such as *The Call of the Wild* (1903) and *The Sea Wolf* (1904), owed their popularity

Thorstein Veblen, in *The Theory of the Leisure Class* (1899), wrote, "Conspicuous consumption of valuable goods is a means of reputability to the gentlemen of leisure." This tendency has more recently been exemplified in the purchase by the newly rich of extravagant motor cars and yachts.

---

* George and Bellamy are discussed earlier, on p. 592.

chiefly to their exciting plots, but on a higher level they were closely related to the current reformist agitation.

Raking Muck with the Muckrakers

By 1902–1903 a group of "Muckrakers"—flaming young reformers with prickly pens—had embarked on a crusade to lay bare the muck of iniquity in American society. They sought not to overthrow capitalism but to cleanse it. They had deep faith in the democratic processes, and earnestly believed that the evils afflicting the country flowed not from democracy but from the absence of enough democracy.

The zealous Muckrakers, who became a front-page sensation, were given their nickname in 1906 by President Roosevelt. Annoyed by their excess of zeal, he compared them to the man in Bunyan's *Pilgrim's Progress* who was so intent on raking manure that he could not see the celestial crown being held above him. Muckrakers were aided by the rise of ten- or fifteen-cent popular magazines, like *McClure's, Cosmopolitan, Collier's,* and *Everybody's,* all of which catered to the public taste for sensational articles. These revelations not only boomed circulation but some of the most scandalous were published in book form.

In 1902 the muckraking movement began in dead earnest. A brilliant New York reporter, Lincoln Steffens, launched a series of articles in *McClure's* entitled "The Shame of the Cities." He fearlessly unmasked the corrupt alliance between Big Business and municipal government. Steffens was followed in the same magazine by Ida M. Tarbell, a quiet spinster who published a devastating but factual exposé of the Standard Oil Company. (Her father had been ruined by the oil interests.) Fearing legal reprisals, the muckraking magazines went to great pains and expense to check their material—paying as much as $3000 to verify a single Tarbell article. R. S. Baker, who attacked assorted abuses, was successfully sued for $15,000 and costs, but his case was a noteworthy exception.

Muckrakers audaciously tilted their pen-lances at varied targets. They assailed the malpractices of life insurance companies and tariff lobbies. They roasted the Beef Trust, the "Money Trust," the railroad barons, and the corrupt amassing of American fortunes. Thomas W. Lawson, an erratic speculator who had himself made $50,000,000 on the stock market, laid bare the practices of his accomplices in "Frenzied Finance." This series of articles, appearing in 1905–1906, rocketed the circulation of *Everybody's.* Lawson, by fouling his own nest, made many enemies among his rich associates, and he died a poor man.

David G. Phillips shocked an already startled nation by his series in *Cosmopolitan* entitled "The Treason of the Senate" (1906). He

In his Muckraker speech (1906), Roosevelt said, "Now, it is very necessary that we should not flinch from seeing what is vile and debasing. There is filth [manure] on the floor and it must be scraped up with the muck-rake; and there are times and places where this service is the most needed of all the services that can be performed. But the man who never does anything else, who never thinks or speaks or writes, save of his feats with the muck-rake, speedily becomes, not a help to society, not an incitement to good, but one of the most potent forces for evil."

boldly charged that seventy-five of the ninety Senators did not represent the people at all but the railroads and trusts. This withering indictment, buttressed by facts, impressed President Roosevelt. Phillips continued his slashing attacks through novels, and was fatally shot in 1911 by a deranged young man whose family he had allegedly maligned.

Some of the most effective fire of the Muckrakers was directed at social evils. The ugly list included the immoral "white slave" traffic in women, the rickety slums, the appalling number of industrial accidents, and the exploitation of Negroes. The abuses of child labor were brought luridly to light by John Spargo's *The Bitter Cry of the Children* (1906).

Vendors of potent patent medicines (often heavily spiked with alcohol) likewise came in for savage criticism. These conscienceless vultures sold incredible quantities of adulterated or habit-forming drugs, while "doping" the press with lavish advertising. Muckraking attacks in *Collier's* were ably reinforced by Dr. H. W. Wiley, chief chemist of the Department of Agriculture, who with his famous "Poison Squad" performed experiments on himself.

The Patent Medicine Fraud. Kemble in *Collier's*, 1905; copyright 1905 by The Crowell-Collier Publishing Company

Pure-food advocates received unexpected support from Upton Sinclair's socialistic novel *The Jungle*, which was aimed at the nation's heart but hit its stomach. Published in 1906, this best-selling assault on the meat industry was ultimately translated into seventeen languages. It described in nauseating detail the filth, disease, and putrefaction in Chicago's damp, ill-ventilated stockyards. Many readers, including Roosevelt, were so sickened that for a time they found meat unpalatable. The President was moved by the loathsome mess in Chicago to appoint a special investigating commission, whose cold-blooded report almost outdid Upton Sinclair's novel. It related how piles of poisoned rats, rope ends, splinters, and other debris were scooped up and canned as potted ham. A cynical jingle ran:

Mary had a little lamb,
And when she saw it sicken,
She shipped it off to Packingtown,
And now it's labeled chicken.

The Golden Age of Reformers

Roosevelt at first was not hostile to the so-called literature of exposure. But when in 1906 he saw that a debased public taste was beginning to demand dirt for dirt's sake, he denounced the excesses of the muckrakers. Yet these flaming souls, whatever their motives, added to the popularity of T.R.'s trust-busting activities, and helped build up popular pressure behind Congress.

A basketful of badly needed legislation was the result of all this agitation. The Meat Inspection Act, passed by Congress in 1906, decreed that the preparation of meat shipped over state lines would be subject to federal inspection from hoof to can. The Pure Food and Drug Act of 1906 was designed to prevent the adulteration and mislabeling of foods and drugs. Like many "firsts," this long-overdue law was riddled with loopholes that had to be plugged later. Both these pieces of legislation encountered bitter resistance, particularly from those special interests or quacks who found it profitable to cheat or poison the public. The White Slave Act (Mann Act), aimed at preventing the interstate transportation of women for immoral purposes, received Congressional approval in 1910.

These reformers actually achieved their most sweeping gains at the state and local levels, for Congress was too much under the influence of lobbyists paid by "the interests." Public-spirited city dwellers were making promising headway in halting the corrupt sale of franchises for street cars and other public utilities. The "invisible government" of trusts and bosses received a damaging blow when the city-manager type of municipal self-rule was devised. Until then, government by experts, sneered at as contrary to the Jacksonian ideal, had gained little ground.

Embattled urban reformers launched house-cleaning assaults on additional evils. These included the stinking tenements, the unhealthful sweatshops, juvenile delinquency, and wide-open prostitution (vice-at-a-price), which flourished in red-light districts unchallenged by the bribed police. Substantial gains were chalked up among the cities in public health, housing, and sanitation. Civil service reform was likewise making encouraging strides, and the confusing "long ballot," overloaded with lists of candidates, was being shortened. A determined campaign was also under way in many localities to achieve equality before the law for the rich and the poor, the powerful and the powerless, the white and the black.

"Mr. LaFollette's Strongest Card" (reform government in Wisconsin). Reprinted, Courtesy of the Chicago *Tribune*

Pioneers of the Progressive Movement

Muckrakers were the godfathers of the pent-up pressure for reform called Progressivism, which gathered tremendous momentum in the early 1900's, and spanned the years 1898 to 1914. This crusade was part of a world-wide movement, for there were similar crosscurrents in many foreign countries at the same time. In America, progressives were to be found in both major parties, and at all levels of government. Conspicuous among them were the long-suffering white-collar workers who, at long last, were joining the farmers in demands for relief from abuses.

Progressivism first bubbled up in individual states like Wisconsin, which became a yeasty laboratory of reform. The governor of the state, pompadoured Robert M. ("Fighting Bob") La Follette, was an undersized but overengined crusader who emerged as the most militant of the Progressive Republican leaders. After a desperate fight with entrenched monopoly, he reached the governor's chair in 1901. Routing the lumber and railroad "interests," he wrested considerable control from the crooked corporations and returned it to the people. He also perfected a scheme for regulating public utilities, while laboring in close association with experts on the faculty of the state university at Madison.

Other states marched steadily toward the Progressive camp, as they undertook to regulate railroads and trusts, chiefly through public utilities commissions. Oregon was not far behind Wisconsin, and California made giant-boot strides under the stocky Hiram W. Johnson. Elected Republican governor in 1910, this dynamic prosecutor of grafters helped break the dominant grip of the Southern Pacific Railroad on California politics and then, like La Follette, set up a political machine of his own. Heavily whiskered Charles Evans Hughes, the able and fearless reformist Republican governor of New York, had earlier gained national fame as an investigator of malpractices by gas and insurance companies and by the coal trust.

Political Progressivism

Ingenious schemes to insure popular control of the government were being seized upon. They were most numerous in the states of the more liberal West, which had inherited the Populist tradition. Newfangled devices were adopted to regain the power that had slipped from the hands of the people into those of the "interests." The "initiative" permitted the voters to initiate needful legislation themselves, especially that which the trust-dominated state legislatures had refused to enact. The "referendum" placed laws on the ballot for approval or veto by the people—laws that in many instances had been lobbied through by glib spokesmen for Big Business. The "recall" enabled the voters in special elections to remove faithless elected officials, particularly those who had become tainted by bosses or lobbyists.

Rooting out graft also became a prime goal of earnest progressives. A number of the state legislatures passed corrupt-practices acts, which limited the amount of money that a candidate might spend for his election. Such legislation also restricted huge gifts from corporations, for which the donors would expect favors. The secret Australian ballot was likewise being introduced more widely in the states to counteract boss rule. Bribery was less feasible when the briber could not tell if he was getting his money's worth from the bribed.

Ex-President Roosevelt wrote of reform in 1913, "It is vitally necessary to move forward and to shake off the dead hand, often a fossilized dead hand, of the reactionaries; and yet we have to face the fact that there is apt to be a lunatic fringe among the votaries of any forward movement."

A swelling demand for popular control of government extended to the "quadrennial madhouses" known as national nominating conventions. Voters realized that they had no real hand in selecting the presidential candidate, who all too often was chosen in smoke-filled and boss-ruled hotel rooms. The presidential preferential primary, adopted by some of the states, was designed to give the mass of the people an effective voice in making nominations. But in actual practice the party wire-pullers managed to retain a large measure of dominance.

Direct election of United States Senators became a favorite goal of progressives, especially after the Muckrakers had exposed the scandalous tie-in between greedy corporations and Congress. By 1900 the Senate contained so many rich men that it was often referred to as "the Millionaires' Club." Too many of the prosperous-appearing solons, elected as they were by trust-dominated legislatures, heeded the voice of their "masters" rather than that of the masses.

A constitutional amendment to bring about the popular election of Senators had rough sledding in Congress, for the plutocratic members of the Senate were happy with existing methods. But a number of states established primary elections in which the voters expressed their preferences for the Senate. The local legislatures, when choosing Senators, found it politically wise to heed the voice of the people. Partly as a result of such pressures, the 17th Amendment to the Constitution, approved in 1913, established the direct election of Senators. (See Appendix.) But the expected improvement in caliber proved somewhat disappointing.

Woman suffrage, the goal of feminists for many decades, likewise received powerful new support from the progressives early in the 1900's. Political reformers believed that the petticoat vote would ele-

WOMAN SUFFRAGE BEFORE THE 19th
AMENDMENT (1920)

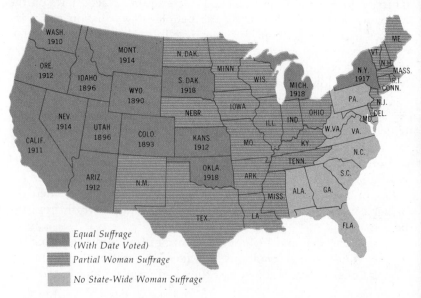

Equal Suffrage
(With Date Voted)

Partial Woman Suffrage

No State-Wide Woman Suffrage

vate the political tone; foes of the saloon felt that they could count on the support of enfranchised females. The "suffragists," crying "Votes for Women" and "Equal Suffrage for Men and Women," protested bitterly against "Taxation without Representation." Many of the states, especially the more liberal ones in the West, gradually extended the vote to women. But by 1910 nationwide female suffrage was still a decade away; and a suffragist could still be sneeringly defined as "One who has ceased to be a lady and has not yet become a gentleman."

Landmarks in Social Progress

Fired-up progressives, working through their state legislatures, tackled head-on a series of social problems. Noteworthy were safety and sanitation codes which, among other safeguards, closed dangerous trades to minors. The enacting of workingmen's compensation laws, or the bolstering of existing laws, provided many toilers with reasonably adequate protection. Heretofore they had often been forced into costly and futile lawsuits to prove negligence on the part of the employer. In addition, some forward-looking states adopted eight-hour laws; and Roosevelt himself inaugurated the eight-hour day on government jobs.

Other social evils clamored for attention. The steaming and unsanitary sweatshops were a public scandal in the urban areas. Some of the states, lashed by public outcries, passed laws regulating the hours of labor by women in such hives, as well as the conditions under which they toiled. Prisons and "reform" schools likewise came under sharp scrutiny, as the public increasingly accepted the view that these institutions were primarily for reformation rather than punishment.

Crusaders for these humane measures did not always have smooth sailing. One dismaying setback came in 1905, when the Supreme Court invalidated a New York law establishing a ten-hour day for bakers. Yet the reformist Progressive wave finally washed up into the judiciary, and in 1917 the Court upheld a ten-hour Oregon law for factory workers. Gradually the concept of the employer's responsibility to society was replacing the old dog-eat-dog philosophy of unregulated free enterprise.

Corner saloons, with their shutter doors, attracted the ire and fire of progressives. Alcohol was intimately connected with prostitution in "red-light districts," with the drunken voter, with crooked city officials dominated by "booze" interests, and with the blowsy "boss," who counted poker chips by night and miscounted ballots by day (including the "cemetery vote"). By 1900 cities like New York and San Francisco had one saloon for about every two hundred people.

In 1908 President Roosevelt wrote prophetically, "Personally I believe in woman's suffrage, but I am not an enthusiastic advocate of it, because I do not regard it as a very important matter. I am unable to see that there has been any special improvement in the position of women in those states in the West that have adopted woman's suffrage, as compared with those states adjoining them that have not adopted it. I do not think that giving the women suffrage will produce any marked improvement in the condition of women. I do not believe that it will produce any of the evils feared, and I am very certain that when women as a whole take any special interest in the matter they will have suffrage if they desire it."

"The Sentinel" (Taking the Names of Saloon Patrons). *Harper's Weekly*, 1874

Anti-liquor campaigners received powerful support from several militant organizations, notably the Woman's Christian Temperance Union (W.C.T.U.). Saintly Frances E. Willard, one of its founders, would fall on her knees in prayer on saloon floors. She found a vigorous ally in the Anti-Saloon League, which was aggressive, well organized, and well financed. The Prohibition Party, which had put a presidential ticket in the field as early as 1872, was similarly snowballing strength.

Caught up in the crusade, some states and numerous counties passed "dry" laws which controlled, restricted, or abolished alcohol. The big cities were generally "wet," for they had a large immigrant vote accustomed in the Old Country to the free flow of wine and beer. When World War erupted in 1914, nearly one-half of the population lived in "dry" territory, and nearly three-fourths of the total area had outlawed the saloon. (See map, p. 786.) Demon Rum was groggy, and he was to be floored—temporarily—by the 18th Amendment in 1919.

The Taft-Bryan Presidential Sweepstakes of 1908

Roosevelt was still so immensely popular in 1908 that he could easily have won a second presidential nomination, and almost certainly the election. Although at loggerheads with Congress and hated by Big Business, he almost hypnotized the masses. The Benéts have captured his appeal:

T.R. is spanking a Senator,
T.R. is chasing a bear,
T.R. is busting an Awful Trust
And dragging it from its lair.

They're calling T.R. a lot of things
—The men in the private car—
But the day-coach likes exciting folks
*And the day-coach likes T.R.**

Roosevelt did not really want to leave the White House; he had enjoyed a "bully time" in the presidential goldfish bowl. But he felt bound by his impulsive post-election promise after his victory in 1904.

The departing President naturally sought a successor who would carry out "my policies"—that is, the forward-looking Roosevelt program. The man of his choice was his amiable, ample-girthed, and huge-framed (six feet tall) Secretary of War, William Howard Taft, a

* Rosemary and Stephen Vincent Benét, *A Book of Americans* (Rinehart and Company, copyright 1933), p. 111. Reprinted by permission.

moderate progressive. Taft had made an admirable record under T.R. as an administrator in subordinate capacities. As an heir apparent, he had often been called upon to "sit on the lid"—all 350 pounds of him—when Roosevelt was absent.

Big-stick methods were much in evidence at the Republican convention of 1908 in Chicago. Roosevelt, wielding his enormous influence backstage, had lined up enough delegates behind his handwritten platform and hand-picked candidate. He also employed the convention machinery—the "steam roller"—to push Taft's nomination through on the first ballot, thus heading off a possible stampede to himself. The Republican (Roosevelt) platform, pointing with pride in all directions and praising T.R.'s policies, declared against monopoly, while promising both tariff revision and currency reform.

Three weeks later in July, 1908, the Democrats met at mile-high Denver, in the heart of the silver country. The Bryanites, who had returned to the driver's seat, had no stomach for another drubbing under a stodgy candidate like Judge Parker. Twice-beaten Bryan, the hardy quadrennial, was nominated with uproarious enthusiasm on the first ballot. His platform condemned the flighty personal rule of Roosevelt, as well as the alleged stranglehold of the trusts on American life.

The campaign of 1908 was even duller in some ways than that of 1904, though both the portly Taft and the balding "Boy Orator" took to the stump. Taft, who read cut-and-dried speeches to large crowds, made a fence-straddling effort to present himself as a progressive in the West and a conservative in the East. Four "P's" helped the Republican ticket: prosperity, progressivism, prosecution of the trusts, and personalities—Taft and Roosevelt, largely Roosevelt. The progressive Bryan, attempting to capitalize on the President's popularity, endorsed many Rooseveltian policies. Alleging that they had been stolen from him, he not illogically represented himself as the logical man to carry them out.

A prosperous country was quite content to accept the stable leadership of Taft—the man so emphatically endorsed by Roosevelt, who in a sense was running again. "Shall the people rule?" cried the silver voice of Bryan. They decided to do so with solid Judge Taft, who polled 321 electoral votes to 162 for the "Peerless Leader." The victor's popular count was 7,678,908 to 6,409,104. Bryan garnered fewer votes than in 1896, despite the increase in population, though he fared much better than the colorless Parker four years earlier. The Socialists amassed a surprising tally of 420,793 for Eugene V. Debs, the "hero" of the Pullman strike of 1894.

Bryan, apostle of lost causes, was finished as a presidential possibility. Yet a number of ideas that he sponsored were seized upon and put into operation by the Republicans. He once quipped that he was the only man who could rule the nation by losing the Presidency.

T.R. Engineers Taft's Nomination at Chicago. Harding in the Brooklyn *Eagle*, 1908

The Rough Rider Thunders Out

Roosevelt, who preached the doctrine of the "strenuous life," practiced it until almost the end. In 1913 he sent a political message on a phonograph recording to the Boy's Progressive League, "Don't flinch, don't foul, and hit the line hard."

Roosevelt, ever in the limelight, left early in 1909 for a lion hunt in Africa. His numerous enemies clinked glasses to the toast "Health to the Lions." But the savage beasts failed to "do their duty." To an ex-President all the rest of life is an anticlimax, and the tragedy of Roosevelt is that he left his office too young, at the age of fifty, when still bursting with energy. Ex-Presidents are usually something of a problem, and here was one who did not take kindly to the role of private citizen.

The puzzle is: Was Roosevelt a radical conservative or a conservative radical? One answer would seem to be that he was a progressive "with the brakes on," and that his reputation as a reformer was inflated. "My spear knows no brother!" he cried. But actually he fought many a sham battle. Willing to compromise and settle for half a loaf, he would often fail to drive a reform through to its logical conclusion. The number of laws that he inspired was certainly not in proportion to the amount of noise that he emitted. But in his defense one must note that he was confronted by a conservative, unsympathetic, and often hostile Congress.

What was Roosevelt's great contribution? It was probably not in laws like the Hepburn railway act or in deeds like digging the Panama Canal or crusading for conservation, but in helping to give the people a renewed faith in themselves and their democracy in a troubled time. His enthusiasm and perpetual youthfulness, like an overgrown Boy Scout's, appealed to the young of all ages. As a kind of umpire, he served as a political lightning rod to protect the conservatives against popular indignation. He strenuously sought the middle road between unbridled individualism and paternalistic socialism.

Two other contributions carried over beyond Roosevelt's presidency. First, he helped to direct and make respectable the Progressive movement. His Square Deal, in a sense, was the grandfather of the New Deal later launched by his fifth cousin, Franklin D. Roosevelt. Second, to a greater degree than any of his predecessors, he opened the eyes of the American people to the fact that they lived in the same world with other nations, and that as a great power they had fallen heir to responsibilities from which there was no escaping.

Roosevelt "The Stationary Crusader." *Punch* (London).

SELECT READINGS

Consult lives of Roosevelt by Pringle and Harbaugh, for previous chapter. Incisive introductions are G. E. MOWRY, *The Era of Theodore Roosevelt, 1900–1912* (1958)*; H. U. FAULKNER, *The Quest for Social Justice, 1898–1914* (1931); and J. M. BLUM, *The Republican Roosevelt* (1954).* See also H. U. FAULKNER, *The Decline of Laissez Faire, 1899–1917,* (1951).* On conservation consult S. P. HAYS,

Conservation and the Gospel of Efficiency, 1890–1920 (1959)* and
ELMO RICHARDSON, *The Politics of Conservation* (1962). Recent lives
of Gifford Pinchot are by M. N. MC GEARY (1960) and M. L. FAUSOLD
(1961). On pure food and drugs, see O. E. ANDERSON, *The Health of
a Nation* (1958) and J. H. YOUNG, *Toadstool Millionaires* (1961). For
reformism in general consult E. F. GOLDMAN's racy *Rendezvous
with Destiny* (1952)* and JOHN CHAMBERLAIN's ironical *Farewell to
Reform* (1932).* The Progressive movement is treated in G. E.
MOWRY, *Theodore Roosevelt and the Progressive Movement* (1946)*;
R. S. MAXWELL, *La Follette and the Rise of the Progressives in Wisconsin* (1956); and R. H. WIEBE, *Businessmen and Reform* (1962).*
Classic contemporary accounts are J. A. RIIS, *The Making of an
American* (1901); LINCOLN STEFFENS, *Autobiography* (1931)* and his
The Shame of the Cities (1904)*; and *La Follette's Autobiography*
(1913).* Also *Harvard Guide,** Pt. VI.

34

Taft and the Progressive Revolt

I am in this [Progressive] fight for certain principles, and the first and most important . . . is . . . "Thou shalt not steal." Thou shalt not steal a nomination. Thou shalt neither steal in politics nor in business. Thou shalt not steal from the people the birthright of the people to rule themselves.

Theodore Roosevelt, in Chicago, 1912

Taft: A Round Peg in a Square Hole

William Howard Taft, with his ruddy complexion and upturned mustache, was inaugurated in 1909 during one of the worst sleet storms of the century. He inspired widespread confidence. "Everybody loves a fat man," the saying goes, and the jovial Taft, with "mirthquakes" of laughter bubbling up from his abundant abdomen, was personally popular. He had graduated second in his class at Yale, and had established an admirable reputation as a lawyer and judge, though widely regarded as hostile to labor unions. He had been a trusted administrator under Roosevelt—in the Philippines, at home, and in Cuba, where he had served capably as a "trouble shooter."

But "good old Will" suffered from fatal political handicaps. "Appointed" by Roosevelt, he followed the noise, bluster, and showmanship of T.R.; and any successor was bound to seem a pale anticlimax. Taft could not rush into controversies with gnashing teeth; he could not brand men liars, and then dash off to shoot bears. Instead, he played a little golf, at a time when this pastime was a "dude's game," and his bulging figure looked ridiculous in a golfing outfit.

Roosevelt believed in a government by men—at least by one man, himself. Taft was an ingrained legalist who believed in a government by laws rather than by men. With his careful legal training, he cringed at the offhand Rooseveltian dictum: "Damn the law!" He searched the statutes to find authority for his proposed actions; Roosevelt had scanned them to see if there was anything to stop his actions.

Roosevelt had led the conflicting elements of the Republican Party by the sheer force of his personality. Taft, though talented in other ways, had none of the arts of a dashing political leader, and none of Roosevelt's zest for the fray. "Politics make me sick" is the refrain that runs through his private letters. A better lieutenant than leader, he had permitted himself to be pushed into the presidential "prison" by his ambitious wife and brothers; his own ambition was for membership on the Supreme Court. Recoiling from the clatter of controversy, he generally adopted an attitude of passivity toward Congress. He was a poor judge of public opinion; and his candor made him a chronic victim of "foot-in-mouth" disease.

President William H. Taft (1857–1930), a conservative lawyer-judge, was handicapped by following the dominating Theodore Roosevelt. About two weeks after taking over the Presidency, he wrote to "My dear Theodore," that "When I am addressed as 'Mr. President,' I turn to see whether you are not at my elbow."

Taft was no doubt a mild progressive, but at heart he was more wedded to the status quo than to change. Carried along on the coattails of Roosevelt's vigorous progressivism, he at first seemed to be more progressive than he actually was. The heavy responsibilities of the Presidency sobered him, so that at times he appeared to be downright reactionary.

Taft's official family at the outset was packed with standpatters, including some who suffered from hardening of the intellectual arteries. The Cabinet—an ultra-conservative body—was dominated by six prosperous lawyers. It contained no representative of the party's "insurgent" wing, which was on fire for reform of current abuses. The leading Cabinet member was an able corporation lawyer, Secretary of State Philander C. Knox, known as "Sleepy Phil" because of his weak-kneed prosecution of the trusts as Attorney General under McKinley.

The Payne-Aldrich Tariff Betrayal

Agitation for a sharp reduction of the high Dingley Tariff of 1897 had gained momentum during the "reign" of Roosevelt. But the Rough Rider had been much too adroit, despite his apparent rashness, to tackle this dynamite-laden issue. Outcries for reform finally

Taft the Golfer Hits Tariff Ball.
Contemporary cartoon.

became so overwhelming that the Republican platform of 1908 "unequivocally" pledged a tariff revision, without saying whether the revision would be up or down. Taft interpreted this promise to mean a substantial reduction, and forthrightly announced that he would strive toward that goal.

This clamor for tariff revision was but one aspect of the current Progressive crusade. The existing Dingley Act was thought to be contributing to the high cost of living and to the much-feared expansion of the trusts. Impassioned spokesmen for the agricultural Middle West argued further that tariff walls hampered the importation of cheap manufactured goods, and at the same time hurt the sale of American farm surpluses abroad. But the hidebound Old Guard Republicans, many of them well-fed beneficiaries of protection, were content to let the high Dingley Tariff stand. "Aren't all our fellows happy?" asked one of their leaders, the shrewd, cynical, cigar-chewing Speaker of the House, Joseph G. ("Uncle Joe") Cannon.

But tariff revision could not be sidestepped. A transparently honest Taft, true to his promises, called Congress into special session in March 1909. The so-called Payne Bill, as approved by the House, provided for modest reductions. But these proved distasteful to the Senate, then dominated by a coterie of reactionaries. This group was brilliantly led by multimillionaire Senator Aldrich of Rhode Island who, though personally charming, was dictatorial. With an arrogant display of power, the senatorial Old Guard engineered 847 changes in the Payne Bill, some 600 of which were revisions upward. As a feeble sop to the public, hides and a few other items, including sea moss and canary-bird seed, were put on the free list. "Mr. Dooley" was prompted to remark that "Practically ivrything nicissry to existence comes in free." Actually, the duties were reduced from 46.5% to 40.8%. (See chart on p. 628.)

When it became evident that the Payne-Aldrich Bill would bring no substantial downward revision, alarm and anger swept through the grain-growing Middle West. Frustrated farmers increased their cries for a high tariff on Western agricultural produce and a lowered one on Eastern manufactured articles. A group of a half-dozen or so Middle Western Senators, led by stumpy and grim-faced "Battling Bob" La Follette of Wisconsin, fought the Payne-Aldrich Bill tooth and nail. Unable to prevent its passage, they at least advertised its fraud to the entire country. But the senatorial insurgents did not emerge empty-handed. They did force into the measure a pioneering 1% tax on corporation profits, and they did give added impetus to the move for attaching an income-tax amendment to the federal Constitution.

The Payne-Aldrich hodgepodge put Taft on an awkward spot. He could point to some slight reductions and to other redeeming features, including provision for a fact-finding Tariff Commission. But the measure seemed like a flagrant betrayal of his promise to reduce the tariff substantially. If he signed the Payne-Aldrich Bill, he would solemnize that betrayal. If he vetoed it, he would disrupt a party that was showing dangerous signs of breaking into insurgent and conservative factions. After much hand wringing, Taft signed.

Taft's subsequent apologies for the new tariff were most ill-advised. He might well have said that while the law was bad, it was the best he could wheedle from Congress. But instead he went out on a speaking tour and vigorously defended the Payne-Aldrich monstrosity. At Winona, Minnesota, he went overboard and insisted that the measure was "the best bill that the Republican Party ever passed." In the midst of the resulting uproar, he floundered into hotter water by explaining lamely that he had dictated the speech hurriedly between railroad stations.

Taft Pleads Vainly for a Lower Tariff. T.R. glares from the wall, and the Big Stick gathers cobwebs. Johnson in the Philadelphia *North American*, 1909.

Conservation Controversies under Taft

Taft was a genuine friend of conservation, and his contributions compare rather favorably with his predecessor's. He set up the Bureau of Mines to conserve mineral resources and to safeguard human resources. He secured authority from Congress to rescue from private exploitation millions of acres of coal lands in Wyoming and Montana—a procedure that Roosevelt had rather questionably exercised on his own responsibility. Taft also withdrew water-power sites from private exploitation, in pursuance of legislation passed by Congress in 1910.

The President's praiseworthy steps toward conservation were largely erased in the public mind by the violent Ballinger-Pinchot quarrel, which erupted in 1909. The storm center was Secretary of the Interior Ballinger, an expert on land law from the state of Washington. Roosevelt, prone to be contemptuous of statutes, had achieved much of his success in conservation by stretching existing laws to the limit—and even beyond. Ballinger, a lawyer troubled by legal scruples, reversed this process when he threw open to private exploitation water-power sites in Wyoming and Montana that had been arbitrarily withdrawn under Roosevelt. Valuable coal lands in Alaska were likewise opened to giant corporations, also in accordance with the strict letter of the law.

Ballinger's retreat scandalized ardent Rooseveltian conservationists. The Rough Rider would have burst out, "Damn the law—these natural resources must be preserved for the people!" Spearheading the criticism was a former member of Roosevelt's Tennis Cabinet, Gifford Pinchot, Chief of the Division of Forestry of the Department of Agriculture. In the resulting free-for-all Taft, who was a stickler for administrative efficiency, felt compelled to uphold Secretary Ballinger and dismiss Pinchot for insubordination. A subsequent

Congressional investigation cleared Ballinger, amid angry cries of "whitewash" from the Rooseveltites. A minority report, dictated partly by Republican insurgents, condemned Secretary Ballinger.

Unhappily the bad taste left by the Ballinger uproar lingered. Taft was much too loyal to desert a subordinate under fire, so he kept the Secretary on for a year and a half after the storm broke. Later revelations indicate that the berated Ballinger was on sounder legal ground than many critics believed. But at that time Taft seemed to be handing over to marauding interests those natural resources that T.R. had so spectacularly rescued. The whole unsavory episode widened the growing rift between the President and the ex-President, one-time bosom friends.

The Insurgent Uprising of 1910

The reformist wing of the Republican Party was now up in arms. It had been aroused particularly by the unpopular Payne-Aldrich Tariff and by White House support for Ballinger. Taft was being pushed increasingly into the company of the standpat Old Guard. Its leading mouthpiece in the House of Representatives was the coarse and profane "Uncle Joe" Cannon, who occupied the driver's seat of the well-oiled House machinery. Becoming insufferably dictatorial, he denied places on important committees to members who were so bold as to grumble against his practices.

The Common People Await Teddy's Return. *Herbert Johnson's Scrapbook*

Republican insurgents in the House, many of them Roosevelt worshipers, were all set to stage a spectacular uprising. Led by George W. Norris of Nebraska, they made the exciting discovery that by joining hands with the Democrats they could outvote the standpat Republicans and curb the tyrannical Cannon. Accordingly, in March, 1910, they engineered a memorable revolt against "Cannonism." After tense sessions, one of which lasted about thirty hours, they gained the upper hand. Specifically, they took away Cannon's privilege of appointing the all-important Rules Committee, made that body elective by the House, and excluded the Speaker from it. Cannon, who had blocked reform legislation, now lost his arbitrary power to decide what bills should be presented.

By the spring of 1910 the Grand Old Party was split wide open, owing in part to the clumsiness of Taft. A popular jingle voiced the longing of many Rooseveltians for their hero's return from Africa:

Teddy, come home and blow your horn,
The sheep's in the meadow, the cow's in the corn.
The boy you left to 'tend the sheep
Is under the haystack fast asleep.

A suspicious "Teddy" returned triumphantly to New York in June, 1910, and shortly thereafter stirred up a tempest. He had already heard enough from talebearers to suspect that Taft was carrying out "my policies" on a stretcher. Unable to keep silent, he took to the stump and at Osawatomie, Kansas, shocked the Old Guard with a flaming speech. The doctrine that he proclaimed—popularly known as "the New Nationalism"—urged the national government to increase its power in order to correct crying social and political abuses. In short, Hamiltonian centralization for social betterment.

Mounting dissension within Republican ranks was further exposed by the Congressional elections in November, 1910. In a victory of landslide proportions, the Democrats emerged with 228 seats, leaving the once-haughty Republicans with only 161. Symptomatic of the radical trend of the times was the election of a Socialist Representative, Austrian-born Victor L. Berger of Milwaukee.* The Republicans, by virtue of holdovers, retained the Senate, 51 to 41, but the insurgents in their midst were numerous enough to make that hold precarious.

Taft the Trust Buster

Meanwhile the floundering President had been gaining some fame as a smasher of monopoly. The ironical truth is that colorless Taft caused ninety legal proceedings to be brought against the trusts

---

* He was finally denied his seat in 1919, during a wave of anti-Red hysteria.

"Upset," 1911. Supreme Court Decision Upsets Standard Oil. *Jersey Journal* cartoon, by permission.

during his four years, as compared with forty-four for Roosevelt in seven and one-half years. But the statistics are misleading, for T.R. had generated the anti-trust momentum, and some of his cases were more important than Taft's.

By happenstance the most sensational judicial victories of the Taft regime came during 1911, in two cases that had been initiated under Roosevelt. The Supreme Court ordered the dissolution of the mighty Standard Oil Company, which was adjudged a combination in restraint of trade under the Sherman Anti-Trust Act of 1890. At the same time the Court handed down its famous "rule of reason," namely that the government should prosecute only those combinations suspected of an "unreasonable" restraint of trade. Two weeks later, in May, 1911, the Supreme Court no less dramatically ordered the dissolution of the gigantic American Tobacco Company. But in neither case did the militant progressives feel that the breakup was as effective as it ought to be.

Wall Street "interests" received another rude jolt in 1912–1913. The Pujo Committee, authorized by the now-Democratic House of Representatives, undertook a prolonged probe of the so-called "Money Trust." "The greatest monopoly in this country is the money monopoly," asserted Dr. Woodrow Wilson, a fast rising political star in New Jersey. The Pujo investigators were to find that banking houses dominated by the Morgan and Rockefeller interests held 341 directorships in corporations worth over twenty-two billion dollars.

The Stillborn Canadian Reciprocity of 1911

Bad luck pursued Taft into foreign affairs, especially those involving Canada. For many decades this big but weak northern sister had been seeking a reciprocal tariff arrangement. Her aim was to lower duties on goods coming from the Yankees, in return for corresponding concessions by her wealthy neighbor. With uncharacteristic zeal, Taft threw himself squarely behind this scheme. Reciprocal tariff reductions might quiet the critics who were condemning the distasteful Payne-Aldrich Tariff, and perhaps restore some of his lost luster.

In 1911 a formal agreement was signed with Canada, and Taft summoned Congress in special session to approve it. But far from gaining popularity, he merely stirred up a hornet's nest. The lumbermen and grain farmers of the Middle West, where the Republican insurgents were entrenched, cried out against the loss of their tariff protection. They accused Taft of having "sold out" to the trusts. Many industrialists in truth welcomed free raw materials from Canada, as well as tariff-free new markets for their finished products. But Taft, at last aroused to the point of applying whip and spur, drove the trade agreement through Congress. He left behind a long trail of bruised and bitter feelings.

Champions of reciprocity in Canada, who at first had hailed the agreement with delight, now began to cool off. The new Democratic Speaker of the House, Champ Clark of Missouri, alarmed the Canadians when he suggested, in a highly publicized speech, that reciprocity would be a step toward the inevitable annexation of America's northern neighbor. Taft himself rather clumsily revealed the imperialistic claws of the measure by remarking that under it Canada would become a mere economic satellite of the United States.

Suspicious Canadians had no desire to be a backdoor lumber camp or, worse yet, to be annexed to their powerful neighbor. Many of them cried in alarm, "No truck or trade with the Yankees." A heated special election in Canada, in which the basic issue was the British Union Jack versus Old Glory, was won by the anti-reciprocity party. The agreement with Washington was thereupon repudiated. A tactless Taft, after all his perspiring exertions, had nothing to show but failure.

Speaker Clark's explosive speech in the House favoring reciprocity reads in part, "I am for it because I hope to see the day when the American flag will float over every square foot of the British-North American possessions clear to the North Pole. They are people of our blood. They speak our language. Their institutions are much like ours. They are trained in the difficult art of self-government. . . ."

The Dollar Goes Abroad as a Diplomat

The brand of "Dollar Diplomacy" was stamped, somewhat unfairly, on the foreign affairs of the Taft administration. This concept was two-sided: (a) using foreign policy to protect Wall Street dollars invested abroad, and (b) using Wall Street dollars to uphold foreign policy. The first aspect was grossly overplayed by Taft's critics; the second aspect was widely misunderstood.

Though ordinarily lethargic, Taft bestirred himself to use the lever of American investments to boost American diplomacy. Washington warmly encouraged Wall Street bankers to pump their surplus dollars into foreign areas of strategic concern to the United States, especially in the Far East and in the regions that might menace the Panama Canal. Otherwise investors from rival powers, say Germany, might take advantage of financial chaos and secure a lodgment inimical to Uncle Sam's interests, both physical and commercial. New York bankers would thus strengthen American defenses and foreign policies, while bringing further prosperity to their homeland and to themselves.

The Almighty Dollar thus came to supplant the Big Stick. A peace-loving Taft was not nearly so enthusiastic for military preparedness as the pugnacious T.R., and did not push battleship construction with vigor. The navy, unable to keep up with Britain and Germany in their frantic race, dropped from second to third place, just ahead of France.

China's Manchuria was the object of Taft's most spectacular effort to pump the reluctant dollar into the Far Eastern theater. Ambitious little Japan and imperialistic Russia, recent foes, controlled the railroads of this strategic province. Taft saw in the Manchurian railway monopoly a possible strangulation of Chinese economic interests, and a consequent slamming of the Open Door in the faces of American merchants. In 1909 Secretary of State Knox blunderingly proposed that a group of American and foreign bankers buy the Manchurian railroads, and then turn them over to China under a self-liquidating arrangement. Both Japan and Russia, unwilling to be jockeyed out of their dominant position, bluntly rejected Knox's overtures. Again Taft was showered with ridicule.

Another dangerous trouble-spot was the revolution-riddled Caribbean—now virtually a Yankee lake. Hoping to head off trouble, Washington urged Wall Street bankers to force dollars into the financial vacuums in Honduras and Haiti to keep out foreign funds. The United States, under the Monroe Doctrine, would not permit foreign nations to intervene, and consequently it had some moral obligation to intervene financially to prevent economic and political chaos.

Again necessity was the mother of armed Caribbean intervention. Sporadic disorders in palm-fronded Cuba, Honduras, and Santo Domingo brought American forces in the days of Taft. A revolutionary upheaval in Nicaragua, perilously close to the nearly completed canal, resulted in the landing of 2500 marines in 1912. (See map, p. 740.)

A luckless Taft could point to a few diplomatic triumphs, even though the Big Stick did gather cobwebs. The age-old dispute over the smelly Newfoundland fisheries was finally settled in 1912, when an Anglo-American pact set up a permanent arbitral board. In the previous year an agreement signed by four nations—the United States, Britain, Japan, and Russia—rescued America's North Pacific seal herd. These furry creatures had dwindled from about 4,000,000 to 120,000, but within thirty-five years the new multi-power safeguards raised the figure to around the 3,000,000 mark. (See map, p. 648.)

The Taft-Roosevelt Rupture

The insurgent uprising in Republican ranks had meanwhile been blossoming into a full-fledged revolt. Early in 1911 the National Progressive Republican League was formed, with the fiery, white-maned Senator La Follette of Wisconsin its leading candidate for the Republican presidential nomination. The assumption was that Roosevelt, an anti-third termer, would not permit himself to be "drafted."

But the restless Rough Rider began to change his views about third terms as he saw Taft, hand in glove with the hated Old Guard, discard "my policies." In February, 1912, Roosevelt formally wrote to seven state governors that he was willing to accept the Republican nomination. His reasoning was that the third-term tradition applied to three *consecutive elective* terms. Informally he cried, "My hat is in the ring!" and "The fight is on and I am stripped to the buff!"

"Where Will He Land?"
Steele in the Denver *Post*,
February, 1912

Roosevelt forthwith seized the Progressive banner, while La Follette, who had served as a convenient pathbreaker, was protestingly thrust aside. Girded for battle, the Rough Rider clattered into the presidential primaries then being held in many states. He shouted through half-clenched teeth that the President had fallen under the thumb of the reactionary bosses, and that although Taft "means well, he means well feebly." The once-genial Taft, now in a fighting mood, retorted by branding the supporters of Roosevelt as "emotionalists and neurotics."

As the fight thickened, Roosevelt allowed himself to be carried away by his Progressive zeal for increased popular control of government. He strenuously advocated the "recall," or removal, of judges who might be anti-reformist or "interest-controlled." What was more shocking, he came out flatly for the recall of judicial decisions at the state level, subject to review by the U.S. Supreme Court. This scheme, though not as radical as pictured, was a first-class blunder. It alienated many mild progressives, who now feared they had a wild man on their hands.

Yet Roosevelt, on the surface, seemed to be sweeping all before him. Still the popular idol, he carried most of the presidential primaries in the states that held them. He even captured Taft's Ohio. But the portly President, who had the smooth-running party machinery behind him, was successful in lining up delegates from the Solid South—an area where the Republican ticket had not won an electoral vote for decades.

A Taft-Roosevelt explosion was near in June, 1912, when the Republican convention met in Chicago. The Rooseveltites, who were about 100 delegates short of winning the nomination, challenged the right of some 250 Taft delegates to be seated. Most of these contests were arbitrarily settled in favor of Taft, whose supporters held the throttle of the convention steam roller. The Roosevelt adherents, crying "fraud" and "naked theft," in the end refused to vote.

Taft triumphed, though ironically he won renomination by the same steam-roller tactics that T.R. had used in his behalf four years earlier. But the Republican platform, bending to the breeze of Progressive doctrine, came out for reforming the trusts and the currency. Roosevelt, the good sportsman, proved to be a poor loser. Having tasted for once the bitter cup of defeat, he was in a mood to lead a third-party crusade.

Roosevelt the Indian Giver. Knecht in the Evansville (Indiana) *Courier*

The Emergence of Dr. Woodrow Wilson

Office-hungry Democrats—the "outs" since 1897—were jubilant over the disruptive Republican brawl at Chicago. The party in power, the adage runs, is seldom defeated; it splits into factions and defeats itself.

If the Democrats were to keep abreast of the times and win, they would have to come up with an outstanding reformist leader. Fortunately for them, one appeared in Dr. Woodrow Wilson, once a mild conservative but now a militant progressive. Beginning professional life as a brilliant academic lecturer on government, he had risen in 1902 to the presidency of Princeton University, and there he had achieved some sweeping educational reforms. In the interests of promoting higher education, he had also battled to abolish the snobbish eating clubs and fuse their members with the rest of the student body. But here he had suffered defeat at the hands of the wealthy alumni.

Wilson's final struggle at Princeton involved the proposed graduate school. He was eager to build it in the physical center of the university, and thus elevate the intellectual life of the undergraduates. But the equally stubborn Dean West insisted on locating the structure on the outskirts, where the serious graduates would not be debased by undergraduate frivolity. Dean West finally secured a handsome bequest, with authority to build the school where he chose. From then on Princeton was not big enough for both the President and the Dean.

By 1910 Wilson had emerged as the potential governor of New Jersey. His name was nationally known, largely because his spirited campaign for educational reform chimed in with current progressive thinking. The Democrats of boss-ridden New Jersey, needing a respectable candidate for the governorship, offered the nomination to Dr. Wilson. They reasoned that if they should have the good luck to win, they could privately lead the bespectacled professor around by his long academic nose, while using him as a show-window "front."

Wilson accepted the New Jersey nomination in 1910, and then put on a tremendous fighting campaign. "God! Look at that man's jaw," exclaimed one observer. In a series of eloquent speeches, Wilson boldly assailed the trusts in a state that was known as "the Mother of Trusts," including Standard Oil of New Jersey (1882). He passionately advocated political and social reforms that would return the state government to the people, and thus break the iron grip of selfish minorities and "predatory" interests.

The "Schoolmaster in Politics," riding the crest of the progressive wave, was swept into the governorship. Demanding "pitiless publicity" for wrongdoing, he turned against the bewildered bosses and routed them. He then drove through the legislature a sheaf of forward-looking measures—reforms that were tailored to make reactionary New Jersey one of the more liberal states. Filled with righteous indignation, Wilson was at his best. He revealed irresistible reforming zeal, burning eloquence, superb powers of leadership, and a refreshing habit of appealing over the heads of the scheming bosses to the sovereign people. Now a figure of national eminence, Wilson was being widely mentioned for the Presidency.

When the Democrats met at Baltimore in 1912, Wilson enjoyed im-

Contemporary Caricature of Wilson.

pressive support, though lacking a majority of the delegates. The front-running contender was the Speaker of the House, Champ Clark of Missouri. An experienced legislator and a popular orator of the old-fashioned school, he had displayed only moderately progressive tendencies. The intellectual level of some of his followers is indicated by their popular song: "They Gotta Quit Kickin' My Dawg Aroun'." Clark polled a majority of the votes on some of the early ballots, though falling short of the required two-thirds, while Wilson ran a strong second.

Wilson's cause was unexpectedly supported by the old war horse, Bryan. Presumably willing to have lightning strike him a fourth time, he was present as a delegate from Nebraska pledged to vote for Champ Clark. But when the formidable New York delegation, with its Wall Street connections, suddenly turned to Clark, Bryan no less dramatically switched to Wilson. He proclaimed that he could not support a candidate of the moneyed interests. This spectacular shift possibly helped Wilson. But by then Clark had shot his bolt, and the Princetonian received the nomination on the forty-sixth ballot. The Democratic platform pointed up Wilson's liberalism by coming out emphatically for current progressive reforms, including anti-trust legislation, monetary changes, and tariff reduction.

The "Bull Moose" Campaign of 1912

Surging events had meanwhile been thrusting Roosevelt to the fore as a candidate for the Presidency on a third-party Progressive Republican ticket. The fighting ex-cowboy, angered by his recent rebuff, was eager to lead the charge. A pro-Roosevelt Progressive convention, with about two thousand delegates from forty states, assembled in Chicago during August, 1912. Roosevelt was applauded tumultuously as he cried in a vehement speech, "We stand at Armageddon, and we battle for the Lord!" The hosanna spirit of a revival meeting suffused the convention, while the hoarse delegates sang "Onward, Christian Soldiers" and "Battle Hymn of the Republic." William Allen White, the caustic Kansas journalist, later wrote, "Roosevelt bit me and I went mad."

Fired-up Progressives entered the campaign with both righteousness and high enthusiasm. Their platform—a "Covenant with the People"—endorsed thoroughgoing reforms and struck at "invisible" government. Roosevelt boasted that he felt "as strong as a bull moose," and hence the bull moose took its place with the donkey and the elephant in the American political zoo. As one poet whimsically put it:

I want to be a Bull Moose,
And with the Bull Moose stand
With antlers on my forehead
And a Big Stick in my hand.

G.O.P. Divided by Bull Moose Equals
Democratic Victory, *Puck,* 1912

Roosevelt and Taft were bound to slit each other's political throats; by dividing the Republican vote they guaranteed a Democratic victory. In truth the only question, said one cynic, was which corpse would get the more flowers in the form of ballots. The two antagonists tore into each other as only former friends can. "Death alone can take me out now," cried the once-genial Taft, as he branded Roosevelt "a dangerous egotist" and a "demagogue." Roosevelt, fighting mad, assailed Taft as a "fathead" with the brain of a "guinea pig."

Despite the clashing personalities, the basic emphasis was on Progressivism. All three candidates and all three platforms professed to favor reform in some degree; the chief difference was often over degree. Roosevelt's presumed radicalism, notably his advocacy of the recall of judicial decisions, came in for heavy fire; at the other end of the scale, Taft was denounced as a reactionary. Wilson, who campaigned widely and persuasively, was inclined to ignore his two overheated opponents. Cool, collected, and gentlemanly, he expounded to attentive audiences the forward-looking principles of his New Freedom. In his view the New Freedom meant new opportunities, under government regulation, for free enterprise. He especially stressed the need for fostering competition by reducing tariffs, and also by curbing the power-hungry trusts—"that invisible empire of special interest."

The campaign of 1912 provided abundant color and drama. Political vocalizers hailed Roosevelt with such songs as "We're Ready for Teddy Again" and "The Moose Is Loose," and sang with soulful dedication:

We will follow Roosevelt,
Follow! Follow!
Anywhere! Everywhere,
We will follow on.

Taft's adherents denounced Roosevelt's dictatorial ambitions in songs like "Teddy Must Be King," while gladsome Democrats sang "Row, Row, Woodrow" and "Wilson—That's All." The heat of the campaign cooled a bit when, in Milwaukee, Roosevelt was shot in the chest by a fanatic. The Rough Rider suspended active campaigning for more than two weeks after delivering, with Bull Moose gameness, his scheduled speech.

Woodrow Wilson: A Minority President

Ex-Professor Wilson won handily, with 435 electoral votes and 6,293,454 popular votes. Back in Princeton, Dean West is said to have groaned, "My God, I've made Wilson President of the United States."

"Bull Moose" Roosevelt was the lively corpse that got the more ballot-box flowers. The totals for him stood at 88 electoral votes and 4,119,538 popular votes. Taft carried only two states, Utah and Vermont, with 8 paltry electoral votes, while gathering 3,484,980 popular votes.

The election figures are fascinating. Wilson, with only 41% of the popular vote, was clearly a minority President, though winning a Democratic majority in Congress. His popular total was actually smaller, despite the increase in population, than Bryan had amassed in any of his three defeats. Taft and Roosevelt together polled over a million and a quarter more votes than the Democrats. Progressivism rather than Wilson was the runaway winner. Though the Democratic total obviously included many conservatives in the Solid South, still the combined progressive vote for Wilson and Roosevelt exceeded the tally of the more conservative Taft. To the progressive tally must be added some support for the Socialist candidate, hardy Eugene V. Debs, who rolled up 900,672 votes, or more than twice as many as he

PRESIDENTIAL ELECTION OF 1912 (with electoral vote by state)

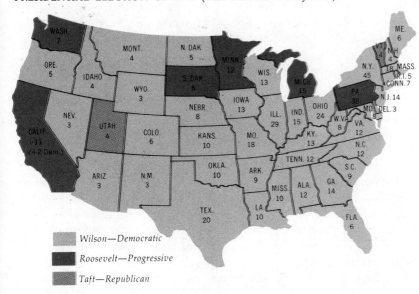

had netted four years earlier. Starry-eyed Socialists saw themselves in the White House within eight years.

The Presidential Vote, 1912

Candidate	Party	Electoral Vote	Popular Vote	Approximate Percentage
Woodrow Wilson	Democratic	435	6,293,454	41%
Theodore Roosevelt	Progressive	88	4,119,538	27%
William H. Taft	Republican	8	3,484,980	23%
Eugene V. Debs	Socialist	—	900,672	6%
E. W. Chafin	Prohibition	—	206,275	1%
A. E. Reimer	Socialist-Labor	—	28,750	.2%

Mortified Republicans were now free to engage in some sorrowful second-guessing. If they had united behind the progressive Roosevelt, they might well have won; if they had united behind the conservative Taft, they might well have lost. But in this event they would have kept their ranks intact, and might have triumphed four years later, instead of losing again.

Roosevelt's lone-wolf course was tragic both for himself and for his former Republican associates. Until 1912 he had set great store by party loyalty; now he had brought untold woes upon himself and his party. Perhaps, to rephrase William Allen White, he had bitten himself and gone mad. The Progressive Party, which was primarily a one-man show, had no future because it had elected few candidates to state and local offices. Without patronage plums to hand out to the faithful workers, death by slow starvation was inevitable. Yet the Progressives made a tremendous showing for a hastily organized third party, and helped spur the enactment of many of their pet reforms by the Wilsonian Democrats.

Taft in Retrospect

An aura of bumble, fumble, and stumble clung to Taft, who left the White House in 1913 after the worst defeat yet suffered by an incumbent. His personal humiliation, combined with the disruption of his party, caused many critics to regard him as a flat failure.

This indictment of Taft is unfair. His achievements in conservation and trust busting were substantial, if lacking in fireworks. In addition, the Mann-Elkins Act of 1910 brought the railroads under a tighter governmental rein, and rather belatedly extended the authority of the Interstate Commerce Commission to the telegraph and cable companies.

Gratifying strides toward better government were made under

Taft. Civil service reform received a strong boost, particularly as more postmasters were added to the classified service. Congress, for its part, enacted significant reform legislation in 1910 and 1911. New laws were specifically designed to give publicity to the campaign funds of Congressmen and to set limits to their political outlays. Finally, a higher degree of administrative efficiency came in 1913, when Congress separated the Department of Commerce and Labor into two departments.

The wondrous West continued to develop. A needed stimulus came when Congress revised the Homestead Act, in 1909 and again in 1912, to square with the realities of farming in arid regions. New Mexico and Arizona were welcomed in 1912 as the forty-seventh and forty-eighth stars. Taft showed his judicial bent when he held up the admission of Arizona until an offensive provision for the recall of judges was removed from her constitution. (Once in the Union, Arizona reinstated this radical provision; and there was nothing that the President or Congress could do about it.)

Additional legislative landmarks dotted the Taft years. The Postal Savings Bank Act of 1910, in the teeth of bitter opposition from the bankers, belatedly provided facilities like those found in many European countries. A parcel-post system, similar to foreign models, was likewise approved in 1912, but not until the express companies had fought it hammer and tongs. An impressive total of some 700,000,000 parcels flooded through the post office during 1913, the first year of operation. Finally, the 16th Amendment, making lawful a federal income tax, was formally riveted to the federal Constitution in February, 1913. (See Appendix.)

All these measures add up to a commendable record of cautious progress, even though some of them were routine or were enacted primarily by Democratic votes. Taft, the amiable misfit, was not only unlucky but a victim of his times. Despite his mildly reformist tendencies, progressive sentiment was sweeping so rapidly past his rotund figure that he seemed to be standing still.

Taft's remaining life was fruitful. He taught law for eight pleasant years at Yale University, and in 1921 became Chief Justice. This exalted post, which he had long coveted, was one for which he was admirably fitted by training and temperament, and in which he was successful. His eight years on the Supreme Bench were among the happiest of his life, just as the four years of his "sentence" in the Big White Jail had proved to be the most unhappy.

Roosevelt wrote privately in May, 1908: "I think that of all men in the country Taft is the best fitted at this time to be President and to carry on the work upon which we have entered during the past six years."

Three years later, in December, 1911, ex-President Roosevelt wrote, "Taft is utterly hopeless. I think he would be beaten if nominated, but in any event it would be a misfortune to have him in the Presidential chair for another term, for he has shown himself an entirely unfit President. . . ."

SELECT READINGS

An able introduction is G. E. MOWRY, *The Era of Theodore Roosevelt, 1900–1912* (1958)*; see also his *Theodore Roosevelt and the Progressive Movement* (1946). Sympathetic biographical coverage is H. F. PRINGLE, *The Life and Times of William Howard Taft* (2 vols.,

1939); also C. G. BOWERS, *Beveridge and the Progressive Era* (1932). The rise of Wilson is described in A. S. LINK, *Wilson: The Road to the White House* (1947).* A penetrating interpretation is RICHARD HOFSTADTER, *The Age of Reform* (1955)*; also E. F. GOLDMAN, *Rendezvous with Destiny* (1952).* Many titles for the previous chapter are relevant, including those by Faulkner (two), McGeary, Fausold, Chamberlain, Wiebe, Riis, Steffens, and La Follette. Consult also AMOS PINCHOT, *A History of the Progressive Party, 1912–1916* (1958) and RICHARD LOWITT, *George W. Norris* (1963). Also *Harvard Guide,** Pt. VI.

RECENT REFERENCES

PAOLO E. COLETTA, *The Presidency of William Howard Taft* (1973); WALTER V. SCHOLES and MARIE V. SCHOLES, *The Foreign Policies of the Taft Administration* (1970).

* Available in paperback.

35

Woodrow Wilson and the New Freedom

*This is not a day of triumph; it is a day of dedication. Here muster
not the forces of party, but the forces of humanity. . . . I summon
all honest men, all patriotic, all forward-looking men, to my side. God
helping me, I will not fail them, if they will but counsel and sustain me!*

Thomas Woodrow Wilson, Inaugural Address, 1913

Wilson: The Idealist in Politics

(Thomas) Woodrow Wilson, the second Democratic President
since 1861, looked like the ascetic intellectual he was, what with
his clean-cut features, pinched-on eye glasses, and trim figure
(five feet eleven and 179 pounds). Born in Virginia shortly before
the Civil War, and reared in Georgia and the Carolinas, the pro-
fessor-politician was the first man from one of the seceded Southern
states to reach the White House since Zachary Taylor, sixty-four
years earlier.

    The impact of Dixieland on young "Tommy" Wilson was pro-
found. His upbringing in the burned-out South caused him to
sympathize with the gallant attempt of the Confederacy to win its
independence in 1861–1865. His later ideal of self-determination
for minority peoples, the world over, was no doubt partly inspired
by these youthful impressions. Wilson was not only born a Southern
Democrat, but he developed into a Democrat steeped in the ultra-

President Woodrow Wilson
(1856–1924), realist-idealist,
wrote some six years before
coming to the White House,
"The President is at liberty,
both in law and conscience, to
be as big a man as he can."
Fighting desperately later for
the League of Nations and
breaking himself down, he said,
"I would rather fail in a cause
that I know some day will
triumph than to win in a cause
that I know some day will
fail." New York Historical
Society, New York City.

liberal Jeffersonian tradition. Like Jefferson, a fellow Virginian, he had strong faith in the judgment of the masses—if they were properly informed.

Son of a Presbyterian minister, Wilson was reared in an atmosphere of extreme piety. He believed devoutly in the power of prayer and in the presence of a personal God. At heart a clergyman, he later used the presidential pulpit to preach his inspirational political sermons.

Wilson was not only a born reformer but an idealist who could radiate righteous indignation. Moved by a stern sense of duty when he saw wrongdoing, he would become "angry for the right." As an earnest Christian who habitually read his Bible and prayed in the bosom of his family, he hated war so intensely that he became a pacifist at heart. Such tendencies were reinforced by his boyhood years in Yankee-gutted Georgia.

A moving orator, Wilson could rise on the wings of spiritual power to soaring eloquence. Yet he was inclined, professor-like, to be more in touch with his subject than with his audience. Skillfully using a persuasive voice, he relied not on arm waving but on sincerity and moral appeal. As a lifelong student of finely chiseled words, he turned out to be a "phraseocrat" who coined many noble epigrams. Someone has remarked that he was born halfway between the Bible and the dictionary, and never got away from either.

A profound student of government, Wilson believed that the Chief Executive should play a dynamic role. He was convinced that Congress could not function properly unless the President, like a kind of prime minister, got out in front and provided leadership. Somewhat paradoxically, this reserved professor of theoretical politics became an astute practical politician. He was often dramatically effective, both as governor and as President, in appealing over the heads of legislators to the sovereign people.

Splendid though Wilson's intellectual equipment was, he suffered from serious defects of personality. Though jovial and witty in private, he could be cold and standoffish in public. Incapable of unbending and acting the showman, like "Teddy" Roosevelt, he lacked the common touch. He loved humanity in the mass rather than the individual in person. His academic background caused him to feel most at home with scholars, although he had to work wry-facedly with politicians. An austere and somewhat arrogant intellectual, he looked down his nose through pince-nez glasses upon lesser minds, including journalists. He was especially intolerant of stupid Senators, whose "bungalow" minds made him "sick."

Wilson's burning idealism—especially his desire to reform ever-present wickedness—drove him forward faster than lesser spirits were willing to go. When concentrating on one problem, he would neglect others; he had what he described as "a single-track mind." His sense of moral righteousness was such that he found compromise difficult: black was black, wrong was wrong, and one should never compromise with wrong. His Scotch Presbyterian ancestors had passed on to him an inflexible stubbornness. When convinced that he was right, he would break before he would bend, unlike Theodore Roosevelt. He tended to make personal enemies of his political foemen; and if he was forced to choose between principle and friend, the friend had to go.

Bryan and Offices for Deserving Democrats

Wilson's inaugural address, delivered before a vast crowd on March 4, 1913, reflected high idealism and deep dedication. It foreshadowed a program of reform designed to achieve the New Freedom of the average man—freedom from exploitation by Big Business and high finance. Wilson forthwith proceeded to push his proposals with unflagging zeal. Few Presidents have come to the White House with a clearer program or one destined to be more completely achieved.

Wilson's Cabinet inspired no great confidence. It was composed largely of "unknowns," principally because the Democrats had been out of power for sixteen years. The sons of the Confederacy had again captured Washington. Five Cabinet members were Southern-born, including the North Carolina newspaperman-politician Josephus Daniels, who became "managing editor of the Navy." He gained considerable publicity by banning alcohol from American warships. The handsome, thirty-one-year-old Franklin D. Roosevelt of New York, who had a passion for ships, was made Assistant Secretary of the Navy.

Bryan, three time loser, fell heir to the Secretaryship of State—the highest appointive post available. He was totally without experience as a diplomat, as were most Secretaries during those years, and he knew little international law. The New York *Sun* thought that he was about as well suited for his position as a "merman to play football." But he was the liberal leader of a strong element in the Democratic Party. The new President, though distrusting Bryan's intellectual furnishings, simply could not leave him out of the Cabinet. As "Mr. Dooley" said, it would be better for Wilson to have Bryan "in his bosom than on his back."

Bryan proved to be something of a problem child, even though he added liberal strength. His reformist zeal even ran to the abolition of liquor at official functions—"grape juice diplomacy." His activities as a political spoilsman unfortunately hampered Wilson's earnest efforts to promote the merit system. Bryan had incurred many political debts over the years, for millions of Democrats had voted for him in three elections. He now eagerly sought gravy jobs for "deserving Democrats"—as he called them. This inept phrase rasped "resolute Republicans," who responded with hypocritical jeers.

"All Ready in the Event of Possible Hostilities," 1913. Byran as Peace-Dove Secretary of State. Courtesy of Philadelphia *Inquirer*

Yet Bryan turned out to be a more useful Cabinet member than cynics had predicted. Buttonholing his Democratic friends in Congress, he used his charm and immense personal influence to speed on its way Wilson's bulging portfolio of reform legislation. An ardent lover of peace, like Wilson, he bestirred himself energetically to negotiate some thirty conciliation treaties. These agreements bound the signatory nations not to begin hostilities for a year after a dispute broke out, by which time their anger presumably would have evaporated. The "cooling-off" or "wait-a-bit" treaties embodied the ancient axiom, "When angry count fifty, when very angry count a hundred." These pacts might have amounted to more if the Great War had not wrapped Europe in flames in 1914.

More influential than any regular member of the Cabinet was another Southerner, Colonel (honorary) Edward M. House. This smallish, self-effacing Texan, who had helped elect Wilson, was a skilled politician and wirepuller. With a judicious rather than a profound mind, he aspired to no formal office but enjoyed the anonymous thrill that came from being the power behind the throne. For nearly seven years he was Wilson's most intimate adviser—a one-man Kitchen Cabinet.

Wilson Tackles the Tariff

Seeking New Freedoms that would free the people from monopoly, Wilson promptly prepared for an all-out assault on what he called "the triple wall of privilege." He meant, of course, the tariff, the trusts, and the archaic system of banking and currency. The first barrier was the unpopular Payne-Aldrich Tariff, which badly needed revamping.

Schoolmaster Wilson Lays
Down the Law to Congress.
New York *Tribune*, 1913

Wilson met the tariff issue head-on, early in 1913, with refreshing decisiveness. First he summoned Congress into special session. Then he prepared an eloquent message against special privilege. But he did not send it over to the Capitol to be read loudly by a bored clerk, as had been the invariable rule since Jefferson's day in 1801. Instead, he appeared before a joint session of Congress and presented the appeal himself with characteristic poise and effectiveness. This precedent-shattering episode further highlighted Wilson's determination to provide aggressive leadership, and to achieve closer cooperation between the President and Congress. Strangely enough, Theodore Roosevelt, the precedent smasher, had not revived the personal appearances of George Washington and John Adams. Wilson remarked smilingly as he rode away from Capitol Hill, "I think we put one over on Teddy that time."

As usual, the new Underwood Tariff Bill ran the familiar gauntlet. Providing for a substantial reduction of existing rates, it passed the House without a serious hitch. But progress was stormy when it reached the Senate, which contained many "tools" of the "special interests." A swarm of lobbyists—"the third house of Congress"—were reportedly about to disembowel the bill, as they had done repeatedly in the past.

This tariff crisis sharply challenged Wilson's leadership. He promptly issued a fighting appeal to the people, with the objective of building up a backfire against the scheming lobbyists. The masses, he insisted, had no agents in Washington to look after their welfare, but the predatory interests did have. Public opinion, aroused by Wilson's eloquence, is believed to have caused the lobbyists to become more discreet. The Senate finally approved the new tariff bill late in 1913, after six months of windy debate.

Fruits of Freer Trade

The Underwood-Simmons Tariff was not a free-trade measure; nor was it really a low-tariff law. Wilson favored not free trade but freer opportunity. Average annual rates were chopped down from 40.8% to 27%. All told, the law reduced the duties on more than nine hundred items, and enlarged the free list by including such basic products as raw wool and steel rails. Increases were tacked on to more than eighty commodities, principally luxuries, and chiefly for revenue. Though still definitely protective, the new measure achieved the first genuine tariff reduction since the Civil War, and thus redeemed Democratic pledges of revision. (See chart, p. 628).

Significantly, the Underwood Act was also a landmark in tax legislation. Under authority recently granted by the 16th Amendment, Congress included a graduated levy, beginning with incomes of $3000 for single persons and $4000 for married couples. A married man earning $5000 would pay about $10. Such painlessly low rates were raised in 1916, owing to the World War emergency, and the next year revenue from the income tax shot ahead of that from the tariff. This gap since then has been vastly widened.

The Underwood Tariff, though acidly criticized, was a giant step toward correcting inequities. It decreased the indirect burden on the poor by lowering the customs duties, and increased the direct burden on the rich by enacting an income tax. Southern Democrats were delighted to shift a part of the tax load onto the backs of their Yankee brethren, many of whom were Big Business Republicans. Northern capitalists, complaining that they had now lost the Civil War, declared that they were the victims of class legislation and sectional discrimination.

Experts regard the Underwood Act as one of the best-balanced tariff measures ever to pass Congress. But how well it would have worked in normal times will never be known. The titanic World War erupted in 1914, before the new law had been on the books a year, and one unhappy result was a sharp reduction of anticipated customs revenue.

"The Funeral Oration," 1913.
Wilson Buries Commercial
Prosperity with Tariff Message.
Courtesy of Philadelphia *Inquirer*

Wilson Battles the Bankers

A second bastion of the "triple wall of privilege" was the banking and currency system, now outgrown. The country's financial structure, still creaking along under the Civil War National Banking Act, revealed glaring defects. Its most serious shortcoming, as laid bare by the Panic of 1907, was the inelasticity of the currency. The amount of money in circulation was heavily concentrated in Wall Street, and could not be speedily expanded in times of financial stress into areas that were badly pinched.

President Taft, for his part, had been content to leave the complicated banking problem to Congress. That body, in 1908, had authorized the National Monetary Commission, headed by a reactionary banker, Senator Aldrich. After more than three years of study, it recommended a gigantic central bank, with numerous branches. This institution would in effect be the Third Bank of the United States. Wall Street financiers would assume the role of long-departed Nicholas Biddle, who in ghostly form struck terror into the hearts of the Bryanites. They feared that through such a monster bank the "Money Trust" would concentrate even more power in the hands of a favored few.

Determined Democrats, with Wilson leading the attack, prepared to battle the bankers. In June, 1913, in a second dramatic appearance before both houses of Congress, the President delivered a stirring plea for genuine banking reform. The legislative machinery then began to grind. Standpat Republicans fought vigorously for a huge private bank with fifteen branches, close to the "Money Trust." But liberal Democrats, with Bryan bustling behind the scenes, demanded a decentralized bank, in government hands, not in those of private money-changers.

Deadlock rapidly developed in Congress. Representative Carter Glass of Virginia, chief sponsor of the administration's banking bill, spoke dejectedly to Wilson of resignation. "Damn it, don't resign, old fellow," rejoined the President in one of his rare outbursts of profanity; "outvote them." The embattled Bryan Democrats finally triumphed over the bankers, and the epochal Federal Reserve Act was signed late in 1913.

Though complex, the Federal Reserve System was efficient. At its head in Washington sat the Federal Reserve Board, appointed by the President. The vesting of such arbitrary power in an inner group alarmed the moneyed men, who naturally distrusted the "politicians." To achieve a compromise between centralization and decentralization, the country was divided into twelve districts, each with a centralized bank owned by the member banks. One result was centralization within decentralization. A network of interconnecting pipelines radiated out from each of the twelve Federal Reserve reservoirs, and these speeded the flow of currency and credit to the

Secretary of the Treasury McAdoo recalled in his autobiography (1931) that many bankers and experts had fought the Federal Reserve Act. "I found that they could take the same set of facts and reach two diametrically opposite conclusions. For example, Forgan [a Chicago banker] estimated that the currency would be contracted to the extent of $1,800,000,000, while Senator Elihu Root, using the same data, predicted an inflation of at least $1,800,000,000."

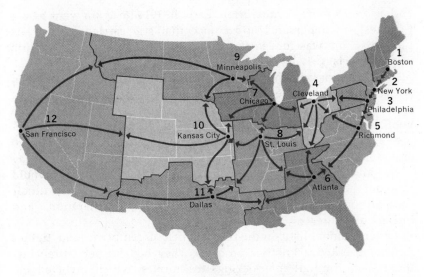

TWELVE FEDERAL RESERVE DISTRICTS AND BANKS
Alaska and Hawaii are included in the Twelfth District.

areas suffering serious financial drought. Congress thus met the long-felt need for a free-flowing currency.

The Federal Reserve Act also tightened the rein on existing institutions. All National Banks were required to join the new system, and others were at liberty to do so, once they had complied with its regulations. The twelve Federal Reserve Banks, which could be used as depositories for government funds, were actually bankers' banks. They dealt not with private individuals but with banking institutions.

An ingenious arrangement provided for expanding the paper money in time of emergency. The Federal Reserve Board was empowered to issue Federal Reserve currency backed by commercial paper —such as the promissory notes of businessmen—held by the member banks in various localities. Thus the amount of money in circulation could be quickly increased to meet the legitimate needs of the business community.

The Federal Reserve Act, which absorbed and ultimately ended the hoary independent treasury system of President Van Buren, was a red-letter achievement. It carried the nation with flying banners through the financial crises of the World War of 1914–1918. Many bankers who at first had viewed the Federal Reserve System with alarm were finally won over completely.

The President Tackles the Trusts

Without pausing for breath, Wilson pushed toward the last rampart in the "triple wall of privilege"—the trusts. He would thus achieve another of his New Freedoms—freedom from monopoly—

and also restore free competition. Early in 1914 he again went before Congress, in a personal appearance that still carried drama. His plea this time was for legislation that would loosen the strangling grip of special privilege.

Nine months and thousands of words later, Congress responded with the Federal Trade Commission Act of 1914. The new law empowered the President, through a bipartisan commission of five men, to turn a searchlight on industries engaged in interstate commerce, such as the meat packers. The commission was expected to crush monopoly in the cradle by careful investigation, followed by "cease and desist" orders where warranted. These presumably would root out harmful practices, including price discrimination, unfair competition, false advertising, misbranding, adulteration, and bribery and threats.

Other monopolistic industries, which urgently needed tighter reins, presented a knottier problem. They had further entrenched themselves through interlocking directorates, which involved the same person serving on different boards of directors. Astute industrialists were now resorting more and more to the device known as the holding company, whose chief business was to hold the stocks or securities of other companies and derive income from them. A corporation produced a useful commodity like harvesters; a holding company produced profits.

The Clayton Anti-Trust Act of 1914 attempted to come to grips with these evils. It forbade practices that lessened competition, created monopoly, or resulted in objectionable price discrimination. It also restricted various types of interlocking directorates and holding companies, provided that they involved monopoly. All this sounded impressive on paper, but actually the Clayton Act suffered from loop-

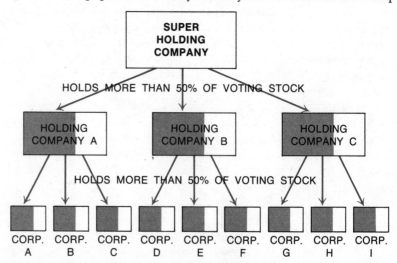

It should be borne in mind that the voting stock of a corporation is often only a fraction of the total stock.

holes and other weak spots. While a definite improvement on the old Sherman Anti-Trust Act of 1890, it disappointed the more zealous foes of monopoly.

Simultaneously the Clayton Act conferred certain benefits, long overdue, on organized labor. The outworn Sherman Anti-Trust Act, toothless though it was in restraining trusts, had been effective in crushing labor organizations. Conservative courts had unexpectedly held that monopolistic unions, like monopolistic corporations, fell under the restraints of the Sherman Act. A classic case in 1908 involved the striking hatters of Danbury, Connecticut. In 1912 they were assessed triple damages of more than $250,000, which resulted in the loss of their savings and homes. The Clayton Act presumably exempted labor and agricultural organizations from anti-trust prosecution, while specifically sanctioning such frowned-upon weapons as strikes and peaceful picketing. It also prohibited court injunctions in labor disputes, except in cases which involved "irreparable injury" to property.

But the gains of labor were illusory. True, workingmen greeted the new law with enthusiasm, partly because it legally lifted human labor from the category of "a commodity or article of commerce." Samuel Gompers, with unjustified praise, even hailed the act as the Magna Charta of labor. But conservative courts in later years, invoking restrictive clauses in the law, often clipped the wings of organized labor.

The trusts, thus partially curbed by Wilsonian legislation, gradually faded from the headlines. Corporations on the whole were inclined to obey the restraining "cease and desist" orders issued by the Federal Trade Commission. Broad-minded courts, for their part, were disposed to follow the "rule of reason," and punish only those combines guilty of unreasonable restraints on trade. The coming of the Great War with Germany in 1917 caused big industry to seem less wicked. With full-scale production desperately needed, Washington was apt to relax prosecutions and wink at technical violations of the anti-trust laws.

"Vindicated," 1914. Fitzpatrick in the St. Louis *Post-Dispatch*

Democratic Doldrums

President Wilson, ramming an impressive sheaf of bills through Congress, was almost irresistible during his first eighteen months. For once, the creed of a political party was matched by deed. The "Schoolmaster President" achieved these legislative victories largely by sheer powers of leadership, with a strong assist from the Democratic Party machinery and the still-vibrant spirit of progressivism. Displaying an unbending backbone, he held Congress in session for over seventy-two weeks. Critics sneered that Professor Wilson was like the teacher, ruler in hand, who keeps the students after school until they have completed their assignments.

But after the initial brilliant successes the Wilsonian spell began to wear off. Ever the idealist, the Princetonian was eager to spur the country into self-improvement more speedily than it wanted to go.

Economic depression further dampened the reformist mood. During the latter part of 1913 and much of 1914, a business recession laid a blighting hand on American industrial life. The dread specter of unemployment again stalked through the land. "Generals" Coxey and Kelly, with down-at-the-heel hoboes and other malcontents, again mobilized "armies" for a descent upon Washington. High-protection Republicans blamed the depression on the Underwood Tariff, which was admitting the handiwork of "cheap foreign labor."

World War, erupting in the summer of 1914, first deepened and then dispelled the depression. The shock resulting from the European blowup, which caused the New York Stock Exchange to close, threatened financial disaster. But gradually orders began to pour in from Europe for American bread and bullets. Business perked up, and before long the nation was basking in the sunlight of unprecedented prosperity.

But before war-boom days fully arrived, the voters had vented some discontent at the polls. The mid-term Congressional elections, held in November, 1914, reduced the margin of the Democratic majority in the House from 147 to 25. But this setback cannot correctly be interpreted as a repudiation of Wilson. His election in 1912 had been a three-party affair. The Congressional canvass of 1914 was the first straight-out two-party contest under Wilson; and as he won a clear majority in the House, the result could be hailed as a victory for the Democrats.

A potent slogan used by the Democrats in their successful mid-term elections (1914) was: "War in the East! Peace in the West! Thank God for Wilson!"

Triumphs for the Toilers

Fretful farmers were generally neglected by pro-business Republican regimes, but the Democratic Congress had enough momentum left to provide them with some relief. The Federal Farm Loan Act of 1916 made credit available to farmers at low rates of interest—a reform that had been demanded long before by the Populists. Notable among the several other attempts at rural relief was the Warehouse Act of 1916, which authorized loans on the security of staple crops. This was also a Populistic scheme. Other laws provided for aid in constructing highways and in establishing agricultural extension work in the colleges.

Laboring men, already benefited by the Clayton Act, received additional aid as the wave of progressive reform continued to foam forward. Common sailors, who had been treated with extreme brutality from cat-o'-nine-tail days onward, were now given welcome relief. The La Follette Seaman's Act of 1915, sponsored by "Fighting Bob" La Follette of Wisconsin, required decent wages, treatment, and food. But while helping mariners, the law hurt the merchant marine.

Standards were pushed so high that American shipping suffered in competition with the low-paying tramp steamers of the world.*

Other enlightened social reforms were signed by Wilson's busy pen. Notable among them was the Workingmen's Compensation Act of 1916, which granted assistance to federal civil service employees during periods of disability. In the same year Wilson approved an act restricting child labor on products flowing into interstate commerce. But this badly needed safeguard, as well as the child-labor law of 1919, was struck down by the Supreme Court as an invasion of states' rights.

Railroad workers, numbering about 1,700,000, were not sidetracked. An imminent strike on the railways threatened a crippling nationwide tie-up in 1916, with a consequent blow at the administration's belated attempts to launch a defense program. The organized Railroad Brotherhoods, pinched by the mounting cost of living, spurned mediation. Wilson then moved. In another surprise appearance before Congress, he urged sweeping concessions to the workers. The response was the Adamson Act of 1916, which established an eight-hour day for all employees on trains in interstate commerce, with extra pay for overtime. Ex-Professor Wilson, though earning the gratitude of the Brotherhoods, was assailed in business circles for his abject "surrender" to union officials.

"Too Cowed [Proud] to Fight," 1916. Congress Passes Adamson Eight-Hour Act. Harding in the Brooklyn *Eagle*.

Undoing Dollar Diplomacy

The quiet scholar-President, dedicated to New Freedoms, recoiled from the aggressive foreign policies of his predecessors. As a lover of peace and a hater of imperialism, he was repelled by the Big Stickism of Roosevelt. As an implacable foe of the big-money interests, he detested the so-called Dollar Diplomacy of Taft. He was convinced that little good could come out of Wall Street.

Wilson had been in office only a week when, in sensational fashion, he declared war on Dollar Diplomacy in Latin America. He announced that his administration would not support American bankers and other "interests" in that area, even though some of them had invested funds there as a result of Taft's promptings.

Shifting his attack from Latin America to the Far East, Wilson further shocked the financial world just a week later, in mid-March, 1913. He proclaimed that he would give no special assistance to American bankers who, under the proddings of Taft, had rather reluctantly embarked upon a six-nation loan in China. Wilson believed that this scheme, designed to finance a strategic Chinese railroad, encroached on the sovereignty of China. Worse yet, it might entangle the United States. The bankers, shivering from this Wilsonian bucket of cold water, pulled out of the project the next day. One critic snarled, "Dollar Diplomacy was at least better than none at all."

* So-called "flags of convenience" largely account for the immense amount of shipping registered in Liberia, Panama, and Greece.

But Wilson soon found, especially in Nicaragua, that his noble ideals clashed with political realities. An incomplete treaty with this banana republic, negotiated under Taft's Dollar Diplomacy, offered splendid strategic advantages. Bryan therefore proceeded to complete a more favorable new one in 1916. It placed Nicaragua even more securely within the orbit of the United States by granting a perpetual option on a Nicaraguan canal route, together with a ninety-nine-year lease on sites for bases near both ends. The pact was so sweeping as to make Taft's Dollar Diplomacy, in the words of one critic, look like mere "ten-cent diplomacy."

Anti-Imperialism Becomes Wilsonian Imperialism

Revolution-rent Haiti likewise forced Wilson to eat his anti-imperialistic words. The climax of disorders came in 1914–1915, when an outraged populace literally tore to pieces the brutal Haitian president. In both years Wilson was reluctantly forced to dispatch marines to protect American lives and property. In 1916 Washington concluded a treaty with Haiti which provided for United States supervision of finances and police, and which made the mulatto republic a protectorate of its giant neighbor. Sovereignty-loving Haitians resented the presence of the Yankees; and various uprisings occurred, in which hundreds of natives were killed.

To Wilson's distress, the story of Santo Domingo seemed like a carbon copy of the Haitian intervention. Serious outbursts in the island republic brought the leathernecked marines in 1916, and the debt-cursed land came under the protecting wings of the American

THE U.S. IN THE CARIBBEAN

eagle. Increasingly the Caribbean Sea, with its vital approaches to the now-completed Panama Canal, was taking on the earmarks of a Yankee preserve.

The purchase of the Danish West Indies (the Virgin Islands), concluded in 1917, tightened the grip of the *Yanqui* in these shark-infested waters. Washington was forced to pay the war-inflated price of $25,000,000, its costliest territorial addition. This fancy figure reflected the fear that these isles might be occupied by the Germans for submarine bases, with disastrous results to American shipping. Uncle Sam thus acquired an expensive Caribbean "poorhouse"— three main islands and some fifty islets, peopled by about 20,000 impoverished blacks.

An embarrassed Wilson, now a prisoner of circumstances, had meanwhile changed his 1913 views on the six-power loan to China. Impelled by American self-interest and the stern realities of international politics after the outbreak of the World War, he did an about-face in 1917. Bewildered Wall Street bankers were now strongly urged to go back into the dubious enterprise. Thus the idealist-President, instead of reversing Taft's Dollar Diplomacy, succeeded in reversing himself.

In the midst of these flip-flops, Wilson and his Democratic following did succeed in steering their traditional course in regard to the Philippines. Ever since Bryan's heyday, the Democrats had favored cutting loose from this burdensome overseas liability. The Filipinos, who panted for complete freedom, were immensely heartened in 1916, when the Democratic Congress passed the Jones Act. It granted the boon of virtual territorial status, and declared flatly that the United States would grant independence as soon as a "stable government" could be established.

Wilson Demands Fair Play for Japan and Britain

The menacing clouds of a crisis with Japan had meanwhile appeared in 1913. California's legislature, seeking to discourage the procreative and acquisitive Japanese, was drafting legislation to debar them from owning land in the Golden State. Tokyo, ever sensitive to slights, lodged vigorous protests, which touched off nasty talk of war. At fortress Corregidor, in the Philippines, American gunners were kept on an around-the-clock alert for six weeks.

Wilson was deeply concerned. As a good Christian, he deplored discrimination against the Japanese in California. As a peace lover, he regretted action by one state that might involve all of the other forty-seven in a bloody conflict. Desperately seeking to avert a clash, he dispatched Secretary Bryan to California to plead with the legislature. The law that finally passed softened the slap somewhat by not mentioning the Japanese by name, but it prevented Oriental ownership of land by discriminating against "aliens ineligible to

"A New Sentry in the Caribbean Sea," 1916. Uncle Sam Sits on the Three Main Virgin Islands. Courtesy of Dayton *News*

citizenship." Nevertheless Wilson's intercession and Bryan's friend-liness helped calm Tokyo, and the crisis was surmounted.

The Japanese, already imperialistic-minded, took advantage of the European conflagration to present to Peking, in 1915, their "Twenty-one Demands." If accepted, these would impinge severely upon China's sovereignty and slam shut the Open Door. Under vigorous protests from Washington, Tokyo finally toned down some of its more offensive terms.

Nearer home, the disputed Panama Canal Tolls Act of 1912 caused Wilson sleepless nights. This law, passed by Congress in the dying months of the Taft regime, specifically exempted American coastwise ships from paying tolls. The Hay-Pauncefote Treaty with Britain in 1901 had granted America a free hand to build and fortify the canal —provided that she would open it to *all* nations on the same tolls-paying terms. Washington interpreted this pact to mean all *other* nations; the British interpreted it to mean *all* nations, including the United States. Downing Street consequently lodged emphatic protests.

Wilson, according to his secretary, J. P. Tumulty, spoke of resigning and making an "appeal to the people" if he did not win on the canal tolls. "In case of failure in this matter," Tumulty quotes Wilson as saying, "I shall go to the country, after my resignation is tendered, and ask it to say whether America is to stand before the world as a nation that violates its contracts as mere matters of convenience, upon a basis of expediency."

Wilson was thus squeezed between international morality and political expediency. The exemption for American ships was popular, especially among the Irish-Americans, who cheered any twisting of the Lion's tail. But the more Wilson read the treaty, the more con-vinced he was that America was breaking her promise to London, no matter what her government's hairsplitting lawyers argued. As a Southern gentleman, he believed that a nation of honor, like a man of honor, should keep its promise—all the more so if it was powerful enough to prevail.

Appearing before Congress in March, 1914, Wilson made a mov-ing plea for a repeal of the exemption. The House and Senate, after a stormy debate, grudgingly granted his request. Grateful Britons, possibly as a result of a tacit understanding, continued to support Wilson's faltering Mexican policy. So it was that less than two weeks before the eruption of World War I, the last serious dispute with London was settled. This fact had an important bearing on the pro-British attitude that prevailed in America at the onset of the conflict.

Revolution below the Rio Grande

Rifle bullets whining across the southern border served as a constant reminder that all was not well in Mexico. Under the three-decade dictatorship of Porfirio Díaz—"Díazpotism"—the natural resources of Mexico had been exploited by foreign investors in oil, railroads, and mines. By 1913 American capitalists had optimistically sunk about a billion dollars into this backward but richly endowed country, and about 50,000 American citizens had taken up residence south of the Rio Grande.

This surface calm to the south merely concealed the combustibles of revolution. For if Mexico was rich, the Mexicans were poor. Most of the 15,000,000 inhabitants—predominantly peons—were landless, while a handful of wealthy landowners and foreign capitalists monopolized the wealth. Little wonder that the masses began to agitate for reform, under the leadership of men like Francisco Madero, a California-educated visionary.

A blowup began in 1910, and the next year the aging Díaz fled the country to escape revolutionary vengeance. President Madero, his successor, proved utterly incapable of controlling the swirling forces thus unleashed. The revolution took an ugly turn in February, 1913, less than two weeks before Wilson entered the White House, when Madero was murdered by a conscienceless clique. It included General Huerta, a full-blooded Indian, who a few days earlier had made himself ruler.

President Wilson, to whom Taft gladly passed on the Mexican muddle, was at the outset presented with a giant-sized headache. The turmoil in Mexico inevitably led to the destruction of American lives and property, and to an angry outcry in the United States for armed intervention. Prominent among those beating the tom-toms for war was the influential chain-newspaper publisher, William R. Hearst, whose views presumably were colored by his owning a Mexican ranch larger than Rhode Island.

Yet Wilson stood firm against intervention. As a peace lover, he was opposed to violent methods, especially in behalf of the greedy "interests" that he distrusted. He persuasively justified his stand in a speech at Mobile, Alabama, in October, 1913, when he declared that it was "perilous" to determine foreign policy "in the terms of material interest." For good measure, he went on to proclaim that the United States would never take "one additional foot of territory by conquest." This reassuring promise was widely heralded as a retreat from the interventionist twist given the Monroe Doctrine by Theodore Roosevelt.

Uncle Sam Refuses Huerta's Blood-Drenched Hand. New York *Daily Tribune*, 1913

General-President Huerta, though bloody-handed, brought a semblance of order to Mexico. His government was gradually recognized by a number of foreign powers, especially after he had shown a tolerant attitude toward their investors. Washington would normally have granted recognition also, for traditional policy had been to recognize firmly entrenched (*de facto*) governments, whether established by bullets or ballots.

But Wilson, dead set against recognizing "government by murder," put idealism above traditionalism. Committed to the New Freedom at home, he would not be a party to crushing freedom abroad. He steadfastly refused to extend the right hand of fellowship to that "desperate brute" Huerta, who seemingly did not have the support of the Mexican masses. "I am going to teach the South American republics to elect good men," the ex-schoolmaster assured a visiting Briton.

Not content with merely holding the line, Wilson next undertook to drive "the unspeakable Huerta" from office. In 1914 he lifted an earlier embargo on arms so that munitions could flow to Huerta's principal rivals, white-bearded Venustiano Carranza and swarthy Francisco ("Pancho") Villa. Drawing a sharp distinction between the poor peons and their ruthless rulers, Wilson insisted that he was trying to help the Mexican people shake off their tyrants. Over in Germany, Emperor Wilhelm II sneered, "Morality [is] all right, but what about the dividends?"

Wilson's policy of "watchful waiting," as he called it, was condemned by Big Business Republicans and other American investors. "Wrathfully waiting," they preferred the brass-knuckled stability that would come with a "strong man" like Huerta. Pressure upon Wilson for forcible intervention mounted, especially when dozens of Americans were killed during recurrent disorders. The President's course was branded as "deadly drifting," while Theodore Roosevelt jeered, "He kissed the blood-stained hand that slapped his face."

Congressman Humphrey voiced Republican complaints against Wilson's Mexican policy in 1916: "It is characterized by weakness, uncertainty, vacillation, and uncontrollable desire to intermeddle in Mexican affairs. He has not had the courage to go into Mexico nor the courage to stay out. . . . I would either go into Mexico and pacify the country or I would keep my hands entirely out of Mexico. If we are too proud to fight, we should be too proud to quarrel. I would not choose between murderers."

American Meddling and Muddling in Mexico

The Mexican volcano erupted at the Atlantic seaport of Tampico, in April, 1914, when a small party of American sailors was arrested and taken from a United States navy launch plainly displaying the Stars and Stripes. Although the captives were promptly released with expressions of regret, the hotheaded American admiral demanded a formal apology and a salute of twenty-one guns. Huerta defiantly refused to salute the flag of a nation that did not even recognize him as the ruler of Mexico.

Wilson, heavy-hearted but stubbornly determined to eliminate Huerta, went before Congress to ask for authority to use force in Mexico. After two days of heated debate, permission was granted, on April 22, 1914. But one day earlier, Wilson had ordered naval units, which were seeking to intercept a German merchantman laden with arms for Huerta, to capture the city of Vera Cruz. The marines and sailors gained their objective, which cost the lives of 19 Americans and some 200 Mexicans, to say nothing of the wounded. War hysteria swept the United States, and a full-dress shooting conflict seemed inevitable.

At this critical juncture Wilson was rescued from a point of no return. The ABC Powers—Argentina, Brazil, and Chile—fearful of another Mexican War, tendered their good offices. Washington promptly and gratefully accepted. The upshot was a meeting at Niagara Falls, in mid-1914, at which the five nations concerned were represented. Although the immediate results were inconclusive, the United States was able to show to the world its determination not to crush Mexico.

Huerta at length collapsed under the pressures from within and without. Resigning in July, 1914, and fleeing to Spain, he was soon succeeded by his arch rival, strong-willed Carranza. Wilson's "watchful waiting," though savagely condemned, was successful at least to this extent.

The sinister figure of "Pancho" Villa had meanwhile stolen the spotlight. A bloodthirsty combination of bandit and Robin Hood, he emerged as the chief rival of President Carranza, whom Wilson reluctantly supported with shipments of arms. Villa showed his contempt and hatred for the "gringos" in January, 1916, when his followers killed eighteen United States citizens in cold blood at Santa Ysabel, Mexico. The culminating outrage occurred in March, 1916, when Villistas shot up Columbus, New Mexico, leaving behind seventeen dead Americans and many others injured, but suffering much heavier losses themselves.

General John J. ("Black Jack")* Pershing, a grim-faced and ramrod-erect veteran of the Cuban and Philippine campaigns, was ordered to break up the bandit band. His hastily organized force of several thousand troops penetrated deep into Mexico with remarkable speed, mauled the Villistas, and narrowly missed capturing Villa. President Carranza permitted the invasion with reluctance, and only after a face-saving agreement that would permit Mexico to invade the United States under reversed conditions.

Pershing's expedition—"the perishing expedition," it was dubbed—at length ran into a blind alley. In the face of clashes with the Carranzista forces and imminent war with Germany, the invading army was withdrawn early in January, 1917.

But the seemingly fruitless foray into Mexico was not without consequence. The confused mobilization of American troops, including the National Guard, advertised military weaknesses and

* So-called from his earlier service as an officer with the crack Negro 10th Cavalry.

THE UNITED STATES AND MEXICO, 1914–1917

helped spur the preparedness movement. The Germans were not impressed with America's armed strength, and the spectacle of the frustrated Pershing expedition was before them when they decided to push Wilson into war with their all-out submarine attacks.

Wilsonian Winnings in Mexico

Wilson's Mexican policy, despite charges of spinelessness, had much to commend it. Elevating human rights above property rights, in the spirit of the New Freedom, the idealist-moralist in the White House strove to leave the masses of Mexico free to reap the fruits of their own revolution. And this they did in the troubled decades that lay ahead.

In dealing with Mexico, Wilson proved to be as much a man of vision as a visionary. He kept his hands free for more pressing crises elsewhere, especially those involving the German submarines. He avoided the vexations and bloodshed of a full-fledged war—a conflict that would have absorbed vast amounts of blood and money. He resisted the clamor for taking over all Mexico—an operation that would have resembled the Philippine vexation, only many times multiplied.

Wilsonian righteousness, despite serious blunders, emerged reasonably clean from the Mexican muddle. "We can afford," the President had told Congress in 1913, "to exercise the self-restraint of a really great nation which realizes its own strength and scorns to misuse it." Even though America's interests elsewhere required a modified use of Dollar Diplomacy, Wilson still tried to steer his stormy course by the far-off stars of idealism.

SELECT READINGS

Ripe scholarship is compressed into A. S. LINK, *Woodrow Wilson and the Progressive Era, 1910–1917* (1954).* A sketchy overview is W. E. LEUCHTENBURG, *The Perils of Prosperity, 1914–1932* (1958).* Social and intellectual currents are described in H. F. MAY, *The End of American Innocence: A Study of the First Years of Our Own Time, 1912–1917* (1959).* A brief biography of Wilson is J. A. GARRATY, *Woodrow Wilson* (1956); more detailed is ARTHUR WALWORTH's Pulitzer-prize *Woodrow Wilson* (2 vols., 1958).* See also J. M. BLUM, *Woodrow Wilson and the Politics of Morality* (1956).* The earlier presidential years are examined in depth by A. S. LINK, *Wilson: The New Freedom* (1956).* Aspects of Wilson's Mexican policy are interestingly presented in R. E. QUIRK, *An Affair of Honor: Woodrow Wilson and the Occupation of Vera Cruz* (1962)* and C. C. CLENDENEN, *The United States and Pancho Villa* (1961). See also P. E. COLETTA, *William Jennings Bryan: Progressive Politician and Moral Statesman* (1969). Also *Harvard Guide,** Pt. VI.

RECENT REFERENCES

P. E. COLETTA, *William Jennings Bryan* (vol. II), *1909–1915* (1969).

* Available in paperback.

36

The Road to World War I

Property can be paid for; the lives of peaceful and innocent people cannot be. The present German submarine warfare against commerce is a warfare against mankind.

Woodrow Wilson, War Message, April 2, 1917

Thunder across the Sea

Europe's powder magazine, long smoldering, blew up in the summer of 1914, when the flaming pistol of a Serb patriot killed the heir to the throne of Austria-Hungary. An outraged Vienna government forthwith presented a stern ultimatum to neighboring Serbia, and war seemed inevitable. Austria-Hungary hoped to localize the conflict between herself and the Serbians, as Germany most ill-advisedly gave her Austro-Hungarian ally a blank-check promise of support.

An explosive chain reaction followed. Tiny Serbia, backed by her powerful Slav neighbor, Russia, refused to bend the knee sufficiently. The Russian Czar began to mobilize his ponderous war machine, menacing Germany on the east. At the same time his ally, France, was confronting Germany on the west. The Germans in alarm suddenly struck at France through unoffending Belgium; their objective was to knock their ancient enemy out of the war so that they would have a free hand to repel Russia. Great Britain, her coastline jeopardized by the assault on Belgium, was sucked into the conflagration on the side of France.

"The Great Wall," 1914. Courtesy of Nashville *Tennessean*

Almost overnight most of Europe was involved in a fight to the death. On one side were arrayed the Central Powers: Germany and Austria-Hungary—and later Turkey and Bulgaria. On the other side were the Allied Powers, principally France, Britain, and Russia—and later Japan and Italy. The network of alliances on which the peace of Europe had been precariously balanced seemed to be pulling the nations into the slippery abyss, much like falling mountain climbers tied to the same rope.

Americans were stunned and bewildered, though not completely surprised. For something like two decades alarmists had predicted a European upheaval, but previous crises had all been surmounted. The cry of "wolf, wolf" had been raised so many times that the American people could hardly believe that the dread beast was at last on the loose. They instinctively thanked God for the ocean moats, and self-righteously congratulated themselves on having had ancestors wise enough to emigrate from the hell pits of Europe. America felt strong, snug, secure.

President Wilson promptly issued the routine proclamation of neutrality, and later warned his countrymen to be neutral in both thought and deed. At heart pro-Ally, he was a lifelong admirer of British civilization and a rather frequent summer visitor to the British Isles. But outwardly he kept his sympathies in check, at least during the early stages of the conflict.

Most Americans, though earnestly desiring to stay out of the blood bath, on the whole sympathized strongly with the Allied camp. Perhaps half of the people, who now numbered about 100,000,000, traced their lineage back to British or Canadian sources. A hundred different cultural and economic ties bound the Republic to Great Britain, while Anglo-American diplomatic relations had recently risen to a new level of friendliness.

But enthusiasm for the Allies would have been much less warm if bleeding France had not been in their ranks. The hearts of many Americans went out to their traditional friend, and a few volunteers entered her armed services, notably the aviation unit known as the Lafayette Escadrille. France had helped to win independence, and Americans felt that they owed her an unrepayable debt. Robert Underwood Johnson prayed:

Forget us, God, if we forget
The sacred sword of Lafayette!

The fate of Belgium deepened pro-Ally sentiment in America. This tiny nation, by an act of unprovoked aggression, had been largely flattened by the German steam roller. Countless Belgians were facing starvation when boyish-faced Herbert Hoover, a spectacularly successful mining engineer who happened to be in London, was chosen to form a relief organization. The young master-organizer, then only forty years of age, did a magnificent job of feeding the Belgians. He was aided by generous gifts from fellow Americans, whose hearts naturally went with their donations.

Wellsprings of Anti-German Animus

When war flamed across Europe, the German-Americans comprised the largest single foreign-born group. Counting persons with at least one foreign-born parent, transplanted peoples from the Central Powers numbered about 11,000,000. Countless thousands of German-Americans and other pro-German "hyphenated" Americans, many of whom had emigrated only physically, expressed noisy sympathy for the Fatherland. They were enthusiastically abetted by numerous Irish-Americans, who naturally cheered any foe of their ancient enemy, Great Britain.

But the American people as a whole were anti-German from the outset. Germany, as a chip-on-the-shoulder newcomer among the powers, had discriminated against America's allegedly diseased pork, and had collided with American expansionist ambitions in Samoa and at Manila Bay. Elbowing for "a place in the sun," the Germans had joined the imperialistic scramble in China, the East Indies, the Pacific, and Africa. Their low-priced goods, bearing the fearsome trademark "Made in Germany," had displaced those of many foreign competitors, including Yankees.

The Germans, moreover, seemed born to the sword. They had recently overtaken the United States in the naval race, and their magnificent army of goose-steppers was reputed to be the most formidable in Europe. In short, the Germans were identified in the American mind with navalism, militarism, and saber-rattling jingoism. And

Herbert Hoover as a Young Mining Engineer. Crandall Collection, Hoover Institution, Stanford, California

Principal Foreign Elements in the United States (*Census of 1910*)
[TOTAL U. S. POPULATION: 91,972,266]

	Country of Origin	Foreign-born	Natives with Two Foreign-born Parents	Natives with One Foreign-born Parent	Total
Central Powers	Germany	2,501,181	3,911,847	1,869,590	8,282,618
	Austria-Hungary	1,670,524	900,129	131,133	2,701,786
Allied Powers	United Kingdom	1,219,968	852,610	1,158,474	3,231,052
	Ireland	1,352,155	2,141,577	1,010,628	4,504,360
	Russia	1,732,421	949,316	70,938	2,752,675
	Italy	1,343,070	695,187	60,103	2,098,360
Total for all foreign countries (including those not listed)		13,345,545	12,916,311	5,981,526	32,243,282

The Kaiser Ravishes Belgium.
New York *World,* 1914

their Emperor, Kaiser Wilhelm II, seemed to be the embodiment of the dangers of German aggression, arrogant autocracy, and decadent monarchism. With villainous upturned mustaches, and a sinister withered arm which suggested degeneracy, he antagonized an America that was traditionally anti-monarchical.

Germany sank even lower in American esteem in 1914, when she seemingly provoked the war with calculated malice. It mattered not that the other major powers, as historians were later to prove, shared some of the blame. Germany's guilt seemed beyond dispute when she assaulted "poor little Belgium," whose neutrality she and the other powers had solemnly guaranteed by treaty as far back as 1839. The misdeed took on a more evil aspect when the German Chancellor blunderingly dismissed the neutrality pact as a mere "scrap of paper."

Atrocities always occur in large-scale wars—and on both sides. Most of this conflict was fought on non-German soil, and the inevitable clashes with civilians dyed the German villains a deeper black. Many Americans even came to believe that the green-clad German warriors thundered through Belgium with babies impaled on their bayonets. The Allies, for their part, were careful not to publicize the rapes and other barbarities committed by their own soldiers.

The brutal execution of Miss Edith Cavell by the Germans in Belgium was one of the worst blunders of the war. Their victim, an English nurse behind German lines, had helped scores of convalescent Allied soldiers to escape so that they might fight another day. Her death before a firing squad was legally defensible, but it was incredibly stupid, for she was a woman and a nurse. The shock to the civilized world was reinforced by such effective propaganda as the American motion picture entitled "Edith Cavell, the Woman the Germans Shot."

Paper Bullets

America was the richest and most powerful of the neutrals. Her open aid, or at least her sympathy, was well worth cultivating.

Allied propagandists, especially the British, enjoyed unusual success in the United States. They were careful to use the tactics of the gentle wooer, partly because they could be sure of a sympathetic hearing. Moreover, most of the transatlantic stories were filtered through British cables, and the scissors of the censors sheared away versions harmful to the Allied cause.

Allied agents drenched the United States with tales of German savagery—tales that stressed the inhuman submarine warfare and the abuse of Belgium. Charges of "Hunnish" barbarity were strengthened by atrocity stories, many of which later proved false. Among these hoaxes were a "crucified Canadian," a "corpse factory" where

Germans supposedly converted human bodies into soap, Belgian babies with their hands amputated, and Belgian maidens with their breasts slashed off.

German propaganda in America fell on much less fertile ground. A hostile reception was almost certain, owing to the long background of Teutonic friction and blundering. German suitors for America's favor, moreover, were inclined to use the crude embrace of the cave man, without sufficient finesse. And what little they did accomplish was largely undone by the ruthlessness of the militarists in the Fatherland.

A dispute persists as to the effectiveness of Allied propaganda. No one can deny that there was a vast amount of it, but no one can measure its effects with precision. Most Americans were undoubtedly pro-Ally from the beginning, and atrocity tales from overseas merely confirmed their existing prejudices. Allied propaganda, though partly fictional, was generally based on facts, notably the invasion of Belgium, the shooting of Edith Cavell, and the sinking of the *Lusitania*.

Pro-Ally sentiment in America deepened as the anxious neutrality period lengthened. Ardent Allied sympathizers declared that only a "moral eunuch" could be neutral in thought, as Wilson had urged. The feeling took root that Britain was "fighting our fight," and that a person was not "100% American" unless he was pro-Ally. But the great majority still fervently hoped that they could stay out of the terrible war.

America Earns Blood Money

When Europe burst into flames in 1914, the United States was still bogged down in the business recession of 1913–1914. The British and French hastened to place huge orders for war materials, and soon American industry pulled itself out of the morass of hard times onto a peak of wartime prosperity.

As the war machine in Europe chewed up munitions, the Allies

U. S. Exports to Belligerents, 1914–1916

	1914	1915	1916	Percentage Relation of 1916 Figure to 1914 Figure
Britain	$594,271,863	$911,794,954	$1,526,685,102	257%
France	159,818,924	369,397,170	628,851,988	393%
Italy*	74,235,012	184,819,688	269,246,105	364%
Germany	344,794,276	28,863,354	288,899	0.08%

* Italy joined the Allies in April, 1915.

began to exhaust their credits in the United States. If the nation were not to be plunged back into the dreary days of depression, so the argument ran, American bankers would have to lend huge sums of money to the Allied governments. The Wilson administration at first frowned upon these loans, for they seemed like a flagrant act of unneutrality. But such objections rapidly faded before the prospect of renewed economic distress.

Private enterprise, notably the Wall Street firm of J. P. Morgan and Company, came to the rescue. Largely through bond sales in the United States, American agencies were able to advance to the Allies during the period of neutrality the enormous sum of $2,300,000,000. At the same time, Wall Street lent only $27,000,000 to the Germans, who were regarded as poor risks. Thus the Americans were not only selling munitions to the Allied camp—munitions that were making thousands of German widows and orphans—but were providing the necessary money.

The Fatherland, the chief German-American propaganda newspaper in the United States, cried, "We [Americans] prattle about humanity, while we manufacture poisoned shrapnel and picric acid for profit. Ten thousand German widows, ten thousand orphans, ten thousand graves bear the legend 'Made in America.'"

Germany and Austria-Hungary protested bitterly against the immense trade in munitions, for America was becoming the chief arsenal of the Allies. But this profitable if bloody business was undoubtedly legal. The Germans themselves, as neutrals, had earlier sold military hardware for a profit. Washington made it clear to Germany and Austria-Hungary that America was showing no favoritism: she would be delighted to make money out of them also, if they would only come and get the munitions. The catch was that the British blockade prevented deliveries.

Germany Seeks to Stop Arms Shipments

German-American groups, raising loud but futile protests, demanded that Washington forbid all shipments of arms abroad. Such a stoppage would have been entirely lawful. But by the time Congress came to grips with the explosive issue, the so-called "merchants of death" were reaping lush profits—and the new prosperity was too precious to be cast aside.

An American embargo on munitions would have been a heaven-sent boon to the Germans. They had built up their vast war machine with adequate stockpiles of military supplies, knowing well that, in the face of a British blockade, they probably could not import armaments from abroad. The sea-controlling Allies had amassed less formidable stockpiles, partly because they knew that they could count on supplementary arms from neutrals, including the United States.

A stoppage of American munitions would have been a signal victory for the Germans, a stunning defeat for the Allies. Whether America did something or nothing about halting arms shipments, she would appear to be unneutral. So she followed the profitable path of doing nothing—a course that was all the easier because her heart was with the Allies. Economically she was thus bound closer and closer to the Allied war chariot by the golden chains of trade.

German and Austrian secret agents, under orders to interrupt the flow of munitions, resorted to violence. They fomented strikes in the arms factories, and plotted fires, explosions, and other acts of sabotage. Their sinister hand was believed to be seen in the wrecking of the New Jersey Black Tom munitions plant, which blew up in 1916 with a loss of $22,000,000. Two German attachés in Washington, as well as the Austro-Hungarian Ambassador, were implicated in such underhanded schemes and were forced to leave the country in 1915.

In the end German plottings backfired badly. In August 1915, Dr. Albert, a key German agent, absent-mindedly left his briefcase on a New York elevated car. It was promptly picked up by an American Secret Service agent, and some of the documents were published in the newspapers. The American imagination was further filled with images of German spies—men with short-cropped square heads and rolls of fat on the backs of their bull necks. Thus American opinion, already ill-disposed, was further turned against the Kaiser and his Fatherland. The result was that much German propaganda had a backlash effect.

Britain's Blockade of Germany

Diplomatic relations with Britain, despite America's pro-Ally bias, were not all smooth sailing. The global struggle, as during the Napoleonic Wars, involved a contest for sea power. And the United States, as earlier, was the most flourishing neutral carrier. The naval blockade, which was still Britain's most potent offensive weapon, was bound to bruise American shippers.

Early in the war, the British inaugurated their slow-strangulation blockade of Germany. Among other steps, they proclaimed the North Sea a military zone and proceeded to mine it heavily. Neutral ships approaching the European coast were forced to stop at the neck of the British bottle for inspection and—if approved—for their sailing directions through the deadly mined area. They would not be approved, naturally, if they carried contraband of war. The British, arbitrarily redefining contraband, included foodstuffs and other items not hitherto regarded as directly useful in waging war. American farmers and manufacturers, feeling the pinch, raised loud and long-familiar cries of protest.

London likewise redefined blockade. A close-in blockade of the German coasts by warships, in the old-fashioned style, was rendered risky by modern long-range guns and by lurking submarines. Alleging "unusual" or "peculiar" conditions in this conflict, the British would force American ships off the high seas into their ports.

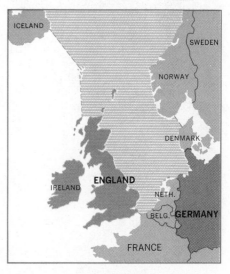

BRITISH MILITARY AREA
(Declared November 3, 1914)

GERMAN SUBMARINE WAR ZONE
(Declared February 4, 1915)

(Lusitania torpedoed, May 7, 1915)

The British-born Secretary of the Interior, Franklin Lane, wrote privately in May, 1915, "There isn't a man in the Cabinet who has a drop of German blood in his veins, I guess. Two of us were born under the British flag. I have two cousins in the British army, and Mrs. Lane has three. . . . Yet each day that we meet we boil over somewhat, at the foolish manner in which England acts. Can it be that she is trying to take advantage of the war to hamper our trade . . . ?"

There a leisurely search could be undertaken, sometimes with X-ray photographs, to inspect cotton bales and other cargo for concealed contraband. This highly irregular procedure, quite different from the offshore blockade sanctioned by international law, evoked emphatic protests from Washington. But since the British paid for many of the cargoes thus confiscated, the edge was taken off the complaints of the shippers.

The British also arbitrarily expanded the doctrine of continuous voyage, as interpreted by the United States during the Civil War. (See p. 455.) Germany's neutral neighbors, like Holland and Denmark, suddenly began to purchase from the United States enormous quantities of hitherto little-used goods. Imports of American lard into Denmark during the first few months of the war, for example, rose from virtually zero to 22,000,000 pounds. Obviously, some of these commodities were slipping into Germany through the neutral "conduit pipes." The British therefore limited such imports to their prewar proportions, and confiscated or diverted the rest. A loud squawk arose from American merchants, but again such complaints were partially quieted when London ultimately provided monetary compensation.

These annoying British practices violated American traditions, especially freedom of the seas. America in 1914–1915 had a powerful navy—the third strongest in the world. If she had used it to escort her merchant ships, the British would have been forced to abandon their objectionable practices, at least against the United States. They simply could not afford to quarrel with their overseas munitions depot.

Why did America fail to take a stronger stand? Her sympathies, including those of the Wilson administration, were with the Allies, and she did not want to drive them into a corner. The American Ambassador in London, editor-writer Walter H. Page, was bewitched by the British—the one race that had "guts." He therefore deliberately removed the sting from some of the official protests from Washington. In addition, American shippers could file claims and collect damages later, even though they might not make as juicy profits as they would have reaped if left alone. Finally, German tactics, especially with the submarine, were so inhumane as to eclipse British offenses.

The German Periscope Emerges

Germany did not tamely consent to being starved out by an illegal blockade—or one she regarded as illegal. Retaliating against the British for mining the North Sea, Berlin announced a submarine war area around the British Isles. The Germans were markedly inferior to Britain in their surface navy, but they had developed the murderous new submarine to a high pitch of efficiency. They therefore proclaimed, in February, 1915, that they would use their cigar-shaped marauders to sink all enemy merchant ships within the proscribed submarine zone.

German U-boat attacks posed a clear threat to the United States. Although Berlin officials declared that they would try not to sink *neutral* shipping, they conceded that mistakes probably would occur. Their aim was partly to frighten away neutral merchant ships, and thus tighten the counter-blockade of Britain. But President Wilson, outraged by the submarine menace, ringingly warned Germany that she would be held to "strict accountability" for any attacks on the American flag.

The submarine, as a commerce destroyer, was a weapon so new that existing international law could not be made to fit it. In the days of the sailing vessel, the rule had been that a warship, upon stopping a merchantman, must first of all dispatch a boarding party to ascertain its nationality and its cargo. If the victim was an enemy vessel—or a neutral vessel carrying contraband of war to the enemy—it might be captured or, if need be, sunk But destruction could not rightfully take place until the passengers and crew had been put in a position of safety—and this did not mean in small boats hundreds of miles from land.

The *Lusitania* leaving New York on her last voyage, 1915. Note that no guns are visible. U.S. Signal Corps, National Archives.

But the old sailing-ship practices were dangerous in the new machine age. If the fragile submarine emerged to give the customary warning, it might be rammed by the prow of the merchantman or sunk by one shot from a six-inch gun. After some disastrous experiences, the Germans became extremely cautious. They concluded that if they were going to use their potent new weapon at all, they had better launch their torpedoes first and write diplomatic notes later. They argued that if the antique rules of international law did not fit their modern weapons, the "unusual" or "peculiar" conditions of the war justified changing the rules.

Beleaguered Britons, who had done some rule changing of their own regarding blockades, heatedly replied that the rules could not be changed in the middle of the game. They insisted that if the submarine could not be used according to the rules, then the submarine, not the rules, ought to be scrapped. In short, the Germans were invited to withdraw their terrible new weapon—and lose the war.

The Lusitania's Last Trip, May 1915

German U-boats began their deadly work on schedule. From February to early May 1915, they sank about ninety ships of various kinds in the war zone. The grisly toll included one British passenger steamer, with the loss of an American life.

Then, on May 7, 1915, stark tragedy struck the England-bound *Lusitania*. This crack passenger liner, a four-funneled British Cunarder, was torpedoed without warning off the coast of Ireland and sank in eighteen minutes. The death roll numbered 1198 persons, 128 of whom were Americans. Many of the victims were women and children.

The salient facts about the *Lusitania* are clear. She was unarmed and unresisting. She was carrying 4200 cases of small-arms ammunition, as well as other munitions of war. Yet the nature of the cargo had no bearing whatever on the rule—long established in international law—that a passenger ship must be warned in advance of sinking.

Countless Germans, quite understandably, rejoiced over the destruction of this death-dealing cargo. One unauthorized German even struck off a fanciful medal showing the *Lusitania* bristling with huge cannon. But the United States, as well as much of the rest of the civilized world, was swept by a wave of shock and anger. This act of "mass murder" was condemned as "piracy," and the New York *Nation* branded the deed as one for which "a Hun would blush, a Turk be ashamed." "Damnable! Damnable! Absolutely hellish!" cried "Billy" Sunday, the acrobatic evangelist. The eastern part of the nation, closer to the war, seethed with talk of fighting. But the rest of the country showed a strong distaste for hostilities.

Wilson, the peace lover, set his jaw against leading a disunited nation into war. He well remembered the mistake in 1812 of his fellow Princetonian, James Madison. Instead, by a series of increasingly strong notes, he attempted to bring the German war lords sharply to book.

Wilson's hand was weakened and the Germans were pleased by these painful signs of disunity. The pacifist Secretary Bryan dramatically resigned rather than sign a protest that might spell shooting. Theodore Roosevelt, again athirst for war, assailed the "flubdubs" and "mollycoddles" who recoiled from fighting. He angrily condemned the "weasel words" of that word-lover in the White House, who had sent toothless note "No. 11,765, Series B."

Yet Wilson, sticking to his verbal guns, made some diplomatic progress. A new crisis developed in August, 1915, when another British liner, the *Arabic*, was sunk with a loss of two Americans. Berlin, responding to outraged protests from Washington, reluctantly agreed not to sink unarmed and unresisting passenger ships *without warning*. By thus partially muzzling the submarine, Wilson won a gratifying diplomatic victory—at least temporarily.

Pressures for Preparedness

Alert citizens had already recognized the need for strengthening the nation's military muscles, for the day might come when America would be sucked into the conflict. The navy was strong, but the army, numbering about 100,000 regulars, was weak. It ranked about fif-

The American Ambassador in Berlin reflected a German point of view on the Lusitania *when he cabled, "Anyway, when Americans have reasonable opportunity to cross the ocean [on American ships] why should we enter a great war because some American wants to cross on a [British] ship where he can have a private bathroom or because Americans may be hired to protect by their presence cargoes of ammunition? . . . Nor can English passenger ships sailing with orders to ram submarines and often armed be put quite in the category of altogether peaceful merchantmen."*

teenth among the armies of the world, in the same bracket with Persia. In 1915 the Secretary of War reported with alarm that he had only a two-day supply of ammunition for the artillery, much of which was obsolete.

Conspicuous among the champions of arming were Colonel Theodore Roosevelt and General Leonard Wood, old-time Rough Riders and now apostles of preparedness. They were largely instrumental in establishing, beginning in 1915, a number of summer training camps for officers, notably the one at Plattsburg, New York. Equipment was so short that trainees sometimes drilled with broomsticks in place of rifles. But even these feeble measures were opposed by the pro-German elements, by confirmed isolationists, and by pacifists. A song that caught the current mood was "I Didn't Raise My Boy to Be a Soldier."

Wilson Pulls Laggard Congress into Preparedness. Kirby in the New York *World,* 1916

President Wilson, still a pacifist at heart, revealed little enthusiasm at the outset for preparedness. His views were generally shared by Secretary Bryan, who proclaimed in 1915 with incredible naïveté that if war should come the President would issue a call and "the sun would go down on a million men in arms." But after repeated sinkings of passenger ships by German U-boats, Wilson gradually edged toward active preparedness. In December, 1915—fifteen long months after war had broken out in Europe—he belatedly urged Congress to roll up its sleeves for defense. Public pressures backed him up. Highlighting the popular agitation was a series of monster parades, one of which was led down Pennsylvania Avenue by a flag-holding Wilson.

The culmination of the preparedness campaign was a series of stop-gap measures passed by Congress, notably the National Defense Act of June, 1916. It was designed to beef up the regular army to 175,000 officers and men, and the National Guard to 450,000 officers and men, with provision for an officers' reserve corps. These increases were a promising step forward, but totally inadequate to meet the storm that was brewing.

Naval preparedness fared better, for the fleet was traditionally regarded as the first line of defense. President Wilson, early in 1916, called for "incomparably the greatest navy in the world." Congress responded, in August, 1916, with a grant of $313,000,000 for new construction—the largest defense appropriation that it had yet passed. Emphasis was mistakenly on big battleships—"white elephants of the sea"—rather than on the smaller and badly needed anti-submarine craft. War ended in Europe before a single new capital ship was completed.

The Council of National Defense, designed to coordinate industry and defense, was likewise created. It consisted of six Cabinet officers and seven unpaid civilians, all of whom did yeoman work in helping to unsnarl the tangled skeins of the national economy as war impended.

An expanded merchant marine, which was urgently needed for naval auxiliary purposes, also claimed attention. In September, 1916, Congress created the Shipping Board and appropriated $50,000,000 for the purchase or construction of urgently needed craft. This program likewise proved to be based upon a shocking underestimate of requirements.

Germany Muzzles the Submarine—Temporarily

Anti-travel legislation was meanwhile being urged, because the only sure way to prevent the killing of Americans on the high seas was to keep them out of submarine-infested waters. Early in 1916 two resolutions came before Congress, each of them designed to prohibit citizens from sailing on armed belligerent merchant ships or passenger liners into the danger zones. Both proposals commanded an impressive amount of support in Congress and throughout the country.

But Wilson, ever the stubborn idealist, was alarmed by these weak-kneed proposals. He argued that if America surrendered her technical rights to sail on belligerent vessels, she would soon be forced to make other concessions. Before long the whole "fine fabric" of international law would break down, as much of it already had. Wilson earnestly believed that to yield such rights, even slightly, would be dishonorable.

"Scant Room for Postscripts." *Sussex* Affair Causes Wilson to Write "Finis." Courtesy of Newark *News*

These two "scuttle" resolutions in Congress were finally side-tracked, as Wilson brandished his presidential club. American citizens continued to sail into the danger zones, where they had a perfect right to go. But when killed, they were just as dead as if they had been wrong.

An alarming new crisis developed with Germany in March, 1916, after she had honored the *Arabic* "muzzling" pledge for six months. A French cross-channel passenger steamer, the *Sussex*, was struck by a German torpedo, with some loss of life and serious injuries to several Americans. This attack, at least outwardly, seemed like a deliberate violation of earlier assurances by Berlin.

Infuriated by the *Sussex* assault, Wilson went out on a limb. He informed the Germans, in angered phrases, that they must renounce the inhuman practice of sinking merchantmen without warning. Otherwise he would have to break diplomatic relations—an almost certain prelude to war.

Germany grudgingly accepted Wilson's *Sussex* ultimatum, thereby agreeing not to sink passenger ships and merchantmen without proper warning. But she attached a long string to her acceptance: America would have to persuade the Allies to respect international law in their blockade. This, obviously, was something that Washington could not or would not do. Wilson promptly accepted the German pledge, without mentioning the "string." He thus won another temporary but precarious diplomatic victory—precarious because Germany could pull the string whenever she chose, and the President would have to sever relations.

Wilson Runs on an Anti-War Ticket (1916)

As the presidential year 1916 loomed, the Bull Moose Progressives of 1912 rallied once again around Roosevelt. Meeting in Chicago in their "swan song" convention, they uproariously renominated the Rough Rider. But Roosevelt, who hated Wilson and all his works, had no stomach for leading another hopeless cause that would again split the Republicans and insure the re-election of the pacifistic professor. He therefore declined the nomination. In doing so he sounded the death knell of the Progressive Party, amid angry charges by Bull Moosers that he had betrayed them for his own selfish purposes.

The Republican convention also met in Chicago at the same time, with admirers of Roosevelt shouting, "Teddy, Teddy, Everybody's for Teddy." But Old Guard Republicans detested the renegade who had ruptured the party in 1912. Instead, they drafted Charles Evans Hughes, a vigorous, outwardly cold, and highly intellectual justice of the Supreme Court who had been loftily remote from the party split of 1912. His character was unimpeachable; his liberal achievements as governor of New York appealed to progressives; and his record as a member of the Supreme Court did not antagonize the Old Guard. The Republican platform condemned the Democratic tariff, Democratic assaults on the trusts, and Wilson's wishy-washiness in dealing with both Mexico and Germany.

The German-American. Only part American. *Life*, 1916. By permission

Wilson, the dominant Democrat, was nominated by acclamation in St. Louis. The most popular theme of the convention was that he had refused to fight at every provocation. In this wildly cheering assemblage, further inspiration was found for the slogan "He Kept Us Out of War."

The richly bewhiskered Hughes ("an animated feather duster") left the bench for the stump, and there he was not at home. In some speeches he assailed Wilson for not having stood up to the Kaiser more menacingly; in other areas, where the German-American vote was vital, he took a less bellicose line. This fence-straddling operation led to the jeer, "Charles Evasive Hughes."

Roosevelt, frothing for war, was a dubious asset to the Republicans. In a series of skin-'em-alive speeches against Wilson, he alienated many German-American voters, whom Hughes badly needed for victory. T.R. not only flayed that "damned Presbyterian hypocrite Wilson" but privately sneered at Hughes as a "bearded iceberg" and as a "whiskered Wilson"—the only difference between the two men being "a shave."

Democratic organizers, concentrating their fire on doubtful districts, played up the pro-Wilson slogan "He Kept Us Out of War." Orators warned the voters that by electing Hughes the nation would be electing a fight—with a certain frustrated Rough Rider leading the charge. A Democratic advertisement appealing to workingmen read:

You Are Working;
      —Not Fighting!
Alive and Happy;
      —Not Cannon Fodder!
Wilson and Peace with Honor?
      or
Hughes with Roosevelt and War?

The West Turns the Tide for Wilson

On election day Hughes, looking like a sure-fire winner, swept the East. This section contained a heavy concentration of voters who were anti-labor, anti-progressive, and pro-Big Business. Wilson went to bed that night prepared to accept defeat, while New York newspapers displayed huge portraits of "THE PRESIDENT-ELECT—CHARLES EVANS HUGHES."

But the rest of the country turned the tide. Middle Westerners and Westerners, attracted by Wilson's progressive reforms and anti-war policies, flocked to the polls for the President. War-boom prosperity also helped his cause. The final result, in doubt for several days, hinged on California, which Wilson carried by some 3800 votes out of about a million cast. The Golden State was lost to Hughes by the

PRESIDENTIAL ELECTION OF 1916 (with electoral vote by state)

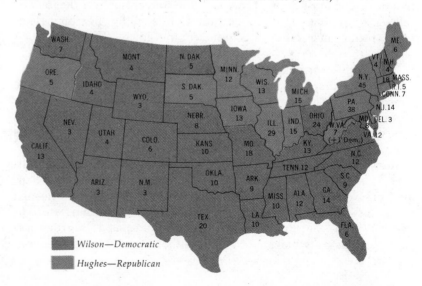

Wilson—Democratic

Hughes—Republican

blunders of his managers, notably the snub known as the "forgotten handshake." Though in the same hotel, Hughes had failed to meet California's favorite son, the fiery Progressive, Governor Hiram W. Johnson, T.R.'s running mate in 1912.

Wilson barely squeaked through, with a final vote of 277 to 254 in the Electoral College, and 9,129,606 to 8,538,221 in the popular column. The pro-labor Wilson, who had backed the eight-hour law for railroad men, received strong working-class support. His liberal reform program also won the votes of many ex-Progressives; the defeat of the Republicans stemmed largely from their failure to lure enough wayward Bull Moosers back into their camp. Wilson had not specifically promised to keep the country out of war, but probably enough people relied on such implicit assurances to insure his victory. The outcome could be written largely in terms of four "P's": peace, prosperity, Progressivism, and pro-laborism.

Germany's Brutal U-Boat Challenge

Wilson, desperately seeking peace, now undertook the role of world mediator. He perceived that the surest way to keep America out of the titanic conflict was to bring it to an end before the nation could become involved. In the hope of securing a negotiated peace, he bluntly called upon the belligerents, in December, 1916, to state their war aims. The Allied response was fuller and franker than that of the Germans, although the Allied leaders were privately annoyed by the efforts of the President to smoke them out. Like the Germans, they cherished secret imperialistic objectives that could not stand the pitiless light of publicity.

But Wilsonian mediation was foredoomed to failure. The simple truth is that by this time so much blood and treasure had been squandered that politicians could not face their people without the fruits of victory. Each side still hoped for a knockout blow.

Undaunted, Wilson next went before the Senate, on January 22, 1917, to deliver one of his most moving addresses. It was an open appeal to world opinion. To the dismay of the Allies, he declared that a victor's peace would not bring peace. "It must be a peace without victory," he insisted. "Only a peace between equals can last. . . ."

Germany's war lords answered Wilson with a blow of the mailed fist. Astounding both him and the civilized world, they announced, on January 31, 1917, that they were going to reopen their submarine campaign. This time they would sink *all* merchant ships, including America's, found within the stipulated danger zone.

American dealings with both Britain and Germany were then such as to increase the force of the U-boat bombshell. Ever since the *Sussex* pledge, some eight months earlier, relations with Berlin had been outwardly calm, while those with the Allies had been stormy.

During the 1916 campaign J. A. O'Leary, the head of a pro-German and pro-Irish organization, sent a scorching telegram to Wilson condemning him for having been pro-British in approving war loans and ammunition traffic. Wilson shot back an answer: "Your telegram received. I would feel deeply mortified to have you or anybody like you vote for me. Since you have access to many disloyal Americans and I have not, I will ask you to convey this message to them." Although Irish-Americans were traditionally Democratic, Wilson's devastating response almost certainly won him votes.

Regarding the British blacklist Wilson wrote to Colonel House (July 23, 1916), "I am, I must admit, about at the end of my patience with Great Britain and the Allies. This blacklist business is the last straw. . . . It is becoming clear to me that there lies latent in this policy the wish to prevent our merchants getting a foothold in markets which Great Britain has hitherto controlled and all but dominated." In later years House stated that if it had not been for Germany's submarine offenses, war might have come with Britain instead of Germany.

Ironically, both Germany and America were contending for freedom of the seas, each in its own way. Especially irritating to Americans was Britain's practice of searching neutral mails for enemy correspondence, allegedly with an eye to trade secrets. London also legally but offensively blacklisted German-tainted firms in the United States—firms with which His Majesty's subjects were forbidden to trade. Even the pro-Ally Wilson burst out that the "poor boobs" in England got on his "nerves."

The momentous U-boat declaration came as no sudden impulse. Fighting in Europe was stalemated on barbed-wire entanglements and in mud-choked trenches; delay meant that the noose of the British blockade was drawing tighter around the necks of 65,000,000 Germans. Germany's naval experts were confident that an all-out submarine campaign would knock Britain out of the war in a few months—as it almost did.

Berlin officials recognized that the U-boat proclamation was a virtual declaration of war. But what of it? The United States boasted a mighty fleet of battleships, yet Britain already dominated the surface of the sea. America had no formidable army, owing in part to Wilson's delay in backing an effective preparedness drive. Even if she had trained a powerful military force, she could not have transported and supplied it with the ships that she had. Seemingly she was already helping the Allies, with shipments of war materials, about all she could. The conflict would presumably be over, with Germany crowned the victor, before America the Unready could throw her full weight into the scales.

The Submarine Causes a Break with Berlin

Wilson, his high hopes for peace torpedoed by the U-boat announcement, was in the position of a poker player whose bluff has been called. In his *Sussex* ultimatum he had proclaimed in effect that if the German militarists should again open their ruthless submarine warfare, he would have to sever relations. This he reluctantly did on February 3, 1917, when the German Ambassador in Washington was handed his passport. There was no other way out—unless a proud, patriotic, and powerful America was to be humiliated in the eyes of the world.

Yet Wilson still nursed one flickering hope for peace. Despite evidence to the contrary, he could not bring himself to believe that the Germans would carry out their threat to sink American ships. Determined not to lead his people into war prematurely, he insisted on awaiting actual "overt" acts by German U-boats against American lives and property.

The issue of arming defenseless American merchantmen now thrust itself forward. As ships continued to cling to port, piled-up surpluses clogged the docks and economic paralysis began to grip the country. Mobs of irate housewives in New York demonstrated angrily for food. Wilson thereupon asked Congress for authority to arm American merchantmen. But a small band of anti-war Senators, conspicuously from the German-populated areas of the Middle West, helped to engineer a filibuster until Congress adjourned, March 3, 1917. Professor Wilson sternly lectured the "little group of willful men" who had rendered a great nation "helpless and contemptible." Then, finding the authority in an almost forgotten law, he sent American ships to sea armed with defensive guns.

Meanwhile the Zimmermann note, hardly less sensational than the U-boat declaration itself, had blazed into the headlines on March 1, 1917. Its author, the German Foreign Secretary, had secretly outlined a course of action pending a shooting war with America. Germany would seek to arrange a German-Mexican alliance, holding out to anti-Yankee Mexico the inducement of recovering Texas, New Mexico, and Arizona. Japan was also to be invited to join in the scheme. Hitherto the anti-Mexican Southwest and the anti-Japanese Pacific Coast had been lukewarm toward war. But this clumsy German note, intercepted by British agents, helped arouse the entire nation.

War by Act of Germany

Those long-dreaded "overt" acts finally came in mid-March, 1917. Four unarmed American merchantmen were sunk on the high seas by German U-boats, with a loss of thirty-six lives. As one Philadelphia newspaper observed, the "difference between war and what we have now is that now we aren't fighting back."

The *Illinois*, one of four unarmed American merchantmen sunk by Germany in mid-March 1917. Photo taken from the German submarine (foreground). Courtesy Department of the Navy

"I Dare You to Come Out."
Richards in the Philadelphia
North American, 1917

In the same March, 1917, the bitter prospect of fighting Germany was sweetened by news from Russia. An epochal upheaval suddenly overthrew Czarist tyranny and established a liberal provisional government. The American people could now look forward to fighting foursquare for democracy on the side of the Allies, without the black sheep of Russian despotism in the Allied fold.

A reluctant Wilson, unable to escape the pressure of "overt" acts, summoned Congress into special session. Pale and erect, he stood before the hushed joint session, on the evening of April 2, 1917, to read an inspired document. In solemn tones he declared that America had no quarrel with the German people, but only with their "military masters." By making war on all mankind they would not permit others to live in peace. Wilson then asked Congress to recognize the state of war "which has thus been *thrust* upon it." "It is a fearful thing," he concluded, to lead the nation into war, but "the right is more precious than peace. . . ."

On Good Friday, April 6, 1917, Congress responded with its fateful war resolution, acknowledging the fact that war had been "thrust" upon the Republic. Debate was brief but heated, with the count 82 to 6 in the Senate, and 373 to 50 in the House. The vote indicated a gratifying degree of unity, especially in the industrial and financial East, which had developed a strong stake in the success of the Allied cause.

Practically all of the dissenters were concentrated in the Middle West—notably in Wisconsin, Illinois, Missouri, and Minnesota—where the German-Americans were numerous and vocal. One of their Senatorial spokesmen, "Fighting Bob" La Follette of Wisconsin, stirred up a storm of protest when he shouted, "I say Germany has been patient with us." Additional members of Congress probably would have voted against war if they had dared defy the whirlwind of popular indignation.

Why War Came to America

Why were the American people finally dragged into the conflagration, despite their two and one-half years of determination to stay out?

The German U-boat was undoubtedly the precipitant. In a figurative sense, America's war declaration bore the well-known trademark "Made in Germany." Take away the submarine and the United States might have stayed out.

Choosing the right foe was not difficult. British and other Allied restrictions on American commerce were galling but endurable; claims for damages could be collected later. But Germany resorted to the mass killing of civilians; and there was no adequate monetary recompense for taking life. One Boston newspaper luridly concluded that while the Allies were "a gang of thieves," the Germans were "a gang of murderers." Many Americans were so deeply disturbed by the U-boat, and by its threat to freedom of the seas, that at the outset they proposed to fight a limited-liability war. They would pull out as soon as the Germans agreed to respect America's rights on the high seas.

But in pointing the finger of accusation solely at the blood-spattered submarine, the American people overlooked their own share of responsibility. Undeniably, the United States was in some degree to blame for inviting these ruthless reprisals. The Germans found it easier to resort to their last desperate throw of the dice because of America's seemingly unfriendly policies. She was sending munitions in vast quantities to their foes; she was advancing credits for such purchases; and she was acquiescing in the "unusual" British blockade that was slowly starving the Fatherland. Bryan charged that the United States had failed to hold the scales of neutrality even —assuming that this was possible.

Once the "overt" acts came, the American people accepted the verdict of war with considerable enthusiasm. At heart they were pro-Ally. They were bound closely to the British and French by profitable golden threads, which were in danger of being cut off by ruthless German tactics. Repelled by German frightfulness, Americans swallowed Allied propaganda the more avidly. They finally came to believe, as one American newspaper headline put it: "ENGLAND'S DEFEAT OUR DEFEAT."

Fear of Germany's militaristic and monarchical threat to democracy was a clincher. Many Americans assumed that if the Kaiser won the war he would dash across the Atlantic, with millions of spike-helmeted soldiers. Hunnish "slitters of babies' throats" would brush aside the Monroe Doctrine, and then crush precious liberties under a Prussian boot heel. Even if there should be no immediate German assault, the triumph of the Kaiser would badly upset the long-established European balance of power. The United States would then, as many apprehensive Americans believed, be placed in ultimate jeopardy.

Dangers of a future attack, either directly or by way of Latin America, appear to have been more grave than those of an immediate invasion. Naval and military difficulties hampering a prompt overseas assault were immense. But countless Americans accepted such an attack as an alarming possibility. They preferred to fight in 1917, when they had European allies afloat, than to wait until they might have to face the wrath of the German militarists alone.

The American people were not duped into war by profit-seeking connivers. They were not dragged in, as later charged, by Wall Street bankers, propagandists, sloganeers, weaponeers, and munitioneers. Although loans for the Allies were not inexhaustible, the munitions

On March 20, 1917, shortly after the news of the sinking of three American ships had arrived, President Wilson met with his Cabinet. Secretary of the Navy Daniels recorded in his diary: "All declared for war except Burleson [Postmaster General] and I, and the President said, 'Burleson, you and Daniels have not spoken.' Burleson said he thought we were already at war [which was true], and that unless President called Congress the people would force action. The President said, 'I do not care for popular demand. I want to do right, whether popular or not.' . . . President was solemn, very sad!!"

makers were reaping indecent profits, unhampered by government restrictions and wartime excess-profits taxes. Their unpublished slogan might well have been "Neutrality Forever."

As the crisis developed early in 1917, America's entrance into the war became inevitable. Desperate German militarists, with confidence in their U-boats, had concluded that they had more to gain than to lose by making the United States an open enemy. Certain defeat was too high a price for them to pay for America's continued "neutrality."

SELECT READINGS

Refer to the previous chapter for the title by A. S. LINK; for full details see his *Wilson: The Struggle for Neutrality, 1914–1915* (1960); *Wilson: Confusions and Crises, 1915–1916* (1964); *Wilson: Campaigns for Progressivism and Peace, 1916–1917* (1965); for outlines, his *Wilson the Diplomatist* (1956).* A first-rate analysis is E. R. MAY, *The World War and American Isolationism, 1914–1917* (1959).* Sympathetic toward the Allies is CHARLES SEYMOUR, *American Diplomacy during the World War* (1934); unsympathetic is C. C. TANSILL, *America Goes to War* (1938). See also D. M. SMITH, *Robert Lansing and American Neutrality* (1958) and his *The Great Departure: The United States and World War I, 1914–1920* (1965).* Racy reading is found in H. C. PETERSON, *Propaganda for War* (1939) and BARBARA W. TUCHMAN, *The Zimmermann Telegram* (1958).* Also *Harvard Guide,*★ Pt. VI.

* Available in paperback.

37

The War to End War, 1917–1918

The world must be made safe for democracy. Its peace must be planted upon the tested foundations of political liberty. We have no selfish ends to serve. We desire no conquest, no dominion. We seek no indemnities for ourselves, no material compensation for the sacrifices we shall freely make.

President Wilson, War Message, April 2, 1917

Wilsonian Idealism Enthroned

In Woodrow Wilson, the man and the hour met. The lover of peace, as fate would have it, emerged as a magnificent leader of war. Flourishing the sword of righteousness, he aroused—almost hypnotized—the nation with his inspirational ideals.

What should be the keynote of the great crusade? German U-boats had unquestionably shoved a reluctant America into the abyss, but Wilson could whip up no enthusiasm, especially in the landlocked Middle West, by fighting to make the world safe against the submarine. He would have to proclaim less localized objectives and more glorified aims.

Wilson's burning idealism led him instinctively to an inspirational decision. Radiating the spiritual fervor of his Presbyterian forebears, he proclaimed the twin goals of "a war to end war"* and

---

* Wilson did not coin the phrase. In 1914 the English author H. G. Wells had published a book entitled *The War That Will End War*.

a crusade "to make the world safe for democracy." He did not believe that the Republic should fight to force its democratic way of life on other peoples. Rather, he sought to create an international atmosphere in which American democracy—any democracy—could prosper without fear of power-crazed autocrats and militarists.

This war, unlike most of its predecessors, was fought with a high degree of unity and enthusiasm. At the outset the nation experienced considerable apathy, confusion, and even downright opposition, especially among the influential German-Americans in the Middle West. But Wilson, holding aloft the torch of idealism, mobilized public emotion into an almost frenzied outburst. "Force, force to the utmost," he cried, while the country responded less elegantly with "Hang the Kaiser."

Selfishness and partisanship took a back seat. Highly paid business executives volunteered their services in Washington as "dollar-a-year men." Many Republicans in Congress, loyally subordinating politics, voted for Democratic measures. In fact, at times Republicans supported Wilson's proposals more strongly than the Democrats themselves.

The entire nation, catching the spirit of a religious revival, burst into song. This was undoubtedly America's singingest war. Popular on the serious side were "Keep the Home Fires Burning," "The Long, Long Trail," and above all George M. Cohan's spine-tingling "Over There":

Over there, over there.
  Send the word, send the word over there,
That the Yanks are coming, the Yanks are coming,
  *The drums rum-tumming ev'rywhere.**

Fourteen Potent Wilsonian Points

Wilson quickly came to be recognized as the moral leader of the Allied cause and the spokesman for it. His early speeches, though eloquent, were rather vague and overlong. Advisers urged him to boil down his main objectives into inspirational, placard-like paragraphs that would be effective propaganda. This he did admirably in his Fourteen Points Address, delivered on January 8, 1918, before an enthusiastic Congress. A primary purpose was to keep reeling Russia in the war. The general effect was to inspire the drooping Allies to mightier efforts, while demoralizing the war-weary enemy nations by holding out alluring promises to their dissatisfied minorities.

The first five of the Fourteen Points were broad in scope. (1) A proposal to abolish secret treaties pleased liberals of all countries.

---

* "Over There" by George M. Cohan; copyright 1917; copyright renewal 1945, Leo Feist, Inc. Used by special permission of copyright proprietor.

(2) Freedom of the seas appealed to the Germans, as well as to Americans who distrusted British sea power. (3) A removal of economic barriers among nations was comforting to Germany, which feared post-war vengeance. (4) Reduction of armament burdens was gratifying to taxpayers everywhere. (5) An adjustment of colonial claims in the interests of both the natives and the great powers concerned was reassuring, especially to those people who hated both imperialism and colonialism.

Other points among the Fourteen proved no less seductive. They held out the promise of partial or full independence to oppressed minority groups, such as the Poles, millions of whom lay under the heel of Germany and Austria-Hungary. The capstone point, Number Fourteen, foreshadowed the League of Nations—a hope-fraught international organization that was to provide a system of collective security. Wilson earnestly hoped that this new scheme would effectively guarantee the political independence and territorial integrity of all countries, whether large or small.

"The Message," 1918. Wilson's Fourteen Point Address Gives Hope to Oppressed Peoples. Courtesy of Omaha *World-Herald*

In subsequent addresses, hardly less lofty, Wilson clarified and supplemented his original Fourteen Points. The list finally came to number about twenty-three. With flaming phrases Wilson declared for a just, permanent, and open peace, while stressing the desirability of consulting subject peoples in the forthcoming treaty settlements. This last point—the self-determination "dynamite"—stirred anew many unrealizable hopes.

The so-called Fourteen Points proved to be a mighty engine of propaganda, for they undoubtedly undermined the enemy's "will to victory." In China, a translated volume of Wilson's speeches became a best seller. In lonely huts in the mountains of Italy, candles burned before poster-portraits of the revered American prophet. In Poland, starry-eyed university men would meet on the streets, clasp hands, and utter only one word, "Wilson."

Yet Wilson's appealing points, though raising up hopes the world over, were not everywhere applauded. Certain leaders of the Allied nations, with an eye to territorial booty, were less than enthusiastic. Hard-nosed Republicans at home grumbled, and some of them openly sneered at the "fourteen commandments" of "God Almighty Wilson."

A Nation's Factories Go to War

War began for America with dismal days. On land the Allies definitely were not winning, and on sea the silent submarines took a frightful toll in April and May of 1917. During the most dismaying weeks, merchant ships were being sunk at the rate of nine a day, and at one time England had grain supplies for only six weeks. The tide turned only when the British reluctantly adopted the convoy system and the Allies managed to perfect other anti-sub devices.

GROSS TONS

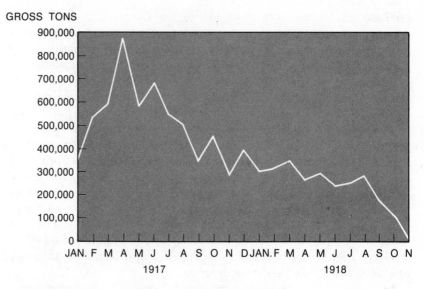

MERCHANT TONNAGE SUNK BY GERMAN U-BOATS
January, 1917–November, 1918

Victory was no foregone conclusion, and at best would involve a herculean effort. It would be achieved only if the country could unsnarl its red tape, reorganize its mighty industrial plant, and retool itself for fighting—while time still permitted. The struggle was a global conflict, which had to be fought as much with big smokestacks as with big guns. "It is not an army that we must train for war," proclaimed Wilson; "it is a nation."

An alarmed Congress conferred virtually dictatorial power on President Wilson, who delegated much of it to subordinates. Conspicuous among them were the members of the War Cabinet, which came to consist of the heads of the six key war boards.

A dictatorship over industry was established by the War Industries Board. This powerful agency was finally headed by silver-thatched Bernard M. ("Barney") Baruch, who had made his millions in stock-market speculation, and who was to become the famed "park-bench philosopher." The Baruch Board fixed prices, established priorities, and reduced waste. It also achieved increased production through standardization. Eight thousand tons of steel were cut each year from women's corsets, and 232 kinds of buggy wheels were reduced to four. Anti-trust legislation was relaxed to increase output. Women were encouraged to enter industry and also agriculture, where they were called "farmerettes." The old saying took a new twist: "A Woman's Place Is in the War."

Brawny-armed workers were urged to put forth their best efforts, spurred by the slogan "Labor Will Win the War." Tens of thousands of Southern Negroes were drawn to the North by the magnet of war industries—the large-scale beginnings of a movement of immense sociological significance. A New Jersey anti-loafing law required all able-bodied males to be regularly employed in some useful occupation, and a "Work or Fight" rule was issued by the War Department in 1918. Fortunately, Samuel Gompers and his powerful American Federation of Labor gave loyal support to the war effort.

Yet labor harbored grievances. Admittedly, the wages of 1914 had nearly doubled by 1918, and many manual laborers could sport gaudy silk shirts. But inflationary prices, boosted by the war, more than kept pace with the wage scale. The pinch of H.C.L.—"high cost of living"—was felt in every modest American home. Not even the call of patriotism and Wilsonian idealism could stifle all labor disputes; and during the conflict there were some six thousand strikes, most of them mercifully brief. The National War Labor Board, with ex-President Taft as co-chairman, was finally established as the supreme court for labor disputes. More than one thousand cases came before it.

Some of the most crippling labor sabotage was engineered by the left-wing Industrial Workers of the World (I.W.W.'s), popularly known as the "I Won't Works" or "Wobblies." Advocating "one big industrial union," and proclaiming the slogan "An injury to one is an injury to all," they chanted:

The hours are long, the pay is small,
So take your time and buck them all.

As transient workers in such industries as fruit and lumber, the "Wobblies" stirred up much trouble. Many of them were arrested, beaten up, or run out of town.

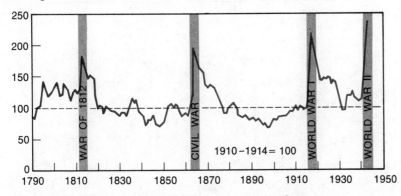

IMPACT OF U.S. WARS ON WHOLESALE PRICES

Hooverizing on Food and Fuel

Members of the War Trade Board became the leading "economic warriors" of the United States. By issuing the proper licenses to maritime shippers, they controlled exports and imports. The Board also continued the Allied practice of rationing imports of the neutral countries adjacent to Germany, and published a "blacklist" of enemy-tainted firms in neutral countries with which American citizens were forbidden to trade. Ironically, Washington had vigorously opposed both rationing and blacklisting in its protests to London during its years of neutrality. But these weapons, though disagreeable, could be employed within the framework of international law.

"Fuel Will Win the War" was another popular slogan. The Fuel Administration was headed by Harry A. Garfield, president of Williams College and a son of the murdered President. Spurred by the slogan "Mine More Coal," production was ultimately increased by about two-fifths. Despite these heroic efforts, the chilled public schools of New York had to close during one critical period for lack of coal, and certain factories were temporarily shut down.

Significant economies in fuel were achieved by voluntary self-sacrifice. There were "heatless Mondays" and "lightless nights," the latter produced by turning off electrical displays. "Daylight saving time" was introduced to conserve power. Similar efforts were made to economize on petroleum, including the voluntary "gasless Sundays."

Food was an even more pressing problem. As the larder of democracy, America not only had to feed herself but produce enough surplus for her allies. By a happy inspiration, the man chosen to head the Food Administration was the Quaker-humanitarian Herbert C. Hoover, already world-famous for his success in saving starving

Food Administrator Hoover Mobilizes His Army. Darling in the Des Moines *Register*, 1917

Belgium. A letter was promptly delivered to him which bore the sole address: "Miracle Man, Washington, D.C."

A superb organizer, Hoover mobilized the nation for less waste and more production. "Food Will Win the War—Don't Waste It" became a favorite slogan, as the Food Administration waged a whirlwind propaganda campaign through posters, billboards, newspapers, pulpits, and movies. Loyal citizens were urged to "use all leftovers," to observe "the gospel of the clean plate," and to practice "the patriotism of the lean garbage can." "Full Garbage Pails," the slogan ran, "Mean Empty Dinner Pails." Even children, when eating apples, were urged to be "patriotic to the core."

An incredible spirit of self-sacrifice aided Hoover's program. So inspiring was the spell of Wilsonian idealism that people voluntarily restricted themselves; no ration cards were issued to consumers, as was done in Europe. "To Hooverize" became a patriotic household synonym for "to economize." In order to save food for export, Hoover proclaimed wheatless Mondays and Wednesdays, meatless Tuesdays, and porkless Thursdays and Saturdays—all on a voluntary basis. Curious and unappetizing substitutes were found in wheatless bread ("Victory bread"), sugarless candy, and vegetarian lamb chops. A popular verse ran:

My Tuesdays are meatless,
My Wednesdays are wheatless,
I'm getting more eatless each day.
My coffee is sweetless,
My bed it is sheetless,
All sent to the Y.M.C.A.

Food surpluses were piled up in still other ways. The country soon broke out in a rash of vegetable "Victory gardens," as perspiring patriots hoed their way to victory in back yards or on vacant lots. Congress severely restricted the use of foodstuffs for manufacturing alcoholic beverages, and the war-born spirit of economy and self-denial helped accelerate the wave of prohibition that was sweeping the country. Many leading brewers were German or German-descended, and this taint made the drive against alcohol all the more popular.

Hoover's work was sensationally successful. Farm products were increased one-fourth, and food shipments to the hard-pressed Allied countries mounted to three times America's pre-war exports.

America's Bridge of Boats

The Atlantic Ocean was in some respects Germany's most effective ally. An anxious question was: Could America transport enough troops and supplies, in view of scanty shipping and grievous losses

Food Administration Poster.
Hoover Institution, Stanford
University California

to submarines, to turn the tide of battle? "Ships, Ships, and More Ships" was the desperate call of the Allies.

The Shipping Board, farsightedly created in 1916, was supplemented in 1917 by the Emergency Fleet Corporation. These two agencies bestirred themselves mightily to increase available tonnage. Among other steps, enemy merchant ships in American harbors were seized and put into operation, despite efforts by their crews to wreck the machinery. Conspicuous among these craft was the gigantic German *Vaterland* which, renamed the *Leviathan*, served as a transatlantic troop carrier. Neutral ships tied up in American harbors were at length requisitioned, with compensation to the owners. In this haul were eighty-seven Dutch vessels.

More vital was a gigantic drive to construct new tonnage. A few concrete vessels were launched, including one appropriately named *Faith*. A wooden-ship program was undertaken, although birds were still nesting in the trees from which they were to be hammered. Prefabricated steel ships were built for the first time on a large scale, with much of the construction undertaken in shipyards on the Great Lakes, far distant from the sea. The accent was on speed, and the staccato of the riveters ("Rivets Are Bayonets—Drive Them Home") announced that "The Ships Are Coming." One frantically built vessel was launched in twenty-seven days.

Although the huge ships-for-victory program was painfully slow in gathering momentum, ship construction finally far outran tonnage destruction by the U-boats. Long before the war ended the nation was laying down two keels for every one lost. On a glorious July 4, 1918, ninety-five vessels were launched in the various American yards. All told, the Shipping Board built and delivered in 1918 a total

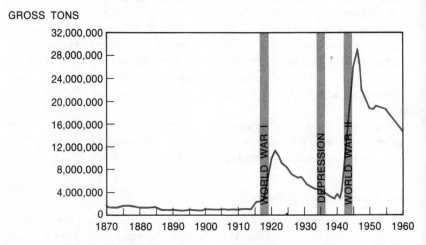

GROSS TONS

U.S. MERCHANT MARINE IN FOREIGN COMMERCE, 1870–1960
For earlier years see p. 336.

of 533, many of which splashed into the water after the Armistice. The largest shipyard, the Hog Island plant near Philadelphia, alone had some eighty miles of railroads. When the war ended there were 350,000 workers in 341 shipyards—or two times the shipbuilding capacity of the rest of the world.

America's railroads, which fed the transatlantic "bridge of ships," creaked badly. No two lines were organized quite alike, and the thirty-odd systems were soon working at cross-purposes. So serious became the snarl that, in December, 1917, Wilson placed the entire network under government control. Director General of Railroads was the tall, hawk-nosed Secretary of the Treasury, William G. McAdoo, who had married Wilson's daughter Eleanor in the White House and who was dubbed "the Crown Prince."

Washington ran the railroads at a loss, partly because it kept the rates low and the financial guarantee to the owners high. Economy was no object. Speed and the winning of the war were the major aims, and here McAdoo succeeded, even though he incurred a deficit of $862,000,000. But the charge that he had "McAdoodled" the railroads was thereafter used as a strong argument against government ownership. Washington likewise took over the telephones, the telegraphs, and the cables.

"Over the Top" with Dollars

Tax burdens added to the other unpleasant war burdens. The conflict was fantastically expensive, judged by previous American experience, and in the closing stages cost $44,000,000 a day. About one-third of this total outlay was handled by a pay-as-you-go policy. Increased taxes brought increased revenue through the income tax, the corporation tax, the excess profits tax, the luxury taxes—the so-called "nuisance taxes" on theater tickets and similar items.

Most of the money for financing victory was borrowed directly from the citizen in huge bond "drives." The Treasury, in line with its policy of making the war a personal effort, abandoned the Civil War practice of marketing bonds through profit-taking banking houses. Bonds were issued in denominations as low as $50, and Thrift Stamps could be purchased by children for as little as twenty-five cents. The appeal was to both profit and patriotism. Interest rates were attractive, and the bond purchaser could proudly display a button on his lapel to prove that he was neither un-American nor pro-German.

Four great Liberty Loan drives, followed by a Victory Loan drive in 1919, netted the impressive total of $21,448,120,300. About 65,000,000 persons contributed from their savings to make "silver bullets." The drives involved much emotional appeal through monster parades and slogans like "Halt the Hun" and "Remember: It's Cheaper to Win Than to Lose." All five of the huge loans were

Liberty Loan Poster. Hoover Institution, Stanford University, California

Hanging the Kaiser—A Favorite Sport. *Life,* 1918

oversubscribed—"went over the top," in the current trench-warfare phrase. Cities and regions vied with one another in competitive outbursts of patriotism.

Pressures of various kinds, patriotic and otherwise, were used to sell bonds. The unfortunate German-American who could not display a Liberty Bond button might find his house bedaubed with yellow paint. A number of luckless persons, suspected of being pro-Germans, were roughly handled, and there was at least one instance of a man who signed for a bond with a rope around his neck.

The Red Cross and other private agencies of benevolence simultaneously staged smaller drives of their own. Slogans that they used with great effectiveness were "Give Until It Hurts" and "Think What You Can Afford to Give—Then Double It."

Creel Manipulates Minds

Mobilizing the mind for war, both in America and abroad, was an urgent task facing the Washington authorities. For this purpose, the Committee on Public Information was created. It was headed by a youngish journalist, George Creel, who, though outspoken and tactless, was gifted with zeal and imagination. His job was to "sell" America on the war, and "sell" the world on Wilsonian war aims.

The Creel organization, employing 150,000 workers at home and overseas, proved that words were weapons. It sent out an army of 75,000 "Four-Minute Men"—often longer-winded than that—who delivered over 7,500,000 speeches containing much "patriotic pep."

Creel's propaganda took varied forms. Posters were splashed on billboards in the "Battle of the Fences," as artists "rallied to the colors." Millions of leaflets and pamphlets, which contained the most pungent Wilsonisms, were showered like confetti upon the world. Special propaganda booklets with red-white-and-blue covers were distributed by the millions, some of them attempting to prove that Germany had started the war with diabolical intent. Hang-the-Kaiser "movies," with such titles as "The Kaiser the Beast of Berlin" and "To Hell with the Kaiser," revealed the "Hun" in his bloodiest colors. Arm-waving song leaders by the thousands led huge audiences in songs that poured scorn on the enemy and glorified the "boys" in uniform.

Creel was unsurpassed as a mobilizer of emotion. Unlike most propagandists, he had merely to tell the truth about America's tremendous war effort—the truth was incredible enough. But he rather oversold the ideals of Wilson, and led the world to expect too much. When the President proved to be a mortal and not a god, the resulting disillusionment at home and abroad was disastrous. Paper bullets can be overdone.

America's most noteworthy contribution to the "science" of warfare was in "mobilizing the mind of the world." Regrettably, some of Creel's techniques were later copied by the master propagandists serving Adolf Hitler and other dictators.

Enforcing Loyalty and Stifling Dissent

A potential source of internal danger was the formidable group of German-Americans. They numbered over 8,000,000, counting those with at least one parent foreign-born, out of a total population of 100,000,000. Before America entered the war, an official in the German Foreign Office boasted that there were 500,000 German army reservists in the United States. The American Ambassador proudly retorted that there were 500,001 lamp posts on which they could be hanged.

German-Americans, on the whole, proved to be gratifyingly loyal. Hundreds of thousands of them not only bought Liberty Bonds but fought bravely under the Stars and Stripes. Yet rumormongers were quick to spread tales of spying and sabotage: even trifling epidemics of diarrhea were blamed on German agents. A few German-Americans were tarred, feathered, and beaten; and in one extreme case a German Socialist in Illinois was lynched by a drunken mob.

As emotion mounted, hate hysteria swept the nation against Germans and things Germanic. Orchestras found it unsafe to present German-composed music, like that of Wagner or Beethoven; and the brilliant Austro-Hungarian violinist, Fritz Kreisler, was forbidden to play in New Jersey. The teaching of the German language was shortsightedly discontinued in many high schools and colleges. Sauerkraut became "Liberty cabbage," Hamburg or Hamburger steak became "Liberty steak," German measles became "Liberty measles," and dachshunds became "Liberty pups," that is, if one were unpatriotic enough to own them.

"Making His Dollars Fight," 1917. German-American Forced to Buy Bonds. Courtesy Baltimore *American*

Both the Espionage Act of 1917 and the Sedition Act of 1918 reflected current fears. These twin measures were inspired partly by hatred of the Germans, partly by a desire to prevent obstruction of the war effort. Over 1900 prosecutions were undertaken under both laws.

Socialists fell under strong suspicion of pro-Germanism, for a majority went on record as opposing this "capitalistic war." A minority, stirred by patriotic impulses, seceded from the party. Eugene V. Debs, kingpin Socialist, continued to speak out violently against American participation. Convicted in 1918 under the Espionage Act, he was sentenced to ten years in a federal penitentiary. After he had served about two years, President Harding granted him a Christmas-present pardon.

A number of I.W.W.'s were likewise prosecuted during the war under the Espionage Act. In 1918 William D. ("Big Bill") Haywood, a one-eyed giant of a man, and ninety-nine associates were convicted. Haywood himself received a twenty-year sentence. (His ashes were later buried in the Kremlin with those of other famous revolutionaries.) In all, there were 1532 arrests under the Sedition Act for disloyal utterances, 65 for threats against Wilson, and 10 for sabotage.

Censorship of a mild sort was occasionally imposed on the press. A Socialist newspaper, *The Masses* (New York), was denied second-class mailing privileges, and at one time an issue of the liberal New York *Nation* was held up.

These prosecutions form an ugly chapter in the history of American civil liberty. Though flouting traditional freedoms, they seemed justified by the national emergency. With the dawn of peace, presidential pardons were rather freely granted, and the nation gradually got back on even keel. Yet a few victims lingered behind bars into the 1930's.

The Navy Brought Them Over

Already cleared for action, the navy got into the war first—though belatedly. Early in May, 1917, an initial flotilla of six destroyers arrived in Ireland for desperately needed anti-submarine operations.

Navy Recruiting Poster. World War I. Courtesy Department of the Navy.

All in all, the American sailors had their hands full. They helped the British battleships hem in the German high-seas fleet; they played a leading role in laying down a 230-mile mine barrage from Scotland to Norway, designed to bottle the deadly U-boats in the North Sea. This gigantic operation, involving 70,000 contact mines, was a not-too-successful scheme of young Assistant Secretary of the Navy Franklin D. Roosevelt, who even this early "thought big."

Simultaneously the navy assisted in tightening the British blockade noose around Germany. America did not violate international law flagrantly, but she did cooperate with the British in enforcing practices against the neutrals to which she had strongly objected while a neutral.

The navy's muscles, though strong, bulged in the wrong places. Wilson's naval preparedness act of 1916 had authorized huge battleships, which were almost useless for anti-submarine operations. After America's entry into the conflict the construction of capital ships was halted, and in the first nine months of 1918 no fewer than eighty-three destroyers were launched. A popular cry was "Help Muzzle the Mad Dogs of the Sea." Responding to the call, the navy did yeoman work by destroying German U-boats with depth bombs and other devices.

Most spectacular of the navy's achievements was the escorting to France of scores of troop transports, American and Allied. More than 2,000,000 soldiers were taken "over there," but only one Europe-bound transport was torpedoed. Six vessels were lost on their way home.

"Yanks" to the Rescue in France

Long regarded as quickly expandable, the army was more of a problem than the navy. The nation, in every one of its major conflicts, had been confronted with two tasks: first to raise an army, and second to fight the war. This emergency was no exception.

Most citizens, at the outset, did not dream of sending a mighty force to France. As far as fighting went, America would use her navy to uphold freedom of the seas. She would continue to ship war material to the Allies and supply them with loans, which finally totaled nearly ten billion dollars. But in April and May of 1917, the European associates laid their cards on the table. They confessed that they were not only scraping the bottom of their money chest, but, more ominously, of their manpower barrel. A huge American army would have to be raised, trained, and transported, or the whole Western front would collapse.

Some kind of token force was necessary at once for European morale. The command of the American Expeditionary Forces (A.E.F.) was entrusted to efficient and stubborn General John J. ("Black Jack") Pershing, who had chased Villa into Mexico. On the Fourth of July, 1917, he led a tiny ill-trained force of khaki-clad Americans through the streets of Paris, amid frenzied cries of "Vive l'Amérique." One of Pershing's subordinates, touching on the debt-to-France theme, remarked, "Lafayette, we are here."

The "Yanks" were coming—slowly. Not until October 23, 1917, nearly seven months after Congress had formally declared hostilities, did the first small detachments of American troops see battle action. "We are at war but not in it," ran a current quip.

Fight-thirsty Theodore Roosevelt, still dreaming of Rough Rider days despite his sixty years, was eager to raise a volunteer division and take it to France. Such a unit would have bolstered Allied morale, but it would also have drawn off the cream of American military leadership. This conflict was a global struggle, with no place for Rough Rider heroics, and Wilson icily rebuffed Roosevelt's offer. It was probably the bitterest disappointment of the ex-President's eventful life.

Army Recruiting Poster. World War I. Hoover Institution, Stanford University, California

Making Plowboys into Doughboys

Conscription was the only answer to the need for raising an immense army with all possible speed. Wilson disliked a draft, as did many other Americans with Civil War memories; such forcible methods were alien to basic traditions. What would be gained, many citizens asked, if the nation militarized itself in order to defeat a militaristic Germany? But Wilson finally accepted and eloquently supported conscription as a disagreeable necessity.

The draft bill immediately ran into a barrage of criticism in

A Universal Draft. Chopin in the San Francisco *Examiner*, 1917

Congress. Champ Clark of Missouri, deploring compulsion, cried out that there was "precious little difference between a conscript and a convict." Prophets of doom predicted that on draft-registration day the streets would run red with blood. At length Congress—six weeks after declaring war—grudgingly got around to passing conscription.

As later amended, the draft act was a true "selective service" law. It required the registration of all males between the ages of eighteen and forty-five. No "draft dodger" could purchase his exemption or hire a substitute, as in the easygoing days of the Civil War. The "selective" idea was that the government would "select" the draftee for duty in those places where he would be most useful. As a result, there were many exemptions for men in key industries, such as shipbuilding.

The draft machinery, on the whole, worked effectively. Registration day proved to be a day of patriotic pilgrimages to flag-draped registration centers, and there was no shedding of blood, as gloomily predicted. Despite all precautions, some 160,000 "slackers" escaped the draft dragnet. Notorious among them was Grover Cleveland Bergdoll, a Philadelphian who, after being given a five-year sentence, escaped to Germany.

New wrinkles were added to the old services. Provision was made for training army and navy officers in the colleges, but in general this program creaked badly. For the first time women were admitted to the armed forces: some 11,000 to the navy ("Yeomanettes") and 269 to the marine corps ("Marinettes").

The draft slipped promptly into high gear, as the singing of "Johnny, Get Your Gun" became the inspiration of the hour. Within a few frantic months the army was increased from about 200,000 men to over 4,000,000. The green draftees ("rookies") were herded into hastily built wooden camps, where they were given heavy doses of high-pressure training. As the popular song ran:

They marched me twenty miles a day to fit me for the war—
I didn't mind the first nineteen but the last one made me sore.

Yet morale was excellent, thanks largely to the ideals of defending democracy and ending war. The hastily trained men, eager to "lick" the Kaiser, were on fire to get "across the pond." After six months of concentrated effort, the "doughboys" might be shipped overseas, singing "Good-bye Broadway, Hello France." Upon arrival, they were normally given about two more months of training before seeing front-line action.

Fighting in France—Belatedly

Russia's collapse underscored the need for haste. The communistic Bolsheviks, after seizing power in Moscow, removed their beaten country from the "capitalistic" war early in 1918. This sudden defection released hundreds of thousands of battle-singed German veterans for the front in France. In the western theater, for the first time in the war, the Germans were developing a dangerous superiority in manpower.

Berlin's calculations as to American tardiness were surprisingly accurate. Germany had counted on knocking Britain out in six months, long before America could get into the struggle. No really effective American fighting force reached France until about a year after Congress declared war. Berlin had also reckoned on the inability of the Americans to transport their army, assuming that they were able to raise one. Here again the German predictions were not far from the mark. Over half of the tonnage for transports was diverted by Britain and her European allies from other pressing tasks, although the United States scraped together about 46% of the needed shipping.

France gradually began to bustle with American "doughboys." The first trainees to reach the front were used as replacements in the Allied armies, and were generally deployed in quiet sectors with the British and French. Enormous supply depots, as well as quarters for officers and men, were constructed in France. Here sprawled an amazing 225 miles of American barracks and 127 miles of hospital wards. The newcomers soon made friends with the French girls— or tried to—and one of the most sung-about women in history was the fabled "Mademoiselle from Armentières." One of the printable stanzas ran:

You might forget the gas and shells,
But you'll never forget the mademoiselles.

Much of America's equipment—in certain categories all of it— was borrowed from the Allies. The list included a large proportion of light artillery, howitzers, tanks, airplanes, and rifles. One explanation is that the American war-production program had lagged dangerously in spots. In addition the Allies, with depleted manpower, preferred to use the available shipping for troops and provide the equipment themselves.

Haste made waste. Hundreds of millions of dollars spent on American artillery were largely thrown away. The Browning machine gun was an excellent weapon, but it was developed too late to be of significant use. An aircraft program was wastefully ineffective to the point of scandal, although the whole effort involved little outright graft. Among other bottlenecks, strikes by the I.W.W. interrupted processing of the lightweight spruce wood, although the day was saved by the L.L.L.L. (Loyal Legion of Loggers and Lumbermen). Altogether, America produced only 12,000 aircraft, not all of which were combat planes.

American airmen—"Cavaliers of the Clouds"—hung up an enviable record in France. In the end the United States could boast

General John J. Pershing (1860–1948), the commander of the Mexican punitive expedition, had earlier served with distinction against the American Indians and the Filipino insurgents, and during World War I became the leader of the American Expeditionary Forces in Europe. National Archives.

twenty-two "aces," or men who had netted five or more enemy craft. The leading hero was indestructible Captain Edward V. ("Eddie") Rickenbacker, later prominent in commercial aviation, whose bag was twenty-two airplanes and three balloons.

America Helps Hammer the Hun*

The dreaded German drive on the Western Front exploded in the spring of 1918. Spearheaded by about half a million troops, the enemy rolled forward with terrifying momentum. So dire was the peril that the Allied nations for the first time united under a Supreme Commander, the quiet French Marshal Foch, whose axiom was: "To make war is to attack." Until then the Allies had been fighting imperfectly coordinated actions.

At last the "Yanks" were finally coming—and not a moment too soon. Late in May, 1918, the forward-rolling Germans, smashing to within forty miles of Paris, threatened to knock France out of the war. Newly arrived American troops, numbering fewer than 30,000, were thrown into the breach at Château-Thierry, where they played a dramatic role in helping to stem the tide. In June the United States marines cleared the Germans from bloody Belleau Wood. The victory was so heroic that appreciative Frenchmen renamed the place "Bois de Marins" (Marine Woods).

American weight in the scales was now being felt. By July, 1918, the awesome German drive had spent its force, and keyed-up American boys participated in a Foch counter-offensive in the Second Battle of the Marne. This engagement marked the beginning of a German withdrawal that was never effectively reversed. As proof of mounting strength, seven American divisions (about 140,000 men) fought in the Second Battle of the Marne, as compared with sixty Allied divisions. In September, 1918, nine American divisions (about 180,000 men) joined four French divisions to dislodge the Germans from the St. Mihiel "hernia" of France.

The Americans, dissatisfied with merely bolstering the British and French, had meanwhile been demanding a separate army. Pride, patriotism, and morale all required that the "Yanks" have their own command, assigned to a specific fighting front. The French, on the contrary, insisted that the American boys be used merely as replacements. But General Pershing, jut-jawed and offense-minded, fought a winning battle against the Allied leaders. The Americans were finally assigned a front of eighty-five miles, stretching northwestward from the Swiss border to meet the French lines.

As a part of the last mighty Allied assault, involving several mil-

* In 1900 the Kaiser had himself used this term in urging German troops to behave like Huns in crushing the Chinese rebels ("Boxers").

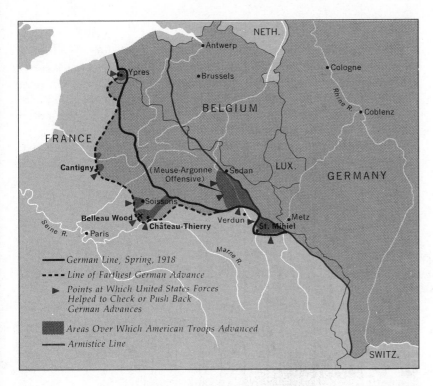

MAJOR U.S. OPERATIONS IN FRANCE, 1918

lion men, Pershing's army undertook the Meuse-Argonne offensive, from September 26 to November 11, 1918. One objective was to cut the German railroad lines feeding the Western Front. This battle, the most titanic thus far in American history, lasted forty-seven days and engaged 1,200,000 American troops. With especially heavy fighting in the rugged Argonne Forest, the killed and wounded mounted to 120,000, or 10% of the total. The slow progress and severe losses resulted in part from inadequate training, in part from dashing open-field tactics, with the bayonet liberally employed. Tennessee-bred Alvin C. York, a member of an anti-war religious sect, became a hero when he singlehandedly killed 20 Germans and captured 132 more.

Victory was in sight—and fortunately so. The slowly advancing American armies in France were eating up their supplies so rapidly that they were in grave danger of running short. But the battered Germans, although their own soil was not being invaded, were ready to raise their arms and cry "Kamerad." Their allies were deserting them; the British blockade was causing critical food shortages; and the German armies were reeling under the sledge-hammer blows of the Allies. Propaganda leaflets, containing seductive Wilsonian promises, were raining upon their crumbling lines from balloons, shells, and rockets.

The Fourteen Points Disarm Germany

Berlin was now ready to hoist the white flag. Warned of imminent defeat by the generals, it turned to the presumably softhearted Wilson in October, 1918, seeking a peace based on the Fourteen Points. In stern responses, the President made it clear that the Kaiser must be thrown overboard before an armistice could be negotiated. War-weary Germans, whom Wilson had been trying to turn against their "military masters," took the hint. The Kaiser was forced to flee to Holland, where he lived out his remaining twenty-three years, "unwept, unhonored, and unhung."

As events proved, the Fourteen Points served better for propaganda than for peacemaking. Allied leaders, whose territorial ambitions were embodied in secret treaties, feared that Wilson's lofty ideals would tie their hands. But they urgently needed the support of rich Uncle Sam for post-war reconstruction. Mystery-man Colonel House, speaking for Wilson, hinted at a separate German-American treaty if the Allies were not reasonable. They finally agreed, with feet-dragging reluctance, to negotiate a peace based on the Fourteen Points. But they insisted on two reservations: one on freedom of the seas that would safeguard British naval power, and one on reparations that would assure France of collecting compensation for damage inflicted by the invading "Hun."

The exhausted Germans were through. They laid down their arms after the Allies had solemnly assured them that the peace treaty would be based on the Fourteen Points—with the two exceptions noted. The Armistice was formally signed at eleven o'clock on the eleventh day of the eleventh month of 1918, and an eerie, numbing silence fell over the Western Front. War-taut America burst into a delirium of around-the-clock rejoicing, as streets were jammed with laughing, whooping, milling, dancing masses. The war to end wars had ended.

Theodore Roosevelt, referring to Wilson's practice of drafting diplomatic notes on his own typewriter, telegraphed several Senators (October 24, 1918), "Let us dictate peace by the hammering guns and not chat about peace to the accompaniment of clicking typewriters. The language of the fourteen points and the subsequent statements explaining or qualifying them are thoroughly mischievous. . . ." Roosevelt favored unconditional surrender.

The Harvest from Global War

Beyond doubt the war effort of the aroused Western giant had been prodigious. America got into the fray, belatedly and awkwardly but full of dash and enthusiasm, just in time to help turn the tide to victory. More than 4,000,000 citizen-soldiers were put into uniform. The total casualties were 320,000, of which 116,000 represented deaths, including disease. Yet these gory losses were minor when bracketed with those suffered by Britain, France, and Russia. As compared with other American wars, death from disease was generally reduced. An exception was the terrible influenza epidemic of 1918, which took a world-wide toll of some 10,000,000 lives, mostly civilians. Direct costs of the war to the United States were staggering, roughly $41,755,000,000, including some of the later pension and "bonus" charges.

Men Killed in Battle		Cost in Money
1,700,000	Russia	$18,000,000,000
1,600,000	Germany	$39,000,000,000
1,385,000	France	$26,000,000,000
900,000	British Empire	$38,000,000,000
800,000	Austria	$21,000,000,000
462,000	Italy	$13,000,000,000
49,000	United States	$22,000,000,000

APPROXIMATE COMPARATIVE LOSSES IN WORLD WAR I

American operations were not confined solely to France; small detachments fought in Belgium, Italy, and notably Russia. The United States, hoping to keep stores of munitions from falling into German hands when Bolshevik Russia quit fighting, contributed some 5000 troops to an Allied invasion of North Russia at Archangel. Wilson likewise sent nearly 10,000 troops to Siberia as a part of an Allied expedition, which included more than 70,000 Japanese. Major American purposes were to prevent Japan from getting a strangle hold on Siberia, to rescue some 45,000 marooned Czechoslovak troops, and to snatch military supplies from Red Bolshevik control. Sharp fighting at Archangel and in Siberia involved casualties on both sides, including several hundred Americans. The Communist rulers of Soviet Russia have never allowed their people to forget these "capitalistic" interventions.

The War of 1917–1918 was America's best-fought war up to that time. Failures stemmed from haste and inexperience; successes sprang from enthusiasm and unity. Every citizen was enlisted "for the duration," whether in fighting, buying bonds, increasing production, or saving fuel and food.

More than 300,000 Negroes were drafted to fight in a war to make the world safe for a democracy that they did not fully enjoy. (Lynchings and race riots during these decades were continuing at an appalling pace.) About two-thirds of the black draftees, often to their discontent, were assigned to labor battalions and other non-combat units. Their morale was not helped by vicious race riots, especially that in East St. Louis in 1917, during which some forty Negroes and eight whites lost their lives. Various kinds of discrimination against the draftees made for inflamed feelings, notably in the South. In 1917 thirteen Negro soldiers were hanged for murder after being provoked into striking back and killing seventeen whites at Houston, Texas. Nevertheless black combat units did reach France, some of which fought with distinction, especially the 369th regiment, dubbed by Germans "Hell Fighters."

No lasting grade-A war heroes, black or white, emerged from this conflict. Stern-faced General Pershing did not radiate the glamor that one associates with presidential timber. The traditional glory of arms was overshadowed by barbed wire, metal monsters called tanks, lethal poison gas, mud, rats, and lice ("cooties"). Master-organizer Herbert Hoover, the so-called "Knight of the Lean Garbage Can," became the outstanding hero—and he was a civilian.

Prohibition was one of two major constitutional amendments floated through by the war emergency. The need for conserving grain and other foodstuffs, combined with an idealistic spirit of self-sacrifice, brought ratification of the 18th Amendment in 1919. (See Appendix.) Most of America had already been voted dry by state action, but the constitutional amendment achieved—on paper—the dream of a saloonless nation.

Woman suffrage, regarded as essential to national unity, was likewise stimulated by the conflict. President Wilson had hitherto opposed it ("He Kept Us Out of Suffrage"), but at last he supported this concession as "a vitally necessary war measure." "Votes for women" achieved a final triumph when, in 1920, the 19th Amendment was written into the Constitution. (See Appendix.) In politics, so the witticism went, the rolling pin now replaced the steam roller. But a sharp elevation of moral tone, so confidently predicted, did not follow the new amendment. Women tended to vote the same way as men.

Constitutional changes were overshadowed by economic dislocations. Swollen war industries brought bulging pay envelopes, but

PROHIBITION ON THE EVE OF
THE 18TH AMENDMENT, 1919

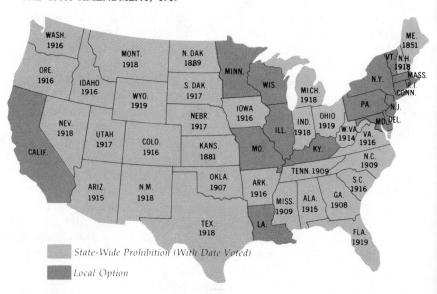

the invisible hand of inflation reached greedily into them. Despite burdensome war taxes, a new crop of profiteers emerged, and the select American millionaire group shot up from 16,000 to 20,000.

But the conflict, above all, was a vindication of American democracy. The German militarists had sneered at America's ability to gird herself for battle while there was yet time. The Republic astonished them—and to some extent itself—when it joined as one people in a mighty crusade for victory. Democracy, after all, did not seem so spineless.

SELECT READINGS

FRANK FREIDEL captures the spirit in *Over There* (1964), stressing photographs and contemporary reactions. MARK SULLIVAN, *Our Times*, volume V (1933) achieves the same effect in greater detail. Solid scholarship is F. L. PAXSON, *America at War* (1939). A perceptive brief analysis of military operations is H. A. DE WEERD, *President Wilson Fights His War* (1968). Behind-the-scenes activities are handled with gusto in the early chapters of P. W. SLOSSON, *The Great Crusade and After, 1914–1928* (1930). American propaganda efforts are colorfully portrayed in J. R. MOCK and C. LARSON, *Words That Won the War* (1939). The abuse of civil liberties is luridly described in H. C. PETERSON and G. C. FITE, *Opponents of War, 1917–1918* (1957)*; more briefly and soberly in H. N. SCHEIBER, *The Wilson Administration and Civil Liberties, 1917–1921* (1960). B. M. BARUCH, chairman of the War Industries Board, reminisces in *Baruch: The Public Years* (1960).* An excellent biography is MARGARET COIT, *Mr. Baruch* (1957). A distinguished ex-foreign service officer, GEORGE F. KENNAN, has given us a perceptive study in *Soviet-American Relations, 1917–1920* (2 vols., 1956, 1958). A useful monograph is BETTY M. UNTERBERGER, *America's Siberian Expedition, 1918–1920* (1956). Also *Harvard Guide,** Pt. VI.

RECENT REFERENCES

EDWARD M. COFFMAN, *The War to End All Wars: The American Military Experience in World War I* (1968).

* Available in paperback.

38

Making and Breaking the Peace

Dare we reject it [the League of Nations] and break the heart of the world?

Woodrow Wilson, 1919

Wilson Steps Down from Olympus

As the war in Europe crashed to a close, Woodrow Wilson towered at the peak of his popularity and power. No other man had ever occupied so dizzy a pinnacle as moral leader of the world; no other man had ever been presented with so breath-taking an opportunity as a peacemaker.

Success seemed assured. Superb as a war leader, Wilson now had behind him the prestige of victory and the economic resources of the mightiest nation on earth. But regrettably his sureness of touch gradually deserted him, and he began to make a series of tragic fumbles.

His first error was the "October Appeal." The war crisis had brought an enforced political unity, and the popular slogan had been "Politics Is Adjourned." Republicans had generally supported the Democratic program for victory, although a few diehards had protested against the dictatorial powers of "Kaiser" Wilson. The Congressional elections of November, 1918, were imminent, and the President believed that his hands would be strengthened at the Paris peace table if the voters should return a Democratic majority.

Urged by anxious politicians, he reverted to his "appeal habit" by publicly calling for a Democratic Congress.

Republicans responded with a bitter cry that the political truce had been broken. Politics, in fact, had never been "adjourned"; partisanship had merely simmered below the surface, with Theodore Roosevelt more than simmering.

On election day the voters tramped to the polls and, by a rather narrow margin, returned a Republican Congress. Whether the result was materially influenced by Wilson's appeal cannot be determined with certainty. But having staked his prestige on the outcome, he suffered a grievous loss of face. At the Paris peace table, he was the only one of the leading statesmen not entitled to be present—that is, on the basis of a legislative majority.

Wilson next infuriated Republicans by announcing that he was going to Paris to help make the peace. At that time no President had ever journeyed to Europe, though Theodore Roosevelt had visited Panama in 1906 to see "the dirt fly." Wilson's critics charged that he had developed a God-complex—a desire, as ex-President Taft put it, "to hog the whole show." The egoist-idealist in the White House was needed at home, so Republicans argued, to grapple with reconstruction. In the hurly-burly of the Peace Conference, this "mushy sentimentalist" would be overwhelmed and "bamboozled." But in Washington, at one end of a wire, he presumably could make his decisions quietly, calmly, and effectively.

The President Snubs the Senate

Renewed outcries burst from Republican lips when Wilson announced the five-man American peace commission. It consisted of himself; the quiet and faithful Colonel House, his second self; Secretary of State Lansing; a military adviser, General T. H. Bliss; and a little-known Republican, ex-career diplomat Henry White. In addi-

The Peace Delegation—A Republican View. *Left to right:* Wilson, House, Lansing, White, Bliss, Baruch, Hoover, Creel. *Harvey's Weekly,* 1919

"The Old Girl Who Wasn't Invited to the Show Turns up her Nose at the Program." Fitzpatrick in the St. Louis *Post-Dispatch*

tion, there were scores of technical advisers, chiefly scholars from quiet campuses whom ex-Professor Wilson regarded as "his kind."

Republicans, now the majority party on the basis of the recent Congressional elections, insisted that they were not represented at all. Henry White, though a Republican, was so minor a one as to be negligible. Republicans had been good enough to fight in the war, they complained; then why should they not have a real place at the peace table? Humorist Will Rogers had Wilson tell them, "We'll split 50–50—I will go and you fellows can stay."

Wilson also snubbed the Senate in making up the peace commission, even though the jealous solons would have to approve the treaty. He did not ask their advice, partly because he had little respect for the "pygmy-minded" Senators. He did not put a single one of them on the peace commission, although there was ample precedent for doing so.

Choosing a Republican Senator presented a problem, for the logical one was slender and aristocratically bewhiskered Henry Cabot Lodge of Massachusetts, Ph.D., Harvard. His mind, quipped one critic, was like the soil of his native New England, "naturally barren but highly cultivated." As the author of many books, Lodge had been known as "the scholar in politics" until Wilson appeared on the scene. The two men came to hate each other passionately and blindly.

But Wilson, in ignoring the Senate, seems to have been primarily preoccupied with global problems. He was like the baseball player, as someone has said, who knocked the ball into the left-field bleachers and then forgot to touch home plate.

The brutal truth is that certain Republican leaders were out to knife Wilson—that "drum major of civilization." He had trampled heavily on the corns of business tycoons with his New Freedom reforms, and the Republican leaders wanted to turn back the clock to the golden days of McKinley standpattism. Wilson must not be permitted to conclude a triumphant peace. If he did, he might—unspeakable thought!—feel that he had to be re-elected for a third term to carry out its provisions.

An Idealist Battles the Imperialists in Paris

Woodrow Wilson, the great prophet arisen in the West, received tumultuous welcomes from the masses of France, England, and Italy late in 1918 and early in 1919. They saw in his idealism the promise of a better world. "Vive l'Amérique!" and "Vive le Président," cried the French, while the Italians no less enthusiastically hailed "Voovro Veelson." But the statesmen of France and Italy were careful to keep the new messiah at arm's length from worshipful crowds. He might so arouse the people as to overthrow their leaders and upset finespun imperialistic plans.

Almost from the outset, the Paris Conference of great and small nations fell into the hands of an inner clique, known as the Big Four. Such inner-sanctum diplomacy was inevitable because the confused multipower gathering was too unwieldy. But behind-the-scenes secrecy seemed to violate the first—and one of the most popular—of the Fourteen Points: "Open Covenants Openly Arrived At." The frustrated journalists were infuriated.

The Big Four proved to be both a powerful and a colorful body. Wilson, representing the richest and freshest great power, more or less occupied the driver's seat. He was joined by genial Premier Vittorio Orlando of Italy and by the brilliant Prime Minister David Lloyd George of Britain. Perhaps the most realistic of the quartet was cynical, hard-bitten Premier Georges Clemenceau of France, the seventy-eight-year-old "organizer of victory" known as "the Tiger."

Speed was urgent when the Conference opened on January 18, 1919. Europe seemed to be slipping into anarchy; the red tide of Communism was licking westward from Bolshevist Russia. A current saying in Paris was "Better a bad treaty today than a good treaty four months hence."

What problem should be tackled first? Wilson had come to Paris with his primary long-run goal the League of Nations, designed to avert future wars. The rest of the Big Four—all Old World realists— were hardly lukewarm about the visionary Wilsonian scheme. They were far more eager to carve up the territorial spoils, as prearranged in secret treaties.

Thoroughly aroused, Wilson opposed with all his Scotch Presbyterian stubbornness an imperialistic parceling out of the booty. Such a division would be an outrageous violation of Point Five, relating to colonies. He finally forced the acceptance of a compromise between naked imperialism and Wilsonian idealism. The victorious powers would not receive the conquered territory outright, but only as trustees or "mandatories" of the League of Nations. Strategic Syria, for example, was awarded to France, and oil-rich Iraq to Britain. This half-loaf solution, as worked out in certain backward areas, proved to be little more than the old pre-war imperialism, thinly disguised.

Meanwhile Wilson had been serving as midwife for the League of Nations. The idea was not original with him; other planners in America had been working on it, as had certain far-visioned British and French thinkers. But Wilson, embracing the scheme with characteristic enthusiasm, made it peculiarly his own. Chosen chairman of the committee that drafted the League Covenant, he labored earnestly on it after conference hours. In ten high-pressure sessions, he drove the document through in reasonably complete form, though it still needed polishing.

Wilson's next task was to get the draft accepted by the entire Conference. Many members, eager to grapple with immediate problems, argued that the League of Nations should be dealt with last. Then, some intriguers hoped, it would be sidetracked, lest it interfere with

"The Race." Fitzpatrick in the St. Louis *Post-Dispatch*.

Grave concern was expressed by General Bliss, one of the five American peace commissioners (December 18, 1918), "I am disquieted to see how hazy and vague our ideas are. We are going to be up against the wiliest politicians in Europe. There will be nothing hazy or vague about their ideas."

imperialistic ambitions. But Wilson gained a signal victory in mid-February, 1919, when he not only won acceptance of the League Covenant by a committee but persuaded the Conference to make it an integral part of the final peace treaty. At one time he spoke so eloquently for his adopted brain child that even the hard-boiled newspaper reporters forgot to take notes.

The Senate Warns Wilson

Wilson, who had done remarkably well for an amateur diplomat, now had to leave the Paris battlefield for a time. Domestic duties required a quick trip back to America, to sign bills passed by Congress and to attend to other pressing business.

"Seein' Things." Brooklyn
Eagle, 1919

An ugly storm was brewing in the Senate. Certain Republican solons were sharpening their knives for Wilson; they distrusted the "League of Denationalized Nations" and the "League of Nations Claptrap." To them the new scheme was either a useless "sewing circle" or an overpotent "super-state." Senator Lodge, jealous and embittered, was active in rallying his Republican following. His ranks were joined by a dozen or so isolationists, mostly Republicans, who were known as "the Battalion of Death." This small group of "irreconcilables" or "bitter-enders" was headed by rabble-rousing orators, notably Senator William E. Borah of Idaho and Senator Hiram W. Johnson of California.

Bitterness against Wilson flared forth ominously in early March, 1919, when Senate Republicans published a Round Robin. This was a sensational manifesto signed by thirty-nine Republican Senators or Senators-elect—enough to defeat the treaty. They proclaimed, for all the world to know, that the Senate would not approve the League of Nations in its existing imperfect form.

Fighting mad, Wilson struck back. On the eve of his return to Paris, he defiantly announced in a New York speech that the League would be inseparably tied into the treaty. The Senators could not cut it out without killing the whole pact—and they dared not, he was confident, break the heart of the world.

The Round Robin, a virtual stab in the back for Wilson, delighted his Allied adversaries in Paris. They were now in a stronger bargaining position. The President would have to come back and beg—as he subsequently did—for changes in the Covenant that would safeguard the Monroe Doctrine and other heritages so precious to the Senators.

Frustrated France Demands Security

Next came the grim battle with the French, who above all sought security against another periodic German invasion. Hardheaded Premier Clemenceau, who remembered that steel bayonets and not paper ideals had repelled the enemy, sneered at the Fourteen Points. "God gave us His Ten Commandments," he reportedly remarked, "and we broke them. Wilson gave us his Fourteen Points—we shall see."

Clemenceau demanded the German Rhineland as a buffer, even though the acquisition of several million Germans by France would be a flagrant violation of self-determination. The heated dispute was complicated by French demands for the coal-rich Saar Valley, inhabited almost solidly by Germans.

At the peak of the French crisis, in early April, 1919, Wilson was prostrated by influenza. Burning with a temperature of 103°, he lay in his bedroom racked by fits of coughing. To every demand of Clemenceau, seated with the rest of the Big Four in the outer chamber, he returned a defiant "no." His patience exhausted, he finally took steps to order the presidential liner, the *George Washington*, to be readied for his return. French newspapers jeered that he was going home to mother.

The Conference was saved when the French deadlock was broken by compromise. Germany's coveted Saar Basin would remain under the League of Nations for fifteen years, and then a vote of the population would determine its fate.* France yielded her demands for the Rhineland buffer state in return for a Security Treaty, signed by Wilson and Lloyd George. By its terms both America and Britain agreed to come to the defense of the French in the event of a future attack by the German invader. This treaty was quickly pigeonholed by the United States Senate, which shied away from all entangling alliances.

For France, which still bore the marks of the Hunnish invader, the outcome was supremely disillusioning. Deprived of both the Rhineland and a feeling of security, she was forced to drink the bitter dregs of betrayal.

Italy and Japan Defy Self-Determination

A clash now loomed with Italy, which demanded the key port of Fiume, near the head of the Adriatic Sea. Unfortunately, this landlocked harbor happened to be the most valuable seaport of the newly created nation of Yugoslavia. The city itself was inhabited predominantly by Italians, but the Yugoslavs were more numerous in the outskirts. To turn over these foreigners to Italy, like cattle in a pasture, would be a glaring violation of self-determination. Wilson, true to principle, fought valiantly for an acceptable alternative. But when the Italian delegates proved stubborn, he reverted to old habits and on April 23, 1919, issued a spectacular appeal over their heads to the masses of Italy.

Colonel House, one of the five American delegates wrote (April 22, 1919), "The whole world is speculating as to whether the Italians are 'bluffing' or whether they really intend going home and not signing the Peace unless they have Fiume. It is not unlike a game of poker."

* The Saar population voted overwhelmingly to rejoin Germany in 1935.

Japan Allegedly Using League to Grab China. San Francisco *Chronicle*.

Wilson's maneuver fell flat, for the Italian delegates went home in a huff. Their people, at heart more interested in booty than in ideals, turned savagely against the once-worshiped "Voovro Veelson." Yet Wilson, while not completely winning his point, kept the Italians from winning theirs—at least temporarily. The result was a hollow victory for self-determination.

The next crucial struggle was with the Japanese, who had been cleverly biding their time. When war broke out in 1914, Japan had joined the Allies and had seized Germany's holdings on China's Shantung peninsula, as well as the German islands in the Pacific. The overcrowded Japanese were naturally eager to keep all these spoils. Their persistence was rewarded when they were allowed to retain the strategic Pacific islands, though only as a mandate from the League of Nations.*

As for German rights in Shantung, Wilson opposed the Japanese claims with set jaw. To turn the fortunes of some 30,000,000 Chinese over to the tender mercies of Japan would be an intolerable violation of self-determination. The politely bowing little delegates from Nippon threatened to walk out, and if they had joined the absent Italians, the Peace Conference might well have dissolved.

In the end Wilson, with a wry face, was forced to accept a compromise on Shantung. Japan would keep Germany's economic holdings, and later return the strategic peninsula to China. The Chinese delegates in Paris, outraged, refused to sign the treaty. This whole solution smelled so much of old-time imperialism as to cause Clemenceau to jeer that Wilson "talked like Jesus Christ but acted like Lloyd George."

The Peace Treaty that Brought a New War

A completed Treaty of Versailles, after more weeks of wrangling, was handed to the Germans in June, 1919—almost literally on the point of a bayonet. They had given up their arms on the strength of assurances that they would be granted a peace based on the Fourteen Points, with two reservations. A careful analysis of the treaty shows that only about four of the twenty-three original Wilsonian points and subsequent principles were fully honored. Loud and guttural cries of betrayal burst from German throats—charges that Adolf Hitler vehemently reiterated during his meteoric rise to power.

Wilson, of course, was guilty of no conscious betrayal. But the Allied powers were torn by conflicting aims, many of them sanctioned by secret treaties. There had to be compromise at Paris—or there would be no agreement. Faced with hard realities, Wilson was forced to compromise away some of his less-cherished Fourteen

* In due time the Japanese illegally fortified these islands—the Marshalls, Marianas, and Carolines—and used them as bases against the United States in World War II.

Points in order to salvage the more precious League of Nations. He was much like the mother who has to throw her sickly younger children to the pursuing wolves in order to save her sturdy first-born son.

A troubled Wilson was not happy with the results. Greeted a few months earlier with frenzied acclaim in Europe, he was now a fallen idol, condemned alike by disillusioned liberals and frustrated imperialists. He was keenly aware of some of the injustices that had been forced into the treaty. But he was hoping that the League of Nations—a potent League with America as a leader—would iron out the inequities.

The Treaty of Versailles, hammered out in a madhouse of clashing ambitions, was clearly vulnerable to criticism. One of its chief weaknesses was that it fell between two stools. It tried to establish a lasting peace, while at the same time punishing the fallen foe. It was too harsh for a peace of accommodation, and too "soft"—thanks in part to Wilson—for a peace of vengeance. The victor may have peace, and he may have vengeance, but he can hardly hope to get both from the same treaty.

Yet the richly condemned Peace of Versailles had much to commend it. Not the least among its merits was its liberation of millions of minority peoples, such as the Poles, from the yoke of an alien dynasty. All the chaotic circumstances considered, the marvel is that any kind of an acceptable pact was signed.

Much—almost everything—depended on the good faith of the men and nations that carried out the treaty. If they had acted in the spirit intended, the results might well have been less tragic. Disappointing though Wilson's handiwork was, he saved the pact from being an old-time peace of imperialism. His critics to the contrary, the settlement was almost certainly a fairer one because he had gone to Paris.

The Domestic Parade of Prejudice

At home in America, breakers loomed. Wilson returned, early in July, 1919, in an uncompromising mood; privately he vowed that he would give no "nosegays" to the Senators whom he scorned. But the nation's temper had been changing while the wheels of the Peace Conference were grinding. The people had been emotionally aroused to march on to Berlin and hang the Kaiser—or perhaps boil him in oil. Wilson had brought a deep feeling of frustration by negotiating a cease-fire before fiery patriots could enjoy their fun. Colonel Theodore Roosevelt, still full of fight at the time of the Armistice, had bitterly condemned all the "peace twaddle."

Victory also brought an emotional letdown. The citizenry, keyed up overlong to a spirit of self-sacrifice, were suffering the inevitable "slump in idealism." It was deepened by a feeling of disillusion-

"Pilgrim Landing in America, 1919." Harding in the Brooklyn *Eagle*, 1919

ment. The world was not "safe for democracy," and just after the costly "war to end war" there were some twenty wars of varying dimensions raging all over the world. America had asked for nothing at the Paris Conference except peace. Instead of that, she was getting nothing but ingratitude from the Allies whom she had strained herself to help—while of course defeating a common enemy.

Disillusion kept pace with demobilization. Homesick "Yanks," pouring back by the hundreds of thousands, added to the national discontent. Sailing to France convinced that the French had wings and the Germans horns, they had been repelled by the ever-present manure piles and the "gouging" of French shopkeepers. The Germans of the Rhineland—especially the blonde girls—seemed so much cleaner and nicer than the French. Perhaps, some of the "doughboys" thought, America had fought the wrong foe. Prolonged delays in getting back to "God's country" had likewise bred nasty tempers among American soldiers. Common complaints were "Let Europe stew in her own juice" and "Lafayette, we are still here." A popular song ran:

We drove the Boche [Hun] across the Rhine,
The Kaiser from his throne.
Oh, Lafayette, we've paid our debt,
For Christ's sake, send us home.

Super-patriots in America, with their strong isolationist convictions, raised a furious outcry against entanglement. Revering the memory of Washington, Jefferson, and Monroe, they were hostile to a newfangled "League of Notions." Why fly the glorious Stars and Stripes below the flag of some internationalized super-state? One rhymester wrote sneeringly:

Our foreign countries, thee,
Lands of the chimpanzee,
Thy names we love. . . .

The Treaty of Versailles, one of the least perused and most abused in history, was showered with brickbats from all sides. Rabid Hunhaters, regarding the pact as not harsh enough, voiced their discontent. Professional liberals, like the New York *Nation*, thought it too harsh—and a gross betrayal to boot. German-Americans, Italian-Americans, and other "hyphenated Americans" were aroused because the peace settlement was not sufficiently favorable to their native lands.

Irish-Americans, traditional twisters of the British Lion's tail, denounced the League. They felt that with the additional votes of the five Dominions it gave Britain undue influence; and they feared that it could be used to force the United States to crush Irish independence. Crowds of Irish-American zealots hissed and booed Wilson's name.

Wilson's Tour and Collapse (1919)

Despite mounting discontent, the President had reason to feel optimistic. When he brought home the treaty, with the "Wilson League" firmly riveted in as Part I, a strong majority of the people still seemed favorable. At this time—early July, 1919—Senator Lodge had no real hope of defeating the pact. His strategy was merely to amend it in such a way as to "Americanize" or "Republicanize" it. The Republicans, still seriously divided, could then claim political credit for the changes.

One potent weapon that Lodge could wield was delay, for delay would confuse and divide public opinion. As chairman of the powerful Senate Committee on Foreign Relations, he read the entire 264-page treaty aloud, even though it had been printed. At one time only the Senator and a clerk occupied the committee room. Protracted hearings were also held by the Committee, and dozens of people of various nationalities aired their grievances. The treaty was in danger of being drowned in a sea of words.

Wilson fretted increasingly as the hot summer of 1919 wore on. The bulky pact was bogged down in the Senate, while the nation was drifting into confusion and apathy. He therefore decided to go to the country in a spectacular speechmaking tour. He would appeal over the heads of the Senate to the sovereign people—as he often had in the past.

This strenuous barnstorming campaign was undertaken in the face of protests by physicians and friends. Wilson had never been robust; he had entered the White House nearly seven years before with a stomach pump and with headache pills for his neuritis. His frail body had begun to sag under the strain of partisan strife, a global war, and a hectic peace conference. But he declared that he was willing to die, like the "doughboys" whom he had sent into battle, for the sake of the new world order.

"Going to Talk to the Boss."
Chicago *News*, 1919

The presidential tour, begun in September, 1919, got off to a rather lame start. The Middle West received Wilson lukewarmly, partly because of strong German-American influence. Trailing after him like bloodhounds came two "irreconcilable" Senators, Borah and Johnson, who used their rabble-rousing talents in the same cities a few days later. Hat-tossing crowds responded to the attacks on Wilson by crying, "Impeach him, impeach him."

But the reception was different in the Rocky Mountain region and on the Pacific Coast. These areas, which had elected Wilson in 1916, welcomed him with heart-warming outbursts. The high point—and the breaking point—of the return trip was at Pueblo, Colorado, September 25, 1919. Wilson, with tears coursing down his cheeks, pleaded for the League of Nations as the only real hope of preventing future wars. That night he collapsed from physical and nervous exhaustion.

Wilson was whisked back in the "funeral train" to Washington, where several days later a stroke paralyzed one side of his body. During the next few weeks he lay in a darkened room in the White House, as much a victim of the war as the unknown soldier buried at Arlington. For seven and one-half months he did not meet his Cabinet. Who ran the government is still something of a mystery, although Mrs. Wilson sifted the few papers that were brought to his attention—"boudoir government." As the tragedy unfolded, second-guessers pointed out that Wilson should never have left Washington. Instead, they argued, he should have tried to work out a compromise with the headstrong Senators, difficult though that course might have been.

Wilson Rejects the Lodge-Reserved Treaty

"Not Room for Both." San Francisco *Chronicle*

Senator Lodge, coldly calculating, was now at the helm. After failing to amend the treaty outright, he finally came up with fourteen formal reservations to it—a sardonic slap at Wilson's Fourteen Points. These safeguards reserved the rights of the United States under the Monroe Doctrine and the Constitution, and otherwise sought to protect American sovereignty. In general, they merely restated the obvious. If the Treaty had been approved with them attached, they probably would have been largely forgotten, as so often happens with reservations.

But Wilson, hating Lodge, saw red at the mere suggestion of the *Lodge* reservations. He was quite willing to accept somewhat similar reservations sponsored by his faithful Democratic followers, but he insisted that the Lodge reservations "emasculated" the entire pact. The truth is that ten of them applied to the League, and only four rather harmlessly to the main body of the treaty.

Public sentiment had meanwhile been shifting. By late November,

1919—two months after Wilson's collapse—popular opinion apparently favored some kind of reservations, whether of the Democratic or of the Lodge stripe. But Wilson, lying in his secluded and darkened sickroom, still had faith that he could get the treaty accepted without reservations. His bedside attendants, fearful of shocking him into a relapse, dared not tell him the disagreeable truth.

Though too feeble to lead, Wilson was still strong enough to obstruct. When the day finally came for the voting in the Senate, he sent word to all true Democrats to vote *against* the treaty with the odious Lodge reservations attached. He hoped that when these were cleared away, the path would be open for ratification without reservations, or with only mild Democratic reservations.

Loyal Democrats in the Senate, on November 19, 1919, blindly did Wilson's bidding. Combining with the "irreconcilables," mostly Republicans, they rejected the treaty with the Lodge reservations appended, 55 to 39. Then the Democrats tried to ram through the pact without any reservations, but mustered only 38 votes to 53. The irreconcilable "Battalion of Death," delighted with the turn of events, had now joined hands with the regular Republicans.

Defeat through the Lodge-Wilson Deadlock

The nation was too deeply shocked to accept the verdict as final. About four-fifths of the Senators professed to favor the treaty, with or without reservations, yet a simple majority could not agree on a single proposition. So strong was public indignation that the Senate was forced to act a second time. In March, 1920, the treaty was brought up again, with the Lodge reservations tacked on.

There was only one possible path to success. Unless the Senate approved the pact with the Lodge reservations, the entire document would be rejected. But the sickly Wilson, still sheltered behind drawn curtains and blind to disagreeable realities, again sent word to all loyal Democrats to vote down the treaty with the obnoxious Lodge reservations. When he signed this letter, he signed the death warrant of the treaty as far as America was concerned.

This time the count was closer. A total of twenty-one realistic Democrats, seeing that the choice was now the reserved pact or none at all, joined forces with the Lodge Republicans. A total of twenty-three loyal Democrats sided with the "Battalion of Death" to cast negative votes. On a fateful March 19, 1920, the treaty netted a simple majority but failed of the necessary two-thirds majority by a count of 49 yeas to 35 nays.

Who defeated the treaty? The Lodge-Wilson personal feud, traditionalism, isolationism, Southern sectionalism, disillusionment, and partisanship all entered the confused picture. Lodge maneuvered astutely to prevent another rupture in the party ranks like the Taft-

Senator Hitchcock, the Democratic leader, later told of one of his brief visits to Wilson and his suggestion of compromise with Lodge.

"'Let Lodge compromise,' he replied. 'Well, of course,' I added, 'he must compromise also, but we might well hold out the olive branch.'

'Let Lodge hold out the olive branch,' he retorted, and that ended it for that day, for he was too sick a man to argue with in the presence of his anxious doctor and his more anxious wife.'"

Roosevelt rift of 1912. But Wilson himself must bear a substantial share of the responsibility. As stubborn as when fighting Dean West at Princeton over the graduate school, he refused to accept a half-loaf. He asked for all or nothing—and got nothing. One Democratic Senator angrily charged that the President had strangled his own brain child with his own palsied hands rather than let the Senate straighten its crooked limbs. Isolationist Republicans jeeringly rewrote the 1916 slogan to read: "He Kept Us Out of Peace." One cynic said he was left "without a League to stand on."

Preparing the "Solemn Referendum" of 1920

Wilson had his own pet solution for the deadlock, and this partly explains why he refused to compromise on Lodge's terms. He proposed to settle the treaty issue in the forthcoming presidential campaign of 1920 by appealing to the people—the old appeal habit again—for a "solemn referendum." This was sheer folly, for a true mandate on the League in the noisy arena of politics was a clear impossibility.

Republican delegates were jubilant when they met in Chicago in June, 1920. Wilson was broken and discredited; the wayward Bull Moosers had wandered back into camp. The Old Guard, spearheaded by the Senate clique, was back in the saddle. Again the saying was current, as in 1896, that all the Republicans had to do was nominate a rag baby or a yellow dog. The platform that the party bosses devised was a masterpiece of ambiguity—a teeter-totter rather than a platform. It appealed to Republicans who favored the League, like ex-President Taft, and to Republicans who derided it, like Senators Borah and Johnson.

The political woods were full of presidential hopefuls. Colorful General Leonard Wood, whom Wilson had snubbed during the war, was the front-running candidate for the nomination. He was opposed, among others, by Senator Johnson of California, who had gained much notoriety by his unbridled assaults on the League.

Harding's windy, alliterative oratory is well exemplified by a famous passage in his "normalcy" speech in Boston (May, 1920): "America's present need is not heroics but healing; not nostrums but normalcy; not revolution but restoration; not surgery but serenity, not the dramatic but the dispassionate, not experiment but equipoise, not submergence in internationality but sustainment in triumphant nationality." The unusual word "normalcy" caught the popular fancy.

As the leading contestants killed one another off, the political weather vane began to veer toward genial Senator Warren G. Harding of Ohio. A group of Senate bosses, meeting rather casually in the historic "smoke-filled" Room 404 of the Hotel Blackstone, informally decided on the affable and malleable Ohioan. Their fair-haired boy was a prosperous, back-slapping, small-town newspaper editor of the "folksy" type, quite the opposite of Wilson, who had earlier noted the Senator's "disturbingly dull" mind. Harding had further increased his acceptability by urging a return to "normalcy" —something that the country ardently desired. Despite grave doubts as to his mentality and morality, certain cigar-chomping bosses helped to engineer his nomination.

When it came to the Vice-Presidency, the perspiring delegates rebelled against domination by the party wheelhorses. Taking the bit in their teeth, they nominated a frugal, grim-faced native of Vermont, Governor Calvin ("Silent Cal") Coolidge of Massachusetts. He had commended himself to the conservative delegates by his recent role, much overrated, in breaking a policemen's strike in Boston.

The Democrats, for the first time in the history of presidential conventions, met in breeze-swept San Francisco. Wilson, ill though he was, secretly angled for a third nomination. But all such maneuvers fell flat. His son-in-law, lanky "Crown Prince" McAdoo, was a leading contender who suffered from the increasing public distaste for both Wilson and his in-laws. At length the convention turned to a wealthy Ohio newspaper editor, the earnest and energetic Governor James M. Cox. The platform came out strongly for the League of Nations, as did the nominee. The vice-presidential nomination went to young Franklin D. Roosevelt, a tall, handsome, vibrant, thirty-eight-year-old New Yorker who had gained some fame as Assistant Secretary of the Navy.

Shortly after the Boston police strike was actually broken despite his own apathy, Coolidge sent a ringing telegram to Samuel Gompers, president of the American Federation of Labor, "There is no right to strike against the public safety by anybody, anywhere, any time."

The Solemn Muddlement of 1920

As campaigns go, this one was rather listless, for the threadbare League issue had been under constant debate for over a year. The Socialist New York *Call* thought that the League of Nations was as "vital as a dead cat in a gutter." A confused Harding, initially kept on his front porch by the party bosses, made a number of contradictory statements about the League. His most consistent theme was that if elected he would work for a vague Association of Nations—*a* league but not *the* League.

PRESIDENTIAL ELECTION OF 1920 (with electoral vote by state)

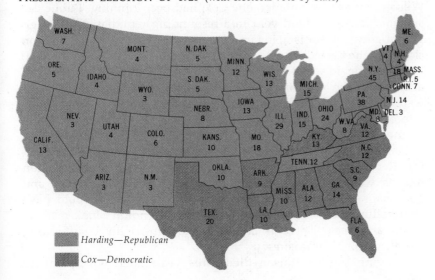

Harding—Republican

Cox—Democratic

Harding's following was badly divided. A group of thirty-one celebrities, mostly Republicans and including Hoover, Root, and Hughes, signed a statement declaring that the election of Harding was the surest way to get America into a reserved League. Bitter-end isolationists like Borah and Johnson insisted, on the contrary, that his election was the surest way to keep out. Republican slogans were "Let's Have Done with Wiggle and Wobble" and "Back to Normalcy."

When the sloganeering and the shouting ended, Harding was swept into the Presidency by a tremendous tidal wave of ballots. The long-frustrated females, given the vote several months earlier by the 19th Amendment, swelled the totals with woman power. Harding polled 16,152,200 votes to 9,147,353 for Cox, thus amassing a prodigious plurality of 7,004,847. The electoral count was 404 to 127. Eugene V. Debs, federal prisoner Number 2253 at the Atlanta Penitentiary, rolled up the largest vote for the Socialist Party in its history—919,799. Much of this left-wing support was doubtless a protest against the ineffective, second-rate Cox and the befuddled, stuffed-shirt Harding. "Thank God only one of them can be elected" was a cynical saying.

Was Harding's smashing victory a popular mandate against the League of Nations? The isolationist Republican wing gloatingly insisted that Wilson had asked for a "solemn referendum"—and now he had it. But there were so many issues that the outcome could not be a clear endorsement of any one proposal. If the electorate had been asked to vote on the League with reservations, they probably would have approved it. But they were never given such an opportunity.

Yet the election of 1920 had deeper meanings. The pendulum had swung back, and the Republicans, normally the majority since the Civil War, were returned to power. A crippled ghost candidate named Wilson, rather than an energetic Cox, had been running. Public desire for a change found vent in a resounding repudiation of "high and mighty" Wilsonism; in fact, "Down with Wilson" was a common slogan of the period. People were tired of professional highbrowism, star-reaching idealism, bothersome do-goodism, moral overstrain, and constant self-sacrifice. Eager to lapse back into "normalcy," they were willing to accept a second-rate President—and they got a third-rate one. It was election "by disgust," with "General Grouch" the winner.

Harding's victory was the death sentence of the League in America. Republican isolationists continued to insist that the election returns were a sweeping mandate against this "superstate," and politicians increasingly shunned the League as they would have shunned a leper. To them the "solemn referendum" looked like a deliberate recall. There is simply no arguing with a suffocating plurality of 7,000,000 votes.

A living legend, Wilson died three years later, with admirers

"He Did It!" Copyright Los Angeles *Times.* Reprinted by permission

kneeling in the snow outside his Washington home. One unsparing critic, the newspaperman William Allen White, wrote:

God gave him a great vision.
The devil gave him an imperious heart.
The proud heart is still.
The vision lives.

The Betrayal of Great Expectations

America's spurning of the League was tragically shortsighted. She had won a costly war, but she blindly kicked the fruits of victory under the table. Whether a strong international organization would have averted World War in 1939 will always be a matter of dispute. But there can be no doubt that the orphaned League of Nations was undercut at the start by the refusal of the mightiest power on the globe to join it. The Allies themselves were largely to blame for the new world conflagration that flared up in 1939, but they found a convenient justification for their own timorous shortcomings by pointing an accusing finger at Uncle Sam.

The ultimate collapse of the Treaty of Versailles must be laid, at least in some degree, at America's doorstep. This complicated pact, tied in with the four other peace treaties through the League Covenant, was a top-heavy structure designed to rest on a four-legged table. The fourth leg, the United States, was never put into place. This rickety structure teetered crazily for over a decade, and then crashed in ruins—a debacle which played into the hands of the German demagogue Adolf Hitler.

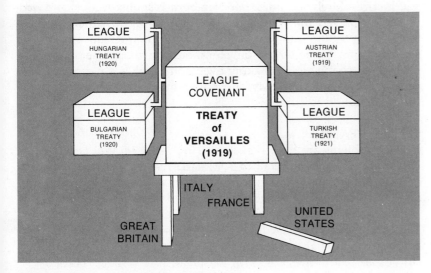

INTERLOCKING TREATY STRUCTURE

America lost moral face by her preach-and-run policy. She claimed advantages and opportunities without duties or responsibilities; she wanted peace—without having to pay for it. Her desertion of her war partners, even granting their imperialistic aims, marked the first serious breach in the ranks of the Allies. This fatal secession indirectly facilitated the ascent of Hitler and his brown-shirted bullies.

The Reparations Commission is a case in point. It had been created under the Treaty of Versailles with the understanding that America would exercise an important moderating influence. When she abdicated, the French secured a dominant voice. The result was an astronomical, trouble-breeding reparations bill of some thirty-two billion dollars, presented to the Germans virtually at pistol point. Although most of it was never paid, it contributed richly to the continuing economic chaos in Germany and elsewhere in Europe. These dangerous dislocations in turn were fuel for the propaganda machine that would promote the rise of Adolf Hitler.

No less ominous events were set in motion when the Senate spurned the Security Treaty with France. The French, fearing that a new generation of Germans would follow in its fathers' goose-steps, undertook to build up a powerful military force. Predictably resenting the presence of strong French armies, Germany began to rearm illegally. This witches' cauldron of uncertainty and suspicion brewed an intoxicant which helped inflame the fanatical following of dictator Hitler.

America, as the tragic sequel proved, hurt her own cause when she buried her head in the sands. Granted that the conduct of her Allies had been disillusioning, she had her own ends to serve by carrying through the Wilsonian program. She would have been well advised if she had resolutely assumed her war-born responsibilities, and had resolutely played the role of global leadership into which she had been thrust by the iron hand of destiny. In the interests of her own security, if for no better reason, she should have used her enormous strength to shape world-shaking events. Instead, she permitted herself to drift along aimlessly and dangerously toward the abyss of international disaster.

SELECT READINGS

The problems are treated sketchily in A. S. LINK, *Wilson the Diplomatist* (1956)*; in detail in T. A. BAILEY, *Woodrow Wilson and the Lost Peace* (1944)* and *Woodrow Wilson and the Great Betrayal* (1945).* The ablest pro-Wilson account is D. F. FLEMING, *The United States and the League of Nations* (1932). HERBERT HOOVER, *The Ordeal of Woodrow Wilson* (1958)* is a somewhat personalized account which is also revealing of ex-President Hoover. Detailed studies are FERDINAND CZERNIN, *Versailles, 1919* (1964)*; HAROLD NICOLSON, *Peacemaking 1919* (1933)*; S. P. TILLMAN, *Anglo-American*

Relations at the Paris Peace Conference of 1919 (1961); L. E. GELFAND, *The Inquiry: American Preparations for Peace, 1917–1919* (1963); R. N. STROMBERG, *Collective Security and American Foreign Policy* (1963); N. GORDON LEVIN, JR., *Woodrow Wilson and World Politics* (1968); and A. J. MAYER, *Politics and Diplomacy of Peacemaking* (1967).* GENE SMITH, *When the Cheering Stopped* (1964)* is a rather lurid journalistic account of the tragedy following Wilson's collapse. Lodge is somewhat rehabilitated in J. A. GARRATY, *Henry Cabot Lodge* (1953). Useful monographs are R. K. MURRAY, *Red Scare: A Study in National Hysteria, 1919–1920* (1955)* and W. M. BAGBY, *The Road to Normalcy: The Presidential Campaign and Election of 1920* (1962).* Also *Harvard Guide,* * Pt. VI.

* Available in paperback.

39

Harding and the Mirage of Normalcy

America's present need is not heroics but healing; not nostrums but normalcy; not revolution but restoration; . . . not surgery but serenity.

Senator Warren G. Harding, 1920

The Republican "Old Guard" Returns

Handsome President Harding, with erect figure (six feet), broad shoulders, high forehead, bushy eyebrows, and graying hair, was one of the best-liked men of his generation. An easygoing, warm-handed first-namer, he exuded graciousness and love of people. So kindly was his nature that he would brush off ants rather than crush them.

Yet the amiable, smiling exterior concealed a weak, flabby interior. With a mediocre mind, Harding quickly found himself beyond his depth in the Presidency. "God! What a job!" was his anguished cry on one occasion.

Harding, like Grant, was unable to detect moral halitosis in his evil associates, and he was soon surrounded by his poker-playing, shirt-sleeved cronies of the "Ohio Gang." "A good guy," Harding was "one of the boys." He hated to hurt people's feelings, especially those of his friends, by saying "no"; and designing political leeches capitalized on this failing. The difference between George Washington and Warren Harding, ran a current quip, was that while Washington could not tell a lie, Harding could not tell a liar.

A darling of the reactionaries, the affable Harding had been put up as a "stooge" by Big Business Republicans. The senatorial clique was tired of a domineering figure in the White House. They wanted a regular party man—a "putty" man—and they thought they had found him in the obliging Ohioan.

Candidate Harding, who admitted his scanty mental furnishings, had promised to gather about him the "best minds" of the party. Charles Evans Hughes—masterful, imperious, incisive, brilliant— brought to the Secretaryship of State a dominating if somewhat conservative leadership. The new Secretary of the Treasury was a lean and elderly Pittsburgh aluminum king, Andrew W. Mellon, multimillionaire collector of the paintings that are now displayed in Washington as his gift to the nation. Chubby-faced Herbert Hoover, famed feeder of the Belgians and "Hooverizer," became Secretary of Commerce. An energetic businessman and engineer, he raised his second-rate Cabinet post to first-rate importance, especially in drumming up foreign trade for American manufacturers.

But the three "best minds" of the Cabinet were partially offset by two of the worst. Senator Albert B. Fall of New Mexico, a scheming anti-conservationist, was appointed Secretary of the Interior. As guardian of the nation's natural resources, he resembled the wolf hired to protect the sheep. Harry M. Daugherty, a small-town lawyer but a big-time crook in the "Ohio Gang," was supposed to prosecute wrongdoers as Attorney General.

G.O.P. Reaction at the Throttle

Well-intentioned but weak-willed, Harding was a perfect "front" for enterprising industrialists. The rigor mortis of reaction slowly set in, as critics raised feeble voices to lament, "You can't teach an Old Guard new tricks." Democrats came to insist that the twelve reactionary Republican years, begun so inauspiciously by Harding, were essentially one administration as far as basic economic philosophy was concerned. Certainly the yeasty progressivism and reformism of the pre-war Wilson era were swept from the White House. A blowsy, nest-feathering crowd moved in and proceeded to hoodwink Harding.

The new Old Guard went the old Old Guard of Mark Hanna one better. Their plea was not for government simply to keep hands off business, but for government to act as an advance agent of business. In short, let Washington assist and protect industry but not regulate or hobble it.

Harding conservatives, though friendly to monopoly, did not try openly to turn back the clock. They made no real attempt to repeal the Clayton Anti-Trust Act or to abolish the Federal Trade Commission, both Wilsonian reforms. They subtly and effectively achieved their

President Warren G. Harding (1865–1923). Calvin Coolidge, Harding's vice-presidential running mate, said in 1920 of him that he was "a fitting representative of the common aspirations of his fellow citizens." The journalist H. L. Mencken wrote, "Put him into the White House, and you will put every president of every Chamber of Commerce into the White House . . ." Harding's reputation with historians has risen slightly in later years with the opening of his White House papers, and with the development of scandals in Washington that make those of his administration seem minor.

ends by putting the courts and the administrative bureaus in the hands of fellow standpatters.

The Supreme Court was a striking example of this trend. Harding lived less than three years as President, but to him fell the task of appointing four of the nine justices. Several of his choices were or became deep-dyed reactionaries, and they held the dike against popular currents for nearly two decades. Harding's fortunate choice for Chief Justice was ex-President Taft, who not only performed his duties ably but was more liberal than some of his associates.

Corporations, under Harding, could once more relax and expand. Anti-trust laws were often ignored, circumvented, or feebly upheld by friendly prosecutors in the Attorney General's office. On paper, the prosecutions under Harding compared not unfavorably in number with those under Taft, Roosevelt, and Wilson. But a zeal to smash monopoly was lacking. The Interstate Commerce Commission, to single out one agency, came to be dominated by men who were personally sympathetic to the managers of the railroads. Harding reactionaries might well have boasted, "We care not what laws the Democrats pass as long as we are permitted to administer them."

Big industrialists, striving to lessen competition, now had a free hand to set up trade associations. Cement manufacturers, for example, would use these agencies to agree upon standardization of product, publicity campaigns, and a united front in dealing with the railroads and labor. Although many of these associations ran counter to the spirit of existing anti-trust legislation, their formation was encouraged by Secretary Hoover. His sense of engineering efficiency was shocked by the waste resulting from cutthroat competition.

America Seeks Benefits without Burdens

Making peace with the fallen foe was the most pressing problem left on Harding's doorstep. The United States, having rejected the Treaty of Versailles, was still technically at war with Germany, Austria, and Hungary nearly three years after the Armistice.

Peace was finally achieved by lone-wolf tactics, for the Senate "irreconcilables" would accept no other. In July, 1921, Congress passed a simple joint resolution which declared the war officially ended. This declaration, at the same time, formally reserved to the United States all the rights and privileges conferred upon it by the yet unratified treaty settlements. In August, 1921, Washington negotiated separate peace pacts with Germany, Austria, and Hungary. These also specifically conferred on America all the advantages of the unratified treaties—without their obligations and responsibilities. Thus was Wilsonian idealism declared bankrupt.

Isolationism was enthroned in Washington. The dominant wing of the Republican Party of McKinley and Hay, though traditionally

Commenting on the separate treaty with Germany, the *London Times* rather sourly remarked that it did not think that the Allies "will be content to do the drudgery of the execution of peace [Treaty of Versailles], while the United States stands at a convenient distance to reap the share of benefits that may emerge."

devoted to mild imperialism and embryonic internationalism, turned its back sharply on the past. "Wobbly Warren" Harding, awed by his immense plurality, dropped his vaguely promised Association of Nations. Unfriendly Republican newspapers sneered at the successes of the infant League of Nations and jeered at its failures.

Official Washington continued to regard the League as a thing unclean. The Harding administration, with the Senate "irreconcilables" holding a hatchet over its head, at first refused even to support the League's world health program, though later taking halting steps toward non-political international cooperation with the new superbody. At one time, partly through inadvertence, the State Department failed to answer a batch of fourteen official communications from the League. All replies, when finally forthcoming, were noncommittal. The mighty Republic, in company with a few other nonjoiners like Ecuador, Mexico, and Hejaz, was content to till its garden alone. But the League was much too important to be completely ignored: "unofficial observers" were sent to its seat in Geneva, Switzerland, to hang around like detectives shadowing a criminal.

Yet Harding's administration could not completely turn its back on the outside world, especially the Middle East. The eagerness of America's recent British ally to secure the lion's share of the oil reserves located there had brought strong remonstrances from Washington. Remembering that the Allies had floated to victory on a flood of oil, experts recognized that liquid "black gold" was as necessary as blood in the battles of tomorrow. Secretary Hughes, dynamically continuing the strong policy of the Wilson regime, at length secured arrangements acceptable to the American oil companies.

"Harding's Way Out of the War," 1921. Fitzpatrick in the St. Louis *Post-Dispatch*

Bolshevist Russia, from the outset, had been getting the cold-shoulder from Washington. Wilson's administration had bluntly refused to recognize the new Communist dictatorship of Moscow. The State Department charged that the bloody-handed Bolsheviks had repudiated their lawful debts; that they had been guilty of bad faith; and that they were propagandizing actively in friendly countries, as they clearly were, for Communist world revolution.

The Harding regime, with its strong conservative coloration, naturally adopted this non-recognition gospel. Viewing the Russian Communists as moral lepers and economic outcasts, succeeding Republican administrations clung tenaciously to their policy for a total of twelve years.

But America's distaste for the Bolsheviks did not stifle her humanitarian impulses. When a calamitous famine struck Russia in 1921, the Republican Congress, seconded by private benefactors, voted $20,000,000 for relief. The huge mission of mercy was administered under the experienced hand of the Great Humanitarian, Herbert Hoover, who received scant appreciation from the suspicious Russian leaders. Perhaps 10,000,000 people were saved, many of whom later held the line against Hitler.

Ship-Scrapping at the Washington Conference

Many Republicans suffered from a guilty feeling that America's rejection of the League had struck a heavy blow at world peace. Once elevated to power, they cast about for some kind of satisfying substitute.

Disarmament was a problem that cried desperately for attention. The earnest attempts of the League in this area were being hampered by the lone-hand course of the United States, which boasted the second mightiest navy in the world, just behind Britain's. Not only that, but when the huge building program projected in 1916 was completed, America would enjoy unquestioned primacy of the waves —provided that rival programs remained unaltered.

The naval race in which Uncle Sam found himself bore all the earmarks of deadly rivalry with Britain and Japan, both recent allies. Competition with Japan was especially dangerous. Tensions had mounted to such a point in the unpacific Pacific as to confront the American people with the grim specter of war.

The son of General Graves, who commanded the American troops in Siberia, wrote for a popular magazine (May, 1921): "Is Japan preparing for a war with America, and was her Siberian expedition the first important step toward the realization of a Pan-Oriental plan calculated to make such a struggle possible and profitable? I am not a jingoist, but twenty months' intimate contact with the problem, as a staff officer of the American expedition, convinces me that such is the case."

Nipponese aggressiveness alarmed many Americans, especially the editors of the "yellow press." The nation had been disturbed by Japan's notorious Twenty-one Demands on China in 1915, and by her additional claims at the Paris Peace Conference regarding Shantung and the German Pacific islands. Friction had also developed with Japan during the Allied intervention in Russia's Siberia. When the American troops departed in 1920, the Japanese band struck up Stephen Foster's "Hard Times, Come Again No More."

The Anglo-Japanese alliance, first launched in 1902, was a further source of anxiety. If an armed clash should break out between America and Japan, British blood brothers would presumably have to shoot white Americans on behalf of yellow Asiatics. Actually, Britain was not so bound, but many people thought otherwise.

Public agitation in America, fed by these perils, brought about the headline-making Washington "Disarmament" Conference in 1921–1922. President Harding, at times a walking mass of indecisions, was almost literally pushed into calling the multi-power parley. The Japanese were reluctant to come, for they feared that they might be forced to disgorge their recent spoils. Bolshevik Russia, blackballed by the "capitalist" nations, defiantly refused to be bound by any of the prospective agreements.

Diplomatic Winnings at Washington

Disarmament on land, though anticipated at Washington, proved to be impossible. Shell-shocked France, rendered insecure by America's spurning the Security Treaty of 1919, not only maintained the finest army in western Europe, but insisted on keeping it. She also vetoed restrictions on submarines—a poor nation's prime naval weapon. Security, she consistently insisted, must precede disarmament.

As for naval disarmament, the spotlight focused on big battleships. Although Britain still had the largest navy, the clatter of American riveters proclaimed that the United States would soon catch up with her. Secretary Hughes dramatically proposed at Washington a holiday in building battleships, and the outright scrapping by the three major powers of dozens built or building. The scaled-down navies of America and Britain were to enjoy parity in battleships and aircraft carriers, with Japan on the small end of a 5–5–3 ratio. This arrangement sounded to the sensitive Japanese ambassador like "Rolls-Royce, Rolls-Royce, Ford."

The Five Power Naval Treaty of 1922 embodied these terms. But they were not agreed upon until face-saving compensation was offered to the insecure Japanese. The British and Americans both agreed, as an important concession, not to build additional fortifications in certain Far Eastern outposts, including the Philippines.

	Battleships	Battleship Tonnage	Aircraft Carrier Tonnage
U. S.	18	525,000	135,000
Britain	22	525,000	135,000
Japan	10	315,000	81,000
France	7	175,000	60,000
Italy	6	175,000	60,000

LIMITS IMPOSED BY WASHINGTON CONFERENCE

Additionally, the Washington Conference sought to soothe American nerves by scrapping the Anglo-Japanese alliance. This pact was finally junked and the Japanese reluctantly accepted the Four Power Treaty—involving America, Britain, France, and Japan—for preserving the status quo in the Pacific. In some respects, this new makeshift was more of an entanglement than the much-feared League of Nations. But because it was sponsored by the reigning Republicans, Senator Lodge gave it his powerful support. One unhappy Japanese diplomat, distressed by this weak substitute for a firm alliance, complained, "We have discarded whiskey and accepted water." Japan got a four-power agreement to talk in place of a two-power agreement to fight.

The Washington Conference also gave chaotic China—"the Sick Man of the Far East"—something of a shot in the arm. In the Nine Power Treaty of 1922, the principal nations concerned with the Far East unanimously agreed to nail wide the Open Door. This pact was the only formal agreement ever entered into by all the major powers, except Russia and Germany, to uphold the principles proclaimed by Secretary John Hay nearly a quarter of a century earlier.

Delusive Disarmament in the 1920's

When the final gavel banged, the Hardingites boasted with much fanfare of their globe-shaking achievement in disarmament. But the results at Washington were, at best, somewhat illusory. As no restrictions whatever were placed on smaller warcraft, the costly naval race went merrily on in cruisers, destroyers, and submarines. In this contest a penny-pinching Uncle Sam was soon lagging dangerously behind. But it is true that the American taxpayer secured substantial relief—temporarily.

As for the burdens of armament, the New York *Independent*, a prominent magazine, noted in January, 1921, that the country was "more afraid of the tax collector than of any more distant foe."

To obtain parity the United States was forced to scrap more than two dozen warships, built or nearing completion. An erroneous sneer was revived: Uncle Sam, the greenhorn at the poker table, wins all his wars but loses all his conferences. In this case he was accused of having "scuttled the navy"—of having scrapped fine big battleships while the other powers scrapped fine big blueprints. Actually, Britain and Japan scrapped both blueprints and battleships.

The truth is that at Washington America yielded *potential* naval superiority. She did so partly because the taxpayers did not want to dig down into their pockets for the money with which to achieve supremacy. American naval experts, of course, were irked by the bar against further fortifications in the Far East. One of them moaned, "Anybody can spit on the Philippines and you can't stop them."

But the Washington treaties were a compromise—and no true compromise is ever completely satisfactory to any party concerned. All three major powers had to give up ships to get a paring down of navies. The Japanese delegates, in their view, sacrificed the most, and their people were acutely distressed by the outcome. Without America's concession to them regarding future non-fortification of Far Eastern outposts, there probably would have been no naval agreement.

A major achievement of the Conference was scrapping distrust. The unpacific Pacific was pacified—temporarily. In the new and less menacing atmosphere, the Japanese grudgingly consented to retire from Siberia and Shantung, and to abandon some of their Twenty-one Demands on China.

But though it afforded short-run relief, the Conference probably hurt long-run arms limitation. It was not, despite boastful Republican claims, a "peace conference" or an adequate substitute for the

League of Nations. The arms-scrapping agreement itself presented dangerous loopholes. It also hampered the earnest efforts of the League to achieve disarmament, partly because it lulled men into a false sense of security. A complete collapse of arms limitation came in the 1930's, thanks partly to America's anti-League policy. This breakdown of disarmament, which resulted in piling up arms while denying them to Germany, was one more rung in the ladder by which Adolf Hitler scrambled to power.

Rousting Out the Reds

A hysterical fear of Red Russia continued to color American thinking for several years after the Communist coup of 1917. Many nervous souls suspected that the Washington government was in danger of being overthrown by the sinister tactics of bomb-and-whisker Bolsheviks. Tensions were heightened by an epidemic of violent strikes that convulsed the Republic shortly after the war, many of them a result of the high cost of living. But upstanding Americans were prone to view these disorders as Red-inspired and Red-led, as indeed a few of them were.

The "Big Red Scare" of 1919-1920 resulted in a nationwide crusade against left-wingers whose Americanism was suspect. Attorney General A. Mitchell Palmer, who perhaps "saw Red" too easily, earned the title of "the Fighting Quaker" by his zeal in rounding up suspects. They ultimately totaled about six thousand. This drive to root out radicals was redoubled in June, 1919, when a bomb shattered both the nerves and the Washington home of Palmer. "The Fighting Quaker" was thereupon dubbed "the Quaking Fighter."

Two other events highlighted the Red Scare. Late in December, 1919, a shipload of 249 alien radicals was deported on the *Buford* ("Soviet Ark") to the "workers' paradise" of Russia. One zealot cried, "My motto for the Reds is S.O.S.—ship or shoot." Hysteria was redoubled in September, 1920, when a still-unexplained bomb blast in Wall Street killed thirty-eight persons and wounded several hundred others.

Bolsheviks Hide Under the Stars and Stripes. Philadelphia *Inquirer*, 1919

Various states joined the pack in the outcry against radicals. In 1919–1920 a number of legislatures, reflecting the anxiety of "solid" citizens, passed criminal syndicalism laws. These anti-Red statutes, some of which were born of the war, made unlawful the *advocacy* of violence to secure social change. Critics protested that mere words were not criminal deeds, and that there was a great gulf between throwing fits and throwing bombs. At all events, violence was done to traditional American concepts of free speech as I.W.W.'s and other radicals were vigorously prosecuted. The hysteria went so far that in 1920 five members of the New York legislature, all lawfully elected, were denied their seats simply because they were Socialists.

Anti-Redism and anti-foreignism were reflected in a notorious case regarded by liberals as a "judicial lynching." Nicola Sacco, a shoe-factory worker, and Bartolomeo Vanzetti, a fish peddler, were convicted in 1921 of the murder of a Massachusetts paymaster and his guard. The jury and judge were probably prejudiced in some degree against the defendants because they were Italians, atheists, anarchists, and draft dodgers.

Liberals and radicals the world over rallied to the defense of the two aliens doomed to die. The case dragged on for six years until 1927, when the condemned men were electrocuted. Communists and other radicals were thus presented with two martyrs in the "class struggle," while many American liberals hung their heads. The evidence against the accused, though damaging, betrayed serious weaknesses. If the trial had been held in an atmosphere less surcharged with anti-Redism, the outcome might have been only a prison term.

Industrial Demobilization

Washington ended its emergency operation of the railroad business in 1920, when the lines were returned to private control. Generous, not to say overgenerous, compensation was paid the owners.

Wartime overuse of the railroads, combined with subsequent labor difficulties, had left the lines in such a snarl that Congress was forced to step in. The Esch-Cummins Transportation Act of 1920 was designed to improve their financial health and provide arbitration of labor disputes. This law differed markedly from previous railroad legislation in that it sought to encourage consolidation rather than to thwart monopoly and enforce competition. The new philosophy was not to save the country from the railroads, as in the days of the Populists, but to save the railroads for the country.

"Low Bridge," 1921. Wartime Freight Rates Due for a Fall. Courtesy of Detroit *News*

Washington also tried to pull up anchor and get out of the shipping business. When the war ended, superfluous ships were sliding down the ways in profusion. The Merchant Marine Act of 1920 authorized the Shipping Board, which controlled about fifteen hundred vessels, to dispose of much of the hastily built wartime fleet at bargain-basement prices. In one instance, two hundred unprofitable wooden ships brought only a little more than the initial cost of building one of them. The Board was also authorized to operate the remaining vessels, and it did so without conspicuous success.

America's sickly merchant marine faced rough seas in the 1920's. It was an important factor in the national economy and, as an auxiliary of the navy, an indispensable prop of the national defense. Yet under the La Follette Seaman's Act American shipping could not thrive in competition with foreigners, who all too often provided wretched food and starvation wages.

During the 1920's successive Republican Congresses attempted to bail out the waterlogged merchant marine, notably with the Jones-

Winslow Homer (1836–1910), **Prisoners from the Front.** 1866
Metropolitan Museum of Art, New York

Boston-born Winslow Homer began his artistic career as a magazine illustrator. Turning to painting, he excelled in folk scenes and in seascapes, notably of the Maine coast, where he rigged up a portable glass studio from which he could paint the fury of the storm. Few American artists have reaped greater acclaim while living, and probably none of them has excelled him in capturing the overwhelming power and majesty of the sea. This painting, exhibited in the Paris International Exposition of 1867, draws upon Homer's wartime observations in recreating with firm outlines and broad planes of light and dark the out-at-the-elbows defiance of the beaten Confederates.

Charles C. Nahl (1818–1897)
Sunday Morning in the Mines. 1872
Collection: E. B. Crocker Art Gallery, Sacramento, California

Born in Germany, Nahl began his painting career in New York City but moved to San Francisco at midcentury to record the drama and excitement of the gold-rush days. He lived close enough in time and place to these stirring times to revive in rich color and picturesque detail the rough vitality of the mining camps and the rugged men who inhabited them. This painting is one of his most ambitious and popular contributions.

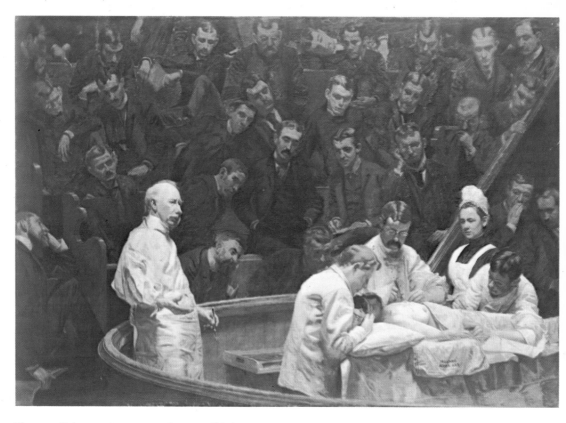

Thomas Eakins (1844–1916), **Agnew Clinic.** 1889
The School of Medicine, University of Pennsylvania

Eakins, a Philadelphian, was trained in Paris and at the Pennsylvania Academy of Fine Arts, where he was to become its greatest teacher and one of America's finest portraitists. Himself a sportsman, he delighted in portraying athletes, and his uncompromising realism is reflected in his mastery of human anatomy. His employment of live nudes for instructional purposes aroused much criticism. One of his most famous paintings depicts with undisguised frankness the surgical clinic of Dr. David H. Agnew, an eminent surgeon at the University of Pennsylvania. This shocking canvas was denied display in the American section of Philadelphia's Centennial Exposition.

Frederic Remington (1861–1909)
The Buffalo Hunt. 1890
The Whitney Gallery of Western Art, Cody, Wyoming

Painter, sculptor, and author (self-illustrated), Remington was born in New York state and studied fine arts at Yale. After unsuccessfully managing a sheep and mule ranch in the West, he found his career in preserving, through hundreds of drawings, paintings, and bronzes, the rough life of the vanishing West—Indians, cowboys, frontiersmen, soldiers, and horses. Considered by many to be the pre-eminent artist of the West, he reveals his mastery of the horse in action in *The Buffalo Hunt.*

John Singer Sargent (1856–1925), **The Crashed Airplane.** 1918
Trustees of the Imperial War Museum, London

Born in Florence to American parents, Sargent studied and painted abroad during most of his life. On his numerous trips to the United States he executed many of the fashionable and near-photographic portraits that made him famous. His rich tonal contrasts rasped some critics, who condemned his bravura brushwork as of "the Slashing School." In later life he turned increasingly to landscapes and everyday scenes. As an official wartime painter for the British government during 1918, he produced this ironical picture of a downed warplane in a pastorally peaceful French setting.

Grant Wood (1892–1942)
Daughters of Revolution. 1932
Cincinnati Art Museum

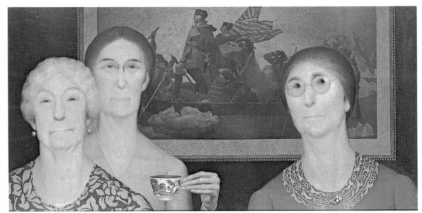

Iowa-born, -bred, and -buried, Wood studied in Chicago, Paris, and Germany. In Europe he was impressed by the harsh and realistic faces he saw in medieval canvases, which reminded him of his own countrymen. He came to reflect the European folk-art technique as one of the foremost "American scene" painters of the 1920's and 1930's. His regionalism was strikingly manifested in the stern and upright visages of the rural Middle West, well exemplified in his famous *American Gothic* (1930). *Daughters of Revolution*, one of his best satirical representations, pillories the smug and conservative D.A.R. type which sometimes grew out of rural parochialism.

Thomas Hart Benton (1889–   )
Boom Town. 1928
The Memorial Art Gallery, University of Rochester

A Missouri grandnephew of Senator Thomas Hart Benton of Missouri, Benton became the best-known American muralist of the 1930's and 1940's. He countered the influence of foreign art movements in America by promoting a distinctive regionalism which relied on a semi-abstract overlapping and a free-flow of figures and objects in highly delineated Americanesque landscapes. Flamboyant in his dramatization of American themes, especially those of the Middle West, he caught the hurly-burly of the hilariously prosperous 1920's in his *Boom Town.*

John Sloan (1871–1951)
Backyards—Greenwich Village. 1914
Oil on canvas. 26 × 32. Collection Whitney Museum of American Art, New York. (Geoffrey Clements, photography)

A Philadelphian by birth, Sloan worked for more than a dozen years as a newspaper illustrator. In New York he became a prominent member of "The Ashcan School," a group of artists who were opposed to melodramatic and superficial estheticism. Sloan found inspiration in the garbage cans, clotheslines, and alley cats of the New York slums, whose streets he loved to walk and whose sights, sounds, and smells he savored for their authenticity. *Greenwich Village Backyards* reveals the direct, unpretentious focus of Sloan's attention on the mundane but thoroughly real experiences of urban life.

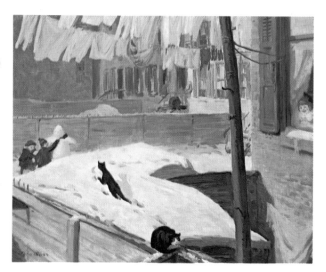

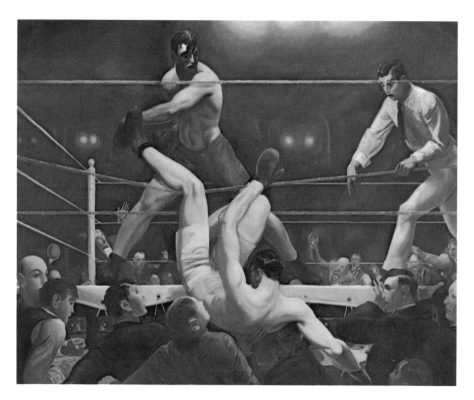

George W. Bellows (1882–1925), **Dempsey and Firpo.** 1924
Oil on canvas. 51 × 63¼ Collection Whitney Museum of American Art, New York
(Geoffrey Clements, photography)

An Ohioan who studied art in New York City, Bellows never visited Europe. His powerful
realism followed the lead of "The Ashcan School," and is strikingly represented in his
bold scenes of big-city ferment and brutality. In a series of six prize-fight paintings,
including *Dempsey and Firpo*, Bellows recaptures the drama of "million-dollar gates" of
the Roaring Twenties. In 1923 the Argentinian Firpo knocked heavyweight champion Jack
Dempsey out of the ring, only to have the crowd boost him back in to win by a knockout.

William Gropper (1897– .), **Migration.**
c. 1932
*Gift of Oliver B. James, University Art
Collections, Arizona State University,
Tempe, Arizona*

Painter, muralist, and cartoonist from New
York City, Gropper supported himself
during his youth by working in restaurants
while studying art at night school. He
became deeply concerned about social
irresponsibility and class inequalities,
especially those magnified by the hardships
of the Depression. His bold, satiric style
is especially effective in *Migration*, which
shows a family in the 1930's being blown
out of the Dust Bowl.

Philip Evergood (1901–   )
American Tragedy. 1937
Collection: Armand G. Erpf
Courtesy: Terry Dintenfass Gallery

Born in New York City, Evergood first
attended Eton and Cambridge in England
and then studied art in London, Paris, and
New York. He painted several murals under
the auspices of the Depression-spawned
Federal Art Project. Evergood's "social
realism" infuses his work with anger directed
at social injustice, such as the killing and
wounding of striking workers during the
1937 Chicago police riot. *American Tragedy,*
with its expressionist distortions of bodies,
details, and perspectives, is Evergood's bitter
reminder of the American dream gone sour.

George Tooker (1920–   ), **The Subway.** 1950
*Egg tempera on composition board. 18⅛ × 36⅛. Juliana Force Purchase. Collection Whitney
Museum of American Art, New York.* (Geoffrey Clements, photography)

Born in Brooklyn and educated at Harvard, Tooker studied art in New York City and has
exhibited his canvases in both America and Europe. He deals with such themes as the alienation
of modern man, notably in *The Subway,* which stresses the mechanistic and depressing urban
routine in which so many people live out their frustrated lives. The painting is compositionally
powerful because of the angular and geometric framework around which Tooker has arranged
the component parts of the scene.

Stuart Davis (1894–1964), **Garage Lights.** 1931
Memorial Art Gallery, The University of Rochester

A native Pennsylvanian, Davis was deeply impressed in 1913 by New York City's Armory Show, which
introduced French impressionism and cubism (with its geometric patterns) to the American public. He
combined the cubist restructuring of form and the expressionist propensity for brilliant color with his
own inclinations toward poster-like and vibrant compositions, thus producing solid and exciting abstract
paintings. His liking for jazz may have contributed a calligraphic tempo to *Garage Lights,* in which he
reduced the electrifying forms of urban life to simplified patterns possessing a unique gaiety, wit, and
freshness.

Jackson Pollock (1912–1956), **The She-Wolf.** 1943
Collection, The Museum of Modern Art, New York

Born in Wyoming, Pollock went to New York and studied under Thomas Hart Benton. Breaking away from regionalism, he turned to surrealism, which was based on the workings of the subconscious mind. The culmination of his bent toward abstraction occurred in the 1950's when he began to lay large canvases on the floor and drip paint in linear rhythms so vigorously as to produce "action painting," in which images are not preconceived but emerge during the expressive action. Pollock had become the high priest of American abstract expressionism when he was killed in an automobile accident at age 44. *The She-Wolf,* in which the outlines of the beast are faintly discernible, was one of Pollock's last barely representational works.

Josef Albers (1888–   ), **Homage to the Square "Ascending."** 1953
Oil on composition board. 43½ × 43½.
Collection Whitney Museum of American Art, New York. (Geoffrey Clements, photography)

Born and educated in Germany, Albers escaped Hitlerian despotism by fleeing to the United States with scores of other artists in the 1930's. He taught art at various institutions, including Yale, and exhibited internationally. Albers' contribution to modern art has been to promote the exploration of pure form in abstract design by turning to geometrical variations, in which his hardedged squares and rigid color areas set up shimmering tensions of space and hue. His famous "homage to the square" series includes this painting, in which his exquisite scientific and artistic precision is displayed with forthright simplicity, yet deep subtlety.

White Act of 1928. Under its provisions shipping was to be encouraged by attractive subsidies, thinly disguised as mail-carrying contracts. Federal loans up to three-fourths of building costs were to be made available at low rates of interest. These arrangements worked reasonably well until the New Deal days of 1936, when Congress abandoned roundabout aid in favor of outright subsidies.

Meanwhile, the return of American business to "normalcy" after the Armistice of 1918 was seriously hampered by inflation and depression. The newly poor far outnumbered the newly rich, for the upward-spiraling cost of living pinched wage earners, white-collar workers, and others on fixed incomes. A major post-war recession, from 1920 to 1922, further aggravated economic conditions. In 1921 alone, about 20,000 business houses went to the wall.

Labor, caught in the middle, on the whole fared badly. A futile strike in the steel industry against the twelve-hour, two-shift day was completely crushed in 1921. A favorite anti-labor device was to accuse the Reds of inspiring these disorders, as in some cases they doubtless did. Violence frequently flared forth, and altogether scores of persons were killed or wounded by factory guards ("goons"). The use of the federal injunction to crush strikes, so bitterly condemned by labor, was conspicuously revived by Attorney General Daugherty, who fully shared Harding's Big Business bias.

Wall Street's Big Bull Market

The Golden Twenties began in 1922, with the end of the post-war depression and the start of the fantastic Long Boom. A theme song of the period was the current tune:

My sister she works in the laundry,
My father sells bootlegger gin,
My mother she takes in the washing,
My God! how the money rolls in!

Yet there was something feverishly unhealthy about the inflationary joy ride; even in the best years of the 1920's several hundred banks failed annually. This something-for-nothing craze was well illustrated by real estate speculation, especially the fantastic Florida boom which culminated in 1925. Numerous underwater lots were sold to eager purchasers for preposterous sums. The whole wildcat scheme collapsed in 1926, when the peninsula was devastated by a West Indian hurricane, which belied advertisements of a "soothing tropical wind."

The stock exchange provided even greater sensations. Speculation ran wild, and an orgy of boom-or-bust trading pushed the bull markets up to dizzy peaks. "Never sell America short" and "Be a bull on America" were favorite catchwords, as Wall Street sharks gouged one

"Just Like Water Off a Duck's Back." Columbus *Dispatch*, 1929

another and fleeced greedy lambs. The stock market became a veritable gambling den.

As the 1920's lurched forward, everybody seemed to be buying stocks "on margin"—that is, with a small down payment. Barbers, stenographers, and elevator boys cashed in on "hot tips" picked up while on duty. One valet was reported to have parlayed his wages into a quarter of a million dollars. "The cash register crashed the Social Register," as rags-to-riches Americans eagerly worshiped at the altar of the ticker-tape machine. So powerful was the intoxicant of quick profits that few heeded the voices raised in certain quarters to warn that this kind of tinsel prosperity could not last forever.

Little was done by Washington to curb money-mad speculators. In the wartime days of Wilson, the national debt had rocketed from the 1914 figure of $1,188,235,400 to the 1921 peak of $23,976,250,608. Conservative financing pointed to a diversion of surplus funds to reduce this financial burden.

A businesslike move toward economic sanity was made in 1921, when a Republican Congress created the Bureau of the Budget. Its Director was to assist the President in preparing careful estimates of receipts and expenditures for submission to Congress as the annual budget. This reform, long overdue, was designed in part to prevent haphazardly extravagant appropriations.

The burdensome taxes inherited from the war were especially distasteful to Secretary of the Treasury Mellon, as well as to his fellow millionaires. Their theory was that such high levies forced the rich to invest in tax-exempt securities, rather than in the factories that provided prosperous payrolls. The Mellonites also argued, with considerable persuasiveness, that high taxes not only discouraged business but also brought a smaller net return to the Treasury than moderate taxes.

Seeking to succor the "poor" rich man, Mellon helped engineer a series of tax reductions from 1921 to 1926. Congress followed his lead by repealing the excess profits tax, abolishing the gift tax, and reducing excise taxes, the surtax, the income tax, and estate taxes. In 1921 a wealthy man with an income of $1,000,000 had paid $663,000 in income taxes; in 1926 he paid about $200,000. Mellon's spare-the-rich policies thus shifted much of the tax burden from the wealthy to the middle income groups.

Mellon, the "greatest Secretary of the Treasury since Hamilton," remains a controversial figure. True, he reduced the national debt by ten billion dollars—from about $26,000,000,000 to $16,000,000,000. But foes of the emaciated multimillionaire charged that he should have bitten a larger chunk out of the debt, especially while the country was pulsating with prosperity. He was also accused of indirectly encouraging the bull market. If he had absorbed more of the national income in taxes, there would have been less money left for frenzied speculation.

The "Bonus Boys" Seek Their Bonus—Prematurely

Needy veterans, no less than greedy millionaires, received generous treatment from the big business administrations of the 1920's. Congress dealt lavishly with the incapacitated ex-soldier when it set up the Veterans' Administration in 1921. The new program—so generous as to promote graft—provided for the building of hospitals and the beginnings of vocational rehabilitation.

Non-disabled veterans, unwilling to be slighted, quickly organized into pressure groups. Noteworthy among them was the American Legion. Founded in Paris in 1919 by Colonel Theodore Roosevelt, Jr., it met periodically to renew old hardships and let off steam in good-natured horseplay. The Legion soon became distinguished for its militant patriotism, its rock-ribbed conservatism, and its zealous anti-Redism.

The chief grievance of the ex-"doughboys" was monetary. Drafted into the army to save their country, they had not only lost their jobs but had got along on the niggardly pay of "buck privates." When arms were grounded, many of them had trouble getting back old jobs or securing new ones. At best, they had lost several costly years in the ruthless economic race. Men exempt from the draft, as well as draft dodgers, had stayed safely at home and waxed fat on war-boom wages. The ex-"doughboys" wanted their "dough"— some kind of additional payment to provide partial compensation for their sacrifices. Critics called this demand a holdup "bonus"; the ex-servicemen called it "adjusted compensation."

The agitation of the organized veterans, manifested colorfully in giant parades, impressed a vote-conscious Congress. In 1922 the legislators passed the first bonus bill, which was designed to grant $50 for each month of service. President Harding, disturbed by what he regarded as a group-interest raid on the Treasury, wielded an emphatic veto. This was one of the few occasions when he displayed real backbone.

Re-forming their lines, the repulsed veterans gathered for a final attack. In 1924 a beleaguered Congress, again hoisting the white flag, passed the Adjusted Compensation Act. Each ex-soldier was to receive a paid-up insurance policy due in twenty years. It would represent $1.25 for every day overseas and $1.00 for each day of home service—altogether a sum that would add about three and a half billion dollars to the total cost of the war. Penny-pinching Calvin Coolidge, who meanwhile had come to the White House, sternly vetoed the measure. But Congress overrode him, leaving the veterans with their deferred bonus.

Calvin Coolidge, while a candidate for the Vice Presidency in 1920, had said, "The nation which forgets its defenders will be itself forgotten." His veto of the bonus in 1924 suggests that he may have been thinking of disabled defenders.

Hiking the Tariff Higher

Businessmen, not to be snubbed, also had their hands outstretched —for a higher protective tariff. They were spurred into action by the prospect of an avalanche of goods from a recovering Europe, and by the blighting post-war depression.

In 1921, less than three months after Harding's inauguration, Congress passed the hastily formulated Emergency Tariff Act. It raised duties on certain agricultural products, including wool and sugar, and clamped an embargo on German dyestuffs.

Emergency legislation was followed the next year by the more comprehensive Fordney-McCumber Tariff Law of 1922. Glib lobbyists once more descended upon Congress and helped boost schedules from the average of 27% under Wilson's Underwood Tariff of 1913 to an average of 38.5%, which was almost as high as Taft's Payne-Aldrich Tariff of 1909. (See graph, p. 849.) More important was the fact that the trend toward high protection was heavily accelerated. Duties on farm produce were increased, and the principle was set forth that the general rates were designed to equalize the cost of American and foreign production. A promising degree of flexibility was introduced for the first time when the President was authorized, with the advice of the fact-finding Tariff Commission, to reduce or increase duties by as much as 50%.

Presidents Harding and Coolidge, true to their big-industry sympathies, were far more friendly to tariff increases than to reductions. In six years they authorized thirty-two upward changes, including on their list vital commodities like dairy products, chemicals, and pig iron. During the same period the White House ordered only five reductions. These included mill feed and such trifling items as bob-white quail, paintbrush handles, phenol, and cresylic acid.

The high-tariff course thus charted by the Republican regimes set off an ominous chain reaction. European producers felt the squeeze, for the American tariff walls prolonged the post-war chaos. An impoverished Europe needed to sell its manufactured goods to the United States, particularly if it hoped to achieve economic recovery and to pay its huge war debt to Washington. America needed the low-cost exports of foreign countries to reduce her current high cost of living. She also needed to give foreign nations a chance to make a profit from her so that they could buy her manufactured articles. International trade, Americans were slow to learn, is a two-way street. In general, they could not sell to others in quantity unless they bought from them in quantity—or lent them more American dollars.

Erecting tariff walls was a game that two could play. The two-edged American example spurred European nations, throughout the feverish 1920's, to pile up higher barriers themselves. These artificial obstacles were doubly bad: they hurt not only American-made goods but the products of neighboring European countries as well. The whole vicious circle further deepened the post-war economic distress, and further disposed the Germans to welcome Hitler as a latter-day messiah.

"It Works Both Ways," 1921. Courtesy of Dallas *News*

Stemming the Foreign Flood

Isolationist America of the 1920's, ingrown and provincial, was hostile to the influx of foreigners, as well as their goods. Hordes of destitute Europeans, uprooted by war, were again flocking to the Promised Land of America. In the one year ending June 30, 1921, some 800,000 stepped ashore, about two-thirds of them from Southern and Eastern Europe. "Refuse the refuse" was a popular outcry of "one-hundred-percent Americans."

Congress temporarily plugged the breach with the Emergency Quota Act of 1921. Newcomers from Europe were restricted in any given year to a definite quota, which was set at 3% of the persons of their nationality who had been living in the United States in 1910. This national-origins system was relatively favorable to the immigrants from Southern and Eastern Europe, for by 1910 immense numbers of them had already arrived.

This stopgap legislation of 1921 was replaced, after more mature reflection, by the Immigration Act of 1924. Quotas for foreigners were cut from 3% to 2%. The national-origins base was shifted from the census of 1910 to that of 1890, when comparatively few South Europeans had arrived.* Great Britain and Northern Ireland, for example, could send 65,721 a year as against 5802 for Italy. South Europeans bitterly condemned the device as unfair and discriminatory—a triumph for the "nativist" belief that blue-eyed and fair-haired North Europeans were of better blood. The purpose was clearly to freeze America's existing racial composition, which was largely North European.

The quota system effected an epochal departure in American practice. It recognized that the nation was filling up and that a "No Vacancy" sign was needed. Immigration henceforth died down to a comparative trickle; the famed melting pot henceforth would operate primarily on the foreigners already present. By 1931, probably for the first time in American experience, more foreigners left than arrived. Quotas thus caused America to sacrifice something of her tradition of freedom and opportunity, as well as much of her color and variety. But the nation gained in racial uniformity.

An ominous section of the Immigration Act of 1924 related to Japan. Relations with the Land of the Cherry Blossoms, following the air-clearing Washington Conference, had been tolerably good. They had markedly improved as a result of the outpouring of American aid to the sufferers from the frightful Tokyo earthquake of 1923, which killed more than 90,000 victims. But now everything was changed.

On paper, the Japanese were not much of a problem, for on a

A recognized expert on American immigration, Henry P. Fairchild, wrote in 1926, "The typical immigrant of the present does not really live in America at all, but, from the point of view of nationality, in Italy, Poland, Czecho-Slovakia, or some other foreign country."

---

* Five years later the Act of 1929, using 1920 as the quota base, virtually cut immigration in half by limiting the total to 152,574 a year.

	Immigrants from N. and W. Europe	Immigrants from Other Countries, Principally S. and E. Europe
Average annual inflow, 1907–1914	176,983	685,531
Quotas under Act of 1921	198,082	158,367
Quotas under Act of 1924	140,999	21,847
Quotas under National-Origins Provision of 1929	132,323	20,251
Quotas under McCarran-Walter Act of 1952	125,165	29,492

ANNUAL IMMIGRATION AND THE QUOTA LAWS

quota basis they would have been able to send only 185 immigrants a year. This handful certainly did not constitute a "yellow horde." Yet insistent outcries from the Pacific Coast demanded that Orientals be completely excluded. The Japanese Ambassador in Washington, hoping to avert this affront, wrote to Secretary Hughes that "grave consequences" would follow the proposed action. No truer words were ever penned, and certain American politicians professed to see in them a threat of war. A spiteful Congress thereupon slammed the door against Asiatics, including Japanese.

The sensitive Nipponese were grievously offended by this re-sounding slap, which constituted an intolerable loss of face. A Jap-anese super-patriot committed suicide near the American Embassy in Tokyo, and "hate-everything-American" mass meetings were widely held. America's friends in Japan were weakened, while out-spoken American militarists and imperialists were strengthened. The military clique ultimately got into the saddle and galloped head-long down the road to Pearl Harbor. America shortsightedly paid much too high a price in ill will for excluding 185 Japanese a year.

Hooded Hoodlums of the KKK

A new Ku Klux Klan, spawned by the post-war reaction, mush-roomed fearsomely in the early 1920's. Despite the familiar sheets and hoods, it more closely resembled the anti-foreign "nativist" movements of the 1850's than the anti-Negro night riders of the 1860's. It was anti-foreign, anti-Catholic, anti-Negro, anti-Jewish, anti-pacifist, anti-Communist, anti-internationalist, anti-evolution-ist, anti-bootlegger, anti-gambling, anti-adultery, and anti-birth control. It was also pro-Anglo-Saxon, pro-native American, and pro-Protestant.

As reconstituted, the Klan spread with astonishing rapidity, especially in the Middle West and the "Bible Belt" South. At its peak in the mid-1920's, it enrolled about five million dues-paying members and wielded potent political influence. It capitalized on the typically American love of excitement, adventure, and joining, to say nothing of the adolescent love for secret ritual. "Knights of the Invisible Empire" embraced among their officials Imperial Wizards, Grand Goblins, King Kleagles, and other horrendous "kreatures." The most impressive displays were "konclaves" and huge besheeted parades. The chief warning was the burning of the fiery cross. The principal weapon was the lash, supplemented by tar and feathers. Relevant songs were "The Fiery Cross on High," "One Hundred Percent American," and "The Ku Klux Klan and the Pope" (against kissing the Pope's toe).

This reign of hooded horror, so repulsive to American ideals, collapsed rather suddenly in the late 1920's. Decent people recoiled from the orgy of ribboned flesh and terrorism, while scandalous grafting by Klan officials launched a Congressional investigation. The bubble was punctured when the movement was exposed, not as a crusade, but as a vicious racket based on a ten-dollar initiation fee. At bottom, the K.K.K. was an alarming manifestation of the intolerance and prejudice so common in the diseased minds of the 1920's. Americanism needed no such cowardly apostles, whose white sheets concealed black purposes.

The Farmer Sons of Wild Jackasses

Sun-bronzed farmers, more conspicuously than any other large group, were excluded from the prosperity of the fabulous 1920's. They were stepchildren of the post-war economic order.

The farmers were caught squarely in the boom-and-bust cycle. During the war they had raked in money hand over gnarled fist; by the spring of 1920 the price of wheat had shot up to an incredible three dollars a bushel. Shortly thereafter government guarantees were withdrawn, prices plummeted, and for about two decades low agricultural prices prevailed.

What ailed the frustrated farmer? For one thing, his grain market abroad was hurt by increasingly efficient foreign production. For another, American tariff walls, by shutting out the manufactured goods of foreigners, cut down the purchasing power of foreigners. But above all, the farmer was raising far more than the available market could absorb; he was in danger of being suffocated by his own golden avalanches.

Basic causes of overproduction were not hard to find. Improved

"The Man with the Hoe."
Courtesy of Muskogee
(Oklahoma) *Phoenix*

seeds and livestock played an important role, but the introduction of the tractor heralded a new day. This steel mule was to cultivation and sowing what the McCormick mower-reaper was to harvesting. A blue-denimed husbandman no longer had to plod after the horse-drawn plow with high-footed gait. He could sit erect on his roaring mechanical chariot and turn under and harrow many acres in a single day. He was thus able to reduce the number of his horses and hired hands, while growing bigger and better crops on larger areas. But such improved efficiency merely piled up more discouraging surpluses.

Overproduction inevitably meant the misery of low prices. The agricultural depression of the 1920's and 1930's turned out to be the most protracted and withering in American history. In the years from 1920 to 1932 one farm in every four was sold for debt or taxes. The renting of farms replaced ownership at an alarming rate, while farmers voiced their complaints with increasing vigor. As a plaintive folk song of the period ran:

No use talkin', any man's beat,
With 'leven-cent cotton and forty-cent meat.

Farm protest, as in the 1880's and 1890's, boiled over in various ways. Political movements of varying significance swept the states of the upper Mississippi Valley, while socialistic enterprises were daringly and desperately launched. Ingenious plans without number were devised for relieving the sorry plight of the farmer, most of them with the aim of jacking up depressed prices. This goal was partially achieved in certain areas through producers' marketing cooperatives.

In 1921 the bipartisan farm bloc was organized in Congress, embracing Republicans and Democrats from the farming areas of the South and the Middle West. Their most persistent proposal for farm relief was the McNary-Haugen Bill, pushed energetically between 1924 and 1928. The objective was to keep agricultural prices high by authorizing the government to buy up price-depressing surpluses and sell them abroad. Losses to the government were to be made up by a special tax on the farmers. The McNary-Haugen Bill finally passed Congress, but frugal Calvin Coolidge, who regarded this boot-strap scheme as expensive, wasteful, and impractical, vetoed it in 1927 and again—this time with finality—in 1928.

As in the days of the Populist "Popocrats," the industrial East showed a distressing lack of sympathy for the plight of the "hicks" who produced its food. Senator Moses of New Hampshire, annoyed by liberal opposition to a higher tariff, branded certain Western progressive Senators as "Sons of the Wild Jackass." Big Business tycoons in the East were a good deal more determined to protect American factories than to protect American farmers.

The Stench of Scandal

Loose morality and get-rich-quickism of the Harding era man-ifested themselves spectacularly in a series of scandals.

Early in 1923 Colonel Charles R. Forbes, one-time deserter from the army, was caught with his hand in the till and resigned as head of the Veterans' Bureau. An appointee of the gullible Harding, he and his accomplices looted the government to the tune of about $250,-000,000, chiefly in connection with the building of veterans' hos-pitals. He was sentenced to two years in a federal penitentiary.

Most shocking of all was the Teapot Dome scandal, an affair which involved priceless naval oil reserves at Teapot Dome (Wyo-ming) and Elk Hills (California). In 1921 the slippery Secretary of the Interior, Albert B. Fall, induced his careless colleague, Secretary of the Navy Denby, to transfer these valuable properties to the Interior Department. President Harding indiscreetly signed the secret order. Fall then quietly leased the lands to oilmen Harry F. Sinclair and Edward L. Doheny, but not until he had received a bribe ("loan") of $100,000 from Doheny and about three times that amount in all from Sinclair.

"Gushing," 1924. Teapot Dome Scandal. Fitzpatrick in the St. Louis *Post-Dispatch*

Teapot Dome finally came to a whistling boil. Details of the crooked transaction gradually began to leak out in March, 1923, two years after Harding took office. Fall, Sinclair, and Doheny were indicted the next year, but the case dragged through the courts until 1929. Finally Fall was found guilty of taking a bribe and was sentenced to one year in jail. By a curious quirk of justice, the two bribegivers were acquitted while the bribetaker was convicted, although Sinclair served several months in jail for having "shadowed" jurors and for refusing to testify before a Senate committee.

The oily smudge from Teapot Dome polluted the prestige of the Washington government. Right-thinking citizens wondered what was going on when public officials could sell out the nation's re-sources, especially those reserved for the United States Navy. The acquittal of Sinclair and Doheny undermined faith in the courts, while giving further currency to the cynical saying, "You can't put a million dollars in jail."

Other scandals erupted, two of them involving suicides. Persistent reports as to the underhanded doings of Attorney General Daugherty brought a Senate investigation in 1924 of the illegal sale of pardons and liquor permits. Forced to resign, the accused official was tried in 1927 but was released after a jury twice failed to agree. During the trial, Daugherty hid behind the trousers of the now-dead Harding by implying that persistent probing might uncover crookedness in the White House.

Harding was mercifully spared the full revelation of these iniqui-ties, though his worst suspicions were aroused. While the scandals were beginning to break, he embarked upon a speechmaking tour across the country all the way to Alaska. On the return trip he died in San Francisco, on August 2, 1923, of pneumonia and thrombosis. His death may have been hastened by a broken heart resulting from the disloyalty of designing friends. Mourning millions, not yet fully aware of the graft in Washington, expressed genuine sorrow.

The brutal fact is that Harding was not a big enough man for the Presidency—as he himself privately admitted. Such was his weakness that he tolerated persons and conditions which subjected the Republic to its worst disgrace since the days of President Grant.

SELECT READINGS

An excellent introduction is J. D. HICKS, *Republican Ascendancy, 1921–1933* (1960).* See also H. U. FAULKNER, *From Versailles to the New Deal* (1950). F. L. ALLEN, *Only Yesterday* (1931)* reads like a novel; likewise Volume VI of MARK SULLIVAN, *Our Times* (1937) and P. W. SLOSSON, *The Great Crusade and After, 1914–1928* (1930). On economics see G. H. SOULE, *Prosperity Decade, 1917–1929* (1947)*; on scandals, S. H. ADAMS, *Incredible Era* (1939)* and the books on Teapot Dome by BURL NOGGLE (1962)* and J. L. BATES (1963). The most recent biographies of Harding are ANDREW SINCLAIR, *The Available Man* (1965)* [rather favorable] and FRANCIS RUSSELL, *The Shadow of Blooming Grove* (1968) [highly critical]. A judicious and scholarly appraisal is R. K. MURRAY, *The Harding Era* (1969). See also A. S. RICE, *The Ku Klux Klan in American Politics* (1962). Also *Harvard Guide,** Pt. VI.

RECENT REFERENCES

ROBERT K. MURRAY, *The Politics of Normalcy: Government Theory and Practice in the Harding-Coolidge Era* (1973); THOMAS H. BUCKLEY, *The United States and the Washington Conference: 1921–1922* (1970).

* Available in paperback.

40

Calvin Coolidge and the Jazz Age

The business of America is business.

Calvin Coolidge, 1925

Calvin Coolidge: A Yankee in the White House

News of Harding's death, in August, 1923, was sped to Vice-President Coolidge, then visiting at the New England farmhouse of his father. By the light of two kerosene lamps the elder Coolidge, a justice of the peace, used the old family Bible to administer the presidential oath to his son.

This homespun setting was symbolic of Coolidge. Quite unlike Harding, the stern-faced Vermonter, with his thin nose and tightly set lips, embodied the New England virtues of honesty, morality, industry, and frugality. As a youth, his father reported, he seemed to get more sap out of a maple tree than any of the other boys. Practicing a rigid economy in both money and words, "Silent Cal" came to be known in Washington conversational circles for his brilliant flashes of silence. His dour, serious visage prompted the acid observation that he had been "weaned on a pickle."

Coolidge seemed to be a crystallization of the commonplace. A painfully shy individual of average height (5 feet 10), he was blessed with only mediocre powers of leadership. He would occasionally flash a dry wit in private; but his speeches, delivered in a nasal New England twang, were invariably boring. A staunch

President Calvin Coolidge (1872–1933) In 1920 Vice President-elect Coolidge asserted, "Civilization and profits go hand in hand."

apostle of the status quo, he was no knight in armor riding forth to tilt at wrongs. His only horse, in fact, was an electric-powered steed on which he took his exercise. True to Republican philosophy, he became the "high priest of the great god Business." He believed that "the man who builds a factory builds a temple."

The hands-off temperament of "Cautious Cal" Coolidge suited the times perfectly. His thrifty, cheeseparing nature caused him to sympathize fully with Secretary of the Treasury Mellon's efforts to reduce both taxes and debts. No foe of industrial bigness, he let business have its head. "Coolidge luck" held during his five and a half prosperity-blessed years, and there were no noteworthy clouds in the American industrial sky, except those caused by factory smokestacks and the farm problem.

Ever a profile in caution, Coolidge slowly gave the Harding regime a badly needed moral fumigation. Yet he did not expel shady characters with undue haste, nor did he strain himself in tracking down crooks. Teapot Dome scalded the Republican Party badly, but so transparently honest was the vinegary Vermonter that the scandalous oil did not rub off on him.

In his easygoing prosecution of offenders, Coolidge chimed in with the relaxed moral standards of the time. The public, though at first shocked by scandal, quickly simmered down; and an alarming tendency developed in certain quarters to excuse some of the wrong-doers on the ground that "they had gotten away with it." Some critics even condemned the government prosecutors for continuing to rock the boat. America's moral sense was evidently being dulled by prosperity.

The Delirious Decade

The Harding-Coolidge era spanned the craziest years of the so-called "Gin and Jazz Age" of the "Roaring Twenties."

A moral sag normally accompanies and follows every great war. The years after 1918 were perhaps more demoralizing than usual, partly because they were shot through with a spirit of disillusionment. The nation had aroused itself to support Wilsonian idealism—to end war and to end the threat to democracy. But its heroic sacrifices had reaped only disappointments. An atmosphere of cynicism and intolerance spread like the poison gas recently released on the battlefields of France. "Oh, yeah?" became a typically popular slang retort. Disillusionment was only deepened by the "revisionist" historians of the 1920's, who published impressive documentary studies to prove that Germany had not been solely responsible for unleashing the dogs of war in 1914. Other European powers were also given a substantial share of the blame.

Materialism was an unlovely offspring of cynicism. Men bowed down and worshiped at the altar of the goddess Success, while seeking quick something-for-nothing riches. "Only suckers work" was a common sneer, while the horse-and-buggy virtues of earnest labor and cautious saving were often greeted with jeers.

An obsession with sex accompanied the materialistic urge. The eminent Viennese physician, Dr. Sigmund Freud, had recently brought out English translations of his earlier findings. Their upshot seemed to be that sex repressions were responsible for various nervous and emotional ills of mankind. Many taboos went out the window as sex-conscious Americans of the turbulent twenties let themselves go. Skirts rose higher and higher, until they hovered above the knee. Semi-nudity became fashionable as non-swimming bathing beauties besported themselves in the new one-piece bathing suits.

Syncopated jazz, up from the Negro quarter of New Orleans, elbowed aside classical music. The blaring saxophone became the trumpet of the new era, while a popular song, "Yes, We Have No Bananas," provided a fitting theme for the lighthearted and light-headed.

The nation more than ever became sports-mad. Baseball heroes like George H. ("Babe") Ruth, who hammered out a record-making sixty home runs in 1927, were far better known than most statesmen. Sports were becoming a big business. In 1921 the slugging heavyweight champion, Jack Dempsey, knocked out the dapper French light heavyweight, Georges Carpentier, before a Jersey City crowd that had paid more than a million dollars—the first in a series of million-dollar "gates" in the golden 1920's.

For Bellows' impression of the Dempsey-Firpo fight, see color portfolio following page 814.

Spiritual life seemed to be retreating before materialism in this "Era of Wonderful Nonsense." The Fundamentalist champions of the old-time religion were losing ground to the Modernists. Some of the churches were even forced to fight the Devil with worldly weapons. Faced with competition from Sunday joy-riding automobiles, to say nothing of golf links and "movie palaces," a few denominations were providing wholesome moving pictures and other attractions for their young people. One uptown House of the Lord in New York even advertised on a billboard: "Come to Church: Christian Worship Increases Your Efficiency."

"Flaming youth" spectacularly reflected the changed standards of the new age of cynicism. The once modest and long-haired maiden blossomed forth shockingly as a "flapper" in bobbed tresses and bobbed dresses. Females saw the further emancipation of their sex in the low-cut gown, the painted lips, the rouged cheeks, the dangling cigarette—all of which had previously been associated with fallen women. The cosmetics industry rapidly blossomed into a billion-dollar business.

The president of the University of Florida condemned the new feminine dress: "The low-cut gowns, the rolled hose and short skirts are born of the Devil and his angels, and are carrying the present and future generations to chaos and destruction."

Teen-agers of the frenzied 1920's, with their gin-filled hip-flasks, cut a wide swath. Glued together in syncopated embrace, they danced to jazz music squeaking from phonographs. In an earlier day a kiss had been the equivalent of a proposal of marriage. But in the new era reckless youth took to the highways and byways in automobiles, there to poach upon the forbidden land of sex as "neckers" and "petters." Alarmed guardians of the public morals decried the careening automobiles as "houses of prostitution on wheels." The ultimate in moral degeneracy was reached in 1924, when two brilliant young college graduates in Chicago, named Loeb and Leopold, kidnapped and killed a boy just for the thrill of it.

Cultural Materialism in "the Age of Wonderful Nonsense"

The spirit of the flask-and-flapper age was partially reflected in the printed word. Cheap, sexy "confession" magazines were now being sold by the hundreds of thousands. The "terrible tabloids," newspapers tailored small for the convenience of subway straphangers, luridly improved on the crime stories of the 19th-Century "penny dreadfuls."

"Flapper," with lipstick, bobbed hair, short skirt, rolled stockings, cigarette, and flask. *Life*, 1926. By permission

The cynical atmosphere of the jazz-and-gin era lent itself to "debunking"—a word appropriately coined in 1923. Noisiest and most influential of the debunkers was Henry L. Mencken, "the Bad Boy of Baltimore." In the green-covered monthly *American Mercury*, which he launched in 1924 and which attained great popularity among young intellectuals, he wielded a meat ax instead of a pen. Sparing nothing, he jibed at marriage, patriotism, democracy, Puritans, prohibition, Rotarians, and the "booboisie" of the Southern "Bible Belt." To him, all idealism was "bilge."

Popular also with college undergraduates was F. Scott Fitzgerald's brilliant and witty novel *This Side of Paradise* (1920). The handsome Minnesota-born author, an alcoholic Princetonian only twenty-four years old, was a sensation with his tale of uninhibited, bewildered youth in the Jazz Age. Catching the spirit of the hour (often about 4 A.M.), he found "All gods dead, all wars fought, all faiths in man shaken."

Other literary contributions mirrored the restlessness of the times. Notorious among writers struggling to find a philosophy to fit the new age was Theodore Dreiser, an Indiana-bred journalist and novelist. His grim realism is perhaps best seen in a novel, *An American Tragedy* (1925), which describes the murder of a pregnant girl by her fickle young lover. Fortunately for sales, the tale was banned in Boston.

Certain American novelists, having emerged before World War I, were carrying on the more conventional tradition. Conspicuous among them were distinguished writers like the well-to-do New Yorker Edith Wharton and Virginia-born Willa Cather, who achieved fame through her delineation of Middle Western prairie life. Notable among the new crop of novelists was spindly, red-haired, heavy-drinking Sinclair Lewis, a violent tempered journalistic product of Sauk Centre, Minnesota. As a master of satire, he sprang into prominence in 1920 with his *Main Street,* an attack on the small-town Middle Western life that he knew so well. His next novel, *Babbitt* (1922), pilloried George F. Babbitt, a prosperous, vulgar, middle-class real estate broker who, under social pressures, conformed to the respectable materialism of his group. The word "Babbittry" was quickly coined to describe his type.

Despite the moan of saxophones, high-quality poetry was still being written. Noteworthy were the poems of skilled craftsmen like Edwin A. Robinson, a reserved New Englander; Ezra Pound, an Idahoan who deserted America for Europe; T. S. Eliot, a Missourian who became a British subject; and Robert Frost, a California-born adopted son of New England. Better known to many contemporaries were less distinguished figures like Chicago's embittered Edgar Lee Masters; Vachel Lindsay, who mixed unconventional poetry with hoboing; and Carl Sandburg, later famed as a folklorist and biographer of Lincoln. These lesser lights were perhaps better known because, like some of the novelists, they were critical of both the social and the economic structure. Edna St. Vincent Millay, a disillusioned Maine poet, described the devil-may-care spirit of rebellious youth.

My candle burns at both ends;
*   It will not last the night;*
But ah, my foes, and oh, my friends—
*   It gives a lovely light!* *

The theater too reflected current modes. Although losing out to the motion picture, it was, as if by compensation, attracting playwrights of genuine distinction. Perhaps the best-known play of the era was *What Price Glory* (1924), written by Maxwell Anderson and Laurence Stallings. Free-living, free-loving marines like Sergeant Quirt and Captain Flagg shocked old-timers by bringing to the stage unrestrained outbursts of soldier-like profanity. Eugene O'Neill, a New York dramatist of globe-trotting background, laid bare Freudian concepts of sex in his plays, notably *Strange Interlude.* He won a Nobel Prize in 1936.

Even architecture married itself to the new materialism and functionalism. The era of machinery continued to lure droves of people to the cities; by 1930 over one-half of the population lived in urban areas. Long-range city planning was being intelligently projected,

* "First Fig" from *A Few Figs from Thistles* (Harper and Brothers, 1918; copyright, 1918, by Edna St. Vincent Millay). Reprinted by permission.

and architects like Frank Lloyd Wright were advancing the theory that buildings should grow from their sites and not slavishly imitate Greek and Roman importations. The Machine Age outdid itself in New York City when it thrust upward the cloud-brushing Empire State Building, 102 stories high. Dedicated in 1931, "The Empty State Building" was partially deserted in the depressed 1930's.

The Prohibition Era

Moral decay in the 1920's was vastly accelerated by prohibition. The arid new order was authorized in 1919 by the 18th Amendment (see Appendix), as implemented by the Volstead Act passed by Congress later that year. Together they made the world "safe for hypocrisy."

The legal abolition of alcohol was fairly popular in the Middle West, and especially so in the South. Southern whites were eager to keep stimulants out of the hands of the Negro, lest he burst out of "his place." But despite the overwhelming ratification of the "dry" amendment, strong opposition persisted in the larger Eastern cities. Concentrated colonies of "wet" foreign-born peoples were loath to abandon their Old World drinking habits. Yet most Americans assumed that prohibition had come to stay. Everywhere there were last wild flings, as the nation prepared to enter upon a permanent "alcoholiday."

"Watcha Got in that Bag?" This slap at the "drys" as snooping killjoys reflected widespread popular sentiment. Weed in the New York *World*

But prohibitionists were naïve in the extreme. They overlooked the tenacious American tradition of strong drink and of weak control by the central government, especially over private lives. They forgot that the federal authorities had never satisfactorily enforced a law where the majority of the people—or a strong minority—were hostile to it. They ignored the fact that one cannot make a crime overnight out of something that millions of people have never regarded as a crime. Legislative bodies cannot legislate away a thirst.

Peculiar conditions hampered the enforcement of prohibition. Profound disillusionment over the aftermath of the war raised serious questions as to the wisdom of further self-denial. Slaking thirst became a cherished personal liberty, and many ardent wets believed that the way to bring about repeal was to violate the law on a large enough scale. Frustrated soldiers, returning from France, complained that prohibition had been "put over" on them while they were "over there." Grimy workingmen bemoaned the loss of their cheap beer, while pointing out that the idle rich could buy all the illicit alcohol they wanted. Flaming youth of the Jazz Age thought it "smart" to swill bootleg liquor—"liquid tonsillectomies." Millions of older citizens likewise found forbidden fruit fascinating, especially when they engaged in "bar hunts."

Prohibition might have started off on a better foot if there had been a larger army of enforcement officials. But the state and federal agencies were understaffed, and their snoopers, susceptible to brib-ery, were underpaid. The public was increasingly distressed as scores of persons, including innocent bystanders, were killed by quick-triggered dry agents.

Prohibition simply did not prohibit. The old-time "men only" corner saloons were replaced by thousands of "speakeasies," with their tiny grilled window through which the thirsty spoke softly before the barred door was opened. Women frequented such dives. Hard liquor, especially the cocktail, was drunk in staggering volume by both sexes. Largely because of the difficulties of transporting and concealing bottles, beverages of high alcoholic content were popular. Foreign rumrunners, even from the West Indies, had their inning, and countless cases of liquor leaked down from Canada. The zeal of American prohibition agents on occasion strained diplomatic rela-tions with Uncle Sam's northern neighbor.

"Home brew" and "bathtub gin" became popular, as law-evading adults engaged in "alky cooking" with toy stills. The worst of the homemade "rot gut" produced blindness, even death. The affable bootlegger worked in silent partnership with the friendly under-taker.

The Golden Age of Gangsterism

Prohibition spawned shocking crimes. The lush profits of illegal alcohol led to bribery of the police, many of whom were induced to see and smell no evil. Violent gang wars broke out in the big cities between rivals seeking to corner the rich market in booze. Rival triggermen used their sawed-off shotguns and chattering "type-writers" (machine guns) to "erase" bootlegging competitors who were trying to "muscle in" on their "racket." In the gang wars of the 1920's in Chicago, about five hundred low characters were murdered. Arrests were few and convictions were even fewer, as the button-lipped gangsters "covered" for one another with the underworld's code of silence.

"The King Still Reigns," 1930. Courtesy of Baltimore *Sun*

Chicago was by far the most spectacular example of lawlessness. In 1925 "Scarface" Al Capone, a greasy and loathsome character, began six years of gang warfare which netted him millions of blood-spattered dollars. He zoomed through the streets in an armor-plated car with bullet-proof windows. A Brooklyn newspaper quipped:

And the pistols' red glare,
Bombs bursting in air
Give proof through the night
That Chicago's still there.

Capone could not be convicted of the cold-blooded massacre, on St. Valentine's Day in 1929, of seven disarmed members of a rival gang.

But he was finally sentenced to a long term in a federal penitentiary for income-tax evasion.

Gangsters rapidly moved into other profitable and illicit activities: prostitution, gambling, and narcotics. Honest merchants were forced to pay "protection money" to the organized thugs; otherwise their windows would be smashed, their trucks overturned, or their employees or themselves beaten up. Racketeers even invaded the ranks of local labor unions as organizers and promoters. Organized crime had come to be one of the nation's most gigantic businesses. By 1930 the annual "take" of the underworld was estimated to be from twelve to eighteen billion dollars—several times the income of the Washington government.

Aside from stimulating gangsterism, prohibition was criticized on other counts. Millions of dollars were spent in semi-enforcement; hundreds of millions of dollars were lost in taxes. The jails were crowded and the courts were clogged, as the result of more than half a million arrests from 1920 to 1930. Hypocritical, hip-flasked legislators spoke or voted dry while privately drinking wet. Europeans were both amused and disgusted by the "silliness" of the Americans. Yet, on the whole, probably less liquor was drunk than in the days before prohibition. As the legendary Irishman remarked, prohibition was "a darn sight better than no liquor at all."

Stern-faced drys decried the lawless traffic in alcohol, as well as the gangsterism that it bred. Voicing alarm lest such widespread flouting of the Constitution and the federal statutes should widen into contempt for all law and order, they loudly demanded an enforcement of the seemingly unenforceable law. In defense of prohibition, they pointed to increased bank savings and decreased absenteeism in industry. They argued that personal liberty to drink was one thing in the oxcart days of Thomas Jefferson, but another in the new machine age. Drunkenness was too high-priced a luxury when the tipsy worker or automobile driver endangered not only himself but the lives of innocent people as well.

Gangster Al Capone, headquartered in Chicago, was reported as saying, "Everybody calls me a racketeer. I call myself a business man. When I sell liquor, it's bootlegging. When my patrons serve it on a silver tray on Lake Shore Drive, it's hospitality."

Expanding Schoolrooms

Education in the 1920's continued to make giant-boot strides. More and more states were requiring their children to remain in school until age sixteen or eighteen, or until graduation from high school. The introduction of the automobile bus made possible the consolidation of one-room bedlams into splendid union schools with excellent facilities for instruction, mental, manual, and physical.

The most revolutionary contribution to educational theory during these yeasty years was made by mild-mannered Professor John Dewey, who served on the faculty of Columbia University from 1904 to 1930. By common consent one of America's few front-rank philosophers, he set forth the principles of "learning by doing" that formed the foundation of so-called "progressive education." He believed that the workbench was as essential as the blackboard, and that "education for life" should be a primary goal of the teacher.

This new emphasis on creating socially useful adults rendered many schools more attractive. No longer was the schoolhouse a kind of educational jail, from which the pupils burst at the end of the year chanting, as had young Dewey when a youngster in Vermont, "Good-bye school, good-bye teacher, damned old fool."

Other educational landmarks were posted. Vocational education was being stressed, at both the juvenile and adult levels. Junior colleges, which provided the first two years of higher education locally, were permitting thousands of youths from poorer families to aspire to college training. University enrollments, appropriations, and endowments continued to soar.

Monkey Business in Tennessee

Science was one of the greatest beneficiaries of modernized university laboratories. New drugs, vitamins, and other wonders were being uncovered. X rays were now being used for cancer treatment and other health-giving purposes, while hospitals were expanding. The great Epsom-salts program of the Rockefeller Foundation, launched in 1909, had virtually wiped out hookworm in the South. Amazing progress was being made in improving the nation's health and in widening the life span of the average citizen. Between 1901 and 1929 the life expectancy of an infant at birth was increased from approximately fifty to fifty-nine years.

Yet science in the universities and schools was still handicapped by a nagging fire from the Fundamentalists. These old-time religionists charged that the teaching of Darwinian evolution was destroying faith in God and the Bible, while contributing to the moral breakdown of youth in the Jazz Age. Numerous attempts were made to secure laws prohibiting the teaching of evolution in the public schools, and three Southern states adopted such shackling measures. The trio included Tennessee, in the heart of the so-called "Bible Belt" South which, ironically enough, was a last refuge of New England Puritanism.

"The Family Tree in Tennessee." The Scopes Trial. Fitzpatrick in the St. Louis *Post-Dispatch*

The stage was set for the memorable "Monkey Trial" at the hamlet of Dayton, eastern Tennessee, in 1925. A likable young high school biology teacher of twenty-four, John T. Scopes, was indicted for teaching evolution. Batteries of newspapermen, armed with notebooks and cameras, descended upon the quiet town to witness the spectacle, as did hundreds of gaping "yokels" from the nearby hills. Scopes was defended by nationally known lawyers, while William Jennings Bryan, an ardent Presbyterian Fundamentalist, joined the prosecution. Taking the stand as an expert on the Bible, he was badly tripped up by the famed criminal lawyer, Clarence Darrow. Five days after the trial was over, Bryan died of apoplexy, no doubt brought on by the heat and strain.

This historic clash between theology and biology proved inconclusive. Scopes, the forgotten man of the drama, was found guilty and fined $100. But the Supreme Court of Tennessee, while upholding the law, set aside the fine on a technicality.* The Fundamentalists at best won only a hollow victory, for the absurdities of the trial cast ridicule on their cause. Increasing numbers of Christians were coming to reconcile the realities of religion with the findings of modern science, and the membership of the churches continued to mount.

A Three-Way Race to the White House in 1924

Hailed as a strong, silent man (and really neither), Coolidge was the clear choice of the Republicans when they met at Cleveland, June, 1924. Although he had been in office less than a year, he had brought respectability to his scandal-besmirched party. He had also proved to be the ideal businessman's candidate. The platform paid lip service to prohibition, and boasted that the nation's jingling cash registers resulted from Republican policies.

The Democrats were much less harmonious. Meeting in Madison Square Garden, New York, they staged one of the most dramatic brawls ever held in that pugilistic amphitheater. Liberal Governor Alfred E. Smith of New York, a Roman Catholic and a wet, locked horns with Woodrow Wilson's son-in-law, "Crown Prince" William G. McAdoo, a Protestant and a dry. After 102 indecisive ballots—the most protracted balloting marathon in American presidential history —the convention wearily, sweatily, and unenthusiastically turned to white-haired John W. Davis. A wealthy New York corporation lawyer connected with the Wall Street firm of J. P. Morgan and Company, the polished nominee was no less a conservative than cautious Calvin Coolidge.

Predictably, the Democratic platform attacked the Harding scandals, and attempted to wave the oil-stained linen of the Republicans in public. Backing Wilson's pro-League ideals, the assembled Democrats condemned what they regarded as the cowardly isolation, vacillation, and indecision of the Washington regime. Favorite Democratic slogans were "Honesty at Home—Honor Abroad" and "Remember the Teapot Dome."

The field was now wide open for a liberal candidate. White-pompadoured Senator ("Fighting Bob") La Follette of Wisconsin, perennial aspirant to the Presidency and now sixty-nine years of age, sprang forward to lead a new Progressive grouping. Its appeal to farm-labor elements was strong. La Follette's platform advocated government ownership of railroads and relief for farmers, lashed out

---

* The Tennessee law was not formally repealed until 1968.

against monopoly and anti-labor injunctions, and urged a Constitutional amendment to limit the Supreme Court's power to invalidate laws passed by Congress. In his fight against "entrenched greed" La Follette gained support from the Socialist Party, and even from elements of the American Federation of Labor. Yet he lacked money, organization, and newspaper backing.

Prosperity Overpowers Progressivism at the Polls

The campaign of 1924 was of the "ho-hum" variety. Voters were prosperity-drugged, and the experts regarded a Republican triumph as inevitable. Popular G.O.P. slogans were "Keep Cool with Coolidge" and "Keep Cool and Keep Coolidge." La Follette, ever the crusader, provided some fireworks by his attacks on the Supreme Court. Republicans assailed his alleged socialism, and played upon the fear that he might win enough electoral votes to throw the decision into the House of Representatives, with attendant uncertainties. "Coolidge or Chaos" cried Coolidgeites in alarm—or pretended alarm.

Democrats noisily hammered on Teapot Dome and other scandals, which ordinarily would have been enough to sink the party in power. They sardonically sang a parody of a popular song:

But how 'n the 'ell kin the country tell,
"You ain' gwine steal no mo'?"

"Cautious Cal" and the oil-bespattered Republicans rode into office on the crest of a landslide—a landslide which overwhelmed Davis, 15,725,016 votes to 8,386,503. The electoral count stood at 382

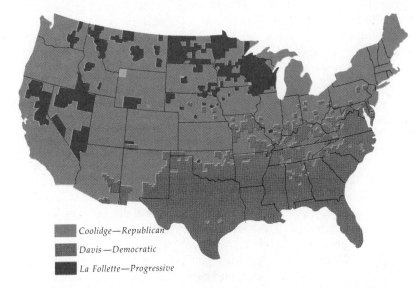

Coolidge—Republican

Davis—Democratic

La Follette—Progressive

PRESIDENTIAL ELECTION OF 1924 (showing popular vote by county)

for Coolidge, 136 for Davis, and 13 for La Follette. "Battling Bob" carried only his own Wisconsin, though polling 4,822,856 popular votes.

Yet La Follette's fight was not altogether in vain. Though badly beaten, his Progressive organization was one of the few third-party groupings ever to break into the electoral column. As the so-called conscience of the calloused 1920's, La Follette injected a badly needed liberal tonic into a materialistic America.

Good times are hard to beat. The slogan of Coolidge Republicans might well have been "Why swap horses in the middle of prosperity?" The victory was basically an endorsement of prosperity, though disgruntled Democrats sneered that it was a mandate to go on stealing.

Uncle Sam: World Banker

"Harmony in Europe," 1932. Courtesy of Detroit *News*

World War I, almost overnight, had reversed the international economic position of the United States. In 1914 America had been a debtor nation in the sum of three billion dollars; by 1922 she had become a creditor nation in the sum of sixteen billion dollars. The Almighty Dollar had displaced the pound sterling as the financial giant of the world.

Well-to-do Americans in the 1920's looked hungrily abroad for high-interest investment opportunities. Wall Street bankers, with the blessing of Washington, invested huge sums of money in Europe, Asia, and Latin America. The total outflow of such private capital in the 1920's mounted to more than ten billion dollars, much of which was lost in the 1930's, when the world-wide Great Depression descended. Ironically, Germany used a substantial portion of this sum to rebuild and expand her industrial machine—the very machine that Hitler later used to crush the victims of his ambition.

But the real debt problem of the 1920's was what foreign governments owed the U.S. Treasury. The so-called Allied war debts totaled $10,350,479,074.70, about 90% of which had been incurred by America's wartime Allies—Britain, France, and Italy. Uncle Sam held their I.O.U.'s—and he wanted to be paid.

War debts, to make matters worse, were closely tied up with reparations. The Allied nations, notably ravaged France and Belgium, argued that Germany had forced a terrible conflict upon peaceful neighbors, and should therefore be liable for full damages. Total costs, as finally presented to Berlin, reached the colossal figure of thirty-two billion dollars. The German masses, traditionally industrious, might have buckled down and paid a more reasonable sum, say ten billion dollars. But they recoiled from the crushing burden they were asked to shoulder, and especially from the implication that they alone had been responsible for igniting the conflagration.

Allied insistence on backbreaking reparations contributed heavily to Europe's post-war chaos and depression. Fresh hatreds were aroused, especially when the reparations-collecting French in 1923 sent troops into Germany to seize the industrialized Ruhr Valley. They forgot that one cannot extract both milk and beefsteak from the same cow. Berlin responded to this intervention by permitting inflation of the currency to reach runaway proportions. The wholesale printing of near-worthless paper money not only wiped out the sturdy German middle class, but also helped pave the path for Hitler and his Nazi bullyboys. Altogether the Germans, with dragging feet, paid about four and a half billion dollars on their huge reparations bill. Yet American investors during these post-war years sank about half this amount in Germany.

Reparations were also bound up with the war debts owed by former Allies to the United States. British spokesmen, hoping to avert a sea of troubles, had early suggested an around-the-board cancellation. France owed both Britain and the United States huge sums. The British were willing to forgive the French their debt, provided that America would forgive both the French and the British their debts. If Uncle Sam had fallen in with this scheme, the French would not have been justified in presenting such a crushing reparations bill, and presumably the Germans would have paid a more manageable amount with some degree of willingness. If all this had happened, endless friction would have been avoided.

But Woodrow Wilson and his successors in the White House sternly rejected the plaintive pleas of foreign debtors. The American people, sadly disillusioned by the imperialistic aims of the Allies, were not about to be the "suckers" in the pretty little game of ring-around-a-rosy cancellation. Any thought of wiping the slate clean was highly unpopular with American taxpayers, who perceived that they would have to reach down into their pockets and reimburse the Treasury if the Allies did not pay. Washington therefore continued to insist, unrealistically, that there was no connection whatever between reparations and debts.

Pundit Walter Lippmann wrote in the New York *World* (1926), "... International debts are like bills submitted to pay for the damage done on a wild party by one's grandfather. The payment seems to the debtor like pure loss, and when it is paid by one nation to another it seems like tribute by the conquered to the conqueror. Money borrowed to build a railroad earns money to pay for itself. But money borrowed to fight a war produces nothing. ..."

Uncle Sam Becomes "Uncle Shylock"

What was the nature of the Allied war debts? The money, totaling some ten billion dollars, had been advanced by the Treasury as credits to the Allies after America entered the conflict in 1917. These sums had been used to buy mountains of military supplies in the United States. About one-third of the so-called Allied *war* debt had been incurred *after* the shooting war had stopped, and a large part of this "reconstruction debt" had gone to needy nations formed out of ex-Ally or even ex-enemy states. Relatively little gold had left the

United States during the war for the debtors. Yet the American tax-payer, knowing nothing of international finance, imagined that countless hogsheads filled with gold dollars had been rolled up the gangplanks for Europe. Now that the shooting had stopped, Uncle Sam demanded his gold "back."

The true debt picture was drastically different. America's hard-pressed Allies had not wanted gold as such: they could not fire gold bullets at their German foe. They had needed credits to buy war materials in the United States. Incidentally, these heavy purchases had further boomed America's war-born prosperity, and had poured additional tax revenue into the Treasury. America counted her profits; the Allies counted their dead—so Europeans complained.

France in particular felt that she had a strong moral case for debt cancellation. America the Unready had entered the war in 1917 without a real army. While she was raising one, the Hun had to be held back. The French, at frightful cost, maintained a wall of flesh and blood against the common foe until America could get into the fray. Each nation, argued France, contributed what it had: the Allies gave lives, the Americans gave dollars. Now that the war was over, the French were not asking for the lives of their boys back. Nor should Uncle Sam, in the eyes of France, ask for his dollars back.

The war-shattered Allies employed even more practical arguments. There were only three possible ways to pay their debt to America: in gold, in goods, and, to a relatively minor degree, in services such as shipping. These debtors either did not have enough gold or needed what they had to back their own currency. They would have been willing to ship goods to the United States. But they were hampered by the post-war tariff walls, erected in response to the outcries of American manufacturers.

"Pay anyhow" was the rigid dictum of the Washington regimes in the 1920's. Calvin Coolidge, tight-lipped and tight-fisted, reportedly remarked, "Well, they hired the money, didn't they?" Other American critics contended that the debtors should pay with the money they were squandering in arming themselves to the teeth. This argument ignored the facts that France was rearming because she felt insecure, and that she felt insecure largely because Uncle Sam had walked out on the League of Nations and the French Security Treaty of 1919.

Money-conscious Americans made a strong point of simple honesty. A loan was a loan, they insisted, and faith in international borrowing would be destroyed if the Allies "welshed." "We went across, but they won't come across," cried a prominent Ohio politician in the 1930's. Yet a debt owed the bank by a manufacturer represented a loan from which profits could be made to repay the money. The war debts were unproductive, dead-horse debts: the munitions had long since been shot away.

"Our Collections from France."
Fitzpatrick in the St. Louis
Post-Dispatch

Washington Duns the Debtors

The Allied debtors were finally beaten into line, but not until Washington began to exert painful economic pressures on them. The war loans had originally been made with the understanding that they would be repaid at 5% interest. This was clearly too heavy a burden, so Congress created the World War Foreign Debt Commission in 1922 to negotiate more favorable terms.

Uncle Sam, from his point of view, showed unexampled generosity toward the debtors. All were required to return the principal. But all of them, on the basis of ability to pay, received reduced interest rates over a protracted repayment period, which was sixty-two years for all except one. Final interest figures ranged from 3.3% for the British to 0.4% for the impoverished Italians. Reductions in interest for all the debtors resulted in about 50% cancellation of the entire indebtedness, counting both principal and interest spread over many years. The assumption—a naive one indeed—was that generations unborn would cheerfully pay for the follies of their fathers.

	Debt	Interest Rate in Repayment Period
Britain	$4,277,000,000	3.3%
France	$3,404,818,945	1.6%
Italy	$1,648,034,050	0.4%
Belgium	$379,087,200	1.8%
Russia	$192,601,297	Repayment never arranged

The figures show both pre-Armistice and post-Armistice loans of credit and supplies. There were twenty debtor countries.

PRINCIPAL ALLIED DEBTORS

By May, 1930, seventeen of the reluctant debtor nations had signed agreements with the United States. The pact with France, concluded in 1926, was violently unpopular in the land of Lafayette. Irate French crowds on occasion would attack American tourists. In the eyes of patriotic Frenchmen, Uncle Sam the Savior had now become Uncle Shylock, greedily whetting his knife for the last pound of French flesh.

In a class by herself was "brave little Finland," recently a part of Czarist Russia. For purposes of rebuilding after the war, she had secured from Washington a relatively tiny post-Armistice commercial loan of $8,281,926. Although not a former Ally, her industry and honesty in making her payments on time won acclaim in America. She invited misleading comparisons with wartime Allies, who had incurred far heavier obligations.

Uncle Sam collected in all about two and three-fourths billion dollars, mostly interest, on the debt of ten billion. Yet he harbored resentment toward the European "ingrates" because they were resentful. Many Americans, in a curious reversal of sympathies, felt more kindly toward their fallen German foe than toward their late comrades-in-arms. This backlash contributed powerfully to the storm-cellar neutrality legislation passed by Congress in the 1930's.

The debt controversy similarly left a bad aftertaste in Europe. American stevedores may not have rolled hogsheads of gold dollars up the gangplanks, but the American people did collect hogsheads of ill will. Washington's insistence on repayment further snarled the reparations tangle and contributed powerfully to the post-war economic dislocations of Europe, including Germany. These ominous trends all provided ammunition for a fast-emerging demagogue, Adolf Hitler.

Uncle Sam Sidles toward World Responsibilities

America's look-under-the-bed fear of the League gradually began to wear off as the 1920's advanced. President Harding had stoutly asserted in 1923 that America would not enter "by the side door, or the back door, or the cellar door." But the League was much too significant to be dismissed, and American unofficial observers continued to hang around Geneva, as scarcely befitted a great power.

Peace Mourns Defeat of World Court. Kirby in the New York *World,* 1935

Gradually, under Presidents Coolidge and Hoover, the Republic began to sidle toward the back door. To an increasing degree, Americans participated as consultants in the non-political functions of the League, such as conferences to control opium and prostitution. By March, 1930, Washington had sent official delegates to more than forty such parleys; and in some respects the nation was a member of the League in all but name. Yet unfriendly critics in America, chiefly isolationists, continued to sneer at the successes and jeer at the failures of the "League of Hallucinations."

The World Court—the judicial arm of the League—inspired much less fear. All Presidents from Wilson through Franklin D. Roosevelt urged that America join it. Despite outcries from the isolationists against the "League Court" or the "League Trap," the Senate approved adherence to the World Court in 1926, though only after tacking on five reservations. One of these proved unacceptable to the League, so negotiations ended. After another futile effort in the Senate to secure ratification in 1935, the United States washed its hands of the World Court.

Naval disarmament also demanded attention, for a race in smaller craft not limited by the Washington Conference was going merrily on—while Uncle Sam lagged far behind. Calvin Coolidge, economy-minded, was eager to repeat the presumed success of Harding at Washington. Hasty plans were finally completed for a three-power conclave at Geneva, Switzerland, in 1927. But inadequate ground-work was done, and the conference broke up in complete futility after an unseemly quarrel between the Americans and the British over the size of cruisers. Isolationists in the United States, aroused by all this bickering, were more determined than ever to plow a lonely furrow.

A tidal wave of public opinion had meanwhile been welling up in America for what was known as "outlawry of war." The conviction spread that if the quarreling nations would solemnly take the pledge to forswear war as an instrument of national policy, swords could be beaten into plowshares. Coolidge's Secretary of State Kellogg, who later won the Nobel Peace Prize for his role, was lukewarm about the idea. But after petitions bearing more than two million signatures had poured in on Washington, he signed with the French foreign minister in 1928 the famed Kellogg-Briand Pact. Officially known as the Pact of Paris, it was ultimately ratified by sixty-two nations, in-cluding all the major powers.

Overpraise came to the Kellogg-Briand pact. The Boston *Herald* announced, "It is a thing to rejoice over, it is superb, it is magnificent. We should sing the *Te Deum Laudamus. . . .*"

The new parchment peace was misleading. Although outlawing war as an instrument of national policy, it permitted defensive war. And what scheming aggressor could not rig up the excuse of self-defense? Lacking both muscles and teeth, the pact was branded by critics "an international kiss" or "a letter to Santa Claus." The Senate nevertheless approved it by an overwhelming margin. One unfor-tunate effect was to lull the American people into a false sense of security—a state of mind that found an outlet in the ostrich-like iso-lationism and neutralism of the 1930's. As events turned out, the new pact did not abolish war: it merely abolished, in some instances, formal declarations of war.

Coolidge Moves toward Good Neighborism

Despite current anti-war sentiment, the United States was reluc-tantly forced to adopt warlike measures in Latin America. Disorders in Nicaragua, perilously close to the Panama Canal, had jeopardized American lives and property, and in 1927 President Coolidge dis-patched over 5000 troops to this troubled land. His political foes, decrying mailed-fist tactics, accused him of waging a "private war," while critics south of the Rio Grande loudly assailed *Yanqui* im-perialism.

Mexican friction, at the same time, came to a boil over oil. The gov-ernment in Mexico City was attempting to wrest from American petroleum companies the private properties which, under the new constitution of 1917, were now legally vested in the Mexican nation. Relations between the two neighbor republics deteriorated alarmingly.

Then the clouds rather suddenly began to lift. In 1927, Coolidge adopted the happy suggestion that he send to Mexico as an amateur ambassador his old Amherst College classmate, Dwight W. Morrow, a Wall Street banker. By a combination of tact and charm, Morrow succeeded where others had failed. He was conspicuously aided by the good-will tour of aviator Charles A. Lindbergh, hero-conqueror of the Atlantic, who on this trip met his future bride, Morrow's daughter. So successful was Lindbergh as "Ambassador of the Air" that one American newspaper suggested as a new variant of an old floral theme: "Say it with fliers."

Under such promising auspices, Morrow finally worked out a temporarily acceptable compromise. The American oil companies were permitted to retain the rights they had secured prior to the constitution of 1917, but not those obtained later. Thus the Coolidge years ended with a bright new day dawning in relations with Latin America.

Farm Boy Hoover vs. City Slicker Smith

Poker-faced Calvin Coolidge, the prosperity President, could probably have won renomination and re-election in 1928 with relative ease. But the close-mouthed "Sphinx of the Potomac" bowed himself out of the race—or apparently did—when he tersely announced: "I do not choose to run for President in 1928."

His logical successor was Secretary of Commerce Hoover, a Quaker orphan from an Iowa farm. Already a living legend as a result of his spectacular work in Belgian relief and wartime food conservation, the "Boy Wonder" had done wonders with the Department of Commerce. Never elected to a public office, he was unpopular with the professional politicians, to whom he was an interloping "Herbie come lately." But he was popular with the masses, who asked, "Who but Hoover?" The object of their devotion was nominated by the Republican convention in Kansas City on the first ballot. His platform clucked contentedly over prosperity and the tariff, and promised enforcement of the unenforceable prohibition amendment.

Most conspicuous of the Democratic contenders was Alfred E. Smith, four-time governor of New York. An engaging, smiling, wise-cracking personality, he had proved himself to be both an outstanding liberal leader and a phenomenal vote-getter, especially with the working classes.

But Smith suffered from fatal political handicaps. He was wet—outspokenly and drippingly wet—at a time when the country was

Hoover recorded in his *Memoirs* (1952) that Old Guard Republicans in the Senate tried to head off his nomination with "smears." "Their favorite name for me was 'Sir Herbert,' a reference to my periodic residence in England. They also 'found' I had robbed a Chinaman some twenty-six years before and had been convicted in a British court."

not yet ready to abandon the "noble experiment." He seemed not quite "one hundred percent American," for though both parents were native New Yorkers, his mother's parents had been born in Ireland. He was a Roman Catholic—and no Catholic had yet been elected President. His formal education had ended with a Catholic parochial school. Sprung from the sidewalks of New York City, "Newsboy Al" was also an alumnus of the Fulton Fish Market, with an informal F.F.M. degree. He was also a political protege, though personally honest, of unsavory Tammany Hall.

Smith was the top-heavy favorite when the Democrats met in Houston, Texas. Franklin D. Roosevelt of New York, now polio-crippled, eloquently nominated his good friend "Al," whom he hailed as "the Happy Warrior." The Southern wing of the party—dry, rural, and Protestant—struggled vainly against the wet, urban, Catholic contender. But Smith sewed up the nomination on the first ballot.

At Houston the divided Democrats awkwardly presented their wet candidate with a dry platform. Smith, undaunted, made a valiant attempt to carry alcohol on one shoulder and water on the other. He sent a telegram to the convention promising to enforce the dry Volstead Act, but declaring that he would work for its moistening in accord with states' rights.

"Double, Double, Toil and Trouble; Fire Burn and Cauldron Bubble." The Campaign of 1928. Fitzpatrick in the St. Louis *Post-Dispatch*

Presidential Mudslingers of 1928

Radio had now come to be an important vote-getting device, but it helped Hoover more than Smith. The ex-fish-peddler, jauntily sporting a brown derby and a long cigar, had more personal sparkle, but he could not project it through the microphone. Many snobbish voters were repelled by his East-side pronunciation ("radd-dee-o" for "radio"), by his free-and-easy manner, and by his breezy, off-the-cuff speeches.

Iowa-born Herbert Hoover, with his double-breasted dignity, inspired confidence. He came out of the microphone better than he went in. Though rather dull and monotonous, he sounded grass-rootish and statesmanlike. Decrying un-American "socialism" and preaching "rugged individualism," he played up the benefits of Republican prosperity. His speech of acceptance smugly proclaimed, "The poorhouse is vanishing from among us." His supporters echoed this sentiment, and, recalling the full dinner pail, proclaimed that victory would bring "A Chicken in Every Pot, a Car in Every Garage." (Cynics later rewrote this to read "Two families in every garage.")

As bands blared Smith's theme song, "The Sidewalks of New York," the campaign sank into the sewers below the sidewalks. Despite the best efforts of Hoover and Smith, below-the-belt tactics were employed to a disgusting degree by lower-level campaigners.

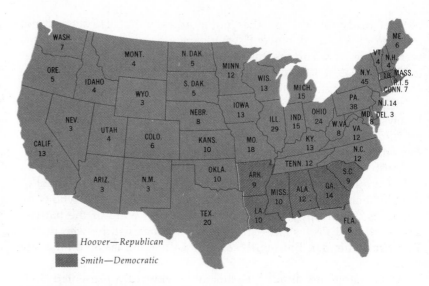

Hoover—Republican

Smith—Democratic

PRESIDENTIAL ELECTION OF 1928 (with electoral vote by state)

A Happy Hoover in 1928.
Crandall Collection, Hoover
Institution, Stanford University,
California

Religious bigotry raised its hideous head over Smith's Catholicism. An irresponsible whispering campaign claimed that "A Vote for Al Smith Is a Vote for the Pope," and that the White House, under Smith, would become a branch of the Vatican—complete with "Rum, Romanism, and Ruin." Hoover's attempts to quash such "smears" were in vain.

The proverbially Solid South—"one hundred percent American" and a stronghold of Protestant Ku Klux Klanism—shied away from Al Smith. It might have accepted a Catholic, or a wet, or the descendant of Irish grandparents, or an urbanite. But a mixture of Catholicism, wettism, foreignism and liberalism brewed on the sidewalks of New York was too bitter a dose for Southern stomachs. Smith's theme song was a constant and rasping reminder that his upbringing had not been convincingly American.

Hoover triumphed in a landslide. He bagged 21,391,381 popular votes to 15,016,443 for his embittered opponent, while rolling up an electoral count of 444 to 87. A huge Republican majority was returned to the House of Representatives. Tens of thousands of dry Southern Democrats—"Hoovercrats"—rebelled against Smith, and Hoover proved to be the first Republican candidate in fifty-two years, except for Harding's Tennessee victory in 1920, to carry a state that had seceded. He swept five states of the former Confederacy, as well as all the Border States.

Yet Smith, in defeat, ran ahead of his ticket and polled almost as many votes as the victorious Coolidge had in 1924. By attracting to the party an immense urban or "sidewalk vote," the New Yorker foreshadowed Roosevelt's New Deal victory in 1932, when the Democrats patched together the Solid South and the urban North.

Six "P's" largely accounted for Hoover's victory: personal prestige, prosperity, prohibition, Protestantism, Popery, and prejudice. (A cruel joke had Smith cabling the Pope a single word after the election, "Unpack.") The satisfaction of the country with prosperity was reflected in the dwindling of the third-party protest vote. The strength of all such groups combined dropped from 4,978,689 in 1924, to a mere 337,125 in 1928.

It so happened that 1928 was a "Republican year." The Democrats probably would have lost with any nominee—even a polished Protestant of English stock, college-bred, farm-domiciled, bone-dry, Boston-accented, and descended from old Plymouth Rock.

SELECT READINGS

A lucid overview is J. D. HICKS, *Republican Ascendancy, 1921–1933* (1960).* See also books by Faulkner, Sullivan, Allen, Slosson, and Soule for the previous chapter. Biographies of Coolidge are C. M. FUESS, *Calvin Coolidge* (1940) and W. A. WHITE's cynical *A Puritan in Babylon* (1938),* both outmoded by D. R. MCCOY, *Calvin Coolidge: The Quiet President* (1967). See also MARVIN BARRETT, *The Jazz Age* (1959) and G. H. KNOLES, *The Jazz Age Revisited* (1955).* On culture, consult R. S. and H. M. LYND's classic *Middletown* (1929)* and *Middletown in Transition* (1937).* Prohibition is handled in ANDREW SINCLAIR, *Prohibition* (1962)* and CHARLES MERZ, *The Dry Decade* (1931); see also J. H. LYLE, *The Dry and Lawless Years* (1960). Revealing on the Scopes trial are RAY GINGER, *Six Days or Forever?* (1958)* and L. W. LEVINE, *Defender of the Faith* [Bryan], *1915–1925* (1965).* Foreign policy is treated in L. E. ELLIS, *Frank B. Kellogg and American Foreign Relations, 1925–1929* (1961); R. H. FERRELL, *Peace in Their Time: The Origins of the Kellogg-Briand Pact* (1952); and J. C. VINSON, *William E. Borah and the Outlawry of War* (1957). On the 1928 election consult E. A. MOORE, *A Catholic Runs for President* (1956); OSCAR HANDLIN, *Al Smith and His America* (1958)*; and Smith's colorful autobiography, *Up to Now* (1929). Also *Harvard Guide,** Pt. VI.

* Available in paperback.

41

Hoover and the Onset of the Depression

. . . I am willing to pledge myself that if the time should ever come that the voluntary agencies of the country together with the local and state government are unable to find resources with which to prevent hunger and suffering in my country, I will ask the aid of every resource of the federal government because I would no more see starvation amongst our countrymen than would any Senator or Congressman. . . .

President Hoover, 1931

Hoover: the Great Engineer in Politics

Chubby-faced and ruddy-complexioned Herbert Hoover, a living example of the American success-story, was an intriguing mixture of two centuries. As a poor orphan boy who had worked his way through Stanford University, he had absorbed the 19th-Century copybook maxims of industry, thrift, and self-reliance. As a fabulously successful mining engineer and a brilliant business man, he had adopted to a high degree the efficiency-expertism of the 20th Century. Yet in his thinking, as well as in his dignified reserve and painfully high starched collar, he reminded one of William McKinley.

Even before entering the White House, Hoover had become world-famous as the "Great Humanitarian." No President had yet entered office with more international renown; certainly none had ever traveled abroad more extensively. "Sir Herbert Hoover" he was dubbed by those who sneered at his protracted residence as an engineer under the British flag. Yet long years of self-imposed exile had not weakened his grass-roots Americanism or his determination, abundantly supported by national tradition, to avoid foreign entanglements.

Hoover, with double-breasted dignity, was a far cry from the ordinary back-slapping politician. Though a citizen of the world and loaded down with international honors, he was shy, standoffish, and stiff. Personally colorless in public, he had been accustomed during much of his life to giving orders to subordinates and not to soliciting votes. Never before elected to public office, he was thin-skinned in the face of criticism, and he did not adapt himself readily to the necessary give-and-take of political accommodation. His real power lay in his integrity, his humanitarianism, his passion for assembling the facts, his efficiency, his talents for administration, and his ability to inspire loyalty in close associates.

As befitted America's newly mechanized civilization, Hoover was the ideal businessman's President. A millionaire in his own right, he found that his conservative instincts recoiled from anything suggesting socialism, paternalism, or "planned economy."

Hoover's Cabinet, which reflected his innate conservatism, carried on unbroken the big industry tradition of Harding and Coolidge. Aging Andrew W. Mellon was kept on in the Treasury Department, partly to retain the confidence of the business world. The regular Cabinet was supplemented by a group of Hoover's more vigorous intimates, who would periodically meet and toss around a medicine ball—hence "the Medicine Ball Cabinet."

The Heyday of Bootleggers and Kidnappers

President Hoover was a darling of the drys. He had referred to prohibition in 1928 as a "far-reaching" "experiment, noble in motive"—hence the popular expression the "noble experiment." Yet lofty though its purposes might be, prohibition was sinking to the ignoble level of lawlessness and gangsterism.

Early in his administration Hoover attempted to grapple with crime and the liquor problem by appointing the Wickersham investigating commission. This group of eleven prominent citizens, after two years of probing, submitted a report in 1931 that was a masterpiece of contradiction. A majority of the members reported that all was not going well, but the commission as a whole recommended that the experiment be continued, with modifications. A writer in a New York newspaper poked fun at the inability of this group to liquidate the liquor problem:

"Fine Opportunity for a Modern Engineer." Darling in the Des Moines *Register,* 1929

Prohibition is an awful flop.
  We like it.
It can't stop what it's meant to stop.
  We like it.
It's left a trail of graft and slime,
It's filled our land with vice and crime,
It don't prohibit worth a dime,
  Nevertheless we're for it.

Lawlessness spawned by prohibition and bootlegging manifested itself further in the "snatch racket"—or kidnapping for ransom. In the early 1930's alone there were several hundred notorious cases. The entire nation was inexpressibly shocked in 1932, when the infant son of aviator-hero Colonel Charles A. Lindbergh was kidnapped and killed in New Jersey. An aroused public opinion caused Congress in 1932 to pass the so-called Lindbergh Law (modified in 1934), making interstate abduction in certain circumstances a death-penalty offense. (In 1968 the death penalty was dropped.) Gradually "snatching" tapered off, owing largely to the vigilance of the Federal Bureau of Investigation (F.B.I.), under J. Edgar Hoover.

Federal Favors for Farmers

Prosperity in the late 1920's smiled broadly as the Hoover years began. Soaring stocks on the bull market continued to defy the laws of financial gravitation. But two immense groups of citizens were not sharing proportionately in the riches flowing from the national horn of plenty: the unorganized wage earners and especially the disorganized farmers.

For Benton's painting "Boom Town," see color portfolio following page 814.

Hoover's administration, contrary to its philosophy of hands-off individualism, was forced to respond to the outcry of the farmers with legislative aspirin. The Agricultural Marketing Act, passed by Congress in June, 1929, was designed to help the farmers help themselves, largely through producers' cooperatives. It set up a Federal Farm Board, with a revolving fund of half a billion dollars at its disposal. Money was lent generously to farm organizations seeking to buy, sell, and store agricultural surpluses. Four years later, in 1933, the Farm Board closed its books with the red figures showing a loss of $345,000,000, and with farm prices still dismayingly low.

In 1930 the Farm Board itself created both the Grain Stabilization Corporation and the Cotton Stabilization Corporation. The prime goal was to bolster sagging prices by buying up surpluses. But the two agencies were soon suffocated by an outpouring of farm produce, as wheat dropped to fifty-seven cents a bushel and cotton to five cents a pound.

Farmers had meanwhile clutched at the tariff as a possible straw to help keep their heads above the morass of starvation prices. During the recent presidential campaign, Hoover, an amateur in politics, had been stampeded into a politically unwise pledge. He had promised to call Congress into special session to consider agricultural relief and, specifically, to bring about "limited" changes in the tariff. These hope-giving assurances no doubt won many votes for Hoover in the Middle Western farm belt.

Hoover's Tariff Tribulations

The Hawley-Smoot Tariff of 1930 followed the well-worn pattern of legislative horse trading. It started out in the House as a fairly reasonable protective measure, designed to assist the farmers. But by the time the high-pressure lobbyists had pushed it through the Senate, it had acquired about a thousand amendments. It thus turned out to be the highest protective tariff in the nation's peacetime history. The average duty on non-free goods was raised from 38.5%, as established by the Fordney-McCumber Act of 1922, to nearly 60%.

Countless protests against the Hawley-Smoot hodge-podge poured in on Congress and the White House. The deluge of telegrams included frantic pleas from American exporters worried about overseas markets and from bankers concerned about international payments. More than one thousand economists, mostly college professors, signed a manifesto urging Hoover to veto the bill. But high-protection industrialists and many agricultural groups supported it.

TARIFF TRENDS, 1920–1960*

Average Annual Percentage Rates on Dutiable Goods

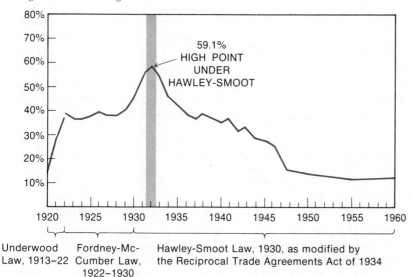

59.1%
HIGH POINT
UNDER
HAWLEY-SMOOT

Underwood Law, 1913–22   Fordney-Mc-Cumber Law, 1922–1930   Hawley-Smoot Law, 1930, as modified by the Reciprocal Trade Agreements Act of 1934

* See p. 628 for earlier tariff levels.

Hoover was placed in an awkward spot. If he wielded the veto, he would disrupt his party and throw away the few desirable features of the bill. These included one for which he had resolutely fought: the 50% flexible rate provision, to be adjusted by him up or down, upon recommendation of the Tariff Commission. He therefore signed the controversial bill, and defended it then and later with dogged vigor.

Foes of the law marshaled formidable arguments. They charged that it would not benefit the farmer who, as an exporter of surpluses, did not really need protection. It would raise commodity prices at home and hurt export business abroad. Foreigners could not buy American goods unless they piled up dollars, and they could not pile up dollars unless they could boost their goods over America's frowning tariff walls. Hawley-Smootism, the argument further ran, would make even more difficult the payment of Allied war debts and further retard Europe's post-war recovery. Finally, the law would invite reprisals from those countries that suffered from Uncle Sam's short-sighted selfishness.

To angered foreigners, the Hawley-Smoot Tariff was a blow below the trade belt. It seemed like a declaration of economic warfare on the entire outside world. It reversed a promising world-wide trend toward reasonable tariffs and widened the yawning trade gaps. It plunged both America and other nations deeper into the terrible depression which had already begun. It increased international financial chaos, and forced the United States further into the bog of economic isolationism. And economic isolationism, both at home and abroad, was playing directly into the hands of a wild-eyed German demagogue, Adolf Hitler.

Reprisals, as threatened, came quickly. Canada, America's next-door neighbor and best two-way customer, pushed up her customs duties on many articles from the United States. Scores of American factories moved into Canada to escape the new barriers. By the end of 1931, twenty-five foreign countries had taken active steps to retaliate against the Hawley-Smoot Tariff. American import and export trade, already languishing under the depression, suffered further losses.

Putting America on Rubber Tires

Descending like a suffocating smog, the Great Depression was the baffling perplexity of the 1930's. It grew basically out of the malfunctioning of America's enormous industrial and agricultural machine.

The New Industrial Revolution had slipped into high gear in America during the first two decades of the 20th Century. Thrusting out steel tentacles, it had changed the daily life of the people in unprecedented ways. Machinery was the new messiah.

"Mr. Hoover: Leave it to Willie." Flexible Clause Designed to Curb Tariff. Acid-tongued H. L. Mencken called Hoover "a fat Coolidge." Omaha *World Herald.* By permission.

Of all the inventions of the era, the automobile left the deepest mark. It became the fountainhead of an amazing industrial mechanism, with its assembly-line methods and other mass-production techniques.

Americans adapted rather than invented the gasoline engine; Europeans can claim the original honor. By the 1890's a few daring American inventors and promoters, including Henry Ford and Ransom E. Olds (Oldsmobile), were developing the infant automotive industry. By 1910 there were sixty-nine companies, with a total annual production of 181,000 units. The early contraptions were neither speedy nor reliable. Many a stalled motorist, profanely cranking his balky car, had to endure the jeer "Get a horse" from the occupants of a Dobbin-drawn carriage.

An enormous industry sprang into being, as Detroit became the motor-car capital of America. The mechanized colossus owed much to the stop-watch efficiency techniques of Frederick W. Taylor, a prominent inventor, engineer, and tennis player, who sought to eliminate waste motion. His epitaph reads: "Father of Scientific Management."

Best-known of the new crop of industrial statesmen was Henry Ford, who more than any other man put America on rubber tires. His high and hideous Model T ("Tin Lizzie") was cheap, rugged, and reasonably reliable, though rough and clattering. The parts of Ford's "flivver" were highly standardized, but the behavior of this "rattling good car" was so individualized that it became the butt of numberless jokes.

Lean and silent Henry Ford, who was said to have wheels in his head, erected an immense personal empire on the cornerstone of his mechanical genius, though his associates provided much of the organizational talent. Ill-educated, this multimillionaire mechanic was socially and culturally narrow; "History is bunk," he once

Henry Ford in his First Car, Built in 1896. Courtesy of Ford Motor Company.

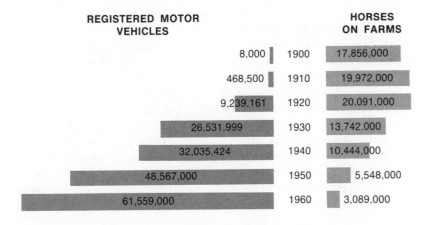

REGISTERED MOTOR VEHICLES		HORSES ON FARMS
8,000	1900	17,856,000
468,500	1910	19,972,000
9,239,161	1920	20,091,000
26,531,999	1930	13,742,000
32,035,424	1940	10,444,000
48,567,000	1950	5,548,000
61,559,000	1960	3,089,000

Henry Ford was accused of invading privacy in 1922, when this notice was posted in his Detroit factory: "From now on it will cost a man his job . . . to have the odor of beer, wine or liquor on his breath, or to have any of these intoxicants on his person or in his home. The Eighteenth Amendment is a part of the fundamental laws of this country. It was meant to be enforced.

Politics has interfered with the enforcement of this law, but so far as our organization is concerned, it is going to be enforced to the letter."

testified. But he devoted himself with one-track devotion to the gospel of standardization. After two early failures, he grasped and applied fully the techniques of assembly-line production—"Fordism." He is supposed to have remarked that the purchaser could have his automobile any color he desired—just as long as it was black. So economical were his methods that in the mid-1920's he was selling the Ford roadster for $260—well within the purse of a thrifty workingman.

The flood of Fords was phenomenal. In 1914 the "Automobile Wizard" turned out his five hundred thousandth Model T; in 1925 he was completing one gasoline buggy every ten seconds of the day. By 1930 his total had risen to 20,000,000, or, on a bumper-to-bumper basis, more than enough to encircle the globe. A national newspaper and magazine poll conducted in 1923 revealed Ford to be the people's choice for the presidential nomination in 1924.

By 1929, when the Great Bull Market collapsed, there were 26,000,000 motor vehicles registered in the United States. This figure, averaging one for every 4.9 Americans, represented far more automobiles fhan existed in all the rest of the world.

The Advent of the Gasoline Age

The impact of the self-propelled carriage on various aspects of American life was tremendous. A gigantic new industry emerged, dependent on steel, but displacing steel from its kingpin role. Employing directly or indirectly about six million men by 1930, it was a major prop of the nation's prosperity. Thousands of new jobs, moreover, were created by supporting industries. The lengthening list would include rubber, glass, and fabrics, to say nothing of thousands of service stations and garages. America's standard of living, responding to this infectious prosperity, rose to an enviable level.

New industries spurted forth; older ones grew sickly. The petroleum business experienced a phenomenal development. Hundreds of new oil derricks mushroomed forth in California, Texas, and Oklahoma, as these states expanded wondrously and the new frontier became an industrial frontier. The once-feared railroad octopus, on the other hand, was hard hit by the competition of passenger cars, buses, and trucks. An age-old story was repeated: one industry's gains were another industry's pains.

Other effects were widely felt. Speedy marketing of perishable foodstuffs, such as fresh fruits, was accelerated. A new prosperity enriched outlying farms, as city dwellers were provided with produce at attractive prices. Countless new roads ribboned out to meet the demand of the American motorist for smoother and faster highways, often paid for by taxes on gasoline. The Era of Mud ended as the nation made haste to construct the finest network of hard-surfaced roadways in the world. Lured by new seductiveness in advertising, and encouraged by the perfecting of installment-plan buying, countless Americans with short purses acquired the habit of riding as they paid.

Zooming motor cars were agents of social change. At first a luxury, they rapidly became a necessity. Essentially devices for needed transportation, they soon developed into a badge of freedom and equality—a necessary prop for self-respect. Leisure hours could now be spent more pleasurably, as tens of thousands of cooped-up souls responded to the call of the open road on joyriding vacations. Women were further freed from clinging-vine dependence on males. Isolation among the sections was broken down, while the less attractive states lost population at an alarming rate. America was becoming a nation of nomads.

Other social byproducts of the automobile were visible. Autobuses made possible the consolidation of schools, and to some extent of churches. The trend toward hive-like urbanization was partially slowed. City workers could now live in the suburbs and commute by motor car or bus to railroad stations, there to catch the 7:52 for work.

The demon machine, on the other hand, exacted a terrible toll by catering to the American mania for speed. Citizens were becoming statistics. Not counting the hundreds of thousands of injured and crippled, the one millionth American had died in a motor accident by 1951—more than all those killed on all the battlefields of all the nation's wars to that date. "The public be rammed" seemed to be the motto of the new age.

Virtuous home life partially broke down as joyriders of all ages forsook the ancestral hearth for the wide open spaces. The morals of flaming youth sagged correspondingly—at least in the judgment of their elders. Even the disgraceful crime waves of the 1920's and 1930's were partly stimulated by the motor car, for gangsters could now make quick getaways.

Yet no sane American would plead for a return of the old horse and buggy, complete with fly-breeding manure. Life might be cut short on the highways, and smog might poison the air, but the automobile brought its satisfactions and telescoped more convenience, pleasure, and excitement into a shorter period than ever before.

A Farewell to the Horse as Early as 1899. Davenport in the New York *Journal*

Man Develops Wings

Gasoline engines also provided the power which enabled man to fulfill his age-old dream of sprouting wings. After near-successful experiments by others with heavier-than-air craft, the Wright brothers, Orville and Wilbur, performed "the Miracle at Kitty Hawk,"

North Carolina. On a historic day—December 17, 1903—Orville Wright took aloft a feebly engined plane that stayed air-borne for 12 seconds and 120 feet. Thus the Air Age was launched by two obscure bicycle repairmen.

As aviation gradually got off the ground, the world slowly shrank. The public was made increasingly air-minded by unsung heroes—often martyrs—who appeared as stunt flyers at fairs and other public gatherings. Airplanes—"flying coffins"—were used with marked success for various purposes during the Great War of 1914–1918. Shortly thereafter private companies began to operate passenger lines with air-mail contracts, which were in effect a subsidy from Washington. The first transcontinental air-mail route was established from New York to San Francisco in 1920.

In 1927 modest and skillful Charles A. Lindbergh, the so-called "Flyin' Fool," electrified the world by the first solo west-to-east conquest of the Atlantic. Seeking a prize of $25,000, the lanky stunt flyer courageously piloted his single-engined plane, "The Spirit of St. Louis," from New York to Paris in a grueling 33 hours and 39 minutes.

Lindbergh's exploit swept Americans off their feet. Fed up with the cynicism and debunking of the Jazz Age, they found in this wholesome and handsome youth a genuine hero. They clasped the fluttering "Lone Eagle" to their hearts much more warmly than the bashful young man desired. In the words of Angela Morgan:

Lindbergh and His "Spirit of St. Louis." National Archives.

Lad, you took the soul of me
That long had lain despairing,
Sent me Heaven-faring
*Gave me wings again.**

"Lucky Lindy" received an uproarious welcome in the "hero canyon" of lower Broadway, as 1800 tons of ticker tape and other improvised confetti showered upon him. Lindbergh's achievement—it was more than a "stunt"—did much to dramatize and popularize flying, while giving a strong boost to the infant aviation industry.

The impact of the airship was tremendous. It provided the soaring American spirit with yet another dimension. At the same time, it gave birth to a giant new industry. Unfortunately, the accident rate in the pioneer stages of aviation was high, though hardly more so than on the early railroads. But by the 1930's and 1940's, travel by air on regularly scheduled air lines was markedly safer than on overcrowded highways.

Man's new wings also increased the tempo of an already breathless civilization. The floundering railroad received another sharp set-

* "Lindbergh," in *The Spirit of St. Louis,* ed. Charles Vale (George H. Doran Company, 1927).

back through the loss of passengers and mail. A lethal new weapon was given to the gods of war; and with the coming of city-busting aerial bombs men could well debate whether the conquest of air was a blessing or a curse. The Atlantic was shriveling to about the size of the Aegean Sea in the days of Socrates, while isolation behind ocean moats was becoming a bygone dream.

The Radio Revolution

The speed of the airplane was far eclipsed by the speed of radio waves. Guglielmo Marconi, an Italian, invented wireless telegraphy in the 1890's, and his brain child was used for long-range communication during World War I.

Next came the voice-carrying radio, a triumph of many minds. A red-letter day was posted in November, 1920, when the Pittsburgh station KDKA broadcast the news of the Harding landslide. Later miracles were achieved in transatlantic wireless photographs, radio telephones, and television. In harmony with American free enterprise, radio programs were generally sustained by bothersome "commercials," as contrasted with drabber government-owned systems of Europe.

Like other marvels, the radio not only created a new industry, but added richness to the fabric of American life. More joy was given to leisure hours, and many children who had been lured from the fireside by the automobile were brought back by the radio. The nation was better knit together. Various sections heard Americans with standardized accents, and countless millions "tuned in" on perennial comedy favorites like "Amos 'n' Andy." Advertising was further perfected as an art.

Educationally and culturally, the radio made a significant contribution. Sports were further stimulated. Politicians had to adjust their speaking techniques to the new medium, and millions rather than thousands of voters heard their pleas. A host of listeners swallowed the gospel of their favorite newscaster, or were even ringside participants in world-shaking events. Finally, musical taste was distinctly elevated, as the strains of famous artists and symphony orchestras were beamed into countless homes.

Radio came in with a bang in the winter of 1921–1922. A San Francisco newspaper reported a discovery that countless citizens were making, "There is radio music in the air, every night, everywhere. Anybody can hear it at home on a receiving set, which any boy can put up in an hour."

Hollywood's Filmland Fantasies

The flickering movie was the fruit of numerous geniuses, including Thomas A. Edison. As early as the 1890's this novel contraption, though still in crude form, had attained some popularity in the naughty peep-show penny arcades. The real birth of the moving picture came in 1903, when the first story sequence reached the screen. This breathless melodrama—"The Great Train Robbery"—

was featured in the five-cent theaters, popularly called "nickelodeons." Spectacular among the first full-length classics was D. W. Griffith's "The Birth of a Nation," which glorified the Ku Klux Klan of Reconstruction days and defamed the blacks.

A fascinating industry was thus launched. Hollywood, in southern California, quickly became the movie capital of the world, for it enjoyed a maximum of sunshine and other advantages. Early producers featured nudity and heavy-lidded female vampires ("vamps"), and an outraged public forced the screen magnates to set up their own rigorous code of censorship. The motion picture really came into its own during the World War of 1914–1918, when it was used as an engine of anti-German propaganda. Specially prepared "hang the Kaiser" films aided powerfully in selling war bonds and in boosting morale.

A new era began in 1927 with the success of the first "talkie"— "The Jazz Singer," starring Al Jolson in blackface. The age of the "silents" was ushered out as theaters everywhere were "wired for sound." At about the same time reasonably satisfactory color films were being produced.

In the face of protests against sex in the movies, the industry appointed a "Movie Czar," Will H. Hays, who issued the famous "Hays Code" in 1934. As he stated in a speech, "This industry must have toward that sacred thing, the mind of a child, toward that clean virgin thing, that unmarked slate, the same responsibility, the same care about the impressions made upon it, that the best clergyman or the most inspired teacher of youth would have."

Movies eclipsed all other new forms of amusement in the phenomenal growth of their popularity. Tens of thousands of actors and "extras" were employed in the cardboard cities behind Hollywood's high wooden fences, to say nothing of additional thousands engaged in exhibiting the films and selling noisy popcorn. Movie "stars" of the first pulchritude commanded much larger salaries than the President of the United States, in some cases as much as $100,000 for a single picture. Many actors and actresses were far more widely known than most statesmen.

The "movie habit" rapidly created a nation of "cinemaniacs." By 1930 weekly admissions totaled 100,000,000—a large number of them "repeaters"—in a population of 122,775,000. Many of the moviegoers were openmouthed children, much of whose education, not all of it wholesome, was derived from this new type of textbook.

Other social consequences of the silver screen were incalculable. Attendance at movie "palaces" provided an escape from drab reality; filmland became the standard for taste, styles, songs, and morals. Newsreels, travelogues, and other informative "shorts" offered infinite possibilities for education, but they constituted only a tiny part of the total offering. Two by-products of the industry were the cheap movie magazine and the no less cheap keyhole commentator, both unduly concerned with the foibles and "sex-capades" of the "stars."

Nor did the influence of the moving picture end here. It almost exterminated vaudeville, and robbed the footlighted theater of much patronage. It no doubt hurt attendance at religious services. Like the radio and the motor car, it contributed to the further standardization of America, for the mass of the people idolized the same actors and heard the same "hit" tunes. Hollywood dominated not only the domestic but the foreign movie market, and regrettably provided potent anti-American propaganda. There was an unwholesome over-emphasis on the idle rich, the plush boudoir, the glowering gangster, and the quick-shooting cattle rustler.

The Great Crash of 1929

When Herbert Hoover confidently took the presidential oath, on March 4, 1929, there were few black clouds on the economic horizon. One painful exception was the debt-blanketed farm belt. America's productive colossus—stimulated by the automobile, radio, movie, and other new industries—was roaring along at a dizzy speed that suggested a permanent plateau of prosperity. Few men sensed that it might smother its own fires by pouring out too much.

The speculative bubble was actually near the busting point. Prices on the stock exchange continued to spiral upward and create a fool's paradise of paper profits, despite Hoover's early but fruitless efforts to curb speculation through the Federal Reserve Board. A few prophets of disaster were bold enough to raise warning voices, but they were drowned out by the mad chatter of the ticker-tape machine.

A catastrophic crash came in October, 1929. It was partially trig-gered by the British, who raised their interest rates in an effort to bring back capital lured abroad by American investments. Foreign investors and wary domestic speculators began to dump their "insecurities," and an orgy of selling followed. Tensions built up to

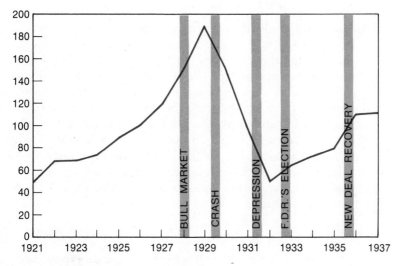

INDEX OF COMMON STOCK PRICES (1926 = 100)

the panicky "Black Tuesday" of October 29, 1929, when 16,410,030 shares of stocks were sold in a save-who-may scramble. Wall Street became a wailing wall as gloom and doom replaced boom, and suicides increased alarmingly.

Losses, even in blue-chip securities, were fantastic. By the end of 1929—two months after the initial crash—stockholders had lost forty billion dollars in paper values, or more than the total cost of World War I to the United States. Typical prices of stocks per share were:

	Adjusted High Price	**Low Price**
	Sept. 3, 1929	*Nov. 13, 1929*
American Can	$181⅞	$ 86
General Electric	396¼	168⅛
Montgomery Ward	137⅞	49¼

The stock-market collapse heralded a business depression, at home and abroad, which was the most prolonged and withering in American or world experience. No other industrialized nation suffered so severe a setback. By the end of 1930 about six or seven million workers in the United States were jobless; two years later the figure had about doubled. Hungry and despairing men pounded pavements in search of non-existent jobs ("We're firing, not hiring"). Where employees were not discharged, wages and salaries were often slashed. A current jingle ran:

Mellon pulled the whistle,
Hoover rang the bell
Wall Street gave the signal
And the country went to hell.

The misery and gloom were incalculable, as forests of dead chimneys stood starkly against the sky. Over five thousand banks collapsed in the first three years of the depression, carrying down with them the life savings of tens of thousands of widows and retired citizens. Countless thousands of honest, hard-working people lost their homes and farms to the forecloser's hammer. Bread lines formed, soup kitchens dispensed food, and apple sellers stood shivering on street corners trying to peddle their wares for five cents. Foreign trade faded badly, for the worldwide depression dried up purchasing power. As cash registers gathered cobwebs, the song "My God, How the Money Rolls In" was replaced with "Brother, Can You Spare a Dime?"

Hooked on the Horn of Plenty

What caused the Great Depression? One basic explanation was overproduction by both farm and factory. Ironically, the depression of the 1930's was one of abundance, not want. It was the "Great Glut" or the "Plague of Plenty."

The nation's ability to produce goods had clearly outrun its capacity to consume them or pay for them. Too much money was going into the hands of a few wealthy people, who in turn invested it in factories and other agencies of production. Not enough was going into salaries and wages, where revitalizing purchasing power could be more quickly felt.

Other maladies were at work. Overexpansion of credit through installment-plan buying overstimulated production. Paying on so-called "easy" terms caused many a consumer to plunge in beyond his depth. Normal technological unemployment, resulting from new labor-saving machines, also added its burden to the abnormal unemployment of the "threadbare thirties."

This already bleak picture was further darkened by economic anemia abroad. Britain and the Continent had never fully recovered from the upheaval of World War I. Depression in America was given a further downward push by a chain-reaction financial collapse in Europe, following the failure in 1931 of a prominent Vienna banking house. A drying up of international trade, moreover, had been hastened by the shortsighted Hawley-Smoot Tariff of 1930. European uncertainties over reparations, war debts, and defaults on loans owed to America caused tensions that reacted unfavorably on the United States. Many of these conditions had been created or worsened by Uncle Sam's own narrow-visioned policies, but it was now too late to unscramble the omelet.

As if man-made disasters were not enough, a terrible drought scorched the Mississippi Valley in 1930. Thousands of farms were sold at auction for taxes, though in some cases kind neighbors would intimidate prospective buyers, bid one cent, and return the property to its original owner. Farm tenancy or rental—a species of peonage—was spreading at an alarming rate among both whites and blacks.

By 1930 the depression had become a national calamity. Through no fault of their own, a host of industrious citizens had lost everything. They wanted to work—but there was no work. The blighting effect of all this dazed despair on the spirit was incalculable and long lasting. America's "uniqueness" no longer seemed so unique or her manifest destiny so manifest. Hitherto the people had grappled with Indians, trees, stones, and other physical obstacles. But the depression was a baffling wraith they could not grasp. Initiative and self-respect were stifled, as panhandlers begged for food or "charity soup." In extreme cases "ragged individualists" slept under "Hoover blankets" (old newspapers), fought over the contents of garbage cans, or cooked their findings in old oil drums in tin-and-paper shantytowns cynically named "Hoovervilles." The very foundations of America's social structure trembled.

Farm Depression and Industrial Expansion in the 1920's. Fitzpatrick in the St. Louis *Post-Dispatch.*

Shivering men sold apples on the street corners of the big cities at five cents apiece. Hoover, in his *Memoirs* (1952), claims that the apple growers shrewdly and profitably capitalized on "the sympathy of the public for the unemployed." He further states, with obvious exaggeration, "Many persons left their jobs for the more profitable one of selling apples. When any left-winger wishes to indulge in scathing oratory, he demands, 'Do you want to return to selling apples.'"

Soup Kitchen Relief. Fitzpatrick in the St. Louis *Post-Dispatch*.

Hoover spoke approvingly in a campaign speech in 1928 of "The American system of Rugged Individualism." In 1930 he referred to a veto in 1887 by Cleveland of a bill to appropriate seed grain to the drought-striken farmers of Texas: ". . . I do not believe that the power and duty of the General Government ought to be extended to the relief of individual suffering. . . . The lesson should be constantly enforced that though the people support the Government the Government should not support the people." This could better be left to the states.

Rugged Times for Rugged Individualists

Hoover's exalted reputation as a wonder-worker and efficiency engineer crashed hardly less dismally than the stock market. He doubtless would have shone in the prosperity-drenched Coolidge years, when he had foreseen the abolition of poverty and poorhouses. But damming the Great Depression proved to be a task beyond his engineering talents.

The perplexed President was thus impaled on the horns of a cruel dilemma. As a deservedly famed humanitarian, he was profoundly distressed by the widespread misery about him. Yet as a staunch individualist, deeply rooted in an earlier era of free enterprise, he shrank from the heresy of government handouts. Convinced that industry, thrift, and self-reliance were the virtues that had made America great, he feared that a government "dole" would weaken, perhaps destroy, the national fiber.

Hoover had deep faith in the efficiency of the industrial machine, which itself was undamaged by depression. He urged business to share some of the unemployment burden by not laying off men, and by reducing wages and hours in an effort to spread the available work among more people. From time to time he would attempt to encourage the public by issuing optimistic statements, which often were followed by a fresh decline. He was accused of saying, although he did not use these precise words, that prosperity was hovering—"Hoovering," critics jibed—just around the corner.

The President at length conceded that the deserving unemployed and hungry should be given a boost during the emergency, but he insisted that such aid should come from local government, not from Washington. He would thus remain true to the American tradition of home responsibility and local self-rule. He would also reduce misrepresentation and graft, for the funds would be handed out by neighbors who knew intimately the needs of the recipients. And, with good reason, he sought to avoid the danger of having "pork barrel" politicians build up in Washington a huge, self-perpetuating bureaucracy, involved in what was later cynically called "givernment."

As the depression nightmare steadily worsened, relief by local government agencies broke down. For one thing, the burden was overwhelming; for another, taxes could not be squeezed from money-less people. Hoover was forced to turn reluctantly from his doctrine of log-cabin individualism and accept the proposition that the welfare of the people in a nationwide depression is a direct concern of the national government.

Hoover at last worked out a compromise between the old hands-off philosophy and the "soul-destroying" direct dole then being used in England. He would assist the hard-pressed railroads, banks, and rural credit corporations, in the hope that if financial health were restored at the top of the economic pyramid, unemployment would be relieved at the bottom.

Partisan critics sneered at the "Great Humanitarian"—he who had fed the faraway Belgians but would not use federal funds to feed needy Americans. Hostile commentators remarked that he was willing to lend government money to the big bankers, who allegedly had plunged the country into the mess. He would likewise lend money to agricultural organizations to feed pigs—but not people. Pigs, cynics noted, had no character to undermine.

Much of this criticism was unfair. Though continued suffering seemed to belie the effectiveness of Hoover's measures, his efforts probably prevented a more serious collapse than did occur. And his expenditures for relief, revolutionary for that day, paved the path for the enormous federal outlays of his successor, Franklin Roosevelt. Hoover proved that the old bootstrap-pulling techniques would no longer work in a crisis of this magnitude.

"It Seems There Wasn't any Depression at All!" Fitzpatrick in the St. Louis *Post-Dispatch*

Herbert Hoover: Forerunner of the New Deal

President Hoover, in line with his "trickle down" philosophy, at last recommended that Congress vote immense sums for useful public works. Though at heart an anti-spender, he secured from Congress appropriations totaling two and one-quarter billion dollars for such projects. To alarmists, the Washington ship of state seemed in danger of sinking in a red-ink sea of unbalanced budgets and mounting debts.

Most imposing of the public enterprises was the gigantic Hoover Dam—originally called Boulder Dam—on the Colorado River. Voted by Congress in the days of Coolidge, it was begun in 1930 under Hoover and completed in 1936 under Roosevelt. It succeeded in creating a huge man-made lake for purposes of irrigation, flood control, and electric power.

But Hoover sternly fought all schemes that he regarded as "socialistic." Conspicuous among them was the Norris Muscle Shoals Bill, which foreshadowed Franklin Roosevelt's Tennessee Valley Authority. Hoover emphatically vetoed this measure, primarily because he opposed the government's selling electric power in competition with its own citizens in private companies.

Early in 1932 Congress, responding to Hoover's belated appeal, established the Reconstruction Finance Corporation (R.F.C.). With an initial working capital of half a billion dollars, this agency became a government lending bank. It was designed to provide indirect relief by assisting insurance companies, banks, agricultural organizations, railroads, and even hard-pressed state and local governments. But to preserve individualism, there would be no loans to individuals.

"Pump-priming" loans by the R.F.C. were no doubt of widespread benefit, though the organization was established many months too late for maximum usefulness. Projects that it supported were largely self-liquidating, and the government as a banker actually profited to the tune of many millions of dollars. Giant corporations so obviously benefited from this assistance that the R.F.C. was dubbed—rather unfairly—"the millionaires' dole." The irony is that the thrifty and individualistic Hoover had sponsored the project, though with initial reluctance, and that it actually had a strong New-Dealish flavor.

Hoover's administration also provided some indirect benefits for labor. After stormy debate, Congress passed the Norris-La Guardia Anti-Injunction Act in 1932, and Hoover signed it. The measure outlawed "yellow dog" (anti-union) contracts, and forbade the federal courts to issue injunctions to restrain strikes, boycotts, and peaceful picketing.

The truth is that Herbert Hoover, despite criticism of his "heartlessness," did inaugurate a significant new policy. In previous panics the masses had been forced to "sweat it out." Slow though Hoover was to abandon this 19th-Century bias, by the end of his term he had traveled a long way toward government assistance for needy citizens —a road that Franklin Roosevelt was to take all the way.

Hoover's woes, one should note, were increased by a hostile Congress. At critical times during his first two years, the Republican majority proved highly uncooperative. Friction worsened during his last two years. A depression-cursed electorate, rebelling in the Congressional elections of 1930, so reduced the Republican majority that Democrats controlled the new House and almost controlled the Senate. Insurgent Republicans could—and did—combine with opposition Democrats to harass Hoover. Some of the President's troubles were deliberately manufactured by Congressmen who, in his words, "played politics with human misery."

"Nothing Else Left for Him to Do," 1932. Omaha *World-Herald*

Routing the Bonus Army in Washington

Many veterans of World War I were numbered among the hard-hit victims of the depression. Industry had secured a "bonus"—though a dubious one—in the Hawley-Smoot Tariff. So the thoughts of the ex-"doughboys" naturally turned to what the government owed them for their services in 1917–1918, when they had "saved" democracy. A drive developed for the premature payment of the deferred bonus voted by Congress in 1924 and payable in 1945.

Hoover was icily unsympathetic to a bonus. As a sound-money man, he emphatically opposed all suggestions from pressure groups for further unbalancing the budget and inflating the currency. But a vote-conscious Congress proved more responsive. It passed a bill in 1931 enabling veterans to borrow up to 50% on their bonus (adjusted compensation), instead of 22%. This concession would impose an additional burden on the Treasury, already in the red, of from one to two billion dollars. Hoover's vigorous veto was so much wasted ink.

Thousands of impoverished veterans, both war and unemployment, were now prepared to move on to Washington, there to demand of Congress the immediate payment of their *entire* bonus. The "Bonus Expeditionary Forces," which mustered about twenty thousand souls, converged on the capital in the summer of 1932. These supplicants promptly set up unsanitary public camps and erected shacks on vacant lots—a gigantic "Hooverville." They thus created a menace to the public health, while attempting to intimidate Congress by their presence in force. After the pending bonus bill had failed in Congress by a narrow margin, Hoover arranged to pay the return fare of about six thousand bonus marchers. The rest refused to decamp, though ordered to do so.

Following riots that cost two lives, Hoover responded to the demands of the Washington authorities by ordering the army to evacuate the unwanted guests. A sprinkling of them were ex-convicts and Communist agitators. The eviction was carried out by General Douglas MacArthur with bayonets and tear gas, and with far more severity than Hoover had planned. A few of the ex-soldiers were injured as the torch was put to their pathetic shanties in the inglorious "Battle of Anacostia Flat."

Hoover claimed in his *Memoirs*, with probable exaggeration, that the ejected Bonus Army consisted of "mixed hoodlums, ex-convicts, Communists, and a minority of veterans. . . ." He complained, "I was portrayed as a murderer and an enemy of the veterans." Actually, there were some non-fatal injuries on both sides.

This brutal episode brought down additional condemnation on the once-popular Hoover, who by now was the most loudly booed man in the country. The Democrats, not content with his vulnerable record, employed professional "smear" artists to drive him from office. Cynics sneered that the "Great Engineer"—a stationary engineer—had in a few months "ditched, drained, and damned the country." The existing panic was unfairly branded "the Hoover Depression." In truth, Hoover had been oversold as a superman—and the public grumbled when his magician's wand failed to produce rabbits.

The Diplomacy of Naval Disarmament

As a Quaker and famed humanitarian, Hoover embraced peace as the keynote of his foreign policy. He cooperated with the non-political activities of the League of Nations as fully as American public opinion would permit. Peace and disarmament were unusually popular themes in those depression days, partly because costly war preparations would further unbalance national budgets.

Arms limitation had a strong appeal to Hoover, whose efficient nature recoiled from the waste of war. Much remained to be done. The Washington Conference of 1921–1922 had tabooed more big battleships and aircraft carriers, but the race was wide open in cruisers, destroyers, submarines, and other smaller craft. America, economy-minded and depression-ridden, was falling alarmingly behind in construction.

The Naval Race, 1922–1929

Warships Laid Down or Appropriated For	
Japan	125
France	119
Italy	82
Britain	74
U.S.	11

The multi-power Naval Conference of 1930, meeting with fanfare in London, was hailed as one of the signal achievements of the Hoover years. Upper limits were placed not only on battleships and carriers but on the construction of smaller vessels. The Americans were formally conceded parity with Britain in all categories of ships; the Japanese were left with the small end of a 10–10–6 ratio in capital ships and heavy cruisers. But Japan did succeed in raising the formula to 10–10–7 in light cruisers and other auxiliary craft, while attaining parity in submarines.

Despite all the ballyhoo, the London Conference was only a paper victory for disarmament. America did win naval parity with the British, but to achieve it she would have to construct about a billion dollars' worth of additional warships. Such a program could hardly be regarded as either disarmament or economy, but the London Conference at least established a ceiling. A tax-conscious America, during the apathetic 1930's, fell far short of building the tonnage to which it was entitled.

The Allied War Debtors Default

The debt-reparations problem also felt the pressure of the global depression. American investors no longer had millions to invest in Europe. Private loans from the United States to Germany dried up; German reparations payments to the Allies consequently dried up. Allied debt payments to Washington were about to dry up—thus ending the fantastic cycle of borrowing from America to pay America. If Europe went completely to pot financially, the billions of dollars in private American investments might be lost, perhaps forever.

In this critical hour—June, 1931—Hoover proposed a financial blood transfusion in the form of a moratorium. It would provide a one-year suspension of European war-debt payments, both principal and interest, to Washington. The "Hoover holiday" was naturally acclaimed in the debt-cursed European countries, but

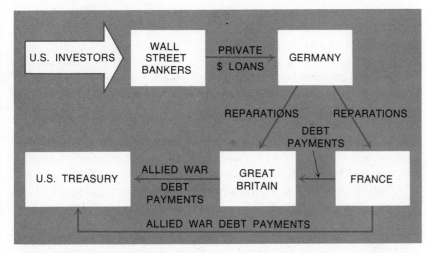

ASPECTS OF THE FINANCIAL MERRY-GO-ROUND, 1921–1933

Hoover ran into difficulty in "selling" the idea to Congress. Suspicions were general that once the one-year period of grace had ended, the emphasis would be on the "more" in "moreatorium." Finally, however, Congress voted its approval.

The debt crisis now came rapidly to a boil. In 1932 representatives of the ex-Allied European powers met at Lausanne, in Switzerland, and agreed to scale down Germany's reparations bill from the original $32,000,000,000 to $714,000,000. The catch was that there would have to be a satisfactory Allied debt readjustment with Washington, and this in turn meant cancellation. But the American public—and Hoover—still strongly opposed cancellation; hence Washington promptly rejected the scheme. To the bitter end the administration argued that there was no connection between Allied debts and German reparations. But saying so did not make it so.

Hoover's breathing-spell moratorium ended in 1932, but only six of the debtors paid their installments. Five nations defaulted outright, including France, and by mid-1934 all the others had followed, except "honest little Finland." By this time America had her choice between cancellation and just not getting the money—and Washington chose the second course. Within a few years, as interest mounted, the original debt was much larger than it had been when the payments started. In less than ten years the financial burdens of a new world war caused the country to write off the defunct debts of the old one.

Japanese Militarists Attack China

The Great Depression, which brewed enough distress at home, added immensely to difficulties abroad.

Rampaging Japan stole the Far Eastern spotlight. In September,

1931, the Japanese imperialists, noting that the Western World was badly mired down in depression, lunged into Manchuria. Alleging provocation, they rapidly overran China's rich province, and proceeded to bolt shut the Open Door in the conquered area.

Civilized peoples were stunned by this act of naked aggression. It was a flagrant violation of the League of Nations covenant, as well as of various other international agreements solemnly signed by Tokyo. Far-visioned observers feared that unless the major powers, acting through the League of Nations, could force Japan to disgorge, the League would perish. Failure would kill collective security, and wipe out the best hope of averting another global conflagration.

Meeting in Geneva, the League was eager to strengthen itself by luring Uncle Sam into its camp. In response to an urgent invitation, an American sat for the first time, though unofficially, with the Council of the League during its discussions of the Manchurian crisis. An American also served on the firsthand investigating commission appointed by the League.

Intervention by the League availed nothing. Its five-man commission of probers reported in 1932 that the Japanese incursion was unjustified. But this condemnation, instead of driving Japan out of Manchuria, merely drove Japan out of the League. Another nail was thus hammered into the coffin of collective security.

Numerous red-blooded Americans, though by no means a majority, urged strong measures, ranging from boycotts to blockades. Possibly a tight blockade by the League, backed by the United States, would have brought Japan sharply to book. But Hoover reflected the isolationist sentiments of most Americans, who wanted no part of the Far Eastern mess. One newspaper remarked that America did not "give a hoot in a rain barrel" about who controlled Manchuria.

The League was handicapped in taking two-fisted action by the non-membership of the United States. Washington flatly rebuffed initial attempts in 1931 to secure American cooperation in applying economic pressures. But Secretary of State Stimson, who was much more internationalist-minded than Hoover, indicated that the United States probably would not interfere with a League embargo. The next year Stimson was more eager to take vigorous steps, but the President cautiously restrained him.

Washington in the end decided to fire only paper bullets at the Japanese aggressors. The so-called Hoover-Stimson doctrine, proclaimed in 1932, declared that the United States would not recognize any territorial acquisitions achieved by force. Collective indignation would substitute for collective security.

This verbal slap on the wrist from America did not deter the march of the Japanese militarists. Smarting under a Chinese boycott, they bombed Shanghai in 1932, with shocking losses to the civilians. Outraged Americans launched informal boycotts of Japanese goods,

Hoover later wrote of his differences with Secretary Stimson over economic boycotts: "I was soon to realize that my able Secretary was at times more of a warrior than a diplomat. To him the phrase 'economic sanctions' was the magic wand of force by which all peace could be summoned from the vasty deep. . . . Ever since Versailles I had held that 'economic sanctions' meant war when applied to any large nation."

chiefly dime-store knickknacks. But there was no real sentiment for armed intervention among a depression-ridden people who were isolation-inclined during the 1930's. President Hoover, who fully shared their views, believed that boycotts and embargoes spelled bayonets and bombs.

In a broad sense, collective security died and World War II was born in 1931 on the wind-swept plains of Manchuria. The League members had the economic and naval power to halt Japan, but lacked the courage to act. One reason—though not the only one—was that they could not count on America's support. Even so, the Republic came closer to stepping into the chill waters of internationalism than American prophets would have dared to predict in the early 1920's.

Hoover Pioneers for the Good Neighbor Policy

Hoover's arrival at the White House brought a more hopeful turn to relations with the southern neighbors. The new President was deeply interested in the colorful lands below the Rio Grande; shortly after his election in 1928 he had undertaken a good-will tour of Latin America on an American battleship.

World depression gave birth to a less aggressive attitude in the United States toward weak Latin neighbors. Following the stock-market collapse of 1929, Americans had less money to invest abroad. As millions of dollars' worth of investments in Latin America went sour, many Yankees felt that they were more preyed upon than preying. Economic imperialism—so called—became much less popular in the United States than it had been in the Golden Twenties.

As an advocate of international good will, Hoover strove to abandon the interventionist twist given to the Monroe Doctrine by Theodore Roosevelt. In 1932 he negotiated a new treaty with the mulatto republic of Haiti, and this pact, later supplanted by an executive agreement, provided for the complete withdrawal of American bayonets by 1934. Further pleasing omens came early in 1933, when the last marine "leathernecks" sailed away from Nicaragua after an almost continuous stay of some twenty years.

Herbert Hoover, the Engineer in Politics, thus happily engineered the foundation stones of the "Good Neighbor" policy. Upon them rose an imposing edifice in the days of his successor, Franklin Roosevelt.

"The Light of Asia," 1933. Japan Sets Fire to Treaty Commitments. Reprinted with permission of Washington *Daily News*

SELECT READINGS

Clear-cut introductions are J. D. HICKS, *Republican Ascendancy, 1921–1933* (1960)* and W. E. LEUCHTENBURG, *The Perils of Prosperity, 1914–1932* (1958).* See also F. L. ALLEN's colorful *Since Yesterday* (1939)*; and the titles by Faulkner, Sullivan, and Soule for Chapter 39. Social and economic conditions are developed in DIXON WECTER,

The Age of the Great Depression, 1929–1941 (1948); G. V. SELDES, *The Years of the Locust* (1933); BROADUS MITCHELL, *Depression Decade* (1947); J. K. GALBRAITH, *The Great Crash, 1929* (1955)*; and in CABELL PHILLIPS, *From the Crash to the Blitz: 1929–1939* (1969). A colorful account is ANDREW SINCLAIR, *Prohibition* (1962).* A. M. SCHLESINGER, JR., *The Age of Roosevelt: The Crisis of the Old Order, 1919–1933* (1957)* is brilliantly unsympathetic toward Hoover. More favorable are H. G. WARREN, *Herbert Hoover and the Great Depression* (1959)* and A. U. ROMASCO, *The Poverty of Abundance* (1965).* Hoover's own memoirs are marred by excessive self-justification: *The Cabinet and the Presidency, 1920–1933* (1952) and *The Great Depression, 1929–1941* (1952).

On foreign affairs consult R. H. FERRELL, *American Diplomacy in the Great Depression* (1957); E. E. MORISON, *Turmoil and Tradition: A Study of the Life and Times of Henry L. Stimson* (1960)*; ARMIN RAPPAPORT, *Henry L. Stimson and Japan, 1931–1933* (1963); and DONALD M. DOZER, *Are We Good Neighbors? Three Decades of Inter-American Relations, 1930–1960* (1959). Also *Harvard Guide,* Pt. VI.

RECENT REFERENCES

JORDAN A. SCHWARZ, *The Interregnum of Despair: Hoover, Congress, and the Depression* (1970).

* Available in paperback.

42

Franklin D. Roosevelt and the New Deal

The country needs and . . . demands bold, persistent experimentation. It is common sense to take a method and try it. If it fails, admit it frankly and try another. But above all, try something.

Franklin D. Roosevelt, 1932 campaign speech

FDR: a Politician in a Wheel Chair

Voters were in an ugly mood as the presidential campaign of 1932 neared. Countless factory chimneys remained ominously cold, while more than eleven million unemployed workers and their families sank ever deeper into the mire of poverty. The "chicken in every pot" of 1928 had seemingly become a discharge slip in every pay envelope.

Herbert Hoover, sick at heart, was renominated by the Republican convention in Chicago without undue enthusiasm. Not to run him again would be a suicidal confession of failure. The platform indulged in extravagant praise of Republican anti-depression policies, while halfheartedly promising to repeal national prohibition and return control of liquor to the states.

The rising star in the Democratic firmament was Governor Franklin Delano Roosevelt of New York, a fifth cousin of Theodore Roosevelt. Like the Rough Rider, he had been born to a wealthy

New York family, had graduated from Harvard, had been elected as a kid-glove politician to the New York legislature, had served as governor of the Empire State, had been nominated for the Vice-Presidency (though not elected), and had served capably as Assistant Secretary of the Navy. Though both men were master politicians, adept with the colorful phrase, F.D.R. was suave and conciliatory, while T.R. was pugnacious and denunciatory.

Infantile paralysis, while putting steel braces on Franklin Roosevelt's legs, put additional steel into his soul. Until 1921, when the dread disease struck, young Roosevelt—tall (6 feet 2), athletic, classic-featured, and as handsome as a Greek god—impressed observers as charming and witty yet at times a supercilious and arrogant "lightweight." But suffering humbled him and brought him down to the level of common clay. In courageously fighting his way back from complete helplessness to a hobbling mobility, he schooled himself in patience, tolerance, compassion, and strength of will. He once remarked that after trying for two years to wiggle one big toe, all else seemed easy.

In his successful campaign of 1928 for the governorship of New York, Roosevelt had played down alleged Democratic "socialism": "We often hear it said that government operation of anything under the sun is socialistic. If that is so, our postal service is socialistic, so is the parcel post which has largely taken the place of the old express companies; so are the public highways which took the place of the toll roads."

Roosevelt's political appeal was amazing. His commanding presence and his golden speaking voice, despite a sophisticated accent, combined to make him the premier American orator of his generation. He could turn on charm in private conversations as one would turn on a faucet. As a popular depression governor of New York, he had sponsored heavy state spending to relieve human suffering. Though favoring frugality, he believed that money, rather than humanity, was expendable. He revealed a deep concern for the plight of the "forgotten man"—a phrase he used in a 1932 speech—although he was assailed by the rich as a "traitor to his class."

In truth, Roosevelt's remarkable qualities of leadership were more apparent later than when the exuberant Democrats met in Chicago in June, 1932. Al Smith felt entitled to a second chance; and a beautiful friendship between the two men wilted when he was pushed aside for Franklin Roosevelt, the choice of the convention on the fourth ballot. The Democratic platform came out more flat-footedly than the Republican for repeal of prohibition, assailed the so-called "Hoover depression," and promised not only a balanced budget but sweeping social and economic reforms.

Presidential Hopefuls of 1932

In the campaign that followed, Roosevelt assumed the offensive with a slashing attack on the Republican Old Dealers. In all, he traveled about 25,000 miles. He was especially eager to prove that he was not an invalid ("Roosevelt Is Robust"), and to display his magnificent torso and radiant personality to as many voters as possible.

Roosevelt consistently preached a New Deal for the "forgotten man," but he was annoyingly vague and somewhat contradictory. Many of his speeches were "ghost-written" by the "Brains Trust," (popularly the "Brain Trust"), a small group of reform-minded intellectuals, predominantly youngish college professors, who, as a kind of Kitchen Cabinet, later authored much of the New Deal legislation. Roosevelt rashly promised a balanced budget and berated heavy Hooverian deficits, amid cries of "Throw the Spenders Out!" All this made ironical reading in later months.

The high spirits of the Democrats found vent in the rallying cry "Everything Will Be Rosy with Roosevelt," and in the catchy air "Happy Days Are Here Again." This theme song fitted F.D.R.'s indestructible smile, his jauntily angled cigarette holder, his breezy optimism, and his promises to do something even at the risk of bold experimentation.

Grim-faced Herbert Hoover remained in the White House, conscientiously battling the depression through short lunches and long hours. Out on the firing line his supporters halfheartedly cried, "The Worst Is Past," "It Might Have Been Worse," and "Prosperity Is Just around the Corner." Faint blushes of returning prosperity did become visible in the early months of the campaign, but these gradually faded as election day neared. Hoover never ceased to insist that the uncertainty and fear produced by Roosevelt's impending victory plunged the nation back into the depression.

With the campaign going badly for the Republicans, a weary and despondent Hoover was persuaded to take to the stump. He stoutly reaffirmed his faith in American free enterprise and individual initiative, and gloomily predicted that if the Hawley-Smoot Tariff were repealed, the grass would grow "in the streets of a hundred cities." Such down-at-the-mouthism contrasted sharply with Roosevelt's tooth-flashing optimism.

Franklin Roosevelt at Hyde Park. As late as January, 1932, before the presidential nomination, pundit Walter Lippmann could write that the candidate was "a pleasant man who, without any important qualifications for the office, would very much like to be President." Justice Oliver W. Holmes was more farsighted in 1933: "A second-class intellect. But a first-class temperament." Franklin D. Roosevelt Library.

The Humiliation of Hoover in 1932

Hoover had been swept into office on a landslide; he was swept out on one. The avalanche of votes totaled 22,821,857 for Roosevelt and 15,761,841 for Hoover; the electoral count stood at 472 to 59. In all, the loser carried only six rock-ribbed Republican states.

One striking feature of the election was the beginning of a heavy shift of Negroes, traditionally grateful to the Republican Party of Lincoln, over to the Roosevelt camp. As the "last hired and first fired," the blacks had been among the worst sufferers from the depression. Beginning with the election of 1932, they were to comprise, especially in the great urban centers of the North, a vital element in the Democratic Party.

Hard times unquestionably ruined the Republicans, for the electoral upheaval in 1932 seems to have been more anti-Hoover than pro-Roosevelt. Democrats had only to harness the national grudge and let it pull them to victory. "A Vote for Roosevelt Is a Vote against Hoover," ran the saying. An overwhelming majority appear to have voiced a demand for a change: *a* new deal rather than *the* New Deal, for the latter was only a gleam in the eyes of its sponsors. Any upstanding Democratic candidate probably could have won.

The pre-inauguration "lame duck" period now ground slowly to an end. Hoover, though defeated and repudiated, continued to be President for four long months, until March 4, 1933. But he was helpless to embark upon any long-range policies without the cooperation of Roosevelt—and the victorious President-elect proved rather uncooperative. Hoover at length succeeded in arranging two meetings with him to discuss the war-debt muddle. But Roosevelt, who airily remarked to the press, "It's not my baby," was loath to assume responsibility without authority. Hoover, so he privately confessed, was trying to bind his successor to an anti-inflationary policy that would have made impossible many of the later New Deal experiments.

With Washington deadlocked, the vast and vaunted American economic machine clanked to a virtual halt. Banks were locking their doors all over the nation, as people nervously stuffed paper money under their mattresses. Hooverites, then and later, accused Roosevelt of deliberately permitting the depression to worsen, so that he could emerge the more spectacularly as a savior.

F.D.R. and the Three R's: Relief, Recovery, Reform

Great crises often call forth gifted leaders; and the hand of destiny tapped Roosevelt on the shoulder. On a dreary inauguration day, March 4, 1933, his vibrant voice, broadcast nationally from a bullet-proof stand, provided the American people with electrifying new hope. He denounced the "money changers" who had brought on the calamity, and declared that the government must wage war on the Great Depression as it would wage war on an armed foe. His clarion note was: "Let me assert my firm belief that the only thing we have to fear is fear itself."

Roosevelt moved decisively. Now that he had full responsibility, he boldly declared a nationwide banking holiday, March 6–10, preliminary to opening most of the banks on a sounder basis. He then summoned the overwhelmingly Democratic Congress into special session to cope with the national emergency. Members stayed at their task for the so-called "Hundred Days" (March 9–June 16, 1933), hastily grinding out an unprecedented basketful of remedial legislation.

Roosevelt's New Deal program was sparked by three R's—relief, recovery, and reform. Short-range goals were relief and immediate

"It's Been in the Family for a Long Time," 1933. Gale in the Los Angeles *Times*

Principal New Deal Acts During Hundred Days Congress, 1933
[ITEMS IN PARENTHESES INDICATE SECONDARY PURPOSES.]

Recovery	Relief	Reform
F.D.R. closes banks, March 6, 1933		
Emergency Banking Relief Act, March 9, 1933		
(Beer Act)	(Beer Act)	Beer and Wine Revenue Act, March 22, 1933
(CCC)	Unemployment Relief Act, March 31, 1933, creates Civilian Conservation Corps (CCC)	
F.D.R. orders gold surrender, April 5, 1933		
F.D.R. abandons gold standard, April 19, 1933		
(FERA)	Federal Emergency Relief Act, May 12, 1933, creates Federal Emergency Relief Administration (FERA)	
(AAA)	Agricultural Adjustment Act (AAA), May 12, 1933	
(TVA)	TVA	Tennessee Valley Authority Act (TVA), May 18, 1933
		Federal Securities Act, May 27, 1933
Gold-payment clause repealed, June 5, 1933		
(HOLC)	Home Owners' Refinancing Act, June 13, 1933, creates Home Owners' Loan Corporation (HOLC)	
National Industrial Recovery Act, June 16, 1933, creates National Recovery Administration (NRA), Public Works Administration (PWA)	(NRA; PWA)	(NRA)
(Glass-Steagall Act)	(Glass-Steagall Act)	Glass-Steagall Banking Reform Act, June 16, 1933, creates Federal Deposit Insurance Corporation

(For later New Deal measures, see p. 878.)

recovery, especially in the first two years. Long-range goals were permanent recovery and reform of current abuses, particularly those that had produced the boom-and-bust catastrophe. The three-R objectives often overlapped and got in one another's way. But amid all the haste and topsy-turvyism, the gigantic New Deal program lurched forward.

Firmly ensconced in the driver's seat, Roosevelt cracked the whip. A green Congress so fully shared the panicky feeling of the country that it was ready to rubber-stamp bills drafted by White House advisers—measures that Roosevelt called "must legislation." More than that, Congress gave the President extraordinary blank-check powers: some of the laws that it passed expressly delegated legislative authority to the Chief Executive. One Senator complained that if F.D.R. asked Congress "to commit suicide tomorrow, they'd do it."

Roosevelt was delighted to accept executive leadership, and Congress responded to it, although he did not always know precisely where he was going. He was inclined to do things by intuition—off the cuff. He was like the quarterback, as he put it, whose next play depends on the success of the previous play. So desperate was the mood of an action-starved public that movement, even in the wrong direction, seemed better than no movement at all.

The frantic Hundred Days Congress passed many essentials of the New Deal "three R's," though important long-range measures were added in later sessions. These reforms, already foreshadowed by the Democratic platform of 1932, were generally in tune with the earlier Progressive–New Freedom tradition. Many of them were long overdue, sidetracked by World War I and the Old Guard reaction of the 1920's. The New Dealers, sooner or later, embraced such old-hat schemes as unemployment insurance, old-age insurance, minimum-wage regulations, and restrictions on child labor. Most of these forward-looking measures had already been adopted a generation or so earlier by the more enlightened countries of Western Europe. A few such reforms had been accepted on a limited basis by some of the states, chiefly during the Progressive era. But in general the United States, in the eyes of many Europeans, was a "backward nation."

"The Galloping Snail." Thomas in the Detroit *News*. By permission

Roosevelt Tackles Money and Banking

Banking chaos cried aloud for immediate action. Congress pulled itself together, and in an incredible eight hours had the Emergency Banking Relief Act of 1933 ready for Roosevelt's busy pen. The new law clothed the President with power to regulate banking transactions and foreign exchange, and to reopen solvent banks.

Roosevelt, the master showman, next turned to the radio to deliver the first of his thirty famous "Fireside Chats." As some 35,000,000 people hung on his soothing words, he gave assurances that it was now safer to keep money in a reopened bank than "under the mat-tress." Confidence returned with a gush, and the banks began to unlock their doors.

The Emergency or Hundred Days Congress buttressed public re-liance on the banking system by enacting the memorable Glass-Steagall Banking Reform Act. This measure provided for the Federal Deposit Insurance Corporation, which insured individual deposits up to $5000 (later raised). Thus ended the disgraceful epidemic of bank failures, which dated back to the "wildcat" days of Andrew Jackson.*

Roosevelt moved swiftly elsewhere on the financial front, seeking to protect the melting gold reserve and to prevent panicky hoarding. He ordered all private holdings of gold to be surrendered to the Treasury in exchange for paper currency, and then took the nation

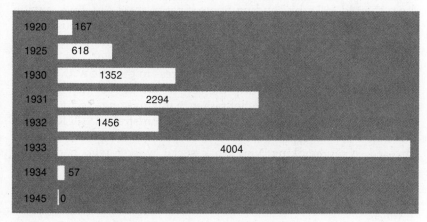

Year	Bank Failures
1920	167
1925	618
1930	1352
1931	2294
1932	1456
1933	4004
1934	57
1945	0

BANK FAILURES AND THE BANKING ACT of 1933

off the gold standard. The Emergency Congress responded to his rec-ommendation by canceling the gold-payment clause in all contracts and authorizing repayment in paper money. A "managed currency" was well on its way.

Early in 1934 Roosevelt reduced the value of the gold content of the dollar to 59.06 cents, in accordance with authority granted by Con-gress. His theory was that this tinkering with the currency would stimulate business through controlled inflation. Prices did rise some-what, but not in proportion to the change in the value of the currency. Alarmed conservatives, like the now "unhappy warrior" Al Smith, assailed "the baloney dollar" and accused the government of rob-bing the people of forty cents on every dollar they owned. Actually, the purchasing power of the newly·shrunken dollar was not sub-stantially inferior to that of the old.

* When FDR was inaugurated in 1933, not a single Canadian bank had failed.

Creating Jobs for the Jobless

Overwhelming unemployment, perhaps even more than banking, clamored for prompt remedial action. Roosevelt had no hesitancy about using federal money to assist the unemployed, and at the same time to "prime the pump" of industrial recovery. A farmer has to pour a little water into a dry pump to start the flow.

The Hundred Days Congress responded to Roosevelt's spurs when it created the Civilian Conservation Corps (CCC), which proved to be perhaps the most popular of all the New Deal "alphabetical agencies." This law provided employment in fresh-air government camps for about three million uniformed young men, many of whom might have been driven into criminal habits. Their work was useful—including reforestation, fire fighting (47 lost their lives), flood control, and swamp drainage. The recruits were required to help the old folks by sending home most of their pay. Both human resources and natural resources were thus conserved, though there were minor complaints of "militarizing" "bums" and "loafers" who would later claim pensions for exposure to poison ivy.

The first major effort of the new Congress to grapple with the millions of adult unemployed was the Federal Emergency Relief Act. Its chief aim was immediate relief rather than long-range recovery. The resulting Federal Emergency Relief Administration (FERA) was handed over to zealous Harry L. Hopkins, a rail-thin, shabbily dressed, chain-smoking New York social worker who had earlier won Roosevelt's friendship and who became one of his most influential advisers. Hopkins' agency finally granted about three billion dollars to the states for direct dole payments or for wages on work projects.*

Immediate relief was also given two large and hard-pressed spe-

PER THOUSAND FARMS

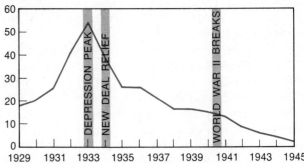

FARM FORECLOSURES AND DEFAULTS, 1929–1945

* A boast attributed to Hopkins in 1938 was: "We will spend and spend, tax and tax, and elect and elect."

cial groups by the Hundred Days Congress. One section of the Agricultural Adjustment Act made available many millions of dollars to help farmers meet their mortgages. Another law created the Home Owners' Loan Corporation (HOLC). Designed to refinance mortgages on non-farm homes, it ultimately assisted about a million badly pinched households.

Harassed by continuing unemployment, FDR himself established the Civil Works Administration (CWA) late in 1933. As a branch of the Federal Emergency Relief Administration, it also fell under the direction of Hopkins. Designed to provide purely temporary jobs during the cruel winter emergency, it served a useful purpose. Tens of thousands of jobless were employed at leaf raking and other make-work tasks, which were dubbed "boondoggling." As this kind of labor put a premium on shovel-leaning slow motion, the scheme was widely criticized. "The only thing we have to fear," scoffers remarked, "is work itself."

Direct relief from Washington to needy families helped pull the nation through the ghastly winter of 1933–1934. But the disheartening persistence of unemployment and suffering demonstrated that emergency relief measures must be not only continued but supplemented. One danger signal was the appearance of various demagogues, notably a magnetic "microphone Messiah," Father Coughlin, a Catholic priest in Michigan who began broadcasting in 1930 and whose slogan was "Social Justice." His anti-New Deal harangues to some 40 million radio fans finally became so anti-semitic, fascistic, and demagogic that he was silenced in 1942 by his superiors.

Also notorious among the new brood of agitators were those who capitalized on popular discontent to make pie-in-the-sky promises. Most conspicuous of these gentry was a United States Senator, Huey P. ("Kingfish") Long of Louisiana, whose brassy, rabble-rousing talents publicized his "Share Our Wealth" program. Every family was to receive $5000, supposedly at the expense of the prosperous. Another Pied Piper was gaunt Dr. Francis E. Townsend of California, a retired physician whose savings had recently been wiped out. He attracted the pathetic support of perhaps five million "senior citizens" with his fantastic plan. Each oldster sixty years of age or over was to receive $200 a month, provided that he spent it within the month.

Partly to quiet the groundswell of unrest produced by such crack-brained proposals, Congress authorized the Works Progress Administration (WPA) in 1935. The objective was employment on useful projects. Launched under the supervision of the ailing but energetic Hopkins, this remarkable agency ultimately spent about eleven billion dollars on thousands of public buildings, bridges, and hard-surfaced roads. It controlled crickets in Wyoming and built a monkey

Madame Frances Perkins (1882–1965), the first woman cabinet member, served with marked ability as Secretary of Labor under Roosevelt for twelve years. Although she had become an expert in New York state on industrial hazards, hygiene, and health, she was subjected to much undeserved criticism from male businessmen, laborites, and politicians. Print from Franklin D. Roosevelt Library, owned by U.P.I.

After Roosevelt's election in 1936, Father Coughlin reportedly said in an interview: "One thing is sure. . . . Democracy is doomed. This is our last election. It is Fascism or Communism. We are at the crossroads. . . . I take the road of Fascism."

Later Major New Deal Measures, 1933–1939

[ITEMS IN PARENTHESES INDICATE SECONDARY PURPOSES.]

Recovery	Relief	Reform
F.D.R. establishes Civil Works Administration (CWA), Nov. 9, 1933	(CWA)	
Gold Reserve Act, Jan. 30, 1934, authorizes F.D.R.'s devaluation, Jan. 31, 1934		
		Securities and Exchange Commission (SEC) authorized by Congress, June 6, 1934
(Reciprocal Trade Agreements)	(Reciprocal Trade Agreements)	Reciprocal Trade Agreements Act, June 12, 1934
(FHA)	National Housing Act, June 28, 1934, authorizes Federal Housing Administration (FHA)	(FHA)
(Frazier-Lemke Act)	Frazier-Lemke Farm Bankruptcy Act, June 28, 1934	
(Resettlement Administration)	F.D.R. creates Resettlement Administration, April 30, 1935	
(WPA)	F.D.R. creates Works Progress Administration (WPA), May 6, 1935, under act of April 8, 1935	
(Wagner Act)	(Wagner Act)	(Wagner) National Labor Relations Act, July 5, 1935
		Social Security Act, August 14, 1935
		Public Utility Holding Co. Act, Aug. 26, 1935
(Soil Conservation Act)	Soil Conservation and Domestic Allotment Act, Feb. 29, 1936	
(USHA)	(USHA)	U.S. Housing Authority (USHA) established by Congress, Sept. 1, 1937
(Second AAA)	Second Agricultural Adjustment Act, Feb. 16, 1938	
(Fair Labor Standards)	(Fair Labor Standards)	Fair Labor Standards Act, June 25, 1938
		Reorganization Act, April 3, 1939
		Hatch Act, Aug. 2, 1939

pen in Oklahoma City. Critics sneered that WPA meant "We Provide Alms," but the fact is that over a period of eight years nearly nine million persons were given jobs.

We work all day
For the WPA.
Let the market crash,
We collect our cash.

Agencies of the WPA also found part-time occupations for needy high school and college students, and for such unemployed white-collar workers as actors, musicians, and writers. John Steinbeck, future Nobel prize novelist, counted dogs in his California county. Cynical taxpayers condemned lessons in tap dancing, as well as the painting of scenes on post-office walls. But much precious talent was nourished, self-respect was preserved, and more than a million pieces of art were created, many of them publicly displayed.

A Helping Hand for Industry and Labor

A daring attempt to stimulate a nationwide comeback was initiated when the Emergency Congress authorized the National Recovery Administration (NRA). This ingenious scheme was by far the most complex and far-reaching effort by the New Dealers to combine immediate relief with long-range recovery and reform. Triple-barreled, it was designed to assist industry, labor, and the unemployed.

Individual industries—over two hundred in all—were to work out codes of "fair competition," under which hours of labor would be reduced so that employment could be spread over more men. A ceiling was placed on the maximum hours of labor; a floor was placed under wages to establish minimum levels.

Labor, under the NRA, was granted additional benefits. Working-men were formally guaranteed the right to organize and bargain collectively through representatives *of their own choosing*—not through hand-picked agents of the company's choosing. The hated "yellow dog" or anti-union contract was expressly forbidden, and certain safeguarding restrictions were placed on the use of child labor.

Industrial recovery through the NRA fair codes would at best be painful, for these called for self-denial by both management and labor. Patriotism was appealed to by mass meetings and monster parades, which included 200,000 marchers on Fifth Avenue. A handsome Blue Eagle was designed as the symbol of the NRA, and merchants subscribing to a code displayed it in their windows with the slogan "We Do Our Part." A newly formed professional football team was christened the Philadelphia Eagles. Such was the enthusiasm for the NRA that for a brief period there was a marked upswing of business activity.

"But Oh, The Sweet Clover!"
Democratic Donkey Savors
Political Jobs. Courtesy Newark
Evening News

Big Business Holds the Line
Against NRA. Knott in the
Dallas *News*, 1933

But the high-flying Blue Eagle gradually fluttered to earth. Too much self-sacrifice was expected of labor, industry, and the public for such a scheme to work. A new "Age of Chiselry" dawned as certain unscrupulous businessmen ("chiselers") publicly displayed the blue bird on their windows but secretly violated the codes. Complete collapse was imminent when, in 1935, the Supreme Court shot down the dying eagle in the famed Schechter "sick chicken" decision. The learned justices *unanimously* held that Congress could not "delegate legislative powers" to the Executive. They further declared that Congressional control of interstate commerce could not properly apply to a local poultry business, like that of the Schechter brothers in Brooklyn and New York. Roosevelt was incensed by this "horse and buggy" interpretation of the Constitution, but actually the Court helped him out of a bad jam.

The same act of Congress that hatched the blue-eagled NRA also authorized the Public Works Administration (PWA), likewise intended both for industrial recovery and for unemployment relief. The agency was headed by the Secretary of the Interior, acid-tongued Harold L. Ickes, a free-swinging ex-Bull Mooser. Long-range recovery was the primary purpose of the new agency, and in time over four billion dollars was spent on some 34,000 projects, which included public buildings, highways, and parkways. One spectacular achievement was the Grand Coulee Dam on the Columbia River—the largest structure erected by man since the Great Wall of China. Speed was essential if the jobless were to be put back to work, but "Honest Harold" Ickes was so determined to prevent waste and extravagance that he blocked maximum relief.

Special stimulants aided the recovery of one segment of business—the liquor industry. The imminent repeal of the prohibition amendment afforded an opportunity to raise needed federal revenue and at the same time to provide some employment. Prodded by Roosevelt, the Hundred Days Congress in one of its earliest acts legalized light wine and beer with an alcoholic content (presumably nonintoxicating) not exceeding 3.2% by weight, and levied a tax of five dollars on every barrel so manufactured. Disgruntled drys, unwilling to acknowledge the breakdown of law and order begotten by bootlegging, damned Roosevelt as "a 3.2% American." Prohibition was officially repealed by the 21st Amendment late in 1933 (see Appendix)—and the saloon returned.

Furnishing Relief for Farmers

A radical new approach to farm recovery was embraced when the Emergency Congress established the Agricultural Adjustment Administration (AAA). Through "artificial scarcity" this agency was to establish "parity prices" for basic commodities. "Parity" was the price set for a product that gave it the same real value, in purchasing power, that it had enjoyed during the period from 1909 to 1914. The AAA would eliminate price-depressing surpluses by paying growers to reduce their crop acreage. The millions of dollars needed for these payments were to be raised by taxing processors of farm products, such as flour millers, who in turn would shift the burden to consumers.

Unhappily, the AAA got off to a wobbly start. It was begun after much of the cotton crop for 1933 had been planted, and balky mules, trained otherwise, were forced to plow under countless young plants. Several million squealing pigs were purchased and slaughtered. Much of their meat was distributed to persons on relief, but some of it was used for fertilizer. This "sinful" destruction of food, at a time when thousands of citizens were hungry, increased condemnation of the American economic system by Communists and other left-wingers.

"Subsidized scarcity" did have the effect of raising farm income, but the whole confused enterprise met with acid criticism. Farmers, food processors, consumers, and taxpayers were all in some degree unhappy. Paying the farmers not to farm actually increased unemployment, at a time when other New Deal agencies were striving to decrease it. When the Supreme Court finally killed the AAA in 1936 by declaring its regulatory taxation provisions unconstitutional, loud rejoicing was heard among foes of the plow-under program.

Quickly recovering from this blow, the New Deal Congress hastened to pass the Soil Conservation and Domestic Allotment Act of 1936. The withdrawal of acreage from production was now achieved by paying the farmer to plant soil-conserving crops, like soya beans, or to let his land lie fallow. With the emphasis thus on conservation, the Supreme Court placed the stamp of its approval on the revamped scheme.

"Eliza Crossing the Ice."
Business Crosses Ice of New Deal Alphabetical Agencies.
Courtesy San Francisco *Chronicle*

The Second Agricultural Adjustment Act of 1938, passed two years later, was a more comprehensive substitute, although it continued conservation payments. If the grower observed acreage restrictions on specified commodities like cotton and wheat, he would be eligible for parity payments. Other provisions of the new AAA were designed to give farmers not only a fairer price but a more substantial share of the national income. Both goals were partially achieved.

Dust Bowls and Black Blizzards

Dame Nature meanwhile had been providing some unplanned scarcity. Late in 1933 a prolonged drought struck the states of the trans-Mississippi Great Plains. Rainless weeks were followed by furious, whining winds, while the sun was darkened by millions of tons of powdery topsoil torn from once-fertile areas. Despondent cit-

For Gropper's painting of the Dust Bowl, see color portfolio following page 814.

izens sat on front porches with protective masks on their faces, watching the farms swirl by. Some of the dust darkened faraway Boston.

Burned and blown out of the Dust Bowl, tens of thousands of refugees fled their ruined acres. In five years about 350,000 Oklahomans and Arkansans—"Okies" and "Arkies"—trekked to southern California in "junkyards on wheels." Their dismal story was realistically portrayed in John Steinbeck's best-selling novel, *The Grapes of Wrath* (1939), which proved to be the *Uncle Tom's Cabin* of the Dust Bowl.

Zealous New Dealers, sympathetic toward the soil tillers, made various efforts to relieve their burdens. The Frazier-Lemke Farm Bankruptcy Act, passed in 1934, made possible a suspension of mortgage foreclosures for five years, but it was voided the next year by the Supreme Court. A revised law, limiting the grace period to three years, was unanimously upheld. In 1935 the President set up the Resettlement Administration, charged with the task of removing near-farmless farmers to better land. And more than 200 million young trees were successfully planted on the bare prairies as windbreaks by the young men of the Civilian Conservation Corps, even though one governor jeered at trying to "grow hair on a bald head."

Battling Bankers and Big Business

Family of "Okies" stalled on the desert near the California border. Franklin D. Roosevelt Library.

Reformist New Dealers were determined from the outset to curb the "money changers" who had played fast and loose with gullible investors before the Wall Street crash of 1929. The Hundred Days Congress passed the "Truth in Securities Act" (Federal Securities Act), which required promoters to transmit to the investor sworn information regarding the soundness of their stocks and bonds. An old saying was thus reversed to read: "Let the seller beware."

In 1934 Congress took further steps to protect the public against fraud, deception, and inside manipulation. It authorized the Securities and Exchange Commission (SEC), which was designed as a watchdog administrative agency. Stock markets henceforth were to operate more as trading marts and less as gambling casinos.

New Dealers likewise directed their fire at public-utility holding companies, those super-super-corporations. Citizens had received an object lesson in the scandalous crash, during the spring of 1932, of Chicagoan Samuel Insull's multi-billion-dollar financial empire. Possibilities of controlling, with a minimum of capital, a half-dozen or so pyramided layers of big business suggested to Roosevelt "a ninety-six-inch dog being wagged by a four-inch tail." The Public Utility Holding Company Act of 1935 finally delivered a "death sentence" to this type of fatty growth, except where it might be deemed economically needful.

The TVA Harnesses the Tennessee River

Inevitably, the sprawling electric-power industry attracted the fire of New Deal reformers. Within a few decades it had risen from nothingness to a colossus, which represented an investment of thirteen billion dollars. As a public utility, it reached directly and regularly into the pocketbooks of millions of consumers for vitally needed services. Ardent New Dealers accused it of gouging the public with excessive rates, especially since it owed its success to having secured, often for a song, priceless water-power sites from the public domain.

The tempestuous Tennessee River provided New Dealers with a rare opportunity. With its tributaries, the river drained a badly eroded area about the size of England, and one containing some 2,500,000 of the most poverty-stricken people in America. The federal government already owned valuable properties at Muscle Shoals, where it had erected plants for needed nitrates in World War I. By developing the hydroelectric potential of the entire area, Washington could combine the immediate advantage of putting thousands of men to work with a long-term project for reforming the power monopoly.

An act creating the Tennessee Valley Authority (TVA) was passed in 1933 by the Hundred Days Congress. This far-ranging enterprise was largely a result of the steadfast vision and unflagging zeal of Senator George W. Norris of Nebraska, after whom one of the mighty dams was named. From the standpoint of social reform and "planned economy," the TVA was by far the most revolutionary of all New Deal schemes.

This new agency was determined to discover precisely how much the production and distribution of electricity cost, so that a "yardstick" could be set up to test the fairness of rates charged by private companies. Utility corporations lashed back at this entering wedge of

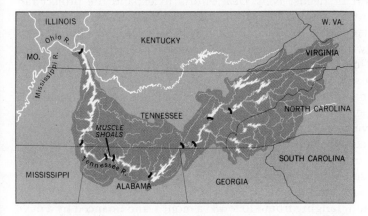

TVA AREA (Only the nine dams on the Tennessee River are shown here. There are more than twenty on the tributaries.)

In flooding the Tennessee valleys to build the dams, the TVA authorities had to provide new houses for the lowland poor folk. According to one account, "When Ezra Hill saw the plans for the home which was to replace his old one in the flood area, he pointed to the place on the print showing the circles and ovals of bathroom fixtures. 'What's all this? . . . I won't have it! I guess a privy [outside] is still good enough for me.'"

governmental control, charging that the low cost of TVA power was due to dishonest bookkeeping and the absence of taxes. Critics complained that the whole dream was "creeping socialism in concrete."

But the New Dealers, shrugging off such outcries, pointed a prideful finger at the amazing achievements of the TVA. The gigantic project had brought to the area not only full employment and the blessings of cheap electric power, but low cost housing, abundant cheap nitrates, the restoration of eroded soil, reforestation, improved navigation, and flood control. Rivers ran blue instead of brown; and a once poverty-cursed area was being transformed into one of the most flourishing regions in the country. Foreigners were greatly impressed with the possibilities of similar schemes in their own lands, and exulting New Dealers agitated for parallel enterprises in the valleys of the Columbia and Missouri Rivers. But conservatives in Congress, growing bolder, confined this particular type of socialism to the Tennessee Valley.

Passing Housing Reform and Social Security

Gratifying beginnings had meanwhile been made by the New Deal in slum clearance. To speed recovery and better housing, Roosevelt set up the Federal Housing Administration (FHA) as early as 1934, under authority granted by Congress. The building industry was to be stimulated by small loans to householders, both for improving their homes and completing new ones. So popular did the FHA prove to be that it was one of the few alphabetical agencies to outlast the Age of Roosevelt.

Congress bolstered the program in 1937 by authorizing the United States Housing Authority (USHA)—an agency designed to lend money to states or communities for low-cost construction. Though units for about 650,000 persons were started, new building fell tragically short of needs. New Deal efforts to expand the project ran headon into vigorous opposition from real-estate promoters, builders, and landlords, to say nothing of anti-New Dealers who attacked what they considered down-the-rathole spending. Nonetheless, for the first time in a century the slum areas in America ceased growing and even shrank.

Incomparably more important was the success of New Dealers in the field of unemployment insurance and old-age pensions. Their greatest victory was the epochal Social Security Act of 1935—one of the most complicated and far-reaching laws ever to pass Congress. To cushion future depressions, the measure provided for federal-state unemployment insurance. To provide security for old age, specified categories of retired workers were to receive regular payments from Washington, ranging from $10 to $85 a month, and financed by a payroll tax on both employers and employees. Provision was also made for the blind, cripples, delinquent children, and other dependents.

Republican opposition to the sweeping new legislation was bitter. "Social Security," insisted Hoover, "must be builded upon a cult of work, not a cult of leisure." The G.O.P. National Chairman falsely charged that every worker would have to wear a metal dog tag for life.

Social Security was largely inspired by the example of some of the more highly industrialized nations of Europe. In the agricultural America of an earlier day, there had always been farm chores for all ages, and the large family had cared for its own dependents. But in an urbanized America, at the mercy of boom-and-bust cycles, the government was now recognizing its responsibility for the welfare of its citizens. By 1939 over 45,000,000 persons were eligible for social-security benefits, and in subsequent years further categories of workers were added and the payments to them were periodically increased.

A New Deal for Unskilled Labor

The NRA Blue Eagles, with their call for collective bargaining, had been a godsend to organized labor. As New Deal expenditures brought some slackening of unemployment, labor began to feel more secure and hence more self-assertive. A rash of walkouts occurred in the summer of 1934, including a paralyzing general strike in San Francisco (following a "Bloody Thursday") which was broken only when outraged citizens resorted to vigilante tactics.

When the Supreme Court axed the Blue Eagle, a Congress sympathetic to labor unions undertook to fill the vacuum. The fruit of its deliberations was the Wagner or National Labor Relations Act of 1935. This trail-blazing law created a powerful new National Labor Relations Board for administrative purposes, and reasserted the right of labor to engage in self-organization and to bargain collectively through representatives of its own choice. The Wagner Act proved to be one of the real milestones on the rocky road of the American labor movement.

Under the encouragement of a highly sympathetic National Labor Relations Board, a host of unskilled workers began to organize themselves into effective unions. The leader of this drive was beetle-browed, domineering, and melodramatic John L. Lewis, boss of the United Mine Workers. In 1935 he succeeded in forming the Committee for Industrial Organization (C.I.O.) within the ranks of the skilled-craft American Federation of Labor. But skilled workers, ever since the days of the ill-fated Knights of Labor in the 1880's, had shown only lukewarm sympathy for the cause of unskilled labor, especially Negroes. In 1936, following inevitable friction with the C.I.O., the older federation suspended the upstart unions associated with the newer organization.

Nothing daunted, the rebellious C.I.O. moved on a concerted scale

"The Great Divide," 1936. Steel Industry as a Factor in Splitting Labor. Fitzpatrick in the St. Louis *Post-Dispatch*

into the huge automobile industry. Late in 1936 the workers resorted to a revolutionary technique (earlier used in both Europe and America) known as the sit-down strike: they refused to leave the factory buildings of General Motors, at Flint, Michigan, and thus prevented the importation of strikebreakers. Conservative respecters of private property were scandalized. The C.I.O. finally won a resounding victory when its union, after heated negotiations, was recognized by General Motors as the sole bargaining agency for its employees.

Roosevelt's "Coddling" of Labor

Unskilled workers now pressed their advantage. The United States Steel Company, hitherto an impossible nut for labor to crack, averted a costly strike when it voluntarily granted rights of unionization to its C.I.O.-organized employees. But the Little Steel Companies fought back savagely. Citizens were shocked in 1937 by the Memorial Day massacre at the plant of the Republic Steel Company in South Chicago. There, in a bloody fracas, police fired upon pickets and workers, leaving the area strewn with several score dead and wounded.

For Evergood's painting of the Chicago worker-police riot, see color portfolio following page 814.

A better deal for labor continued when Congress, in 1938, passed the memorable Fair Labor Standards Act (Wages and Hours Bill). Industries involved in interstate commerce were to set up minimum-wage and maximum-hour levels. Though not immediately established, the specific goals were forty cents an hour (later raised) and a forty-hour week. Labor by children under sixteen was forbidden;

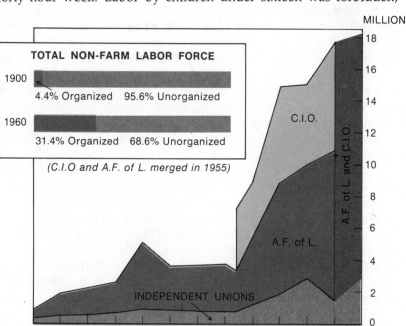

THE RISE OF ORGANIZED LABOR, 1900–1960

under eighteen, if the occupation was dangerous. These reforms were bitterly though futilely opposed by many industrialists, especially by those Southern textile manufacturers who had profited from low-wage labor.

In later New Deal days, labor unionization flourished like crab grass; "Roosevelt wants you to join a union" was the rallying cry of professional organizers. The President received valuable support at ballot-box time from labor leaders and many appreciative working-men. One mill worker remarked that Roosevelt was "the only man we ever had in the White House who would know that my boss is a skunk." F.D.R. was indeed the Forgotten Man's man.

The C.I.O. surged forward, breaking completely with the A.F. of L. in 1938. On that occasion the *Committee* for Industrial Organization was formally reconstituted as the *Congress* of Industrial Organizations (the new C.I.O.), under the highhanded presidency of John L. Lewis. By 1940 the C.I.O. could claim about four million members in its constituent unions, including some 200,000 Negroes. Nevertheless bitter and annoying jurisdictional feuding, involving strikes, continued with the A.F. of L. At times labor seemed more bent on costly civil war than on its age-old war with management.

John L. Lewis (1880–1969) became a miner and worked his way up to the presidency of the United Mine Workers of America. He once remarked of strike-breaking soldiers, "You can't dig coal with bayonets." He testified in 1939 before a Congressional committee, "The genesis of this campaign against labor in the House of Representatives is not hard to find . . . It runs across to the Senate . . . and emanates there from a labor-baiting, poker-playing, whiskey-drinking, evil old man whose name is Garner [Vice President]."

Landon Challenges "The Champ" in 1936

As the presidential campaign of 1936 neared, the New Dealers were on top of the world. They had achieved considerable progress, and millions of "reliefers" were grateful to their bountiful government. The exultant Democrats, meeting in Philadelphia, pushed through the renomination of Roosevelt in a brief rubber-stamp ceremony. Their platform stood squarely on the record of the New Deal years.

The Republicans, assembling in Cleveland, were hard pressed to find someone to feed to "the Champ." They finally settled on the colorless and mildly liberal Governor Alfred M. Landon of the Sunflower State Kansas, a wealthy oil man, whose chief claim to distinction was that he had balanced the budget of his state in an era of unbalanced budgets. The Republican platform, though promising relief benefits that would cost many millions, condemned the New Deal of Franklin "Deficit" Roosevelt—its radicalism, experimentation, confusion, and "frightful waste." Popular watchwords were "Defeat the New Deal and Its Reckless Spending," "Let's Get Another Deck," "Life, Liberty, and Landon," and "Let's Make it a Landon-slide."

Landon—"the Kansas Coolidge"—was honest, sincere, home-spun, "common-sensical," and as American as cherry pie. But he had a poor radio voice and seemed schoolboyish on the stump. Surrounded by imitation Kansas sunflowers, he stressed "deeds, not deficits," and condemned New Deal highhandedness. Though

Three days before the 1936 election Roosevelt sounded positively dictatorial in his speech at New York's Madison Square Garden, "I should like to have it said of my first Administration that in it the forces of selfishness and of lust for power met their match. I should like to have it said of my second Administration that in it these forces met their master."

Mrs. Eleanor Roosevelt voting at Hyde Park, November 1936. Mrs. Roosevelt was certainly the most visible and probably the most energetic of all the First Ladies. Among varied activities, she wrote a daily newspaper column and traveled and lectured widely while promoting many causes, mainly those affecting human welfare. After her husband's death she continued to work for numerous reforms, and served as a U.S. delegate to the United Nations. Franklin D. Roosevelt Library.

opposing the popular Social Security Act, he advocated just enough reform to cause the Democrats to retort that he would continue the New Deal—a second-hand New Deal—in his own way. He was, they sneered, "the poor man's Hoover."

Democrats denounced the G.O.P. as the party of the Big Moneyed Interests and the Big Depression, and amid loud choruses of boos cried, "Remember Hoover!" The embittered ex-President called for "a holy crusade for liberty." A group of wealthy Republicans and conservative Democrats had in 1934 formed the American Liberty League, and they vented their reactionary spleen against "that man" Roosevelt, "the New Dealocrat." But they hurt their own cause by becoming a made-to-order target for FDR. His dander aroused, he took to the stump and denounced the "economic royalists" who sought to "hide behind the flag and the Constitution." "I welcome their hatred," he proclaimed.

A landslide overwhelmed Landon, as the demoralized Republicans carried only two states, Maine and Vermont. This dismal showing caused political wiseacres to make the old adage read: "As Maine goes, so goes Vermont."* The popular vote was 27,751,597 to 16,-679,583; the electoral count was 523 to 8—the most lopsided in 116 years. Democratic majorities, riding in on Roosevelt's magic coattails, were again returned to Congress. Jubilant Democrats could now claim more than two-thirds of the seats in the House, and a like proportion in the Senate.

The battle of 1936, perhaps the most bitter since Bryan's in 1896, partially bore out Republican charges of class warfare. Even more than in 1932, the needy economic groups were lined up against the so-called greedy economic groups ("Tories"). C.I.O. units contributed generously to F.D.R.'s campaign chest. Many left-wingers turned to Roosevelt, as the customary third-party protest vote sharply declined. The Negroes, several million of whom had enjoyed welcome relief handouts, had by now largely shaken off their traditional allegiance to the Republican Party. To them, Lincoln was "finally dead."

F.D.R. won primarily because he appealed to the "forgotten men," whom he never forgot. But much of the President's support was only pocketbook-deep: "reliefers" were not going to bite the hand that doled out the government checks. No one, as Al Smith remarked, "shoots at Santa Claus."

Nine Old Men on the Supreme Bench

Bowing his head to the sleety blasts, Roosevelt took the presidential oath on January 20, 1937, instead of the traditional March 4. The

* Maine, which traditionally held its state elections in September, was long regarded as a political weather vane. Hence the expression "As Maine goes, so goes the nation."

20th Amendment to the Constitution, sponsored by Senator Norris of TVA fame, had been ratified in 1933. (See Appendix.) It swept away the post-election "lame duck" session of Congress, and shortened by six weeks the awkward period before inauguration.

Flushed with victory, Roosevelt interpreted his re-election as a mandate to continue New Deal reforms. But in his eyes the cloistered old men on the Supreme Bench, like fossilized stumbling blocks, stood stubbornly in the pathway of progress. In nine major cases involving the New Deal, the Roosevelt administration had been defeated seven times. The Court was ultra-conservative, and six of the nine oldsters in black were over seventy. As luck would have it, not a single member had been appointed by F.D.R. in his first term.

Roosevelt—his "Dutch up"—viewed with mounting impatience what he regarded as the obstructive conservatism of the court. Some of these Old Guard appointees were hanging on with a senile grip, partly because they felt it their patriotic duty to curb the "socialistic" tendencies of that radical in the White House. Roosevelt believed that the voters in three successive elections—the presidential elections of 1932 and 1936 and the mid-term Congressional elections of 1934— had returned a smashing verdict for *a* new deal—though perhaps not *the* New Deal. Democracy, in his view, meant rule by the people. If the American way of life was to be preserved, Roosevelt argued, the Supreme Court ought to get in line with the supreme court of public opinion.

Roosevelt finally hit upon a Court scheme that he regarded as "the answer to a maiden's prayer." When he sprang it on a shocked nation, early in 1937, he caught the country and Congress completely by surprise. One basic reason was that the proposition had never been mentioned in the recent campaign. Roosevelt bluntly asked Congress for legislation to permit him to add a new justice to the Supreme Court for every member over seventy who would not retire. The maximum membership could then be fifteen. Roosevelt pointed to the necessity of injecting vigorous new blood, for the Court, he alleged, was far behind in its work. This charge, which turned out to be false, brought heated accusations of dishonesty. At best, Roosevelt was headstrong and not fully aware of the fact that the Court, in popular thinking, had become something of a Sacred Cow.

The Supreme Court Under Pressure. Seibel in the Richmond *Times-Dispatch*, 1937

The Court Changes Course

Congress and the nation were promptly convulsed over the scheme to "pack" the Supreme Court with a "dictator bill," which one critic called "too damned slick." Franklin "Double-crossing" Roosevelt was savagely condemned for attempting to break down the delicate checks and balances among the three branches of the government. He was accused of grooming himself as a dictator by trying

In a radio address (March, 1937) Roosevelt expressed some startling thoughts about the Supreme Court, "We have . . . reached the point . . . where we must take action to save the Constitution from the Court and the Court from itself. We must find a way to take an appeal from the Supreme Court to the Constitution itself. We want a Supreme Court which will do justice under the Constitution—not over it."

to browbeat the judiciary. In the eyes of countless citizens, mostly Republicans but including many Democrats, basic liberties seemed to be in jeopardy. "God Bless the Supreme Court" was a fervent prayer.

The Court had meanwhile not been unaware of the ax hanging over its head. Whatever his motives, Mr. Justice Roberts, formerly regarded as a conservative, began to vote on the side of his liberal colleagues. "A switch in time saves nine" was the classic witticism inspired by this change. By a five-to-four decision the Court, in March, 1937, upheld the principle of a state minimum wage for women, thereby reversing its stand on a different case a year earlier. In succeeding decisions, a Court more sympathetic to the New Deal upheld the National Labor Relations Act (Wagner Act) and the Social Security Act. Roosevelt's "court packing" scheme was further undermined when Congress voted full pay for Justices over seventy who retired, whereupon one of the oldest conservative members resigned, to be replaced by a New Dealer, Mr. Justice Black.

Congress finally passed a court reform bill, but this watered-down version applied only to the lower courts. Roosevelt, the master politician, thus suffered his first major legislative defeat at the hands of his own party in Congress. Americans have never viewed lightly a tampering with the Supreme Court by the President, no matter how popular he may be. Yet in losing this battle, Roosevelt incidentally won his campaign. The Court, as he had hoped, became markedly more friendly to New Deal reforms. Furthermore, a succession of deaths and resignations enabled him to make nine appointments to the tribunal—more than any of his predecessors since George Washington. Father Time "unpacked" the Court.

Yet in a sense F.D.R. lost both the court battle and the war. He so aroused conservatives of both parties in Congress that few New Deal reforms were passed after 1937, the year of the fight to "pack" the Supreme Court.

The Twilight of the New Deal

From 1933 to 1937 the country had been gradually inching its way out of the depression, largely because of the billions of dollars injected by Congress into the economic bloodstream. Although millions of dejected souls remained unemployed, gratifying gains had been registered. "We planned it that way," remarked Roosevelt cheerily.

But in 1937 a sharp recession set in which hit bottom in 1938. The President's critics, branding this setback "the Roosevelt Depression," asserted that if F.D.R. could plan upward spirals he must also have planned the downward dip. This particular recession was probably due basically to an overrapid cutting back of "pump-priming" spending by Washington.

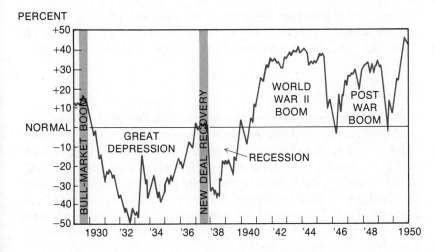

PERCENT

U.S. BUSINESS ACTIVITY, 1928–1950

Undiscouraged, Roosevelt had meanwhile been pushing the remaining measures of the New Deal. Early in 1937 he urged Congress —a Congress growing more conservative—to authorize a sweeping reorganization of the national administration in the interests of streamlined efficiency. But the issue became tangled up with his presumed dictatorial ambitions in regard to the Supreme Court, and he suffered another stinging defeat. Two years later, in 1939, Congress partially relented and in the Reorganization Act gave him limited powers for administrative reforms, including the key new Executive Office in the White House.

The New Dealers were accused of having the richest campaign chest in history; and in truth government relief checks had a curious habit of coming in bunches just before balloting time. To remedy such practices, which tended to make a farce of free elections, Congress adopted the much-heralded Hatch Act of 1939. It debarred federal administrative officials, except the highest policy-making officers, from active political campaigning and soliciting. It also forbade the use of government funds for political purposes, as well as the collection of campaign contributions from persons receiving relief payments. The Hatch Act was broadened in 1940 to place limits on campaign contributions and expenditures, but such clever ways of getting around it were found that on the whole the legislation proved disappointing.

By 1938 the New Deal had clearly lost most of its early momentum. Magician Roosevelt could find few spectacular new reform rabbits to pull out of his tall silk hat. In the Congressional elections of 1938 the Republicans, for the first time, cut heavily into the unwieldy New Deal majorities in Congress, though failing to gain control of either house. The international crisis which came to a boil in 1938–1939 shifted public attention away from domestic reform, and no doubt helped save the political hide of the Roosevelt "spendocracy." The New Deal, for all practical purposes, had shot its bolt.

New Deal or Raw Deal?

Foes of the New Deal condemned its alleged waste, incompetence, confusion, contradictions, and cross-purposes, as well as the chiseling and graft in the alphabetical agencies—"alphabet soup," sneered Al Smith. Roosevelt had done nothing, cynics said, that an earthquake could not have done better. Critics deplored the employment of "crackpot" college professors, leftist "pinkos," and outright Communists. Such subversives, it was charged, were trying to make America over in the Bolshevik-Marxist image under "Rooseveltski." The Hearst newspapers assailed

The Red New Deal with a Soviet seal
  Endorsed by a Moscow hand,
The strange result of an alien cult
  In a liberty-loving land.

Roosevelt was further accused by conservatives of being Jewish ("Rosenfeld"), and of tapping too many bright young Jewish leftists ("The Jew Deal") for his "Drain Trust."

Hardheaded businessmen, who "had met a payroll," were shocked by the leap-before-you-look, try-anything-once spirit of Roosevelt, the gay improviser. They accused him of confusing movement with progress. Humorist Will Rogers, the rope-twirling "poet lariat" of the era, remarked that if Roosevelt were to burn down the capitol, people would say, "Well, we at least got a fire started, anyhow."

"Bureaucratic meddling" and "regimentation" were also bitter complaints of anti-New Dealers; and in truth bureaucracy did blossom. The federal government, with its hundreds of thousands of employees, became incomparably the largest single business on earth, as the states faded farther into the background. Unhappily, many of the ill-trained newcomers to the political payroll represented a setback for the merit system. (See chart p. 539.)

Promises of budget balancing, to say nothing of other promises, had flown out the window—so foes of the New Deal pointed out. The national debt had skyrocketed from the already enormous figure of $19,487,000,000 in 1932 to $40,440,000,000 by 1939. America was becoming, its critics charged, a "handout state" trying to squander itself into prosperity—U.S. stood for "unlimited spending." Such lavish benefactions were undermining the old virtues of thrift and initiative. Ordinary Americans, once self-reliant citizens, were getting a bad case of the "gimmies": their wishbones were larger than

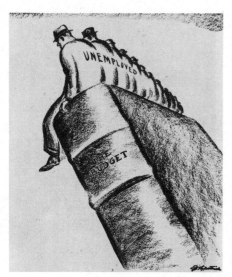

"Keeping It Out of Balance," 1935. Fitzpatrick in the St. Louis *Post-Dispatch*

their backbones. In the 19th Century, hard-pressed workers went West; now they went on relief.

Business was bitter. Accusing the New Deal of fomenting class strife in a once middle-class America, conservatives insisted that the laboring man and the farmer—especially the big operator—were being pampered. Why "soak the successful?" Countless businessmen, especially Republicans, declared that they could pull themselves out of the depression if they could only get the federal government—an interventionist Big Government—off their backs. Private enterprise, they charged, was being stifled by "planned economy," "planned bankruptcy," "creeping socialism," and the philosophy "Washington can do it better," with a federal pill for every ill. States' rights were being ignored, while the government was competing in business with its own citizens.

The aggressive leadership of Roosevelt—"one-man super-government"—also came in for denunciation. Heavy fire was especially directed at his attempts to browbeat the Supreme Court and to create a "dummy Congress." He had even tried in the 1938 elections, with backfiring results, to "purge" members of Congress who would not lock-step with him. The three Senators whom he publicly opposed were all triumphantly re-elected.

The most damning indictment of the New Deal was that it had failed to cure the depression. Afloat in a sea of red ink it had merely administered aspirin and sedatives. Despite some twenty billion dollars poured out in six years of spending and lending, of leaf raking and pump priming, the gap was not closed between production and consumption. There were even more mountainous farm surpluses under Roosevelt than under Hoover. Millions of dispirited men were still unemployed in 1939, after six years of drain, strain, and pain. Not until World War II blazed forth in Europe with Hitler—the greatest pump primer of all—was the unemployment headache solved.

A basic objective of the New Deal was featured in Roosevelt's second inaugural address (1937): "I see one-third of a nation ill-housed, ill-clad, ill-nourished. . . . The test of our progress is not whether we add more to the abundance of those who have much; it is whether we provide enough for those who have too little."

FDR's Balance Sheet

New Dealers, on the other hand, staunchly defended their record. Admitting that there had been some waste, they pointed out that relief—not economy—had been the primary object of their multi-front war on the depression. Conceding also that there had been some graft, they argued that it had been trivial in view of the immense sums spent and the obvious need for haste.

Apologists for Roosevelt further declared that the New Deal had relieved the worst of the crisis in 1933. It promoted the philosophy of "balancing the human budget," and accepted the principle that the federal government was bound to prevent mass hunger and starvation by "managing" the economy. The Washington regime was to be used, not feared. America's economic system was kept from collapse;

MILLIONS

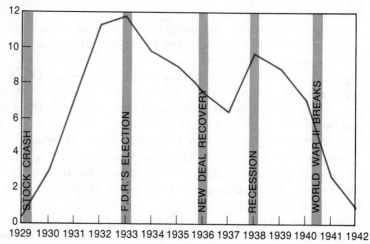

UNEMPLOYMENT, 1929–1942

a fairer distribution of the national income was achieved; and the citizens were enabled to retain their self-respect. "Nobody is going to starve" was Roosevelt's promise.

Though hated by business tycoons, F.D.R. should have been their patron saint, so his admirers claimed. He deflected popular resentments against business, and may have saved the American system of free enterprise. Roosevelt's quarrel was not with capitalism but with capitalists; he purged American capitalism of some of its worst abuses so that it might be saved from itself. He may have headed off socialism and socialist dogma by a mild dose of what was condemned as "socialism." He did not hate rich men; he merely wanted "to skin them," it was said.

Roosevelt, like Jefferson, provided reform without a bloody revolution—at a time when some foreign nations were suffering armed uprisings and when many Europeans were predicting either communism or fascism for America. He was upbraided by the left-wing radicals for not going far enough; by the right-wing conservatives for going too far. Choosing the middle road, he has been called the greatest American conservative since Hamilton. He was in fact Hamiltonian in his espousal of big government, but Jeffersonian in his concern for the forgotten man. Demonstrating anew the value of powerful presidential leadership, he exercised that power to relieve the erosion of the nation's greatest physical resource—its people. He helped preserve democracy in America at a time when democracies abroad were disappearing down the dictatorial drain. And in playing this role he unwittingly girded the nation for its part in the titanic war that hung on the horizon—a war in which democracy the world over would be at stake.

SELECT READINGS

A masterly summation is W. E. LEUCHTENBURG, *Franklin D. Roosevelt and the New Deal, 1932–1940* (1963).* See also the books by Leuchtenburg, Allen, Wecter, Seldes, and Mitchell cited for previous chapter. A readable one-volume biography is J. M. BURNS, *Roosevelt: The Lion and the Fox* (1956).* Brilliantly pro-F.D.R. are A. M. SCHLESINGER, JR., *The Coming of the New Deal* (1959)* and *The Politics of Upheaval* (1960).* An unfavorable appraisal is E. E. ROBINSON, *The Roosevelt Leadership, 1933–1945* (1955). See also RICHARD HOFSTADTER, *The Age of Reform* (1955)* and BASIL RAUCH, *The History of the New Deal, 1933–1938* (1944).* Roosevelt's years as governor are analyzed in FRANK FREIDEL, *Franklin D. Roosevelt: The Triumph* (1956). Contemporary glimpses are provided by FRANCES PERKINS, *The Roosevelt I Knew* (1946)*; JOHN M. BLUM, *From the Morgenthau Diaries: Years of Crisis, 1928–1938* (1959) and *Years of Urgency, 1938–1941* (1965); *The Journals of David E. Lilienthal* (2 vols., 1964); R. G. TUGWELL, *FDR: Architect of an Era* (1967) and *The Brains Trust* (1968); and RAYMOND MOLEY, *The First New Deal* (1966). A high-quality biography is T. H. WILLIAMS, *Huey Long* (1969). Also *Harvard Guide,** Pt. VI.

RECENT REFERENCES

FRANK FREIDEL, *Franklin D. Roosevelt: Launching the New Deal* (1974).

* Available in paperback.

43

Franklin Roosevelt and Foreign Affairs

The epidemic of world lawlessness is spreading. When an epidemic of physical disease starts to spread, the community approves and joins in a quarantine of the patients in order to protect the health of the community against the spread of the disease. . . . There must be positive endeavors to preserve peace.

President Roosevelt, Chicago Quarantine Speech, 1937

The London Conference and Russian Recognition

The 66-nation London Economic Conference, meeting in the summer of 1933, revealed how intimately Roosevelt's early foreign policy was entwined with his schemes for domestic recovery. This distinguished assemblage, to which America sent delegates, had as its major purpose a frontal attack on the global depression. It was particularly eager to stabilize national currencies on a world-wide front; and to such a course Washington had apparently committed itself in advance.

But Roosevelt began to have second thoughts. He evidently believed that his gold-juggling policies were stimulating faint blushes of returning prosperity. An international agreement on currency might tie his hands; and, as an astute politician, he was unwilling to sacrifice probable recovery at home for possible recovery abroad. While vacationing on a cruiser in the North Atlantic, he dashed off a radio message to London, scolding the Conference for trying to stabilize currencies, and urging it to turn to more basic economic ills.

Roosevelt's bombshell message blew the rug from under the London Conference. It adjourned virtually empty-handed, amid angry cries of American bad faith. The delegates, in any event, probably would have failed to produce a wonder drug for the world's economic maladies. But the devil-take-the-hindmost attitude of Roosevelt plunged the world even deeper into the morass of narrow isolationism and extreme nationalism. This unfortunate trend, as fate would have it, played directly into the hands of power-mad dictators.

Less spectacular than Roosevelt's "torpedoing" of the London Conference was his formal recognition of the Soviet Union, late in 1933. Disagreeable though the thought might be to conservative Americans, the Bolshevik government had fastened itself securely on the backs of the Russian masses, and had won recognition from other great powers. There was a certain unreality in America's refusing to recognize, after sixteen long years, the official existence of the Moscow government—a regime representing 160,000,000 people and holding sway over one-sixth of the earth's land surface. Washington's cold-shoulder treatment, moreover, had not caused the Soviet Union to collapse, or induced the Bolsheviks to abandon their insidious propaganda for world revolution.

Why did Roosevelt extend the right hand of recognition? He was first of all an outspoken liberal, not bound by the conservatism of his Republican predecessors. Hitler was on the rise in Germany, land-hungry Japan was on the rampage in the Far East, and many Americans believed that the recognition of Moscow might bolster the Russians against the Nipponese. Finally, a depression-ridden United States was willing to gamble that an enriching trade would develop with the Soviet Union.

Horse-trading negotiations with the Russians were concluded in Washington during November, 1933. The Soviets formally promised, among other assurances, to refrain from revolutionary propaganda in America. They promptly broke this pledge. Large-scale trade with the U.S.S.R. did not develop, primarily because a huge American loan, which the Russians had expected, was not granted. Russia was regarded as a poor credit risk. Uncle Sam was to some extent duped by Moscow, but at least he was now on official speaking terms—or name-calling terms—with the rulers of the largest and most populous of the white nations. Roosevelt remarked that while Russia was not yet "housebroken," she was still a good breed of dog.

"Just Another Customer," 1933. The U.S. Recognizes Russia. Courtesy of the Dallas *News*

Freedom for (from?) the Filipinos

The Great Depression, usually a blight, actually brightened hopes of Philippine independence. McKinley's imperialistic dream-bubble in the Far East had burst, and American taxpayers were eager to throw overboard their expensive tropical liability. Organized labor clamored for the exclusion of low-wage Filipinos, while American producers of sugar and other products were eager to restrict competition from the Philippines.

In 1934 Congress, remembering its earlier promises of Philippine independence, responded to the prodding of such self-seeking groups. It passed a bill under which the potentially rich islands were to become free, but only after a ten-year period of economic and political tutelage. Uncle Sam's military establishments were to be relinquished, but naval bases were to be reserved for future discussion.

Rather than freeing the Philippines, the American people tried to free themselves *from* the Philippines. With a selfish eye to their own welfare, they imposed upon the Filipinos economic terms so ungenerous as to threaten the islands with prostration. American isolationists, moreover, rejoiced to be rid of this Far Eastern heel of Achilles—so vulnerable to Japanese attack. Yet these turn-tail-and-run tactics, though applauded by anti-colonialists in Eastern Asia, cost America "face" in the Far East. Certainly abandoning the Filipinos did nothing to discourage the barefaced aggressions of the Japanese militarists.

The Flowering of Good-Neighborism under F.D.R.

A refreshing new era in relations with Latin America was heralded when Roosevelt ringingly proclaimed in his inaugural address, ". . . I would dedicate this nation to the policy of the Good Neighbor."

Old-fashioned intervention by bayonet in the Caribbean had not paid off, except in an evil harvest of resentment, suspicion, and fear. The Great Depression had cooled off Yankee economic aggressiveness, as thousands of investors in Latin American "securities" became sackholders rather than stockholders. There were now fewer dollars to be protected by the rifles of the hated marines.

Roosevelt has generally received extravagant credit for the Good Neighbor policy. Actually, the retreat from economic imperialism in Latin America had already been foreshadowed under Harding and Coolidge, and particularly under Hoover. But F.D.R. went the whole way, partly because of his liberal tendencies, and partly because global politics were shifting. With war-thirsty dictators seizing power in Europe and Asia, he was eager to line up the Latin Americans to help defend the Western Hemisphere. Embittered neighbors would be potential tools of transoceanic aggressors.

President Roosevelt made clear at the outset that he was going to renounce armed intervention, particularly the vexatious corollary of the Monroe Doctrine devised by his cousin, Theodore Roosevelt.

President-elect Hoover, during his good will trip to Latin America (1928–1929) repeatedly referred in speeches to "good neighbor" and "good neighbors." In Uruguay he declared, "I have hoped that I might by this visit symbolize the courtesy of a call from one good neighbor to another, that I might convey the respect, esteem and desire for intellectual and spiritual co-operation." Roosevelt did not invent the phrase "Good Neighbor."

Late in 1933, at the Seventh Pan-American Conference in Montevideo, the American delegation formally accepted non-intervention, and this doctrine was speedily adopted by Washington.

Deeds followed words. The last marines embarked from Haiti in 1934. In the same year restive Cuba was released from the hobbles of the Platt Amendment, under which Uncle Sam had been free to intervene. Tiny Panama received a similar uplift in 1936, when the leading strings of Washington were partially unfastened.

The hope-inspiring Good Neighbor policy, with the accent on consultation and non-intervention, received its acid test in Mexico. A seizure of Yankee oil properties in 1938, under the constitution of 1917, brought vehement demands for armed intervention from American investors. But Roosevelt successfully resisted the clamor, and a settlement was finally threshed out in 1941, even though the oil companies lost much of their original stake.

Spectacular success crowned Roosevelt's Good Neighbor policy. His earnest attempts to inaugurate a new era of friendliness, though hurting some Yankee bondholders, paid rich dividends in good will among the peoples to the south. No other citizen of the United States has ever been held in such high esteem in Latin America during his lifetime. Roosevelt was cheered with tumultuous enthusiasm when, as a "traveling salesman for peace," he journeyed to the special Inter-American Conference at Buenos Aires in 1936. The Colossus of the North now seemed less a vulture and more an eagle.

Secretary Hull's Reciprocal Trade Agreements

Intimately associated with the Good Neighbor, and also popular in Latin America, was the reciprocal trade policy of the New Dealers. Its chief architect was high-domed Secretary of State Cordell Hull, a homespun Tennessean of the low-tariff school. Like Roosevelt, he believed that trade was a two-way street; that a nation can sell abroad only as it buys abroad; that tariff barriers choke off foreign trade; and that trade wars beget shooting wars.

Responding to the Hull-Roosevelt leadership, Congress passed the Reciprocal Trade Agreements Act in 1934. Designed in part to lift American export trade from the depression doldrums, this far-visioned measure was aimed at both relief and recovery, while putting into active operation the low-tariff policies of the New Dealers. (See chart, p. 849.)

The Trade Agreements Act avoided the dangerous uncertainties of a wholesale tariff revision; it merely whittled down the most objectionable schedules of the Hawley-Smoot law by amending them. Roosevelt was empowered to lower existing rates by as much as 50%, provided that the other country involved was willing to reciprocate with similar reductions. The resulting pacts, moreover, were to be-

"Sounding the Dinner Gong for World Trade," 1933. Fitzpatrick in the St. Louis *Post-Dispatch*

"One of Our Quaint Ideas
About Foreign Trade."
Fitzpatrick in the St. Louis
Post-Dispatch

come effective without the formal approval of the Senate. This novel feature not only insured speedier action, but sidestepped the evils of logrolling and high-pressure lobbying in Congress.

Secretary Hull, whose zeal for reciprocity was unflagging, succeeded in negotiating pacts with twenty-one countries by the end of 1939. During these same years American foreign trade increased somewhat and the depression eased appreciably, all presumably in part as a result of the Hull-Roosevelt policies. Trade agreements undoubtedly bettered economic and political relations with Latin America, and proved to be an influence for peace in a war-bent world.

The Reciprocal Trade Agreements Act, with modifications, was renewed periodically by Congress—but invariably in the teeth of heated protests from high-tariff Republicans. James G. Blaine, Republican Secretary of State of yesteryear, had fathered the reciprocal trade policy. But dyed-in-the-wool Republicans were loath to recognize the Blaine baby in Democratic diapers. Manufacturers were not alone in their opposition; they were joined by many Middle Western farmers who were hurt by lowered duties on meat and other foreign imports. But a majority of the New Deal Congress felt that the interests of special groups, however important, should be sacrificed to those of the nation as a whole.

Impulses Toward Storm-Cellar Isolationism

Post-1918 chaos in Europe, followed by the Great Depression, fostered the ominous concept of totalitarianism. The individual was nothing; the state was everything. Communist Russia led the way, with the crafty and ruthless Joseph Stalin finally emerging as dictator. Blustery Benito Mussolini, a swaggering Fascist, seized the reins of power in Italy during 1922. And Adolf Hitler, a fanatic with a toothbrush mustache, plotted and harangued his way into control of Germany in 1933.

Hitler was the most immediately dangerous, because he combined tremendous power with great impulsiveness. A frustrated Austrian painter, with hypnotic talents as an orator and a leader, he had secured control of the Nazi Party by making political capital of the Treaty of Versailles and the depression-spawned unemployment. He was thus a misbegotten child of the shortsighted post-war policies of the victorious Allies, including the United States. The desperate German people had fallen in behind the new Pied Piper, for they saw no other hope of escape from the plague of economic chaos and national disgrace. In 1936 the Nazi Hitler and the Fascist Mussolini allied themselves in the Rome-Berlin Axis.

International gangsterism was likewise spreading in the Far East, where the Nipponese were on the make. Like Germany and Italy, Japan was a so-called "have-not" power. Like them, she resented the ungenerous Treaty of Versailles. Like them, she demanded additional space for her teeming millions.

Japanese navalists were not to be denied. Determined to find a place in the Asiatic sun, Tokyo gave notice in 1934 of the termination of the twelve-year-old Washington Naval Treaty. A year later at London, the Japanese torpedoed all hope of effective naval disarmament: upon being denied complete parity, they walked out on the multi-power conference.

Jut-jawed Mussolini, seeking both glory and empire in Africa, brutally attacked Ethiopia in 1935 with bombers and tanks. The black defenders, armed with spears and ancient firearms, were speedily crushed. Members of the League of Nations could have caused Mussolini's war machine to creak to a halt—if they had only dared to embargo oil. But when the League quailed rather than risk global hostilities, it merely signed its own death warrant.

Isolationism, long festering in America, received a strong boost from these alarms abroad. Though disapproving of the dictators, Americans still believed that their encircling seas conferred a kind of mystic immunity. They were continuing to suffer disillusionment born of their participation in World War I, which they now regarded as a colossal blunder. They likewise cherished bitter memories of the ungrateful and defaulting debtors. As early as 1934 a spiteful Congress had passed the Johnson Debt Default Act, which prevented debt-dodging nations from borrowing further in the United States. If attacked again by aggressors, these delinquents could "stew in their own juice."

Mired down in the Great Depression, Americans had no real appreciation of the revolutionary forces being harnessed by the dictators. The "have-not" powers were out to become "have" powers. Americans were not so much afraid that the totalitarian aggression would cause trouble as they were fearful that they might be drawn into it. Strong nationwide agitation welled up for a constitutional amendment to forbid a declaration of war by Congress—except in case of invasion—unless there was first a favorable popular referendum. With a mixture of seriousness and frivolity, a group of Princeton University students began to agitate in 1936 for a bonus to be paid to the Veterans of Future Wars (V.F.W.'s) while still alive.

Mussolini's thirst for national glory in primitive Ethiopia is indicated by his remark in 1940, "To make a people great it is necessary to send them to battle even if you have to kick them in the pants." (The Italians were notoriously unwarlike.) In 1934 Mussolini proclaimed in a public speech, "We have buried the putrid corpse of liberty."

Congress Legislates Neutrality

As the gloomy 1930's lengthened, an avalanche of lurid articles and books poured from American presses condemning the munitions manufacturers as war-fomenting "merchants of death." A Senate committee, headed by Senator Nye, was appointed in 1934 to investigate these charges. By sensationalizing evidence regarding America's entry into World War I, the senatorial probers tended to shift the blame away from the German submarine to the American bankers and arms manufacturers. As the munitions-makers had obviously made money out of the war, many a naïve soul leaped to the illogical conclusion that these soulless scavengers had caused the war in order to make money. This kind of reasoning suggested that if the profits could only be removed from the arms traffic—"one hell of a business"—the country could keep out of any world conflict that might erupt in the future.

Responding to overwhelming popular pressure, Congress made haste to legislate the nation out of war. Action was spurred by the danger that Mussolini's Ethiopian assault would plunge the world into a new blood bath. The Neutrality Acts of 1935, 1936, and 1937, taken together, stipulated that *when the President proclaimed* the existence of a foreign war, certain restrictions would automatically go into effect. No American could legally sail on a belligerent ship, or sell or transport munitions to a belligerent, or make loans to a belligerent.

This head-in-the-sands legislation marked in effect an abandonment of the traditional policy of freedom of the seas—a policy for which America had professedly fought two full-fledged wars and several undeclared wars. The Neutrality Acts, so called, were specifically tailored to keep the nation out of a conflict like World War I. If they had been in effect at that time, America probably would not have been sucked in—at least not in April, 1917. Congress was one war too late with its legislation. What had seemed dishonorable to Wilson seemed honorable and desirable to a later disillusioned generation.

Storm-cellar neutrality proved to be tragically shortsighted. America falsely assumed that the decision for peace or war lay in her own hands, not in those of the satanic forces already unleashed in the world. Prisoner of her own fears, she failed to recognize that she should have used her enormous power to control international events in her own interest. Instead, she remained at the mercy of events controlled by the dictators.

Statutory neutrality, though of undoubted legality, was of dubious morality. America served notice that she would make no distinction whatever between the brutal aggressor and his innocent victims. By striving to hold the scales even, she actually overbalanced them in favor of the dictators who had armed themselves to the teeth. By declining to use her vast industrial strength to aid her democratic friends and defeat her totalitarian foes, she helped spur the aggressors along their blood-spattered path of conquest.

"The Jig-Saw Puzzle," 1939. Cassel in the Brooklyn *Eagle*

America Dooms Loyalist Spain and Delights Franco

The Spanish Civil War of 1936–1939—a proving ground and dress rehearsal in miniature for World War II—was a painful object lesson in the folly of neutrality-by-legislation. Spanish rebels, who rose against the republican government in Madrid, were headed by dictator-minded General Francisco Franco. Generously aided by his fellow conspirators, Hitler and Mussolini, he undertook to overthrow the established Loyalist regime, which in turn was assisted on a smaller scale by the Soviet Union. This pipeline from Communist Moscow chilled the natural sympathies of many Americans, especially those of Roman Catholic faith.

Washington continued official relations with the Loyalist government. In accordance with previous American practice, this regime should have been free to purchase desperately needed munitions in the United States. But Congress, with the encouragement of Roosevelt and with only one dissenting vote, amended the existing neutrality legislation so as to apply an arms embargo to both Loyalists and rebels. "Roosevelt," remarked dictator Franco, "behaved in the manner of a true gentleman." F.D.R. later regretted being so gentlemanly.

Uncle Sam thus sat on the sidelines while Franco, abundantly supplied with arms and men by his fellow dictators, strangled the republican government of Spain. The democracies, including the United States, were so determined to stay out of war that they helped to condemn a fellow democracy to death. In so doing, they further encouraged the dictators to take the dangerous road which led over the precipice of World War II.

Such peace-at-any-price-ism was further cursed with illogic. While determined to stay out of war, America declined to build up her armed forces to a point where she could deter the aggressors. In fact, she allowed her navy to decline in relative strength. She had been led to believe that huge fleets cause huge wars; she was also trying to spare the complaining taxpayer during the grim days of the Great Depression. When President Roosevelt repeatedly called for preparedness, he was branded a warmonger. Not until 1938, the year before World War II exploded, did Congress come to grips with the problem when it passed a billion-dollar naval construction act. The calamitous story was repeated of too little—and that too late.

Claude Bowers, the U.S. Ambassador in Spain, deplored neutrality and favored support for the defeated Loyalists. When he returned to America and met with Roosevelt, the President's first words were, "We've made a mistake. You've been right all along." At least this is what Bowers states in his memoirs.

Appeasing Japan and Germany

Sulphurous war clouds had meanwhile been gathering in the tension-taut Far East. In 1937 the Japanese militarists, at the Marco Polo bridge near Peiping, touched off the explosion that led to a full-dress invasion of China. In a sense this attack was the curtain raiser of World War II.

Roosevelt declined to invoke the recently passed neutrality legislation, noting that the so-called "China incident" was not an officially declared war. If he had put the existing restrictions into effect, he would have cut off the tiny trickle of munitions on which the Chinese were desperately dependent. The Japanese, of course, could continue to buy mountainous war supplies in the United States.

The U.S.S. *Panay* with Decks Awash. Courtesy Navy Department

In Chicago—unofficial isolationist "capital" of America—Roosevelt delivered his sensational "Quarantine Speech" in the autumn of 1937. Alarmed by the recent aggressions of Italy and Japan, he called for "positive endeavors" to "quarantine" the aggressors—presumably by economic embargoes. One immediate result was a cyclone of protest from isolationists and other foes of involvement; they feared that a moral quarantine would lead to a shooting quarantine. Startled by this angry response, Roosevelt sought by less direct means to curb the dictators.

America's isolationist mood deepened, especially in regard to China. In December, 1937, Japanese aviators bombed and sank an American gunboat, the *Panay*, in Chinese waters, with a loss of two killed and thirty wounded. In the days of 1898, when the *Maine* went down, this outrage might have provoked war. But after Tokyo hastened to make the necessary apologies and pay a proper indemnity, the American public breathed an audible sigh of relief. Japanese militarists were thus encouraged to vent their anger against the "superior" white race by subjecting American civilians in China, both male and female, to humiliating slappings and strippings.

More immediately menacing was Adolf Hitler. In 1935 he had openly flouted the Treaty of Versailles by introducing compulsory military service in Germany. The next year he boldly marched into the demilitarized German Rhineland, likewise contrary to the detested treaty, while France and Britain looked on in an agony of indecision. Lashing his following to a frenzy, Hitler undertook to liquidate the Jewish population under his control. In the end, he wiped out about six million innocent victims. Calling upon his people to sacrifice butter for guns, he whipped the new German air force and mechanized ground divisions into the most devastating machine the world had yet seen.

Suddenly, in March, 1938, Hitler bloodlessly seized German-speaking Austria. The democratic powers, wringing their hands in despair, prayed that this last grab would satisfy his passion for conquest.

But Hitler could not stop. Later in 1938 he continued his "war of nerves" by his bullying demands for the German-inhabited Sudetenland of his neighbor, tiny Czechoslovakia. The leaders of Britain and France, eager to appease Hitler, sought frantically to bring the dispute to the conference table. President Roosevelt, also deeply alarmed, kept the wires hot with personal messages, to both Hitler and Mussolini, urging a peaceful settlement.

A conference was finally arranged in Munich, Germany, in September, 1938. The Western European democracies, badly unprepared for war, betrayed Czechoslovakia to Germany when they consented to the shearing away of the Sudetenland. They hoped—and these hopes were shared by the American people—that the concessions at the conference table would appease the power-lust of Hitler and bring "peace in our time."

"Appeasement" of the dictators, symbolized by the ugly word "Munich," turned out to be merely surrender on the installment plan. In March, 1939, scarcely six months later, Hitler suddenly erased the rest of Czechoslovakia from the map, contrary to his solemn promises. The democratic world was again stunned.

Hitlerian Belligerency and U.S. Neutrality

Joseph Stalin, the Sphinx of the Kremlin, was a key to the peace puzzle. In the summer of 1939 the British and French were busily negotiating with Moscow, hopeful of securing a treaty that would halt Hitler. But mutual suspicions proved insuperable. Almost overnight the Soviet Union astounded the civilized world by signing, on August 23, 1939, a non-aggression treaty with the German dictator.

The notorious Hitler-Stalin pact was epochal. It meant that the Nazi German leader now had a green light to make war on Poland and the western democracies, without fearing a stab in the back from Russia —his Communist archfoe. Consternation struck those wishful thinkers in Western Europe who had fondly hoped that Hitler might be egged upon Stalin so that the twin menaces would bleed each other to death. It was as plain as the mustache on Stalin's face that the wily Soviet dictator was plotting to turn his German accomplice against the western democracies. The two warring camps would kill each other off—and leave him bestriding Europe like a colossus.

World War II was only hours away. Hitler, intensifying the pressure, demanded from neighboring Poland a return of the areas wrested from Germany after World War I. Failing to secure satisfaction, he sent his mechanized divisions crashing into Poland at dawn on September 1, 1939.

Britain and France, honoring their commitments to Poland, promptly declared war. At long last they perceived the folly of continued appeasement. But they were powerless to aid Poland, which succumbed in three weeks to Hitler's smashing strategy of terror. Stalin, as prearranged secretly in his fateful pact with Hitler, came in on the kill for his share of old Russian Poland. Long-dreaded World War II was now fully launched, and the Long Truce of 1919–1939 had ended.

President Roosevelt speedily issued the routine proclamations of neutrality. The American people were overwhelmingly anti-Nazi and anti-Hitler; they fervently hoped that the democracies would win; they fondly believed that the forces of righteousness would again triumph, as in 1918. But they were desperately determined to stay out: they were not going to be "suckers" again.

Neutrality promptly became a heated issue in the United States.

European War Narrows the Atlantic. Courtesy of the Washington (D.C.) *Star*

Ill-prepared Britain and France urgently needed American airplanes and other weapons, but the Neutrality Act of 1937 raised a sternly forbidding hand. Roosevelt summoned Congress in special session, shortly after the invasion of Poland, to consider a lifting of the arms embargo. After six hectic weeks of debate, a makeshift law emerged.

The Neutrality Act of 1939 provided that henceforth the European democracies might buy American war materials, but only on a "cash and carry" basis. This meant that they would have to transport the munitions in their own ships, and pay for them in cash. America would thus avoid loans, war debts, and the torpedoing of American arms-carriers. While Congress thus loosened former restrictions in response to interventionist cries, it added others in response to isolationist fears. Roosevelt was now authorized to proclaim danger zones into which American merchant ships would be forbidden to enter.

This unneutral neutrality law clearly favored the democracies against the dictators—and was so intended. As the British and French navies controlled the Atlantic, the European aggressors could not send their ships to buy America's munitions. The nation not only improved its moral position, but simultaneously helped its economic position. An overseas demand for war goods brought a sharp upswing from the recession of 1937–1938, and ultimately solved the decade-long unemployment crisis. (See charts, pp. 891, 894.)

Aftermath of the Fall of France

The months following the collapse of Poland, while France and Britain marked time, were known as the "phony war." An ominous silence fell on Europe, as Hitler shifted his victorious divisions from Poland for a knockout blow at France. Inaction during this anxious period was relieved by the Soviets, who wantonly attacked neighboring Finland in an effort to secure strategic buffer territory. The debt-paying Finns, who had a host of admirers in America, were speedily granted $30,000,000 by an isolationist Congress for *non-military* supplies. But despite heroic resistance, Finland was finally flattened by the Russian steam roller.

An abrupt end to the "phony war" came in April, 1940, when Hitler, again without warning, overran his weaker neighbors, Denmark and Norway. Hardly pausing for breath, the next month he launched an unannounced assault on Holland and Belgium, followed by a paralyzing blow at France. By late June, France was forced to surrender, but not until Mussolini had pounced on her rear for a jackal's share of the loot. Only by the so-called "miracle of Dunkirk" did the British manage to evacuate to England the bulk of their shattered and partially disarmed army. The crisis providentially brought forth an inspired leader in Prime Minister Winston Churchill, the bulldog-

In 1924, while briefly imprisoned, Hitler dictated a remarkable book, *Mein Kampf* (*My Struggle*), which brazenly set forth his objectives and techniques. He was a past master of the "Big Lie." As he wrote, "The primitive simplicity of their minds [the masses] render them a more easy prey to a big lie than a small one, for they themselves often tell little lies but would be ashamed to tell big ones." He also said, "The victor will never be asked if he told the truth" and "Success is the sole earthly judge of right and wrong."

jawed orator who nerved his people to fight off the fearful air bombings of their cities.

France's sudden collapse shocked Americans out of their daydreams. Stout-hearted Britons, singing "There'll Always Be an England," were all that stood between Hitler and the end in Europe of constitutional government. If Britain went under, Hitler would have at his disposal the workshops, shipyards, and slave labor of Western Europe. He might even have the powerful British fleet as well. This frightening possibility, which seemed to pose a dire threat to American security, steeled the American people to a tremendous effort.

Roosevelt moved with electrifying energy and dispatch. He called upon an already debt-burdened nation to build huge airfleets and a two-ocean navy, which could also check Japan. Congress, jarred out of its apathy toward preparedness, within a year appropriated the astounding sum of $37,000,000,000. This figure was more than the total cost of fighting World War I.

Congress also passed a conscription law, approved September 6, 1940. Under this measure—the first peacetime draft in American history—provision was made for training each year 1,200,000 troops and 800,000 reserves. The act was later adapted to the requirements of a global war.

The Latin American bulkhead likewise needed bolstering. Holland, Denmark and France, all crushed under the German jackboot, had orphaned colonies in the New World. Would these fall into German hands? At the Havana Conference of 1940 the United States, by implication, agreed to share with its twenty sister republics the responsibility of upholding the Monroe Doctrine. This ancient dictum, hitherto unilateral, had been a bludgeon brandished only by the hated Yankee colossus. Now multilateral, it was to be wielded by twenty-one pairs of American hands—at least in theory.

"Just So There'll be No Misunderstanding," Hitler and Mussolini warned. Ray in the Kansas City *Star*.

Bolstering Britain with the Destroyer Deal (1940)

Before the fall of France, Washington had generally observed a technical neutrality. But now Americans had to choose between neutrality and unneutral assistance to Britain before she fell under the heel of Hitler. Neutrality gradually went into the ash can.

Roosevelt at first arranged to transfer surplus federal arms to private American concerns ("dummies"), through which the weapons could be sent to bomb-blasted Britain. Thus airplanes, rifles, mortars, artillery, and ammunition were shipped in a technically legal way.

Advocates of aid to England formed propaganda groups, the most potent of which was the Committee to Defend America by Aiding the Allies. Its argument was double-barreled. To interventionists, it could appeal for direct succor to the British by such slogans as "Britain Is Fighting Our Fight." To the isolationists, it could appeal for

DESTROYER DEAL BASES

assistance to the democracies by "All Methods Short of War," so that the terrible conflict would be kept in faraway Europe.

The isolationists, both numerous and sincere, were by no means silent. Determined to avoid bloodshed at all costs, they organized the America First Committee and proclaimed, "England Will Fight to the Last American." They contended that America should concentrate what strength she had to defend her own shores, lest a victorious Hitler, after crushing Britain, successfully assault her. Their basic philosophy was "The Yanks Are Not Coming," and their most effective speechmaker was the famed aviator, Colonel Charles A. Lindbergh who, ironically, had narrowed the Atlantic in 1927.

Britain was in critical need of destroyers, for German submarines were again threatening to starve her out with attacks on shipping. Roosevelt moved boldly when, on September 2, 1940, he agreed to transfer to Great Britain fifty old-model, four-funnel destroyers left over from World War I. In return, the British promised to hand over to the United States eight valuable defensive base sites, stretching from Newfoundland to South America. These strategically located outposts were to remain under the Stars and Stripes for ninety-nine years.

Transferring fifty destroyers to a foreign navy was a highly questionable disposal of government property, despite a strained interpretation of existing legislation. The exchange was achieved by a simple presidential agreement, without so much as a "by your leave" to Congress. Applause burst from the aid-to-Britain advocates, many of whom had been urging such a step. But condemnation arose from "America Firsters" and other isolationists, as well as from anti-administration Republicans. Some of them approved the transfer but decried Roosevelt's secretive and highhanded methods. Yet so grave was the crisis that the President was unwilling to submit the scheme to the uncertainties and delays of a full-dress debate in Congress.

Shifting warships from a "neutral" United States to a belligerent Britain was, beyond question, a flagrant violation of neutral obligations—at least neutral obligations that had existed before Hitler's barefaced aggresssions rendered dangerous such old-fashioned concepts of fair play. Public opinion polls demonstrated that a majority of Americans were determined, even at the risk of armed hostilities, to provide the battered British with "all aid short of war."

F.D.R. Shatters the Two-Term Tradition (1940)

A distracting presidential election, as fate decreed, came in the midst of this crisis. The two leading Republican aspirants were round-faced and flat-voiced Senator Robert A. Taft of Ohio, son of the ex-President, and an energetic boy-wonder, lawyer-prosecutor, Thomas E. Dewey of New York. But in one of the miracles of American political history, the Philadelphia convention was swept off its feet by an interventionist latecomer, Wendell L. Willkie, a German-descended son of Hoosier Indiana. This dynamic lawyer—tousle-headed, long-lipped, broad-faced, and large-framed—had until recently been a Democrat and the head of a huge public-utilities corporation. A complete novice in politics, he had rocketed from political nothingness in a few short weeks. His great appeal lay in his personality, for he was magnetic, transparently sincere, and honest in a homespun, Lincolnesque way.

With the galleries in Philadelphia wildly chanting "We Want Will-kie," the delegates finally accepted this political upstart as the only candidate who could possibly beat Roosevelt. The Republican platform condemned F.D.R.'s alleged dictatorship, as well as the costly and confusing zigzags of the New Deal. Willkie, an outstanding liberal, was not so much opposed to the New Deal as to its extravagances and inefficiencies. Democratic critics branded him "the rich man's Roosevelt" and "the simple barefoot Wall Street lawyer."

While the rumor-pot boiled, Roosevelt delayed to the last minute the announcement of his decision to challenge the sacred two-term tradition. Despite what he described as his personal yearning for retirement, he avowed that in so grave a crisis he owed his experienced hand to the service of his country and humanity. The Democratic delegates in Chicago, realizing that only with "the Champ" could they defeat Willkie, drafted him by a technically unanimous vote. "Better a Third Term than a Third-Rater" was the war cry of many Democrats.

Burning with sincerity and energy, Willkie launched out upon a whirlwind, Bryanesque campaign in which he delivered over five hundred speeches. At times his voice became a hoarse croak. The country was already badly split between interventionists and isolationists, and Willkie might have widened the breach dangerously by a violent attack on Roosevelt's aid-to-Britain policies. But seeing eye to eye with F.D.R. on the necessity of bolstering the democracies, he refrained from assailing the President's interventionism, though objecting to his methods.

In the realm of foreign affairs, there was not much to choose between the two candidates. Both promised to stay out of the war; both promised aid to the victims of aggression; both promised to strengthen the nation's defenses. Yet Willkie, with a mop of black hair in his eyes, hit hard at Rooseveltian "dictatorship" and the third term. His enthusiastic followers cried, "Win with Willkie," "No Fourth Term Either," and "There's No Indispensable Man."

Roosevelt, busy at his desk with mounting problems, made only a few speeches. Stung by taunts that he was leading the nation by the back door into the European slaughterhouse, he repeatedly denied any such intention. His most specific statement was at Boston, where he emphatically declared, "Your boys are not going to be sent into

The old-line Republican bosses were not happy over having a recent Democrat head their ticket. Ex-Senator James Watson reportedly told Willkie to his face, "You have been a Democrat all your life. I don't mind the church converting a whore, but I don't like her to lead the choir the first night."

F.D.R. before microphones campaigning for a third term in 1940. Franklin D. Roosevelt Library.

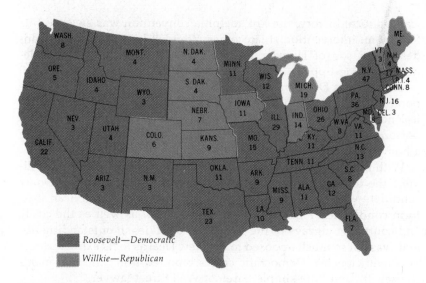

PRESIDENTIAL ELECTION OF 1940
(with electoral vote by state)

any foreign wars"—a pledge that later came back to plague him. He and his henchmen vigorously defended the New Deal, as well as all-out preparations for the defense of America and aid to the Allies.

Roosevelt triumphed in an unprecedented turnout of the voters, although Willkie ran a strong race. The popular total was 27,244,160 to 22,305,198, and the electoral count was 449 to 82. This contest was much less of a walkaway than in 1932 or 1936; Democratic majorities in Congress remained about the same.

Jubilant Democrats hailed their triumph as a mandate to abolish the two-term tradition. But the truth is that Roosevelt won in spite of the third-term handicap. Voters generally felt that, should war come, the experienced hand of the tried leader was needed at the helm. Less appealing was the completely inexperienced hand of the well-intentioned Willkie, who had never held public office.

The hoary argument that one should not change horses in the middle of a stream was strong, especially in an era of war-spawned prosperity. Roosevelt might not have won if there had not been a war crisis. On the other hand, he probably would not have run if foreign perils had not loomed so ominously. In a sense, his opponent was Adolf Hitler, not Willkie.

Congress Passes the Landmark Lend-Lease Law

By late 1940 embattled Britain was nearing the end of her financial tether; her credits in America were being rapidly consumed by insatiable war orders. But Roosevelt, who had bitter memories of the wrangling over the Allied debts of World War I, was determined, as he put it, to eliminate "the silly, foolish, old dollar sign." He finally hit on the scheme of lending or leasing American arms to the reeling democracies. When the shooting was over, to use his comparison, the guns and tanks could be returned, just as one's next-door neighbor would return a length of garden hose when a threatening fire was put out. But isolationist Senator Taft retorted that lending arms was like lending chewing gum: "You don't want it back."

The lend-lease bill was entitled "An Act Further to Promote the Defense of the United States." Sprung on the country after the election was safely over, it was praised by the administration as a device that would keep the nation out of the war, rather than get it in. America, so Roosevelt promised, would be the "arsenal of democracy." She would send a limitless supply of arms to the victims of aggression, who in turn would finish the job and keep the war on their side of the Atlantic. Accounts would be settled by equivalents, not gold.

Lend-lease was heatedly debated throughout the land and in Congress. Most of the opposition came, as might be expected, from isolationists and anti-Roosevelt Republicans. The scheme was assailed as "the blank-check bill" and, in the words of isolationist Senator Wheeler, as "the new Triple-A bill"—a measure designed to "plow under every fourth American boy." Nevertheless lend-lease was finally approved in March, 1941, by sweeping majorities in both houses of Congress.

Lend-lease was one of the most momentous laws ever to pass Congress; it was a challenge hurled squarely into the teeth of the Axis dictators. America pledged herself, to the extent of her vast resources, to bolster those nations that were indirectly defending her by fighting aggression. When the gigantic operation ended in 1945, she had sent about fifty billion dollars' worth of arms and equipment—much more than the cost to her of World War I—to those nations fighting

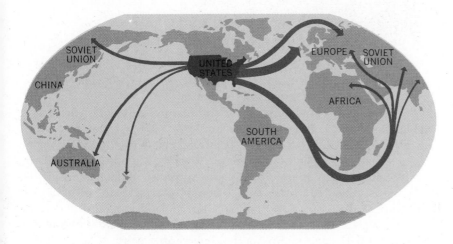

MAIN FLOW OF LEND-LEASE AID
(width of arrows indicates relative amount)

aggressors. The passing of lend-lease was in effect an economic declaration of war; a shooting declaration could not be very far around the corner.

By its very nature, lend-lease marked the abandonment of any pretense of neutrality. It was no destroyer deal arranged privately by Roosevelt. It was universally debated, over drugstore counters and cracker barrels, from California to Maine; and the sovereign citizen at last spoke through convincing majorities in Congress. Most people probably realized that they were tossing the old concepts of neutrality out the window. But they also recognized that they would play a suicidal game if they bound themselves by the oxcart rules of the 19th Century—especially while the aggressors themselves openly spurned international obligations. Lend-lease would admittedly involve a grave risk of war, but most Americans were prepared to take that chance, rather than see Britain collapse and then face the dictators alone.

Lend-lease had the somewhat incidental result of gearing the nation's own factories for all-out war production. The enormously increased capacity thus achieved helped to save America's own skin when, at long last, the shooting war burst around her head.

Hitler himself evidently recognized lend-lease as an unofficial declaration of war. Until then, Germany had avoided attacking American ships; memories of Uncle Sam's decisive intervention in 1917–1918 were still fresh in German minds. But after the passing of lend-lease there was less point in trying to curry favor with the United States. On May 21, 1941, the *Robin Moor,* an unarmed American merchantman, was torpedoed and destroyed by a German submarine in the South Atlantic, outside a war zone. The sinkings had started, but on a limited scale.

Hitler's Assault on Russia and the Atlantic Charter

Two globe-shaking events marked the course of World War II before the assault on Pearl Harbor in 1941. One was the fall of France; the other was Hitler's invasion of Russia.

The scheming dictators, Hitler and Stalin, had been uneasy yokefellows under the ill-begotten pact of 1939. As masters of the double-cross, neither trusted the other. They engaged in prolonged dickering in a secret attempt to divide potential territorial spoils between them, but Stalin gagged on dominant German control of the Balkans. Hitler thereupon decided to crush his co-conspirator, seize the oil and other resources of Russia, and then have a free hand to snuff out Britain. He assumed that his all-conquering armies would subdue the "Mongol half-wits" of Russia in a few short weeks.

Out of a clear sky, on June 22, 1941, Hitler launched a devastating attack on his Soviet neighbor. This timely assault was an incredible

Senator Harry S. Truman (later President) had a common reaction to Hitler's invasion of Russia in 1941, "If we see that Germany is winning, we ought to help Russia, and if we see Russia is winning, we ought to help Germany, and that way let them kill as many as possible."

stroke of good fortune for the democratic world—or so it seemed at the time. The two menaces could now slit each other's throats on the icy steppes of Russia. Or they would if the Soviets did not speedily collapse, as many military experts predicted.

Sound American strategy seemed to dictate speedy aid to Russia while she was still afloat. Roosevelt immediately promised assistance, and backed up his words by making military supplies available. Several months later, interpreting the lend-lease law to mean that the defense of Russia was essential for the defense of the United States, he extended one billion dollars in lend-lease—the first installment on an ultimate total of eleven billions. Meanwhile the valor of the Red Army, combined with the white paralysis of an early Russian winter, had halted the Hitlerian invaders at the gates of Moscow.

With the collapse of the Soviets still a dread possibility, the drama-charged Atlantic Conference was held in August, 1941. British Prime Minister Winston Churchill, with cigar embedded in his cherubic face, secretly met with Roosevelt on a warship off the foggy coast of Newfoundland. This was the first of a series of history-making conferences between the two statesmen for the discussion of common problems, including the menace of Japan in the Far East.

The most memorable offspring of this get-together was the eight-point Atlantic Charter. It was formally accepted by Roosevelt and Churchill, and endorsed by the Soviet Union later that year. Suggestive of Wilson's Fourteen Points, the new covenant outlined the aspirations of the democracies for a better world at war's end.

Surprisingly, the Atlantic Charter was rather specific. While opposing imperialistic annexations, it promised that there would be no territorial changes contrary to the wishes of the inhabitants (self-determination). It further affirmed the right of a people to choose their own form of government and, in particular, to regain the governments abolished by the dictators. Among various other goals, the Charter declared for disarmament and a peace of security, pending "a permanent system of general security" (a new League of Nations).

Liberals the world over took heart from the Atlantic Charter. It was especially gratifying to subject populations, like the Poles, who were then ground under the iron heel of a conqueror. But the agreement was roundly condemned in the United States by isolationists and others hostile to Roosevelt. What right, they charged, had "neutral" America to confer with belligerent Britain on common policies? Such critics missed the point: the nation was no longer neutral.

"Unexpected Guest," 1941. Russia Joins the Democracies. Courtesy Detroit *News*

U.S. Destroyers and Hitler's U-Boats Clash

Lend-lease shipments of arms to Britain on British ships were bound to be sunk by German wolf-pack submarines. If the intent was to get the munitions to England, not to dump them into the ocean, the freighters would have to be escorted by American warships. Britain simply did not have enough destroyers. The dangerous possibility of being "convoyed into war" had been mentioned in Congress during the lengthy debate on lend-lease, but administration spokesmen had brushed the idea aside. Their strategy was to make only one commitment at a time.

The fateful decision to convoy was taken in July, 1941. Roosevelt, by virtue of his authority as Commander-in-Chief of the armed forces, issued orders to the navy to escort lend-lease shipments to Iceland. The British would then shepherd them the rest of the way.

Inevitable clashes with submarines ensued on the Iceland run, even though Hitler's orders were to strike American warships only in self-defense. In September, 1941, the U.S. destroyer *Greer*, provocatively trailing a German U-boat, was attacked by the undersea craft, without damage to either side. Roosevelt then proclaimed a shoot-on-sight policy. On October 17, the escorting destroyer *Kearny*, while engaged in a battle with U-boats, lost eleven men when it was crippled but not sent to the bottom. Two weeks later the destroyer *Reuben James* was torpedoed and sunk off southwestern Iceland, with the loss of about one hundred officers and men.

Neutrality was still inscribed on the statute books, but not in American hearts. Congress, responding to public pressures and confonted with a shooting war, voted in mid-November, 1941, to pull the teeth from the now-useless Neutrality Act of 1939. Merchant ships could henceforth be legally armed, and they could enter the combat zones with munitions for Britain. Americans braced themselves for wholesale attacks by Hitler's submarines.

A Damaged U.S.S. *Kearny (left)* Towed into Iceland Port. U.S. Army Signal Corps Photo, courtesy Navy Department

Heading for the Surprise Assault at Pearl Harbor

The blowup came, not in the Atlantic, but in the faraway Pacific. This explosion should have surprised no close observer, for Japan, since September of 1940, had been a formal military ally of Nazi Germany—America's shooting foe in the North Atlantic.

Japan's position in the Far East had grown more perilous by the hour. She was still mired down in the costly and exhausting "China incident," from which she could extract neither honor nor victory. Her war machine was fatally dependent on immense shipments from the United States of steel, scrap iron, oil, and aviation gasoline. Such assistance to the Japanese aggressor was highly unpopular in America. But Roosevelt had resolutely held off an embargo, lest he goad the Tokyo warlords into a descent upon the oil-rich and weakly defended Dutch East Indies.

Washington, late in 1940, finally imposed the first of its embargoes on Japan-bound supplies. This blow was followed in mid-1941 by a "freezing" of Nipponese assets in the United States and a cessation of all shipments of gasoline and other sinews of war. As the oil gauge dropped, the squeeze on Japan grew steadily more nerve-racking: protracted delay was on the side of the United States. Japanese leaders were faced with two painful alternatives. They could either knuckle under to the Americans, or break out of the embargo ring by a desperate attack on the oil supplies and other riches of Southeast Asia. The ticking of the clock, while soothing to American ears, drove the Japanese to madness.

Final tense negotiations with Japan took place in Washington during November and early December of 1941. The State Department insisted that the Japanese clear out of China but, to sweeten the pill, offered to renew trade relations on a limited basis. Japanese imperialists, after waging a bitter war against the Chinese for more than four years, were unwilling to lose face by withdrawing at the behest of the United States. As between capitulation and continued conquest, they chose the sword. They had to put up or shut up, as the American press noted. They put up.

Officials in Washington, having "cracked" the top secret code of the Japanese, knew that Tokyo's decision was for war. But the United States, as a democracy committed to public debate and action by Congress, could not shoot first. Roosevelt, misled by Japanese ship movements in the Far East, evidently expected the blow to fall on British Malaya or perhaps on the Philippines. No one in high authority in Washington seems to have believed that the Japanese were either strong enough or foolhardy enough to lash out at Hawaii.

December 7, 1941, U.S.S. *Cassin* and U.S.S. *Downes* Damaged by Japanese Attack on Pearl Harbor. From the National Archives, courtesy Navy Department

But the paralyzing blow struck Pearl Harbor, while Tokyo was deliberately prolonging negotiations in Washington. Japanese bombers, winging in from distant aircraft carriers, attacked without warning on the "Black Sunday" morning of December 7, 1941. It was a date, as Roosevelt told Congress, "which will live in infamy." About three thousand casualties were inflicted on American personnel; many aircraft were destroyed; the battleship fleet was virtually wiped out when all eight of the craft were sunk or otherwise immobilized; and numerous small vessels were damaged or destroyed. Fortunately for America, three priceless aircraft carriers happened to be outside the harbor.

An angered Congress, the next day, officially recognized the war that had been "thrust" upon the United States. The roll call in the Senate and House lacked only one vote of unanimity. Germany and Italy, allies of Japan, spared Congress the indecision of debate by declaring war on December 11, 1941. This challenge was formally accepted on the same day by a unanimous vote of both Senate and House. The unofficial war, of many months' duration, was now official.

America's Transformation from Bystander to Belligerent

Roosevelt's war message to Congress began with these famous words, "Yesterday, December 7, 1941—a date which will live in infamy—the United States of America was suddenly and deliberately attacked by naval and air forces of the Empire of Japan."

Japan's hara-kiri gamble in Hawaii paid off only in the short run. True, the Pacific fleet was largely destroyed or immobilized, but the sneak attack aroused and united America as almost nothing else could have done. To the very day of the blowup, a strong majority of Americans still wanted to keep out of war. But the bombs that pulverized Pearl Harbor blasted the isolationists into silence. The only thing left to do, growled Senator Wheeler, was "to lick hell out of them."

But Pearl Harbor was not the full answer to the question as to why the United States went to war. This treacherous attack was but the last explosion in a long chain reaction. Following the fall of France, Americans were confronted with a devil's dilemma. They desired above all to stay out of the conflict; yet they did not want Britain to be knocked out. They wished to halt Japan's conquests in the Far East —conquests that menaced not only American trade and security but international peace as well. To keep Britain from collapsing, the Roosevelt administration felt compelled to extend the unneutral aid that invited attacks from German submarines. To keep Japan from expanding, Washington undertook to cut off vital Japanese supplies and invite possible retaliation. Rather than let democracy die and dictatorship rule supreme, a strong majority of citizens were evidently determined to support a policy that might lead to war. It did.

Clearheaded Americans had come to the conclusion that no nation was safe in an era of international anarchy. Appeasement—the process of throwing the weaker persons out of the sleigh to the pursuing wolves—had been tried, but it had merely whetted dictatorial appetites. Power-drunk dictators had flouted international law and decency. Pursuing the philosophy that might makes right, they had cynically negotiated non-aggression treaties with their intended victims, merely to lull them into a false sense of security. Most Americans were determined to stand firm—and let war come if it must—because they were convinced that with ruthless dictators on the loose the world could not long remain half enchained and half free.

SELECT READINGS

Useful overviews are provided by R. A. DIVINE, *The Reluctant Belligerent: American Entry into World War II* (1965)* and DEXTER PERKINS, *The New Age of Franklin Roosevelt, 1932–1945* (1957).* More detailed are D. F. DRUMMOND's incisive *The Passing of American Neutrality, 1937–1941* (1955) and the classic volumes of W. L. LANGER and S. E. GLEASON, *The Challenge to Isolation, 1937–1940* (1952)* and *The Undeclared War, 1940–1941* (1953).* A Pulitzer-prize interpretation by one of FDR's ghost writers is R. E. SHERWOOD,

Roosevelt and Hopkins (1948).* See also J. W. PRATT, *Cordell Hull, 1933–1944* (2 vols., 1964). On Good Neighborism consult BRYCE WOOD, *The Making of the Good Neighbor Policy* (1961)* and D. M. DOZER, *Are We Good Neighbors?* (1959). Aspects of isolation are ably handled in R. A. DIVINE, *The Illusion of Neutrality* (1962),* W. S. COLE, *Gerald P. Nye and American Foreign Relations* (1962), and MANFRED JONAS, *Isolationism in America, 1935–1941* (1966).*

Regarding the rise of the dictators see F. J. TAYLOR, *The United States and The Spanish Civil War* (1956); ALLEN GUTTMANN, *The Wound in the Heart* [Spanish Civil War] (1962); and DOROTHY BORG, *The United States and the Far Eastern Crisis of 1933–1938* (1964). Revealing is R. H. DAWSON, *The Decision to Aid Russia, 1941* (1959). Aspects of relations with Japan are treated in W. L. NEUMANN, *America Encounters Japan* (1963)*; P. W. SCHROEDER, *The Axis Alliance and Japanese-American Relations, 1941* (1958); and R. J. C. BUTOW, *Tojo and the Coming of the War* (1961).* The preliminaries to war with Japan are well presented in HERBERT FEIS, *The Road to Pearl Harbor* (1950)* and ROBERTA WOHLSTETTER, *Pearl Harbor: Warning and Decision* (1962).* Also references for preceding chapter and *Harvard Guide,** Pt. VI.

* Available in paperback.

44

America in World War II

Never before have we had so little time in which to do so much.

President Roosevelt, 1942

The Allies Trade Space for Time

America was plunged into the inferno of World War II with the most stupefying and humiliating military defeat in her history. In the dismal months that ensued, the democratic world teetered on the edge of disaster.

Japan's fanatics forgot that when one stabs a king, one must stab to kill. A wounded but still potent American giant pulled himself out of the mud of Pearl Harbor, grimly determined to avenge the bloody treachery. "Get Hirohito first" was the cry that rose from millions of infuriated Americans, especially on the Pacific Coast. These outraged souls regarded America's share in the global conflict as a private war of vengeance in the Pacific, with the European front a kind of holding operation.

Washington, in harmony with the British, had wisely adopted the grand strategy of "getting Hitler first." If America diverted her main strength to the Pacific, Hitler might crush both Russia and Britain, and then emerge unconquerable in Fortress Europe. But if Germany was knocked out first, the combined Allied forces could be concentrated on Japan, and her daring game of conquest would be up. Meanwhile enough American strength would be sent to the Pacific to prevent the Nipponese from digging in too deeply.

The get-Hitler-first strategy was retained. But it encountered much ignorant criticism from two-fisted Americans who, according to opinion polls, at one time constituted a plurality. Aggrieved protests were also registered by shorthanded American commanders in the Pacific, and by Chinese and Australian allies. But Roosevelt, a competent strategist in his own right, was able to resist these pressures.

Given time, the Allies seemed bound to triumph. But would they be given time? True, they had on their side the great mass of the world's population, but the wolf is never frightened by the number of the sheep. The United States was the mightiest military power on earth—potentially. But wars are won with weapons, not blueprints. Indeed, America came perilously close to losing the war to the well-armed aggressors before she could begin to throw her full weight into the scales.

Time, in a sense, was the most-needed munition. Expense was no limitation. The overpowering problem confronting America was to retool herself for all-out war production, while praying that the dictators would not meanwhile crush the democracies. Haste was all the more imperative because the highly skilled German scientists might turn up with unbeatable secret weapons—as they almost did.

America's task was far more complex and backbreaking than during World War I. She had to feed, clothe, and arm herself, as well as transport her forces to regions as far separated as Britain and Burma. More than that, she had to send a vast amount of food and munitions to her hard-pressed allies, who stretched all the way from Russia to Australia. Could the American people, reputedly "gone soft," measure up to this colossal responsibility? Was democracy "rotten" and "decadent," as the dictators sneeringly proclaimed?

"All Tangled Up." Wartime Priorities and Shortages. Courtesy Richmond *Times-Dispatch*

Unity at Home and Abroad

National unity was no worry, thanks to the electrifying blow of the Japanese at Pearl Harbor. The cynical aggressions of the dictators had laid nakedly bare the issue of survival. This time America was not out to make the world safe for democracy, but to make the world safe—for decency. The handful of strutting pro-Hitlerites in the United States melted away, while millions of Italian-Americans and German-Americans loyally supported the nation's war program. Communists and "fellow travelers," who had decried the Anglo-French "imperialist war" before Hitler attacked Stalin in 1941, now clamored for an all-out assault on the Axis powers. There was no witch-hunting persecution of dissenting groups, as in World War I.

About 110,000 Japanese-Americans, concentrated on the Pacific Coast, provided a painful exception. The Washington top command, fearing that they might act as saboteurs for the Mikado in case of invasion, decided to herd them together in concentration camps,

Japanese Evacuation Sale.
Library of Congress.

American song titles aimed at the Japanese after Pearl Harbor were "Slap the Jap Right Off the Map," "We'll Knock the Japs Right into the Laps of the Nazis," "You're a Sap, Mr. Jap," "We're Gonna Have to Slap the Dirty Little Jap," "They're Going to be Playing Taps for the Japs," "The Japs Haven't Got a Chinaman's Chance," "Goodbye, Momma, I'm Off to Yokohama," "We are the Sons of the Rising Guns," "Oh, You Little Son of an Oriental," "To be Specific, It's Our Pacific," "When Those Little Yellow Bellies Meet the Cohens and the Kelleys," and "The Sun will Soon be Setting on the Land of the Rising Sun."

though about two-thirds of them were American-born citizens. This brutal precaution turned out to be unnecessary, for the loyalty and combat record of the Japanese-Americans, especially those from Hawaii, proved to be admirable.* Partial financial compensation after the war did something to recompense these uprooted citizens for their sufferings and losses.

Black Americans generally supported the war effort. Though resenting inequalities at home, including segregated blood banks, they saw no future in Hitler's cremation-camp "final solution." Nearly 700,000 Negro draftees were serving in the army at the war's end, or about one-ninth of the total. Less discriminated against than in World War I, they were still generally assigned to service branches rather than combat units. Some of them saw bloody action in Europe and the Pacific. As during 1917–1918, tens of thousands of civilians migrated from the South to the North and West to work in war industries, and explosive tensions developed over housing and segregated facilities. The worst of a series of outbursts was the frightful race riot which rocked Detroit in 1943, resulting in the death of twenty-five blacks and nine whites. Disorders were finally quelled by federal troops.

World War II was no idealistic crusade, as in 1917–1918. The appropriate agencies in Washington did make some effort to propagandize abroad with the Atlantic Charter, as well as with other hope-giving Rooseveltian pronouncements. But the accent was on action. Americans realized that they had before them a dirty job, and that the only way out was forward. They did their killing coldly, methodically, calculatingly, efficiently. It was not a singing war, as in 1917–1918. "Praise the Lord and Pass the Ammunition" enjoyed some vogue, as did "God Bless America." But the latter was a song of consecration rather than of excitation.

An unexpected degree of unity was also achieved among the Allies, thanks in part to the jolting effect of Pearl Harbor. On January 1, 1942, the representatives of twenty-six countries, including the United States, signed in Washington the Declaration of the United Nations. This group, which formed the nucleus of the yet unborn United Nations Organization, pledged itself to fight four-square, under the principles of the Atlantic Charter, and not to make separate peaces.

Latin American republics, their largest sister the victim of a treacherous attack, rallied behind the once-hated Colossus of the North. The one conspicuous exception was Fascist-inclined Argentina, with its large Italian and German population and with its burning jealousy of rich Uncle Sam, a competitor in beef and grain. Yet the Good

* A future U.S. Senator from Hawaii, Senator Inouye, lost an arm in Italy while fighting with a much-decorated Japanese-American unit.

Neighbor policy of the 1930's reaped a happy harvest during these anxious years. Pan-Americanism became more a fact than a phrase, as the Yankees spent billions of dollars in Latin America for tin, nitrates, and other urgently needed materials.

Aid to the ever-suspicious Soviets claimed a high priority. Dedicated to the destruction of capitalism through Communism, the Russians accepted distrustfully the vast amount of munitions provided by their American stepbrothers-in-arms. Lend-lease materials from the United States in time made up only about 10% of the total military equipment of the Soviet Union. But these contributions came in the form of desperately needed trucks, automobiles, military aircraft, and other equipment, without which the Russians probably could not have smashed their way to Berlin.

Smokestacks Go to War

America was already partially geared for a war economy when the galvanizing blow fell at Pearl Harbor. Allied orders for munitions, plus lend-lease operations and defense appropriations, had all contributed to the chassis of a mighty war-production machine. But at the outset the nation was only ankle-deep in the conflict.

Vital materials were in dangerously short supply, partly because the Republic had failed to stockpile enough needed commodities. When the Japanese overran British Malaya and the Dutch East Indies, shortly after Pearl Harbor, they snapped America's lifeline of natural rubber, and cut off most of her essential tin and quinine. Supplements or substitutes for these critical items, especially rubber, were urgently needed—and eventually were found. Most spectacular of all was the creation of a huge synthetic rubber industry, which had to be started from scratch. After much fumbling, it was brought into production just in the nick of time by "Rubber Czar" William M. Jeffers, president of the Union Pacific Railroad.

First things had to come first. The War Production Board, under genial Donald M. Nelson, vice-president of Sears, Roebuck and Company, halted non-essential building in order to conserve materials for war purposes. Priorities were set up for most industries. "Dollar-a-year men" in Washington worked at a desperate pace, and as the red tape slowly unwound they did not even have time, quipsters said, for a nervous breakdown.

Rationing goods to the consumer was undertaken on a huge scale for the first time in American experience. Voluntary "Hooverizing," as in 1917–1918, was not enough. Ration tickets were issued for butter, meat, gasoline, and other necessities; and on the whole the system worked well. But a minority of selfish souls patronized illegal sellers of goods, known as "black marketeers" and "meatleggers."

A booming wartime economy boosted prices somewhat, as the

"The Three Musketeers," F.D.R., Stalin, and Churchill, drawn by Manning in the Phoenix *Arizona Republic*; reprinted by permission of the McNaught Syndicate, Inc.

sneaky hand of inflation robbed every pay envelope. Among various agencies, the Office of Price Administration was set up, and it helped to keep rents and commodity prices within reasonable bounds.

America's Prodigies of Production

Labor, which felt the pinch of mild inflation, had to be kept happy if high production quotas were to be attained. The A.F. of L. and the C.I.O. were among the important groups that joined in no-strike pledges, with the understanding that the government would hold the lid on the cost of living. Yet prices continued to inch upward, and a rash of strikes broke out, some of them "wildcat" strikes, not authorized by union leaders. Noteworthy among the troublemaking groups were the United Mine Workers, who several times were called out on strike against the coal operators by their crusty and iron-willed leader, John L. Lewis. The accident-ridden miners, who harbored genuine grievances, finally won coveted concessions after Lewis had defied Washington and had temporarily jeopardized the war effort.

Threats of lost production through strikes became so serious that Congress, in June, 1943, passed the Smith-Connally Anti-Strike Act. It authorized the seizure and operation by the federal government of tied-up industries. Strikes against any industry thus operated were made a criminal offense. Under the Smith-Connally Act, Washington seized and ran the coal mines and, for a brief period, the railroads. Yet work stoppages, dangerous though they were, actually accounted for less than 1% of the total working time of the nation's laboring force during the war—a record better than blockaded Britain's. American workingmen, on the whole, were magnificently efficient.

Agricultural production was one of the miracles of these anxious years. Though shorthanded because of the armed services, the farmers rolled up their sleeves and produced bumper crops. Providentially, as in 1917–1918, weather conditions were unusually favorable. Farm income, despite price controls, more than doubled, as countless mortgages were joyously paid off. The blue-jeaned farmers had probably never before been so prosperous, though they had to labor long hours to provide "food for freedom." Their sweat was supplemented, as in 1917–1918, by countless volunteer green-thumbers, who hopefully planted "victory gardens" in back yards and vacant lots.

The Battle of Production was clearly won by 1943. Unemployment became only a bad dream, as such agencies as the Civilian Conservation Corps and the Works Progress Administration received an "honorable discharge." President Roosevelt, in fact, declared that "Dr. New Deal" had given way to "Dr. Win the War." But the abounding prosperity was in some degree misleading. The inflation

"What Price Ceiling?" 1942. Labor Costs Rise Before Controls Imposed. Los Angeles *Times*, copyright Los Angeles *Times*. Reprinted by permission

squeeze, though fairly well controlled, was pinching white-collar workers and others on fixed incomes.

Warriors, Women, and War Bonds

All told, the armed services enrolled more than 15,000,000 men and women. The draft was tightened after Pearl Harbor, as millions of young men were plucked from their homes and clothed in "G.I." (government issue) outfits. Scores of training camps peppered the land, while the training of officer material went forward rapidly in the colleges. With an eye to the long pull, draft deferments were often granted to key workers in industry and agriculture, as in World War I.

Women desk-warriors came into their own. They had been used sparingly in 1917–1918, but now some 216,000 of them were efficiently employed for non-combat duties, chiefly clerical. Best-known of these "women in arms" were the WACS (Army), WAVES (Navy), Marines,* and SPARS (Coast Guard).

The "War for Survival" of 1941–1945, more than that of 1917–1918, was an all-out conflict. Old folks came out of retirement "for the duration" to serve in industry, or as air-raid wardens in civilian defense. Western Union telegraph "boys" were often elderly men. Women were drawn from the home into war work, even into the heavier industries such as shipbuilding, where "Rosie the Riveter" won laurels. But Rosie's untended children, many with the home door key tied to a string around their necks, were inclined to run wild. An alarming wave of juvenile delinquency—often caused by parental delinquency—accompanied and followed the war.

Shipbuilding, as in 1917–1918, was pressed at a frantic pace in an effort to outrace the deadly submarine. The output of the shipyards, partly as a result of the use of prefabricated materials, was no less phenomenal than that of the industrial plants. A leading miracle-man shipbuilder was Henry J. Kaiser, who was dubbed "Sir Launchalot": one of his ships was assembled within five days, complete with life belts and coat hangers. In 1943 alone American shipyards produced a formidable navy. Long before the shooting stopped, the United States had incomparably the mightiest merchant fleet the world had ever seen. (See chart, p. 774).

The conflict proved to be prodigiously expensive. The total bill was about $330,000,000,000—or many times the cost of World War I—and this figure ran the total national debt from $48,961,000,000, in June, 1941, to $258,682,000,000 in June, 1945. When production finally got into high gear, the war was costing about a quarter of a billion dollars a day.

A strict pay-as-you-go policy was clearly too burdensome.

Poster appeals and slogans urging women to enlist in the WAAC's (Women's Army Auxiliary Corps) were, "Speed Them Back, Join the WAAC," "I'd Rather Be with Them—than Waiting for them," "Back the Attack, Be a WAAC! For America is Calling," and (a song throwback to World War I) "The WAACS and WAVES Will Win The War, Parlez Vous."

* The U.S. Marine Corps refused to use the designation "Marinettes."

Borrowing was the answer. About three-fifths of the total war costs were raised by selling interest-bearing bonds, redeemable by the Treasury in the future, as in 1917–1918. Altogether, there were eight high-pressure War Bond drives, all of them oversubscribed. An effective new wrinkle was added when regular deductions, with the consent of the worker, were taken from pay envelopes for bond purchases.

About one-third of the colossal war cost was paid by the government out of current revenue. This achievement was not unduly difficult, for the national income shot up to about $200,000,000,000 a year and taxes generally received a sharp boost. The list included income taxes, corporation taxes, excess profits taxes, and "nuisance" taxes on various luxuries, like diamonds and furs. Some slight but welcome relief was afforded the American taxpayer by "reverse lend-lease"—a process by which the Allies supplied about $7,819,000,000 in goods and services against their total lend-lease bill of $50,692,000,000.

The Rising Sun in the Pacific

Early successes of the efficient Japanese militarists were breathtaking: they realized that they would have to win quickly or lose slowly. Seldom, if ever, has so much been conquered so rapidly with so little loss.

Simultaneously with the assault on Pearl Harbor, the Japanese launched widespread and uniformly successful attacks on various Far Eastern bastions. These included the American outposts of Guam, Wake, and the Philippines. In a dismayingly short time, the Nipponese invader seized not only the British-Chinese port of Hong Kong but also British Malaya, with its critically important supplies of rubber and tin.

Nor did the Nipponese tide stop there. The undersized but over-ambitious soldiers of the Emperor, plunging into the snake-infested jungles of Burma, cut the famed Burma road. This was the route over which the United States had been trucking a trickle of munitions to the armies of the Chinese Generalissimo Chiang Kai-shek, who was still resisting the Japanese invader in China. Thereafter intrepid American aviators were forced to fly a handful of war supplies to Chiang "over the hump" of the towering Himalaya Mountains from the India-Burma theater. Meanwhile the Japanese had lunged southward against the Dutch East Indies, with their rich oil resources. The jungle-matted islands speedily fell to the assailant, after the combined British, Australian, Dutch, and American naval and air forces had been smashed by their numerically superior foe.

Better news came from the Philippines, which succeeded dramatically in slowing down the Mikado's warriors for five months. The

Japanese promptly landed a small but effective army, and General Douglas MacArthur, the statuesque American commander, withdrew to a strong defensive position at Bataan, not far from Manila. There about 20,000 American troops, supported by a much larger force of ill-trained Filipinos, held off violent Japanese attacks until April 9, 1942. The defenders, reduced to eating mules and monkeys, heroically traded their lives for time in the face of hopeless odds. They grimly felt while vainly hoping for reinforcements:

We're the battling bastards of Bataan;
No Mamma, no Papa, no Uncle Sam. . . .

Before the inevitable American surrender, General MacArthur was ordered by Washington to depart secretly for Australia, there to head resistance against the Japanese. Leaving by motorboat and airplane, he proclaimed, "I shall return." After the battered remnants of his army had hoisted the white flag, they were treated with vicious cruelty in the infamous 85-mile Bataan death march. The island fortress of Corregidor, in Manila Harbor, held out until May 6, 1942, when it surrendered and left Japanese forces in control of the Philippine archipelago.

CORREGIDOR–BATAAN

Japan's High Tide at Midway

The aggressive little men from Nippon, making hay while the Rising Sun shone, pushed relentlessly southward. They invaded the turtle-shaped island of New Guinea, north of Australia, and landed on the Solomon Islands, from which they threatened Australia itself. Their onrush was finally checked by a crucial naval battle fought in the Coral Sea, in May, 1942. An American carrier task force, with Australian support, inflicted heavy losses on the victory-flushed Nipponese. For the first time in history the fighting was all done by carrier-based aircraft, and neither fleet saw or fired a shot at the other.

Japan next undertook to seize Midway Island, more than a thousand miles northwest of Honolulu. From this strategic base, she could launch devastating assaults on Pearl Harbor, and perhaps force the weakened American Pacific fleet into destructive combat. A crucial naval battle was fought near Midway, June 3–6, 1942. Admiral Chester W. Nimitz, a high-grade naval strategist, directed a skillfully maneuvered but inferior carrier force, under Admiral Raymond A. Spruance, against the powerful invading fleet. The fighting was all done by aircraft, and the Japanese broke off action after losing four vitally important carriers.

The smashing success at Midway, combined with the Battle of the Coral Sea, turned the tide of Japan's conquest. But the thrust of the Nipponese into the eastern Pacific did net them America's fog-girt islands of Kiska and Attu, in the Aleutian archipelago, off Alaska.

Japanese Cruiser Sinking at Midway, June, 1942. Courtesy Navy Department, National Archives 80–G–414422

This easy conquest aroused fear of an invasion of the United States from the northwest. Much American strength was consequently diverted to the defense of Alaska, including the construction of the "Alcan" highway through Canada.

Yet the Japanese imperialists, overextended in 1942, suffered from "victory disease." Their appetites were bigger than their stomachs. If they had only dug in and consolidated their gains, they would have been much more difficult to dislodge.

American Leapfrogging toward Tokyo

Following the exhilarating victory at Midway, the United States for the first time was able to seize the initiative in the Pacific. In August, 1942, American ground forces gained a toe hold on Guadalcanal Island, in the Solomons, in an effort to protect the lifeline from America to Australia through the Southwest Pacific. An early naval defeat inflicted by the Japanese shortened American supplies dangerously, and for weeks the United States troops held onto the

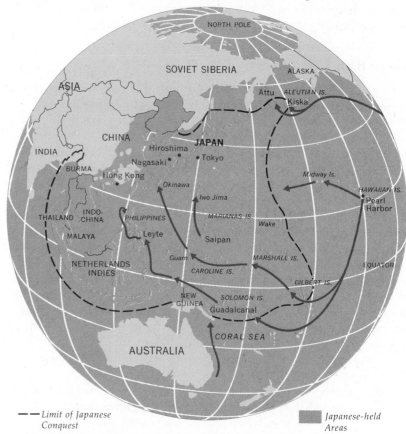

— —Limit of Japanese Conquest

Japanese-held Areas

UNITED STATES THRUSTS IN THE PACIFIC, 1942–1945

malarial island only by their fingernails. After four desperate sea battles for naval control, the Japanese troops evacuated Guadalcanal in February, 1943.

American and Australian forces, under General MacArthur, meanwhile had been hanging on grimly to the southeastern tip of New Guinea, the last buffer protecting Australia. The scales of war gradually began to tip as the American navy, including submarines, inflicted lethal losses on Japanese supply ships and troop carriers. Conquest of the north coast of New Guinea was completed by August, 1944, after General MacArthur had fought his way westward through green jungle hells. This hard-won victory was the first leg on the long return journey to the Philippines.

The United States navy, with marines and army divisions doing the meat-grinder fighting, had meanwhile been leapfrogging the Japanese islands in the Pacific. Old-fashioned strategy required that the American forces, as they drove toward Tokyo, should reduce the fortified Japanese outposts on their flank. This course would have taken many bloodstained months, for the holed-in defenders were prepared to die to the last man in their caves. The new strategy of island hopping ("leapfrogging") called for bypassing some of the most heavily fortified Japanese posts, capturing nearby islands, setting up airfields on them, and then neutralizing the enemy bases through heavy bombing. Deprived of supplies from the homeland, the Mikado's outposts would slowly wither on the vine—as they did.

Admiral Chester W. Nimitz. National Archives.

Brilliant success crowned the American attacks on the Japanese island strongholds in the Pacific, where Admiral Nimitz skillfully coordinated the efforts of naval, air, and ground units. In May and August of 1943, Attu and Kiska in the Aleutians were easily retaken. In November, 1943, "bloody Tarawa" and Makin, both in the Gilbert Islands, fell after suicidal resistance. In January and February, 1944, the key outposts of the Marshall group succumbed after savage fighting.

Especially prized islands were the Marianas, of which America's conquered Guam was one. They were spacious enough to provide abundant airfields for American super-bombers, and they were close enough to Japan to permit round-trip bombing. After fanatical resistance, the major islands fell to the American attackers in July and August, 1944. With these unsinkable aircraft carriers now available, the first sustained air attacks on Japan were launched by giant bombers in November, 1944.

The Allied Halting of Hitler

Early setbacks for America in the Pacific were paralleled in the Atlantic. Hitler had entered the war with a formidable fleet of ultra-modern submarines, which operated in "wolf packs" with frightful

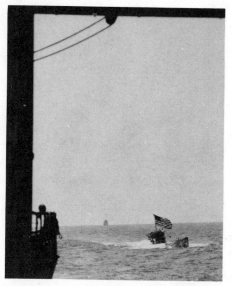

Captured German Submarine
Being Towed (1944). Courtesy
Navy Department, National
Archives 80–G–446950

effect, especially in the North Atlantic, the Caribbean, and the Gulf of Mexico. During ten months of 1942 more than 500 merchantmen were reported lost—111 in June alone—as ship destruction far outran construction.

The tide of subsea battle turned with agonizing slowness. Old techniques, such as escorting convoys of merchantmen and dropping depth bombs from destroyers, were strengthened by air patrol, radar, and the bombing of submarine bases. "Keep 'Em Sailing" was the motto of begrimed merchant seamen, hundreds of whom perished as unsung heroes in icy seas.

Not until the spring of 1943 did the Allies clearly have the upper hand against the U-boat. If they had not won the Battle of the Atlantic, Britain would have been forced under, and a second front could not have been launched from her island springboard. Victory over the undersea raiders was nerve-rackingly narrow. When the war ended, Hitler was about to mass-produce a fearsome new submarine—one that could remain under water indefinitely and cruise at seventeen knots when submerged.

Meanwhile, the turning point of the land-air war against Hitler had come late in 1942. The British, who had launched a 1000-plane raid on Cologne in May, were now cascading bombs, with American help, on German cities. The Germans under Marshal Rommel—"the Desert Fox"—had driven across the hot sands of North Africa into Egypt, perilously close to the Suez Canal. A break-through would have spelled disaster for the Allies. But late in October, 1942, the

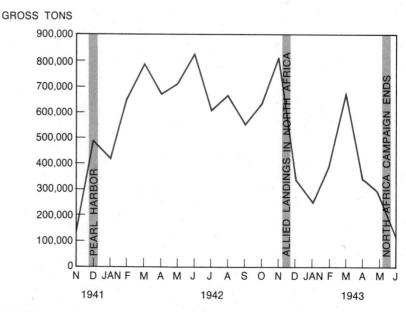

MERCHANT TONNAGE SUNK BY U-BOATS, NOV., 1941–June, 1943

British General Montgomery delivered a withering attack. With the aid of several hundred hastily shipped American Sherman tanks, he speedily drove the enemy back to Tunis, more than a thousand miles away.

On the Soviet front, the unexpected successes of the Red Army gave a new lift to the Allied cause. In September, 1942, the Russians halted the German steam roller at rubble-bestrewn Stalingrad, graveyard of Hitler's hopes. More than a score of invading divisions, caught in an icy noose, later surrendered or were "mopped up." In November, 1942, the elated Russians unleashed a crushing counter-offensive, which was never seriously reversed. A year later, Stalin had regained about two-thirds of the blood-soaked Russian motherland wrested from him by the Teutonic invader.

Prime Minister Churchill observed in a speech (May, 1943), "The proud German Army has by its sudden collapse, sudden crumbling and breaking up . . . once again proved the truth of the saying, 'The Hun [German] is always either at your throat or at your feet.'"

The North African Second Front

Soviet leaders meanwhile had never ceased to clamor for an Anglo-American second front—a demand stridently supported by American Communists. Red divisions were doing practically all of the mud-and-blood fighting against Hitler's armies, and Moscow insisted that the Allies get into the war and drain off their fair share of the invader's strength. Russian officials did not regard the American operations in the Pacific as helpful, nor did they look upon the allied aerial blasting of Germany as a second front at all.

Many Americans were eager to begin a diversionary invasion of France in 1942 or in 1943, while Russia was still afloat. Fears prevailed that the Soviets, unable to hold out against Germany, might make a separate peace, as they had in 1918, and leave the western Allies to face the fury of Hitler alone. The British, remembering their fearful losses in 1914–1918, were not enthusiastic about a frontal assault on German-held France. It might end in complete disaster. They preferred to attack Hitler's Fortress Europe through the "soft underbelly" of the Mediterranean, while gathering strength for a cross-channel thrust.

An invasion of French-held North Africa was a compromise second front. It seemed less risky than a premature descent upon the coast of France, yet it would serve as a partial answer to the demands of the Russians for a diversion. If successful, it would open the Axis-dominated Mediterranean to life-line communication with India and other parts of Asia.

The highly secret Allied attack on North Africa, launched in November, 1942, was headed by a gifted and easy-smiling American general, Dwight D. ("Ike") Eisenhower, a master of organization and conciliation. As a joint Allied operation ultimately involving some 400,000 men (British, Canadian, French, and chiefly American), the invasion was the mightiest water-borne effort up to that time in history. About 850 ships of various sorts were employed.

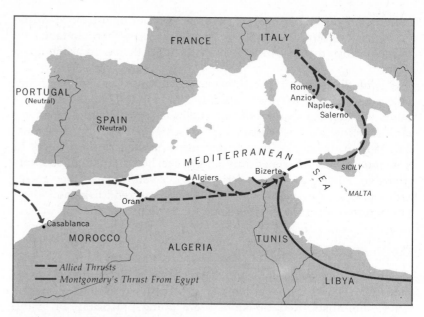

ALLIED THRUSTS IN NORTH AFRICA
AND ITALY, 1942–1945

At the outset, the surprise landing in North Africa was highly successful. The neutralized French, both anti-Hitler and pro-Ally, put up only a token resistance. After savage fighting with the Germans, who inflicted one sharp setback on the green Americans, the remnants of the German-Italian army were finally trapped in Tunis. Some 266,000 dazed survivors surrendered in May, 1943.

The North African campaign, though redeeming one continent, in itself was not conclusive. It was not the beginning of the end, but "the end of the beginning." Certain Russian spokesmen scoffed at this second-rate second front, but valuable lessons were learned for the full-fledged invasion of France.

The Rough Road to Rome

New blows were now planned by the Allies. At Casablanca, in newly occupied French Morocco, President Roosevelt, who had boldly flown the Atlantic, met in a historic conference with Winston Churchill in January, 1943. The Big Two agreed to step up the Pacific war, invade Sicily, increase pressure on Italy, and insist upon an "unconditional surrender" of the enemy—a phrase popularized by General Grant during the Civil War. Such an unyielding policy would presumably hearten the ultra-suspicious Soviets, who professed to fear separate Allied peace negotiations. It would also forestall charges of broken armistice terms, such as had come after 1918.

Proclaiming "unconditional surrender" was one of the most controversial moves of the war. The main criticism was that it steeled the enemy to fight to a last-bunker resistance, while discouraging anti-war groups in Germany from revolting. Although there was no doubt some truth in these charges, no one can prove that "unconditional surrender" either shortened or lengthened the war. But by helping to destroy the German government utterly, the harsh policy immensely complicated the problems of reconstruction.

The victorious Allied forces—American, British, and Canadian—now turned against the not-so-soft underbelly of Europe. Sicily fell, in August, 1943, after sporadic but sometimes bitter resistance. Shortly before the conquest of the island, Mussolini was deposed and a new Rome government was set up. Italy surrendered unconditionally early in September, 1943, while Allied troops were pouring onto the toe of the Italian boot. President Roosevelt, referring to the three original Axis accomplices—Germany, Italy, and Japan—joked grimly that it was now one down and two to go. Two years later Mussolini, together with his attractive mistress, was brutally lynched by his own people. Both bodies were ingloriously hung up by the heels for public display.

But if Italy dropped out of the war, the Germans did not drop out of Italy. Hitler's well-trained troops resisted the Allied invaders with methodical and infuriating stubbornness. The luckless Italians, turning their coats, declared war on Germany in October, 1943. "Sunny Italy" proceeded to belie her name, for in the snow-covered and mud-caked mountains of her elongated peninsula occurred some of the muddiest, bloodiest, and most frustrating fighting of the war.

For many months Italy seemed to be a dead end. After a touch-and-go assault on the Anzio beachhead, Rome was taken on June 4, 1944. Two days later, when the tremendous cross-channel invasion of France began, Italy became a kind of sideshow. But the Allies, with limited manpower, continued to fight their way slowly and painfully into northern Italy. On May 2, 1945, only five days before Germany's official surrender, several hundred thousand Axis troops laid down their arms.

The Italian campaign, though agonizingly slow, was by no means fruitless. It opened the Mediterranean, diverted some German divisions from the blazing Russian and French fronts, and provided air bases for bombing assaults on German Austria and southern Germany.

At a Washington press conference (May 25, 1943), visiting Prime Minister Churchill was asked how collapsing Italy should be treated. He replied, "All we can do is to apply the physical stimuli which we have at our disposal to bring about a change of mind in these recalcitrant persons. Of this you may be sure: we shall continue to operate on the Italian donkey at both ends, with a carrot and with a stick."

Eisenhower's D-Day Invasion of France

The Russians had never ceased their clamor for an all-out second front, and the time rapidly approached for the coordination of promised efforts. Marshal Joseph Stalin, with a careful eye on Russian military operations, was loath to leave the Soviet Union. President Roosevelt, who jauntily remarked in private, "I can handle that old buzzard," was eager to confer with him. The President seemed confident that Rooseveltian charm could woo the hardened conspirator of the Kremlin from his nasty Communist ways.

Teheran, the capital of Iran, was finally chosen as the meeting place. To this ancient city Roosevelt riskily flew, after a stop-over conference in Cairo with Britain's Churchill and China's Chiang Kai-shek regarding the war against Japan. At Teheran the discussions between Stalin, Roosevelt, and Churchill—November 28 to December 1, 1943—progressed smoothly. Perhaps the most important achievement was agreement on broad plans, especially those for launching Russian attacks on Germany from the east simultaneously with the prospective Allied assault from the west.

Preparations for the cross-channel invasion of France were gigantic. Britain's fast-anchored isle virtually groaned with munitions, supplies, and troops, as nearly 3,000,000 fighting men were readied. As the United States was to provide most of the Allied warriors, the over-all command was entrusted to an American, General Eisenhower. He had already distinguished himself in the North African and Mediterranean campaigns, not only for his military capacity but also for his gifts as a conciliator of clashing Allied interests.

French Normandy, less heavily fortified than other beaches, was pinpointed for the invasion assault. On D-Day, June 6, 1944, the

Allies Landing in Normandy, June 6, 1944. Wide World, Inc. photo

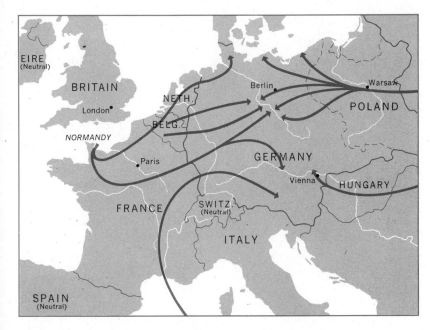

FINAL ALLIED THRUSTS IN EUROPE, 1944–1945

enormous operation, which involved some 4600 vessels, unwound. Stiff resistance was encountered from the Germans, who had been misled by a feint into expecting the blow to fall farther north. The Allies quickly achieved mastery of the air over France. They were thus able to block reinforcements by crippling the railroads, while increasing fuel shortages by bombing gasoline manufacturing plants in Germany.

The Allied beachhead, at first clung to with finger tips, was gradually enlarged, consolidated, and reinforced. After desperate fighting, the invaders finally broke out of the German iron ring at the base of the Normandy peninsula. Most spectacular were the lunges across France by American armored divisions, brilliantly commanded by blustery and profane General George S. ("Blood 'n' Guts") Patton. The retreat of the German defenders was hastened when an American-French force landed in August, 1944, on the southern coast of France and swept northward. With the assistance of the French "underground," Paris was liberated in August, 1944, amid exuberant manifestations of joy and gratitude.

Allied forces rolled irresistibly toward Germany, and many of the Americans encountered places, like Château-Thierry, familiar to their fathers in 1918. "Lafayette, we are here again," proclaimed some of the American soldiers jocosely. The first important German city (Aachen) fell to the Americans in October, 1944, and the days of Hitler's "Thousand-Year Empire" seemed to be numbered.

F.D.R.: The Fourth-Termite of '44

The presidential campaign of 1944, which was bound to divert energy from the war program, came most awkwardly as the titanic conflict roared to its climax. But the normal electoral processes continued to function, despite some loose talk of suspending them "for the duration."

Victory-starved Republicans met in Chicago with hopeful enthusiasm. They quickly nominated the short, mustached, and dapper Thomas E. Dewey, popular vote-getting governor of New York. Regarded as a liberal, he had already made a national reputation as a prosecutor in New York City of grafters and racketeers. His shortness and youth—he was only forty-two—had caused Harold Ickes to sneer that the candidate had cast his diaper into the ring. To offset Dewey's anti-isolationism, the convention nominated for the Vice-Presidency a strong isolationist, handsome and white-maned Senator John W. Bricker of Ohio. Yet the platform called for an unstinted prosecution of the war, and for the creation of a new international organization to maintain peace.

Franklin Roosevelt, obviously aging under the strain, was the "indispensable man" of the Democrats. No other major figure was available, and the war was apparently grinding to its grand finale. He was nominated at Chicago on the first ballot by acclamation. But in a sense he was the "forgotten man" of the convention for, in view of his age, an unusual amount of attention was focused on the Vice-Presidency.

The scramble for the vice-presidential plum turned into something of a free-for-all. Henry A. Wallace, one-time "plow 'em under" Secretary of Agriculture, had served four years as Vice-President and desired a renomination. But conservative Democrats distrusted him as an ill-balanced and unpredictable liberal. A "ditch Wallace" move developed tremendous momentum, despite the popularity of Wallace with large numbers of voters and many of the delegates. With Roosevelt's blessing, the vice-presidential nomination finally went to smiling and self-assured Senator Harry S. Truman of Missouri ("the new Missouri Compromise"). Hitherto inconspicuous, he had recently attained national fame as the efficient chairman of a Senate committee conducting an investigation of wasteful war expenditures.

At the Chicago convention of 1944 Roosevelt's pre-Pearl Harbor policies came under sharp attack from Congresswoman Clare Boothe Luce (the "Blonde Bombshell"), who violently charged Roosevelt with having "lied us into war because he did not have the political courage to lead us into it."

Roosevelt Defeats Dewey

A dynamic Dewey took the offensive, for Roosevelt was too busily involved in directing the war to spare much time for speechmaking. The vigorous young "crime buster," with his beautiful baritone voice and polished diction, denounced the tired and quarrelsome "old men" in Washington. He proclaimed repeatedly that after "twelve long years" of New Dealism it was "time for a change." As for the war, Dewey would not alter the basic strategy but would fight it better—a type of "me-tooism" ridiculed by the Democrats. The fourth-term issue did not figure prominently, now that the ice had been broken by Roosevelt's third term. But "Dewey-eyed" Republicans, half-humorously, professed to fear fifth and sixth terms by the "lifer" in the White House.

In the closing weeks of the campaign, Roosevelt left his desk for the stump. He was stung by certain Republican charges, including alleged aspersions on his pet Scottie dog, Fala. He was also eager to show himself, even in chilling rains, to spike well-founded rumors of failing health.

Substantial assistance came from the new Political Action Committee of the C.I.O., which was organized to get around the law banning the direct use of union funds for political purposes. Zealous C.I.O. members, branded as Communists by the Republicans, rang countless doorbells and asked, with pointed reference to the recent depression, "What were you doing in 1932?" At times Roosevelt seemed to be running again against Hoover.

Roosevelt, as customary, won a sweeping victory: 432 to 99 in the Electoral College; 25,602,504 to 22,006,285 in the popular totals. Elated, he quipped that "The first twelve years are the hardest." As in every one of his previous three campaigns, he was opposed by a majority of the newspapers, which were owned chiefly by Republicans. His popular majority declined from 1940, partly because of the absence of many soldiers. Younger people tended to support Roosevelt; and consequently a Democratic Congress had passed a law making it possible for service personnel to vote. But only about one-fourth of them did so, and their absentee ballots did not affect the result materially.

It seems clear that Roosevelt won primarily because the war was going well. A winning pitcher is not ordinarily taken out. Foreign policy was a decisive factor with untold thousands of voters, who concluded that Roosevelt's experienced hand was needed in fashioning a future organization for world peace. Dewey, whom Ickes dubbed "the little man on top of the wedding cake," spoke smoothly of international cooperation, but his isolationist running mate, Bricker, implanted serious doubts. The Republican Party was still suffering from the taint of isolationism fastened on it by the Hardingites.

The Last Days of Hitler

By mid-December, 1944, the month after Roosevelt's fourth-term victory, Germany seemed to be wobbling on her last legs. The Soviet surge had penetrated eastern Germany. Allied aerial "blockbusters,"

Dewey *vs* F.D.R. The People Return a Verdict. Courtesy Washington *Evening Star*

on an around-the-clock schedule, were falling like giant hailstones on cities, factories, and transportation arteries. The German western front seemed about to buckle under the sledge-hammer blows of the Americans and their allies.

Hitler then staked everything on one last throw. Secretly concentrating a powerful force, he hurled it, on December 16, 1944, against the thinly held American lines in the heavily befogged and snow-shrouded Ardennes forest. Caught off guard, the outmanned Americans were driven back, and the key Belgian port of Antwerp was menaced. The ten-day penetration was finally halted after the 101st Airborne Division had stood firm at the vital bastion of Bastogne. The commander, Brigadier General A. C. McAuliffe, defiantly answered the German demand for surrender with one word, "Nuts." Reinforcements were rushed up, and the last-gasp Hitlerian offensive was at length bloodily stemmed in the Battle of the Bulge.

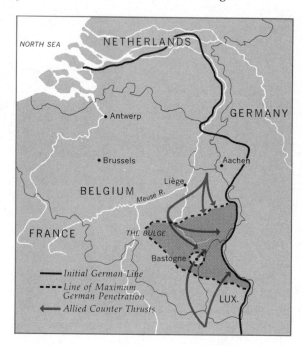

BATTLE OF THE BULGE

In March, 1945, forward-driving American troops reached Germany's Rhine River, where, by incredibly good luck, they found one strategic bridge undemolished. Pressing their advantage, General Eisenhower's troops reached the Elbe River in April, 1945. There, some sixty miles south of Berlin, American and Russian advance guards dramatically clasped hands, amid cries of "*Amerikanskie tovarishchi"* (American comrades). The conquering Americans were horrified to find blood-bespattered and still-stinking concentration camps, where the German Nazis had engaged in scientific mass murder. These horrors, for once, far exceeded the lurid reports of propagandists.

The vengeful Russians, clawing their way forward from the east, reached Berlin in April, 1945. After desperate house-to-house fighting, accompanied by an orgy of pillage and rape, they captured the bomb-shattered city. Adolf Hitler, after a hasty marriage to his mistress, committed suicide with her in a burned-out bunker, April 30, 1945.

Tragedy had meanwhile struck the United States. President Roosevelt, while relaxing at Warm Springs, Georgia, suddenly died from a massive cerebral hemorrhage on April 12, 1945. The crushing burden of twelve years in the White House had finally taken its toll. Knots of confused and leaderless citizens gathered to discuss the future anxiously, as a bewildered and unbriefed Vice-President Truman took the helm.

On May 7, 1945, what was left of the German government surrendered unconditionally. The next day was officially proclaimed V-E Day—Victory in Europe Day—and it was greeted with frenzied rejoicing in the Allied countries.

American and Russian Soldiers Meet in Germany, 1945. U.S. Army photo

Japan Dies Hard

Japan's rickety bamboo empire meantime was tottering to its fall. American submarines—"the silent service"—were sending the Japanese merchant marine to the bottom so fast that they were running out of prey. All told, these underseas craft destroyed 1042 ships, or about 50% of Nippon's entire life-giving merchant fleet.

Giant bomber attacks were more spectacular. Launched from Saipan and other captured Marianas, they were reducing the enemy's fragile cities to cinders. The massive fire-bomb raid on Tokyo, March 9–10, 1945, was annihilating. It destroyed over 250,000 buildings, gutted a quarter of the city, and killed an estimated 83,000 persons— a loss comparable to that later inflicted by atomic bombs.

General MacArthur was also on the move. Completing the conquest of the jungle-cursed New Guinea, he headed northwest for the Philippines, en route to Japan, with 600 ships and 250,000 men. In a scene well staged for the photographers, he splashed ashore at Leyte Island, October 20, 1944, with the summons: "People of the Philippines, I have returned. . . . Rally to me."

Nippon's navy—still menacing—now made one last-chance effort to destroy MacArthur by wiping out his transports and supply ships. A gigantic clash at Leyte Gulf, fought on the sea and in the air, was actually three battles (October 23–26, 1944). The Americans won all of

The Flag Raising at Iwo Jima. Admiral Nimitz said that in the capture of this island, "Uncommon valor was a common virtue." National Archives.

them, though the crucial engagement was almost lost when Admiral William F. ("Bull") Halsey was decoyed away by a feint.

Japan was through as a seapower: she had lost about sixty ships in the greatest naval battle of all time. American fleets, numbering more than 4000 vessels, now commanded Asiatic seas. Several battleships, raised from the mud of Pearl Harbor, were finding belated but sweet revenge.

Overrunning Leyte, MacArthur next landed on the main Philippine island of Luzon, in January, 1945. Manila was his major objective. The ravaged city fell in March but the Philippines were not conquered until July. Victory was purchased only after bitter fighting against holed-in Japanese, who took a toll of over 60,000 American casualties.

America's iron ring was tightening inexorably around Nippon. The tiny island of Iwo Jima, needed as a roosting place for damaged American bombers returning from Japan, was captured in March, 1945. This desperate twenty-five-day assault cost over 4000 American dead.

Okinawa, a well-defended Japanese island, was next on the list: it was needed for closer bases from which to blast and burn enemy cities and industries. Fighting dragged on from April to June of 1945. Nipponese soldiers, fighting with cornered-rat courage from their caves, finally sold Okinawa for 80,000 American casualties, while suffering far heavier losses themselves.

The American navy, which covered the invasion of Okinawa, sustained severe damage. Japanese suicide pilots, in an exhibition of mass hara-kiri for their god-emperor, crashed their bomb-laden planes onto the decks of the invading fleet. All told, they sank over thirty ships and badly damaged scores more. The navy farsightedly had developed floating repair ships and other time-saving new techniques, all of which helped it to keep up the pressure.

Atomic Awfulness

Strategists in Washington were meanwhile planning an all-out invasion of the main islands of Japan—an invasion that presumably would cost hundreds of thousands of American (and Japanese) casualties. Tokyo, recognizing imminent defeat, had secretly sent peace feelers to Russia, which had not yet entered the Far Eastern war. But bomb-scorched Japan still showed no outward willingness to surrender *unconditionally*.

The Potsdam conference, held near Berlin in July, 1945, sounded the death knell of the Japanese. There President Truman, still new on his job, met in a seventeen-day parley with Joseph Stalin and the British leaders. The conferees issued a stern ultimatum to Japan: surrender or be destroyed. American bombers showered the grim warning on Japan in tens of thousands of leaflets, but no encouraging response was forthcoming.

America had a fantastic ace up her sleeve. Early in 1940, after Hitler's wanton assault on Poland, Roosevelt was persuaded by American scientists to push ahead with gigantic preparations for unlocking the secret of an atomic bomb. Congress, on Roosevelt's blank-check request, blindly made available nearly two billion dollars. Many military minds were skeptical of this "damned professor's nonsense," but fear of well-known German scientific progress provided an additional spur.

The huge atomic project was pushed feverishly forward, as American know-how and industrial power were combined with the most advanced scientific knowledge. Much technical skill was provided by British and Continental scientists, some of whom ironically had been forced to flee the torture chambers of the dictators. Finally, in the desert near Alamogordo, New Mexico, July 16, 1945, the experts detonated the first awesome atomic bomb.

With Japan still refusing to surrender, the Potsdam threat was fulfilled. On August 6, 1945, a lone American bomber dropped one atomic bomb on the military-base city of Hiroshima, Japan. In a blinding flash, followed by a funnel-shaped cloud, 180,000 persons were left killed, wounded, or missing. Some 70,000 of them were dead or presumed dead.

Two days later, on August 8, Stalin entered the war against Japan, exactly on the deadline date previously agreed upon with his allies. Regrouped Soviet armies speedily overran the depleted Japanese defenses in Manchuria and Korea in a six-day "victory parade" which involved several thousand Russian casualties. Stalin was evidently determined to be in on the kill, lest he lose a voice in the final division of Japan's holdings.

Fanatically resisting Japanese, though facing atomization, still did not surrender. American airmen, on August 9, dropped a second atomic bomb, on the naval-base city of Nagasaki, home of the fictional "Madam Butterfly." The explosion took a horrible toll of 80,000 persons killed or missing.

Japan could endure no more. On August 10, 1945, Tokyo sued for peace on one condition: that Hirohito, the bespectacled Son of Heaven, be allowed to remain on his ancestral throne as nominal Emperor. Despite their "unconditional surrender" policy, the Allies accepted this condition on August 14. The Japanese, though losing face, saved both their exalted ruler and their skins.

The formal end came, with dramatic force, on September 2, 1945. Official surrender ceremonies were conducted by General MacArthur on the battleship *Missouri* in Tokyo Bay. At the same time Americans at home hysterically celebrated V-J Day—Victory in Japan Day—after the most horrible war in history had ended in a mushrooming atomic cloud.

The Bomb at Nagasaki. U.S. Air Force photo

The Allies Triumphant

World War II proved to be terribly costly. American forces suffered some one million casualties, about one-third of which were deaths. Compared with other wars, the proportion killed by wounds and disease was sharply reduced, owing in part to the use of blood plasma and of miracle drugs, notably penicillin. Yet heavy though American losses were, the Russian allies suffered casualties many times greater.

America was fortunate in emerging with its mainland virtually unscathed. Two Japanese submarines, using shells and one submarine-based bomber, had rather harmlessly attacked the California and Oregon coast, and a few balloons, incendiary and otherwise, had drifted across the Pacific. But that was about all. Much of the rest of the world was bomb-pocked, rubble-strewn, and impoverished. Yet America's natural resources, magnificent though they were, had been seriously depleted by the ravenous war machine.

This incredibly complex conflict was the best-fought war in America's history. Though far from prepared for it at the outset, she was better prepared than for the others, partly because she had begun to buckle on her armor about a year and a half before the war officially began. She was actually fighting German submarines in the Atlantic months before the final explosion in the Pacific at Pearl Harbor. In the end, she proved herself to be resourceful, tough, adaptable—able to accommodate herself to the tactics of an enemy who was relentless and ruthless.

American military leadership proved to be of the highest order. A new crop of war heroes emerged in brilliant generals like Eisenhower, MacArthur, and Marshall (Chief of Staff), and in imaginative admirals like Nimitz and Spruance. President Roosevelt and Prime Minister Churchill, as kindred spirits, collaborated closely in planning over-all strategy. "It is fun to be in the same decade with you," FDR once added to a long cablegram.

Industrial leaders were no less skilled, for marvels of production were performed almost daily. Assembly lines proved no less important than battle lines; and victory went again to the side with the big smokestacks. The enemy was almost literally smothered in an avalanche of bayonets, bullets, bazookas, and bombs. Hitler and his Axis co-conspirators had chosen to make war with machines, and the ingenious Yankees could ask for nothing better. From 1940 to 1945, American factories rolled out an incredible 300,317 airplanes. As Winston Churchill remarked, "Nothing succeeds like excess."

Hermann Göring, a Nazi leader, had sneered, "The Americans can't build planes—only electric iceboxes and razor blades." Democracy had given its answer, as the dictators, despite long preparation, were overthrown and discredited. It is true that an unusual amount

"Well—?" 1945. Fitzpatrick in the St. Louis *Post-Dispatch*

of direct control was exercised over the individual by the Washington authorities during the war emergency. But the American people preserved their precious liberties without serious impairment. The outcome was another vindication of the American democratic system —a system founded on faith in the power and courage of free men.

SELECT READINGS

The picture is painted with bold strokes in ALLAN NEVINS, *The New Deal and World Affairs* (1950). The United States is given due consideration in L. L. SNYDER's popularly written *The War: A Concise History, 1939–1945* (1960)*; the main outlines also appear in R. W. SHUGG and H. A. DE WEERD, *World War II, A Concise History* (1946). Abundant detail is provided by A. R. BUCHANAN, *The United States and World War II* (2 vols., 1964)* and K. S. DAVIS, *Experience of War: The U.S. in World War II* (1965). The naval side is handled masterfully in Admiral S. E. MORISON, *The Two-Ocean War* (1963), a one-volume condensation of his monumental twelve-volume history of the United States Navy in World War II. High strategy is developed in K. R. GREENFIELD, ed., *Command Decisions* (1959) and in his *American Strategy in World War II* (1963). See also GADDIS SMITH's succinct *American Diplomacy during the Second World War, 1941–1945* (1965).* More detailed are HERBERT FEIS' three volumes: *Churchill, Roosevelt, Stalin* (2nd. ed., 1967)*; *Between War and Peace: The Potsdam Conference* (1960)*; and *The Atomic Bomb and the End of World War II* (1966). A pro-Soviet interpretation is GAR ALPEROVITZ, *Atomic Diplomacy* (1965),* as is GABRIEL KOLKO, *The Politics of War: The World and United States Foreign Policy, 1943–1945* (1968). See also J. L. SNELL, ed., *The Meaning of Yalta* (1956)*; ANNE ARMSTRONG, *Unconditional Surrender* (1961); R. A. DIVINE, *Second Chance: The Triumph of Internationalism in America during World War II* (1967); and *Roosevelt and World War II* (1969).

The more important biographical or autobiographical works are H. L. STIMSON (then Secretary of War) and M. BUNDY, *On Active Service in Peace and War* (1947); E. E. MORISON, *Turmoil and Tradition* (1960) [life of Stimson]*; General D. D. EISENHOWER's best-selling *Crusade in Europe* (1948)*; General DOUGLAS MACARTHUR, *Reminiscences* (1964); General L. R. GROVES, *Now It Can Be Told* (1962) [the atomic bomb project]; and ROBERT MURPHY, *Diplomat Among Warriors* (1964).* Also *Harvard Guide,* Pt. VI.

RECENT REFERENCES

JAMES M. BURNS, *Roosevelt: The Soldier of Freedom* (1970); JOHN L. GADDIS, *The United States and the Origins of the Cold War, 1941–1947* (1972).

* Available in paperback.

45

Truman and the Cold War

I believe that it must be the policy of the United States to support free peoples who are resisting attempted subjugation by armed minorities or by outside pressures.

President Truman, "Truman Doctrine" Message, 1947

Truman: The Man from Missouri

Trim and owlishly bespectacled Harry S Truman, with his graying hair and friendly, toothy grin, was called "the average man's average man." Even his height—five feet nine—was average. The first President in many years without a college education, he had farmed, served as an artillery officer in France during World War I, and failed at haberdashery. He then tried his hand at precinct-level Missouri politics, through which he rose from a judgeship to the United States Senate. Though a protégé of a notorious political machine in Kansas City, he had managed to keep his own skirts clean.

The roof caved in on Truman with Roosevelt's sudden death. Problems were overpowering, and the firm-mouthed new President approached his tasks with becoming humility. Gradually gaining confidence to the point of cockiness, he displayed courage, decisiveness, and a willingness to fight. Although high-schoolish as a speaker at first, he finally developed into one of the most effective "give 'em hell" speakers of his generation.

Yet by degrees the defects of Truman's common clay became painfully apparent. A smallish man suddenly thrust into an overwhelming job, he was inclined to go off half-cocked or to stick mulishly to some wrongheaded notion. On occasion, he would dash off hot-tempered and highly indiscreet s.o.b. letters. Worst of all, he permitted designing old associates of the "Missouri gang" to gather around him and, like Grant, was stubbornly loyal to them when they were caught with the cream on their whiskers. "To err is Truman" was a cynical explanation.

This was the man on whom Roosevelt's oversize mantle fell in April, 1945, when victory over Hitler was in view. Truman's most pressing task was to follow through and win both the war and the peace. Fortunately, he developed a surprising capacity to seize the tiller with bold hand in time of crisis. If he was sometimes small in small things, he was often big in the big things. A motto on the White House desk read, "The buck stops here." A favorite saying of his was, "If you can't stand the heat, get out of the kitchen."

Yalta: Bargain or Betrayal?

Vast and silent, the Soviet Union continued to be the Great Enigma. The conference at Teheran in 1943, where Roosevelt had first met Stalin on a man-to-man basis, had done something to clear the air, but much had remained unsettled.

A final fateful conference of the Big Three had taken place in February, 1945, at Yalta. At this former Czarist resort on the relatively warm shores of the Black Sea, Stalin, Churchill, and the fast-failing Roosevelt reached momentous agreements, after pledging their faith with vodka. Final plans were laid for smashing the buckling German lines and shackling the beaten Axis foe. Stalin agreed that Poland, with revised boundaries, should have a representative government based on free elections—a pledge that he soon broke. Bulgaria and Romania were likewise to have free elections—a promise also flouted. The Big Three further announced that they had decided to hold a multi-power conference, this time in San Francisco, for the purpose of fashioning a new international organization for peace.

Of all the painful decisions at Yalta, the most controversial concerned the Far East. The atomic bomb had not yet been tested, and Washington strategists expected frightful casualties in the projected assault on Japan. From Roosevelt's standpoint it seemed highly desirable that Stalin should enter the Far Eastern war, pin down Japanese troops in Manchuria and Korea, and lighten American losses. Russian casualties had already been enormous, and the Soviets presumably needed inducements to bring them into the Far Eastern conflagration.

Horse-trader Stalin was in a position at Yalta to exact a high price.

President Harry S. Truman (1884–1972). Regarded as one of the "guttier" Presidents, he remarked regarding the pressure of politics, "If you can't stand the heat, get out of the kitchen." As for passing decisions up to higher authority, he kept on his White House desk the motto, "The buck stops here." When his Republican opponents complained that he was giving them "hell," he replied, "I don't give 'em hell, I just tell the truth and they think it's hell."

He agreed to attack Japan within two to three months after the collapse of Germany; and he later redeemed his pledge in full. In return, the Soviets were promised the southern half of Sakhalin Island, lost by Russia to Japan in 1905, and Japan's Kurile Islands as well. The Soviet Union was also granted joint control over the railroads of China's Manchuria and, in a revival of Czarist imperialism, received special privileges in the two key seaports of that area, Dairen and Port Arthur. These concessions evidently would give Stalin control over vital industrial centers of America's weakening Chinese ally.

Russia's last-minute entry into the war against Japan was hailed in America with delight. But critics quickly concluded that Stalin's aid had not been needed, and that in any case his desire to grab his share of the spoils would have brought him into the conflict without concessions. Foes of the dead Roosevelt charged angrily that he had sold Chiang Kai-shek down the river when he conceded control of China's Manchuria to Stalin. The consequent undermining of Chinese morale, so the accusation ran, contributed powerfully to Chiang's overthrow by the Communists four years later.

Defenders of the departed Roosevelt were not silent. They argued that if Stalin had kept his promise to support free elections in Poland and the liberated Balkans, the sorry sequel would have been different. They also contended that Stalin, with his mighty Red Army, could have secured much more of China, and that the Yalta conference really set limits to his ambitions. He actually pledged himself to make a treaty of friendship and alliance with Chiang's government, and he carried through his promise later in 1945.

A myth took root—especially in the Soviet Union—that Russian-American relations would not have gone sour if Roosevelt had only lived. The truth is that several weeks before his death, he was shocked to learn that Moscow was about to violate its free-election pledges at Yalta concerning Poland and the Balkans. He died knowing that his charm and generous treatment had failed to lure the Russian Communists away from their menacing goal of world revolution.

"Uncorked at Last!" Secret Yalta Papers Released Ten Years Later, 1955. The *Knickerbocker News* (Albany). By permission

Birth Pangs of the United Nations

As flags wept at half-mast, the United Nations Conference met in San Francisco, on the scheduled April 25, 1945, despite Roosevelt's dismaying death thirteen days earlier. Groundwork had been laid for the historic gathering over a period of several years. The sobered Republicans, in sharp contrast with 1919, had shown a strong disposition to go along with Democratic leadership. Roosevelt, in turn, had displayed more tact than Wilson. He had chosen both Democrats and Republicans for the American delegation, and in addition had included Senators on it. He had also avoided Wilson's mistake of riveting the new world organization to the dead weight of an unpopular peace treaty.

With a drizzling rain outside, the delegates from nearly fifty nations assembled in the classic-style San Francisco War Memorial Opera House. The United Nations Charter, as finally whipped together after nine weeks of hectic debate, bore strong resemblances to the old League of Nations Covenant. Two kingpin bodies were set up. One was the Security Council, dominated by the Big Five Powers —the United States, Russia, Britain, France, and China. The other was the Assembly, which could be controlled by the smaller countries. A new International Court of Justice was patterned after the old World Court under the League of Nations.

The response of the Senate to the United Nations Charter in 1945 contrasted strikingly with its chilly reception of the League of Nations Covenant in 1919. After a brief flurry of debate, the final vote was taken on July 28, 1945. Impressed by an overwhelmingly favorable public opinion, the Senators approved the document by a vote of 89 to 2.

The U.N.'s Early Successes and Failures

The United Nations, which ultimately erected its permanent glass home in New York City, soon disappointed the hopes of those who had cried for One World. The Soviet bloc, a suspicious and outvoted minority, deliberately employed obstructionist tactics. As time passed, the conviction deepened that the Russians had not joined the U.N. in good faith. Evidently they had entered with the intention of snarling it up, and of using it as a megaphone for their incendiary propaganda. Particularly harsh were their wild charges of "warmongering" against America and her "capitalistic" associates.

The built-in big-power veto in the Security Council proved to be a near-fatal stumbling block. At San Francisco this device had been adopted in the expectation that it would be used sparingly, but the Soviets invoked it routinely to block any action that might thwart their schemes for world revolution. Within a few years they had wielded this potent hatchet scores of times.

"Wearied and Getting Nowhere." Bishop in the St. Louis *Star-Times*, 1947

Despite these setbacks, the U.N. could point to success in varied theaters. It played a praiseworthy role in helping to preserve peace in Iran, in Kashmir (India), in Indonesia, and elsewhere. It was largely instrumental in creating the new Jewish state of Israel, and in temporarily dampening the subsequent hostilities that broke out between the Jews and their resentful Arab neighbors. The mediatory work of Dr. Ralph J. Bunche, grandson of an American Negro slave, won for him the Nobel Peace Prize in 1950. But peace did not come to the Holy Land.

Under the Trusteeship Council, the U.N. set up trust territories that resembled the old League of Nations mandates. In 1947 the United States insisted on—and received as a trustee—the strategic Japanese-mandated islands in the Pacific. These insular outposts, already dearly purchased with American blood, were deemed essential to America's future defense plans.

Another significant agency of the U.N. was the Economic and Social Council. Elected by the General Assembly, it achieved substantial gains in world health and in social, cultural, and economic betterment. Prominent among its far-reaching arms was the United Nations Educational, Scientific, and Cultural Organization (UNESCO), which sought to promote a more wholesome understanding among the nations. But certain ultra-nationalistic groups in the United States condemned the experiment as internationalist and un-American.

Yet more disheartening were the failures of the U.N. in the larger area of disarmament. The new organization was unable to create an international police force, in order to guarantee a warless world. It was likewise unable to achieve international control of the atomic bomb. The United States, feeling temporarily secure in its presumed monopoly, had established the Atomic Energy Commission to stockpile nuclear explosives, and to explore possible peacetime uses of the atom. America was quite willing to share its atomic secrets with the rest of the world, provided that there was a foolproof system of international control and inspection.

But the Soviets defiantly refused to tie their hands with any such atomic agreement. They did not want capitalistic "spies" snooping around Mother Russia, and they evidently expected to make their own city-wrecking bombs in due course. As the atomic clock ticked steadily away, the Russians came ever nearer their goal.

Bernard Baruch, in presenting his plan for the control of atomic energy to the United Nations, in June, 1946, said, "We are here to make a choice between the quick and the dead. That is our business. Behind the black portent of the new atomic age lies a hope which, seized upon with faith, can work our salvation. If we fail, then we have damned every man to be the slave of fear. Let us not deceive ourselves; we must elect world peace or world destruction." The Soviets found his plan unacceptable, and the nuclear race was on full blast.

America Retools for Peace

After the war ended with an atomic bang, America was again confronted with the familiar pattern of demobilization. Millions of men and women in the armed forces had to be put back into civilian clothes—a process that went forward fairly rapidly. Congress made generous financial provision for readjustment to non-military life. Several million ex-service men and women, whose schooling in many instances had been interrupted, took advantage of the educational benefits provided by Congress in the so-called "G.I. Bill of Rights." Colleges during the post-war years were crowded to the blackboards, as more than a million eager veterans entered halls of higher learning.

But the demobilization of laurel-laden warriors was conducted with indecent haste, and without proper regard for America's new power position. When the enemy collapsed, the Republic had the most potent striking force ever assembled—and it was relatively fresh. To wipe it out would create a power vacuum into which the aggressive men of Moscow would be tempted to move. Yet tremendous pressure converged on Washington from sweethearts, parents, and children ("Bring-Daddy-Back-Home Clubs"). These earnest souls were loudly supported by homesick and mutinous G.I.'s themselves, who staged incredible "I wanna go home" demonstrations all the way from Germany to India. The shortsighted views of the American people finally prevailed, and the costly tools of victory were tossed away. "Nothing recedes like success," ran a current quip.

BILLIONS OF DOLLARS

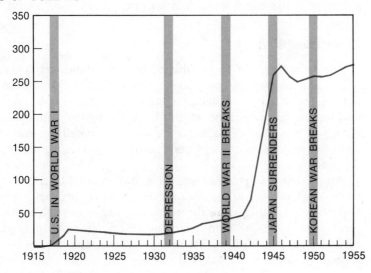

NATIONAL DEBT, 1915–1955

Dismantling the enormous war-production machine was a formidable task. In response to another insistent public clamor, wartime taxes were reduced—perhaps too rapidly in view of America's heavy financial obligations. The war had caused the national debt to shoot up to an astronomical $260,000,000,000. Conservative economists were disturbed because the richest nation in the world, during the years after military victory, could not or would not balance its budget, at a time when high income and inflationary pressures seemed to call for balancing.

On other fronts, economic demobilization lurched forward. War factories and other installations owned by the government were disposed of at fire-sale prices, partly in the misplaced hope that there could never be another war. Price controls were removed, except for rents, although not until President Truman had waged a slam-bang losing fight with Congress for continued restrictions. Manufacturers and retailers were eager to get back to the old law of "supply and demand"—and they did. With rationing ended, demand outran supply: people were tired of substituting liver for steak. By December, 1946, prices were about one-third higher than in the previous year.

Inflationary pressures were almost irresistible. During the war automobiles, refrigerators, stoves, and other appliances had been in short supply, owing chiefly to the ravenous appetite of the munitions industries for scarce metals. When the shooting stopped, the people had amassed fat savings—an estimated $44,000,000,000—and they were starved for consumers' goods. With the purchasers bidding competitively, and with the government making heavy shipments of supplies to devastated Europe, prices were bound to soar.

Labor Tramps Ahead

The "working stiff" was pinched by the inflationary spiral, which had about halved the purchasing power of the Depression dollar. During the war he had been restrained from striking by high wages and high-pressure patriotism. But when the fighting ended and overtime pay was sharply reduced, he was in a rebellious mood, especially when he saw management raking in profits from the pent-up demand.

An epidemic of strikes swept the country, and during 1946 alone some 4,600,000 laborers downed their tools for varying periods. Especially crippling were the work stoppages in such industries as steel and motor-car manufacturing. Stark drama unfolded in the bituminous coal industry when iron-willed John L. Lewis, defying a court injunction in 1946, led out his faithful miners. The strikers were forced to return to their pits, but not until a federal court had fined Lewis $10,000 and the union a whopping $3,500,000 (later reduced).

Embattled laborers were usually successful in winning wage increases, largely because the order-swamped manufacturers could pass the additional costs on to the consumer. But as prices continued to creep upward, further rounds of strikes resulted, followed by new price rises—in a dog-chasing-its-tail cycle. Yet employment continued full, and during the early post-war years attained the amazing total of 60,000,000 jobs.

Labor, on the whole, registered significant gains during these feverish post-war years. The workingman, to an increasing degree, was winning vacation allowances, old-age pensions, and other unaccustomed welfare benefits. A trail-blazing contract, signed by giant General Motors in 1948, included a clause to the effect that wages would rise and fall automatically with the rise and fall of the cost-of-living index.

Underprivileged Negro laborers, to an increasing degree, were

John L. Lewis, leader of the accident-cursed coal miners, told a House Labor Committee (April, 1947), "If we must grind up human flesh and bones in an industrial machine . . . then, before God, I assert that those who consume coal, and you and I who benefit from that service . . . owe protection to those men first, and we owe security to their families after, if they die. I say it! I voice it! I proclaim it! And I care not who in heaven or hell oppose it."

sharing the war-spawned prosperity. Southern Congressmen were blocking President Truman's recommendations for a national fair employment practices law and for civil rights legislation. But the plight of black "second-class citizens" was being generally improved by state legislation and changing public attitudes. Symptomatic of a new day for Negroes was the breaking of the color bar in big-league baseball. Amid less controversy than predicted, the Brooklyn "Dodgers" led the way in 1947, when they signed a star Negro second baseman, Jack Roosevelt ("Jackie") Robinson, a former college football player.

Labor Curbs and Housing Programs

The growing power of organized workingmen had meanwhile proved deeply disturbing to many conservatives. Asserting that Big Labor was now as much a menace as Big Business had ever been, diehard industrialists demanded a showdown. The Republicans gained control of Congress in 1947, for the first time in fourteen years, and proceeded to call the tune. Balding, blunt-spoken Robert A. Taft of Ohio, son of the former President and one of the Republican big guns of the Senate, became co-sponsor of a controversial new labor law known as the Taft-Hartley Act. It was passed in June, 1947, over President Truman's vigorous veto.

The Taft-Hartley law promptly became a storm center. Partly designed to protect the public, it contained a number of provisions that were not highly objectionable to open-minded workingmen. But the curbs on unions caused labor leaders to condemn the entire act as a "slave labor law." Especially irksome were the provisions outlawing the closed (all-union) shop, while making unions liable for damages resulting from jurisdictional disputes among themselves. Union leaders were required to take a non-Communist oath, though employers were not forced to do so. Despite labor's pained outcries, Taft-Hartleyism, while annoying, did not cripple the labor movement. The A.F. of L. by 1950 could boast 8,000,000 members and the C.I.O. 6,000,000.

Wretched housing was another grievance of labor, as indeed of much of the population. New construction had been slowed or halted by the war, while at the same time the country had experienced a baby-boom. Tens of thousands of migrant workers, moreover, had hived around war industries. This trend was most conspicuous in the northern industrial areas, like Detroit, and on the Pacific Coast, notably in California, which experienced a spectacular increase of population.

In response to Truman's persistent proddings, Congress finally tackled the housing problem. Laws were passed in 1948 and 1949 to provide federally financed construction, despite the outraged pro-

"Where Does He Fit In?" Doubts About Taft-Hartley Act, 1949. The *Knickerbocker News* (Albany). By permission

tests of real-estate promoters and other conservative groups. But these measures, though promising steps forward, fell far short of pressing needs. Hundreds of thousands of additional structures would have to be built if the nation was going to wipe out its disgraceful slums and provide homes to match its fabulous wealth.

Reconstruction and De-Nazification Abroad

At the close of the war America, rich and unscarred, had a moral obligation to help her less fortunate sisters—or so many of her citizens felt. "It is now 11:59 on the clock of starvation," warned Herbert Hoover.

Aid of a non-military nature continued to flow to Europe, even though the end of the shooting brought an abrupt end to lend-lease. The United States simply could not afford to see the ravaged peoples of Europe fall prey to creeping Communism. Wealthy Uncle Sam carried the heavy end of the log in financing short-term relief, chiefly through the United Nations Relief and Rehabilitation Administration (UNRRA). This organization did life-saving work from 1943 to 1947 by providing succor for many destitute countries in both Europe and Asia. Official relief was supplemented by personal gifts, particularly the private packages of food and clothing sent by Americans to starving families in Europe under the auspices of CARE.

Displaced persons—"D.P.s," or "Delayed Pilgrims," they were called—numbered several million unfortunates uprooted by the war. Large numbers of them were anti-Communists who did not dare return to their Red-dominated homelands. America had room for many of these rootless souls, but Congress moved slowly and halfheartedly in the face of possible unemployment, maladjustment, or the importation of dangerous foreign doctrines. An act as finally passed in 1948—expanded in 1950—made provision for the admission of 205,000 carefully selected persons in two years.

Two wartime associates received special attention. The prostrate Philippines, in accordance with the act of Congress in 1934, were formally awarded independence in 1946 on America's Independence Day—July 4. The United States agreed to provide substantial financial assistance, and in return received leases on more than a score of military, naval, and air-base sites.

Impoverished Britain was grudgingly voted a low-interest loan in 1946 of $3,750,000,000. Much opposition was registered, especially on the floor of Congress, by the isolationists, the anti-British, and the economy-minded, who feared that the money would never be repaid. A cynical jingle ran:

There will always be a U.S.A.
If we don't give it away.

Ex-President Truman wrote in his memoirs (1956), "The American approach to world affairs was best demonstrated by the manner in which we treated conquered nations. . . . We set up the means to feed and clothe and take care of the physical needs of the people. We rehabilitated the conquered nations instead of attempting to keep them conquered and prostrate. . . . This was something new in the history of nations."

Germany presented especially thorny problems. Policy-makers in Washington were determined that she should not rise in her industrial and military might, again to menace the peace of the world. Multiple goals were therefore adopted: de-Nazification, de-militarization, de-industrialization, and democratization. Some Hitler-haters in America, remembering that an industrialized Germany had been an aggressor, were determined to reduce the German Fatherland to a potato patch. But in the end less harsh courses were adopted, partly because Germany was the key to the economic recovery of Europe.

De-Nazification involved punishing Nazi German leaders for war crimes. The Allies joined in trying twenty-two leading culprits at Nuremberg, Germany, during 1945–1946, with Associate Justice Jackson of the United States Supreme Court serving as a special prosecutor. Accusations included committing crimes against the laws of war and humanity, and plotting aggressions contrary to solemn treaty pledges.

Justice, new style, was harsh. In 1946, nineteen of the accused Nazis were convicted: twelve were sentenced to the gallows and seven to jail terms. "Foxy Hermann" Göring, whose blubbery chest had once blazed with ribbons, cheated the hangman by swallowing a hidden cyanide capsule a few hours before his scheduled execution. The trials of scores of small-fry Nazis continued for several years. Legalistic critics in America condemned these proceedings as judicial lynchings, for the victims were tried for offenses that had not been clearcut crimes when the war began. In any event, future aggressors were warned that they might expect the noose instead of the halo.

"Witnesses for the Prosecution," 1945. Fitzpatrick in the St. Louis *Post-Dispatch*

Russian Roadblocks to Peace in Germany and Japan

Allied efforts to make a peace treaty with Germany and Austria speedily ran onto the rocks of Soviet obstruction. Germany and Austria, as previously agreed, were arbitrarily broken into four military zones, and one of them was assigned to each of the Big Four powers: France, Britain, America, and Russia. But the ever-suspicious Russians did not work well in multi-power harness. Besides, they were eager to bleed Germany with heavy reparations—in money, goods, and factories—and leave her so desperately impoverished that her people would fall prey to the seductive promises of Soviet Communism.

An ominous gulf between the Russians and the western Allies gradually widened. The Soviet Zone in eastern Germany was turned into a Communist puppet, even though the three-power Potsdam agreement of 1945 had stipulated that the German Reich was to be treated as an economic whole. Moscow was reluctant to conclude

POST-WAR PARTITION OF GERMANY

multi-power settlements with Germany and Austria, lest these two conquered nations wriggle out from under the Soviet heel. But there were no insuperable obstacles to peace pacts with Italy, Bulgaria, Hungary, Romania, and Finland; and treaties were formally signed with these defeated countries in 1947.

Reconstruction in Japan was simpler than in Germany, primarily because it was largely a one-man show. The occupying American army, under the Supreme Allied Commander, five-starred General Douglas MacArthur, sat in the driver's seat. In the teeth of violent protests from the Soviet officials, he went inflexibly ahead with his program for the democratization of Japan. Following the pattern in Germany, top Japanese "war criminals" were tried in Tokyo from 1946 to 1948. Eighteen of them were sentenced to prison terms and seven were hanged.

General MacArthur, as a kind of Yankee Mikado, enjoyed phenomenal success. He made a tremendous impression on the Japanese with his aloof, Greek-god bearing; and the vanquished sons of Nippon cooperated with their conqueror to an unbelievable degree. They were clever enough to see that good behavior and the adoption of "de-mok-las-sie" would speed the end of the occupation—as it did.

The non-Communist powers, fed up with Soviet obstruction, at length concluded a separate treaty with Japan at San Francisco in 1951—six years after the surrender ceremonies. With passions cooled, it was essentially a "soft peace," designed to help the Nipponese get back on their sandaled feet and stand as a bulwark against Communism in Eastern Asia.

Soviet Aggressiveness and the Rift with Moscow

Tensions between the Soviet Union and the free world, multiplying in many quarters, finally flared into an open quarrel. This was the overshadowingly ominous development of the post-war years.

When World War II burned itself out, a vast reservoir of good will existed in the United States for the resolute Russians. Even though they had been ultra-suspicious associates, they had helped America save her skin while saving their own. If the men in the Kremlin had sung a sweeter tune, they probably could have borrowed billions of American dollars to assist in the task of picking up the pieces left by Hitler.

Instead of milking America, the Russian rulers kicked her in the teeth. In doing so, they all too openly revealed that they had not abandoned their zeal for Communist world revolution. They further revealed their aggressive aims by crying "capitalist encirclement"— at the very time when America was hastily demobilizing her armed forces and they were bolstering theirs.

The Soviets forthwith proceeded to clang down the "iron curtain" over their smaller neighbors like Poland and Hungary—in violation of the Atlantic Charter and the Yalta pledges. Presumably the Kremlin wanted to bring these nations securely into its own camp as buffers against a future invasion from the capitalistic world—a capitalistic world which, in its view, was "rattling" the atomic bomb and practicing "atomic blackmail."

Moscow's iron-fisted policy wrought a psychological Pearl Harbor. The eyes of the people were jarred wide open by the unmistakable hostility of the Kremlin toward the democratic nations. Many Americans had experienced grave misgivings ever since the Bolshevik revolution in 1917, but now even the wishful thinkers were deeply disturbed. They were profoundly alarmed by Soviet sabotaging of the United Nations, and especially by the seeming determination of Moscow to Communize both Italy and France and sweep to the English Channel. "I'm tired of babying the Soviets," wrote Truman privately in 1946.

Russian aggressiveness thus aroused and forewarned America. She was once more forced, though reluctantly, to shoulder the heavy burdens of rearmament. The supreme irony is that Americans not only ceased to dismantle German war-industry factories, but before long were trying to induce Germany to rearm. Her manpower seemed indispensable in halting the westward surge of Soviet Communism.

Marshaling Marshall Dollars

Truman, backed by an aroused public opinion, formally adopted a "get-tough-with-Russia" policy in 1947. His first dramatic move was triggered by word that Britain, heavily burdened, could no

Ex-Prime Minister Churchill, in a highly controversial speech at Fulton, Missouri (March, 1946), warned of Communist Russia's expansiveness, "From Stettin in the Baltic to Trieste in the Adriatic an iron curtain has descended across the Continent."

The Communists stereotyped Truman as an arrogant autocrat, with money bags and atomic bombs, defiantly backed by the West European capitalistic statesmen. From the Soviet satirical magazine *Krokodil*.

longer bear the financial and military load of defending Greece against Communist pressures. If Greece fell, Turkey would presumably collapse and the strategic Eastern Mediterranean would be lost to the free world.

In a surprise appearance, the President went before Congress, on March 12, 1947, and urged it to support what came to be known as the Truman Doctrine. America, he felt, should attempt to halt or "contain" Communist aggression wherever it threatened free peoples. Specifically, he asked Congress to appropriate $400,000,000 for the economic and military bolstering of both Greece and Turkey. The legislators, reflecting the changed public mood, responded with lopsided votes of approval. American aid was rushed to the troubled spots, and Greece and Turkey, Truman believed, were saved from the clutches of Communism.

But Truman's countermoves against outside aggression proved far too limited in scope. Western Europe—especially Italy, France, and western Germany—was still suffering from the hunger and economic chaos spawned by the war. These key nations were in grave danger of being taken over from the inside by the "stomach Communists"— that is, by desperate people to whom any change would seem a change for the better.

Secretary of State George C. Marshall, the most distinguished desk-general of the recent war, was delegated to step into the breach. In a commencement address at Harvard University on June 5, 1947, he broadly hinted that the countries of Europe should get together and work out plans for their economic recovery. If they did so, Washington might help them with adequate financial assistance, pending that day when they could support themselves and consequently strengthen American policy.

The democratic nations of Europe rose to the life-giving bait with enthusiasm and in July, 1947, a conference was held in Paris to thrash out details. The Soviets muffed a priceless opportunity to snarl the Marshall Plan hopelessly when they walked out of the conference. They branded the whole scheme an "imperialist" plot, cooked up by the Wall Street "Knights of the Dollar" for "the enslavement of Europe."

The next move was up to Congress, which had to vote the money. As outlined by President Truman, the plan was to spend the enormous sum of $17,000,000,000 over four years in sixteen cooperating countries. Uncle Sam was already tax-burdened and debt-ridden, and critics of the Marshall scheme, chiefly old-line isolationists, branded it "the Martial Plan," "Operation Rathole," and "the Share-the-American-Wealth Plan."

Finally, in April, 1948, Congress voted the initial appropriation— with evident reluctance. A few voices were raised to say that as good Samaritans America owed help to her distressed neighbors and

"Where To?" Truman Doctrine, 1947. Courtesy of Richmond *Times-Dispatch*

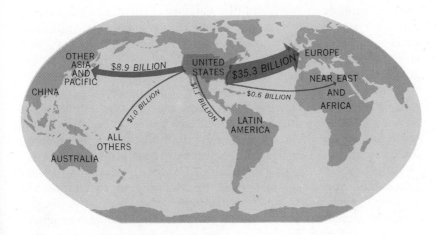

UNITED STATES FOREIGN AID, MILITARY
AND ECONOMIC, 1945–1954

recent allies. But the clincher turned out to be the naked aggression
of Soviet Communism. The Marshall Plan appropriation was
languishing in Congress when a Communist coup in Czechoslovakia,
involving the suicide (or murder?) of its Foreign Minister, provided
a frightening new object lesson in how a democracy could be enchained overnight.

Truman's Marshall Plan on the whole proved to be a spectacular
success. The billions voted by Congress were administered by the
Economic Cooperation Administration, headed by Paul G. Hoffman,
former president of the Studebaker automobile corporation. Life-
giving American dollars pumped a blood transfusion into the
economic veins of the anemic Western European nations, and within
a few years most of them were approaching or even exceeding their
pre-war production output. The Reds in Italy and France lost some
ground, and these two keystone countries were saved from the claws
of Communism.

American Rearmament and Propaganda

The struggle to stem Soviet Communism resulted in what came to
be known as "the Cold War." It was not war—yet it was not peace.
The alarming tactics of the Kremlin completely banished the dreams
of tax-weary Americans that arms could be beaten into automobiles.

Unification of the armed services, long argued, was spurred on
by the Soviet menace. In 1947 Congress passed an act which created
a Department of Defense, headed by a new Cabinet member called
the Secretary of Defense. Under him, but without Cabinet status,
were the Secretary of the Navy, the Secretary of the Army (replacing

"American Motor of the Latest
Type." The conquering Truman
uses U.S. money bags to induce
dollar-hungry European nations
to draw the U.S. capitalistic
chariot. From the Soviet
satirical magazine *Krokodil*.

the old Secretary of War), and the Secretary of the Air Force (a recognition of air power). Unification unhappily generated continuing friction, largely because of traditional service rivalries, some of which were reflected in the annual football classics between the academies at West Point and Annapolis.

Rearmament in the United States was pushed with vigor. American military men, viewing with alarm the growing might of the Soviet colossus, urged Universal Military Training. But they had to settle in 1948 for a less sweeping new draft law, which provided for the conscription of youths from eighteen to twenty-five.

Large-scale official propaganda, for the first time in the nation's peacetime experience, was used by Washington to counter the powerful blasts from Moscow. Through "The Voice of America," which was formally authorized by Congress in 1948, radio programs were beamed beyond the Iron Curtain. Management of the enterprise at first suffered from serious shortcomings, and Congress half-choked "The Voice" with niggardly appropriations and a barrage of criticism. But the efforts of the Soviets to "jam" the program indicated that it was of some effect in trumpeting abroad American democratic ideals.

Ferreting Out Alleged Communists

One of the most active Cold-War fronts was at home, where a new anti-Red chase was in full cry. Many nervous citizens feared that Communist spies, paid with Moscow gold, were undermining the government and treacherously misdirecting foreign policy. In 1947 Truman ordered a loyalty investigation of federal employees, and as a result a number of possible "security risks" were dropped. The Attorney General in the same year issued a long list of allegedly subversive organizations, membership in which would cause one's loyalty to be suspect.

Individual states likewise became intensely security-conscious. Loyalty oaths in increasing numbers were demanded of employees, educational and otherwise. Disagreeable incidents involving freedom of speech and teaching burst into the headlines. The gnawing question to many earnest Americans was: could the nation continue to enjoy to the fullest extent traditional freedoms in the face of a ruthless international conspiracy known as Soviet Communism?

In 1949 eleven Communists were brought before a New York jury for violating the Smith Act of 1940, the first peacetime anti-sedition law since 1798. Hiding behind the very Constitution they were attempting to destroy, the defendants were convicted of advocating the overthrow of the American government by force, and were sent to prison.

In his inaugural address, Jan. 1949, Truman said: "Communism is based on the belief that man is so weak and inadequate that he is unable to govern himself, and therefore requires the rule of strong masters.
"Democracy is based on the conviction that man has the moral and intellectual capacity, as well as the inalienable right, to govern himself with reason and justice."

The House Committee on Un-American Activities had meanwhile thrown out a dragnet for disloyal citizens. Its most sensational catch, thanks to the alertness of young Congressman Richard M. Nixon, was Alger Hiss, once a highly trusted second-drawer employee of the Department of State. A New York jury in 1950 found him guilty of perjury, after he had denied under oath passing State Department secrets on to Moscow agents in 1938. He was sentenced to five years in prison, though continuing to protest his innocence.

President Truman, who had launched his own security program, jibed that the Republicans were trying to cover up their own shortcomings in Congress by dragging in "Red herrings." He regarded the sensationalized findings of the inquisitors as a reflection on the vigilance and competence of his Democratic administration, as to some extent they were. But his cover-up policy merely played into the hands of avid Red-hunters like Senator Joseph R. McCarthy of Wisconsin, a Republican who recklessly charged in 1950 that there were scores of known Communists in the Department of State. Not a single one was found.

"Protecting the Baby." An Anti-McCarthyite Cartoon. Justus in the Minneapolis *Star*

The Berlin Airlift and NATO

The cold war had meanwhile come perilously close to flaring into a hot war in the rubble heap known as Berlin. Lying deep within the Soviet Zone of Germany (see map, p. 952), this democratic isle in a Red sea had been broken into four sectors, each of which was occupied by troops of one of the four great powers. Yet no provision had been made for guaranteeing joint control of the roads and railroads approaching Berlin through the Soviet-controlled zone. In 1948, following angry controversies over German currency reform and four-power control, the Russians sprang the trap. They abruptly choked off land and water routes to Berlin, no doubt reasoning that the Allies would be starved out.

Rather than turn tail and run, the British and Americans, chiefly Americans, organized a gigantic airlift in the midst of trigger-finger tension. For nearly a year intrepid aviators, summer and winter, flew in the necessities of the Berliners, including coal—expensive coal. At its peak the airlift ("Operation Vittles") was ferrying some 4500 tons of supplies a day to more than two million people, at the rate of one plane every three minutes. The Berliners, though former enemies, were heartened and grateful.

Moscow, taken aback, was sobered by the determination of the Allies to stand firm. The democracies at length won an impressive moral victory when the Russians, their fingers burned by an Allied counter-blockade, formally lifted their ban on surface shipments in May, 1949.

Two Germanies thus emerged from the Soviet-engineered dead-

Even the U.S. Navy helped in the Berlin airlift. National Archives.

lock: the Communist-dominated East Germany and the democratically organized West Germany. The government of the West German Republic was formally and hopefully set up in 1949 at the historic Rhine city of Bonn, birthplace of Beethoven.

Soviet menaces meanwhile had been forcing the divided democracies of Western Europe into an unforeseen degree of unity, both economic and political. In 1948, Britain, France, Belgium, the Netherlands, and Luxemburg signed a pathbreaking defensive alliance at Brussels. A security-seeking America, despite a deep-seated prejudice against peacetime entanglements, was drawn irresistibly toward the new grouping.

The alliance negotiations reached their climax in Washington. There, on April 4, 1949, the representatives of twelve nations, with white-tie pageantry, signed the historic North Atlantic Pact. It stipulated that an attack on one member by an aggressor would be an attack on all, and that the signatories would then take such action as they deemed necessary, including "armed force."

Would the United States Senate, despite a strongly favorable public opinion, reject the treaty? Last-ditch isolationists insisted that the scheme was a dangerous involvement which would cause the Republic to become a kind of helpless tail to the European kite. But security came before tradition, and the Senate registered its approval, on July 21, 1949, by a vote of 82 to 13.

The pact was truly epochal. Uncle Sam did not assume a hard-and-fast commitment to rush to the aid of any one of the signatories assaulted by Soviet Russia—but there was clearly a moral commitment. Due notice was served on the men of Moscow that they attacked at their peril, and preparations were pushed by the North Atlantic Treaty Organization (NATO) to build up an army for defensive purposes. Membership was boosted to fourteen in 1952 by the inclusion of Greece and Turkey.

It seemed evident to Americans that the free nations would have to stand together, or they would be picked off one by one—in artichoke-eating fashion. A willingness to join a peacetime military alliance, despite hoary tradition, revealed a tormenting concern over Soviet aggressions. The Cold War had forced the nation to face cold facts.

Democratic Dissensions and Divisions in 1948

Republican prospects had seldom looked rosier as the presidential campaign of 1948 neared. The G.O.P. could point happily to the Congressional elections of 1946, when the voters, responding to the slogan "Had Enough?" had elected a Republican Congress. Seemingly the country was fed up with New Deal spending, high prices, and "High-Tax Harry" Truman.

Jubilant Republicans, meeting in Philadelphia, departed sharply from previous practice. They noisily renominated a warmed-over candidate, the once-defeated Thomas E. Dewey, governor of New York, still as debonair as if he had stepped out of a bandbox. The platform listed in detail the shortcomings of the New Deal, and revived the threadbare theme that it was "time for a change." "Save What's Left" became a popular Republican slogan.

Democratic politicos, also gathering in Philadelphia, worked up no real enthusiasm for their hand-me-down President, Harry S Truman. An effort had been made to draft war-hero General Dwight D. Eisenhower, and when he continued to turn a deaf ear, the "dump Truman" movement collapsed. The peppery President, unwanted but undaunted, was then chosen in the face of violent opposition from the Southern delegates. They were alienated by his strong stand in favor of civil rights for Negroes, who now mustered many votes in the big-city ghettos of the North. The song "I'm Just Wild about Harry" became "I'm Just Mild about Harry."

Truman's nomination split the party wide open. Embittered Southern Democrats from thirteen states, like their fire-eating forebears of 1860, next met in their own convention, in Birmingham, Alabama, with Confederate flags in evidence. Amid scenes of heated defiance, these "Dixiecrats" nominated Governor J. Strom Thurmond of South Carolina on a States' Rights Party ticket.

To add to the confusion within Democratic ranks, former Vice-President Henry A. Wallace threw his hat into the ring. Having parted company with the Administration over its get-tough-with Russia policy, he was nominated at Philadelphia by the new Progressive Party—a bizarre collection of disgruntled ex-New Dealers, starry-eyed pacifists, progressives, well-meaning liberals, and Communist-fronters, who chanted:

One, two, three, four,
We don't want another war.

Wallace, a vigorous if misguided liberal, assailed Uncle Sam's "dollar imperialism" from the stump. Drenched with rotten eggs in hostile cities, this so-called "Pied Piper of the Politburo" took a pro-Soviet line that undoubtedly weakened America's diplomatic posture.

Democratic Split Raises G.O.P. Hopes. Bishop in the St. Louis *Star-Times.* 1948

Truman Achieves the "Miracle" of 1948

Truman's chances seemed desperate. A party is ordinarily doomed when it splits in half: this time it had split three ways. It had been in power for sixteen long years, had made many well-publicized mistakes, had incurred a host of enemies, and had lost the Congress to the Republicans in 1946. The Democrats were vulnerable, moreover, to the charge of "Communist coddling."

Dewey, riding a "Victory Special" train, fell victim to overconfidence, especially after the public-opinion polls and the political experts had him winning in a walk. To many voters he seemed cold, smug, superior, arrogant, and evasive. Non-committal in the extreme, he engaged in dispensing soothing-syrup generalities, including "Our future lies before us." Democrats jeered that G.O.P. spelled "Grand Old Platitudes." But Dewey's strategy was basically sound: if victory is certain, why tie one's hands by making any more positive commitments than one has to?

Harry Truman—"the forgotten man"—was left almost alone, with little money and few active supporters. But his instincts as a "gut-fighter" were aroused. Rolling up his sleeves, he put on a furious, free-swinging, one-man campaign. Touring the country and showing his "folksy" personality to advantage, he delivered some 300 "give 'em hell" speeches at numerous whistle-stops. He condemned the Taft-Hartley "slave labor" law, and lashed out at the "notorious" record of the "do nothing," "good for nothing," Republican Eightieth Congress—the "worst in history." That body, he shouted to a roaring mass of 100,000 people in Iowa, had "stuck a pitchfork in the farmer's back." He airily waved aside the findings of the pollsters as "sleeping polls," designed to lull the voters to sleep. The crowds, growing increasingly large and enthusiastic, cried back, "Pour it on 'em Harry!"

"That Ain't the Way I Heard It!"
(Truman). UPI photo

Only a Republican genius, it was said, could lose this election; and "President" Dewey succeeded brilliantly in snatching defeat from the jaws of victory. Truman swept to a stunning triumph, to the complete bewilderment of the politicians, pollsters, prophets, and pundits. The chagrined Chicago *Tribune* had overconfidently run off an edition with the headline "DEWEY DEFEATS TRUMAN." The statistical results are most revealing:

	Popular Vote	Electoral Vote	
Truman (Democratic)	24,105,812	303	(chiefly South, Middle West, and West)
Dewey (Republican)	21,970,065	189	(chiefly New England, Middle Atlantic states)
Thurmond (States' Rights Democratic)	1,169,063	39	(Ala., Miss., La., S.C.)
Wallace (Progressive)	1,157,172	0	

To make victory all the sweeter, the Democrats regained control of Congress, fully prepared to continue New Deal spending under "Roosevelt's fifth term."

Why the sensational upset? High among the reasons must rank Republican overconfidence, fed by the poll-takers and reflected in the light turnout, smaller than in 1940. Farmers found Truman's promises of price supports more reassuring than Dewey's; labor opposed the Republican-sponsored Taft-Hartley law; and the massed Negro vote in the large Northern cities naturally turned to Truman as a result of his pro-civil rights stand. The country was prosperous, and government checks were still flowing out from the Treasury to various voters. Finally, Truman's lone-wolf, never-say-die campaign won him the support of many Americans who admired "guts." No one wanted him, someone remarked, except the mass of the voters.

New Dealers Become Fair Dealers

Smilingly confident, Truman sounded a clarion note, in the fourth point of his inaugural address, when he called for a "bold new program" ("Point Four"). The plan was to lend American money and technical aid to backward lands, so that they might aid themselves. Truman wanted to spend millions to keep underprivileged peoples from becoming Communists, rather than to spend billions to shoot them after they had become Communists. This far-seeing program was officially launched in 1950, and it brought badly needed assistance to impoverished countries, notably in Latin America, Africa, the Near East, and the Far East.

A Fair Deal, aimed at helping poverty-stricken peoples at home, was fully outlined in Truman's annual message to Congress in January, 1949. The President issued an appeal for a sweeping program that would embrace badly needed housing, full employment, higher minimum wages, better price supports for farmers, new TVA's for other major river valleys, and an extension of social security. This Fair Deal program went further in some respects than the New Deal itself, and the Republicans condemned these "Fear Deal" proposals as designed to create a socialistic and spendthrift "welfare state."

The Fair Dealers, despite Truman's zeal, achieved only a small part of their program. A filibuster by Southern members of the 81st Congress—the "eighty-worst"—blocked a federal anti-poll-tax law and a fair employment practices act. But in 1949 Congress, bowing to inflation, did boost the minimum wage to 75 cents an hour from the 40 cents set in 1940. Progress was also made toward slum clearance and public housing in the Housing Act of 1949. Perhaps the greatest success of Truman's Fair Deal came in the Social Security Act of 1950, which broadened the old-age insurance benefits of the original law of 1935. It added some 9,700,000 beneficiaries to the 35,000,000 already covered.

The Nuclear Arms Race and China's Collapse

President Truman shocked the nation by announcing in September, 1949, that the Soviets had exploded an atomic bomb—approximately three years earlier than the experts had thought possible. American strategists since 1945 had counted on keeping the Soviets in line by threats of a one-sided aerial attack with nuclear weapons. America's monopoly of this lethal weapon may in fact have restrained the Russians from launching out on a course of armed aggression. But atomic bombing was now a game that two could play.

The stunning success of the Soviet scientists was presumably due, at least in part, to the cleverness of Communist spies in stealing American secrets. Notorious among those Americans and Britishers who had allegedly "leaked" atomic data to Moscow were two American citizens, Julius and Ethel Rosenberg. They were convicted in 1951 of espionage, and after prolonged appeals went to the electric chair in 1953—the first peacetime American spies to be executed. The activities of such disloyal citizens, combined with fear of the A-bomb, gave strong public support to look-under-the-bed Congressional Red-hunters.

Bad news of a different sort came in 1949 with the catastrophic fall of China to the Communists. Since the end of the war, and even earlier, Washington had halfheartedly supported the Nationalist government of Chiang Kai-shek in his bitter civil war with the Communists. But the Generalissimo gradually began to forfeit the confidence of his people, owing to the ineptitude and corruption within his

In August, 1949, Secretary of State Acheson explained publicly why America had "dumped" Chiang Kai-shek: "The unfortunate but inescapable fact is that the ominous result of the civil war in China was beyond the control of the government of the United States. Nothing that this country did or could have done within the reasonable limits of its capabilities could have changed that result; nothing that was left undone by this country has contributed to it. It was the product of internal Chinese forces, forces which this country tried to influence but could not."

regime. Communist armies swept south overwhelmingly, and late in 1949 Chiang was forced to flee with the remnants of his once-powerful force to the last-hope island of Formosa (Taiwan).

The collapse of Nationalist China was a depressing defeat for America and her allies in the Cold War—the worst to date. At one fell swoop nearly one-fourth of the world's population—some 500,000,000 souls—was swept into the Communist camp. The Republicans, seeking "goats," assailed President Truman and his natty, bristly mustached, British-appearing Secretary of State, Dean Acheson, for having "lost" China. They insisted that Democratic agencies, wormy with Communists, had deliberately withheld aid from Chiang Kai-shek so that he would fall. Democrats heatedly replied that when a regime has forfeited the support of its people, no amount of outside help will save it. Truman, the argument ran, did not "lose" China because he never had China to lose.

The horrifying race in "city-busting" weapons continued at a stepped-up pace. If force was the only language that the Soviets respected, then weakness in the democratic world would invite disaster. Late in 1952, after tests in the South Pacific, word leaked out that an American hydrogen device, many times more lethal than the atomic bomb, had been exploded. The assumption was that the Soviets would soon have one also—and the next year they claimed that they did. If the Cold War should blaze into a hot war, perhaps there would be no world left for the Communists to Communize—a sobering thought that may have given them pause. Peace through mutual terror might yet come to be the best hope of mankind.

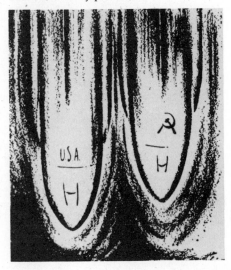

"Look We're Out In Front." Little in the Nashville Tennessean, 1953. By permission

SELECT READINGS

Helpful overviews are WALTER LA FEBER, *America, Russia, and the Cold War, 1945–1966* (1967)*; HERBERT AGAR, *The Price of Power: America since 1945* (1957)*; J. W. SPANIER, *American Foreign Policy since World War II* (1960)*; and W. G. CARLETON, *The Revolution in American Foreign Policy* (1963).* Engagingly written is E. F. GOLDMAN's analysis *The Crucial Decade: America, 1945–1955* (1956).* HARRY TRUMAN's own story is saltily told in his *Year of Decisions* (1955)* and *Years of Trial and Hope* (1956).* See also ALFRED STEINBERG's journalistic *The Man from Missouri* [Truman] (1962) and CABELL PHILLIPS' *The Truman Presidency* (1966).*

Various aspects of foreign policy are revealed in J. A. LUKACS, *A History of the Cold War* (1961)*; M. F. HERZ, *Beginnings of the Cold War* (1966); D. F. FLEMING's pro-Soviet *The Cold War and Its Origins, 1917–1960* (2 vols., 1961); N. A. GRAEBNER, *The New Isolationism* (1956); W. P. DAVISON, *The Berlin Blockade* (1958);

R. E. OSGOOD, *NATO: The Entangling Alliance* (1962); HERBERT FEIS, *The China Tangle* (1953)*; F. S. DUNN, *Peace-Making and the Settlement with Japan* (1963); KAZUO KAWAI, *Japan's American Interlude* (1960); and TANG TSOU, *America's Failure in China, 1941–1950* (1963).* Brilliant observations by an architect of "containment" appear in G. F. KENNAN, *Memoirs, 1925–1950* (1967). The then Secretary of State, Dean Acheson, has published his recollections in *Present at the Creation* (1969).

Aspects of Communism are developed in D. A. SHANNON, *The Decline of American Communism: A History of the Communist Party of the United States since 1945* (1959); D. J. SAPOSS, *Communism in American Politics* (1960); and K. M. SCHMIDT, *Henry A. Wallace: Quixotic Crusade, 1948* (1960). Revealing personal glimpses are found in Secretary J. F. BYRNES, *Speaking Frankly* (1947) and *All in One Lifetime* (1958); also General L. D. CLAY, *Decision in Germany* (1950). Also references for preceding chapter and *Harvard Guide,** Pt. VI.

RECENT REFERENCES

CHARLES E. BOHLEN, *Witness to History, 1929–1969* (1973), by a former Ambassador to Russia; MARGARET TRUMAN, *Harry S. Truman* (1973), a favorable portrait by Truman's daughter.

---

* Available in paperback.

46

Korea and the Challenge to the West

*The attack upon Korea makes it plain beyond all doubt that
Communism has passed beyond the use of subversion to conquer
independent nations and will now use armed invasion and war.*

Harry S. Truman, June 27, 1950

The Korean Volcano Erupts (1950)

Korea, the Land of the Morning Calm, suddenly heralded a new
and more ominous phase of the Cold War—the shooting phase—
in June, 1950.

Following the collapse of Japan's empire in 1945, Korea had been
occupied by Russian and American troops, separated by the 38th
parallel. The Soviets proceeded to Communize their northern half
under a propped-up puppet regime. The Americans attempted to
democratize their southern half—a vastly more difficult task—
under a popularly elected government. In 1949, when order was
sufficiently restored, the United States withdrew its troops.

On June 25, 1950, the dam broke. A North Korean army—Russian-
trained, Russian-equipped, and presumably Russian-inspired—
lunged across the 38th parallel into South Korea. The weaker forces
of the South Koreans crumpled before the overwhelming onslaught.
This sudden attack was presumably made in full confidence, both
in Moscow and in North Korea, that the U.N. would do no more

than express pious indignation. Such a view was strengthened by previous American indifference to Korea, and by an earlier statement of Secretary of State Acheson which seemed to mean, although it did not, that Uncle Sam would never fight to defend South Korea.

The life of the infant U.N. hung by a hair, for it had been frontally challenged by Soviet Communism, acting through North Korean puppets. Once again the events of 1931, when the Japanese plunged into Manchuria, seemed to be repeating themselves like a phonograph record with a needle stuck in one groove. The old League of Nations had faltered, and had ultimately died. If the new U.N. faltered, it probably would die—and with it would perish all hope of collective security for world peace.

But the United Nations Security Council, then meeting at Lake Success, New York, rose magnificently to the challenge. (Ironically, the Soviet Union, which could have cast the usual crippling veto, was boycotting the sessions as a protest against the non-admission of Communist China to the U.N.) On the very day of the invasion, the Council unanimously branded North Korea the aggressor, and called upon all member nations "to render every assistance" to the U.N. in restoring peace.

President Truman would have to act fast, in response to this appeal, if he were to act effectively. To have asked Congress for the usual declaration of war would probably have stirred up enough windy debate to insure the fall of South Korea. So two days after the invasion, on June 27, 1950, Truman seized the bull by the horns. By virtue of his constitutional authority as Commander-in-Chief, he boldly issued the order for American air and naval forces to support South Korea. At the same time he instructed the navy to protect the

THE SHIFTING FRONT IN KOREA

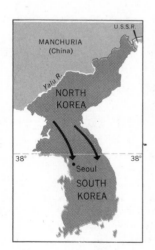   

June 25, 1950   Sept. 14, 1950   Nov. 25, 1950   July 27, 1953

Nationalist Chinese in Formosa against invasion from Communist China. Three days later, when he perceived that a boy had been sent on a man's errand, he ordered to Korea a substantial part of the green American ground troops then occupying Japan.

The President's decisive and courageous action won vigorous applause *at the time* from the public and Congress—quite in contrast with later condemnation when the going got rougher. Fed up with appeasement, the American people were evidently prepared to draw the line somewhere; and that line happened to be the 38th parallel.

Halting Communist aggression in South Korea was officially a United Nations responsibility. Authorized by the U.N., Truman chose General MacArthur, then in Japan, to head the joint forces under the blue and white United Nations flag. The United States provided the overwhelming bulk of the air units, the naval forces, the money, the supplies, and, except for the South Koreans, most of the men.

"History Doesn't Repeat Itself." Truman and the U.N. Rush to the Rescue. Low in the London *Daily Herald*, 1950. Reprinted by special permission; world copyright reserved.

The Military Seesaw in Korea

South Korean and American troops were relentlessly pushed southward by a superior force spearheaded by Russian-made tanks. But the invader was slowed somewhat by American dominance in the air and on the sea. Reinforcements were rushed as speedily as possible from the United States, and these were ultimately joined by tiny contingents from fifteen other members of the U.N.

Unexpectedly, in September, 1950, the tide turned. General Mac-Arthur, in a surprise move, executed a brilliant amphibious attack at Inchon, on the enemy's flank and rear. The North Koreans, their supply lines menaced, fled northward from South Korea in panic, leaving the U.N. victorious in the Korean conflict, first phase.

Should MacArthur pursue the beaten foe across the 38th parallel into North Korea, as South Koreans were already doing? If the U.N. invaded the territory of the aggressor, it would itself become—at least technically—an aggressor. Yet to halt at the boundary would simply permit the beaten Communists to rally and regroup their armies for another assault at their own convenience.

The decision was a momentous one, for the Chinese Communists had threatened to enter the war if North Korea were invaded. In these circumstances the U.N. Assembly rather vaguely authorized MacArthur to proceed, and he prepared to drive to the Yalu River, the northern border of North Korea. Late in November, 1950, he launched a rash all-out assault designed, in his words, to bring the boys "home by Christmas."

The Chinese Reds made good their threat, for MacArthur's forces were approaching too close to their vital hydroelectric power stations on the Manchuria-Korean border. Suddenly a horde of Chinese

"Not Much Help But It's Nice to Have Company." Uncle Sam Short-handed in Korea. Reprinted with permission from the Chicago *Daily News.* Cartoon by Cecil Jensen

"volunteers"—obviously under orders from Communist Peiping—attacked in overwhelming strength. Catching the over-extended U.N. invader on the flank in sub-zero weather, they hurled back their foe in a headlong, frostbitten retreat. Complete disaster threatened; but the shattered South Korean and U.N. forces finally regrouped on the icy terrain south of the 38th parallel. There they held off the Communists, inflicted staggering losses on the "human waves" of Chinese, and retrieved some lost ground.

Five-starred General MacArthur, humiliated by this crushing defeat, pressed for drastic retaliation. He urged a blockade of the Chinese coast, an employment of Chiang Kai-shek's Nationalist troops in Formosa, and a bombing of Red Chinese bases in Manchuria—an area which the enemy was using as a "privileged sanctuary."

MacArthur's desire to fight with both fists, instead of one, was quite understandable. But officials in Washington, where global policy was formulated, were more cautious, as were the U.N. allies. They were unwilling to risk bringing Red China formally into a full-dress conflict and touching off World War III with the Russians, who were bound to the Chinese by the thirty-year mutual aid pact of 1950. The Truman administration, strongly supported by public opinion, regarded the Soviet Union as the main foe, and shied away from pouring American money and manhood down the Chinese rathole. Such a conflict, declared General Omar Bradley of the Joint Chiefs of Staff, would be "the wrong war, at the wrong place, at the wrong time, and with the wrong enemy." Unlimited fighting might be the price of total victory.

Fighting a No-Win War in Korea

A showdown impended with MacArthur, who wrote, "There is no substitute for victory"—even though impermanent. Restive under the restraints imposed by Washington, he sought by various pronouncements to change official policy. An irritated President, alleging insubordination, arbitrarily removed him from all his Far Eastern commands on April 11, 1951. In Truman's eyes the basic issue was: Should military policy be made in Washington, in collaboration with the civilian authorities, or by the general in the field? Yet a flood of telegrams descended upon the White House branding the President a "pig," an "imbecile," and "a Judas." In Congress there was some talk of impeachment.

The deposed hero, who had not seen his country for fourteen years, returned to receive an uproarious welcome. These hysterical reactions resulted partly from gratitude for MacArthur's past services, and partly from Republican resentment against "small-bore" Truman's tactless treatment of a "large-bore" Republican. Even many defenders of Truman believed that he might better have shown the general the stairs, rather than kicking him out the fifth-story window.

War in Korea now turned into a dull, muddy, bloody affair. MacArthur was replaced by General Matthew Ridgway, who regained essentially the 38th parallel after inflicting appalling losses on the Chinese and North Koreans ("Operation Killer"). He was hammering northward when, in June, 1951, the Russian delegate to the U.N. brought new hope to the world by proposing that negotiations be undertaken for a cease-fire.

Truce discussions, which began in a tent a short distance north of the firing line, provided a fantastic charade. Negotiations were dragged out, chiefly by Communist insults and obstructionism, for more than two years. Amid sporadic fighting at the front, the Chinese and North Koreans strengthened their lines and dug in. Probably their initial main goal in seeking a battle of words was to improve their unfavorable position in the battle of weapons.

Outcries against all this shilly-shallying mounted. Americans are not a patient people; they had been accustomed to quick and heady successes. Many red-blooded citizens could see no point in being in a war without striving for a satisfying triumph, even though such action would be costly in lives and might wrap the world in flames.

A Business-as-Usual Conflict

Meanwhile the home-front scenes of World War II were to some extent being re-enacted. The selective service law was extended, and many resentful reservists were torn from their new civilian lives and sent back into action. Soldier morale was sustained by rotating the men home after they had done their required stint. Although about 260,000 United States troops were bolstering the South Korean and U.N. forces at war's end, all told more than a million Americans served in Korea.

Racial integration received a strong boost from the conflict. The Negroes, pursuant to orders issued by Truman, were fully integrated into the army for the first time on a large scale, and they fought well. Many of them, ironically, found the army the most democratic part of America.

Economic pinches from the Korean War were quickly felt at home. Taxes were boosted; buying "scares" necessitated new controls. Congress again set up agencies to impose curbs on installment buying, to establish priorities for scarce materials, and to freeze wages and prices. But such restrictions were not completely effective. The upward-thrusting inflation spiral was stimulated by war purchases, as factories hummed anew with defense orders.

America tried hard to maintain a normal economy while fighting

General Ridgway, writing on the Korean War in 1967, concluded "If the President had failed—after MacArthur's repeated neglect to comply with directives and after the General's public airing of displeasure with approved government policies—to relieve MacArthur from duty, he would have been derelict in his own duty."

Korean War Scene. Grief-stricken American soldier whose buddy has been killed is being comforted, while a medical corpsman fills out casualty tags. U.S. Army Photograph.

the abnormal Korean War. The people sought to have not only new tanks but also new automobiles. Yet occasional strikes hampered the war effort, notably the crippling steel walkout of June and July, 1952.

The prolonged truce talkathon in Korea, at Panmunjom, together with upward-edging prices, hurt the Truman administration. So long as the war to curb aggression and rescue the U.N. went well, the intervention was reasonably popular. But then came heavy reverses, mounting casualty lists, and finally a deadlock which seemed to be a farce. Increasing numbers of action-loving Americans became critical of "Truman's War."

Another disturbing aspect of the talk-fight war in Korea was the fact that only sixteen of the sixty U.N. members sent fighting contingents, mostly pint-sized. Admittedly the other allies were all poorer than rich Uncle Sam, who was left carrying the heavy end of the log. Some of them, conspicuously France and Britain, offered the solid excuse of military commitments elsewhere. Irate American patriots, annoyed by the willingness of the U.N. to "fight to the last American," were demanding that the nation "go it alone." But a disruptive quarrel with allies would have doomed collective security—the very objective for which Truman had intervened in the first place.

McCarthyism and Trial by Slander

One lurid by-product of the Korean War was a stepping-up of the campaign to ferret out Communists. Countless Americans, especially Republicans, believed that the "loss" of China and the Korea "mess" had resulted from the infiltration of Communist agents into the State Department. Republican Senator Joseph R. McCarthy of Wisconsin —"low-blow Joe," some of his foes called him—redoubled his charges, often before whirring cameras. Many of his recklessly unfair accusations, though damaging, were later found to be without substance, but some of them proved embarrassing to a handful of suspected Communists.

A-Bomb Ruins in America. Fitzpatrick in the St. Louis *Post-Dispatch*

All loyal Americans deplored the presence of Communists in the government—provided that they were Communists and not merely non-conformists. But many earnest citizens wondered if McCarthyites were not burning down the barn to get rid of a few rats. Traditional American ideals did not square with the overready assumption of guilt rather than innocence, the use of slander-and-smear tactics, and the making of great reputations by besmirching the reputations of honorable men. Such un-American methods were bringing democracy into disrepute overseas, for they presented unpleasant parallels to the vicious anti-Communist campaigns of Hitler's Germany, including the burning of offensive books. Many Americans, slaves of their suspicions, were evidently willing to yield part of their precious freedom for more security—or fancied security. Some citizens were actually beginning to fear one another more than they feared the Soviets.

The We-Like-Ike Boom of 1952

Morality in American public life had meanwhile been sagging. Washington swarmed with "five-percenter" "influence peddlers," who claimed that they had special "pull" at the White House. A few persons close to the people who were close to Truman suddenly blossomed out in costly fur coats—"the Mink Dynasty." A number of Democratic income-tax collectors were found guilty of favoritism and graft. Yet the President remained stubbornly loyal to his cronies. "Turn the rascals out" was the refurbished cry of the Republicans, who branded the record of the administration as "Plunder at home, blunder abroad."

Republican prospects seemed rosy—but so they had four years earlier. Machine politicians clamored for wheelhorse Senator Robert A. Taft, their ablest leader and a figure long associated as "Mr. Republican" with the isolationist wing of the party. But the blunt and honest Ohioan had made many enemies, especially when his name was attached to the controversial Taft-Hartley labor law. Rank-and-file Republicans were eager for a less vulnerable and more glamorous leader.

By far the most popular American was war hero General Dwight D. ("Ike") Eisenhower, with his ruddy face, glamorous grin, and captivating personality. Though a professional soldier, he had been temporarily demilitarized by post-war service as president of Columbia University. His familiarity with the Communist menace overseas was intimate, for in 1950–1952 he had headed the army in Western Europe under the North Atlantic Treaty Organization (NATO). In January, 1952, he openly declared that he was a Republican (a matter previously in doubt), and that he would be available for the nomination.

Enthusiastic supporters of Eisenhower descended on Chicago in July, 1952, flashing "I Like Ike" buttons. The contest in the convention hall was close and exciting. But grass-roots sentiment for "Ike," who had shown strong appeal in some of the primaries, at length overcame the organization-led support of Taft. The genial general was drafted on the first ballot. His platform assailed corruption and Korea, while stressing the threadbare theme of need for a change.

For Democrats, the race was wide open, since the trim Truman, though full of fight and bounce, chose not to run again. The 22nd Amendment to the Constitution, ratified in 1951 as something of a kick at the corpse of Roosevelt, limited future Presidents to two terms. (See Appendix.) Truman, though specifically exempted from this new restriction, was well aware of his unpopularity in the public

Regarding labor legislation, John L. Lewis, leader of the coal miners, told a convention in 1947, "The Taft-Hartley statute is the first ugly, savage thrust of fascism in America. It came into being through an alliance between industrialists and the Republican majority in Congress, aided and abetted by those Democratic legislators who still believe in the institution of human slavery."

opinion polls. He preferred to pass the torch on to Adlai E. Stevenson, the witty, eloquent, and idealistic governor of Illinois.

Democratic delegates, assembling in Chicago in late July, 1952, were in high spirits. They sang:

The farmer's farmin' every day,
Makin' money, and that ain't hay!
  (Clap, clap)
DON'T LET 'EM TAKE IT AWAY!*

Lanky Senator Estes Kefauver of Tennessee, who had run well in the primaries after heading a highly publicized Senate probe of crime, attracted considerable support from partisans who donned (with him) coonskin caps. But after a tense and noisy struggle on the convention floor, Governor Stevenson was nominated on the third ballot—despite his avowed reluctance to run.

The Eisenhower Landslide

The ensuing campaign was hotly contested. Stevenson—thin, quiet, and intellectual ("egg headed")—was handicapped at the start because he was little known outside Illinois, while the sparkling Eisenhower was a five-starred household word. Television figured prominently in a presidential campaign for the first time. Both candidates appeared to good advantage—Eisenhower with his transparent sincerity, Stevenson with his touch of Wilsonian loftiness leavened by a keen sense of humor. "Eggheads of the world, unite!" he quipped. "You have nothing to lose but your yolks."

Eisenhower, the amateur in politics, embarked upon a rousing "crusade" to overthrow corruptionists and clean up "the mess in Washington." He injected further fireworks when he promised to visit Korea to see what he could do to straighten out the frustrating stalemate; and this hope-inspiring pledge by a distinguished general no doubt won many votes. Democrats deplored this "grandstand gesture," and predicted that a Republican victory would bring back dreary depression days. The slogan "You Never Had It So Good" was an obvious attempt to make political capital once more of the "Hoover Depression."

Seven "C's" hampered the Democrats. Corruption in government, which Truman pooh-poohed out of loyalty to his appointees. Corea (old spelling), with its deadlock and dead-end futility. China, which had gone Communist, allegedly as a result of the Roosevelt-Truman blunderings. Communist-coddling in Washington, with imprisoned Alger Hiss a chief target of attack. Cost of living, which was inching

Republicans applied the sneer of "egghead" to the intellectuals who supported Stevenson, many of whom had high foreheads and semi-bald heads that suggested the egg. Stevenson's quip about "yolks" was evidently inspired by the call of the Communist Manifesto of 1848, usually rendered as "Workers, unite! You have nothing to lose but your yokes."

* "Don't Let 'Em Take It Away!" by Robert Sour and Bernie Wayne, 1952. By permission of Meridian Music Corp.

upward under the pressure of Korean War spending. Controls on wages, buying, and prices, with all the consequent frustrations. All in all, the record of the Truman administration was a burden to Stevenson.

The seventh "C" was Change, which the Republicans—crying "Had Enough?"—claimed was urgently needed. Democrats had been in power for nearly twenty years, and if the two-party system was to survive, so Republicans insisted, there would have to be a thorough housecleaning. Republicans also decried the red tape, the red ink, and the Reds; the New Deal, the Fair Deal, and the Ordeal.

The victorious war hero triumphed in a landslide so massive that the pollsters were again caught off base. He amassed 33,936,234 votes to 27,314,992 for Stevenson—an enormous plurality of more than 6,500,000 votes. He cracked the Solid South wide open, as he rang up 442 electoral votes to 89 for his opponent. His enormous popularity in large areas of the South led to the hope that a genuine two-party system could be established in Dixieland. A Southern Republican could now claim respectability.

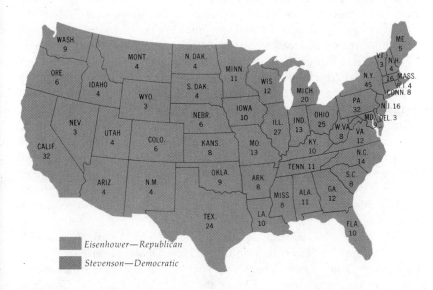

Eisenhower—Republican

Stevenson—Democratic

PRESIDENTIAL ELECTION OF 1952 (with electoral vote by state)

"Ike's" amazing personality told much of the story. Even though the Democrats could point to pulsating prosperity, such was the spell cast by Eisenhower that the voters, for once, voted against their pocketbooks. "Ike" ran far ahead of his ticket, polling several million more votes than all the Republican Congressmen combined, many of whom rode into office on his military coattails. But at that, the victors won control of Congress by only a paper-thin margin.

"Ike" and the New Republicanism

Dwight D. Eisenhower (1890–1969). When General Eisenhower was approached in 1948 regarding the presidential nomination, he wrote, "The necessary and wise subordination of the military to civil power will be best sustained when life-long professional soldiers abstain from seeking high political office." The Democratic Congressman Rayburn remarked, "No, won't do. Good man, but wrong business." The fears of a militaristic regime were not realized. Photo courtesy of Mrs. Eisenhower.

Eisenhower was an erect (5 feet 10½) and balding career soldier who, in the autumn of his public life, had to adjust himself to the give-and-take of politics and the techniques of civilian government. A liberal internationalist in foreign affairs, he was a middle-of-the-road Kansas conservative in domestic affairs. He deeply respected the separation of powers among the three branches of government, as taught in his civics textbooks, and he evidently had no desire to dominate Congress in the Rooseveltian manner. Famed as a conciliator, he undertook to achieve his ends by quiet lunch-table conferences.

As a "team man," Eisenhower earnestly sought party unity. Republicans were divided into two camps: the isolationist or "dinosaur" wing, headed by Senator Taft, and the internationalist wing, headed by men like Governor Dewey. Although Eisenhower's personal sympathies were with the Dewey group, he would have to make both wings flap together if he was to keep his party air-borne.

Eisenhower's Cabinet was noteworthy in several respects. A new post was created when the Republican Congress established the Department of Health, Education, and Welfare, under the second woman Cabinet officer in history, Mrs. Oveta Culp Hobby of Texas, a journalist. Most of the Cabinet positions were filled by big bankers or industrialists, in harmony with the Republican tradition of having big businessmen run the big business of government. A hot controversy preceded the confirmation of the new Defense Secretary, blunt-spoken Charles E. Wilson, ex-president of General Motors, who was forced to sell his heavy holdings of General Motors stock because of his new role in assigning juicy defense contracts. Democrats growled that New Dealers were being replaced by Car Dealers, and that the Cabinet consisted of "eight millionaires and a plumber." (Labor Secretary Durkin had been president of the International Plumbers Union.)

Obviously the triumphant Republicans could not unscramble the eggs that had been scrambled by New Dealers and Fair Dealers in twenty long years. The TVA, social security, and other deep-reaching changes would have to stand; in fact, the new Congress extended social security benefits to an additional ten million persons. But the Republicans were pledged to make reforms relating to a balanced budget, reduced federal outlays, lowered taxes, free enterprise, less government in business, and fewer curbs on industry. Eisenhower's own preoccupation with fiscal responsibility led Democrats to jeer, "Better dead than in the red."

Eisenhowerites took their economy pledges seriously. Their ax fell painfully on many a Democratic neck as they lopped off superfluous offices and found many places for faithful followers—so far as they could under existing civil service regulations. Some 183,000 officeholders were dropped during the first year—cynically dubbed F.B.I.'s ("fired by 'Ike'"). The Republicans likewise wielded a meat ax on Truman's proposed budget, slashing more than twelve billion dollars from his estimates, and proceeded to reduce taxes sharply.

Nor did the Republicans overlook their promises to shake off governmental restrictions. Despite a temporary boost to inflation, they wiped out the price and wage controls imposed by the Truman administration during the Korean War. The Republican Congress also limited a public housing program to one year, and permitted the Hoover-sponsored Reconstruction Finance Corporation to die a natural death.

Republican efforts toward enlarged free enterprise continued in other areas. Offshore oil lands, despite a record-breaking twenty-two-hour filibustering speech by Senator Morse of Oregon, were handed over to the coastal states to facilitate private rather than federal exploitation. Naturally the new administration showed a strong preference for private as against public hydroelectric power, and shepherded through Congress an act authorizing a private atomic-energy industry to generate electricity. The traditionally high-tariff Republicans, influenced to some extent by Europe's cry of "Trade, Not Aid," reluctantly renewed for one year a limited Reciprocal Trade Agreements Act, pending a full study.

Cease-Fire in Korea

Eisenhower at the outset attempted to fashion a bipartisan foreign policy—a goal only partially achieved by his immediate predecessors. Democrats in Congress, steeped in the internationalism of Franklin Roosevelt and Harry S Truman, on the whole supported "Ike" more effectively than his own followers.

Korea, the "forgotten war," remained a Chinese puzzle. President-elect Eisenhower had redeemed his campaign promise by making a flying three-day visit to that war-ravaged land in December, 1952. But the stalemated truce negotiations continued on dead center. The sticking point was the demand of the Communists that the U.N. return all prisoners, willing or not, including those anti-Communists to whom America had promised asylum if they surrendered.

A new chapter of the cold war was opened on March 5, 1953, when Moscow announced that Joseph Stalin (the Man of Steel) had died. Shortly thereafter the Kremlin began to adopt—for a brief period—a less bellicose attitude toward the Western World in what was branded by cynics a "peace offensive." The Soviets presumably were hoping to trick the democratic nations into dropping their guard and slackening preparations for the NATO army; and in this respect they were partially successful. But while the tongues of the Russians talked peace, their hands continued to build up a powerful force on land, on sea, and in the air.

While the truce negotiations were being prolonged, many Americans urged complete military victory. General Ridgway, who had succeeded MacArthur in Korea, wrote in 1967, "No one who was conscious of the military facts could have believed that with the limited forces at our disposal, we could have won anything resembling a total victory."

Moscow's "peace offensive" was reflected in the truce negotiations in Korea, where armistice terms were finally signed on July 27, 1953, after Washington had hinted at the use of atomic bombs. The United Nations won a victory for human dignity when the Communists agreed that prisoners who did not want to go home would be processed by neutral countries. It was further stipulated that a subsequent political conference (never held) would arrange for the evacuation of foreign troops, as well as for the peaceful settlement of the whole Korean question.

After more than three years of shooting (including two of talking), the brutal and futile fighting stopped. Americans, breathing a sigh of relief, accepted but did not celebrate the armistice. There was no dancing in the streets. America had not lost; yet she had not won a satisfying victory, such as she had traditionally come to expect. The outcome was more like that of the frustrating War of 1812.

Korean costs had been high. Though never officially declared by Congress, the conflict ranked as the nation's third largest foreign war until then in outlay and losses. Over fifteen billion dollars had been spent; more than 157,000 American casualties had been suffered, over 33,000 of them deaths. These losses amounted to about 95% of those of the sixteen participating U.N. members. The Republic of South Korea (not a U.N. member) was the most seriously hurt of all, not only at the battle front but even more grievously among civilians. Yet the casualties inflicted on the Communist armies were estimated to be far heavier than those suffered by the United Nations and South Korea combined. Counting both sides, more than a million people probably perished.

"The Paper Cornerstone." Hesse in the St. Louis Globe-Democrat, 1953

Disheartening though the losses were, certain gains were evident. America had shown unexpected decisiveness as a global leader; no one could now say that the U.N. had died in the rice paddies of Korea in 1950 because Uncle Sam failed to measure up to his responsibilities. The infant organization had been saved—at least temporarily. It had halted the aggressor through joint police action—the first time in history that an international combination had thus acted collectively and effectively. The North Koreans, their fingers badly burned, had been taught the harsh lesson that aggression did not pay. Their own land devastated, they had wound up with 1500 square miles less territory than when the war started.

Eisenhower's Debits and Credits—and School Desegregation

At home, the "honeymoon period" of the Eisenhower administration was rapidly passing. Senator Taft died of cancer in July, 1953; and with his expert hand gone, Congress became progressively more unruly. The isolationist wing of the Republican Party began to flop even more vigorously. Noteworthy was the determined attempt of

Senator Bricker of Ohio to curb the treaty-making power of the President by constitutional amendment—a move that failed in the Senate by the narrowest of margins.

A somewhat balky Republican Congress was slow to follow Eisenhower's leadership in the "great crusade." Such issues as the tariff, revision of the Taft-Hartley labor law, health reinsurance, and the admission of Hawaii and Alaska to statehood were not acted upon at all, or were dealt with unsatisfactorily. Congress finally responded to decades-long prodding from the White House when, in May, 1954, it authorized American participation with Canada in the construction of the Great Lakes–St. Lawrence Seaway. This "socialistic ditch" would turn lake ports into seaports. But favorable action did not come until Canada had threatened to go it alone.

The eagerness of Congress to encroach on Executive authority was glaringly revealed in the angry dispute between Senator Mc-Carthy and the Army. Touched off by the Communists-in-government issue, the quarrel resulted in one of the most highly publicized television shows of 1954. Democrats, now turning the tables, were speaking cynically of the "mess in Washington." But in this latest episode, a bullying McCarthy overreached himself before millions of television viewers, and his influence rapidly declined.

A business recession, accompanied by considerable unemployment, followed the heavy spending of the Korean war. Administration spokesmen referred delicately to "the slide" rather than "the slump." Farm income was sharply down, largely as a result of lower prices and extensive drought. Yet Secretary of Agriculture Benson —a hard-working, hard-praying Mormon of the old economic school—was reluctant to continue generous handouts. A vexing problem was to secure adequate parity payments for the farmer without boosting federal price supports. The latter had proved excessively costly, and had left the government knee-deep in the butter, eggs, and other produce which it had purchased to bolster prices.

On the education front, a sensational decision burst into the headlines on May 17, 1954. The Supreme Court ruled unanimously that the long-established "separate but equal" school facilities granted to Negroes violated the 14th Amendment. (They were always separate, seldom equal.) But the Court indicated that so drastic a social revolution as school desegregation would have to be worked out gradually, "with all deliberate speed."

Opposition in the South to the integration decision mounted with burning intensity. Just as the North had denounced the Dred Scott decision of 1857 as a political dictum by an anti-Northern court, so the South denounced the ruling of 1954 as a sociological decision by an anti-Southern court. To millions of Southerners this decree represented an unwarranted invasion of states' rights and an intolerable interference with purely local affairs. The gravest constitutional crisis

In the desegregation decision of 1954, the Supreme Court quoted approvingly from a lower court: "Segregation of white and colored children in public schools has a detrimental effect upon the colored children. The impact is greater when it has the sanction of the law; for the policy of separating the races is usually interpreted as denoting the inferiority of the Negro group. A sense of inferiority affects the motivation of a child to learn. Segregation . . . has a tendency to retard the educational and mental development of Negro children. . . ."

since the Civil War came to a head as massive resistance to desegregation formed in the Deep South, and conspicuously also in Arkansas and Virginia. But in many other peripheral areas integration in the schools went forward slowly and without disagreeable incident.

Republican Setbacks and Laborite Gains

Hotly contested Congressional elections, in November, 1954, resulted in a stinging setback for the Republicans. Eisenhower, standing on his record of achievement, bluntly appealed for a Republican Congress. But the Democrats carried the Senate by a margin of one vote, and the House by a more comfortable majority. The results were widely regarded as a protest against lowered farm income and spotty unemployment, as well as a rebuke to McCarthyism and big-businessism. But—presumably as a result of Eisenhower's still-great personal popularity—the Republican losses were not so large as those ordinarily suffered by the party in power during the mid-term slump.

Curiously, the Senate "condemned" McCarthy, not for assailing fellow Americans, but for failing to cooperate with a Senate investigating committee regarding matters which "affected the honor of the Senate and instead, repeatedly abused members who were trying to carry out assigned duties, thereby obstructing the constitutional processes of the Senate. . . ." On the other hand, a Fort Worth, Texas, newspaper wrote, "Joe McCarthy was slowly tortured to death by the pimps of the Kremlin."

Conservative Republican right-wingers lost ground as a result of this setback at the polls, and in the ensuing calmer atmosphere fairer methods were devised for dealing with "security risks." With the Democrats now in power, Red-hunting Senator McCarthy, already discredited by his backfiring attack on the Army, lost the chairmanship of his investigating committee early in 1955. Late in the preceding year he had been soundly spanked when the Senate, by a bipartisan vote of 67 to 22, agreed to "condemn" him for his abuse of fellow Senators, while overlooking more serious offenses. He took heavily to drink and died three years later, apparently without having rooted out a single Communist from a sensitive governmental agency.

The new Democratic 84th Congress cooperated unexpectedly well with Eisenhower, especially in foreign policy. While shying away from many of the President's recommendations, the legislators did pass a law in 1955 authorizing 45,000 housing units, and a three-year extension of the reciprocal trade agreements act. A surprising development occurred when much of the newly industrialized South, reversing its historic low-tariff position, held out vainly for higher protection.

Labor chalked up significant gains, both in Washington and elsewhere. The Democratic Congress boosted the legal hourly minimum wage from seventy-five cents to one dollar. Although failing to secure a revision of the Taft-Hartley Act, labor won a resounding victory over itself early in 1955. At Miami, Florida, representatives of the feuding A.F. of L. and C.I.O. agreed to bury the hatchet and unite their total membership of some 15,000,000. The merger could only mean greater strength for organized labor.

Symptomatic of a growing assertiveness among workers were

the mounting demands, particularly in the automobile industry, for a "guaranteed annual wage" as a cushion against unemployment. A long stride toward this goal was taken in June, 1955, when the United Auto Workers wrested highly favorable unemployment-wage contracts from the Ford Motor Company and General Motors.

Hydrogen Bombs and German Rearmament

A mushroom-shaped nuclear cloud continued to hang over foreign relations. Eisenhower spectacularly proposed to the U.N. in December, 1953, that the nations pool their atomic resources for peaceful purposes. When this scheme received the usual cold shoulder from the Soviets, the United States nevertheless launched it on a limited basis. Moscow later expressed a willingness to go along.

In March, 1954, American experts detonated in the Pacific two hydrogen bombs, both of them hundreds of times more powerful than the obsolete Hiroshima model. The Soviets, it was revealed, had also devised a hydrogen bomb. Before 1945 the United States, with billowing oceans east and west, never had reason to fear an overnight intercontinental attack. Now, with power relationships radically changing, it was vulnerable to a sudden and perhaps crippling blow.

"Russia Presiding." (Soviet Obstruction in U.N.) Pletcher in the Sioux City, Iowa *Journal*. By permission

Eisenhower, faced with overpowering military costs in fending off Communism all over the world, committed himself to a "New Look" defense policy. The army and navy would be shown the back seat, and the air force would be built up to deter aggressors with the threat of "massive retaliation." At the same time the Republic would strive to beef up the armed forces being amassed by its NATO allies in Europe.

Fateful progress had meantime been made toward the rearmament of West Germany, as well as her inclusion in the camp of the western allies as a buffer against Soviet Communism. After the French had stubbornly vetoed one ambitious plan, the powers threshed out new arrangements at Paris in the autumn of 1954—arrangements designed to give West Germany her sovereignty and to admit her to NATO with a contribution of 500,000 troops. The members of NATO, including the United States, subordinated their misgivings and concluded ratification of the agreements in April, 1955. West Germany thus became the fifteenth partner.

Growing Dangers in Vietnam and Formosa (Taiwan)

A crisis in the Far East had meanwhile been coming to a boil. The multi-nation Geneva Conference of 1954, called to deal with Korean and Indochinese problems, resulted in another stunning reverse for the free world. With French forces in northern Indochina crumbling before Communist rebels, the conferees agreed to cut Vietnam provisionally at the waist, and turn over the 13,000,000 inhabitants

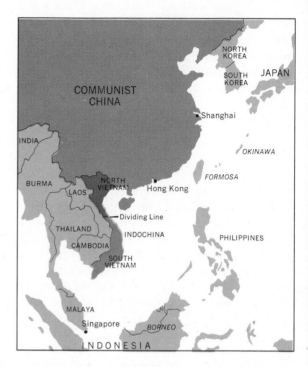

THE FAR EAST, 1955–1956

north of that line to the Communists. A free election scheduled for 1956 (but never held) would determine the fate of all Vietnam. Uncle Sam, though acquiescing, was not an official party to this surrender, which was widely condemned in America as "appeasement." Late in 1954, as a countermeasure, Washington did take the lead in organizing the free nations of Southeast Asia into the eight-country Southeast Asia Treaty Organization (SEATO).* It was designed as a weaker Far Eastern counterpart of the defensive North Atlantic Treaty Organization (NATO).

Despite these efforts at unity, the upsurging Communists continued to show their contempt for Western weakness. Americans were aroused in 1954 when the Peiping regime, contrary to the Korean armistice, sentenced as spies eleven uniformed American airmen who had been forced down on Communist territory. Further evidence of an aggressive attitude by the Chinese Communists came with a stepping-up of preparations for attacking Chiang's refuge on Formosa, which was a vital bastion of anti-Communist strength in the Far East.

Tensions became so acute that early in 1955 Eisenhower took an unparalleled step. He flatly asked Congress for advance authorization to use armed forces to repel a Communist assault on Formosa.

---

* Signatories were Australia, France, Great Britain, New Zealand, Pakistan, the Philippines, Thailand, and the U.S.

Such a blank check would enable him to avoid the agonizing responsibility that had fallen to Truman at the time of the North Korean invasion of 1950. Congress, impressed with the desirability of keeping Formosa afloat, approved this pre-dated war resolution by an overwhelming vote of 85 to 3 in the Senate and 409 to 3 in the House. The initiative now lay in the hands of the Communists.

Soviet Wiles and "Ike's" Recovery

With the world braced for an explosion, the grim-faced Soviet leaders suddenly and unexpectedly put on a smiling countenance in the spring and summer of 1955. Experts could only speculate as to the motivation. Perhaps it was fear of a rearmed Germany; or internal strain within the Soviet economy; or friction among the successors of Stalin; or fear of a terrible hydrogen-bomb war; or a desire to lull the democracies into slackening their defense preparations.

Whatever the cause, the Soviet change of front was unmistakable. After ten years of obstruction, Moscow suddenly gave way and signed a treaty in May, 1955, to end the four-power occupation of Austria. The Moscow Communists then humbled themselves when they patched up their noisy feud with Tito of Yugoslavia. In May, 1955, the Red Chinese government, presumably acting in concert with the Kremlin, released four of the imprisoned American airmen, preparatory to releasing the remaining seven a month later. In a striking reversal of policy, the Russians began to lift their iron curtain to permit a few foreign visitors to enter the U.S.S.R., and a few selected Russian tourists to leave.

Highly encouraging was the acceptance by the Soviets of a meeting at the "summit" by the heads of state of the Big Four at Geneva in July, 1955. Eisenhower's radiant personality dominated the sessions, and he spectacularly seized the initiative in the propaganda war by proposing that the Soviets and the United States exchange their military blueprints and permit mutual "open skies" flights over their installations. A Soviet acceptance in good faith seemed highly improbable, but the sessions at Geneva adjourned in a new spirit of friendliness—at least outwardly. Soviet and Western leaders had talked freely, and apparently had convinced one another of the sincerity of their desire for peace. An atmosphere of cautious optimism began to pervade the Western World.

But a bucket of cold water suddenly descended on September 24, 1955, when Eisenhower, then vacationing in Colorado, was stricken with a heart attack. Republican leaders had been counting heavily on running him for a second time, for they feared that they could not win again without his immense popularity. Resulting uncertainties touched off a series of downward plunges in the stock market reminiscent of 1929.

Prospects abroad were even more disquieting. In view of Mos-

When Eisenhower proposed his Open Skies scheme at Geneva, he found the chairman of the Soviet delegation, Bulganin, not altogether hostile. Shortly thereafter, so Eisenhower records in his memoirs, he met Nikita S. Khrushchev, a member of the delegation who was soon to be formally elevated to power. "'I don't agree with the chairman,' he said, smiling—but there was no smile in his voice. . . . He said the idea was nothing more than a bold espionage plot against the U.S.S.R., and to this line of argument he stubbornly adhered. He made his points laughingly—but his argument was definite and intractable."

cow's deeds, it quickly became evident that the new Soviet smile was merely a painted mask. A meeting of foreign ministers at Geneva in October, 1955, speedily ran into the usual deadlock, chiefly over disarmament and Soviet unwillingness to permit Germany to become both united and free. While proclaiming peace and disarmament, the Communists were shipping huge quantities of arms to the Arabs in the explosive Middle East, where Israel was in imminent danger of being attacked by her neighbors.

Yet at home confidence returned with Eisenhower's steady recovery. An unprecedented 65,000,000 persons were gainfully employed, and the administration could soon claim that the budget was in balance. With much justification, and with a pointed allusion to the recent Korean War, the Republicans could boast, "Only the guns are not booming."

SELECT READINGS

The era is surveyed readably in E. F. GOLDMAN, *The Crucial Decade: America, 1945–1955* (1956)*; more sketchily in HERBERT AGAR, *The Price of Power: America since 1945* (1957).* President D. D. EISENHOWER tells his own story (blandly) in *Mandate for Change, 1953–1956* (1963).* Interesting insights into politics are found in WALTER JOHNSON, *1600 Pennsylvania Avenue: Presidents and the People, 1929–1959* (1960).* A solid study is L. L. GERSON, *John Foster Dulles* (1967). Journalistic analyses of a controversial Secretary of State are J. R. BEAL, *John Foster Dulles* (1957); ROSCOE DRUMMOND and GASTON COBLENTZ, *Duel at the Brink* (1960). Also journalistic are M. J. PUSEY, *Eisenhower, the President* (1956) and R. J. DONOVAN, *Eisenhower* (1956). Less friendly are M. W. CHILDS, *Eisenhower: Captive Hero* (1958) and E. J. HUGHES' indiscreet *The Ordeal of Power* (1963).* For a critical appraisal of McCarthyism consult R. H. ROVERE, *Senator Joe McCarthy* (1959).* See also H. M. HYMAN, *To Try Men's Souls: Loyalty Tests in American History* (1959).

The Korean War is discussed in DAVID REES, *Korea: The Limited War* (1964). General MacArthur is criticized in HARRY TRUMAN, *Years of Trial and Hope* (1956)*; in J. W. SPANIER, *The Truman-MacArthur Controversy and the Korean War* (1965)*; in TRUMBULL HIGGINS, *Korea and the Fall of MacArthur* (1960); in R. H. ROVERE and A. M. SCHLESINGER, JR., *The General and the President* (1951); and in General M. B. RIDGWAY, *The Korean War* (1967).* He is defended by C. A. WILLOUGHBY and J. CHAMBERLAIN in *MacArthur, 1941–1951* (1954); by COURTNEY WHITNEY in *MacArthur* (1956); and by the General himself in *Reminiscences* (1964). See also SELECT READINGS of preceding and succeeding chapters.

* Available in paperback.

47

The End of the Eisenhower Era

In all those things which deal with people, be liberal,
be human. In all those things which deal with people's money, or
their economy, or their form of government, be conservative.

REPUBLICAN PLATFORM, 1956, quoting President Eisenhower

The Voters Still Like Ike in 1956

President Eisenhower, the magnetic general, was still immensely popular despite Democratic sneers that the only order he ever gave was to mark time. The Republicans, now a minority party, had to run him again if they hoped to win in 1956. Many voters wondered if he had recovered sufficiently from his recent heart attack to risk re-election. The doctors finally gave him a clean bill of health, despite a major abdominal operation (for ileitis) in June, 1956. He was unanimously renominated in San Francisco, as was Vice-President Nixon.

Adlai E. Stevenson, beaten by Eisenhower in 1952, wanted the nomination again, but this time he did not receive it on a silver platter. After a grueling struggle in the state primaries, he won easily on the first ballot at Chicago. Voters were thus presented with two warmed-over candidates—the first such pair since 1900 —running on middle-of-the-road platforms.

The mood of the country was moderation. No one, with the notable exception of the farmers, was "mad at anybody." Jobs, wages, and profits were at record levels, as indeed were inflated prices. Republicans preened themselves on being "the party of peace." Proud of having ended the Korean deadlock in 1953, they condemned the Democrats as "the party of war" by pointing to the Democrat-led World War I, World War II, and Korean War. They conveniently overlooked the Spanish-American War and the Civil War (the bloodiest of all to America), both of them fought under Republican auspices. Democrats, attacking President "Eisenhoover," no less unfairly branded the Republicans as "the party of depression." A reversible salesman's "safety pin" button proved popular: on one side was "I like Ike," on the other "All the Way with Adlai."

In the campaign of 1956 the Republicans used "Truth Squads," each consisting of about four Congressmen or Senators, to follow the principal Democratic speakers around and hold press conferences by way of rebuttal. Stevenson quipped that each squad bore the same relation to truth that a fire department did to a fire. "It will," he said, "extinguish it if it can."

Stevenson, though still urbane, witty, and idealistic, seemed less freshly appealing than four years earlier. Eisenhower's health was a prime issue; and Stevenson (who was to die first) bluntly warned that his opponent probably would not live out another term. In that event the country would inherit Vice President Nixon, whose earlier anti-Communist campaigning had raised doubts as to his statesmanship and had caused irate Democrats to dub him "Tricky Dick." Stevenson finally injected some fireworks when he urged a unilateral halting of nuclear bomb tests, in the interests of both disarmament and an unpolluted atmosphere. Eisenhower branded this scheme "incredible folly," although he embraced it himself two years later.

In the last week of the campaign a four-nation collision in Egypt over the Suez crisis aided Eisenhower's cause. If World War III erupted, as seemed quite possible, the country preferred a military hero in the White House to a less experienced "egghead."

The election was a resounding endorsement of the amiable general with a glamorous grin. He had candidly told the voters that his health would permit him to be only a part-time President, but such was the "national love affair" that the people were willing to take him on his own terms. His landslide was even more awesome than that four years earlier; only Franklin Roosevelt's popular majority of 1936 exceeded it. The popular count was 35,590,472 to 26,022,752; the electoral count 457 to 73. Eisenhower was the first Republican to be re-elected since McKinley in 1900; the oldest incumbent ever to be re-elected; and probably the poorest life insurance risk to re-enter the White House. "Any jockey would look good riding Ike," replied the Republican national chairman when congratulated on the victory. To many voters the President seemed like a kindly "father image" on whom they might lean for comfort in a troubled world.

But the President's popularity did not rub off on those politicians who had hoped to slide into office by clinging to his coattails. Democrats retained both houses of Congress, though by relatively narrow

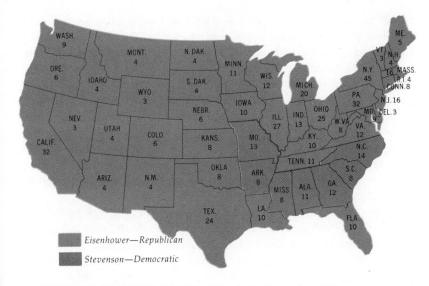

Eisenhower—Republican

Stevenson—Democratic

PRESIDENTIAL ELECTION OF 1956 (with electoral vote by state)

margins. For the first time since Zachary Taylor's election in 1848—
one hundred and eight years earlier—a victorious President had
failed to carry with him either the House or the Senate. The vote was
more one of adoration for Eisenhower than admiration for his party.

Ike Resorts to Government by Proxy

At the outset Eisenhower's second administration marked no
sharp break with the past. Suffering a mild stroke three weeks after
reelection, the President resorted more than ever to golfing and quail
shooting. By now an avowed partisan, rather than a referee between
parties, he got along surprisingly well with the Democratic majorities in Congress. Liberal Democrats joined with liberal Republicans
to pass much of his middle-of-the-road legislation. The conservative
wing of the Republican Party showed a marked distaste for Eisenhower's liberal-tinged "Modern Republicanism," so much so that
the President had earlier thought seriously of forming a new party.

Flanked by big-business advisers, Eisenhower was deeply concerned about "fiscal integrity"—that is, balancing the budget and
halting inflation. Liberal Democrats, reared on the "damn the deficits" attitude of the New Dealers, sneered at this "piggy-bank"
concept, and insisted that Eisenhower was still more concerned
with General Motors than with General Welfare. To such "budget
busters," urgent human needs seemed more important than bookkeeping needs, especially in an era of rapidly rising national income.
Spurred by the Cold War, Democratic Congresses annually appropriated for defense some forty-five billion dollars of the national

"Humpty Dumpty." Eisenhower Republicanism Takes a Fall. Justus in the Minneapolis *Star*

budget of nearly eighty billion dollars. They would have voted even more but were restrained by the aging general. Fearing that the nation would spend itself into bankruptcy, he argued that he knew more about military needs than Congress. The Democrats contended that a balanced budget was out of place in an unbalanced world.

Handicapped as he was by precarious health, Eisenhower was evidently more willing than even before to reign rather than rule. Increasingly he entrusted foreign affairs to his hard-working, far-flying Secretary of State, John Foster Dulles. At the same time he delegated important domestic decisions to his presidential assistant, Sherman Adams, the tough-minded ex-governor of New Hampshire who had publicly condemned Democratic corruption.

Adams fell from grace in 1958, when a House investigation revealed that he had accepted expensive gifts from a Boston industrialist, on whose behalf he had thrice interceded with federal agencies. Eisenhower, conceding that Adams had been imprudent, responded to cries for his resignation with a curt "I need him." But the need became less apparent when Adams proved to be a political liability, and Eisenhower finally accepted his resignation "with sadness" in September, 1958. With his right-hand man gone, Eisenhower did less golfing and more governing, and partly silenced demands for more vigorous leadership.

The Adams scandal highlighted an alarming moral sag throughout the country. Congressmen were paying their relatives handsome salaries; certain members of the Eisenhower administration were being forced to resign because of their intimacy with persons or firms seeking government contracts or other favors. In 1959 the nation was shocked to learn that big-money television contests had been "rigged," and that "disc jockeys" playing records on radio had "plugged" certain recordings after receiving under-the-table payments ("payola").

Economic Cross Currents under Eisenhower

Secretary of Agriculture Benson, who was hanged by Iowa farmers in effigy, continued to be a highly controversial figure. But with Eisenhower's backing he resigned himself to his duty rather than resigning. A bumper crop of agricultural headaches included declining farm income (despite general prosperity), the bankruptcy of smaller farmers, the costly price-support payments by Washington (averaging over three billion dollars a year), and the fantastic farm surpluses (valued at about nine billion dollars), stored in silo-shaped containers over the land. Storage alone was costing the taxpayers about $2,000,000 a day.

There were no simple solutions. Democrats generally advocated high and inflexible parity price supports; Republicans favored somewhat lower and more flexible payments. Some farmers wanted to end price supports; others clamored for them. Congressmen feared punishment at the polls if they took away these handouts. Communist propagandists, proclaiming that half the world went to bed hungry, hammered ceaselessly at the stored (and spoiling) surpluses. Washington's giveaway program to needy nations made only a dent in the towering pile.

The prosperity joyride suffered a severe jolt late in 1957, when a serious business "recession" set in, the third and severest since World War II. Republicans called it a "dip"; Democrats called it a "depression," especially when unemployment reached its peak in June, 1958, with 5,437,000 workers out of jobs. Democrats demanded a drastic tax reduction to increase purchasing power and spur recovery. But Eisenhower refused to push the panic button. A huge highway-building program, costing some thirty-three billion dollars and financed by state-federal funds, had been authorized by Congress in 1956, and though it crept forward with disappointing slowness, it helped take up some of the slack.

Eisenhower's optimism was rewarded when boom times began to return late in 1958, and his economic advisers could warn, "Inflation is the problem." The cost of living continued to edge upward to an all-time high late in 1960, although at a much slower rate than during the preceding Democratic administrations.

Paraphrasing the maxim that war is too important to be left to the generals, General Eisenhower declared in a campaign speech in New York in 1952, "Inflation is too critical a matter to be left to the politicians."

For three of the eight Eisenhower fiscal years, the budget was balanced. The administration could even boast a surplus of more than one billion dollars for the fiscal year 1960. Yet American expenditures abroad were so heavy that the nation was showing an adverse balance of payments ("flight of gold"), and by 1960 was having to export about four billion dollars annually to plug the gap. Alarmed budget-parers in Congress looked with growing hostility on the yearly four billion dollars flowing to various "backward" nations as military and economic aid, primarily to keep them out of the Communist camp.

Congress Cracks Down on Labor

Labor unrest persisted throughout the later Eisenhower years. Mechanization (automation) was throwing thousands of men out of jobs, and hundreds of thousands of young people were being pitchforked annually onto the labor market. Discontent with closed-shop union tactics led to much agitation in the states for right-to-work laws—that is, the right to take a job without having to join a union. Under sanction of the Taft-Hartley "slave-labor" Act of 1947, about a score of states had adopted such legislation by 1957.

Organized labor was flexing its muscles awesomely, especially after the merger of the A. F. of L. and the C.I.O. in 1955. A series of strikes partially paralyzed production, notably in the steel industry, which suffered its sixth and most serious tie-up since World War II in 1959–1960. At a time when the nation was struggling to keep well ahead of the Russians, the steel stalemate lasted one-third of a year (116 days) and idled over a half million men. It finally ended early in 1960 with wage increases and other worker benefits.

Labor demanded a larger share of lush profits; management wanted to hold the line against rising costs—and inflation. The workers would strike and win higher wages; management would raise prices correspondingly; and the workers would again strike because of higher prices. This dog-chasing-its-tail cycle sparked charges that labor and management had entered into a conspiracy to cheat the public. In vain did President Eisenhower appeal to both management and labor to be reasonable, but neither wanted to be the sacrificial goat.

A reported tie-in between gangsters and certain labor leaders broke into the headlines in 1956, when an extortionist threw acid into the eyes of a journalist exposing racketeering. The next year a Senate committee began its spectacular probe of corruption in labor-management relations. Investigators were especially concerned with the use of brass knuckles and explosives to dragoon employers into accepting certain unions, and with the misuse of pension funds and other benefits. Millionaire "Dave" Beck, president of the gigantic Teamsters' Union (1,500,000 members), invoked the Fifth Amendment against self-incrimination 209 times to avoid telling what he had done with $320,000. He was later sentenced to prison for embezzlement. When his union defiantly elected the headstrong James R. Hoffa as his successor, the A. F. of L.–C.I.O. expelled the teamsters, and court-appointed monitors attempted to ride herd on the new teamster leader. The Senate committee finally reported that in fifteen years union officials had stolen or otherwise misused some $10,000,-000.

George Meany, president of the A.F.L.-C.I.O., while favoring the elimination of crooks and racketeers from organized labor, opposed the Landrum-Griffin Bill, claiming in a radio address (1959): "It is a blunderbuss that would inflict grievous harm on all unions. It is supported by the very elements in Congress which have consistently through the years voted for the program of big business and against every progressive measure that would benefit the American people."

Legislation was clearly needed to prevent collective bargaining from becoming collective bludgeoning, and to permit rank-and-file union men to have a voice in the running of their organizations without being beaten up. Teamster-boss Hoffa threatened to defeat for re-election those Congressmen who dared to vote for a "tough" labor bill. His arrogance, combined with a dramatic television appeal by President Eisenhower, spurred a drastic labor-reform bill through Congress by wide margins in September, 1959. The Landrum-Griffin Act was specifically tailored to make labor officials responsible for their financial stewardship, to prevent bully-boy tactics, to insure democratic practices within the unions, to outlaw "secondary boycotts," and to restrict picketing.

The Negro, Little Rock, and Civil Rights

The "Black Monday" decision of the Supreme Court in 1954, ordering desegregation in the public schools, disappointed reformers. It continued to encounter "massive resistance" in the states'-rights Deep South. Resourceful Southerners devised various schemes, such as closing public schools, only to open them as private schools supported by state funds. In 1956 white rioters drove a Negro girl from the University of Alabama amid a shower of stones. A few fanatics, condemned by decent Southerners, dynamited schools, notably the high school in Clinton, Tennessee. But Northern hands raised in horror were not completely clean, for anti-Negro discrimination in housing and jobs was still widely prevalent.

Little Rock, Arkansas, cast a big shadow in 1957. Governor Faubus summoned the state-controlled National Guard to prevent court-ordered integration at Central High School, where nine Negro students were seeking to enroll with two thousand whites. He alleged that their exclusion was necessary to avert violence. Reacting to mob defiance of federal authority, Eisenhower ordered a thousand federal paratroopers to Little Rock, and under their protection the nine Negro children attended the high school. "Military occupation," cried Governor Faubus, who accused the federal soldiers of invading the girls' rest rooms. Memories of bayonet-supported Reconstruction were revived as a new wave of states'-rights bitterness swept over the South. "Little Rock" became a big catchword of Communist propaganda all over the world, even though Washington was trying to protect, not persecute, the Negro.

Massive resistance to integration in the Deep South was still continuing as the Eisenhower era ended. But considerable desegregation had occurred in the Border states and in some of the Southern states. Many Southerners, when forced to choose between integration and no education for their children, reluctantly chose integration.

On a historic day in December, 1955, Mrs. Rosa Parks, a college-educated Negro seamstress, boarded a bus in Montgomery, Alabama, took a seat in the section reserved for whites, and refused to give it up to a white man who entered later. This incident touched off a year-long boycott of the city buses, during which the Negro leader, the Reverend Martin Luther King, Jr., first sprang into prominence. The boycotting Negroes, suffering great inconvenience, won a resounding victory in December 1956, when the Supreme Court declared Alabama's bus-segregation laws unconstitutional.

Other struggles for Negro rights involved equal recreational opportunities (golf courses), non-discrimination in jobs, and the elimination of the poll tax. Massive "sit-in" demonstrations by Southern Negroes at segregated lunch counters began as a Gandhi-like type of passive resistance. They were launched in February, 1960, by four college students in Greensboro, North Carolina, and they achieved extraordinary success, especially when supported in the North by sympathetic demonstrations against Woolworth's and other chain stores.

Strenuous endeavors to safeguard the Negro in his civil rights,

"Deadlock at the Intersection." The Supreme Court and Virginia Meet Head-on Over States' Rights. Seibel in the Richmond *Times-Dispatch.* By permission

especially voting rights, bore fruit in two laws. The first passed Congress in 1957, after a record twenty-four-hour "filibuster" by Senator Thurmond of South Carolina. As the first civil-rights bill enacted since Reconstruction days, it set up new federal machinery to protect Southern Negroes seeking to vote. The second bill, passed in 1960, made further progress toward guaranteeing voting rights.

Civil rights for whites were meanwhile winning more recognition. As the McCarthyite hysteria faded away, the courts were accused of leaning over backward to insure the constitutional guarantees of alleged Communists or Communist sympathizers ("Comsymps"). A determined effort by strong anti-Communist elements in Congress to clip the wings of the Supreme Court narrowly missed success in 1958.

The Soviet "Butchers" of Budapest

Cold War relations with Russia continued strained at the highest levels, while more relaxed at the lower. Increasing numbers of American tourists were being allowed to enter Russia following Stalin's death in 1953. Cultural exchanges featured reciprocal exhibits in New York and Moscow, as well as tours by assorted artists. The brilliant Bolshoi ballet took America by storm in 1959; tickets were reportedly "scalped" in New York for $150 each.

Nikita Khrushchev, a burly, earthy ex-coalminer, continued to tighten his grip as the top Communist official in Russia. Alternately growling and grinning, he sought to defrost the Cold War and lull the free world by coos of peaceful co-existence. At a Communist party congress early in 1956 he sensationally denounced Stalin as a murderer and a blunderer, assailed "the cult of personality," and lightened somewhat the police-state atmosphere.

The "softer" Khrushchev line triggered unexpected explosions among the Russian satellite nations, notably Poland and Hungary. Partly swayed by unofficial American radio propaganda featuring "liberation," the liberty-loving Hungarians revolted in 1956. After initial successes, they were treacherously overpowered by Soviet troops and tanks, which turned Budapest into a slaughterhouse.

Startled by the unreliability of their satellites, the Soviets embarked upon a sterner policy. Khrushchev abandoned de-Stalinization for limited re-Stalinization, thus indicating that his recent peace offensive was only smile-deep. Soviet brutality shocked "neutralist" countries like India, and prompted many foreign Communists to tear up their party cards. But the moral black eye to Russia was largely offset by the simultaneous assault of France, Britain, and Israel upon Egypt late in 1956.

Both the United Nations and the United States lost face over Hungary. The Russians defied U.N. resolutions calling upon them

"Do These Men Look Like Slave Workers?" A View of Russia's Khrushchev. Little in the Nashville *Tennessean.* By permission

to withdraw and to permit an on-the-spot investigation. Embittered Hungarians accused the Americans of promising liberation and then "welshing" when the chips were down. But armed intervention probably would have ignited World War III, and Washington reasoned that it was better for a nation to lose its liberties than for a planet to die. Uncle Sam to some extent redeemed himself by dispatching medical aid and other supplies, and by lifting immigration bars to permit over 30,000 Hungarians to enter.

Crises in the Middle East and Asia

The Suez crisis proved even more explosive. President Nasser of Egypt, an ardent Arab nationalist, was seeking funds to build an immense dam on the upper Nile for urgently needed irrigation and power. America and Britain tentatively offered financial help, but when Nasser began to flirt openly with the Communist camp, Secretary of State Dulles dramatically withdrew the dam offer. Thus slapped in the face, Nasser promptly regained face by nationalizing the Suez Canal, owned chiefly by British and French stockholders.

Nasser's stroke placed a razor's edge at the jugular vein of Western Europe's oil supply. Secretary Dulles labored strenuously to ward off armed intervention, which was forbidden by the U.N. charter. But America's apprehensive British and French allies, after deliberately keeping Washington in the dark and coordinating their blow with one from Israel, staged a joint assault on Egypt late in October, 1956. They were evidently determined to internationalize the canal and eliminate Nasser as a potential Middle Eastern Hitler.

For a breathless week the world teetered on the edge of the abyss. President Eisenhower, reluctantly siding against Britain and France, honored the non-aggression commitment of the U.N. charter and supported a cease-fire resolution. Russia, which for once voted with the Americans, threatened to pour "volunteers" into Egypt. Bending to such pressures, Britain, France, and Israel resentfully withdrew their troops, and for the first time in history a U.N. police contingent was sent to maintain order.

As the United Nations emerged with new laurels, the North Atlantic Treaty Organization (NATO) tottered. Britain and France were angered by America's willingness to turn against old friends and join the Soviet "butchers of Budapest." The United States, irritated by the behind-the-back aggression of its NATO allies, rather grudgingly supplied them with oil during the five months when the Suez Canal was being cleared of sunken ships.

Increasing Communist pressures on the oil-rich Middle East prompted Washington to seek a new protective parasol. The instrument seized upon was the so-called Eisenhower Doctrine, approved overwhelmingly by Congress in March, 1957. It formally empowered

"I'll Be Glad To Restore Peace to the Middle East, Too." (Soviet Ruthlessness.) From Herblock's *Special for Today* (Simon and Schuster, 1958)

the President to extend economic and military aid to the nations of the Middle East, provided that they desired it and were threatened by aggression from a Communist-controlled country. But a doctrine designed to halt military invasion proved ineffective in combatting Communist infiltration.

Secretary of State Dulles, determined "to go to the brink," took a strong position in the Far East as well as in the Middle East in 1958. Chinese Communists began to shell the tiny Nationalist-held island of Quemoy, to which Chiang Kai-shek had rashly committed about one-third of his entire Formosan army. Washington, brandishing the big stick of the Seventh Fleet, backed him in his determination to hang on. At the same time, Dulles partially quieted Communist fears by flying to Formosa and inducing Chiang to renounce the use of force in regaining the Chinese mainland.

The Chinese Reds, now in a position to trigger World War III, continued to be a menace. Their brutalities in Tibet and their aggression against India's borders strengthened Washington in its determination to withhold recognition and to oppose their admission to the U.N. But the effort to keep one-fourth of the world's population out of a world organization became increasingly difficult. With the admission of fifteen new African nations to the U.N. in 1960, the balance was gradually tipping toward the Afro-Asian bloc, while the Communists turned the Assembly floor into a circus for their propaganda. The Daughters of the American Revolution and other highly nationalistic groups increased their clamor for taking the U.S. out of the U.N. and the U.N. out of the U.S.

The Race with Russia into Space

Soviet scientists astounded the world, on October 4, 1957, by lofting into orbit around the globe a beep-beeping "baby moon" (Sputnik I), weighing 184 pounds. A month later they topped their own ace by sending aloft a larger satellite (Sputnik II) weighing 1120 pounds and carrying a dog.

This amazing scientific breakthrough was a psychological Pearl Harbor. The Soviets had long been trying to convince the uncommitted nations that the shortcut to industrial production and riches lay through Communism—and the Sputniks bolstered their claim. America had seemingly taken a back seat in scientific achievement. Envious "backward" nations laughed at Uncle Sam's discomfiture, all the more so because the Soviets were occupying outer space while American troops were occupying the high school in Little Rock.

Military implications of these man-made satellites proved sobering. If the Russians could fire heavy objects into outer space, they certainly could reach America with intercontinental ballistic mis-

"Different Worlds." From Herblock's *Special for Today* (Simon and Schuster, 1958).

siles. Old-soldier Eisenhower, adopting a father-knows-best attitude toward the Soviet "gimmick," remarked that it should not cause "one iota" of concern. Others, chiefly Republicans, blamed the Truman administration for having spent more for supporting peanuts than for supporting a missile program at an early date. Agonizing soul-searching led to the conclusion that while the United States was well advanced on a broad scientific front, including color television, the Soviets had gone all-out for rocketry. Experts testified that America's manned bombers were still a powerful deterrent, but heroic efforts were needed if the alleged "missile gap" was not to widen.

"Rocket fever" swept the nation. The government embarked upon a "crash program," amidst the confusion generated by interservice rivalries. After humiliating and well-advertised failures (the Soviets concealed theirs), the Americans regained some prestige four months after the initial Soviet triumph. They managed to put into orbit a grapefruit-sized satellite weighing two and one half pounds. By February 5, 1961, the United States had successfully sent aloft thirty-two satellites, as compared with seven for the U.S.S.R. American efforts in general were less spectacular but their scientific contributions were heralded (in America) as greater.

The Sputnik spur led to a critical comparison of the American educational system, already under fire as too easy-going, with that of the Soviet Union. A strong move developed to replace "frills" with solid subjects—to substitute square root for square dancing. Congress rejected demands for federal scholarships, but late in 1958 authorized $887,000,000 in loans to needy college students and in grants for the improvement of teaching the sciences and languages. Exploring space between the ears seemed necessary if America was going to "catch up with the Russians" in exploring outer space.

Alan Shepard, Jr., pioneer American astronaut. Courtesy NASA.

Nuclear Bombs, Lebanon, and Berlin

The fantastic race toward nuclear annihilation continued unabated. Emboldened by his Sputniks, Premier Khrushchev boasted openly that he would shower rockets on America. Humanity-minded scientists urged that nuclear tests be stopped before the atmosphere became so polluted as to produce generations of deformed monsters. The Soviets, after completing an intensive series of exceptionally "dirty" tests, proclaimed a suspension in March, 1958, and urged the Western world to follow. Beginning in October, 1958, Washington did halt both underground and atmospheric testing. But all attempts to regularize such suspensions by proper inspection sank on the reef of mutual suspicions. "Bargain-basement bombs" were meanwhile in the making, with every prospect that lesser powers would soon join the exclusive nuclear club.

In a radio-television address, at the time of the Lebanon invasion, Eisenhower said: "I am well aware of the fact that landing . . . troops . . . could have some serious consequences. That is why this step was taken only after the most serious consideration and broad consultation. . . . It was required to support the principles of justice and international law upon which peace and a stable international order depend."

Thermonuclear suicide seemed nearer in July, 1958, when both Egyptian and Communist plottings threatened to engulf Western-oriented Lebanon. After its president had called for aid under the Eisenhower Doctrine, the United States boldly landed several thousand troops (ultimately about 14,000) and helped restore order without taking a single life. This energetic action, in the teeth of Soviet condemnation and threats, served notice that Washington was unwilling to travel the well-rutted road to appeasement.

Khrushchev, no doubt feeling his missile-muscles, deliberately provoked an even more ominous crisis over Berlin—"a bone in the throat," he said—in November, 1958. Annoyed by this pro-Western oasis in a Communist desert, he gave the three Western powers (Britain, France, the United States) six months in which to pull their troops out of West Berlin. The Soviet East German satellite would then take over, and if the West resisted, Moscow would rush to the aid of its puppet. This could only mean World War III. But Eisenhower and Dulles, again remembering the perils of appeasement, staunchly refused to yield well-established rights. The six-month deadline passed almost unnoticed.

Good Will Diplomacy and the Spy Plane

Secretary Dulles, who had traveled over 500,000 miles by air, died of a recurring cancer in 1959. His successor, Christian A. Herter, did not enjoy the President's confidence to the same degree, and Eisenhower—"the new Eisenhower"—assumed a far more active role in directing foreign policy. Taking his cue from the highly publicized tours of Khrushchev and other Russian leaders, he embarked upon a whirlwind eleven-nation good-will trip in December, 1959, all the way from Europe to India. Early in 1960 he staged a repeat performance in Latin America. Grinning his way through showers of confetti and shouts of "Eekay" (Ike), he scored a great personal triumph. He no doubt generated good will, but Democratic critics charged that stagecraft was no substitute for statecraft.

The burly Khrushchev, seeking new propaganda laurels, was eager to meet with Eisenhower and pave the way for a "summit conference" with Western leaders. Despite grave misgivings as to any tangible results, the President invited him to America in 1959. Arriving in New York, Khrushchev appeared before the U.N. General Assembly and dramatically resurrected the ancient Soviet proposal of complete disarmament. But he offered no practical means of achieving this end. He then journeyed out to the Pacific Coast and returned by way of Iowa, where he approvingly patted a prize pig. But the smiling, kewpie-doll exterior concealed a steely, bellicose interior, which occasionally erupted in bullying denunciations.

A noteworthy result of this tour was a meeting at Camp David, the President's rustic retreat in Maryland. Khrushchev emerged saying that his ultimatum for the evacuation of Berlin would be extended indefinitely. The relieved world gave prayerful but premature thanks for the "spirit of Camp David."

The Paris "summit conference," scheduled for May, 1960, turned out to be an incredible fiasco. Both Moscow and Washington had publicly taken a firm stand on the burning Berlin issue, and neither could risk a public backdown. Luckily for Soviet propaganda, an American U-2 spy plane was shot down deep in Russian territory on the eve of the conference. (The Soviets, whose world-wide espionage was notorious, later admitted that Khrushchev had known at Camp David of many such flights.) After bungling bureaucratic denials in Washington, Eisenhower took the unprecedented step of assuming personal responsibility. Professing to be insulted by his "fishy friend," Khrushchev stormed into Paris filling the air with invective and demanding that Eisenhower not only apologize for the spy flights but punish those responsible for them. The President obviously would not punish himself, so the conference collapsed before it could get off the ground.

"What's So Funny?" (Premier Khrushchev Gloats over Ike's Spying Discomfiture.) Copyright 1960 by Herblock in *The Washington Post*

Khrushchev's "diplomacy by tantrum" virtually ended Eisenhower's "diplomacy by good-will tour." Moscow abruptly canceled its invitation to Eisenhower to visit Russia. Communist agents, playing upon resurgent Japanese nationalism, helped engineer such violent demonstrations in Japan that the President was forced to abandon a trip to the Flowery Kingdom during his Far Eastern tour. America's slipping prestige received yet another body blow.

Cuba's Castroism Spells Communism

Soviet propagandists had meanwhile been making alarming inroads below the Rio Grande. Latin Americans bitterly resented Uncle Sam's lavishing billions of dollars on Europe, while doling out only millions to the poor relations to the south. Liberals everywhere were outraged by Washington's willingness to support— even decorate—bloody dictators who would insure the sanctity of dollar investments. And the American recession-depression of 1957–1958, combined with Yankee tariff barriers, further tightened the screws.

An ill-timed "good will" tour of Vice-President Nixon through South America in 1958 reaped a harvest of spit and spite. Communist agitators and others became increasingly violent. After being stoned, spat upon, and shouted down at Lima (Peru), Nixon narrowly escaped serious injury at Caracas (Venezuela). Decent Latin Americans were apologetic, but one of them explained that since the masses could not vent their anger by spitting on the United States, they spat on the Vice-President of the United States.

Most ominous of all was the Communist beachhead in Cuba. The iron-fisted dictator Batista had encouraged huge investments of American capital, and Washington in turn had given him some support. When black-bearded Dr. Fidel Castro engineered a revolution early in 1959, he denounced the Yankee imperialists and began to expropriate valuable American properties in pursuing a land-distribution program. Washington, finally losing patience, released Cuba from "imperialistic slavery" by cutting off the heavy imports of Cuban sugar. Castro retaliated against this "imperialistic aggression" with further wholesale confiscations of Yankee property, and in effect made his left-wing dictatorship an economic and military satellite of Moscow. Further deliberate affronts prompted Washington to break diplomatic relations with Cuba early in 1961.

Americans talked seriously of invoking the Monroe Doctrine before the Russians set up a Communist base only ninety miles from their shores. Khrushchev angrily proclaimed that the Monroe Doctrine was dead, and indicated that he would shower missiles upon the United States if it attacked his good friend Castro. Soviet spokesmen later softened this threat.

The Cuban revolution, which Castro sought to "export" to his neighbors, brought other significant responses. At San José, Costa Rica, in August, 1960, the United States induced the Organization of American States to condemn (unenthusiastically) Communist infiltration into the Americas. President Eisenhower, whom Castro dubbed "the senile White House golfer," hastily proposed a long-deferred "Marshall Plan" for Latin America. Congress responded to his recommendation with an initial authorization of $500,000,000. The Latin Americans had Castro to thank for attention which many of them regarded as too little and too late.

"We Stand on our Own Two Feet." Soviets Support Castro. Don Hesse in the St. Louis *Globe-Democrat*

Kennedy Challenges Nixon for the Presidency

Republicans faced up to the presidential campaign of 1960 without undue optimism. They had taken a bad beating in the mid-term Congressional elections of 1958, even though both President Eisenhower and Vice-President Nixon had lashed out against the "radicals" and "high spenders." Voters had been especially disturbed by the recession of 1957–1958, the Sherman Adams scandal, farm problems, and foreign tensions. Not only had the Republicans suffered the heaviest losses in the history of Senate elections, but the casualties were especially heavy among ultraconservative Republican Senators. A crestfallen Eisenhower was dismayed that his "New Republicanism" had not taken root.

Vice-President Nixon was the Republican heir apparent. An ever-popular Eisenhower, nearing seventy and soon to be the oldest President in American history, was barred by the 22nd Amendment from serving a third term. To many, Nixon was a gifted party leader;

to others, a ruthless opportunist. The "old" Nixon had been a no-holds-barred campaigner, especially in assailing Democrats and left-wingers. The "new" Nixon was represented as a mature, seasoned statesman. More in the limelight than any earlier Vice-President, he had shouldered heavy new responsibilities and had traveled globally as a "trouble shooter" in various capacities. He had vigorously defended American democracy in a famous "kitchen debate" with Khrushchev in Moscow in 1959. His supporters, flourishing a telling photograph of this finger-pointing episode, claimed that he alone knew how to "stand up to" the Russians.

Nixon's nomination in Chicago—one hundred years after Lincoln's in the same city—was in effect a coronation. Liberal and personable Governor Nelson A. Rockefeller of New York had thrown his hat into the ring, but had withdrawn it in the face of strong support by the "regulars" for the safe-and-sane Nixon. But the Rockefeller revolt did force a more liberal platform upon the Republican convention, to the acute dissatisfaction of the stand-pat wing of the party. Nixon was nominated unanimously on the first ballot. His running mate was handsome Henry Cabot Lodge, Jr., of Massachusetts (grandson of Woodrow Wilson's archfoe), who had served conspicuously for seven years as American representative to the United Nations.

By contrast, the Democratic race for the presidential nomination started as a free-for-all. Supporters of Adlai Stevenson cried "We're Madly for Adlai," but hard-headed politicians shied away from a two-time loser. John F. Kennedy, a tall (6 feet), youthful, dark-haired, and tooth-flashing millionaire Senator from Massachusetts, won impressive victories in the primaries. He then scored a first-ballot triumph in Los Angeles over his closest rival, Senator Lyndon B. Johnson, the Senate majority leader from Texas. A disappointed South was not completely appeased when Johnson accepted second place on the ticket in an eleventh-hour marriage of convenience. Kennedy's challenging acceptance speech called upon the American people for sacrifices to achieve their potential greatness, which he hailed as the New Frontier.

The Presidential Issues of 1960

Bigotry, as was inevitable, showed its snarling face. Senator Kennedy was a Roman Catholic, the first to be nominated since Al Smith's ill-starred campaign in 1928. Smear artists revived the ancient charges about the Pope's controlling the White House. Kennedy pointed to his fourteen years of service in Congress, denied that he would be swayed by Rome, and asked if some 40,000,000 Catholic Americans were to be condemned to second-class citizenship from birth.

Kennedy's Catholicism aroused misgivings in the Protestant,

Candidate Kennedy, in a speech to a Houston group of Protestant ministers (Sept. 12, 1960), declared, "I believe in an America where the separation of church and state is absolute—where no Catholic prelate would tell the President, should he be a Catholic, how to act, and no Protestant minister would tell his parishioners for whom to vote . . . and where no man is denied public office because his religion differs from the President who might appoint him or the people who might elect him. . . ."

Bible-belt South, which was ordinarily Democratic. "I fear Catholicism more than I fear Communism," declaimed one Baptist minister in North Carolina. But the religious issue largely canceled itself out. If many Southern Democrats supported Nixon because of Kennedy's Catholicism, many Northern Republicans supported Kennedy because of the bitter attacks on their Catholic faith.

Also vital was the international crisis, which focused attention on the "experience" of the candidates. Khrushchev made no bones about his dislike of Nixon—that "fumbler" and "grocery clerk"—although he dismissed both candidates as "lackeys of imperialism." Unable to secure a summit conference, the rotund Russian journeyed to New York, unwanted and uninvited, to head the Soviet delegation in the U.N. Assembly and woo the new Afro-Asian delegates. He violently attacked the handling of the Congo crisis by the U.N. Secretary General, demanded an unworkable revamping of the U.N. structure, denounced the Security Council as a "cuspidor," and insisted that the U.N. be moved to some other country. His purple-faced presence in New York forced all the prominent leaders of the world, including Eisenhower, to put in an appearance. His boorish table pounding, fist shaking, shoe waving, and rocket rattling shocked many delegates, while his balcony harangues with newsmen and his clownish bear hugs with Cuba's Fidel Castro turned the star-studded assemblage into a colossal propaganda arena.

"Listen,—When I Get Through With It, It Won't Be Worth Belonging To." (Khrushchev, Communist China, and the U.N.) From *Straight Herblock* (Simon and Schuster, 1964)

Khrushchev's bulldozing antics in New York temporarily stole the spotlight from the Presidential election, but they gave added point to the Republican slogan "Experience Counts." Republicans harped on the fact that both Nixon and Lodge were old hands at talking back to Moscow. (Slogan: "They Understand What Peace Demands.") The forty-seven-year-old Nixon emphasized the youth, immaturity, and naïveté of his forty-three-year-old opponent.

Kennedy struck back by attacking the do-nothingism of the Eisenhower administration in the face of alarming Soviet progress. He insisted that the Russians, with their nuclear bombs and Sputniks, had gained on America in prestige and power. Nixon, forced to defend the dying administration, replied that the nation's prestige had not slipped, although Kennedy was causing it to do so by his unpatriotic talk. The aged but amazingly energetic Eisenhower, stung by these gloom-and-doom reflections on his stewardship, took to the stump in the closing days of the campaign, thereby prompting the Democrats to charge that he was trying to carry Nixon "piggyback" into the White House. But the preachments of both Nixon and Eisenhower rang a bit hollow when the State Department refused to release a secret report which allegedly proved that in foreign eyes America's prestige had slipped badly.

Kennedy's "get America moving" theme, with its call to action and sacrifice, struck a rather depressing note of self-disparagement.

Ordinarily, as the politicians know, the people want tranquilizers, not challenges. But the nation has often demonstrated that when faced with the harsh realities of an international crisis it can be trusted to choose the harder road. In any case, Nixon's contention that "we never had it so good" was belied by a deepening business recession ("inventory readjustment" to the Republicans), which may well have proved decisive in the election.

A Catholic Wins the White House

Personalities swayed countless voters in 1960. Nixon, realizing that the Republicans were outnumbered about 60 to 40, urged the electorate to support, not the party, but the better man—that is, himself. With great energy and increasing hoarseness, he barnstormed in all fifty states. Kennedy, campaigning no less strenuously, revealed his youthful magnetism to millions of voters.

Television may well have tipped the scales. Nixon agreed to meet Kennedy in four so-called "debates"—probably a strategic error. A public figure as well known as Vice-President Nixon should never share his large following with a less well-known man. The contestants crossed words in millions of living rooms before audiences estimated at sixty million or more. Nobody "won" the debates, but Kennedy at least held his own and did not suffer by comparison with the more "experienced" Nixon.

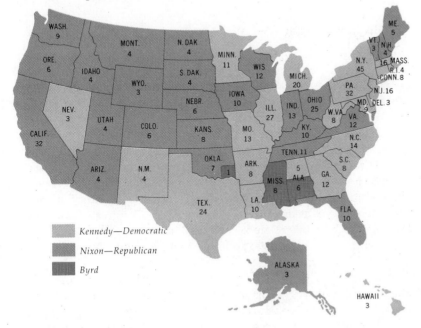

Kennedy—Democratic

Nixon—Republican

Byrd

PRESIDENTIAL ELECTION OF 1960 (with electoral vote by state)

Kennedy squeezed through by the rather comfortable margin of 303 electoral votes to 219, but with the breathtakingly close popular margin of only 118,574 votes out of over 68,000,000 cast. Like Franklin Roosevelt, Kennedy ran well in the large industrial centers, where he had strong support from laborites, Catholics, and Negroes. (He had solicitously telephoned the pregnant Mrs. Martin Luther King, Jr., whose husband was then imprisoned in Georgia for a sit-in.) But Kennedy lost several states of the Bible-belt South that were presumably repelled by his Catholicism. Nixon, although not inheriting Eisenhower's popularity, ran well in the less populous states of the trans-Mississippi area, especially in the Protestant farm belt. Kennedy's Catholicism both hurt and helped him, but on balance may have helped him. The Democratic Party has been traditionally the refuge of Catholics, and the passing of "Ike" marked the return of many Catholic "Eisenhower Democrats" to the Democratic fold.

Although losing a few seats, the Democrats swept both houses of Congress by wide margins, as was a foregone conclusion. The possibility of another Republican President handcuffed by an opposition Congress definitely hurt Nixon. Many voters were weary of government by deadlock. John Fitzgerald Kennedy—the youngest man and the first Catholic to be elected President—was free to set out for his New Frontier, provided that the die-hard conservatives in his party would join the wagon train.

An Old General Fades Away

President Eisenhower, the aging progressive-conservative, continued to enjoy extraordinary popularity to the final curtain. Despite Democratic jibes about "eight years of golfing and goofing," of "putting and puttering," he was universally admired and respected for his dignity, decency, sincerity, good will, and moderation.

Pessimists had predicted that Eisenhower would be a seriously crippled "lame duck" during his second term, owing to the barrier against re-election erected by the 22nd Amendment. In truth, he displayed more vigor, more political know-how, and more aggressive leadership during his last two years than ever before. For an unprecedented six years, from 1955 to 1961, Congress remained in Democratic hands, yet he established unusual control over it. He wielded the veto 169 times, and only twice was he overridden by the required two-thirds vote.

America was generally prosperous, despite pockets of poverty and unemployment, recurrent recessions, and perennial farm problems. The budget was in balance, the treasury showed a surplus, and the up-creep in prices was being slowed. To the north the vast St. Lawrence waterway project, constructed jointly with Canada and

In his Farewell Address on radio and television, Jan. 17, 1961, Eisenhower warned against a potent new menace, "This conjunction of an immense military establishment and a large arms industry is new in the American experience. . . . In the councils of government, we must guard against the acquisition of unwarranted influence, whether sought or unsought, by the military-industrial complex."

completed in 1959, had turned the cities of the Great Lakes into bustling ocean seaports.

"Old Glory" could now proudly display fifty stars. Alaska attained statehood in 1959, as did Hawaii. Alaska, though gigantic, was thinly populated and non-contiguous, but these objections were overcome in a Democratic Congress that expected Alaska to vote Democratic. Hawaii had ample population (largely of Oriental descent), advanced democratic institutions, and more acreage than Rhode Island, Delaware, or Connecticut. But Democrats objected to admitting a potentially Republican state; Southerners wanted no more non-whites; and apprehensive citizens opposed statehood for a military base whose labor force was allegedly infiltrated by Communists. With the Alaska log jam broken, however, progress finally triumphed in 1959, and the island paradise sent three able representatives to Congress, two of them of Oriental extraction.

Eisenhower had clearly grown during his eight momentous years, despite political inexperience, advancing age, three major illnesses, and often lackadaisical leadership—"the bland leading the bland." He had mounted no flaming moral crusade for civil rights or related issues. Yet he was obviously far more than an "honest Harding," and he had done more than "grin away" problems and tread water. He had acquitted himself far better than any other professional military man in the White House, including his fellow West Pointer, General

"What's So Lame [Duck] About It?" Alexander in the Philadelphia *Bulletin*

Grant, the only other Republican ever to serve two full terms. He had ended one war and avoided all others. He had helped preserve the two-party system by merely getting elected. But whether or not his middle-of-the-roadism was enough, remained a subject for partisan debate.

SELECT READINGS

An excellent brief analysis of the Eisenhower years appears in WALTER JOHNSON, *1600 Pennsylvania Avenue: Presidents and the People, 1929–1959* (1960).* Intimate observations may be found in Presidential Assistant SHERMAN ADAMS, *Firsthand Report* (1961)*; Vice President R. M. NIXON, *Six Crises* (1962)*; and speech-writer E. J. HUGHES, *The Ordeal of Power* (1963).* D. D. EISENHOWER concluded his memoirs in *The White House Years: Waging Peace, 1956–1961* (1965).* A systematic study is C. A. H. THOMSON and F. M. SHATTUCK, *The 1956 Presidential Campaign* (1960). On foreign affairs consult J. W. SPANIER, *American Foreign Policy since World War II* (1960).* A diplomatic-economic achievement of vast significance is described in W. R. WILLOUGHBY, *The St. Lawrence Waterway* (1961). On Secretary Dulles, see references for preceding chapter and also RICHARD GOOLD-ADAMS, *John Foster Dulles* (1962), an appraisal by a Britisher. Of the numerous books on the rise of Castro one may single out R. F. SMITH, *The United States and Cuba: Business and Diplomacy, 1917–1960* (1960).* Among the more noteworthy books to come out of the election of 1960 are EARL MAZO, *Richard Nixon* (1959), J. M. BURNS, *John Kennedy* (1960),* and particularly T. H. WHITE, *The Making of the President, 1960* (1961).* Also SELECT READINGS for preceding chapter.

RECENT REFERENCES

HERBERT S. PARMET, *Eisenhower and the American Crusades* (1972).

* Available in paperback.

48

New Frontiersmen on the Potomac

In the long history of the world, only a few generations have been
granted the role of defending freedom in its hour of maximum danger.
I do not shrink from this responsibility—I welcome it.

John F. Kennedy, Inaugural Address, 1961

The Coming of the Kennedys to Washington

A breezy new atmosphere swept through Washington—22° above
zero—as the New Frontiersmen rode into power, January 20, 1961.
Hatless and topcoatless, President Kennedy delivered with vigor a
stirring inaugural address, in which he called for sacrifice at home
and steadfastness abroad. From the outset of his Administration
his emphasis was on energy, brains (especially Harvard-trained),
and youth. As the youngest President ever elected, he assembled
one of the youngest Cabinets. It included his younger brother
Robert, whom he named Attorney General despite outcries against
favoritism and inexperience. He quipped that "Bobby" would
find the experience "useful" when he began to practice law.

A stellar member of the Cabinet proved to be Defense
Secretary Robert S. McNamara. A walking computing machine,
he sacrificed a $400,000-a-year position with the Ford Motor
Company to become a public servant at $35,000 a year. Trampling
on sensitive toes, he achieved many economies among the jealous
armed services that were squabbling for their cut of the prodigious

Kennedy's inaugural address foreshadowed a strong foreign policy, "Let every nation know, whether it wishes us well or ill, that we shall pay any price, bear any burden, meet any hardship, support any friend, oppose any foe, in order to assure the survival and the success of liberty."

defense pie. More important, he supervised a reversal of the grim Eisenhower–Dulles doctrine of "massive [nuclear] retaliation." With adequate ground forces, Washington would have more options in a crisis than a world-wide blowup or a humiliating backdown. A balanced military arm could presumably dampen brushfire wars before they broke dangerously out of control.

Breakers loomed ahead in Congress, despite a lopsided Democratic majority in both branches. Southern Democrats held a lion's share of the all-important committee chairmanships, thanks to the operation of seniority ("rule by senility," critics said). Thus entrenched, these "mossbacks" could bottle up or strangle legislation they disliked. On the floor of Congress conservative Southern Democrats, repeatedly lining up with conservative Northern Republicans, watered down or defeated bills desperately desired by Kennedy.

After much arm-twisting, Kennedy's first Congress honored about the average number of White House requests. But the President suffered stinging rebuffs in pushing some of his pet programs, including hospital insurance for the aged under Social Security (Medicare) and large-scale federal aid for the overflowing public schools. Medicare was assailed as a foot in the door for socialized medicine by the powerful American Medical Association; aid for the public schools sank on the rock of parochial schools. Many Americans, including the ultra-cautious Catholic Kennedy, believed that support for religious schools violated the First Amendment, which decreed separation of church and state. Yet supporters of private schools were potent enough to block all general aid to public schools unless they shared it.

Congress also had its butcher knife sharpened for Kennedy's foreign-aid request of $4.7 billion, which was slashed by half a billion dollars. Taxpayers were becoming increasingly critical of the more than $100 billion disbursed in assorted global grants since 1945, especially to dictators who grabbed dollars with one hand and slapped Uncle Sam with the other.

Kennedy's Initial Accomplishments

Early in the game Kennedy brought a warm heart to the Cold War when he established the Peace Corps. The peace corpsmen (and women) were dedicated Americans who volunteered to go out to about fifty backward countries and show the impoverished people how to improve their lot. At first scorned as "Kennedy's Kiddie Corps," this relatively inexpensive organization proved so useful in cultivating good will that Congress enthusiastically put it on a permanent basis in September, 1961.

Much more costly and much less successful was the Alliance for

Progress (*Alianza para el Progreso*), of which fear-arousing Dr. Fidel Castro of Cuba was an unwitting father. With a ten-year, ten-point, twenty-billion-dollar program, it was designed to provide a kind of Marshall plan for Latin America. A primary goal was to help the Good Neighbors decrease the ghastly gap between the calloused rich and the wretchedly poor, and thus head off Castro-like Communism. Congress passed the initial appropriation by lopsided majorities in May, 1961, but the Alliance proved to be no alliance and progress was painfully slow. Short-sighted greed was reluctant to embrace overdue reforms, in Latin America as elsewhere in the world.

President Kennedy's most spectacular legislative triumph was the Trade Expansion Act of October, 1962. One of the boldest strokes of its kind in American history, it empowered the President to slash existing tariffs at least fifty percent in the interests of promoting trade. In some cases he could eliminate them entirely.

Kennedy also induced Congress to pass the initial appropriations for his man-on-the-moon program. The estimated overall cost was some $25,000,000,000; the goal was an American on the moon by 1970. Skeptics, who saw the desperate need for such money on this planet, cried "lunar lunacy." Yet the costly space-race with the Russians continued. In April, 1961, the Soviets successfully orbited the first man. America was unable to match this achievement until some ten months later, February, 1962, when Lt. Colonel John H. Glenn, Jr., circled the earth three times, and became the most idolized of a group of daring American astronauts. In October, 1964, Russians lofted three men into orbit, and revealed that, with superior booster power, they were then well ahead in the race for the moon, at least temporarily.

In his inaugural address, Kennedy struck a lofty note: "And so, my fellow Americans, ask not what your country can do for you: Ask what you can do for your country.
"My fellow citizens of the world: Ask not what America will do for you, but what together we can do for the freedom of man."

But American space men, more concerned with science than showmanship, managed to shoot aloft a good many more satellites than the Soviet Union. Their total scientific contribution was hailed (in America) as greater than that of the Soviets. Especially noteworthy was the Telstar communications satellite, designed for transatlantic telephone and television transmission. A fierce battle developed in Congress between anti-monopoly liberals, who demanded government ownership of Telstar, and the conservatives, who demanded private ownership. After a fiery filibuster by the liberals, a compromise bill emerged, in August, 1962, which provided for a private corporation under government regulation.

Kennedy, who was determined to check creeping inflation, ran afoul of the powerful steel companies. Early in 1962 they had negotiated a wage contract, under which the workers agreed to no increase in wages, merely fringe benefits totaling about ten cents an hour. The assumption was that the companies would also hold the line on inflation. But when, ten days later, the leading producers suddenly announced identical increases in prices, Kennedy reacted angrily to what he deemed a collusive "double cross." He immediately put into motion the awesome investigative and judicial machinery of the federal government, including anti-trust action and F.B.I. agents.

Overawed, the steel operators rescinded their price increases, and Kennedy chalked up a spectacular victory. But he was savagely criticized for using dictatorial tactics, and he earned the undying hostility of the free-enterprise business community, especially after he stated that his father had long branded the steel moguls as "sons of bitches." In this hostile atmosphere the stock market nosedived, wiping out paper profits of some $20,000,000,000. About a year later the steel companies quietly raised their prices, without objectionable evidences of conspiracy. Kennedy this time remained silent, and the inflationary spiral continued to edge upward.

The Bay of Pigs Blunder

Castro's Communist Cuba continued to be a thorn in the underbelly of the United States, and plans for an invasion by Cuban refugees had long been brewing. With the secret encouragement of the Eisenhower administration, a group of some 1400 exiles was being trained in Guatemala with American arms and American advisers. Shortly after his election, Kennedy learned of these preparations. The invasion of a sovereign nation in peacetime was plainly a violation of both American domestic law and international obligations. Yet Castro was growing stronger by the week with Soviet arms, and his overthrow seemed urgent.

Kennedy finally decided to back the invasion attempt with one crippling reservation. He announced that in no circumstances would the United States become *directly* involved. Then followed a tragedy of errors in mid-April, 1961. Three air strikes by Cuban exiles, flying from Central America with obsolete United States planes, were to destroy Castro's air power. The first strike was only partially effective, and world opinion reacted so violently that Kennedy called off the second one. The third was ineffective. Castro retained control of the air and was thus able to destroy invading aircraft and supply vessels, while pressure mounted in the United States for direct help. Finally the bullet-riddled band of exiles, who had counted on American intervention, was forced to surrender.

Seldom has Washington bungled anything more badly. Its "indirect" involvement was so deep as to amount to futile "direct" involvement. Premier Khrushchev of Russia, denouncing American "gangsterism," pledged all necessary military assistance to his Cuban puppet. Kennedy, who might easily have found scapegoats, manfully assumed full responsibility for the failure. But his conscience troubled him, and he arranged through private contribu-

"It Certainly Was Loaded!"
The Bay of Pigs Affair. Justus
in the Minneapolis *Star*

tions for the "ransoming" of the 1100 survivors in Cuba with some $62,000,000 worth of American drugs and other supplies.

The Berlin Wall and the Congo Imbroglio

Partly to dispel the impression of spinelessness left by the Bay of Pigs, Kennedy journeyed to Europe in June, 1961, for conferences with leading statesmen. A crucial meeting with Khrushchev occurred in Vienna. Kennedy emerged grim and visibly shaken. The tough-fisted Russian adopted a belligerent attitude on Germany and West Berlin, and threatened to turn the whole city over to the Communist East Germans, with all the explosive possibilities of World War III.

But Kennedy refused to be bullied out of Berlin. He secured from Congress authority to beef up the armed forces, and he summoned to active duty some 80,000 reservists and National Guardsmen. This time the Russians backed off. Their response was the Berlin Wall, hastily begun in August, 1961, and then extended along the entire border of East Germany. Constructed of barbed wire and concrete, it was designed to prevent the heavy drainage of population from the East German "paradise" to West Germany.

A monument to failure, the Berlin Wall was something of a propaganda victory for the West. It advertised the glaring disparity between blighted East Germany and booming West Germany, as well as the necessity of keeping some sixteen million people in a barbed-wire jail. Kennedy was condemned by many red-blooded Republicans for not having ordered American tanks to topple the Wall of Shame before it could be completed. But naked force would probably have provoked counterforce—and possibly World War III.

Meanwhile the Belgian Congo had exploded with the butchering and raping of whites, following the overhasty withdrawal of Belgian colonialist overlords. The United Nations became deeply involved when, in July, 1960, the Security Council voted to send in neutral troops to avert civil war. Surprisingly, the Soviets at first supported intervention, evidently concluding that it would bolster pro-Communist elements. But when leading left-wingers were exiled or murdered, Moscow reversed its position and tried to throw a monkey wrench into the whole "illegal" operation. Like France and numerous other nations, Russia flatly refused to pay its assessments for military ventures of which it disapproved. Washington kept the Congo campaign afloat by authorizing a loan of $100 million, but a shortage of funds finally forced the peace-keeping troops of the UN to withdraw, after a temporary pacification in January, 1963.

The Congo operation stirred up a hornets' nest. In the interests of unification, the United Nations forces had crushed the anti-Communist leader of the mineral-rich Katanga Province. American foes of the United Nations, chiefly extreme right-wingers, con-

Speaking at a press conference shortly after the Bay of Pigs disaster, Kennedy whimsically assumed the responsibility that was technically his with the remark, "There's an old saying that victory has a hundred fathers and defeat is an orphan."

U.S. Naval Reservists at Berlin Wall. Naval Photographic Center.

"New Balance of Power." (In the U.N.) Crawford for the N.E.A.

demned this blow against freedom. Permanent financial paralysis also threatened the UN as many members continued to default on their financial obligations, and as Uncle Sam grew increasingly weary of picking up the tab.

As these ominous cracks were developing in the glass house of the United Nations, its whole complexion was changing. When launched in 1945, it had 51 members; by 1965 it had 115. Most of the newcomers hailed from once-colonial Asia and Africa—such as Uganda, Somalia, and Rwanda. The bitter anti-white memories of these peoples endured, and the United States faced the disagreeable possibility of being outvoted by tiny young nations not far removed from barbarism. All this provided further ammunition for American right-wingers, many of whom called for abandoning the leaky UN ship.

Soviet Nuclear Missiles in Cuba

A crowing Castro continued to annoy his powerful Yankee neighbor. Washington persisted in its partial embargo on goods to Cuba, and tried without conspicuous success to persuade other nations to follow suit. But Castro, with generous financial aid from Russia, clung to power and continued to strengthen his armed forces with made-in-Moscow muscle, presumably defensive.

Official Washington was stunned in October, 1962, when aerial photographs revealed that Russian technicians were secretly and hastily emplacing forty-two missiles in Cuba. Armed with nuclear warheads, these weapons could incinerate most of America's major cities with a push of the button. By this sneak violation of the Monroe Doctrine the Soviets were evidently attempting to create a blackmail bludgeon—one that would force the United States to back down in Berlin and elsewhere in threatened hot spots.

Quite in contrast to the Bay of Pigs, which probably had misled Moscow, Kennedy played this game of "nuclear chicken" in a masterly fashion. While quietly making large-scale preparations for an invasion of Cuba, he proclaimed, on October 22, 1962, a naval and aerial "quarantine" of all offensive weapons being shipped into the island. Seizing or sinking Soviet ships in peacetime on the high seas would unquestionably be an act of war, but Kennedy was prepared to face up to the consequences.

In the breathless week of this eyeball-to-eyeball confrontation, Khrushchev finally flinched. On October 28, 1962, he agreed to a face-saving compromise, by which he would pull his missiles out of Cuba. The United States, in turn, would pledge itself to lift the "quarantine" and not invade the island. Withdrawal of the missiles was to be certified by UN inspectors.

Neither side won a clear-cut victory, but Kennedy gained the essential point—after going to the brink of global atomization. The checkmated Russians ostensibly shipped their missiles out of Cuba, but suspicious Americans feared that some were hidden in caves. A crestfallen Castro flatly refused to permit UN verifiers to pollute his soil. (Kennedy was thereupon released from his tentative pledge not to invade Cuba.) Moscow propagandists, now cooing like doves of peace, proclaimed that the Soviets had won their objective because they had forced the Americans to keep their hands off the Cubans. But it was as plain as the beard on Castro's face that the bold Soviet coup had backfired badly.

After the first heartfelt sigh of relief, thoughtful Americans saw that Kennedy's victory was far from complete. A resentful Castro was still there—and growing stronger militarily. In flagrant violation of the Monroe Doctrine, thousands of Russian troops and technicians lingered in Cuba. But the Soviet backdown did restore some confidence among Allies who had been appalled by the Bay of Pigs. It also silenced cries that a "Castro-coddling" administration was doing nothing about the Communist arms buildup.

In the Congressional elections of November, 1962, the Democrats gained four seats in the Senate while losing four in the House. As the party in power normally suffers a sharp decline in mid-term elections, Democrats hailed this stand-off as a signal gain. "We were Cubanized," complained rueful Republicans.

Two years after the Cuban missile crisis Chairman Khrushchev was deposed, presumably in part because of his costly blunder. Yet in his so-called memoirs, he implausibly insists that he saved "Socialist Cuba" from an imperialistic American invasion: "The Caribbean crisis was a triumph of Soviet foreign policy and a personal triumph in my own career as a statesman and as a member of the collective leadership. We achieved, I would say, a spectacular success without having to fire a shot!"

The Test-Ban Treaty and the Soviet Wheat Deal

The Cuban missile crunch focused attention anew on the terrifying race in nuclear weapons. About a year earlier, in September, 1961, the Soviets, spurning all pleas, had set off a number of air-polluting explosions. Kennedy in turn felt compelled to resume nuclear testing in the atmosphere lest the Russians gain an overwhelming superiority.

Nerve-shattering crisis in Cuba was followed by relaxation of tensions with the Soviets. They now revealed active interest in a nuclear test-ban treaty, which they had previously spurned. Prolonged negotiations were completed in Moscow, on August 5, 1963, with a pact that prohibited nuclear explosions in the atmosphere, under water, and in outer space. Only underground testing was permitted. The United States Senate, after voicing misgivings as to possible Soviet "cheating," approved the treaty with crossed fingers, 80 to 19, on September 24.

The nuclear test-ban treaty proved more important for what it promised in disarmament than for what it performed. No existing stocks of bombs were to be destroyed, and the signatories could pull out after giving three months' notice. Most of the other nations speedily subscribed to the ban. Conspicuous exceptions were

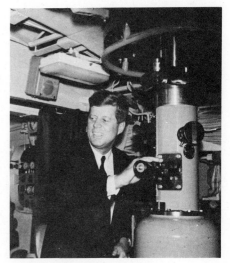

President Kennedy at submarine periscope. He had commanded and lost, with serious injury, a PT (torpedo) boat in the South Pacific in World War II. Naval Photographic Center.

France, which was developing a tiny nuclear arsenal, and China, which had not yet exploded its first nuclear device and which branded the Moscow pact a "dirty fraud." But the test-ban treaty, while reducing pollution of the atmosphere, also reduced international friction, and to this extent created a more favorable climate for disarmament negotiations.

Two other barometers reflected a warmer atmosphere in the Cold War. In August, 1963, Moscow and Washington opened a direct "hot line" which permitted immediate teletype communication should an accidental explosion or similar catastrophe occur. Two months later, Kennedy authorized the sale of $250 million worth of surplus wheat to the Soviets, who had suffered crippling crop failures.

Anti-Russian elements in the United States condemned the folly of strengthening the hand that was trying to strangle them, but most Americans apparently favored the wheat deal. Humanitarianism pricked many consciences, and the nation was staggering under grain surpluses that were costly to store. Besides, Russian gold would partially check the alarming hemorrhaging of bullion to Europe to cover the balance of payments deficit—that is, the difference between what Americans expended or invested abroad and sold or earned abroad.

Balance of Payments Deficits (in millions)

	1955	1959	1960	1961	1962	1964
Gold Stock	$21,753	$19,507	$17,804	$16,947	$16,057	$15,550
Annual Deficit	$−1,145	$−3,743	$−3,881	$−2,370	$−2,186	$−2,660

Note: The maximum gold stock of the United States had been $24 billion in 1949; there had been a net drain on it every year since 1957.

Le Grand Charles de Gaulle of France

If relations with Moscow were visibly thawing, those with America's fourteen NATO allies were audibly chilling. Yet the growing independence of Western European nations was in some respects a healthy sign. It indicated that these war-ravaged peoples had so far recovered, economically and psychologically, as to want to shake off the guiding hand of Big Brother in Washington.

President Kennedy nevertheless had ambitious designs for the Mother Continent. He envisioned an economically and politically united Western Europe, with Uncle Sam the dominant partner, standing as a bulwark against a westward thrust by the Communists. But stiff-backed President de Gaulle of France, a towering nationalist fanatically determined to recapture the Napoleonic *grandeur* of yesteryear, refused to permit his beloved France to play second fiddle to the dominating Yankee. He therefore undertook to build a small nuclear force ("farce," his critics said), despite pressures from Washington. As a lone-wolf general of World War II, he argued that in a future crisis the Americans, rather than risk the destruction of their own cities, might leave France naked in the face of the Soviets. Instead of an interdependent partnership between Europe and the United States, he would have a France-led Europe, independent of transatlantic ties and capable of defending itself.

De Gaulle also resented efforts by the British (who had the nuclear bomb) to join hands with the Americans in providing leadership for Europe, with France in the backseat. He brusquely rejected all attempts to work out a joint nuclear force for NATO, with Uncle Sam's solo finger on the trigger. In January, 1963, with a haughty *"non,"* he vetoed Britain's application for membership in the Common Market, a spectacularly successful union of the nations of Western Europe for the mutual lowering of tariff barriers. Kennedy, though visibly annoyed, could only pocket his pride and await future developments.

President de Gaulle: "Why Do You Americans Stay Where You're Not Wanted?" Mauldin in the Chicago *Sun-Times*

The Chinese Dragon Breathes Fire on India

Red China and Red Russia were meanwhile noisily parting company. Moscow was gradually veering away from Leninism toward coexistence with the West ("creeping capitalism"), except for "wars of liberation." Peking clung to the tough old Lenin line of world revolution, even at the cost of wrapping the world in thermonuclear flames. Chinese Reds assailed Russia's backdown in Cuba before the American "paper tiger," as well as the Kremlin's subsequent tendency to be "soft on capitalism." Premier Khrushchev, faced with the problem of coexistence with China, sternly reminded Peking that the American "tiger" might be "paper" but he had nuclear teeth.

As if to show their toughness, the Chinese Communists suddenly began to pour troops over the mountainous approaches to India, late in October, 1962. The Indians, alarmed by what they called "yellow rats," besought American aid, ironically after having long assailed America's buildup against Communism. Washington responded by air-lifting large quantities of arms. The Red assault mysteriously ceased a month after it had begun, and a troubled truce settled over the Indian border.

The alarming behavior of the Red Dragon raised anew the question of continuing the nonrecognition of Communist China and her nonseating in the U.N. Many Europeans argued that the 700,000,000 Chinese (who were about to explode a nuclear bomb) would be easier to control within the family of nations than outside it. But most

Americans, loyal to frozen policies, argued otherwise. They insisted that the U.N. by its very charter consisted of peaceloving nations, and that China should not be allowed to shoot her way in, especially after invading India. To deepen the deadlock the Red Chinese insisted that they would accept no seat in the U.N. unless the exiled regime of Chiang Kai-shek were unseated—and this the Americans were unwilling to do.

Deepening Involvement in Laos and Vietnam

In Southeast Asia the menace of Chinese Communism was less open but hardly less alarming. Fears still persisted that if Laos and South Vietnam fell to the Reds, the remainder of the area would collapse like a row of falling dominoes. The jungle kingdom of Laos, which Washington had drenched with dollars, was in grave danger of a Communist takeover; Peking was allegedly sending arms to battling pro-Communist elements. But Kennedy was unwilling to get bogged down in a Korea-type slaughterpen in an area that adjoined the teeming manpower of China. Seeking an escape hatch, the United States participated in a fifteen-month, fourteen-power conference at Geneva which, on July 23, 1962, agreed on the neutralization and independence of Laos. But continued violations of this agreement by neighboring Reds led to repeated American aerial bombardment of supply lines, beginning late in 1964.

VIETNAM AND
SOUTHEAST ASIA

Kennedy finally decided to take a firm stand in South Vietnam. Red China's countless millions were not contiguous, and overwhelming American sea and air power could be employed with far greater effectiveness. But the Communist warriors of South Vietnam (Viet Cong), supplied in part by Communist North Vietnam and China, used deadly guerrilla tactics to take over increasingly large areas. The Eisenhower administration had committed the United States to heavy support of the anti-Communist regime in South Vietnam with money and military hardware, together with about 700 noncombatant advisers. But all this did not turn the trick.

Late in 1961, in a fateful decision, Kennedy undertook to increase many fold the number of American military advisers in Vietnam. At the time of his murder in November, 1963, the total had risen to about 15,500, and much deeper involvement seemed almost inevitable. With corrupt and collapsible governments in South Vietnam succeeding one another with monotonous regularity, defeat was evidently coming on the installment plan.

The Warren Court under Fire

As if the threat from Communism abroad were not enough, many Americans viewed with alarm "Communist coddling" by the Supreme Court at home. The "Earl Warren Court"—so named after the big, jovial, white-haired Chief Justice appointed in 1953—handed down a long series of controversial decisions. These interpreted basic American freedoms so broadly as to provide loopholes through which alleged Communists escaped the clutches of the law. In the conflict between individual rights and national security, the Court upheld traditional American rights, and in so doing invalidated numerous state laws. It even decreed in 1964 that the State Department could not deny passports to known Communists who sought to travel abroad, even for subversive activity.

Other decisions of the Supreme Court reflected its deep concern for the individual, no matter how lowly. In 1963 it held (Gideon *vs.* Wainwright) that all defendants in serious criminal cases were entitled to legal counsel, even if they were too poor to afford it. More controversial were the rulings in two cases—Escobido (1964) and Miranda (1966)—which insured the right of the accused to remain silent and to enjoy other protections when accused of a crime. In this way safeguards were erected against confessions extorted under torture. Critics of these decisions were loud in their condemnation of "crook coddling," and demanded that the courts handcuff criminals, not the "cops."

Nor did the Court shy away from explosive religious issues. In two shocking decisions, in 1962 and 1963, it voted against required prayers and Bible reading in the public schools. These rulings were

"Backbone." U.S. Supports South Vietnam. Copyright © 1964. The Chicago *Sun-Times*. Reproduced by courtesy of Will-Jo Associates, Inc. and Bill Mauldin

based on the First Amendment, which required the separation of church and state, but they seemed to put the justices in the same bracket with atheistic Communists. Cynics predicted that the "old goats in black coats" would soon be erasing "In God We Trust" from all coins.

Infuriating to many Southerners was the determination of the Court, following the school desegregation decision of 1954, to support Negroes in civil rights cases. Five Southern state legislatures officially nullified the "sociological" Supreme Court decision, but they in turn were overruled by the high tribunal. In general, it held that the states could not deny to Negroes rights that were extended to white men. States'-rights Southerners complained bitterly that the Warren Court was not interpreting the Constitution but rewriting it, at the expense of states' rights. It was acting more like a legislative and not enough like a judicial body.

The Court also developed the philosophy that where the states permitted notorious evils to persist, it should step in. Of special concern was the over-representation in state legislatures of cow-pasture agricultural areas, especially where urban areas were bursting their boundaries. Adopting the principle of one-man-one-vote, the Court intervened in 1962 and again more emphatically in 1964. It ruled that the state legislatures, both upper and lower houses, would have to be reapportioned according to the human population, irrespective of cows. States'-righters and assorted right-wingers, pointing to the non-population representation in the United States Senate, raised anew the battle cry, "Impeach Earl Warren." But the legislatures grudgingly went ahead with reapportionment.

From 1954 onward the Court came under endless criticism, the bitterest since New Deal days. Its foes made numerous but unsuccessful efforts to clip its wings through bills in Congress or through Constitutional amendments. But the Court reflected perhaps not so much its own philosophy as the necessity of grappling with persistent new problems spawned by mid-century tensions. The black-robed justices were evidently determined to protect the rights of the individual, white or black, against the tyranny of the majority, even if the individuals in some cases were "not very nice people."

"You Mean These Apply To The Riff-Raff Too?" From *The Herblock Gallery* (Simon and Schuster, 1968)

Kennedy and the Black Revolution

School desegregation, though ordered by the Supreme Court in 1954, continued to be slow-motion desegregation in the Deep South. No less annoying to Negroes was discrimination in voter registration, transportation, public accommodations, housing, and job opportunities ("first-class taxes, second-class jobs"). Some of these grievances were even more galling in the North than in the South.

Kennedy, though committed to civil rights for Negroes, proceeded gingerly. Eager to steer his New Frontier schemes through

Congress, he feared the tomahawks of Southern members if he pushed too hard for civil rights. But he did appoint a few Negroes to prominent office, and arranged for many more to be put on federally financed jobs. Somewhat belatedly, on November 20, 1962, he issued an executive order barring racial discrimination in housing constructed with federal funds.

In truth, Kennedy was suddenly caught up in a frightening revolution by aroused blacks. Weary of waiting one hundred years for justice, and chanting "Jim Crow"—clap, clap—"must go," they were adopting the nonviolent tactics of massive civil disobedience that had been employed so effectively by Mohandas Gandhi in India in the 1940's. In so doing the blacks incurred economic discrimination (loss of jobs), jailings, shootings and other forms of physical abuse. Their most distinguished leader was an eloquent young Negro clergyman, the Reverend Dr. Martin Luther King, Jr., who was awarded the Nobel Peace Prize in 1964. Resorting to sit-ins, lie-ins, wade-ins, and pray-ins, the Negroes and their white associates made substantial progress in compelling the desegregation of Southern busses, stores, restaurants, and other public accommodations, while enlarging job opportunities, North and South. On August 28, 1963, some 200,000 demonstrators, about four-fifths of them Negroes, gathered peaceably at the Lincoln Memorial in Washington to demand better jobs and a comprehensive civil rights law.

Integrating the Southern universities almost brought wholesale slaughter. Some of them desegregated without any fuss, but the University of Mississippi ("Old Miss") became a volcano. A twenty-nine year old Negro veteran of the air force, James Meredith, attempted to register in October, 1962, pursuant to a federal court order. Such violent disorders erupted that President Kennedy was forced to send in some four hundred marshals and three thousand troops. Two men were killed and scores were injured in some fifteen hours of rioting, but Meredith attended class in the custody of federal marshals. He ultimately graduated—with a sheepskin that cost some four million dollars.

Violence begets violence, and "the long hot summer" of 1963 will long be remembered in the South. White Southern lawmen used billy clubs, high-pressure fire hoses, and electric cattle prods on Negroes who were demonstrating for their rights. In the "Battle of Birmingham," Alabama, the police turned savage dogs on defenseless Negroes.

As the white-sheeted Ku Klux Klan rode again, dozens of Negro churches were burned or bombed in Mississippi and Alabama ("Bombingham"). In September, 1963, an explosion wrecked a Baptist Church in Birmingham, killing four Negro girls who had just finished their lesson, "The Love That Forgives." Three "freedom riders" working for civil rights in Mississippi (two whites and one black) were brutally murdered and then buried under an earthen

In a message to Congress supporting a civil rights bill (1963), Kennedy said, "No one has been barred on account of his race from fighting or dying for America—there are no 'white' or 'colored' signs on the foxholes or graveyards of battle."

dam. Subsequent investigations by the F.B.I. implicated the sheriff, his deputy, and sixteen others, none of whom could be convicted of murder by white juries. Mob violence also erupted in Northern cities in the summer of 1964, notably in Harlem, Rochester, and Jersey City.

Negroes were clearly making substantial gains. Whites were beginning to appreciate the explosiveness of the problem and the mounting impatience of blacks who were outcasts within their own country. The rather hollow Twenty-third Amendment, effective in 1961, permitted the predominantly Negro population of Washington, D.C., to vote in presidential elections. (Yet the ballot was still withheld from some 800,000 inhabitants in local elections—a classic example of "taxation without representation.") Also designed to help poor Southern Negroes to vote was the anti-poll-tax Twenty-fourth Amendment, effective in 1964, and forbidding the assessment of a tax on voters in presidential or congressional elections. (See Appendix.) But the reform did not apply to state and local elections, where poll taxes still kept many poor blacks (and whites) from voting.

The Killing of Kennedy

The New Frontiersmen continued to encounter hostile hatchets in Congress. Kennedy was making little or no progress with Medicare, aid to secondary education, the pending civil rights bill for Negroes, or the proposed tax cut. The last of these was a daring scheme to reduce taxes, while incurring a planned deficit of $13.6 billion over a period of several years. Dollars that would otherwise pour into the Treasury would presumably be spent to revive the economy, avert depression, and relieve the four million or so unemployed, many of them Negroes. An increased national income would presumably wipe out the deficit, despite lower taxes. But conservatives, both Republicans and Democrats, objected that only a madman would slash his income when he was already deep in the red.

U.S. Public Debt

	Amount in millions	Per capita		Amount in millions	Per capita
1800	$ 83	$ 15.87	1945 (postwar)	$258,682	$1,848.60
1860	65	2.06	1956 (Cold War)	276,200	1,624.71
1865 (postwar)	2,678	75.01	1961	296,170	1,611.65
1900	1,263	16.60	1962	303,470	1,625.08
1920 (postwar)	24,299	228.23	1963	309,350	1,633.49
1929 (post-Coolidge)	16,931	139.04	1969	353,720	1,741.00
1939 (New Deal)	$ 40,440	$ 308.98			

Note: Except for 1956, 1957, 1960, and 1969, there were actual or projected deficits for the years from 1956 to 1969. Owing to the increase in population, the per capita debt remained about the same.

Kennedy scheduled a political fence-mending tour in Texas for November, 1963. Bitterness had boiled up against him as a result of his armed intervention on behalf of civil rights: KKK stickers ("Kayo Kennedy Klan") were insultingly in evidence. Then the unbelievable happened. On November 22, while riding in an open limousine in downtown Dallas, Kennedy was shot in the head by a concealed rifleman and died within minutes. The alleged assassin, Lee Oswald, a left-wing malcontent, was quickly apprehended. Within hours he was shot and killed by a self-appointed avenger, Jack Ruby. Both men had acted alone and not as a part of a conspiracy, according to the controversial findings of an elaborate official investigation headed by Chief Justice Warren. Vice President Johnson was promptly sworn in on a waiting airplane and flown back to Washington with Kennedy's corpse.

The murder of this young, eloquent, vibrant, and personable President evoked an amazing outpouring of grief at home and abroad. Not until then did many Americans realize how fully their attractive leader and his bewitching young wife had cast a spell over them. Chopped down in his prime after only slightly more than a thousand days in the White House, he was acclaimed more for the ideals he had enunciated and the programs he had advocated than for a large sheaf of legislative reforms. Not only had he grown impressively in office but he had silenced the charge that a Catholic could not be entrusted with the presidency of the United States. Mass was celebrated only once in the White House—the day of his funeral.

Kennedy's administration lasted a little more than 1,000 days, and his death recalled the words of his inaugural address. In outlining the goals that he sought he said, "All this will not be finished in the first 100 days. Nor will it be finished in the first 1,000 days, nor in the life of this administration, nor even perhaps in our lifetime on this planet. But let us begin."

Johnson Imprints the LBJ Brand

A remarkably smooth transfer of power to President Lyndon B. Johnson, the towering (6 feet 3) Texan, impressed critical observers. A so-called "wheeler dealer" who had become famous as a high-powered persuader and compromiser while Senate majority leader, he took hold with whirlwind vigor. Capitalizing on the shock of Kennedy's murder, he galvanized Congress into action with an impressive display of back slapping, arm twisting, "flesh pressing," and telephone pleading ("the fourth arm of government").

Congress responded with a noteworthy legislative output. Kennedy had laid the groundwork for most of these laws, and many of them no doubt would have passed in time. But the daring tax-cut scheme, applying to both personal and corporation incomes, sailed through with a minimum of difficulty. Fiscal orthodoxy flew out the window as planned deficits came in the door.

More significant in many ways was the passage of the Civil Rights Bill, strongly backed by the Southerner Johnson, after a seventy-five-day filibuster by die-hard Southern Senators. Signed on July 2, 1964, it was the most sweeping measure of its kind since Reconstruction days. Highly controversial was the public accommodations clause

In urging civil rights legislation on Congress, late in 1963, President Johnson said, "We have talked long enough in this country about equal rights. We have talked for a hundred years or more. It is time now to write the next chapter—and to write in the books of law."

which, by an unusual interpretation of interstate commerce, required even isolated restaurants and hotels to admit Negroes. Southerners insisted that this provision was unconstitutional, but the Supreme Court unanimously upheld it on the ground that it involved interstate commerce, at least indirectly.

Johnson's honeymoon—the nine "miracle months"—was highlighted by other achievements. As a former New Dealer (F.D.R. was his political "daddy"), he "declared war" on poverty and threw his weight behind a billion-dollar appropriation for the initial phase of the campaign. An estimated thirty million Americans dwelt on the dark side of the poverty line, and he was particularly concerned with the Appalachian poverty belt. There the collapse of the soft-coal industry had left tens of thousands of jobless Americans on the human slag heap. Johnson also asked for a relatively modest appropriation of $3.4 billion for foreign aid, and Congress passed it substantially intact. He also personally and energetically intervened to avert a paralyzing railroad strike over "featherbedding"—that is, the retention of some 65,000 allegedly superfluous jobs.

Bloody riots erupted in Panama in January, 1964, over American occupancy of the Canal Zone under the one-sided treaty of 1903. Johnson temporarily mollified the Panamanian government. Then, in December, he announced that the United States would undertake to renegotiate the objectionable treaty and also construct a new sea-level canal, perhaps in Panama and perhaps by cheaper nuclear excavation. The old waterway was too narrow, too slow, too congested, and too vulnerable to sabotage or bombing. Demands by Panama for more generous concessions delayed a satisfactory solution.

Johnson's Great Society Versus Goldwaterism

The nomination of Lyndon Johnson by the Democrats in 1964 loomed as a foregone conclusion: he had proved to be a "can do" President. He was chosen in August by acclamation in Atlantic City, as his birthday present, by a convention which he had carefully ringmastered. His platform, which outlined what Johnson called the Great Society, stressed five P's: Peace, Prosperity (the tax cut was evidently working), anti-Poverty, Prudence, and Progress. Proclaiming unity and reasonableness, the President's program sprawled so completely over the middle of the road as to leave mostly gutters for the extreme right and the extreme left.

Meeting the month before, the Republicans were bitterly divided as their delegates crowded into San Francisco's famed Cow Palace. Their free-for-all primaries had proved inconclusive. Moderates— a rather silent majority—had been unable to unite behind any one candidate. The leading middle-of-the-roader, Governor Rockefeller of New York, had faded, partly because of a highly-publicized divorce. Box-jawed, bronzed, and gray-haired Senator Barry M. Goldwater of Arizona, the leading right-winger, had managed to pick up enough delegates in conservative state conventions to insure his nomination on the first ballot. His near-fanatical "Barry's Boys," riding roughshod over the moderate "Eastern Establishment," adopted a conservative platform that refused to repudiate right-wing extremists, whether semi-secret John Birchers or besheeted Ku Klux Klanners. Lapel buttons proclaimed "What's Wrong with Being Right?"

Goldwater's candidacy was doomed from the start. The handsome, personable and wealthy Arizonan (a "poor" millionaire), with heavy horn-rimmed glasses, radiated sincerity and charm. But his extreme "rightism" repelled millions of rank-and-file Republicans, most of whom had not favored him in the first place. While promising an aggressive and costly campaign against Communism the world over, he inconsistently urged a meat-ax slash in federal spending. By proposing that American field commanders be given discretionary authority to use tactical nuclear weapons, he had created the image of a reckless, trigger-happy Arizona cowboy who would soon "Barry us" in the debris of World War III. A Democratic slogan jeered, "Help Barry Stamp Out Peace."

The two candidates never really clashed over the issues. Johnson spoke vaguely about his Great Society, and stressed the need for politicians and peoples to "reason together." Goldwater got in some telling blows when he condemned the "no-win war" in South Vietnam, wasteful spending, the excesses of big government, and "Communist coddling." ("In your heart you know he's *right*" became a Goldwater refrain.) He also assailed low ethics in government. Johnson himself, together with his wife, had become a multimillionaire while in public office, and his Senate-employed protégé, young Robert G. ("Bobby") Baker, had become a mystery millionaire under suspicious circumstances. Attempted coverups of Baker from the White House led to sneers about the "Whitewash House."

But Goldwater, who habitually "shot from the lip," failed to rise above his handicaps. The impression of impulsiveness and irresponsibility would not fade. His opposition to the nuclear test-ban treaty had alienated the "mother vote," just as his stand against the Civil Rights Bill had alienated the Negro vote. While "pooping around" the country (as he put it), he had earlier made many statements which were interpreted to mean, whether fairly or not, that he would be a veritable bull in the china shop. Some of these off-the-cuff views he toned down after his nomination, but he failed to erase the impression of recklessness abroad and heartlessness at home. One of his aggrieved supporters urged the newspapers to publish not what he said but what he really meant.

Senator Barry M. Goldwater.
Courtesy Senator Goldwater

In his speech accepting the Republican nomination in 1964, Senator Goldwater frightened many liberals and some moderates when he said, "Extremism in the defense of liberty is no vice. And . . . moderation in the pursuit of justice is no virtue."

Lyndon Johnson Engulfs Goldwater

On November 3, 1964, Johnson swept all sections, except the South, and triumphed by the biggest popular-vote total thus far in American history, 43,129,484, or a monstrous margin of nearly 16,000,000. He received an unprecedented 61% of the total vote, or almost precisely what the pollsters had predicted from the start. The electoral count was 486 to 52. Goldwater carried only five states of the Deep South, plus (narrowly) his home-state Arizona, with about 7,000,000 fewer votes than the losing Republican Nixon had polled in 1960. Democrats moreover swept both houses of Congress. With better than two-to-one majorities in the Senate and House, they enjoyed the most comfortable working majority since Franklin Roosevelt's landslide of 1936. The obstructive coalition of conservative Southern Democrats and conservative Northern Republicans was smashed, and a wide-open legislative road stretched before the Great Society.

For Republicans, Goldwater proved to be not so much a candidate as a catastrophe. Pessimists predicted that the Grand Old Party was

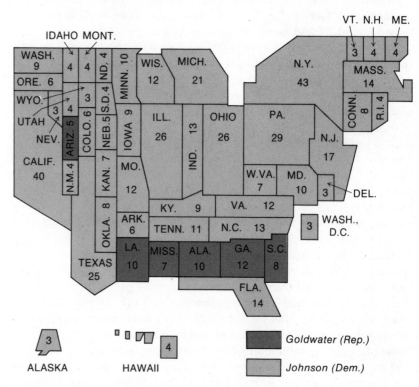

States distorted according to number of electoral votes indicated on each state.

PRESIDENTIAL ELECTION—1964

careening down the road to the Federalist-Whig cemetery. Many able and moderate Republican candidates for lesser offices, though running far ahead of Goldwater, were "buried with Barry." The Negro vote was overwhelmingly pro-Johnson. Oddly enough, the pro-Negro party of Lincoln had found its only solid support in the anti-Negro South, once solidly Democratic.

Lyndon Johnson had won a heady triumph. But the vagueness of the Great Society was such that no one quite knew what mandate he had received: perhaps it was to move ahead—prudently. Countless voters regarded both candidates as distasteful, and thanked God that only one of them could be elected. Probably any well known and respectable Democrat of presidential stature could have won. Millions of split-the-ticket Republicans, distrustful of Goldwater, voted for Johnson while continuing to support state and local Republican candidates. Big Business, normally Republican, was surprisingly friendly to Johnson and his moderate approach. For the first time in many decades a majority of the newspapers that endorsed a candidate supported the Democratic nominee.

Goldwater had declared that the voters, too often confronted with "me-tooism," needed a clear choice between a liberal and a conservative philosophy. "A choice and not an echo" was perhaps his most seductive slogan. But such were his contradictions that the voters had no clear-cut alternatives. His critics claimed that he was offering a choice between the 19th and the 20th Centuries in his opposition to social welfare, big government, racial equality, and concern for the poor. "Goldwater in 1864" was another satirical slogan.

Overseas crises during the electoral campaign had contributed heavily to Johnson's advantage. On August 2 and 4, 1964, the month after Goldwater's nomination, North Vietnamese torpedo boats reportedly attacked two American destroyers in the international waters of the Gulf of Tonkin. President Johnson, then under fire from Republicans for being "soft on Communism," promptly ordered retaliatory bombings of North Vietnam naval bases. On August 7, at his request, Congress speedily handed him a fateful blank check, with only two dissenting votes. This Tonkin Gulf resolution authorized him to take any action, including the use of armed forces that he might deem necessary in the Southeast Asia crisis.

Then a chain of spectacular developments occurred two weeks before the election. Premier Khrushchev of Russia was sacked and made an "un-person"; a Socialist (Labour) government attained office in Britain; and the Red Chinese exploded their first nuclear bomb. They thus became Member Five—the only non-white member —of the exclusive Nuclear Club, with terrifying prospects for the future. These alarming events provided further ammunition for those

Senator Wayne Morse of Oregon was one of the two members of Congress who voted against the Tonkin Gulf resolution. He opposed a blank check for war, favored intervention by the UN, and predicted the bottomless pit that developed. "It makes no difference who says that our objective is peace," he told Congress, "even if he be the President. Our actions speak louder than words; and our actions in Asia today are the actions of warmaking."

who argued that the country needed to retain in the White House an experienced President of Johnson's proven prudence. Had he not repeatedly assured the voters during the campaign that American boys should not be used to "do the fighting for Asian boys"?

In the light of subsequent developments, countless voters were to complain that they voted for Johnson but got Goldwater.

SELECT READINGS

Favorable and detailed overviews of the Kennedy years by participants are A. M. SCHLESINGER, JR., *A Thousand Days* (1965)* and T. C. SORENSEN, *Kennedy* (1965).* More general is T. C. SORENSEN, *The Kennedy Legacy* (1969). On foreign affairs consult ROGER HILSMAN, *To Move a Nation* (1967).* The Bay of Pigs fiasco is described in TAD SZULC and K. E. MEYER, *The Cuban Invasion* (1962).* For details of the Cuban crisis with Russia see ELIE ABEL, *The Missile Crisis* (1966) and R. F. KENNEDY, *Thirteen Days* (1969). Kennedy's assassination is reported meticulously in *The Official Warren Commission Report,* published in 1964 in various editions. The best book on the Goldwater-Johnson election is T. H. WHITE, *The Making of the President, 1964* (1965).* On aspects of the Negro revolution consult M. L. KING, JR., *Why We Can't Wait* (1964)*; J. W. SILVER, *Mississippi: The Closed Society* (1964)*; WILLIAM BRINK and LOUIS HARRIS, *The Negro Revolution in America* (1964)*; *Report of the National Advisory Commission on Civil Disorders* (1968)*; and *The Autobiography of Malcolm X* (1966).* For Vietnam, see next chapter.

* Available in paperback.

49

Lyndon Johnson and the Great Society

*What really matters is not the ultimate judgments that historians
will pass but whether there was a change for the better in the way
our people live.*

President Johnson, 1969

Johnson's "Hip-Pocket Congress" of 1965

A victory-flushed Lyndon B. Johnson (LBJ) unveiled his Great
Society program for the 89th Congress in January, 1965. The
heavily Democratic majorities responded to his urgings and arm-
twistings with an avalanche of legislation that compared favorably
with Franklin Roosevelt's Hundred Days Congress of 1933.
Johnson, in fact, regarded his Great Society as a logical
extension of the New Deal.

Poverty figured prominently in the first major legislation of
1965. One appropriation of more than a billion dollars was aimed
at hilly Appalachia, where gutted sections were suffering from
economic anemia. Later in the same session Congress doubled the
general anti-poverty program with a sweetener of $1.8 billion.
Unhappily, hoped for progress was hampered by inept
administration, graft, and insufficient funds.

More successful was the long-blocked Medicare scheme,
also enacted in 1965. It provided, under Social Security, for the
medical treatment and hospitalization of persons, whether mil-

lionaires or paupers, who had reached the age of sixty-five. As a tribute to ex-President Truman, a pioneer promoter, Johnson journeyed to Independence, Missouri, to sign the bill in his presence. Although "socialistic" Medicare was a bitter pill for the American Medical Association, the program got off the ground with unexpected smoothness as some 17 million oldsters gradually signed up. Fears of socialism were considerably calmed when physicians raised their fees and discovered that collections from Uncle Sam were more reliable than those from impoverished patients.

Congress also enheartened voteless Negroes by coming to grips with the Voting Rights Act of 1965. This measure was designed to put more teeth into the Civil Rights Act of the previous year by arming Washington officials with power to end discrimination against Negroes in registering and voting. Directed principally at the Deep South, the new law was spurred on its way by a massive Freedom March in Alabama, led by Dr. Martin Luther King, Jr. The subsequent injuring or murdering of a number of civil rights workers, both white and black, brought out federal troops, while back in Washington die-hard Southerners launched a furious but futile filibuster. Keenly aware of the historical nature of the bill, Johnson rode up to the Capitol to sign it in the same "President's room" where, 104 years earlier, President Lincoln had signed a law freeing certain slaves.

Low-rent urban housing remained a pressing concern of both blacks and whites. A major breakthrough came with the Housing Bill of 1965, which authorized the expenditure of $7.8 billion over four years. It included for the first time rent subsidies ("renticare") for poor families, but Congress failed to vote the recommended funds, much to Johnson's chagrin.

Dr. Martin Luther King, Jr. In 1964, King wrote, "Nonviolent resistance paralyzed and confused the power structures against which it was directed." Courtesy NAACP.

Education, Immigration, and Reorganization

Of immense importance to education was the passage in 1965 of two red-letter laws. The first provided $1.3 billion for elementary and secondary schools, both public and private, in proportion to the number of children from poor families. The second made available $2.3 billion for higher education, plus scholarships for needy students. Aid to non-public schools raised anew the thorny question of the separation of church and state (First Amendment), which had previously been a roadblock. But Johnson arranged for such ingenious wording of the bill that the funds could be legally shared by Catholic and other hard-pressed parochial schools. With a sure eye for the dramatic, he traveled to the one-room schoolhouse in Texas which he had attended, and there signed the elementary education bill in the presence of his first teacher, now a 72-year-old matron.

Johnson's "hip-pocket Congress" of 1965 also tackled immigration. Its great achievement was abolishing the long-criticized quota system based on national origins, which had discriminated heavily against newcomers from southern and eastern Europe. Henceforth quotas of 170,000 persons a year could enter from outside the Western Hemisphere, plus 120,000 from the Western Hemisphere. This was the first time that Congress had imposed such a restriction on migrants from nations within the Americas, such as Canada and Mexico. All told, about 50,000 more foreigners a year could enter than previously had been admitted. With his flair for the theatrical, President Johnson traveled to New York and signed the bill at the base of the welcoming Statue of Liberty.

Congress in 1965 also took the needed steps to insure smooth presidential succession. The recent death of John F. Kennedy, who was shot in the brain, raised anew the specter of an incapacitated President incapable of declaring himself incapable. Congress enacted a constitutional amendment, the twenty-fifth, which was approved in 1967 by the required three-fourths of the states (see Appendix). It stipulated that the Vice President should take the helm in the event of the President's disability, and it also set up machinery for quickly filling the vice-presidential vacancy upon the death of the President.

Recognizing the growing sickness of the cities, Congress in 1965 established a Department of Housing and Urban Development, the 11th with Cabinet status. Named to the new post was Dr. Robert C. Weaver, a distinguished Negro economist who had written several books on urban problems. He became the first Negro Cabinet member in the nation's history.

President Lyndon B. Johnson Five days after Kennedy's death, President Johnson told Congress in person, "All I have I would have given gladly not to be standing here today." Courtesy of Mr. Johnson.

The Great Society Sags

Johnson's magic touch was beginning to weaken as the second session of the 89th Congress met, early in 1966. Mass Negro demonstrations, which resulted in violence and counterviolence, were creating a "white backlash" against further legislation for civil rights. The fearful drain caused by the Vietnam War, in both gore and gold, was deepening nationwide disenchantment, while diverting energy and funds from the War on Poverty and urban blight. Enormous military expenditures were overheating the economy, with a consequent inflationary spurt in the cost of living. Overseas commitments were coming under increasing fire, especially those that involved the heavy leakage of gold abroad. Demands were also rising for meat-axing foreign aid, which had siphoned off more than one hundred billion dollars since the end of World War II.

LBJ suffered several stinging setbacks in the Congressional session of 1966. One casualty was the new civil rights bill, which included a ban on racial discrimination in the sale or rental of housing.

It slipped through the House by a comfortable margin, but temporarily died in the grip of a filibuster in the Senate, where opponents branded it unconstitutional. The real bugbear was the fear of white property owners that their homes would sink in value if Negroes moved into the neighborhood. One popular slogan was: "Your home is your castle—protect it."

Another reverse for Johnson was the failure of Congress, after a Senate filibuster, to amend the Taft-Hartley Act. Debate focused on Section 14 (b), which established the principle of "right to work" without joining a union. Though embittered by this defeat, organized labor was to some extent mollified by a bill passed in 1966 which boosted the nationwide minimum wage from $1.25 to $1.60 an hour. It brought more than 8 million additional toilers under the umbrella of the minimum wage, including certain agricultural workers.

Highway slaughter also commanded legislative attention. Ralph Nader, a lawyer-crusader, had burst into the headlines in 1965–1966 by blaming the manufacturers for their flimsy, chrome-plated death traps. In their cutthroat competition auto-makers had discovered that buyers seemed less interested in safety than in style and speed. Congress in 1966 enacted two significant measures: the Traffic Safety Act, aimed chiefly at establishing safety standards for automobiles, and the Highway Safety Act, requiring the states to adopt safety programs. The growing concern of Congress was further manifested by the creation of a new Cabinet-level Department of Transportation in 1966, thus adding a twelfth member to the Cabinet.

The Republican Resurgence in Congress

Normally the party in power loses some Congressional seats in the "off year" elections, but in November of 1966 the Republicans bounced back with surprising gains. They added three new Senators and 47 House members, thus more than regaining the 38 House seats lost during the Goldwater disaster. They were unable to control either house of Congress, but they could link arms with conservative Democrats to slow down Johnson's Great Society legislation.

The Republican revival was also evident at the state and local levels. Far from being dead, the GOP was in a strong position to make a run for the White House in 1968. Much of this upsurge was a return of moderate Republicans to the party fold, but some of it was doubtless due to deepening discontent with Johnson's Vietnam War, with crime in the streets, and with racial rioting. But even the "backlash vote" against blacks proved less pronounced than expected. Edward W. Brooke, the able Republican attorney general of Massachusetts, was elected to the United States Senate. He thus became the first Negro member of that body since Reconstruction days.

Senator Edward W. Brooke of Massachusetts.
Courtesy Senator Brooke

As anticipated, the 90th Congress was harder for Johnson to manipulate. He sought to cool off inflation by securing a ten percent surtax on income taxes, but his request was denied until he had agreed to make slashes in the heavily unbalanced budget. One of the severest cuts hit foreign aid, which in 1968 sank to about $1.7 billion. This was the lowest figure in the twenty-one-year history of the program, and a poorer showing relatively than several other nations were making. A sharp slap came in 1968 when the Senate voiced bitter opposition to the elevation of Justice Fortas to the Chief Justiceship, following the tentative resignation of Chief Justice Warren. LBJ at length was forced to withdraw the nomination, at Fortas's request. (The next year Fortas resigned from the Court under fire after further revelations of improper financial dealings.)

Several Great Society measures did manage to pass through the Congressional grinder in 1968. One was the Omnibus Social Security Bill, which raised the payments of some 24 million inflation-pinched pensioners by about thirteen percent. Another was the long-deferred Civil Rights Bill, filibustered to death in 1966 but now sped on its way by the recent assassination of the Negro leader Dr. King. This measure, which contained the controversial open housing provision, was designed to topple racial barriers in about eighty percent of the nation's dwellings by 1970. The Housing and Urban Development Act, a complementary bill, earmarked $5.3 billion over a period of three years. Johnson also signed a broad crime control law. It bore scant resemblance to what he had sought but it brought some hope of stemming the mounting wave of lawlessness.

"Bookmarks." Copyright © 1968. The Chicago *Sun-Times.* Reproduced by Courtesy of Will-Jo Associates, Inc. and Bill Mauldin

The murder of President Kennedy in 1963, followed by that of Dr. King and other prominent persons,* built up strong public pressure for limiting the sale and ownership of firearms. Such weapons, through accident or design, had taken over 750,000 civilian lives since 1900, or more than all of America's battle deaths to that date.

President Johnson favored the registering and licensing of guns, but the powerful National Rifle Association, with some 900,000 members, sprang to arms. It was backed by insecure citizens, black and white, who felt the need for weapons in the face of racial rioting. "When Guns Are Outlawed, Only Outlaws Will Have Guns" ran a pointed bumper sticker. Radical rightwing organizations, organizing "minute men" to preserve order and repel Communism, feared that a totalitarian government might confiscate their weapons, if registered. The upshot was a watered-down bill, grudgingly signed by Johnson as the first major gun-control law in thirty years. It placed relatively weak restrictions on the mail-order purchase of rifles, shotguns, hand-guns, and ammunition, while curbing the out-of-state purchase of such firearms.

* The list included Negro leaders Malcolm X (1965) and Dr. Martin Luther King, Jr. (1968); George Lincoln Rockwell, head of the American Nazi party (1967); and Senator Robert F. Kennedy (1968).

The Black Revolution

Johnson's last four years were marked by a new and alarming phase of the Negro uprising: a shift from massive peaceful protest to outright violence. Outspoken black militants like H. Rap Brown and Stokely Carmichael were springing to the fore, impatient with snaillike progress toward equality, in jobs, education, and housing, and urging extreme methods. "Black Power" became a watchword: that is, consolidating culturally, politically, and militantly behind Negro leaders so that, in the words of Carmichael, "they can bargain from a position of strength."

Special circumstances popularized "Black Power." Unemployment among Negroes persisted, partly because the more automated American society became, the less room there was for unskilled labor by black dropouts. To many Negroes the white man's schools seemed "irrelevant," with a resulting "cultural castration" and feeling of hopelessness. Accompanying the increase of ignorance, joblessness, idleness, and drug addiction came a rise in the Negro crime rate. The police ("pigs") were the enemy, who all too frequently overreacted with "police brutality." Housing, especially in the smelly ghettoes, was shamefully dilapidated, unsanitary, overpriced, and dangerous, with rats gnawing unattended babies. While white college boys secured draft deferments, a disproportionate number of Negro youths, not enjoying full freedom at home, were being drafted for service abroad. Shipped off to Vietnam, these black men were killing yellow men, it was said, in an attempt to bring freedom to other yellow men and thus protect an America that white men had "stolen" from red men.

In the late 1960's an overwhelming majority of Negroes were still hoping for integration into American society. But extremists like the Black Muslims and Black Panthers, despairing of fair treatment in a white-dominated society, were preaching self-segregation. Rising bitterness among Negroes themselves was highlighted when Malcolm X, a magnetic Black Muslim leader, was shot in 1965 by a fellow black as he addressed his followers in New York City.

An appalling outburst convulsed Watts, the ghettoized area of Los Angeles, in August, 1965. Rioting was triggered by a routine arrest of a young black by white policemen. Nearly a week of burning, looting, and shooting resulted in a toll of 34 dead, over 800 injured, over 3500 arrested, and over $140,000,000 in property damage. In venting their frustration and anger by burning their own buildings the Negroes focused attention on their grievances. Conservatives, representing the "white backlash," demanded a harsher application of force to preserve law and order; liberal whites (and blacks) insisted that the only lasting solution would be an elimination of discrimination and other root causes of unrest.

Fortunately, the "long hot summer" of 1966 passed without a

"You Don't Understand Boy—You're Supposed To Just Shuffle Along." From *Straight Herblock* (Simon and Schuster, 1964)

comparable explosion, but 1967 was another story. Detroit blew up in July, with widespread burning and looting, costing some $200 million, and with forty-three deaths. President Johnson was compelled to summon army units to restore order. Other cities suffered similar agonies, conspicuously Newark, Rochester, Milwaukee, and Washington. One of the most frightening aspects of these outbreaks was the rifle fire directed at the police and firemen who were trying to restore order or extinguish blazes. This was guerrilla warfare with a vengeance.

A new wave of violence was touched off by the murder of the non-violent Negro leader, Dr. Martin Luther King, Jr., by a white rifleman in Memphis, Tennessee, April 4, 1968. Infuriated blacks broke loose in nationwide orgies of arson and pillaging, all told costing forty-six lives. A heavy pall of smoke hung over the Negro section of the capital ("the second burning of Washington"), as the army was called in and a curfew was imposed. Dr. King's mantle as leader of the Southern Christian Leadership Conference fell on the Reverend Dr. Ralph D. Abernathy, who in 1969 led a Poor People's March to Washington from Memphis, Tennessee. Tens of thousands of blacks (with some whites) converged on the capital, there to be housed in a shantytown "Resurrection City." Torrential rains turned it into an impossible "Mudsville," and the sodden marchers were finally driven out with tear gas in pathetic disarray.

> The irony is that the violent death of King, a preacher and practitioner of non-violence, touched off an orgy of violence. As he wrote in 1964, "Nonviolent action, the Negro saw, was the way to supplement, not replace, the process of change. It was the way to divest himself of passivity without arraying himself in vindictive force."

Despite these unlovely spectacles, the black man was making some progress toward controlling his own destiny. In the elections of November, 1967, prominent Negroes were elected mayors of Cleveland, Ohio, and Gary, Indiana. Within four years after the Voting Rights Act of 1965, more than four hundred Negroes were holding public office in the South, in positions ranging from state legislator and mayor to aldermen and town councilmen. A few white juries were even convicting white men of crimes against blacks.

Colleges in Convulsion

A revolt of American youth in the late 1960's was clearly a phase of a world-wide movement, involving mass violence by college students all the way from Tokyo to Paris. Collegians in the United States, traditionally identified with goldfish swallowing and "panty raids," were bestirring themselves to achieve less frivolous goals.

Basic causes of youthful unrest in America were thought to be lack of parental discipline (Dr. Spock's best-selling baby book was blamed); excessive permissiveness in the schools (Dr. John Dewey and progressive education were condemned); dissatisfaction with the mismanagement of the world by older folks ("The Generation Gap"); the murder of youthful leaders like the Kennedy brothers; resentment against "The Establishment," whether educational or governmental; the inequities and uncertainties of the draft (scores of eligibles were fleeing to Canada); the existence of glaring social and economic inequalities (starvation in The Land of Plenty); a break-down of respect for law and law enforcers; and the widespread use of illegal, mind-warping drugs, even by grade schoolers. Among immediate spurs to action were beliefs that the draft-supported Vietnam War was "immoral" and that mass demonstration tech-niques, used so effectively by blacks, could be employed successfully in the colleges. "Draft Beer, Not Students" became a common demand.

A nationwide left-wing group—Students for a Democratic Society (SDS)—emerged as a principal spearhead of the movement. It agitated for such goals as the abolition of campus Reserve Officer Training Corps (ROTC), an end to war-related research for the gov-ernment, and a greater voice in shaping university policies, curricula, faculties, administrators, and boards of trustees.

Referring to underprivileged blacks, President Johnson told Congress, in January, 1964, "Unfortunately many Americans live on the outskirts of hope —some because of their poverty, some because of their color, and all too many because of both. Our task is to help replace their despair with opportunity."

Negro militants concurrently presented long lists of "non-nego-tiable demands" in both white and black colleges. A prime objective was an autonomous or semi-autonomous "black studies" program— black-taught and black-administered—which many Negroes be-lieved they needed to establish pride in their "cultural identity" and an awareness of their African inheritance. Conservative Negro leaders, like Roy Wilkins, argued that in general black studies were desirable for whites, especially if run by blacks and whites. But he believed that blacks should also acquire skills in such areas as law, accounting, medicine, and engineering, to be able to live usefully in the predominantly white society in which they were trapped. By 1970 only about one student in fifty in the non-black colleges was a Negro, and the pressure was on to admit more, even those whose underprivileged background had left them inadequately prepared.

Initial demonstrations at the colleges by both white and black militants were generally non-violent, consisting often of peaceful picketing and sit-ins. But such tactics led inevitably to tear gassing and forcible evictions, followed by window smashings, burnings, bombings, and shootings, amid familiar charges of "police bru-tality." A frightening outburst occurred at Columbia University, in New York City, during the spring of 1968, when the police were sum-moned to clear five university buildings that had been occupied for several days. The resulting injuries (about 150) and arrests (over 600) created an uproar so disruptive that this great university was forced to cancel classes for the remainder of the school year.

Fair-minded observers were quick to concede that the huge, im-personalized universities were in need of reform, that many more Negroes ought to be admitted, and that expertly taught black studies had a legitimate place in a scholarly curriculum. But a Harvard dean remarked, following a violent confrontation in 1969, that if a university community could not resolve its problems by rational discussion and not rioting, it was no longer a university. One consoling thought was that the great bulk of the nation's colleges had not experienced serious disorders, and that the hard-core militants represented only a tiny percentage of the student bodies where trouble had erupted.

Anti-Communism in the Caribbean and Vietnam

Disorders at home paralleled and interacted with disorders abroad. These, in turn, did much to eclipse Johnson's noteworthy legislative triumphs.

Discontented Dominicans rose in revolt against their military government in April, 1965. With American lives in jeopardy, President Johnson reluctantly dispatched a small contingent of troops for their protection—ultimately about 25,000 men. A few days later he declared that he had also acted to avert a Castro-like takeover by "Communist conspirators." Evidence of such a coup seemed exaggerated, and liberals everywhere, especially in Latin America, reacted angrily against a return to "gunboat diplomacy."

LBJ's military intervention, for the first time, broke Franklin Roosevelt's Good Neighbor pledges of 1933. It also violated Washington's obligations under the United Nations and the Organization of American States (OAS). Fortunately for Johnson, the OAS finally agreed to sanction the occupation, and five Latin American nations ultimately dispatched troop contingents, mostly tiny. Fair elections were held; the moderates were victorious; and all foreign forces were withdrawn in 1966. But the President incurred much criticism from liberals for his alleged haste, slipperiness, and willingness to back right-wing regimes with bayonets.

On the other side of the globe, Johnson had sunk ever deeper into the monsoon mud of Vietnam. He had conveniently at hand the blank-check Tonkin Gulf Resolution, voted by Congress in August, 1964. It clothed him with authority to take necessary military measures against the Communist North Vietnamese, who were supporting the Communist Viet Cong guerrillas in South Vietnam against the American-backed Saigon government. In February, 1965, in response to a Viet Cong attack on the American base at Pleiku, in South Vietnam, LBJ ordered large-scale retaliatory bombing of installations in North Vietnam.

Another crucial decision now had to be made. With the Viet Cong gaining strength, the Americans would either be thrown out of South Vietnam or they would have to pour in massive troop reinforcements. The South Vietnamese alone could not hold the line, cursed as they were with disunity and a succession of military governments that were unpopular, corrupt, autocratic, and collapsible. America had already sunk billions of dollars into South Vietnam, to say noth-

"There's Been a Change in Plans —Turn Around." (Johnson's Anti-Castro Intervention.) Brooks in the Birmingham *News*

ing of providing some 20,000 military "advisers" for the South Vietnamese army. This investment would be completely lost if South Vietnam went under. Worse yet, all the other nations of Southeast Asia might topple into the Communist camp like so many "falling dominoes." American forces, alarmists predicted, might even be driven back to Waikiki Beach, in Hawaii.

There was moreover a moral commitment, for Presidents Eisenhower and Kennedy had promised, in the expectation of overdue reform, to support the Saigon regime, primarily with money. Both men had reflected an American determination to prevent the southward spread of Soviet–Chinese Communism, while guaranteeing to the South Vietnamese the right to establish their own government without interference from foreign (Communist) aggressors.

Vietnam Quicksands

Johnson's fateful decision to employ combat units, contrary to his 1964 campaign promises, was reluctantly taken. The first sizeable contingents of marines stepped ashore in March, 1965. Three years later, by mid-1968, America was spending about thirty billion dollars annually, had committed about 550,000 men, had incurred over 25,000 fatalities and nearly 200,000 casualties, and had lost several thousand aircraft. So heavy was the American involvement that the operation was becoming Americanized. The South Vietnamese, whose army did not show a strong will to fight, were becoming spectators in their own war. Frontless and rearless, this brutal and futile struggle had become America's largest foreign war and the most unpopular overseas conflict in her history. By far more tons of explosives were dropped on tiny Vietnam than on all enemy territory during World War II. And by 1968 countless thousands of Vietnamese civilians, South and North, were being killed or wounded annually as a result of all phases of the fighting on both sides.

America's aerial bombing of civilian centers in North Vietnam merely strengthened the Communists' will to resist. Armed with abundant antiaircraft weapons and other equipment from Red China and Russia, the enemy struck back savagely. To many Americans this war seemed unwinnable by any conventional means that the public was willing to support in effective quantity.

Nuclear bombing would perhaps have been effective, but unthinkable: a civilized people cannot create a desert and call it peace. From time to time the United States would order a bombing halt, hoping to lure the enemy to the peace table; and from time to time the North Vietnamese put out peace feelers. But Washington either doubted their sincerity or hoped that it could get better terms than monotonous North Vietnamese demands for unconditional withdrawal of all foreign forces.

Marines splash ashore in South Vietnam. Naval Photographic Center

America's "no win" Vietnam War produced profound side effects. World opinion was generally hostile: the blasting of a primitive people by a mighty power struck many critics as obscene. Neighboring nations were also involved. Thailand became a U.S. bombing base, while "neutral" Cambodia and Laos both suffered from un-neutral American bombing incursions. The enormous costs unbalanced the national budget, accelerated the disturbing drain of dollars abroad, reduced foreign aid appropriations, further inflated inflation, and diverted funds from welfare programs ("Make War on Poverty, not People"). Finally, the war increased resentment among draftees, actual and prospective, white and black.

Overcommitment in the Far East also tied America's hands in the Middle East, while exposing a critical weakness. The desert sands exploded in June, 1967, when tiny Israel attacked and defeated her menacing Arab neighbors in a devastating six-days war. Happily for America, the conflict ended before serious involvement was required, but the powder keg remained.

The hulking shadow of Red China likewise loomed large. Repeated bombings close to the Chinese border, with several American aircraft shot down in China's air space, created the ever-present danger of provoking another World War—or at least a Korean-sized war. As if to give point to this peril, the North Koreans seized and kept an American intelligence ship ("spy ship"), the *Pueblo*, in January, 1968, evidently in international waters. They retained the crew of some eighty men for eleven months, after subjecting them to inhuman tortures. This humiliating episode aroused patriotic fury in America, but negotiation seemed the only alternative to a conflagration at a time when one Asiatic war was more than enough.

The Militant "Doves" on Vietnam

Public condemnation in America of the Vietnam meatchopper finally mounted to tidal-wave proportions. It began on a menacing scale in 1965, after the first commitment of U.S. troops, and it found a conspicuous outlet in the colleges. There "teach-ins" on the war issues were widely held by "Vietniks." Young men of draft age were especially concerned over the moral questions involved, including the use of "improved napalm" on women and children. Common slogans were "Make love, not war" and "Hell no, we won't go," accompanied by the burning or returning of draft cards.

Opposition in Congress to the Vietnam involvement centered in the powerful Senate Committee on Foreign Relations, headed by a former Rhodes Scholar, Senator Fulbright of Arkansas. A constant thorn in the side of the President, he staged a series of widely televised public hearings in 1966 and 1967, during which prominent personages aired their views, largely anti-war.

"It's Hopeless." A Chinese Cartoonist Views Vietnam

"Doves," or opponents of the conflict, advanced numerous arguments. They denounced America's participation as unconstitutional because only Congress can declare war, and the Tonkin Gulf Resolution, they claimed, was never meant to apply to an intervention of this magnitude. The conflict was immoral, they charged, because it involved propping up a corrupt regime, supporting a military clique rather than a democracy, and bombing tens of thousands of men, women, and children (on both sides). ("Hey, Hey, LBJ, How Many Kids Did You Kill Today", ran a sardonic chant.)

The tragic Vietnam trap involved America's interference in a civil war against Viet Cong rebels who were striving to overthrow an oppressive regime. Such action, the "doves" argued, thwarted the principle of self-determination, betrayed America's revolutionary tradition, and flouted the President's no-war electoral pledges of 1964.

The Hard-Nosed "Hawks"

"Hawks," or belligerent backers of the war, had ready replies. They contended that America's interference was constitutional, for the Tonkin Gulf Resolution of 1964 had authorized it. If Congress did not like that resolution, it could repeal it (a refusal to support the soldiers in the field would have been political suicide). America had made commitments under three Presidents to uphold the non-Communist regime in Saigon against the aggressions of Communism under North Vietnam's Ho Chi Minh. To cut and run now would destroy all faith in the nation's word, undermine the forty or so alliances that Washington had made all over the world, and leave to Communist slaughter tens of thousands of innocent people who had put their faith in America. Uncle Sam, as a policeman of the planet, must stop aggression all over the globe, and demonstrate that it did not pay. "Appeasement" would merely postpone the day of reckoning.

The "hawks" advanced additional arguments. If America turned tail now, the billions of dollars and tens of thousands of American lives would have been sacrificed in vain. To surrender would ruin the nation's perfect record of never having failed to win a war (although the War of 1812 and the Korean War had been neither "won" nor "lost"). Finally, the "hawks" claimed, victory was possible by conventional means if the United States would only pour in enough men and bombers. All-out assaults would destroy North Vietnamese cities and seaports, through which military supplies were funneling from Chinese and Russian ships. Of course, China and Russia might jump in and touch off World War III, but that was a calculated risk.

Hawkish illusions that the struggle was about to be won were rudely shattered by the Communist Tet offensive, launched late in

"Onward and Upward." (Johnson and Vietnam.) Crawford for the NEA. Reproduced by permission of the Newspaper Enterprise Association

January, 1968. At a time when the Viet Cong guerrillas were supposedly licking their wounds, they suddenly launched blistering
attacks on twenty-seven key cities, including the capital, Saigon.
Although eventually beaten off with heavy losses, they demonstrated anew that victory could not be gained with such forces as
the American taxpayers were willing to supply. With an increasingly
insistent voice, American public opinion began to demand that the
war be ended as speedily as possible, and on terms that would
enable America to "de-Americanize" the conflict and withdraw with
honor. Opposition finally became so vehement that President
Johnson could feel the very foundations of government shaking
under his feet.

Johnson's "Abdication" and its Aftermath

Political experts had confidently predicted that President Johnson
would run for a second elective term. He loved power; he was not
one to quit under fire; and he desperately hoped to crown his administration with peace in Vietnam. And there was no one in the Democratic camp who could wrest the nomination from him. Senator
Robert F. Kennedy of New York, the murdered President's younger
brother and a "dove" on Vietnam, was urged by opponents of the
war to challenge the incumbent. But recognizing the hopelessness of
such an effort, Kennedy declared that he would support Johnson.

An unlikely challenger did appear in the person of "dovish" Senator Eugene ("Clean Gene") McCarthy of Minnesota, an idealistic
and quiet-spoken ex-professor. Few people took his candidacy
seriously, except an idealistic group of anti-war college students
("The Children's Crusade") who flooded New Hampshire and rang
doorbells on the eve of that state's presidential primary, on March 12,
1968. The little-known McCarthy won an incredible 42 percent of
the Democratic votes and 20 of the 24 delegates, although President
Johnson, only a write-in candidate, received 48 percent. Sentiment
against both the war and Johnson was evidently much stronger than
realized, and four days later Senator Kennedy belatedly threw his
hat into the ring.

This startling turn of events was not lost on LBJ. He would evidently have to fight for the nomination, and if he won it, he might
lose to the Republicans. Why not bow out, reunite the country, and
run for his place in history rather than for a second elective term?

Johnson exploded his bombshell on March 31, 1968, two weeks
after Senator Kennedy entered the race. Appearing on nationwide
television, he announced that he would de-escalate the war in Vietnam, as the "doves" were demanding. The rumored massive troop
reinforcements would not be sent, and the bombing of North Vietnam would be limited to the scantily populated southern sector,

Senator Eugene McCarthy.
Courtesy Senator McCarthy

Quite in contrast with Coolidge's ambiguous "I do not choose to run for President in 1928," President Johnson was crystal clear: "Accordingly, I shall not seek, and I will not accept, the nomination of my party for another term as your President."

through which enemy soldiers and supplies were leaking. Johnson evidently hoped that this unilateral olive branch would lure the enemy to the peace table. After an earnest plea for national unity, he stunned his vast audience by declaring firmly that he would not be a candidate for the presidency in 1968.

North Vietnam responded somewhat encouragingly three days later, when it expressed a willingness to talk about peace. After a month of haggling over the site, the adversaries agreed to meet in Paris. The succeeding months were consumed by bickering over procedural matters, including the shape of the conference table.

After Johnson's dramatic "abdication," the heir apparent was liberal Vice President Hubert H. Humphrey—a former druggist, college teacher, mayor and Senator. As a thick-and-thin supporter of the President's Vietnam policies, he received the machine support of the Democratic Party, while Senators McCarthy and Kennedy battled in the primaries (only 14 states had them). The late-coming Kennedy, capitalizing on his brother's fame, the Kennedy name, and his own record as a liberal, made a remarkable showing, outpolling McCarthy in all but one of the half-dozen or so primaries that the two men entered. But on the night of an exciting victory in the California primary, he was fatally shot by a young Arab immigrant who resented his pro-Jewish views.

Presidential Gladiators of 1968

Scenting victory as the Democrats divided, the Republicans jubilantly convened in plush Miami Beach, Florida, early in August, 1968. Richard M. Nixon, the former Vice President whom John F. Kennedy had narrowly defeated eight years earlier, had the nomination sewed up on the first ballot. He had won impressively in all of the Republican primaries that he had officially entered.

Nixon, with his "loser's image," was fighting history. Not since 1840 had a candidate won the presidency for a first term after a previous electoral defeat for that office. But as a "hawk" on Vietnam and as a middle-of-the-roader with leanings toward the right, he was capable of uniting the party and winning the support of moderates, as well as Goldwater conservatives. His backers claimed that the "New Nixon" was more mature, more experienced, and better poised than the anti-liberal, anti-Communist, "Old Nixon."

Nixon surprised the convention by his choice of a vice presidential running mate. Seeking to mollify Southern elements of the party who were demanding tougher enforcement of "law and order," he tapped Maryland's Governor Spiro T. Agnew, hitherto little known.

As expected, the Republican platform assailed the Democratic administration. It demanded that the war in Vietnam be fought to an honorable conclusion, with an accompanying de-Americanization.

Closer to home it urged an all-out attack on crime (while seeking to remove its basic causes); an elimination of urban decay; and an improvement of the economy, with less inflation and more expansion.

To their lasting regret, the Democrats met in Chicago late in August, 1968. Young anti-war zealots, including "hippies" and "yippies," had threatened to disrupt proceedings. Mayor Daley consequently arranged for barbed-wire barricades ("Fort Daley") and thousands of police and troop reinforcements. The militants poured in by the thousands, some of them tauntingly waving Viet Cong flags and chanting "Ho, Ho, Ho Chi Minh." Many baited the police ("pigs"), shouting obscenities and hurling bags and cans of human filth. Large numbers of infuriated policemen "went animal," clubbing and manhandling innocent and guilty alike. Hundreds of demonstrators were arrested, scores were hospitalized (including police), but no one was killed except, as cynics said, the Democratic Party and its candidate.

Within the besieged convention hall, Vice President Humphrey was unstoppable on the first ballot. His chief challenge came from Senator McCarthy, who simply did not have the machine-marshaled votes. The bitterest battle involved a three-hour debate over the plank in the platform regarding Vietnam. McCarthyites demanded an unconditional halt in the bombings, followed by negotiations for the withdrawal of all foreign troops. Humphreyites, echoing the President, rammed through their own plank. It called for an end of the bombing only when such action would not endanger American troops, and when there was evidence of an appropriate response from the enemy.

On three key issues—Vietnam, the urban crisis, and law and order—the Democratic platform rather closely paralleled the middle-road Republican platform. The sharpest difference was that one praised while the other pilloried the Johnson administration.

The Triumph of Nixon

A "spoiler" third-party ticket—the American Independent Party —added confusion and color to the campaign. It was headed by ex-pugilist George C. Wallace, former governor of Alabama, a vehement right-winger and racist. His new grouping was anti-Negro, anti-rioter, anti-Communist, anti-dove, anti-intellectual, and pro-states rights. Wallace would put the Negroes and other demonstrators in their place, with bayonets if necessary. He would also smash the North Vietnamese into smithereens and bring the boys home victorious. Speaking behind a bullet-proof screen, he drew unexpectedly large crowds in the North, despite screaming disruptions by masses of hecklers.

Vietnam did not prove to be as crucial an issue in the campaign as

Vice President Hubert H. Humphrey Senator Humphrey said after his close defeat for the Presidency in 1968, "I think we ought to remember one thing. The Republicans did not win this election. We defeated ourselves." Courtesy Mr. Humphrey.

expected. Wallace, with his hard-nosed line, had no real chance of winning. Between the positions of the Republicans and Democrats there was not much to choose: both candidates were committed to keeping on with the war until the enemy would settle for an "honorable peace." The millions of "doves" had no place to roost. Humphrey, a prisoner of LBJ's policies, was unwilling to soften his stance perceptibly until late in the campaign. About a week before the election McCarthy, with evident distaste, came out lukewarmly for Humphrey.

Early opinion polls showed Nixon far out in front. He ran a rather relaxed campaign, promising, without specifics, to "end" the war in Vietnam and "win" the peace. Humphrey began to catch fire toward the end. His stock took a sharp rise on October 31, 1968, when Johnson exploded a final bombshell by announcing that he had ordered a halt to *all* bombing of North Vietnam. He explained that the North Vietnamese, in return, had agreed to permit the South Vietnamese to take part in the Paris talks. The effect of this announcement was dampened when the South Vietnamese indicated that they were not yet ready to go to Paris.

Nixon, who had lost a cliffhanger to Kennedy in 1960, won one in 1968. He garnered 302 electoral votes,* with 43.4 percent of the

* In the Electoral College one North Carolina elector pledged to Nixon voted for Wallace.

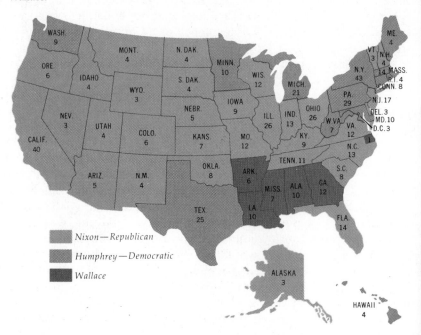

PRESIDENTIAL ELECTION OF 1968 (with electoral vote by state)

popular vote (31,785,480) as compared with 191 electoral votes and 42.7 percent of the popular vote (31,275,166) for Humphrey. Not since Woodrow Wilson in 1912 had the victor received so small a percentage. Nixon was also the first President-elect since 1848 not to bring in on his coattails at least one house of Congress for his party in an initial presidential election. The victor did not carry a single major city, thereby attesting to the continuing urban strength of the Democrats, who also won about 95% of the Negro vote. Nixon had received no clear mandate to do anything: his victory was in large part a protest vote against high prices, high taxes, the bottomless war, the unfair draft, big spending, rampant crime, and riotous turmoil.

Wallace did more poorly than expected. Yet he won an impressive 9,906,473 popular votes and 45 electoral votes, all from five states of the Deep South, four of which the Republican Goldwater had carried in 1964. "Why waste your vote?" was an argument that sent many of Wallace's followers over into the ranks of the major parties. Even so, he remained a formidable force, for he had amassed the largest third-party popular vote in American history.

The Wallace "scare" had one constructive consequence. Fears that no candidate would receive a majority in the Electoral College, and that the issue would be thrown into the House of Representatives, revived serious work in Congress on a corrective Constitutional amendment. In an atomically-triggered world, the dangers of perpetuating an oxcart system were painfully apparent.

Uneasy Soviet-American Relations

Friction with Russia seemed less acute after the removal of Khrushchev in 1964: his successor, Premier Kosygin, was less given to bombast, bullying, and bomb-rattling. The fifteen-nation NATO defensive alliance, never built up to specifications, appeared to be less imperatively necessary.

President de Gaulle of France, the go-it-alone nationalist, continued to resent outside control over forces on French soil. In 1966 he announced that the NATO central command would have to leave France, although the French would still retain a partial connection with the Alliance. With great reluctance, the allies moved their headquarters from France to cramped Belgium—at a cost of hundreds of millions of dollars.

Rivalry with Russia in the planetary race continued at a frantic pace and with astronomical expense. Both nations in the 1960's lofted various unmanned and manned vehicles into space, or orbited them around the moon. The Americans in 1968 (Apollo 8) and in 1969 (Apollo 10) sent three-man space vehicles hurtling around the moon, in preparation for a manned lunar landing, in July, 1969. At

In March, 1968, candidate Nixon had declared, "I pledge to you the new leadership will end the war and win the peace in the Pacific." Many voters expected a relatively rapid pullout from Vietnam, but American ground troops were not withdrawn until the beginning of Nixon's second term, more than four years and thousands of casualties later. And the fighting between North and South Vietnam continued on a bloody scale.

Mercury-Atlas 6 carrying Astronaut John H. Glenn on first U.S. orbital flight. NASA

"Frightening Delivery System."
Don Hesse in the St. Louis
Globe-Democrat

this stage the United States seemed to be well ahead in the celestial competition.

Spectacular flights into outer space were closely related to long-range nuclear weapons. During the Johnson years, despite mutual misgivings, appreciable progress was made toward some limitation on such armaments. In January, 1967, Russia and America, and about 60 others, signed a treaty banning weapons of mass destruction in outer space. And in June, 1968, the General Assembly of the UN adopted a nuclear nonproliferation treaty, subject to ratification by individual nations. Under it the signatories agreed not to supply nuclear weapons to countries not possessing them. The assumption was that the fewer nuclear weapons there were, the less likely a war was to start by an accidental explosion. A half dozen or so other nations refused to go along, conspicuously France and Red China, both of which were latecomers to the exclusive Nuclear Club.

Fears on all sides were clearly stimulating the upward spiraling race in nuclear weapons. A new and even more expensive phase loomed with prospective systems of anti-missile missiles, variously estimated to cost the U.S. from $40 to $400 billion. Hopes persisted that the Soviets and the Americans, the only two peoples financially able to build such shields, could work out a mutual moratorium before either side became too deeply involved. At least Moscow showed some faint signs of interest.

After years of name-calling, the Chinese Communists, more red than the Russian Reds, developed a violent ideological rift with Moscow in the mid-1960's. By 1969 Soviet and Chinese armed forces were killing each other in small-scale border skirmishes. This ominous clash presented Washington with a priceless opportunity to drive a wider wedge between these erstwhile "comrades." But America's unending war against Communist North Vietnam tended to push the two Red giants together.

The Czech Checkmate in 1968

Hopes that the Soviets would cooperate in arms limitation were shattered in August, 1968, when Moscow cracked down on Czechoslovakia. This prosperous little Soviet satellite, edging toward more freedom and democracy, threatened to infect the neighboring satellite states—and even Russia itself. In a lightning move, the Soviets rumbled into Czechoslovakia with tanks and troops. The luckless Czechs were forced to turn back the hands of the freedom clock.

Afterclaps of the Czech coup were far-reaching. Instantly the Cold War became hotter, for the Kremlin was clearly putting the preservation of its own harsh regime above everything else. Faltering NATO received a shot in the arm: the rickety alliance did not seem like excess baggage after all. The untrustworthiness of the Soviets lent further support to demands by American "hawks" that the anti-Communist war in Vietnam, supported by Russian and Chinese Communists, be fought through to victory. Demands for pushing ahead with the costly anti-missile defensive system became more insistent.

The tragic story of Hungary, crushed by Russia in 1956, was thus repeated with variations in Czechoslovakia. As in 1956, the Western world could do nothing effective, short of sparking World War III. Again the United Nations revealed its impotence: an ineffective resolution was effectively vetoed by the Soviets. President Johnson issued a solemn protest over television, but critics were quick to point out that his hands were not completely clean. He had sent troops into the Dominican Republic and into South Vietnam in 1965, and they were still in Vietnam after four bloody years.

The LBJ Obituary

Elected in 1964 but rejected in 1968, the tall, talented Texan returned to his ranch in January, 1969. His party was defeated, and his "me-too" Hubert Humphrey was repudiated. His popularity remained low in the opinion polls ("The Affection Gap"), although it had risen somewhat after his "great renunciation"—ironically one of his most popular acts.

Yet Johnson's legislative leadership had been remarkable. No President since Lincoln had worked harder or done more for civil rights. None had shown more compassion for the poor, the ill-educated, and the black. The halfway gains for the Negro had in fact stimulated discontent among many Negroes, while adding to white fears and racial turmoil, and contributing to Johnson's undoing. His War on Poverty was a humanitarian concept, but here too the enemy was as stubborn as the Viet Cong. Great want persisted alongside great wealth, although unemployment was substantially down. Prosperity, unbroken and unprecedented, had continued. But the price the public had to pay was ever-creeping inflation, which the President had fought with all the weapons at his command.

Johnson had crucified himself on the cross of Vietnam. Committed to some degree by his two predecessors, he had chosen to defend American bases and enlarge the conflict rather than be run out. He was evidently persuaded by his advisers, both civilian and military, that a "cheap" victory was possible by aerial bombing. Repeated assurances by the administration that the conflict could be won with just a little more effort widened the "Credibility Gap" in Washington, and further convicted the President of deceiving the people. His decision not to enlarge the war offended the "hawks," and his refusal to back down antagonized the "doves," including many intellectuals who had never taken to his breezy Texan ways.

Of all the words that most came back to haunt President Johnson, those that he uttered during the presidential campaign of 1964 about "American boys" took high rank. For example, at Akron, Ohio, October, 1964, he said, "But we are not about to send American boys nine or ten thousand miles away from home to do what Asian boys ought to be doing for themselves." When he left office more than four years later, more than 500,000 American boys were there.

Johnson wrote in his memoirs, "When we made mistakes, I believe we erred because we tried to do too much too soon, and never because we walked away from challenge. If the Presidency can be said to have been employed and to have been enjoyed, I had employed it to the utmost, and I had enjoyed it to the limit."

Close associates testified that Johnson was a highly intelligent human dynamo whose mind had not been honed by the best formal education. He relied heavily on energy, cajolery, and wizardry. Clearly his high-pressure and secretive methods of arm-twisting and horse trading, which had proved so effective in the Senate, did not work so well with the press and public. Looking like everybody's grandfather, he lacked glamor on television. He seemed to suffer from a kind of inferiority complex growing out of his arid cultural background, and he strove furiously to prove that he could be a great President in the image of his political idol, Franklin Roosevelt. At his Farewell Dinner Address, in New York, he closed by saying simply, ". . . we tried." Perhaps he tried too hard.

SELECT READINGS

A critical appraisal by a first-hand historian observer is ERIC GOLDMAN, *The Tragedy of Lyndon Johnson* (1969).* High-quality journalism is evident in ROWLAND EVANS and ROBERT NOVAK, *Lyndon B. Johnson: The Exercise of Power* (1966). T. H. WHITE has continued his exhaustive analyses in *The Making of the President, 1968* (1969). On the Negro see references in the previous chapter and the extremist views presented in STOKELY CARMICHAEL and C. V. HAMILTON, *Black Power: The Politics of Liberation in America* (1967).* A journalistic survey of foreign problems is P. L. GEYELIN, *Lyndon B. Johnson and the World* (1966). On the Dominican intervention consult JOHN B. MARTIN, *Overtaken by Events* (1966), by the ex-ambassador. Of the enormous literature on Vietnam, probably the most useful single overview is G. M. KAHIN and J. W. LEWIS, *The United States in Vietnam* (1967). See also ROBERT SHAPLEN, *The Lost Revolution: The U.S. in Vietnam, 1946–1966* (rev. ed., 1966) and BERNARD FALL, *Two Viet Nams: A Political & Military Analysis* (2nd. rev. ed., 1967). G. W. BALL, former Undersecretary of State, is perceptive in *The Discipline of Power* (1968). Two of the best books to emerge on the Vietnam War are DAVID HALBERSTAM, *The Best and the Brightest* (1972) and FRANCES FITZGERALD, *Fire in the Lake* (1972). Lyndon B. Johnson's *The Vantage Point: Perspectives of the Presidency, 1963–1969* (1971) contains the President's own favorable view of his administration, including its handling of the Vietnam war.

* Available in paperback.

50

The Nixon Years

*I have never been a quitter. To leave office before my term is
completed is abhorrent to every instinct in my body. But as President
I must put the interest of America first.*

President Nixon, Televised Farewell Address, August 8, 1974

Nixonian Beginnings

Inaugurated on January 20, 1969, a calm and confident President
Nixon urged a people torn with dissension over Vietnam and
racism to lower their voices and "stop shouting at one another."
Elected as a plurality President by only a 43 percent minority and
confronted by a strongly Democratic Congress, he obviously could
launch no reformist crusade. His early moves were characterized
by coolness and caution. The basic political strategy was not to
move too far to the right or left, but to enlarge the "silent center,"
while courting further Republican support in the South. To this
end Nixon soft-pedaled civil rights and desegregation, openly
opposed school busing to achieve racial balance, and gave the
blacks, who had voted overwhelmingly against him, only token
representation in high office. His Attorney General, a former New
York law partner, was grim-faced John N. Mitchell, who could be
counted on to fulfill Republican promises of law and order.
Federal prosecution of the radical Chicago rioters of 1968 resulted in

a protracted trial (the Chicago Seven) in 1969–1970 which further widened the "Generation Gap." Their conviction was finally overturned on appeal.

Conservatism characterized Nixon's early appointments, even though he was soon advocating such basic reforms as overhauling the scandal-ridden welfare program, guaranteeing a minimum income, and handing back to the states a portion of federally collected revenues (the "New Federalism"). He finally succeeded with revenue sharing. Fulfilling recent campaign promises, he undertook to conservatize the Supreme Court by seeking appointees who would strictly interpret the Constitution and not coddle radicals and criminals. The promotion of Warren E. Burger from a lower federal court to the Chief Justiceship (recently vacated by Earl Warren) received speedy Senate confirmation in June, 1969. But the successive nominations of two Southern judges, vulnerable to charges of racism, were both narrowly defeated amid bitter accusations. A third choice, Harry A. Blackmun of Minnesota, was unanimously approved in May, 1970. Before the end of the next year, two new conservative justices were added, making a total of four Nixon appointees out of nine members of the Court.

Nixon gave high priority to the task of cooling down the overheated economy, which had produced the insidious inflationary spiral of the "soaring sixties." Living costs were rising so alarmingly as to inspire serious talk of wage-price controls. In the early stages of his administration, Nixon tackled the problem in part by cutting back on government expenditures and defense contracts, with a consequent rise in unemployment. His purpose was to halt inflation by producing a recession that was mild enough not to qualify as a depression. But creating unemployment proved easier than stemming inflation, which, when combined with stagnation, produced alarming "stagflation."

An important part of the fiscal problem was the necessity of tax reform, and here Congress took the lead. The records showed that twenty-one persons with over a million dollars in annual income had legally avoided paying any federal income tax whatever in 1966. A sweeping tax reform bill passed Congress early in 1970. Though plugging some loopholes, it proved to be a disappointing mass of compromises and contradictions, including a 15 percent increase in Social Security benefactions. It required the President, who signed with reluctance, to raise several billion additional dollars from other sources to compensate for enlarged exemptions.

The national budget for the year ending June 30, 1970, was just under $200 billion. Although the Treasury's books finally balanced with an excess of some $3 billion in 1970—the first surplus in nine consecutive years—the overall increase was fantastic. The defense budget gouged out over 40%, or about 50% if one counted veteran

President Richard M. Nixon. Reversing Kennedy's inaugural plea to "bear any burden," Nixon told Congress in February, 1970, "America cannot—and will not—conceive all the plans, design all the programs, execute all the decisions and undertake all the defense of the free nations of the world." White House photo.

benefits and interest payments for past wars. New weapons were proving frightfully costly, with unexpected budget overruns of billions of dollars, and the vast military-industrial complex, with powerful lobbies in Washington, was reluctant to lose business. Military expenses were so high, including some $25 billion a year for the stalemate in Vietnam, as to make virtually impossible sufficient tax money for waging an all-out war on such varied fronts as the urban ghettos and the pollution of air, earth, and water.

Nixon's first budget, for the year beginning July 1, 1970, called for expenditures of $200.8 billion, with the allocation to national defense dropping from 40% to 36%, but still an enormous sum. The burden was made all the heavier by the collapse of the stock market in 1969–1970, partially in response to the Vietnam War, with a consequent wiping out of more than $200 billion in paper values. Sickly stocks generally predominated during the remainder of the Nixon years.

Vietnamizing the Vietnam War

At the outset, President Nixon enjoyed gratifying success in quieting the public uproar over Vietnam. His announced policy, foreshadowed in a televised address on May 14, 1969, was to withdraw the 540,000 American troops in South Vietnam, over an extended period. The South Vietnamese, with American money, weapons, training, and advice, could then gradually take over the burden of fighting their own war. In pursuance of this objective, Nixon flew out to Midway Island, in June, 1969, there to confer with President Thieu of South Vietnam. Following top-secret discussions, Nixon announced the scheduled withdrawal of the initial contingent of 25,000 troops. Two subsequent pronouncements, in September and December of 1969, were designed to bring total withdrawals to 110,000 men.

The so-called "Guam Doctrine" or "Nixon Doctrine" thus evolved. It embraced the concept that the United States would honor its existing defense commitments, but that henceforth Asiatics would have to fight their own wars without the support of large bodies of American ground troops.

As for Vietnam, Nixon's policy was not so much to end the conflict as to "Vietnamize" it by gradually turning it over to South Vietnam. His hope was that in time the North Vietnamese would be willing to end this seemingly endless war, which would meanwhile continue without American troops but with American support— aerial, naval, financial, and advisory. But even this much involvement was distasteful to American "doves," many of whom demanded a withdrawal that was prompt, complete, unconditional, and irreversible.

"Cold War? Not for Some."
Brimrose in the Portland
Oregonian. By permission

Opposition to the bottomless war entered upon a new phase in October, 1969, when the protesters staged a massive national Vietnam moratorium. In contrast to previous outbursts of violence, it featured peaceful, almost prayerful, demonstrations by several million people. An estimated 100,000 jammed the Boston Common, and some 50,000 filed by the White House carrying lighted candles.

Confident that the marchers represented only a highly vocal minority, Nixon, on November 3, 1969, delivered a dramatic televised appeal to the great silent majority. The response was overwhelmingly favorable to his gradual Vietnamization, and his poll-popularity, which had been sagging, rose sharply. In harsher tones than Nixon, Vice President Agnew, soon to become a household word as the President's hatchet man, lashed out at the "misleading" news media and the "effete corps of impudent snobs" who demanded quick withdrawal from Vietnam.

By early 1970 the Vietnam issue had become partially eclipsed by such burning domestic problems as inflation, racism, and pollution. Some of the tensions had been eased, especially on the college campuses, by reducing the draft calls and by shortening the period of draftability, on a lottery basis, from eight years (18 to 26) to one year (the 19th). This change was instituted by President Nixon, pursuant to an act of Congress passed in November, 1969.

Disgust with the bloody mess in Vietnam was further deepened by shocking reports, especially those involving the massacre of innocent women and children by American troops in the village of My Lai. Only one officer, an obscure Lieutenant Calley, was convicted by a U.S. military court of murder (some twenty victims), but his sentence was progressively lightened from twenty to ten years. By January, 1970, the Vietnam conflict had become the longest in American history, and with over 40,000 killed and over 250,000 wounded, the third most costly foreign war in the nation's experience.

Foreign Affairs and Moon Landings

Jet-plane diplomacy characterized Nixon's early months, and he soon became by far the most airborne President in history. In February, 1969, he embarked upon an eight-day tour of five foreign capitals, in an effort to improve relations with the European allies, especially France. His task was made easier by the resignation of President de Gaulle several weeks later, following a stinging rebuke at the polls. In July, 1969, Nixon undertook a quick tour of East Asia, including Thailand, and returned by way of Communist Romania. There he received an uproarious welcome, to the obvious discomfiture of Communist Moscow.

At Nixon's invitation, Governor Nelson Rockefeller in 1969 made four trips to Latin America, where he received riotously unfriendly receptions, which cost more than a half-dozen lives. Uncle Sam's existing Alliance for Progress program was evidently proving inadequate to combat rampant poverty, upper-class greed and graft, armed insurrection by leftists, and takeovers by military dictatorships.

As for East Asia, Japan won the "second battle of Okinawa," when President Nixon agreed, in November, 1969, to return the blood-bought island chain by 1972. Although America retained certain non-nuclear military privileges, this concession, as finally ratified, quieted Japanese nationalists. As regards the Asiatic mainland, the United States, after about twenty years of rejection, was showing more willingness to deal with Communist China, partly because of the rift between Peking and Moscow. In July, 1969, Washington partially relaxed the embargo on American purchases of Chinese goods and on travel to China.

Intimately connected with the costly arms race was the space race, which attained a fantastic climax on July 20, 1969. On that historic day two American astronauts, Neil A. Armstrong and Edwin E. Aldrin, Jr., reached the moon (mission Apollo 11). The venture had been launched by President Kennedy in 1961, and the price tag turned out to be about $24 billion. Critics charged that the money could better have been used for needed projects that were of some earthly use, but the moon-glow accompanying this astonishing feat inflated the national pride and impressed peoples the world over. The simultaneous failure of an unmanned rocket-ship from the

Astronaut Aldrin poses with stretched U.S. flag on windless moon. Photo taken by Armstrong. Courtesy NASA

Soviet Union to achieve its supposed goal of scooping up lunar material made the victory over the Russians in the moon-race all the sweeter. Two more American moon men achieved another lunar landing on November 19, 1969, and other space spectaculars continued, including orbiting skylabs and the photographic probing of the privacy of Mars.

The Shadow of Nuclear Incineration

The Soviets, who had quarreled noisily with their Chinese neighbor in the mid-1960's, were obviously worried by Red China's emergence as a nuclear power. Probably as a consequence, they began to adopt a less bellicose tone toward the United States. The oppressive problem facing these two mighty nuclear powers was limiting the mad momentum of the nuclear arms race, which threatened to bankrupt both. President Nixon favored a compromise Sentinel ABM (Anti-Ballistic Missile) system, which involved setting up missile sites in America to protect the weapons already emplaced. The strategy was to have enough offensive missiles undamaged after a Soviet first strike to be able to inflict unacceptable damage on the Russians. Opponents of the proposed ABM criticized its cost, which was estimated to be about $8 billion initially but which could swell to tens of billions more. Others argued that the scheme was misdirected (why not more offensive missiles?), unworkable, ineffective, and so provocative as to chill all hope of nuclear limitation. But Nixon threw his weight behind the ABM proposal, and it narrowly passed Congress in October, 1969. He thus had one more "bargaining chip" in his arms negotiations with Russia.

Nixon had meanwhile lent his support to the UN-sponsored nuclear nonproliferation treaty, which needed the ratification of some forty nations. The Senate approved it in March, 1969, although France and Red China, piling up their own atomic arsenals, held aloof. Finally, long-awaited preliminary talks with the Soviets regarding the limitation of nuclear weapons got under way in Helsinki, Finland, in November, 1969. The Russians seemed somewhat more willing to come to grips with the problem than previously. Further sessions of these so-called SALT talks (Strategic Arms Limitation Talks) were deferred to the spring of 1970.

"O.K., Now Let's Talk!" Nixon Confronts Soviet Spokesman (Brezhnev). Brooks in the Birmingham *News.* Courtesy Mr. Brooks

Cambodianizing the Vietnam War

For several years the North Vietnamese and Viet Cong had been using "neutral" Cambodia, bordering South Vietnam on the west, as a springboard for troops, weapons, and supplies. Suddenly, on April 29, 1970, without consulting Congress, Nixon ordered American forces, joining with the South Vietnamese, to clean out these havens. In announcing this bold stroke, he assured the nation that the incursion would be limited to the borderland area. He further declared that the American (but not South Vietnamese) troops would be speedily withdrawn, and that the "boys" would be brought home on schedule.

At the time of this sensational announcement, massive dissent in the colleges was manifesting itself in student-faculty "strikes," accompanied by wholesale rock-throwing, window-smashing, and arson. Nixon's coup, which seemed to spell deeper involvement rather than withdrawal, fanned the flames nationwide. At Kent State University, in Ohio, National Guardsmen fired into an angry crowd, killing four and wounding many more; at Jackson State College, in Mississippi, the highway patrol discharged volleys at a student dormitory, killing two black students. The nation was in turmoil as rioters and arsonists convulsed the land. Any serious attempt to prosecute the trigger-happy Guardsmen was deferred for several years.

Nixon's assurances that he was invading Cambodia to save lives and shorten American involvement was evidently persuasive with the great silent majority. In the short run, at least, the stroke was a mild success, for it resulted in the capture of some stores of weapons, ammunition, and rice. The larger objective of eliminating the enemy base was not achieved. The American troops were withdrawn on June 29, 1970, after only two months, and with assurances to Cambodia of continued aerial, naval, and financial support. At the same time Nixon publicly promised to reduce, by the spring of 1971, the American contingent in Vietnam to 285,000, as contrasted with some 540,000 men when he took office.

Supporters of Nixon argued that he had gained at least eight months for the South Vietnamese to strengthen themselves, but many of the immediate results were disturbing. Communist forces, in reaction, overran large areas of Cambodia, while threatening the remainder. Bitterness in America between the "hawks" and "doves" deepened, as right-wing groups physically assaulted leftists. Disillusionment among the blacks with "whitey's war" increased, ominously in the armed forces. The youth of America, further aroused, were only slightly mollified when Congress, in June, 1970, passed a law of dubious constitutionality which lowered the voting age to eighteen. It was superseded by the 26th Amendment in 1971. The Senate (though not the House) overwhelmingly repealed the Gulf of Tonkin blank check given President Johnson by Congress in 1964, while seeking other ways to restrain Nixon. The President's dramatic call (October 7, 1970) for a standstill cease fire in Indochina, as a preliminary to the peace conference, was flatly rejected by the Communists as a capitalistic trick.

At a press conference in May, 1970, President Nixon explained why he had called student rioters "bums." He stated that he had always upheld the right of nonviolent dissent, but . . . "When students on university campuses burn buildings, when they engage in violence, when they break up furniture, when they terrorize their fellow students and terrorize the faculty, then I think 'bums' is perhaps too kind a word to apply to that kind of person."

Congressional Politics and Antiwar Agitation

Veto hatchet in hand, Nixon continued to be at odds with Congress throughout his troubled years. Both houses, strongly Democratic, shied away from heaping political credit on the President by enacting his programs. For his part, Nixon opposed, at least initially, an unbalanced budget and an increased national debt. When he disapproved of what he regarded as "budget busting" legislation, he would impound billions of dollars appropriated by Congress for specific purposes, even over his veto. Other presidents had occasionally failed to spend surplus money, but Nixon engaged in this practice repeatedly and on an enormous scale, despite a series of court decisions overruling him. Impoundment was but one example of the presidential expansion of constitutional powers at the expense of the legislative branch.

With Congress often in a balky mood, Nixon enjoyed scant success in 1970 with his legislative program, and none at all in his attempts to overhaul the scandalously wasteful welfare system. One landmark law turned the nation's mail over to a federal but independent U.S. Postal Service, which proved less efficient but more expensive than its predecessor. As a staunch law-and-order man, Nixon gained some ground when Congress passed the Omnibus Crime Control Act, which especially sought to stamp out college arsonists and bombers. The District of Columbia Crime Control Act was largely inspired by repeated muggings within sight of the capitol dome.

Nixon was grimly determined to secure the election of a Republican Congress and defeat "obstructionists" of both parties. In the autumn of 1970 he embarked upon a nationwide barnstorming tour against the "rising tide of terrorism," and his effort was undoubtedly the most farflung ever undertaken by an incumbent President in a midterm election. He encountered boisterous heckling from "thugs and hoodlums" opposed to the Vietnam war, and in San Jose, California, a small but violent group of "hippie"-type "bums" shouted epithets and threw eggs and stones that narrowly missed injuring him. Decent Democrats, who bitterly resented Nixon's accusations of violence and criminality, charged that such demonstrations were staged by Republican "dirty tricksters" to discredit their opponents and the antiwar movement. Whatever the truth, in November the President could claim a victory of sorts at the polls. He did not dislodge the Democratic majority in Congress, but the Republicans won nine extra seats in the House of Representatives and two in the Senate. Yet this nominal gain was actually a loss because in the midterm elections the party out of power normally picks up at least several times this number of members. The Republican cause was doubtless hurt by declining employment, rising

In a tape-recorded White House conversation of March 27, 1973, Nixon remarked, "I believe in playing politics hard, but I am also smart."

prices, spiraling inflation, and the slow-motion withdrawal of troops from the Vietnam death trap.

Public demonstrations against the Asian war crested again in late April and early May, 1971, when mass rallies and marches again erupted from coast to coast. Belligerent "doves" attempted to shut down the government in Washington by blocking bridges, streets, and intersections with their bodies, stalled cars, and other objects. In subsequent clashes with the authorities, scores of demonstrators, as well as some police, suffered injuries. Thousands of activists and spectators alike were arrested and held a day or so in the football stadium of the Washington Redskins. The detention of citizens without charge was clearly a violation of their constitutional rights, but the authorities argued that the dangers of the situation took clear priority over individual liberties. President Nixon, stout champion of law and order, had no sympathy with "pampering punks" and "coddling criminals."

New combustibles fueled the fires of antiwar discontent in June, 1971, when *The New York Times* began publishing a top-secret study of America's involvement in the Vietnam war, prepared by officials in the Pentagon. These purloined Pentagon Papers laid bare the miscalculations, blunders, and deceptions of the Kennedy and Johnson administrations, especially the provoking of the North Vietnamese in 1964 into the attack in the Gulf of Tonkin, which sparked the blank-check war resolution passed by Congress. The individual most responsible for this leak to the press was Dr. Daniel Ellsberg, who had worked on these same papers in the Pentagon and who subsequently photocopied them. Despite his breach of the law in thus exposing state secrets, he evidently believed that his patriotic duty required him to reveal to the public the cynicism and trickery involved. He was subsequently indicted for theft and conspiracy, but his case was finally dismissed because of a counter-illegality by the prosecuting Washington government. The White House not only arranged for a burglary of the office of Ellsberg's psychiatrist, but was also guilty of a crude attempt to influence the presiding judge.

New Directions in China and India

The burdensome Vietnam war was intimately related to President Nixon's increasing interest in Red China, a chief supplier of the North Vietnamese Communists. For some while the administration had been making conciliatory noises through the Bamboo Curtain toward Peking, especially in regard to easing official trade restrictions. The Chinese responded by inviting American table tennis players to China, where, as expected, they suffered a sound beating by the world champions. "Ping pong diplomacy" thus led to a further relaxation of tensions, and in July, 1971, Nixon startled a huge television audience by announcing that he had accepted with pleasure an invitation to visit Red China the next year. This unexpected move, which was bound to infuriate Republican right-wingers and other conservatives, presented a sharp contrast to Nixon's previous record. He owed his early rise in politics to being one of the most persistent and consistent Communist baiters in American public life— "a card-carrying anti-Communist."

The two great Communist powers, Red China and Red Russia, were now at each other's throats over their clashing interpretations of Marxism. Balance-of-power strategy dictated that the United States should play one antagonist off against the other, rather than face both united, especially if Washington expected to enlist the aid of both the Soviet Union and China in pressuring North Vietnam into peace. With such objectives in view, Nixon announced in October, 1971, that he was going to visit Russia during the following May. Soviet-American tensions had been eased somewhat during the previous month by a major four-power pact which finally defused the Berlin bomb by permitting unhindered civilian access to the isolated city.

America had long blackballed Red China as a prospective member of the United Nations, but now Nixon neatly reversed himself and opted for a two-China policy. This course involved the admission of mainland China and the continued membership of offshore China (Taiwan), a charter member. But many of the less-developed countries of the United Nations, delighted to slap the rich and capitalistic Uncle Sam while welcoming a Communist regime, gleefully joined the majority that voted to admit Red China and expel tiny Taiwan, October 25, 1971. One Tanzanian delegate danced an impromptu jig in the aisle.

The health of American foreign relations was intimately related to the health of the American economy, particularly the drooping dollar, officially devalued in 1972 and again in 1973. In the area of "Nixonomics," as in the overseas theater, the President executed some spectacular flipflops. Although his distaste for economic controls was well known, in August, 1971, he announced with fanfare his New Economic Policy, which included an initial wage-price freeze for ninety days in an effort to hold down the fast-spiraling inflation. (Price-fixing had not been undertaken since the Korean war in 1951.) All these changes came at a time when the nation's balance of trade was showing a distressing deficit, and the once Almighty Dollar was being pounded down and scorned in the world markets, as American tourists quickly discovered. The national debt continued to mount alarmingly as Nixon backed away from his balance-the-budget philosophy.

Uncle Sam suffered yet another black eye in December, 1971, when war broke out anew between India (backed by Russia) and neighboring Pakistan (backed by China) over Pakistan's seceding Bangladesh.

Washington not only branded India the "main aggressor" and cut off $87 million in development loans, but menacingly rushed a naval force to Indian waters. Pakistan collapsed in only ten days, and the Americans, with their money on the losing horse, managed to offend both combatants. India resented too much interference, and Pakistan not enough. Nearly a year later the disgruntled Pakistanis withdrew from the American-sponsored South East Asia Treaty Organization (SEATO alliance).

Nixon in Peking and Moscow

An airborne President and his party, including Mrs. Nixon, made an historic visit to China during the last eight days of February, 1972. Between glass-clinking toasts, Nixon engaged in extended conferences with Chairman Mao and Premier Chou En-Lai, and walked on the fabled Great Wall of China. A joint statement issued at the end did little more than reaffirm the fixed positions of both powers, although the United States declared its "ultimate" objective to be withdrawal of its armed forces and installations from offshore China (Taiwan). Diplomatically the visit only established a face-to-face dialogue between both nations, while opening the door for more extended contacts, including possible formal recognition. The Russians were obviously displeased to see Nixon snuggling up to their sworn enemy, while America's valuable Japanese ally, which had not been consulted in advance, experienced a severe loss of face, known as the "Nixon shock" (*shokku*).

As was true of the earlier Peking visit, Dr. Henry A. Kissinger, Nixon's special adviser on national security affairs, had prepared the path to Moscow. Smiling, bespectacled, and German-accented, he had reached America as a youth when his parents fled Hitler's anti-Jewish persecutions. Becoming a brilliant professor of government at Harvard, he subsequently served Nixon with numerous intercontinental flights ("shuttle diplomacy"), and with a high degree of tireless diplomatic skill and persistence. Although without cabinet rank, he was sometimes referred to as "the most powerful number-two man in American history."

President Nixon's extended talks in Moscow, featuring an unprecedented television address to the Russian (and American) people, resulted in a number of significant agreements late in May, 1972. A primary goal was to cut the colossal costs of the frantic race in nuclear arms. The first major achievement was a treaty, subsequently approved by the Senate, which limited each nation to two defensive clusters of Anti-Ballistic Missiles, each with 100 units. One would protect the respective capitals and the other would safeguard an offensive missile complex. The second significant pact was an executive agreement to freeze long-range nuclear missiles, built or build-

Dr. Kissinger denied that the U.S. was making advances to China for the purpose of blackmailing Russia. "We are pursuing our policy . . . on the ground that a stable peace . . . is difficult to envisage if 800 million people are excluded from a dialogue with the most powerful nation in the world. . . ."

"Henry Kissinger, Diplomat with a Global Vision." Robert Graysmith, San Francisco *Chronicle*, by permission.

ing, at their existing levels for a period of five years. Additionally, there were various pacts of lesser importance that related to such matters as health, space exploration, safety at sea, and environmental protection.

The agreement to freeze the number of missiles at existing levels caused much uneasiness, for the Russians deployed bigger and more powerful weapons, and they could ultimately add a larger number of independently targeted warheads to each monster. Clearly the bankrupting race in nuclear arms would continue in certain categories. But one result of the eased relations with food-short Russia was the great grain deal of July, 1972—a three-year arrangement by which the food-rich United States agreed to sell at least $750 million worth of wheat, corn, and other cereals. Using clever capitalistic tricks, the Russian Communists bought up the desired grain in America quietly and cheaply. As a consequence, prices for the now scarce commodity rose sharply and American bread-eaters were forced to pay millions of dollars more than if there had been no "great grain steal." For the first time in decades, the United States could see the end of its stored surplus of cereals. Only one year of bad crops in America would leave the nation in real trouble, along with much of the rest of the grain-hungry world.

McGovern Challenges Nixon

Vietnam was bound to be a burning issue in President Nixon's campaign for re-election. Nearly four years had passed since he had promised, as a presidential candidate, to end the war and "win" the peace. Yet in the spring of 1972 the fighting escalated anew to alarming levels when the North Vietnamese, heavily equipped with foreign tanks, burst through the demilitarized zone (DMZ) separating the two Vietnams. Nixon reacted promptly by launching massive bombing attacks on strategic centers in North Vietnam, including Hanoi, the capital. Gambling heavily on foreign forbearance, he also ordered the dropping of contact mines to blockade the principal harbors of North Vietnam. Either Russia or China or both could have responded explosively, but neither did, and the North Vietnamese offensive finally ground to a halt.

The vexatious Vietnam issue was bound to have a political impact at home. During a grueling fight in the Democratic primaries, Senators Humphrey and Muskie, running mates on the same presidential ticket four years earlier, undercut each other, and Governor George C. Wallace of Alabama was almost killed when shot and paralyzed by a deranged young man in Maryland. Senator McGovern of South Dakota ("Senator who?"), the earnest and indefatigable "Prairie Populist," managed to line up enough delegates to ensure his lop-sided nomination at the Miami convention of the Democrats in July, 1972. Dedicated to pulling the remaining 30,000 or so American troops out of Vietnam in ninety days, he issued a clarion call in his speech of acceptance, "Come Home America!"

McGovern undoubtedly had the backing of the large and respectable antiwar element in ·the Democratic Party, with its leaning toward liberalism and idealism. He also appealed to the racial minorities, the feminists, the youth, and the leftists. But in enlisting this oddly assorted following McGovern managed to snub and alienate the conservative backbone of his party, as well as numerous independents. The recent revolt of youth had brought a hasty enactment and ratification of the 26th Amendment (1971), which lowered the voting age to eighteen years, and McGovern was counting on about three-fourths of the youthful vote. Less than half of the group from 18 to 21 bothered to go to the polls or even registered, and the percentage of their support for McGovern was disappointing to him.

Late the next month, August, 1972, the exultant Republicans, all set to renominate Nixon and Agnew, also met in Miami, where they chanted "Four More Years, Four More Years," as they acclaimed their leader's so-called triumphs for peace in China and Russia. They condemned the "crackpot" welfare schemes of McGovern, his proposed slashing of defense funds, and his alleged intention of reducing America to a "second class power." They demanded a negotiated "peace with honor" rather than a "peace with surrender"

Shirley Chisholm. A woman candidate for the Democratic presidential nomination in 1972, she received an unprecedented 152 votes at the national convention. Courtesy Congresswoman Chisholm

in Vietnam. Using eye-catching charts, they showed how Nixon (in nearly four years) had wound down "the Democratic war" in Vietnam from some 540,000 troops to about 30,000, with more to come home shortly. There was no boasting about a concurrent windup of aerial and naval forces, which now totaled 100,000 men. Outside the convention hall, police arrested some three hundred of the most militant antiwar demonstrators.

McGovern's candidacy was perhaps doomed from the outset. The nominee hastily tapped Senator Eagleton of Missouri as his running mate, after several other invitees had declined. Word soon leaked out that Eagleton, over a period of years, had received psychiatric care, including electric shock treatments. McGovern loyally declared that he was behind Eagleton "1,000 percent," but soon concluded that it would be better to dump him. This he arranged to do, in favor of the Catholic Sargent Shriver, former President Kennedy's brother-in-law. This act of expediency shattered one of McGovern's best assets—a reputation for decisiveness, candor, and credibility.

The Nixon Landslide of 1972

President Nixon subsequently remarked that "the election was over the day he (McGovern) was nominated." This statement was probably true, because the Democratic party had already torn itself to pieces in the bitter primary fights. Their candidate only made matters worse by dumping Eagleton and proposing impractical schemes for curing economic ills, including his soon-withdrawn proposal of $1,000 for every American (more than $200 billion). His strongest talking point was his promise to bring the boys home from the blood-soaked jungle trap in Vietnam. Even this appeal was largely canceled out when, twelve days before the balloting, the high-flying Dr. Kissinger returned from the Vietnam negotiations in Paris to proclaim that "peace is at hand." He explained that a few minor details would be settled in "three or four days." The Democrats could only reply lamely that if peace was at hand, it should have come four years and thousands of casualties sooner.

The Republican landslide of November, 1972, was superficially awesome, despite a relatively light turnout of voters. Many were discouraged by the public opinion polls, which with uncanny accuracy predicted the lopsided victory. Nixon swept every state except Massachusetts and the nonstate District of Columbia, piling up 520 to 17 electoral votes and a popular majority of 47,000,000 to 29,000,000, or an almost unprecedented 60.7 percent. Although in a sense he won by default, Nixon claimed a mandate, as politicians do, for his policies—past, present, and future. But if it was a mandate, it was not for his party. The Republicans not only failed to recapture Congress but gained only twelve new seats in the House and lost

Presidential candidate George McGovern. Courtesy Senator McGovern

two in the Senate—an unexampled rebuke to the head of the ticket in a presidential victory of this magnitude. Few candidates rode into power on the President's coattails. Many voters, deluded into thinking that the war in Vietnam had just ended, regarded the candidates as a choice of evils. Much of the pro-Nixon vote was a vote by ticket-splitting Democrats against McGovern, as further attested by the election of a majority of Democratic state governors—who now totaled 31 to 19.

Nixon's success at the polls was partially attributable to his legislative program in 1972. He had approved a revenue-sharing bill which provided for a return of $30.2 billion in federal revenues to the state and local governments over a period of five years. The assumption was that these funds would assist the localities with such social service problems as mass transit, education, and housing. Congress increased Social Security benefits by raising the contributions of employees and employers by 20 percent, and by providing for automatic increases when the cost of living rose more than 3% in any calendar year. Feminists were enheartened when, after about a half-century of pressure, Congress completed action in 1972 on a sex-equality amendment to the Constitution. Designed to be the 27th amendment, and sent to the states for approval, it encountered stubborn resistance with victory almost in sight. Opponents, both male and female, objected to the imposition of equal physical burdens, especially in regard to the military draft.

Bombing North Vietnam to the Peace Table

The dove of peace, "at hand" in Vietnam just before the balloting, took flight after the election, when Nixon refused to be stampeded into accepting terms that had obvious loopholes. After the fighting on both sides had again escalated, he launched a furious two-week bombing ("the Christmas blitz") of North Vietnam, which appeared to be an iron-handed effort to drive the North Vietnamese back to the conference table. The attack was the heaviest of the war and resulted in substantial losses of America's big B-52 bombers. Evidently this merciless pounding had the desired effect, because the North Vietnamese negotiators returned to Paris and agreed to cease-fire arrangements on January 23, 1973, nearly three months after peace was prematurely proclaimed. In essence, the United States within sixty days would withdraw its remaining 27,000 or so troops, but would be allowed to provide South Vietnam with replacements of worn-out weapons. Prisoners of war on both sides would be released, including some 560 Americans for whom the bombing had largely been continued. The government of South Vietnam would be permitted to remain under the autocratic President Thieu, with American support. Other stipulations called for a future election, which the Communists expected would enable them to take over the entire country. Oddly enough, the North Vietnamese were permitted to retain some 145,000 troops in South Vietnam, where they could be used to spearhead a powerful new offensive when the time seemed ripe. Significantly, the North Vietnamese still occupied about thirty percent of South Vietnam.

President Nixon, optimistically interpreting retreat as no defeat, hailed the face-saving cease-fire agreements as "peace with honor." What he evidently meant was that the United States had not simply withdrawn completely, as McGovern had advocated, and left American prisoners and all of South Vietnam to the Communists. Nixon did not want the United States, while he was in office, to be charged with having lost a war, with consequent weakened credibility. The nation had poured into this Asian quagmire more than 50,000 American lives, to say nothing of some 300,000 casualties and some $125 billion, and the President felt the United States should emerge on its feet rather than on its knees. Yet America was heavily committed to sustaining indefinitely an independent but authoritarian South Vietnam with continuing billions of dollars in financial assistance, military supplies, advisory personnel, and long-range aerial support. Such was the high cost of leaving. Repeated Republican boasts that Nixon had ended the war rang hollow, because the cease-fire agreements were daily violated, heavy fighting continued, and at least 50,000 Vietnamese, North and South, were reportedly killed in the year following "peace with honor." In a sense there were no winners or losers—just victims. The long list included draft-dodgers and deserters, for whom the "doves" raised a mounting cry for amnesty, despite strong opposition from the hard-line "hawks," including the President.

Watergate Woes

Nixon did not have long to enjoy his recent electoral triumph, which was soon sullied by a flood of so-called Watergate scandals. On June 17, 1972, some two months before his renomination, a bungled burglary had occurred in the Democratic headquarters, located in the Watergate apartment-office complex in Washington. Five men were arrested inside the building with electronic "bugging" equipment in their possession. They were working for the Republican Committee for the Re-election of the President—popularly known as CREEP—which had managed to raise tens of millions of dollars, often by secretive, unethical, or unlawful means. Large corporate contributions, some in the range of $100,000 or more, resembled bribes or extortion money paid in the expectation of future or continued favors from the Nixon administration. CREEP had also engaged in a "dirty-tricks" campaign of unethical espionage and sabotage, including faked documents, directed against Democratic candidates in the campaign of 1972.

The Watergate break-in proved to be only the tip of an iceberg in a slimy sea of corruption that made the Grant and Harding scandals look almost respectable. A number of the highest placed White House aides and advisers were forced to resign. Many were involved in a criminal obstruction of justice through tangled cover-ups or payment of hush money. By early 1974, twenty-nine people had been indicted, had pleaded guilty, or had been convicted of Watergate-related crimes. Additionally, about ten corporations had been convicted of making illegal contributions. Other guilty persons and companies surfaced in the months ahead.

The scandalous mess in Washington also involved the improper or illegal use of the Federal Bureau of Investigation and the Central

"The Ancient Mariner." Nixon troubled by Watergate albatross. Courtesy SCRAWLS and the Palm Beach *Post*

Intelligence Agency. Even the Internal Revenue Service was called upon by Nixon's aides to audit or otherwise harass political opponents and others who had fallen into disfavor. A White House "enemies list" turned up which included innocent citizens who were to be hounded or prosecuted in various ways—as though the government were the persecutor rather than the protector and servant of the sovereign people. In the name of national security, Nixon's aides had authorized a burglary of the files of Dr. Daniel Ellsberg's psychiatrist, so great was the determination to convict the man who had leaked the Pentagon Papers. This was the most notorious exploit of the White House "plumbers unit," created to plug up leaks of confidential information that might be useful to foreign powers.

A select Senate committee, headed by the aging Senator Ervin, of North Carolina, conducted a prolonged and widely televised series of hearings in 1973–1974. The avowed purpose was not to convict anyone, but to secure information on which to base remedial legislation. Before long the most crying need became apparent: tough new laws to control the raising of immense sums of money from wealthy and self-seeking individuals and corporations. John Dean III, a former White House lawyer with a remarkable memory, testified glibly and at great length as to the involvement of the top echelons in the White House, including the President, in the cover-up of the Watergate break-in. If true, this was an obstruction of justice, in itself a crime, but the committee then had only the unsupported word of Dean against White House protestations of innocence.

The Great Tape Controversy

A bombshell exploded before Senator Ervin's committee in July, 1973, when a former presidential aide reported the presence of "bugging" equipment in the White House, installed under the President's authority. Nixonian conversations, in person or on the telephone, had been recorded on tape without notifying the other party or parties that electronic eavesdropping was taking place.

Nixon had emphatically denied prior knowledge of the Watergate burglary or involvement in the cover-up. Now Dean's sensational testimony could be checked against the White House tapes, and the Senate committee could better determine who was telling the truth. But for months Nixon flatly refused to produce the taped evidence, partly on the grounds that he would weaken the presidential office for his successors (and himself). He took refuge in various principles, including separation of powers and executive privilege (confidentiality). But all of them were at least constitutionally arguable, especially when used to cover up crime or obstruct justice. A common conclusion was that if Nixon were innocent, he would strengthen the presidency by promptly making available the evi-

GRAYSMITH

"Tapeworm." Republican elephant suffers from a strange disease. Robert Graysmith, San Francisco *Chronicle*, by permission.

dence that would prove his innocence. Not to do so was widely interpreted as a confession of guilt or a defiant affirmation that the President held himself above the law.

The anxieties of the White House deepened when Vice President Agnew, whom Nixon had lifted from relative obscurity in 1968, was forced to resign in October, 1973. Although evidently not involved in the Watergate-related crimes, he was accused of taking bribes or "kickbacks" from Maryland contractors while Governor and also as Vice President. The case against him proved so overwhelming that, rather than go to jail, he pleaded "no contest" to a charge of income tax evasion. His plea in these circumstances amounted to an admission of guilt. Fined $10,000 and placed on three-year probation, he fell even further when disbarred as a lawyer. With President Nixon himself in danger of being removed by the impeachment route, Congress invoked the 25th Amendment to replace Agnew with a twelve-term congressman from Michigan, Gerald ("Jerry") Ford. As a former football star at the University of Michigan, he had achieved fame in college for brawn rather than brains, but his record in public life was politically respectable and his financial affairs proved to be above suspicion at a time when unquestioned honesty was in short supply. He was hailed as "Mr. Clean."

Ten days after Agnew's resignation came the famous "Saturday

Night Massacre" (October 20, 1973). Archibald Cox, appointed as a special prosecutor by Nixon in May, had been assured of a free hand in securing relevant tapes and other documents from the White House. After encountering stubborn resistance, he finally issued a subpoena for what he required. Nixon thereupon fired Cox, and then accepted the resignations of the Attorney General and the Deputy Attorney General because they would not fire Cox. The outraged public outcry, especially as expressed in a flood of telegrams to the White House, brought such strident demands for impeachment or resignation that Nixon backed down. Although he agreed to comply with demands for tapes and documents from the new special prosecutor and the House Judiciary Committee, such materials were forthcoming only partially and after foot-dragging delays. Word gradually leaked out of the White House that some of the tapes were missing, that others had never been recorded, and that portions of key conversations had been mysteriously blotted out, perhaps deliberately "sanitized."

In a Florida speech to newsmen in 1973 Nixon declared: ". . . In all my years of public life, I have never obstructed justice. People have got to know whether or not their President is a crook. Well, I'm not a crook, I earned everything I've got."

The House Judiciary Committee now faced up more resolutely to an investigation of impeachment charges. Such activity intensified after revelations that Nixon's income tax returns in recent years had benefited from astonishingly large but unallowable deductions, some of which more than suggested fraud. To quiet the uproar, the White House announced that Nixon would pay back taxes and interest penalties of $465,000, newly assessed by the Internal Revenue Service.

The Secret-Open Bombing of Cambodia

As if Watergate were not enough, the constitutionality of Nixon's continued aerial battering of Cambodia came under increasing fire. In July of 1973 America was shocked to learn that the U.S. Air Force had already secretly conducted some 3,500 bombing raids against North Vietnamese positions in Cambodia, beginning in March, 1969, and continuing for some fourteen months prior to the open American incursion in May, 1970. Evidently the Cambodian government proved cooperative and President Nixon had privately notified a few hawkish leaders of Congress whose approval could be expected. But perhaps the most disturbing feature of these sly sky forays was that while they were going on, American officials, including the President, were avowing that Cambodian neutrality was being respected. Countless Americans began to wonder what kind of representative government they had if they were fighting a war which they knew nothing about and would have opposed if they had known of its existence.

Defiance followed secretiveness. Nixon's large-scale bombing of Communist forces in Cambodia after the Vietnam cease-fire went into effect in 1973 was in the open, and was carried on in the teeth of furious public opposition. Many Americans, especially after Vietnam, abhorred the philosophy of destroying a country in order to save it. Such bombing assaults grew more devastating in the early summer of 1973, and were designed to help the rightist Cambodian government against Cambodian Communists. The President stretched his war-making powers (he had no war-declaring powers under the Constitution) when he argued that crushing the Communists in Cambodia was one way of supporting the Vietnam cease-fire, to which the United States was a party. A clear majority in both houses of Congress favored an end to the bombing, but repeated efforts to achieve a stoppage by adding amendments to essential appropriation bills fell before the President's veto pen. There were always enough hawkish votes in the House, at least one-third plus one, to prevent Congress from overriding the Nixonian negative. But appropriations were running short, the power of the purse finally prevailed, and in June, 1973, the President was forced to accept a compromise. He would reluctantly end the bombing and other military operations in Cambodia on August 15—some six weeks later—and thereafter would seek Congressional approval of any future activity in that blasted country. Yet he regarded this enforced cessation of bombing as an act of great weakness that would undermine "the prospect for world peace."

The New Isolationism

The "doves" in Congress had long protested the expansion of war-making powers by Presidents Johnson and Nixon, especially in Indochina. Johnson had operated under authority hastily voted by Congress in the blank-check Tonkin Gulf resolution; Nixon no longer enjoyed this sanction because Congress had repealed it in June, 1971. Then, after failing eight times to override Nixon's veto, Congress finally mustered enough votes to pass its own restriction on the war-making powers in November, 1973. Under the new law the President was required to report to Congress within 48 hours after committing troops to a foreign conflict or "substantially" enlarging American combat units in a foreign country. Such a limited authorization would have to end within sixty days unless Congress extended it for thirty more days. Yet the President could still commit troops, and after sixty days the involvement could be so deep that a graceful withdrawal would be extremely difficult, if not impossible.

Compelling Nixon to end the bombing of Cambodia in August, 1973, was but one manifestation of what came to be called the New Isolationism. It was largely a child of the ugly war in Vietnam and the subsequent "peace" that demanded open-ended monetary and other material support. The detested draft ended in January, 1973, although retained on a stand-by basis. Future members of the armed forces were to be well-paid volunteers—a change that greatly eased tensions among the youth, especially in the colleges. Insistent demands arose in Congress for reducing American armed forces abroad, especially since some 300,000 remained in Europe more than a quarter of a century after Hitler's downfall. The argument often heard was that the Western European countries, with more population than Russia, ought by now to be willing and able to provide for their own defense against the forces of Communism. But President Nixon, fearful of a weakened hand in the high-stakes game of power politics, headed off all serious attempts at troop reduction. The patchwork North Atlantic Treaty Organization continued, with many of the fifteen members unreliably dragging their feet.

Dr. Kissinger, Nixon's adviser on national security affairs, proclaimed in April, 1973, "The Year of Europe," with a stronger NATO alliance occupying center stage. Such hopes were dashed, yet 1973 turned out to be "The Year of Kissinger," for the German-born emigré officially became Secretary of State in September, 1973 —a post that he had already held in all but name. The next month he was awarded one-half of the $122,000 Nobel Peace Prize for his role in negotiating the Paris accords which had brought a "cease-fire" to Vietnam—a cease-fire that had already claimed some 50,000 lives. The other half went to the chief North Vietnam negotiator at Paris, Le Duc Tho. He refused his share for the reason that "peace" had never come to Vietnam. Dr. Kissinger donated his half to provide educational scholarships for the children of American servicemen who had lost their lives in the war.

The Yom Kippur War

The long-rumbling Middle East erupted anew in October, 1973, when the rearmed Syrians and Egyptians unleashed crushing surprise attacks on Israeli forces. They were obviously seeking to regain the extensive territory lost in the so-called Six Day War of 1967, which had never officially ended, although brought to a halt by an uneasy cease-fire agreed upon in 1970. The Israelis, though attackers in the earlier conflict, were caught off guard while celebrating their most sacred holiday, Yom Kippur. Battles flamed furiously on both fronts as the Egyptians stormed across the Suez Canal and attacked Israeli fall-back positions.

Pinched between Syria on the north and Egypt on the south and west, Israel was caught in a desperate bind. Few observers believed that her vengeful Arab enemies, if overwhelmingly victorious, would stop at regaining only lost land. Dr. Kissinger hastily flew to Moscow in a last-ditch effort to restrain the Soviets, who had provided the attackers with the great bulk of their tanks, aircraft, and other sophisticated weapons. Nixon hastily placed America's armed forces on a precautionary alert when he learned, whether correctly or not, that the Russians were poised to fly combat troops into the Suez area. The deterrent effect of the President's bomb-rattling is unknown, but in any event the Russians did not intervene and America's NATO allies drew back in alarm. The Israelis suffered such heavy losses of arms in the initial surprise onslaught that Nixon ordered a gigantic airlift of nearly $2 billion in war materials, which undoubtedly saved the day. Included was a gift of 1,000 tanks.

At a crucial phase of the fighting along the Suez Canal, the Israelis executed a brilliant thrust across the waterway to the rear of the enemy, thereby threatening destruction of the Egyptian armies and the capture of Cairo. Egypt, which had regained much self-respect by its temporary successes, was now in a position to accept terms "with honor." Thanks largely to the tireless efforts of Secretary Kissinger, a cease-fire along the Suez was arranged, to be policed by a small force of truce observers from certain smaller countries of the United Nations. The combatants were gradually disentangled, and the Israelis were induced to accept a new defense line somewhat farther back from the canal. But the Syrians, though hard pressed, refused to stop fighting on their front. Hope continued that Washington could apply enough pressure on Israel to induce her, dependent as she was on American financial and material support, to consent to some kind of compromise arrangement that would still leave her with defensible borders.

The Energy Crisis

America's policy of backing Israel against her oil-rich neighbors exacted a heavy penalty. Late in October, 1973, the Arab countries suddenly clamped an embargo on oil for the United States and other Israel-supporting countries. The oil-thirsty American people, numbering about six percent of the world's population but consuming some thirty percent of its energy, derived only about six percent of their petroleum supply from Arab lands, but this deficiency was enough to create a fuel crisis. The United States, though abundantly forewarned by experts, overnight discovered that the age of cheap and abundant oil had ended. Nixon, though opposing rationing, enthroned an energy czar, William E. Simon, and the American people suffered through a long winter of lowered thermostats and speedometers. Lines of automobiles at service stations lengthened as tempers shortened and an incipient business recession deepened.

The "energy crisis" suddenly energized a number of long-deferred

"Hat in Hand." Editorial cartoon by Lou Grant of the Oakland *Tribune*. Copyright, Los Angeles *Times* Syndicate. Reprinted with permission.

projects. The costly pipeline from northern to southern Alaska received Congressional approval in 1974, over the protests of conservationists and environmentalists, who feared oil spills and the destruction of flora and fauna, including caribou. President Nixon urged a crash program to make America self-sufficient in energy by the target date 1980. Proposals multiplied for utilizing energy from the sun, wind, thermal heat, shale, and untapped coal deposits, of which the United States had more than half of the world's known reserves—or enough to last for an estimated several hundred years. Yet heavy coal consumption would increase air pollution. The result was that agitation increased for relaxing standards for clean air and water, as well as for pushing ahead with more nuclear power stations, despite their ever-present threat of catastrophic radioactivity. A clamor likewise developed for nationalizing or at least heavily taxing the profiteering oil companies, while leaving them with enough surplus to encourage the development of additional oil reserves. The energy crisis further emphasized the need for improving the mass transportation of people, especially in the urban areas. Congress had belatedly made a major departure in this direction in 1973 by voting to permit some funds earmarked for highways to be used for urban transportation systems.

The Arab "blackmail" embargo, partially leaky, was lifted in March, 1974, after five months of anxiety, and after the Egypt-Israeli cease-fire had taken effect. Countless Americans, especially those in big gas-gulping cars, reverted thoughtlessly to their speeding and other wasteful practices. The Middle Eastern sheiks had about quadrupled their price of crude oil, and their inevitable accumulation of tens of billions of dollars jeopardized the American balance of trade and payments. Additionally, the Arab nations were amassing enormous sums which could flood and dislocate the international investment market.

The United States continued by mid-1974 to be cursed simultaneously with a heavily unbalanced budget, a high national debt, high interest rates for borrowers, high unemployment, high inflation, and high prices, especially in food. The new price controls, adopted in successive phases since 1971, had not proved effective, and in April, 1974, were almost entirely abandoned in favor of a free-market economy. The hope was that the ancient law of supply and demand would create equilibrium. One source of consolation was that while America suffered from inflation, most of the countries of the Western world complained of the same fever, in many cases in a more advanced stage.

Impeachment Politics

The continuing impeachment inquiry reached a new climax on

April 29, 1974, when Nixon belatedly responded to the demand of the House Judiciary Committee for 42 tapes by making a dramatic appearance on television. Exuding confidence, and with a huge pile of manuscript folders at his elbow, he staged a virtuoso performance. He announced that he was not submitting the requested Watergate tapes to the House, but only typed transcripts of those portions that he, though under investigation, deemed relevant to the impeachment proceedings. At the same time he was in effect appealing over the head of Congress to the sovereign people by making the White House conversations public, thus completely destroying their confidentiality. He further declared that "everything that is relevant" was included, including some material not subpoenaed, and that this mass of documentary evidence would further prove his innocence. He also stated that the "rough" language thus submitted would embarrass him, but that he was including it because he had "nothing to hide."

"The truth, the hole truth . . ." Nixon presents tape transcripts to Congress and the public. Reprinted by permission of Newspaper Enterprise Association.

Publication of the bulky transcripts in one printed volume stirred up a storm of criticism. Readers, including Congressmen, quickly perceived that Nixon had not provided the tapes or even the contents of all the 42 requested. He had, in fact, cut out substantial portions of those presented. Moreover, the typists had transcribed inaccurately or incompletely the contents of the tapes; within parentheses there appeared scores of "unintelligibles," especially in Nixon's remarks. Much of the "rough" language had been replaced with the phrases "expletive deleted" or "characterization deleted." In one uncensored passage Nixon described President Truman as an "old bastard" whom many had admired for "standing by people . . . who were guilty as hell." Even more shocking to many readers was the low tone of the White House conversations: cynical, amoral, vindictive, self-serving, and conspiratorial. Some of the President's former defenders were reminded of the secret plottings of gangsters.

A releasing of the tapes, many of them diffuse and ambiguous, deepened grave suspicions about the President's role in the Watergate cover-up and related crimes. His supporters in Congress, mostly Republicans, insisted that the documents proved no indictable or impeachable offense. But many of his critics, after reading the same evidence, thought otherwise. Nixon temporarily rode out the storm by what he called "stonewalling," that is, by flatly refusing to turn over any more tapes to the investigators. The issue of withholding "confidential" evidence was finally brought directly to the Supreme Court, which indicated that it could render a decision in July, 1974.

As the summer of 1974 approached, economic problems continued to loom large, especially double-digit inflation, which was gnawing away at an annual rate of about 10 or 11 percent. The President, whose popular approval had sunk to about 24 percent, was so burdened by the investigators that his leadership was plainly suffering. Resorting to age-old strategy, he diverted some of the attention from his domestic shortcomings by focusing on his accomplishments in foreign policy.

Nixon's most spectacular triumph for peace really belonged to Secretary of State Henry Kissinger, who finally arranged for a shaky cease-fire on the Syrian-Israeli front, on May 29, 1974. The breakthrough came after intense negotiations, during which the Secretary shuttled back and forth from Damascus to Jerusalem for 32 days. Although the Kissinger achievement was dazzling diplomacy, it did not settle the basic problems bedeviling Israel and her unhappy Arab neighbors.

The Unmaking of a President

Nixon diverted some attention from the impeachment probe by embarking on two spectacular tours, the first to the Middle East in mid-June, 1974, and the second to the Soviet Union later that month. He received an uproarious welcome in Egypt, whose impoverished people hoped for billions of Uncle Sam's dollars. The reception in Moscow proved disappointing. Some agreements of secondary importance were reached, but the hoped-for breakthrough on the limitation of nuclear arms failed.

The President returned from his modest foreign triumphs to suffer a series of disastrous setbacks. On July 24, 1974, the Supreme Court unanimously ruled that he had no right, under executive privilege, to withhold from the special prosecutor those portions of the 64 tapes that involved relevant criminal activity. Nixon reluctantly agreed to comply with this decision, although his office later reported that a number of the subpoenaed recordings had never been made or were missing.

The House Judiciary Committee pressed ahead with its investigation, which culminated in televised debates on the proposed articles of impeachment. The key vote came late in July 1974, when the committee adopted the first article, which charged obstruction of "the administration of justice," including Watergate-related crimes. The count was 27 to 11, with all of the Democrats and nearly half of the Republican members voting for impeachment. Two other articles were later approved by the committee accusing Nixon of having abused the powers of his office and of having shown contempt of Congress by ignoring lawful subpoenas for relevant tapes and other evidence. Insiders were certain that at least the first of the articles of impeachment would pass the Democratic House by wide margins. The President would then have to subject himself and the nation to a long and disruptive trial in the Senate, all the while hoping that a two-thirds vote for conviction could not be mustered.

Probably to soften the impact of inevitable disclosure, Nixon took a step, on August 5, 1974, that had a devastating effect on what remained of his credibility. He made public three subpoenaed tapes of conversations with his chief aide on June 23, 1972. One of them had him giving orders, six days after the Watergate break-in, to use the Central Intelligence Agency to hold back an investigation by the Federal Bureau of Investigation. Last-ditch defenders of Nixon had hitherto claimed that there was no direct evidence of a crime—no "smoking pistol." Now Nixon's own tape-recorded words convicted him of having been an active party to the attempted coverup, in itself the crime of obstructing justice. More than that, he had solemnly told the American people that he had known nothing of the Watergate coverup until about nine months later.

The public backlash proved to be overwhelming. Republican leaders in Congress frankly informed Nixon that his impeachment by the full House and his removal by the Senate were foregone conclusions. They made it clear that he would best serve his nation, his party, and himself by resigning with honor, or a semblance of it. If convicted by the Senate he would lose all his normal retirement benefits; if he resigned he would retain them—more than $150,000 a year.

Left with no better choice, Nixon choked back his tears and announced his resignation in a dramatic television appearance on August 8, 1974. In this Farewell Address he admitted having made some "judgments" that "were wrong" but insisted that he had always acted "in what I believed at the time to be the best interests of the nation." Ignoring his imminent conviction by the Senate, he declared that he was leaving because he had lost his "political base in Congress," which he needed to carry out his decisions and duties as the leader of the republic. To the bitter end he avowed that he was thinking primarily of the welfare of his country, not of himself.

Richard Milhous Nixon, the first President ever to resign, was succeeded on August 9, 1974, by Gerald Rudolph Ford, the first President or Vice-President ever to be elevated to either of these high offices by a vote of Congress. The nation had survived a wrenching constitutional crisis which proved that the impeachment machinery created by the Founding Fathers could work when public opinion overwhelmingly demanded that it be made to work. The principles were strengthened that no man was above the law, and that the President must be held to strict accountability for his acts. Democracy was still alive when the sovereign people could force out of office the powerful head of the mightiest nation without firing a single shot. The United States of America, on the eve of its 200th birthday as a republic, had given an impressive demonstration of self-discipline and self-government to the rest of the world.

In his resignation speech Nixon referred to his inaugural pledge in 1969 to work for peace "among all nations. . . . I have done my very best in the days since to be true to that pledge. . . . This . . . is what I hope will be my legacy to you . . . as I leave the presidency."

SELECT READINGS

Most of what has been written thus far about the Nixon years is biased contemporary journalism. On the two elections, the best books are THEODORE H. WHITE's *The Making of the President, 1968* (1969) and *The Making of the President, 1972* (1973).* See also ARTHUR M. SCHLESINGER, JR., *The Imperial Presidency* (1973). Among the better received books on Nixon are GARRY WILLS, *Nixon Agonistes: The Crisis of the Self-Made Man* (1970);* JOHN OSBORNE, *The Nixon Watch* (1970);* and RALPH DE TOLEDANO, *One Man Alone: Richard Nixon* (1969). See also DAVID LANDAU, *Kissinger: The Uses of Power* (1972). High-quality journalism may be found in HENRY BRANDON, *The Retreat of American Power* (1973) and ROWLAND EVANS, JR. and ROBERT D. NOVAK, *Nixon in the White House: The Frustration of Power* (1971).* Concerned with the American "empire" are MERLO J. PUSEY, *The U.S.A. Astride the Globe* (1971) and RONALD STEEL, *Imperialists and other Heroes: A Chronicle of the American Empire* (1971).*

* Available in paperback.

51

Society in Flux

We find ourselves rich in goods, but ragged in spirit;
reaching with magnificent precision for the moon, but falling into
raucous discord on earth . . . . The American dream does not
come to those who fall asleep.

President Nixon, Inaugural Address, 1969

The Menace of a Proliferating Population

Glancing back over the three decades since the end of World War II, an observer notes significant, even breathtaking, social, economic, and cultural changes.

Ominously, the nation's facilities were being increasingly burdened by America's contribution to the global "population explosion"—potentially about as dangerous as a nuclear explosion. The world has limited resources but unlimited procreative power. At the current rate of reproduction the nearly four billion of 1970 would become about six billion by the year 2000 and 25 billion by 2070. Mass starvation loomed on the horizon.

In 1950 the United States could count some 150,000,000 inhabitants; in 1970 over 203,000,000. The mixture had become more uniform, owing to the bubbling of the Melting Pot and the continued slowdown of the immigration stream. Among those who were foreign born, or who had at least one foreign-born parent, the largest alien groups were Italian-Americans, German-Americans, Canadian-Americans (many French-Canadian), and Polish-Americans, in that descending order. People with Spanish surnames, numbering over nine million, were becoming increasingly conspicuous and vocal, notably the Puerto Ricans in New York, the Cuban refugees in Florida, and especially the six million or so Mexican-Americans (Chicanos) in the states of the Southwest.

Population pressures had given strong impetus to planned parenthood. Oral contraceptives, notably "the pill," came into wide use during the 1960's, and many state abortion laws were liberalized, with support from the Supreme Court. Despite official frowns from the Pope, countless Catholics were weakening in their opposition to birth control. Black militants, aware that more black bodies meant more Black Power, bitterly rejected "whitey's genocidal" efforts to deny them "the right to breed." In December 1972, the Census Bureau made the significant announcement that at the current rate of reproduction—about two per couple—the nation had achieved Zero Population Growth (ZPG) and, if continued, the increase would level off in due time.

Striking indeed were the shifts of population during these postwar decades. Especially noteworthy was the fantastic growth of states in the "sun belt," notably Florida, Texas, the Southwest, and the Pacific Coast. Incredible California beat out New York as the most populous state in the 1960's, with approximately 20,000,000.

The sick cities, sprawling outward, were losing population to the suburbs ("slurbs") or the "bedroom cities" of commuters. There the harried citizen, gasping from urban smog and jangled by traffic snarls, was finding more elbow room, especially at the convenient shopping centers. The suburban slopover tended to be white and upper middle class, while large black sections of the ghettoized cities were being abandoned to become more ghettoized. This "white flight" left the inner cities more "black, brown, and broke."

Congress made something of a start toward the solution of urban problems in the late 1960's. It provided substantial financial support for improved transportation, publicly financed housing (urban renewal), and the creation of entirely new towns as "model cities." But billions rather than millions of dollars were needed at a time when Washington was spending vast sums trying to get a man on the moon. The only housing surplus was in slums, since federal projects often proved to be costly, run-down disappointments.

Masses of people required mass transit, which featured earth-gobbling freeways, car-clogged cities, infuriating parking problems, and bumper-to-bumper crops of automobiles. By 1970 there were about 100 million motor vehicles in the United States, almost one for every two people.

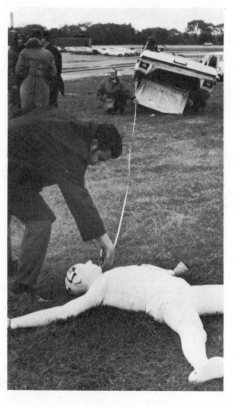

Seat-belt Experiments With Crashed Dummy. Courtesy Ford Motor Co.

Traffic deaths were skyrocketing. By the late 1960's the grim toll, often the result of drunk driving, had mounted to some 55,000 lives a year. This figure did not take into account the hundreds of thousands of injuries, the millions of lost man-hours, and the billions of dollars in damages. Yet this senseless slaughter, totaling more deaths a year than American battle losses in either the entire Korean or Vietnam conflicts, was more or less taken for granted. An automobile safety campaign, launched in the mid-1960's by crusading Ralph Nader, resulted in some safeguarding legislation by Congress and in the subsequent recall of many cars by manufacturers because of possible defects. But the "crashworthy" motor vehicle was still on the drawing boards.

"The Thinker." Osrin in the Cleveland *Plain Dealer*

By the late 1960's travel by airplane, chiefly on rocket-like jets, had reached fantastic proportions. All of the major airports were badly congested. When serious accidents occurred, there were few if any survivors, and jumbo aircraft, with a payload of over 300 passengers, were being produced. Yet, on a per-mile basis, travel by commercial aircraft was about ten times safer than travel by automobile. Passenger trains on many of the railroads were suffering so severely from airline competition that a number of famous runs were being discontinued in favor of profitable freight. In 1971 a quasi-governmental organization called Amtrak was set up to carry intercity passenger traffic, but it continued to pile up heavy financial losses while rendering less than satisfactory service.

Urban blight and suburban sprawl inevitably worsened problems of smog (aerial sewage), water pollution (chlorinated and processed sewage), sound pollution (acoustic garbage), sight pollution ("uglification"), soil pollution (pesticides), and beach pollution (oil slicks). Once-blue rivers (for example, the Potomac) and lakes (for example, Erie) were turning into smelly sewers and cesspools. Occasionally streams became so oily as to pose fire hazards. America the Beautiful was gradually becoming America the Blighted.

Youth in Revolt

The post-1945 baby boom, partly touched off by returning veterans, resulted in a tidal wave of students who overwhelmed the schools in the 1950's and 1960's. Overcrowding contributed to the alarming number of incorrigible "punks" and dropouts. Others were simply "passed through," in many cases graduating from high school as functional illiterates. Totally without saleable skills, these juveniles flooded the labor market, and tens of thousands of them were headed for a life of drug addiction, degeneracy, and dependency.

Rebellious youth was a worldwide phenomenon, fully evident in America even before the 1960's. A "generation gap" had developed, and the day had passed when young folks were to be "seen and not heard." Growing numbers of teen-agers were marrying, producing offspring, and expecting the old folks to provide support or education. The older generation had clearly made a mess of the world, especially in the perpetuation of war and social injustice, and many of the younger generation were rejecting conventional values. "Trust no one over thirty" was a common warning.

Youthful rebellion in the late 1960's manifested itself in varied outbursts. Conspicuous were demonstrations in colleges and high schools, designed to achieve a greater "say" in governing social conduct, morals, curricula, books, and teachers. Radicals of the New Left were accused of not wanting a place at the table but seeking to overturn it. The "hippie" movement of the late 1960's provided the spectacle of long-haired, unwashed youths of both sexes rejecting the materialistic, hypocritical values of society and seeking peace and brotherly love through a simple, more relaxed existence. But in the eyes of many of the contemptuous elders they seemed to be living for marijuana, alcohol, hallucinatory drugs, and sex.

Juvenile delinquency had increased alarmingly in the 1960's and early 1970's, partly as a result of stinking slums, maladjusted minorities, boredom, too much leisure, parental permissiveness, and broken homes. With nearly half of all marriages ending in the courts, couples were evidently uniting "until death or divorce do us part." Floods of pornography were burdening the mails and reaching the newsstands. Teen-age gangs were running wild in the streets of some of the larger cities, knifing rivals and beating up unoffending bystanders "just for kicks." "Adults don't understand us" was the standard complaint of youthful criminals, including murderers. Some critics blamed juvenile crime on the square-eyed monster known as television, with its emphasis on mayhem, manslaughter, and murder. Certainly the movies were not setting much of an example with their growing emphasis on sensation, sadism, and sex.

"Recruiting Office." Crawford, NEA. Reproduced by permission of Newspaper Enterprise Association

Upsurging Crime

Parents were also short of perfection. Alcoholism, drug addiction, and violence were sharply on the increase. In 1968, about one American in 600 was reported as robbed, raped, or murdered, and by 1974 one estimate was that two out of 100 babies would ultimately die at the hands of killers. Adult criminals fattened on illicit gambling, prostitution, narcotics, and racketeering. Syndicated crime was on the upswing, with gangsters routinely eliminating rivals in Chicago and Boston in a monotonous series of unsolved murders. The annual "take" of the underground octopus known as the Mafia was reputed to be many billions of dollars, some of which were being invested in legitimate businesses. America's total crime bill by 1974 was estimated to be about $50 billion annually. Beginning conspicuously in the late 1960's, the international picture was darkened by a wave of terrorist bombings and shootings, the "skyjacking" of airplanes (many from the United States to Cuba), and the kidnapping of diplomats and others for ransom.

An ominous omen was the growing contempt of American citizens for their police. This was notably true of youths, white and black, many of whom habitually "ganged up" on officers who were making arrests. Unfortunately, many of the police had proved to be brutal, sadistic, and notoriously corrupt.

Especially disquieting was the refusal of citizens to play the Good Samaritan and render aid to innocent victims of violence. "We don't want to get involved" was a common excuse, and one justified by unhappy experiences in the courts. A shocking case in 1964 involved a young woman, Kitty Genovese, in a respectable neighborhood of New York City during an early morning hour. Her struggling and outcries while being stabbed to death during a period of half an hour were seen or heard by thirty-eight persons, none of whom interceded or even telephoned the police. On the other hand, volunteer vigilantes in some communities were beginning to patrol the streets, to the horror of professional lawmen. The naked truth was that at night a citizen could not safely walk the streets and parks of many of the larger cities. A pedestrian was much safer in Moscow after dark than in New York or Washington, even in sight of the Capitol dome. Critics sneered that America was trying to police the world but could not even police its own streets.

By 1970 about one-fourth of the states had abolished the death penalty. Opponents of capital punishment argued that it was brutal, demeaning, nondeterring (although it did deter the executed criminal), and racially discriminatory. A disproportionate number of those executed were poor and friendless blacks. Wealthy whites with influential connections and high-priced lawyers seldom went to the electric chair or the gallows. Prisons themselves were failing to reform; in 1971 seething discontent erupted at Attica, New York, with forty-three persons dead, thirty-four of them prisoners.

Life of the Spirit

A curious mix of materialism and idealism marked the years since 1945. Yet some people were turning to the solace of religion because of fear of nuclear annihilation, concern over the inhumanity of war, and guilt feelings regarding social injustices and other tensions.

Church membership in the 1960's and early 1970's embraced about 63 percent of the population—an increase over preceding decades. Protestants continued to outnumber Catholics in the ratio of about

Billy Graham, who declared in 1955, "I just want to lobby for God," used as his favorite benediction, "May the Lord bless you real good." In 1969 he said in a radio address, "There is so much hell in the country because there is not more hell in the pulpit."

three to two. The leading evangelist of the Western world was "Billy" (William Franklin) Graham, who attracted the greatest religious crowds of modern times, at home and abroad. He addressed in person an estimated 40 million people. His enormous audiences filled amphitheaters like Yankee Stadium in New York in 1957 and Madison Square Garden in 1969, and thousands of "sinners" made public "decisions for Christ." Pope Paul VI, during an extraordinary transatlantic tour in 1965, celebrated mass in Yankee Stadium.

Church membership was perhaps never so high as in the 1960's and early 1970's, but church prestige apparently was never so low. In a secular age, religion was becoming more secular. A small percentage of church members were actually atheists, and a "God is dead" movement attracted considerable notoriety in the mid-1960's. Cynics remarked that God was not dead but the church was, and that if God was dead the devil was not.

Currents of liberalism were eddying through the religious world in the 1960's. This was especially true of the Roman Catholic Church, which felt increasing pressures for birth control and for a married priesthood. An encouraging impetus was being given to the world-wide ecumenical movement—that is, bringing closer together the fragmented Christian faiths.

Economic Crosscurrents

The monstrous annual budget of the federal government for fiscal 1974–1975 had skyrocketed to $304.4 billion, with local and state taxes also rising painfully. Uncle Sam was still deeply in debt, for the red-inked figure showed about half a trillion dollars. Balanced budgets were by far the exception rather than the rule during the decades after 1945, while multibillion dollar annual deficits mounted.

Nearly one-half of the enormous federal pie was going to the defense establishment. The military-industrial complex, with sleek lobbyists buttonholing Congressmen, had become frighteningly powerful. Drastic cuts in expenditures for defense were extremely difficult to achieve. Ironically, the more frantic the race in nation-busting weapons became, the less secure Americans felt.

Simultaneously, inflation forced ever upward the cost of living, with mounting hardships to senior citizens, pensioners, and others on fixed incomes. Like an incurable rash, some inflation seemingly was the price that had to be paid for this continuing and unprecedented decade of prosperity. But the mild inflation had become galloping inflation by 1974.

The personal income of all Americans in 1972 had zoomed to nearly one trillion dollars, a prodigious sum even in inflated currency. Still higher peaks were in prospect. Maldistribution of wealth, long a complaint of the Communists, continued to be glaring, especially in the contrast between the gaudy rich and the grubby poor. Yet in 1974 the median income for all American families had risen to above $10,000 for the first time.

Crass materialism inevitably marred a materialistic civilization. An increased income evidently resulted in increasing wants rather than in supplying satisfactions; status seeking was leading to "conspicuous consumption." With increased leisure, vast sums were being poured into swimming pools, three-car garages, boats, mink coats, travel, and summer homes. A lavish distribution of credit cards encouraged the wholesale expenditure of money that people did not possess for luxuries they did not need. "Charge it—and feel like a king" (temporarily) was a slogan of these decades. Several million Americans were working after hours at more than one job—"moonlighting"—in a frantic struggle to keep their heads above water or to keep up with the Joneses.

Farmers continued to raise a lush crop of seemingly insoluble problems. For political as well as economic reasons, Congress was maintaining price supports for cotton, wheat, and other products to the tune of about four billion dollars a year in 1969. Senator Eastland of Mississippi, for example, was paid $116,978 in 1968 not to raise cotton. Yet the enormous wheat surpluses of the 1950's and 1960's were substantially reduced, owing in part to heavy shipments to India, Russia, and other famine-stricken countries. By the early 1970's the United States faced food shortages, and the prices at markets had risen alarmingly.

The rich farmers were getting richer and the poor poorer, or were being squeezed off their land into the already overglutted labor market. In the fifty years from 1920 to 1970, the farm population had been more than cut in half, although the total population had grown by more than 90 million persons. Back in 1790, nine out of ten people were involved in farming; in 1970, more than nine out of ten were involved in other occupations.

"He Don't Plant 'Taters, He Don't Plant Cotton, He Just Digs Subsidies." Editorial Cartoon by Lou Grant (of the Oakland *Tribune*), copyright Los Angeles Times Syndicate. Reprinted with permission.

Labor Problems

Chronic unemployment, paralyzing about four percent of the nation's labor force, remained a nagging headache. Most alarming was the galloping computerizing and mechanizing of industry (automation), with a consequent elimination of jobs at the fearsome rate of many thousands a week. The government at all levels was making some attempt to retrain displaced workers, but such efforts fell far short of needs. By 1974 unemployment had risen above the five percent mark.

Organized labor, grown rich and somewhat complacent, had lost much of its early crusading zeal by the 1960's. Unions that clung to "featherbedding" (superfluous jobs) fought automation tooth and nail. Where they had to yield, they often secured monetary compensation for the uprooted workers. Even before 1970 some labor leaders were seriously advocating a 32-hour week, with no reduction in total pay, plus fringe benefits like profit-sharing and paid vacations. A vast number of wage earners were still unorganized, but in 1974 Congress extended the federal minimum wage law to some seven million additional workers, with raises to come in stages to offset inflation.

Labor racketeering was being partially curbed by the controversial Landrum-Griffin Act of 1959. Tough-fisted James R. Hoffa, president of the potent Teamsters' Union, was twice convicted in 1964 of felonies. He was finally sent to prison to serve an eight-year sentence, later commuted by President Nixon on the eve of the election of 1972.

A disturbing phase of the labor movement was the outbreak in the 1960's of a number of strikes by public service employees: policemen, firemen, nurses, teachers, and garbage collectors ("sanitary engineers"). All of these had previously been regarded as so essential to public safety, health, and welfare as to be barred from striking, in some cases by law. Thus handcuffed, many strikers avoided penalties by slowdowns or "calling in sick." Especially disruptive were the teacher strikes in New York City which in 1967 and 1968 tied up the vast public school system for five weeks. Long-standing grievances related to low salaries and intolerable conditions of employment, ranging from overloaded classes and dilapidated buildings to rowdyism and vandalism growing out of "teen-age tyranny." Teachers had long been regarded as members of an honored profession, not as unionized laborers, and this epidemic of strikes, despite strong justification, seriously damaged their public image. Times had indeed changed when the instructors, not the pupils, seemed to be "playing hookey."

In 1969, Governor Nelson Rockefeller of New York told the Central Labor Council, "We used to think strikes were a weapon of last resort, but some of your powerful unions here seem to be making them a weapon of first resort."

Muses for the Masses

Artistic expression in America, despite much vulgar materialism, never had greater encouragement than in the 1960's and early 1970's. Courses in art appreciation at all levels were attracting thousands of eager learners, and inexpensive painting kits were sending countless amateurs out to the landscapes. The great galleries were being thronged, and the art market reported record auction prices, including several million-dollar paintings. Manufacturers of cheap reproductions of the classical painters were doing a land-office business. Some potential masters, rather than starve in a garret, were being lured away by lucrative "billboard art."

Many of the younger painters, deemphasizing subject matter, were moving away from realism to pure abstraction, with splashes of color and angular designs, all presumably expressive of feeling. Some artists were surrealists, who painted realistic or recognizable objects in unrealistic or exaggerated ways. (See panel after p. 814, herein.) Avant-garde art included experimentation with new media, such as plastics and lights.

Nor was American architecture a pallid prisoner of the past. Stimulated by a vast amount of new construction, it was revealing extraordinary imagination, though often at the cost of convenience. Modern design, which manifested itself in structures ranging from churches to industrial buildings, tended to feature glass and plastic materials and pierced decorative screens. The death of Frank Lloyd Wright in 1959 removed one of the boldest and most controversial of the innovators. "He was more frank than right," remarked one quipster.

The "legitimate" theaters still commanded a large following, although Broadway shows had become a big business—and an infinitely risky one at that. Nudity was gaining acceptance. It was a logical culmination of thigh-high mini-skirts, peek-a-boo dresses, bikinis, topless waitresses, and underground "stag movies," all to be found in the 1960's. Complete nudity came to the "legit" New York stage in 1969 when actors, both male and female, began to appear together totally without clothing.

Not to be outstripped, "adult movies" were stressing nudity and sex, often with nude-lewd foreign imports that were hard-core pornography or "porn." Once the foe of television, the moving picture industry worked hand in glove with its competitor, on the ancient principle "if you can't lick 'em, join 'em."

The Sound of Music

By 1968 sixteen of seventeen homes could boast television sets, more than one-sixth of them in color, reaching ninety-six percent of the population. The fare ran heavily to "old" movies (re-runs of re-runs), Western "horse operas," cheap spy thrillers, and light situation comedy, generously interspersed with commercials. There were enough documentaries, round tables, symphonies, and other intellectually and culturally stimulating programs to whet the appetite for more. Educational television, struggling along on marginal channels in a vast wasteland of rubbish, received a welcome financial boost from Congress in 1968.

About 260,000,000 radios existed by 1967, especially the easily portable transistors, or more than one for every inhabitant. They were featuring "instant news," sports events, and audience-participation "call-in" programs, interspersed with often moronic and overlong singing commercials. Portable radios were piercing the quiet of parks, beaches, and other hitherto secluded places.

Speaking in 1961, Newton Minow urged his hearers to sit at length before a television screen. "I can assure you," he said, "that you will observe a vast wasteland. You will see a procession of game shows, violence, audience participation shows, formula comedies about totally unbelievable families, blood and thunder, mayhem, violence, sadism, murder, Western badmen, Western goodmen, private eyes, gangsters. more violence, and cartoons. And, endlessly, commercials—many screaming, cajoling and offending."

Louis Armstrong, Premier Trumpeter of the Blues. United Press International photo.

Pearl Buck. Photo by Clara E. Sipprell

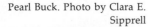

Once fearful of radio, the music industry in the late 1960's and early 1970's was selling about one billion dollars worth of records a year for the more than fifty million recording instruments. Improved techniques of reproduction—such as long-playing records, magnetic tapes, high fidelity sets (hi-fi), and stereophonic reproduction—were adding to the immense popularity of "canned music."

Rock-'n'-roll, derived in part from folk music and the Negro-devised blues, was introduced in the 1950's and came to dominate the musical scene in the 1960's. Immensely popular with gyrating youth, despite the hazard to eardrums, this art form found its most profitable expression in the four Beatles of England ("Beatlemania"). Their recordings, which in part incorporated serious music from the past, had sold over 210,000,000 copies by 1969, barely nosing out Bing Crosby for the premier spot.

Another version of the blues that attained wide acceptance in the 1960's was the adaptation known as "soul music." At a different level, the introduction of computer-programmed and computer-generated music was a significant feature of the mechanized age.

The vitality and virtuosity of local musical organizations in America continued to be most impressive, whether operatic, orchestral, or choral. In 1965 the Ford Foundation granted $85 million to some fifty symphony orchestras. The next year the famed Metropolitan Opera House in New York moved to its palatial new home in the same city. By 1967–1968 the nation could boast 297 opera companies and 325 colleges with productive opera departments.

The World of the Printed Word

American writing had more to offer than critics of Yankee materialism would concede. Beginning with the idol-smashing novelist Sinclair Lewis in 1930, six American citizens won Nobel prizes in literature. The others were the playwright Eugene O'Neill (1936), who attained fame with his gloom-shrouded tragedies; Pearl Buck (1938), whose upbringing as the daughter of missionaries in China provided themes for important novels; William Faulkner (1949), whose tales laid bare the degeneracy of the poor-white life in the South; Ernest Hemingway (1954), who revealed a mastery of realism in a succession of noteworthy books of fiction, including *For Whom the Bell Tolls* (1940), a tale of the Spanish Civil War; and John Steinbeck (1962), most famous for his depression-spawned *The Grapes of Wrath* and other stories depicting life among poor agricultural workers in California.

Lewis died in 1951, O'Neill in 1953, and Faulkner in 1962. Hemingway ended his troubled life with a shotgun blast in 1961, although some of his writings continued to appear subsequently. Steinbeck died in 1968, Mrs. Buck in 1973. But other novelists were coming along, notably Saul Bellow and Norman Mailer, both of whom were distinguished for brutal realism. In 1966 Truman Capote published *In Cold Blood,* a "non-fiction novel" which recreated in lurid detail the actual experiences of two murderers and their victims.

Robert Frost, the New England poet born in San Francisco, died in 1963 after publishing a dozen or so volumes of poetry and winning the Pulitzer Prize four times. But somewhat younger poets were being heard from, notably Robert Lowell, Karl Shapiro, and Allen Ginsberg, who had worked his way up from dishwasher and welder.

Nor were black writers to be ignored, for the momentum of the "Harlem Renaissance" during the 1920's and 1930's carried over into the 1960's. Most of the black spokesmen cried out against the victimization of their people by white society. Probably the most bitter of the group was Newark-born LeRoi Jones (Amiri Baraka), internationally honored as a poet and a playwright. Novelist Richard Wright, born on a Mississippi plantation and self-educated, is perhaps best known for *Native Son* (1940), which lays bare the Chicago ghettoes. James Baldwin, novelist and essayist, won particular distinction for his non-fiction, notably *The Fire Next Time* (1963), which portrays the agony of his native Harlem. Ralph Ellison, an Oklahoman, created a sensation with his novel *Invisible Man* (1952), which describes in lurid detail his young black hero's search for identity in various places, including New York City. The book was voted by a panel of 200 critics in 1965 as the most memorable and enduring work of fiction of the preceding two decades.

Author James Baldwin.
James Baldwin wrote in 1955,
"The wonder is not that so many
Negro boys and girls are ruined
but that so many survive."
Photo by Mottke Weissman

The Roar of the Printing Presses

Significant among the trends of the 1960's was the phenomenal sale of low-priced paperback books. In 1939, 3,000,000 copies had been sold; in 1960, approximately 365,000,000 were sold—or a million a day. Despite the underclad females pictured on much of the trash, millions of volumes of the classics were purchased. Yet in 1969 a Gallup poll found that 58% of the population had never read a book from cover to cover.

Sex censorship received a devastating blow in 1959 when the Supreme Court, in Roth *v.* the U.S., set new low standards for obscenity. It held that for material to be obscene the dominant appeal must be to excite a prurient interest in sex, must affront community standards, and must be utterly without redeeming social value. The floodgates were now open for *Fanny Hill* and other under-the-counter specimens of hard-core pornography, purveyed in enormous quantities by the "merchants of Venus."

In the world of journalism, newspaper publishing was becoming more and more a big business, with competitors gradually dying off or selling out. Many cities were only one-newspaper towns. After a

Erwin Canham, editor of *The Christian Science Monitor*, wrote in 1958, "... The day of the printed word is far from ended. Swift as is the delivery of the radio bulletin, graphic as is television's eyewitness picture, the task of adding meaning and clarity remains urgent. People cannot and need not absorb meanings at the speed of light."

series of costly strikes and unsuccessful mergers, the populous New York Manhattan area was left in 1967 with only one afternoon newspaper of general circulation, plus two morning newspapers.

Among the sensationally successful journals were the human-interest *Reader's Digest* and the picture magazines *Look* and *Life*. A major casualty of 1969 was the *Saturday Evening Post*, after 148 years of continuous publication under that title. Although boasting a circulation of nearly 7 million, it was forced to fold because of inadequate advertising revenue. *Look* died in 1971, and *Life* expired in 1972, both partly the victims of sharply increased postal rates.

Men of Destiny

America's physical growth stands as a near-miracle, without parallel in human history. The nation started as a few struggling colonies; it emerged a vast empire. Its people conquered, cleared, cultivated, and civilized an area nearly as large as all Europe in less than three centuries.

Why this amazing success?

First of all, the new republic was blessed with a semi-isolated, near-empty continent, whose bountiful natural resources lay unscratched and seemingly inexhaustible. Hardly less important than the discovery of America was what Americans discovered in America.

Second, whatever their faults, the Americans were a remarkable people: tough, energetic, ambitious, inventive, efficient, resourceful, and determined. No less important than natural resources were the backs and brains of America's human resources. Soft-muscled descendants of the pioneers who tamed the wilderness will never fully appreciate how much sweat lubricated the process.

Third, the new country developed a marvelous economic productivity. This achievement flowed largely from the industry and efficiency of the people, who took full advantage of their fabulous natural endowment.

Fourth, the nation owed much to "the American way." It encouraged order under liberty and diversity within unity. A soaring release came to the spirit from a system of free enterprise under a representative government. America's overshadowing contribution was not in Panama Canals and Empire State buildings, but in demonstrating that democracy could survive and succeed on a continental scale. And in attaining this goal America served as an exemplar and lodestar for liberals the world over.

Danger Signals

As the 1970's began, Americans had no reason to grow complacent, for their "inexhaustible" natural resources were being exhausted at an alarming rate. World War II had taken a heavy toll of mineral deposits and oil pools. Increasingly the country was being forced to tap new reserves abroad, conspicuously the iron ore of Canada and South America, as well as the oil of the Arab world.

The shortage of fuel reached crisis proportions in 1973–1974. As an exploding population pressed upon available essentials, America was becoming a "have not" nation—on balance an importer rather than an exporter of raw materials.

The good earth is in need of preservation. Much of the world is hungry, and mounting birth rates are taxing tired lands. A frontier farmer of the last century could boast of wearing out three farms and three wives in one lifetime. But he was not thinking of posterity. To America's shame and lasting hurt, she has permitted the topsoil —the national skin—to be eroded from an acreage roughly the size of the thirteen original states. Waves of concrete continue to suffocate much of the fertile suburban land, and surface coal mining (strip mining) is leaving lunar landscapes.

The nation would be wise to continue striving for forest preservation and flood control, while seeking to preserve nature's beauty. Ax and fire have ravaged virgin trees that once sponged up rainfall: the cream-skimming Americans have long been more interested in sawmills than in seedlings. The people would be well advised to change their wasteful habits and intensify programs of reforestation. Rampaging rivers every year wash away millions of dollars worth of property. New Tennessee Valley Authorities (TVA's) in other river valleys, with private and state capital playing proper roles, may hold the key to control of erosion, flood waters, irrigation, and subsoil water depletion.

Americans need to keep their giant productive machine running at full blast. But can they continue to do this with the tax bite—federal, state, county, and city—gouging ever deeper and deeper? Can they shoulder indefinitely the financial burdens imposed by arming themselves against potential enemies—with arms that are becoming crushingly costly? Can they absorb the cutbacks essential to arms reduction or disarmament without ruining the nation's economy? Can they keep employment full or must they again fall victim to the boom-and-gloom cycle of depression? Can labor and management learn to settle their quarrels without forcing a long-suffering public to impose compulsory arbitration or dictatorial controls, especially where transportation and other public utilities are involved?

Thoughtful Americans will have to grapple with other economic problems as well. How can they achieve a maximum of industrial efficiency with a minimum of governmental restriction? How can investors be induced to venture risk capital in new enterprises if taxation takes too deep a bite from prospective profits? How long can

Senator Charles Mathias of Maryland, speaking in Maryland to a soil conservation group, said in 1969, "Along many of our roadsides we can't see the erosion for the trash. At the bottom of many of our streams, where once we found the geologic strata of the ages, we now find inches of muck and the typical fossils of our age, rusty beer cans."

a debt-cursed Treasury support the demands of pressure groups for price supports and other special handouts?

Health Hazards

Speedy steps are imperative to improve and rehabilitate precious human resources—the people whose hands and brains shape the Republic. American scientists have wrought miracles in the field of medicine, notably the Salk anti-polio vaccine introduced in 1953. Life expectancy at birth has increased remarkably in recent decades. Yet the shocking fact remains that from World War I to the Vietnam War hundreds of thousands of young men were rejected as physically or mentally unfit for military service—despite a boasted standard of living. Although Americans, including black Americans, made a brilliant showing in the Olympic games of these years, standard physical tests showed that only about half of American children could pass tests performed by Austrians, Italians, and Swiss of the same age. A soft life, automotive transportation, and a frantic pursuit of happiness have undoubtedly weakened the nation's physical fiber. The consumption of drugs, alcohol, and tobacco, whether by adults or juveniles, has risen sharply.

"Cigarette Box." (Coffin Nails.) From *Straight Herblock* (Simon and Schuster, 1964)

Years of Life Expectation at Birth*

	White Males	White Females	Nonwhite Males	Nonwhite Females
1850	38.3	40.5	No records	No records
1900–02	48.23	51.08	32.54	35.04
1919–21	56.34	58.53	47.14	46.92
1939–41	62.81	67.29	52.26	55.56
1962	67.6	74.4	61.5	66.8
1967	67.8	75.1	61.1	68.2

*The differential between whites and nonwhites was presumed to be caused largely by better food, shelter, and health care for the whites.

Cigarettes first came under heavy fire during the 1960's as a leading suspect in the alarming increase of lung cancer, heart disease, and other afflictions. The Surgeon General's report of 1964, which strongly supported such claims, did not have the deterrent effect that one might have supposed, especially among young people who ignored the warning which Congress voted for each package of cigarettes: "Caution: Cigarette smoking may be hazardous to your health," later changed to: "Warning: The Surgeon General Has Determined That Cigarette Smoking is Dangerous to Your Health."

Statistics pointed unerringly to the need for better health education, an improved diet, and cheaper hospitalization (costs had risen sickeningly). Millions of Americans lacked proper medical and dental care simply because it was too expensive or unavailable. The country was badly underdoctored. Many rural areas had no physicians whatever, and in urban areas house calls were going the way of the horse and buggy. Despite its vaunted medical facilities, the United States ranked about fourteenth among the nations in infant mortality, with the underprivileged minorities contributing heavily to this grim statistic. In about eighteen countries men were living longer than in the United States.

Leading killers continued to be heart disease, cancer, and alcoholism, although hope-giving research was being pursued in all these areas. In the 1960's spectacular breakthroughs occurred in the implanting of artificial organs or the transplanting of human organs, including hearts. Symptomatic of the tensions of American society was the fact that mentally ill patients were occupying about half of the hospital beds in the entire country.

The Dilemmas of Democracy

What of America's cherished political democracy? Signs multiply that her ungainly government is creaking, and cannot continue to function effectively on a colossal scale. Everyone, cynics say, now works for the government, either on the payroll or the tax roll. The need for streamlining and decentralizing the Washington regime is imperative. A conservative bumper sticker of the 1964 presidential campaign proclaimed, "No Thanks Uncle Sam, We'd Rather Do It Ourselves." Voters can keep a more watchful eye on their government, as Thomas Jefferson once observed, when as many functions as feasible are entrusted to the states and the local communities.

The Washington nerve center, already confusingly complex, may break down because of poor or mediocre personnel. Essential government bureaus cannot function without bureaucrats; hence the need for more effective steps in recruiting competent and honest civil servants. Not enough high-caliber men and women are attracted to public life when they are often paid poorly in money and richly in abuse. Too many younger people regard a career in politics as somewhat tainted. This impression was strengthened by the Watergate-related scandals of the Nixon years; they revealed an appalling level of ethics among officials high and low.

In 1969, Senator Erwin, the constitutionalist from North Carolina, told the U.S. Senate, "Crusading bureaucrats are power hungry officers of the executive branch of the Government who steal a mile of authority for every inch given them by the law."

One seldom misses water until the well runs dry, and many apathetic Americans do not appreciate the blessings of democracy. The depressing stay-at-home vote in state and national elections—often running higher than 50 percent—compares most unfavorably with the record of certain "developing" democratic nations.

Americans would do well to give redoubled attention to their schools, for if the educational system breaks down, democracy breaks down. Without effective schools, citizens cannot be trained to assume the heavy obligations of self-government. Without proper schools, the people cannot erect adequate safeguards against the wiles of demagogues and other dangerous self-seekers. Education is costly, but ignorance is infinitely costlier.

Overcrowding in the schools, in the 1960's, resembled a fast-growing boy who is constantly bursting out of his trousers. The question was repeatedly raised as to whether the nation can afford the outlays for maintaining a first-rate educational system in the face of the staggering defense costs imposed by the Cold War. Ready answers were that the people could afford nothing less, and that they would be foolish to pursue a policy of billions for bombs but pennies for progress. New problems were created in the early 1970's when the sharply declining birthrate brought many partially filled classrooms in the lower grades and a large number of unneeded and unemployed teachers.

America's schools have done a praiseworthy job in many respects, but the educational picture reveals dark shadows. About 80 percent of the youth finish high school, at least nominally. But there are still several million adult illiterates, although the official percentage has dropped to about two percent of the population. A distressing number of the ablest high school students are not going on to college, often because they lack funds. The country should beware of a shortage of scientists, engineers, and medical technicians in a day when wars are won in laboratories. Nor can a nation afford to neglect the humanities and social sciences in an era when wars can be averted or shortened by statesmen.

The Submerged Minorities

American democracy—political, social, economic—cannot fulfill its rich promise until its blessings reach every citizen. The plight of minority groups cries aloud for improvement, especially the blacks, who numbered about 23,000,000 in the census of 1970. They constitute a partially submerged twelve percent of the nation—a population group larger than Canada's set down within the United States. To many of them the American dream has long been a nightmare; the escalator is for them still largely a treadmill.

Yet genuine progress has been made, despite dissatisfaction with its glacial slowness. Mob lynching, which blotted out about a hundred blacks a year in the 1880's and 1890's, had fallen off to virtually zero by the 1930's and 1940's. Jim Crow segregation was legally ended by the federal Civil Rights legislation of the 1960's, although some of it informally, and even formally, persists. Black athletes, amateur and professional, are welcomed, even lionized. The integra-

"When Do You Think There'll Be Some Excitement About School DISintegration?" From *Straight Herblock* (Simon and Schuster, 1964)

tion of blacks into the army, achieved under President Truman in the 1950's, resulted in closer race relationships and a better utilization of manpower. North and South, more blacks are voting, more are being elected to public office, and more are enjoying fuller health, better education, and larger incomes. In the elections of 1972, 1144 blacks were elevated to office, including that of mayor in 86 cities.

Yet integration has not proceeded nearly as rapidly as its friends had hoped. Some black militants—representing a small minority—have run counter to this current by demanding self-imposed segregation, in separate dormitories, schools, and even in separate communities. Their view is that a school system designed by whites for whites does not "relate" to the need of their people for developing pride in their African culture and racial identity.

The results of the school-integration decision of the Supreme Court in 1954 have proved disappointing to the integrationists. Last-ditch defenders of separatism in the Deep South have devised ingenious and devious ways of circumventing court decisions. In some areas in 1969 no more than 7 percent of the blacks were integrated. In the North, the wisdom of busing children long distances to achieve racial balance in the schools has encountered violent criticism and opposition. Caught in the middle, significant numbers of blacks who had left the South were returning there in the 1970's.

Pressure continued to mount in the 1960's and 1970's against discrimination in job-giving because of race, color, creed, or sex. One proposed solution lay in fair-employment-practices acts. Increasing numbers of employers were pledging themselves to hire a quota of minorities, even though these were not always the best qualified and even though in some cases they were "token" blacks. In the area of religion, anti-Semitism and anti-Catholicism were markedly less virulent than in previous decades.

America's forgotten minority, the 800,000 or so Indians, have in a sense almost been ignored almost to death. Yet despite neglect, deprivation, illiteracy, disease, suicide, and alcoholism, their number has increased, partially as a result of intermarrying with other races. One noteworthy development of recent years has been the movement from the reservation to the city, where tribal identity tends to be lost. By 1974 the cities contained about 45 percent of the total Indian population.

American women, the largest minority group of all (though a numerical majority by about five percent), were continuing their demands for sex-equality legislation. Until recent decades the traditional house spouse, one of whose main missions was to bear and care for children, often held back from taking a job lest she reflect upon the bread-winning ability of her husband. But this stigma has long since disappeared as millions of women have left mechanized kitchens to seek gainful employment. Many of them aimed either to supplement the family income or keep constructively busy after the children were reared. Increasingly women have entered politics, including Congress, which in 1973 had about fourteen female members. Congresswoman Shirley Chisholm, an eloquent black woman from Brooklyn, made a serious bid for the presidency in 1972.

By the early 1970's the militant leadership of the "woman's movement" or "feminism" had been taken over by the woman liberationists ("Libbers"), headed by outspoken feminists. Urging the use of Woman Power and the utilization of untapped feminine talent, they urged "equal pay for equal work"; indeed in 1973 the average wage of female workers was only 59 percent of that of men in corresponding jobs. Feminists also demanded an affirmative program for hiring women in education and industry, as well as ratification of the sex-equality amendment to the Constitution. Hailing abortion as a "new birth of freedom," they insisted that women had the right of control over their bodies. Despite bitter dissent from Roman Catholics, the Supreme Court, in January, 1973, handed down a landmark decision upholding the right to an abortion.

Militant feminists further insisted that "Ms." be used for Miss and Mrs., and that the language be so changed as to accommodate such words as "chairperson" for "chairman" and other reminders of male dominance. Many liberationists condemned the Miss America Pageant and similar exhibitions as putting emphasis on sex and physical endowments, to the exclusion of inner worth.

Despite much ridicule from "male chauvinists" and considerable opposition from male-supported wives, substantial change could be recorded. In the late 1960's and early 1970 such citadels of masculinity as Yale and Princeton opened their doors to females. Pressure was on for equal participation in physical education and competitive athletics, as well as admission to police forces and the upper echelons of the armed services. By 1970, the records revealed two women brigadier generals. There was almost no formerly male-monopolized activity into which women were not entering on an equal-pay basis, although often in small numbers. By 1973 a total of about 33 million women could be found in the nation's working force, or about 38 percent of the total, with a consequent effect on the employment of male bread-winners.

Increasing sexual freedom in the late 1960's and early 1970's resulted in growing numbers of informal bisexual unions in preference to marriage, especially among the young. Greater public acceptance was also being accorded an outcast minority, the homosexuals of both sexes, who militantly claimed "the right to be different." Calling themselves "gays" and allegedly numbering about 15 million, they and their organizations were increasingly venturing out into the open and combating with some success the kinds of dis-

Senator Margaret Chase Smith of Maine.
(A Woman in Politics.)
Courtesy Senator Smith
At the height of the McCarthy hysteria in 1950, Senator Smith was practically the only Republican in the Senate with enough courage to speak out. In a memorable speech she said, "I think it is high time that we remembered that the Constitution, as amended, speaks not only of the freedom of speech but also of trial by jury instead of trial by accusation."

crimination, in jobs and otherwise, that had traditionally been directed against homosexuals.

Unfinished Business

High though America's standard of living is, it reveals ugly inequalities. By 1970, the poor were estimated to number about 30 million of the nation's total of more than 200,000,000. A better life lay only in the future for the millions of substandard tenant farmers, sharecroppers, migratory fruit-and-vegetable workers, and day laborers, both black and white. An attempt in the late 1960's to organize the grape pickers of California, headed by the Mexican-American Cesar Chavez, led to state and international boycotts of table grapes. Millions of Americans enjoy less than a decent standard of living, and consequently fall victim to malnutrition, illness, crime, and other misfortunes related to low income. For all too many citizens the American way of life is squalor. A high standard of democracy and a high standard of decency inevitably go hand in hand.

Disgraceful slums, whether urban or rural, cry aloud for elimination. Improper shelter contributes to disease, like tuberculosis, and to the mounting crime rate, already appallingly high. Congress in the 1960's made a substantial contribution toward housing improvement. Yet all too often "urban renewal" spelled "Negro removal," or the substitution of an even higher rent (with fewer units) than the poorer people could afford to pay. Many of these "gilded ghettoes" quickly fell into hopeless disrepair.

The perennial poor pose special problems. In 1969 as many as nine million persons were being supported by tax-raised welfare payments, one million of them in the New York City area. Welfare was becoming a way of life. And at one time in the 1960's poverty was the third most important industry in Mississippi, for federal payments outranked the value of cotton.

Social security leaves much to be desired. Millions of citizens still do not enjoy the benefits of the existing law, and for countless others the coverage is inadequate and inflation-shriveled. But if the individual is protected too snugly "from womb to tomb," the government may irreparably undermine his time-honored virtues of thrift, initiative, and self-reliance—the very qualities that built America. The wishbone may permanently replace the backbone. And the rising pressure for increased social services is coupled with a clamor, quite inconsistently, for decreased taxes and a balanced national budget. Many people were beginning to ask, "Can we afford tomorrow?"

New problems are constantly arising in connection with leisure time. In recent decades the coffee-break has become a national institution, quite out of harmony with the nervous-breakdown spirit

In his speech accepting his renomination for the presidency in 1972, Nixon declared, "I say that, instead of providing incentives for more millions to go on welfare, we need a program which will provide incentives for people to get off welfare and go to work. It is wrong for anyone on welfare to receive more than someone who works. . . . Let us never destroy the principle . . . that a person should get what he works for and work for what he gets."

and the Puritan work ethic of the 19th Century. Hours of labor are growing shorter; old folks are retiring earlier and living longer, thanks to the fountains of youth tapped by medical science.

The era of mass leisure has arrived. Americans are now spending about one-seventh of the national income for pleasure. Thousands of homes without indoor plumbing or running water have television antennas towering over leaky roofs. Less than 5 percent of the population lacks a television set. Millions of citizens, including impressionable children, are spending five hours or more a day before the "idiot box."

Americans will have to discover new frontiers in the Land of Limitless Opportunity, now that the westward receding frontier has played out. As long as there is an open mind, there will always be an open frontier; as long as there is resourcefulness, there will be resources. There are unattained horizons in the laboratory, in industry, and in human welfare; in the brain, in the heart, and in the soul. Pioneering is still possible almost anywhere. If one is not content to strike oil, discover uranium, or explore the ocean beds, one can plan a rocket-ship trip to the moon or to Mars.

The United States of America did vastly more than make democracy function for the first time in history on a huge scale. It emerged in the 20th Century as the undisputed leader of the democratic world. Americans did not seek this burdensome new responsibility. In fact, they fled from it in 1919, after World War I. But in the science-shrunken world of today, there is no escape: they are locked on the center of the global stage. Destiny has thrust into their hands the torch of leadership for the free world. If they fall, all the other democratic nations may fall.

The World's Last Hope

Once a revolutionary force in a world of conservatism, America is now a conservative force in a world of revolutionism. In recent decades men have witnessed the Communist revolution; the revolution in Asia and Africa against colonialism, imperialism, and racism; and the Revolution of Rising Expectations everywhere. All of these pressures are hoisting storm warnings. By the 1970's the American people, with about 6 percent of the world's population, were enjoying about 50 percent of its riches. A global "share the wealth movement," coupled with the fearsome world population explosion, is gaining terrifying momentum. The submerged masses are not going to be content to ride forever in oxcarts while a privileged few speed by in Cadillacs. Men are not going to live together in harmony as long as two-thirds of them have to struggle to live at all.

But if the crisis is formidable, so is the Republic. In generations past Americans resolutely confronted and conquered menaces as dangerous as those of today—that is, in relation to their existing strength. They need not yield to a wave of defeatism or hoist the white flag of surrender. They can, if they will, exert leadership commensurate with their enormous strength; they can create events, rather than bow to them.

America can fulfill with flying colors her mission as the foremost champion of the free world—if she will. But she will have to recapture much of the driving faith that she had in democracy during the morning years of the Republic. At that time three "isms" greatly feared by the monarchical world were American constitutionalism, republicanism, and liberalism. One should remember that a people cannot effectively fight dangerous foreign ideologies with inquisitions and bayonets, but only with better ideologies, effectively communicated.

Americans will have to learn to live with chronic crisis. They should seek to reconcile a maximum of liberty with a maximum of security. They should strive to preserve their precious freedoms without strangling them in an effort to protect them from enemies, within or without, Communist or Fascist. They should remember that America was founded and built by generations of nonconformists. They cannot permit truth and thought to become captives in the Land of the Free; they cannot safeguard democracy by shackling democracy. The best way to preserve it is to practice it. As Alfred E. Smith remarked in 1933, "All the ills of democracy can be cured by more democracy."

Finally, the nation will have to keep up its guard against potential foes. Eternal vigilance is still the price that one must pay for liberty. Americans should prepare to sacrifice—even until it hurts—to defend those priceless heritages of freedom and human dignity handed down by the Founding Fathers. To be an American is not only a rare privilege but, in these perilous times, a heavy responsibility.

SELECT READINGS

Relevant titles of interest and value are C. N. DEGLER, *Out of Our Past: The Forces That Shaped Modern America* (rev. ed., 1970)*; H. B. PARKES, *The American Experience* (2nd. ed., 1955)*; D. W. BROGAN, *The American Character* (1944)* and *America in the Modern World* (1960); D. M. POTTER, *People of Plenty* (1954)*; MAX LERNER, *America as a Civilization* (1957)*; ROGER BURLINGAME, *The American Conscience* (1957); E. M. BURNS, *The American Ideal of Mission* (1957); LOUIS HARTZ, *The Liberal Tradition in America* (1955)*; A. A. EKIRCH, *The Decline of American Liberalism* (1955)*; HANS KOHN, *American Nationalism* (1957)*; Y. ARIELI, *Individualism and Nationalism in American Ideology* (1964)*; R. L. BRUCKBERGER,

Image of America (1959)* [by a French Dominican]; L. D. BALDWIN, *The Meaning of America* (1955); MERLE CURTI, *American Paradox: The Conflict of Thought and Action* (1956); R. L. HEILBRONER, *The Future as History: The Historic Currents of Our Time and the Direction in Which They Are Taking America* (1960)*; CLINTON ROSSITER, *Conservatism in America* (1955)*; M. M. AUERBACH, *The Conservative Illusion* (1959); VANCE PACKARD, *The Status Seekers* (1959)* and *The Waste Makers* (1960)*; F. M. JOSEPH, ed., *As Others See Us: The United States Through Foreign Eyes* (1959); J. K. JESSUP, *et al., National Purpose* (1960)*; R. E. SPILLER and ERIC LARRABEE, *American Perspectives* (1961); D. J. BOORSTIN, *America and the Image of Europe: Reflections on American Thought* (1960)* and *The Image: Or, What Happened to the American Dream* (1962)*; OSCAR HANDLIN, *The Americans* (1963)*; C. V. WOODWARD, ed., *The Comparative Approach to American History* (1968)*; and B. J. BERNSTEIN, ed., *Towards a New Past* (1968).* Among the most useful recent appraisals are E. J. KAHN, JR., *The American People* (1974); R. N. GOODWIN, *The American Condition* (1974); and R. L. HEILBRONER, *An Inquiry into the Human Prospect* (1974).

* Available in paperback.

DECLARATION OF INDEPENDENCE

In Congress, July 4, 1776

The Unanimous Declaration of the Thirteen United States of America

[Bracketed material is inserted. For background see pp. 114–115.]

When, in the course of human events, it becomes necessary for one people to dissolve the political bands which have connected them with another, and to assume, among the powers of the earth, the separate and equal station to which the laws of nature and of nature's God entitle them, a decent respect to the opinions of mankind requires that they should declare the causes which impel them to the separation.

We hold these truths to be self-evident: That all men are created equal; that they are endowed by their Creator with certain unalienable rights; that among these are life, liberty, and the pursuit of happiness; that, to secure these rights, governments are instituted among men, deriving their just powers from the consent of the governed; that whenever any form of government becomes destructive of these ends, it is the right of the people to alter or to abolish it, and to institute new government, laying its foundation on such principles, and organizing its powers in such form, as to them shall seem most likely to effect their safety and happiness. Prudence, indeed, will dictate that governments long established should not be changed for light and transient causes; and accordingly all experience hath shown that mankind are more disposed to suffer, while evils are sufferable, than to right themselves by abolishing the forms to which they are accustomed. But when a long train of abuses and usurpations, pursuing invariably the same object, evinces a design to reduce them under absolute despotism, it is their right, it is their duty, to throw off such government, and to provide new guards for their future security. Such has been the patient sufferance of these colonies; and such is now the necessity which constrains them to alter their former systems of government. The history of the present King of Great Britain is a history of repeated injuries and usurpations, all having in direct object the establishment of an absolute tyranny over these states. To prove this, let facts be submitted to a candid world.

He has refused his assent to laws, the most wholesome and necessary for the public good. [See royal veto, p. 93.]

He has forbidden his governors to pass laws of immediate and pressing importance, unless suspended in their operation till his assent should be obtained; and, when so suspended, he has utterly neglected to attend to them.

He has refused to pass other laws for the accommodation of large districts of people [by establishing new counties], unless those people would relinquish the right of representation in the legislature, a right inestimable to them, and formidable to tyrants only.

He has called together legislative bodies at places unusual, uncomfortable, and distant from the depository of their public records, for the sole purpose of fatiguing them into compliance with his measures. [E.g., removal of Massachusetts Assembly to Salem, 1774.]

He has dissolved representative houses repeatedly, for opposing, with manly firmness, his invasions on the rights of the people. [E.g., Virginia Assembly, 1765.]

He has refused for a long time, after such dissolutions, to cause others to be elected; whereby the legislative powers, incapable of annihilation, have returned to the people at large for their exercise; the state remaining, in the mean time, exposed to all the dangers of invasions from without and convulsions within.

He has endeavored to prevent the population [populating] of these states; for that purpose obstructing the laws for naturalization of foreigners; refusing to pass others to encourage their migration hither, and raising the conditions of new appropriations of lands. [E.g., Proclamation of 1763, p. 64.]

He has obstructed the administration of justice, by refusing his assent to laws for establishing judiciary powers.

He has made judges dependent on his will alone, for the tenure of their offices, and the amount and payment of their salaries. [See Townshend Acts, p. 99.]

He has erected a multitude of new offices, and sent hither swarms of officers to harass our people and eat out their substance. [See enforcement of Navigation Laws, p. 99.]

He has kept among us, in times of peace, standing armies, without the consent of our legislatures. [See pp. 96, 99.]

He has affected to render the military independent of, and superior to, the civil power.

He has combined with others to subject us to a jurisdiction foreign to our constitution, and unacknowledged by our laws, giving his assent to their acts of pretended legislation:

For quartering large bodies of armed troops among us [see Boston Massacre, pp. 96, 99];

For protecting them, by a mock trial, from punishment for any murders which they should commit on the inhabitants of these states [see 1774 Act, pp. 102–103];

For cutting off our trade with all parts of the world [see Boston Port Bill, p. 102];

For imposing taxes on us without our consent [see Stamp Act, p. 96];

For depriving us, in many cases, of the benefits of trial by jury;

For transporting us beyond seas, to be tried for pretended offenses;

For abolishing the free system of English laws in a neighboring province [Quebec], establishing therein an arbitrary government, and enlarging its boundaries, so as to render it at once an example and fit instrument for introducing the same absolute rule into these colonies [Quebec Act, p. 103];

For taking away our charters, abolishing our most valuable laws, and altering fundamentally the forms of our governments [E.g., in Massachusetts, p. 102];

For suspending our own legislatures, and declaring themselves invested with power to legislate for us in all cases whatsoever [see Stamp Act repeal, p. 98].

He has abdicated government here, by declaring us out of his protection and waging war against us. [Proclamation, p. 112.]

He has plundered our seas, ravaged our coasts, burned our towns, and destroyed the lives of our people. [E.g., the burning of Falmouth (Portland), p. 112.]

He is at this time transporting large armies of foreign mercenaries [Hessians, p. 105] to complete the works of death, desolation, and tyranny already begun with circumstances of cruelty and perfidy scarcely paralleled in the most barbarous ages, and totally unworthy the head of a civilized nation.

He has constrained our fellow-citizens, taken captive on the high seas, to bear arms against their country, to become the executioners of their friends and brethren, or to fall themselves by their hands.

He has excited domestic insurrection among us [i.e., among slaves], and has endeavored to bring on the inhabitants of our frontiers the merciless Indian savages, whose known rule of warfare is an undistinguished destruction of all ages, sexes, and conditions.

In every stage of these oppressions we have petitioned for redress in the most humble terms; our repeated petitions have been answered only by repeated injury. [E.g., pp. 104, 110.] A prince, whose character is thus marked by every act which may define a tyrant, is unfit to be the ruler of a free people.

Nor have we been wanting in our attentions to our British brethren. We have warned them, from time to time, of attempts by their legislature to extend an unwarrantable jurisdiction over us. We have reminded them of the circumstances of our emigration and settlement here. We have appealed to their native justice and magnanimity; and we have conjured them, by the ties of our common kindred, to disavow these usurpations, which would inevitably interrupt our connections and correspondence. They, too, have been deaf to the voice of justice and of consanguinity [blood relationship; see p. 110]. We must, therefore, acquiesce in the necessity which denounces [announces] our separation, and hold them, as we hold the rest of mankind, enemies in war, in peace friends.

We, therefore, the representatives of the United States of America, in General Congress assembled, appealing to the Supreme Judge of the world for the rectitude of our intentions, do, in the name and by the authority of the good people of these colonies, solemnly publish and declare, That these United Colonies are, and of right ought to be, FREE AND INDEPENDENT STATES; that they are absolved from all allegiance to the British crown, and that all political connection between them and the state of Great Britain is, and ought to be, totally dissolved; and that, as free and independent states, they have full power to levy war, conclude peace, contract alliances, establish commerce, and do all other acts and things which independent states may of right do. And for the support of this declaration, with a firm reliance on the protection of Divine Providence, we mutually pledge to each other our lives, our fortunes, and our sacred honor.

[Signed by]   JOHN HANCOCK [President]
                                           [and fifty-five others]

CONSTITUTION OF
THE UNITED STATES OF AMERICA

[Boldface headings and bracketed explanatory matter have been inserted for the reader's convenience. Passages which are no longer operative are printed in italic type.]

PREAMBLE

On "We the people" see p. 274n.
We the people of the United States, in order to form a more perfect union, establish justice, insure domestic tranquillity, provide for the common defense, promote the general welfare, and secure the blessings of liberty to ourselves and our posterity, do ordain and establish this CONSTITUTION for the United States of America.

Article I. Legislative Department

Section I. Congress

Legislative power vested in a two-house Congress. All legislative powers herein granted shall be vested in a Congress of the United States, which shall consist of a Senate and a House of Representatives.

Section II. House of Representatives

1. The people elect representatives biennially. The House of Representatives shall be composed of members chosen every second year by the people of the several States, and the electors [voters] in each State shall have the qualifications requisite for electors of the most numerous branch of the State Legislature.

2. Who may be representatives. No person shall be a Representative who shall not have attained to the age of twenty-five years, and been seven years a citizen of the United States, and who shall not, when elected, be an inhabitant of that State in which he shall be chosen.

3. Representation in the House based on population; census. Representa-

See 1787 compromise, p. 147
tives and direct taxes[1] shall be apportioned among the several States which may be included within this Union, according to their respective numbers, *which shall be determined by adding to the whole number of free persons, including those bound to service for a term of years* [apprentices and indentured

See 1787 compromise, p. 148
servants], *and excluding Indians not taxed, three-fifths of all other persons* [slaves].[2] The actual enumeration [census] shall be made within three years after the first meeting of the Congress of the United States, and within

[1] Modified in 1913 by the 16th Amendment re income taxes (see p. 727).
[2] The word "slave" appears nowhere in the Constitution; "slavery" appears in the 13th Amendment. The three-fifths rule ceased to be in force when the 13th Amendment was adopted in 1865 (see p. 460 and Amendments below).

every subsequent term of ten years, in such manner as they shall by law direct. The number of Representatives shall not exceed one for every thirty thousand, but each State shall have at least one Representative; *and until such enumeration shall be made, the State of New Hampshire shall be entitled to choose three, Massachusetts eight, Rhode Island and Providence Plantations one, Connecticut five, New York six, New Jersey four, Pennsylvania eight, Delaware one, Maryland six, Virginia ten, North Carolina five, South Carolina five, and Georgia three.*

4. Vacancies in the House are filled by election. When vacancies happen in the representation from any State, the Executive authority [governor] thereof shall issue writs of election [call a special election] to fill such vacancies.

5. The House selects its Speaker; has sole power to vote impeachment charges (i.e., indictments). The House of Representatives shall choose their Speaker and other officers; and shall have the sole power of impeachment.

See Chase and Johnson trials, pp. 198, 505.

Section III. Senate

1. Senators represent the states. The Senate of the United States shall be composed of two Senators from each State, *chosen by the legislature thereof,*[1] for six years; and each Senator shall have one vote.

2. One-third of Senators chosen every two years; vacancies. *Immediately after they shall be assembled in consequence of the first election, they shall be divided as equally as may be into three classes. The seats of the Senators of the first class shall be vacated at the expiration of the second year, of the second class at the expiration of the fourth year, and of the third class at the expiration of the sixth year, so that one-third may be chosen every second year; and if vacancies happen by resignation or otherwise, during the recess of the legislature of any State, the Executive [governor] thereof may make temporary appointments until the next meeting of the legislature, which shall then fill such vacancies.*[2]

3. Who may be Senators. No person shall be a Senator who shall not have attained to the age of thirty years, and been nine years a citizen of the United States, and who shall not, when elected, be an inhabitant of that State for which he shall be chosen.

4. The Vice-President presides over the Senate. The Vice-President of the United States shall be President of the Senate, but shall have no vote, unless they be equally divided [tied].

5. The Senate chooses its other officers. The Senate shall choose their other officers, and also a President *pro tempore,* in the absence of the Vice-President, or when he shall exercise the office of President of the United States.

6. The Senate has sole power to try impeachments. The Senate shall have the sole power to try all impeachments. When sitting for that purpose, they shall be on oath or affirmation. When the President of the United States is tried, the Chief Justice shall preside:[3] and no person shall be convicted without the concurrence of two-thirds of the members present.

See Chase and Johnson trials, pp. 198, 505.

7. Penalties for impeachment conviction. Judgment in cases of impeach-

[1] Repealed in favor of popular election in 1913 by the 17th Amendment (see p. 706).
[2] Changed in 1913 by the 17th Amendment (see p. 706, and Amendments below).
[3] The Vice-President, as next in line, would be an interested party.

ment shall not extend further than to removal from office, and disqualification to hold and enjoy any office of honor, trust or profit under the United States: but the party convicted shall nevertheless be liable and subject to indictment, trial, judgment and punishment, according to law.

Section IV. Election and Meetings of Congress

1. Regulation of elections. The times, places and manner of holding elections for Senators and Representatives shall be prescribed in each State by the legislature thereof; but the Congress may at any time by law make or alter such regulations, except as to the places of choosing Senators.

2. Congress must meet once a year. The Congress shall assemble at least once in every year, and such meeting *shall be on the first Monday in December, unless they shall by law appoint a different day.*[1]

Section V. Organization and Rules of the Houses

1. Each House may reject members; quorums. Each house shall be the judge of the elections, returns and qualifications of its own members, and a majority of each shall constitute a quorum to do business; but a smaller number may adjourn from day to day, and may be authorized to compel the attendance of absent members, in such manner, and under such penalties, as each house may provide.

See "Bully" Brooks case, p. 424

2. Each House makes its own rules. Each house may determine the rules of its proceedings, punish its members for disorderly behavior, and with the concurrence of two-thirds, expel a member.

3. Each House must keep and publish a record of its proceedings. Each house shall keep a journal of its proceedings, and from time to time publish the same, excepting such parts as may in their judgment require secrecy; and the yeas and nays of the members of either house on any question shall, at the desire of one-fifth of those present, be entered on the journal.

4. Both Houses must agree on adjournment. Neither house, during the session of Congress, shall, without the consent of the other, adjourn for more than three days, nor to any other place than that in which the two houses shall be sitting.

Section VI. Privileges of and Prohibitions upon Congressmen

1. Congressional salaries; immunities. The Senators and Representatives shall receive a compensation for their services, to be ascertained by law and paid out of the treasury of the United States. They shall in all cases except treason, felony and breach of the peace, be privileged from arrest during their attendance at the session of their respective houses, and in going to and returning from the same; and for any speech or debate in either house, they shall not be questioned in any other place [i.e., they shall be immune from libel suits].

2. A Congressman may not hold any other federal civil office. No Senator or Representative shall, during the time for which he was elected, be ap-

[1] Changed in 1933 to January 3 by the 20th Amendment (see p. 889 and below).

pointed to any civil office under the authority of the United States, which shall have been created, or the emoluments whereof shall have been increased, during such time; and no person holding any office under the United States shall be a member of either house during his continuance in office.

Section VII. Method of Making Laws

1. Money bills must originate in the House. All bills for raising revenue shall originate in the House of Representatives; but the Senate may propose or concur with amendments as on other bills.

See 1787 compromise, p. 147.

2. The President's veto power; Congress may override. Every bill which shall have passed the House of Representatives and the Senate, shall, before it become a law, be presented to the President of the United States; if he approve he shall sign it, but if not he shall return it with his objections to that house in which it shall have originated, who shall enter the objections at large on their journal, and proceed to reconsider it. If after such reconsideration two-thirds of that house shall agree to pass the bill, it shall be sent, together with the objections, to the other house, by which it shall likewise be reconsidered, and, if approved by two-thirds of that house, it shall become a law. But in all such cases the votes of both houses shall be determined by yeas and nays, and the names of the persons voting for and against the bill shall be entered on the journal of each house respectively. If any bill shall not be returned by the President within ten days (Sundays excepted) after it shall have been presented to him, the same shall be a law, in like manner as if he had signed it, unless the Congress by their adjournment prevent its return, in which case it shall not be a law [this is the so-called pocket veto].

3. All measures requiring the agreement of both houses go to President for approval. Every order, resolution, or vote to which the concurrence of the Senate and House of Representatives may be necessary (except on a question of adjournment) shall be presented to the President of the United States; and before the same shall take effect, shall be approved by him, or being disapproved by him, shall be repassed by two-thirds of the Senate and House of Representatives, according to the rules and limitations prescribed in the case of a bill.

Section VIII. Powers Granted to Congress

Congress has certain enumerated powers:
1. It may lay and collect taxes. The Congress shall have power to lay and collect taxes, duties, imposts, and excises, to pay the debts and provide for the common defense and general welfare of the United States; but all duties, imposts and excises shall be uniform throughout the United States;

2. It may borrow money. To borrow money on the credit of the United States;

3. It may regulate foreign and interstate trade. To regulate commerce with foreign nations, and among the several States, and with the Indian tribes;

4. It may pass naturalization and bankruptcy laws. To establish an uniform rule of naturalization, and uniform laws on the subject of bankruptcies throughout the United States;

For 1798 naturalization see p. 185

5. It may coin money. To coin money, regulate the value thereof, and of foreign coin, and fix the standard of weights and measures;

6. It may punish conterfeiters. To provide for the punishment of counterfeiting the securities and current coin of the United States;

7. It may establish a postal service. To establish post offices and post roads;

8. It may issue patents and copyrights. To promote the progress of science and useful arts by securing for limited times to authors and inventors the exclusive right to their respective writings and discoveries;

See Judiciary Act of 1789, p. 160.

9. It may establish inferior courts. To constitute tribunals inferior to the Supreme Court;

10. It may punish crimes committed on the high seas. To define and punish piracies and felonies committed on the high seas [i.e., outside the three-mile limit] and offenses against the law of nations [international law];

11. It may declare war; authorize privateers. To declare war,[1] grant letters of marque and reprisal,[2] and make rules concerning captures on land and water;

12. It may maintain an army. To raise and support armies, but no appropriation of money to that use shall be for a longer term than two years;[3]

13. It may maintain a navy. To provide and maintain a navy;

14. It may regulate the army and navy. To make rules for the government and regulation of the land and naval forces;

See Whiskey Rebellion, p. 169.

15. It may call out the state militia. To provide for calling forth the militia to execute the laws of the Union, suppress insurrections, and repel invasions;

16. It shares with the states control of militia. To provide for organizing, arming, and disciplining the militia, and for governing such part of them as may be employed in the service of the United States, reserving to the States respectively the appointment of the officers, and the authority of training the militia according to the discipline prescribed by Congress;

17. It makes laws for the District of Columbia and other federal areas. To exercise exclusive legislation in all cases whatsoever, over such district (not exceeding ten miles square) as may, by cession of particular States, and the acceptance of Congress, become the seat of government of the United States,[4] and to exercise like authority over all places purchased by the consent of the legislature of the State, in which the same shall be, for the erection of forts, magazines, arsenals, dock-yards, and other needful buildings;—and

Congress has certain implied powers:

This is the famous "Elastic Clause"; see p. 165.

18. It may make laws necessary for carrying out the enumerated powers. To make all laws which shall be necessary and proper for carrying into execution the foregoing powers, and all other powers vested by this Constitu-

[1] Note that the President, though he can provoke war (see the case of Polk, pp. 309–310) or wage it after it is declared, cannot declare it.

[2] Papers issued private citizens in wartime authorizing them to capture enemy ships.

[3] A reflection of fear of standing armies earlier expressed in the Declaration of Independence.

[4] The District of Columbia, ten miles square, was established in 1791 (see p. 162).

tion in the government of the United States, or in any department or officer thereof.

Section IX. Powers Denied to the Federal Government

1. Congressional control of slave trade postponed until 1808. *The migration or importation of such persons as any of the States now existing shall think proper to admit shall not be prohibited by the Congress prior to the year 1808; but a tax or duty may be imposed on such importation, not exceeding $10 for each person.*

See 1787 slave compromise, p. 148.

2. The writ of habeas corpus[1] may be suspended only in case of rebellion or invasion. The privilege of the writ of habeas corpus shall not be suspended, unless when in cases of rebellion or invasion the public safety may require it.

See Lincoln's suspension, p. 478.

3. Attainders[2] and ex post facto laws[3] forbidden. No bill of attainder or ex post facto law shall be passed.

4. Direct taxes must be apportioned according to population. No capitation [head or poll tax], or other direct, tax shall be laid, unless in proportion to the census or enumeration herein before directed to be taken.[4]

5. Export taxes forbidden. No tax or duty shall be laid on articles exported from any State.

6. Congress must not discriminate among states in regulating commerce. No preference shall be given by any regulation of commerce or revenue to the ports of one State over those of another; nor shall vessels bound to, or from, one State, be obliged to enter, clear, or pay duties in another.

7. Public money may not be spent without Congressional appropriation; accounting. No money shall be drawn from the treasury, but in consequence of appropriations made by law; and a regular statement and account of the receipts and expenditures of all public money shall be published from time to time.

See Lincoln's infraction, p. 478.

8. Titles of nobility prohibited; foreign gifts. No title of nobility shall be granted by the United States: and no person holding any office of profit or trust under them, shall, without the consent of the Congress, accept of any present, emolument, office, or title, of any kind whatever, from any king, prince, or foreign state.

Section X. Powers Denied to the States

Absolute prohibitions on the states:
1. The states are forbidden to do certain things. No State shall enter into any treaty, alliance, or confederation; grant letters of marque and reprisal [i.e., authorize privateers]; coin money; emit bills of credit [issue paper money]; make anything but gold and silver coin a [legal] tender in payment

[1] A writ of habeas corpus is a document which enables a person under arrest to obtain an immediate examination in court to ascertain whether he is being legally held.
[2] A bill of attainder is a special legislative act condemning and punishing an individual without a judicial trial.
[3] An ex post facto law is one that fixes punishments for acts committed before the law was passed.
[4] Modified in 1913 by the 16th Amendment (see pp. 727, 733, and Amendments below).

See Fletcher vs. *Peck, p. 245*

of debts; pass any bill of attainder, ex post facto law,[1] or law impairing the obligation of contracts, or grant any title of nobility.

Conditional prohibitions on the states:

2. The states may not levy duties without the consent of Congress. No State shall, without the consent of the Congress, lay any imposts or duties on imports or exports, except what may be absolutely necessary for executing its inspection laws: and the net produce of all duties and imposts, laid by any State on imports or exports, shall be for the use of the treasury of the United States; and all such laws shall be subject to the revision and control of the Congress.

Cf. Confederation chaos, p. 139.

3. Certain other federal powers are forbidden the states except with the consent of Congress. No State shall, without the consent of Congress, lay any duty of tonnage [i.e., duty on ship tonnage], keep [non-militia] troops or ships of war in time of peace, enter into any agreement or compact with another State, or with a foreign power, or engage in war, unless actually invaded, or in such imminent danger as will not admit of delay.

Article II. Executive Department

Section I. President and Vice-President

1. The President the chief executive; his term. The executive power shall be vested in a President of the United States of America. He shall hold his office during the term of four years,[2] and, together with the Vice-President, chosen for the same term, be elected as follows:

See 1787 compromise, p. 149.

2. The President is chosen by electors. Each State shall appoint, in such manner as the legislature thereof may direct, a number of electors, equal to the whole number of Senators and Representatives to which the State may be entitled in the Congress; but no Senator or Representative, or person holding an office of trust or profit under the United States, shall be appointed an elector.

See 1876 Oregon case, p. 526n.

A majority of the electoral votes needed to elect a President. *The electors shall meet in their respective States, and vote by ballot for two persons, of whom one at least shall not be an inhabitant of the same State with themselves. And they shall make a list of all the persons voted for, and of the number of votes for each; which list they shall sign and certify, and transmit sealed to the seat of government of the United States, directed to the President of the Senate. The President of the Senate shall, in the presence of the Senate and House of Representatives, open all the certificates, and the votes shall then be counted. The person having the greatest number of votes shall be the President, if such number be a majority of the whole number of electors appointed; and if there be more than one who have such majority, and have an equal number of votes, then the House of Representatives shall immediately choose by ballot one of them for President; and if no person have a majority, then from the five highest on the list the said house shall in like manner choose the President. But in choosing the President the votes shall be taken by States, the representation from each State having one vote; a quorum for this purpose shall consist of a member or members from two-thirds of the States, and a majority of all the States shall be necessary to a choice. In every*

See Burr-Jefferson disputed election of 1800, pp. 190–191.

---

[1] For definitions see footnotes 2 and 3 on preceding page.

[2] No reference to re-election; for anti-third term 22d Amendment see p. 971 and below.

case, after the choice of the President, the person having the greatest number of votes of the electors shall be the Vice-President. But if there should remain two or more who have equal votes, the Senate shall choose from them by ballot the Vice-President.[1]

3. Congress decides time of meeting of Electoral College. The Congress may determine the time of choosing the electors and the day on which they shall give their votes; which day shall be the same throughout the United States.

4. Who may be President. No person except a natural-born citizen, *or a citizen of the United States at the time of the adoption of this Constitution,* shall be eligible to the office of President; neither shall any person be eligible to that office who shall not have attained to the age of thirty-five years, and been fourteen years a resident within the United States [i.e., a legal resident].

To provide for foreign-born like Hamilton

5. Replacements for President. In case of the removal of the President from office or of his death, resignation, or inability to discharge the powers and duties of the said office, the same shall devolve on the Vice-President, and the Congress may by law provide for the case of removal, death, resignation, or inability, both of the President and Vice-President, declaring what officer shall then act as President, and such officer shall act accordingly, until the disability be removed, or a President shall be elected.

6. The President's salary. The President shall, at stated times, receive for his services a compensation, which shall neither be increased nor diminished during the period for which he shall have been elected, and he shall not receive within that period any other emolument from the United States, or any of them.

7. The President's oath of office. Before he enter on the execution of his office, he shall take the following oath or affirmation:—"I do solemnly swear (or affirm) that I will faithfully execute the office of the President of the United States, and will to the best of my ability preserve, protect and defend the Constitution of the United States."

Section II. Powers of the President

1. The President has important military and civil powers. The President shall be commander in chief of the army and navy of the United States, and of the militia of the several States, when called into the actual service of the United States; he may require the opinion, in writing, of the principal officer in each of the executive departments, upon any subject relating to the duties of their respective offices, and he shall have power to grant reprieves and pardons for offenses against the United States, except in cases of impeachment.[2]

See Cabinet evolution, pp. 159–160

2. The President may negotiate treaties and nominate federal officials. He shall have power, by and with the advice and consent of the Senate, to make treaties, provided two-thirds of the Senators present concur; and he shall nominate, and by and with the advice and consent of the Senate, shall appoint ambassadors, other public ministers and consuls, judges of the Supreme Court, and all other officers of the United States, whose appoint-

See Jefferson as Vice-President in 1796, p. 182.

[1] Repealed in 1804 by the 12th Amendment (for text, see Amendments below).
[2] To prevent the President's pardoning himself or his close associates.

For President's removal power, see pp. 505–506.

ments are not herein otherwise provided for, and which shall be established by law: but the Congress may by law vest the appointment of such inferior officers, as they think proper, in the President alone, in the courts of law, or in the heads of departments.

3. The president may fill vacancies during Senate recess. The President shall have power to fill up all vacancies that may happen during the recess of the Senate, by granting commissions which shall expire at the end of their next session.

Section III. Other Powers and Duties of the President

For President's personal appearances, see p. 732.

Messages; extra sessions; receiving ambassadors: execution of the laws. He shall from time to time give to the Congress information of the state of the Union, and recommend to their consideration such measures as he shall judge necessary and expedient; he may, on extraordinary occasions, convene both houses, or either of them, and in case of disagreement between them, with respect to the time of adjournment, he may adjourn them to such time as he shall think proper; he shall receive ambassadors and other public ministers; he shall take care that the laws be faithfully executed, and shall commission all the officers of the United States.

Section IV Impeachment

See Johnson's acquittal, p. 506.

Civil officers may be removed by impeachment. The President, Vice-President and all civil officers[1] of the United States shall be removed from office on impeachment for, and on conviction of, treason, bribery, or other high crimes and misdemeanors.

Article III. Judicial Department

Section I. The Federal Courts

See Judiciary Act of 1789, p. 160.

The judicial power belongs to the federal courts. The judicial power of the United States shall be vested in one Supreme Court, and in such inferior courts as the Congress may from time to time ordain and establish. The judges, both of the Supreme and inferior courts, shall hold their offices during good behavior, and shall, at stated times, receive for their services a compensation which shall not be diminished during their continuance in office.

Section II. Jurisdiction of Federal Courts

1. Kinds of cases that may be heard. The judicial power shall extend to all cases, in law and equity, arising under this Constitution, the laws of the United States, and treaties made, or which shall be made, under their authority;—to all cases affecting ambassadors, other public ministers and consuls;—to all cases of admiralty and maritime jurisdiction;—to controversies to which the United States shall be a party;—to controversies between two or more States;—*between a State and citizens of another State;*[2]—

---

[1] I.e., all federal executive and judicial officers, but not members of Congress or military personnel.

[2] The 11th Amendment (see Amendments below) restricts this to suits by a state against citizens of another state.

between citizens of different States;—between citizens of the same State claiming lands under grants of different States, and between a State, or the citizens thereof, and foreign states, citizens or subjects.

2. Jurisdiction of the Supreme Court. In all cases affecting ambassadors, other public ministers and consuls, and those in which a State shall be party, the Supreme Court shall have original jurisdiction.[1] In all the other cases before mentioned, the Supreme Court shall have appellate jurisdiction,[2] both as to law and fact, with such exceptions, and under such regulations, as the Congress shall make.

3. Trial for federal crime is by jury. The trial of all crimes, except in cases of impeachment, shall be by jury; and such trial shall be held in the State where the said crimes shall have been committed; but when not committed within any State, the trial shall be at such place or places as the Congress may by law have directed.

Section III. Treason

1. Treason defined. Treason against the United States shall consist only in levying war against them, or in adhering to their enemies, giving them aid and comfort. No person shall be convicted of treason unless on the testimony of two witnesses to the same overt act, or on confession in open court.

See Burr trial, p. 204

2. Congress fixes punishment for treason. The Congress shall have power to declare the punishment of treason, but no attainder of treason shall work corruption of blood, or forfeiture except during the life of the person attainted.[3]

Article IV. Relations of the States
to One Another

Section I. Credit to Acts, Records, and
Court Proceedings

Each state must respect the public acts of the others. Full faith and credit shall be given in each State to the public acts, records, and judicial proceedings of every other State.[4] And the Congress may by general laws prescribe the manner in which such acts, records, and proceedings shall be proved [attested], and the effect thereof.

Section II. Duties of States to States

1. Citizenship in one state is valid in all. The citizens of each State shall be entitled to all privileges and immunities of citizens in the several States.

2. Fugitives from justice must be surrendered by the state to which they have fled. A person charged in any State with treason, felony, or other crime, who shall flee from justice, and be found in another State, shall on demand of the executive authority [governor] of the State from which he fled, be delivered up, to be removed to the State having jurisdiction of the crime.

[1] I.e., such cases must originate in the Supreme Court.
[2] I.e., it hears other cases only when they are appealed to it from a lower federal court or a state court.
[3] I.e., punishment only for the offender; none for his heirs.
[4] E.g., a marriage valid in one is valid in all.

Basis of fugitive slave laws; see pp. 402–403. **3. Slaves and apprentices must be returned.** *No person held to service or labor in one State, under the laws thereof, escaping into another, shall, in consequence of any law or regulation therein, be discharged from such service or labor, but shall be delivered up on claim of the party to whom such service or labor may be due.*[1]

Section III. New States and Territories

1. Congress may admit new states. New States may be admitted by the Congress into this Union; but no new State shall be formed or erected within *E.g., Maine (1820); see p. 241* the jurisdiction of any other State; nor any State be formed by the junction of two or more States, or parts of States, without the consent of the legislatures of the States concerned as well as of the Congress.

2. Congress regulates federal territory and property. The Congress shall have power to dispose of and make all needful rules and regulations respecting the territory or other property belonging to the United States; and nothing in this Constitution shall be so construed as to prejudice any claims of the United States, or of any particular State.

Section IV. Protection to the States

United States guarantees to states representative government and protection against invasion and rebellion. The United States shall guarantee to every State in this Union a republican form of government, and shall *See Pullman strike, p. 635.* protect each of them against invasion; and on application of the legislature, or of the executive [governor] (when the legislature cannot be convened), against domestic violence.

Article V. The Process of Amendment

The Constitution may be amended in four ways. The Congress, whenever two-thirds of both houses shall deem it necessary, shall propose amendments to this Constitution, or, on the application of the legislatures of two-thirds of the several States, shall call a convention for proposing amendments, which, in either case, shall be valid to all intents and purposes, as part of this Constitution, when ratified by the legislatures of three-fourths of the several States, or by conventions in three-fourths thereof, as the one or the other mode of ratification may be proposed by the Congress; provided *that no amendments which may be made prior to the year one thousand eight hundred and eight shall in any manner affect the first and fourth clauses in the ninth section of the first article;*[2] and that no State, without its consent, shall be deprived of its equal suffrage in the Senate.

Article VI. General Provisions

This pledge honored by Hamilton, p. 161. **1. The debts of the Confederation are taken over.** All debts contracted and engagements entered into, before the adoption of this Constitution, shall be as valid against the United States under this Constitution, as under the Confederation.

[1] Invalidated in 1865 by the 13th Amendment (for text see Amendments below).
[2] This clause, re slave trade and direct taxes, became inoperative in 1808.

2. The Constitution, federal laws, and treaties are the supreme law of the land. This Constitution, and the laws of the United States which shall be made in pursuance thereof; and all treaties made, or which shall be made, under the authority of the United States, shall be the supreme law of the land; and the judges in every State shall be bound thereby, anything in the Constitution or laws of any State to the contrary notwithstanding.

3. Federal and state officers bound by oath to support the Constitution. The Senators and Representatives before mentioned, and the members of the several State legislatures, and all executive and judicial officers, both of the United States and of the several States, shall be bound by oath or affirmation to support this Constitution; but no religious test shall ever be required as a qualification to any office or public trust under the United States.

Article VII. Ratification of the Constitution

The Constitution effective when ratified by conventions in nine states. The ratification of the conventions of nine States shall be sufficient for the establishment of this Constitution between the States so ratifying the same.

See 1787 irregularity, p. 149.

Done in Convention by the unanimous consent of the States present, the seventeenth day of September in the year of our Lord one thousand seven hundred and eighty-seven and of the Independence of the United States of America the twelfth. In witness whereof we have hereunto subscribed our names.

[Signed by]

Gº WASHINGTON
Presidt and Deputy from Virginia
[and thirty-eight others]

AMENDMENTS TO THE CONSTITUTION[1]

Article I. Religious and Political Freedom

Congress must not interfere with freedom of religion, speech or press, assembly, and petition. Congress shall make no law respecting an establishment of religion, or prohibiting the free exercise thereof; or abridging the freedom of speech, or of the press; or the right of the people peaceably to assemble, and to petition the government for a redress of grievances.

For background of Bill of Rights see p. 160.

Article II. Right to Bear Arms

The people may bear arms. A well-regulated militia being necessary to the security of a free State, the right of the people to keep and bear arms [i.e., for military purposes] shall not be infringed.

Article III. Quartering of Troops

Soldiers may not be arbitrarily quartered on the people. No soldier shall, in time of peace, be quartered in any house without the consent of the owner, nor in time of war, but in a manner to be prescribed by law.

See Declaration of Independence, above.

[1] The first ten Amendments (Bill of Rights) were adopted in 1791

Article IV. Searches and Seizures

A reflection of colonial grievances against Crown.

Unreasonable searches are forbidden. The right of the people to be secure in their persons, houses, papers, and effects, against unreasonable searches and seizures, shall not be violated, and no [search] warrants shall issue but upon probable cause, supported by oath or affirmation, and particularly describing the place to be searched, and the persons or things to be seized.

Article V. Right to Life, Liberty, and Property

The individual is guaranteed certain rights when on trial and the right to life, liberty, and property. No person shall be held to answer for a capital, or otherwise infamous crime, unless on a presentment [formal charge] or indictment of a grand jury, except in cases arising in the land or naval forces, or in the militia, when in actual service in time of war or public danger; nor shall any person be subject for the same offense to be twice put in jeopardy of life or limb; nor shall be compelled in any criminal case to be a witness against himself, nor be deprived of life, liberty, or property, without due process of law; nor shall private property be taken for public use [i.e., by eminent domain] without just compensation.

Article VI. Protection in Criminal Trials

See Declaration of Independence, above.

An accused person has important rights. In all criminal prosecutions, the accused shall enjoy the right to a speedy and public trial, by an impartial jury of the State and district wherein the crime shall have been committed, which district shall have been previously ascertained by law, and to be informed of the nature and cause of the accusation; to be confronted with the witnesses against him; to have compulsory process [subpoena] for obtaining witnesses in his favor, and to have the assistance of counsel for his defense.

Article VII. Suits at Common Law

The rules of common law are recognized. In suits at common law, where the value in controversy shall exceed twenty dollars, the right of trial by jury shall be preserved, and no fact tried by a jury shall be otherwise re-examined in any court of the United States, than according to the rules of the common law.

Article VIII. Bail and Punishments

Excessive fines and unusual punishments are forbidden. Excessive bail shall not be required, nor excessive fines imposed, nor cruel and unusual punishments inflicted.

Article IX. Concerning Rights Not Enumerated

The people retain rights not here enumerated. The enumeration in the Constitution, of certain rights, shall not be construed to deny or disparage others retained by the people.

Article X. Powers Reserved to the States and to the People

Powers not delegated to the federal government are reserved to the states and the people. The powers not delegated to the United States by the Constitution, nor prohibited by it to the States, are reserved to the States respectively, or to the people.

A concession to states' rights, p. 165.

Article XI. Suits against a State

The federal courts have no authority in suits by citizens against a state. The judicial power of the United States shall not be construed to extend to any suit in law or equity, commenced or prosecuted against one of the United States by citizens of another State, or by citizens or subjects of any foreign state. [Adopted 1798.]

Article XII. Election of President and Vice-President

1. Changes in manner of electing President and Vice-President; procedure when no presidential candidate receives electoral majority. The electors shall meet in their respective States, and vote by ballot for President and Vice-President, one of whom, at least, shall not be an inhabitant of the same State with themselves; they shall name in their ballots the person voted for as President, and in distinct ballots the person voted for as Vice-President, and they shall make distinct lists of all persons voted for as President, and of all persons voted for as Vice-President, and of the number of votes for each, which lists they shall sign and certify, and transmit sealed to the seat of government of the United States, directed to the President of the Senate;— the President of the Senate shall, in the presence of the Senate and House of Representatives, open all the certificates and the votes shall then be counted; —the person having the greatest number of votes for President shall be the President, if such number be a majority of the whole number of electors appointed; and if no person have such majority, then from the persons having the highest numbers not exceeding three on the list of those voted for as President, the House of Representatives shall choose immediately, by ballot, the President. But in choosing the President, the votes shall be taken by States, the representation from each State having one vote; a quorum for this purpose shall consist of a member or members from two-thirds of the States, and a majority of all the States shall be necessary to a choice. And if the House of Representatives shall not choose a President whenever the right of choice shall devolve upon them, before *the fourth day of March*[1] next following, then the Vice-President shall act as President, as in the case of the death or other constitutional disability of the President.

Forestalls repetition of 1800 dispute, pp. 190–191

See 1876 election, p. 527.

See 1824 election, p. 258.

2. Procedure when no vice-presidential candidate receives electoral majority. The person having the greatest number of votes as Vice-President shall be the Vice-President, if such number be a majority of the whole number of electors appointed; and if no person have a majority, then from the two highest numbers on the list the Senate shall choose the Vice-President; a quorum for the purpose shall consist of two-thirds of the whole number of Senators, and a majority of the whole number shall be necessary to a choice. But no person constitutionally ineligible to the office of President shall be eligible to that of Vice-President of the United States. [Adopted 1804.]

Article XIII. Slavery Prohibited

Slavery forbidden. 1. Neither slavery[2] nor involuntary servitude, except

---

[1] Changed to January 20 by the 20th Amendment (for text, see Amendments below).
[2] The only explicit mention of slavery in the Constitution.

For background see p. 460. as a punishment for crime whereof the party shall have been duly convicted, shall exist within the United States, or any place subject to their jurisdiction.

2. Congress shall have power to enforce this article by apptopriate legislation. [Adopted 1865.]

Article XIV. Civil Rights for Negroes, Etc.

For background see p. 497. **1. Negroes made citizens; U. S. citizenship primary.** All persons born or naturalized in the United States, and subject to the jurisdiction thereof, are citizens of the United States and of the State wherein they reside. No State shall make or enforce any law which shall abridge the privileges or immuni- *For corporations as "persons" see p. 567.* ties of citizens of the United States; nor shall any State deprive any person of life, liberty, or property, without due process of law; nor deny to any person within its jurisdiction the equal protection of the laws.

2. When a state denies Negroes the vote, its representation shall be reduced. *Abolishes three-fifths rule for Negroes, Art. I, Sec. II, para. 3, above.* Representatives shall be apportioned among the several States according to their respective numbers, counting the whole number of persons in each State, excluding Indians not taxed. But when the right to vote at any election for the choice of Electors for President and Vice-President of the United States, Representatives in Congress, the executive and judicial officers of a State, or the members of the legislature thereof, is denied to any of the male inhabitants of such State, being twenty-one years of age and citizens of the United States, or in any way abridged, except for participation in rebellion, or other crime, the basis of representation therein shall be reduced in the proportion which the number of such male citizens shall bear to the whole number of male citizens twenty-one years of age in such State.

3. Certain persons who have been in rebellion are ineligible for federal and state office. No person shall be a Senator or Representative in Congress, or Elector of President and Vice-President, or hold any office, civil or military, under the United States, or under any State, who, having previously taken an oath, as a member of Congress, or as an officer of the United States, or as a member of any State legislature, or as an executive or judicial officer of any State, to support the Constitution of the United States, shall have engaged in insurrection or rebellion against the same, or given aid or comfort to the enemies thereof. But Congress may, by a vote of two-thirds of each house, remove such disability.

4. Debts incurred in aid of rebellion are void. The validity of the public debt of the United States, authorized by law, including debts incurred for payment of pensions and bounties for services in suppressing insurrection or rebellion, shall not be questioned. But neither the United States nor any State shall assume or pay any debt or obligation incurred in aid of insur- rection or rebellion against the United States, or any claim for the loss or emancipation of any slave; but all such debts, obligations, and claims shall be held illegal and void.

5. Enforcement. The Congress shall have power to enforce, by appropriate legislation, the provisions of this article. [Adopted 1868.]

Article XV. Negro Suffrage

For background see pp. 499–500. **Negroes are made voters.** 1. The right of citizens of the United States to vote shall not be denied or abridged by the United States or by any State on account of race, color, or previous condition of servitude.

2. The Congress shall have power to enforce this article by appropriate legislation. [Adopted 1870.]

Article XVI. Income Taxes

Congress has power to lay and collect income taxes. The Congress shall have power to lay and collect taxes on incomes, from whatever source derived, without apportionment among the several States, and without regard to any census or enumeration. [Adopted 1913.]

For background see pp. 636, 727.

Article XVII. Direct Election of Senators

Senators shall be elected by popular vote. 1. The Senate of the United States shall be composed of two Senators from each State, elected by the people thereof, for six years; and each Senator shall have one vote. The electors in each State shall have the qualifications requisite for electors of [voters for] the most numerous branch of the State legislatures.

For background see p. 706.

2. When vacancies happen in the representation of any State in the Senate, the executive authority of such State shall issue writs of election to fill such vacancies: Provided, that the Legislature of any State may empower the executive thereof to make temporary appointments until the people fill the vacancies by election as the Legislature may direct.

3. This amendment shall not be so construed as to affect the election or term of any Senator chosen before it becomes valid as part of the Constitution. [Adopted 1913.]

Article XVIII. National Prohibition

The sale or manufacture of intoxicating liquors is forbidden. 1. *After one year from the ratification of this article the manufacture, sale, or transportation of intoxicating liquors within, the importation thereof into, or the exportation thereof from the United States and all territory subject to the jurisdiction thereof, for beverage purposes, is hereby prohibited.*

For background see p. 786.

2. *The Congress and the several States shall have concurrent power to enforce this article by appropriate legislation.*

3. *This article shall be inoperative unless it shall have been ratified as an amendment to the Constitution by the legislatures of the several States, as provided by the Constitution, within seven years from the date of the submission thereof to the States by the Congress.* [Adopted 1919; repealed 1933 by 21st Amendment.]

Article XIX. Woman Suffrage

Women guaranteed the right to vote. 1. The right of citizens of the United States to vote shall not be denied or abridged by the United States or by any State on account of sex.

For background see p. 786.

2. The Congress shall have power to enforce this article by appropriate legislation. [Adopted 1920.]

Article XX. Presidential and Congressional Terms

1. Presidential, vice-presidential, and Congressional terms of office begin in January. The terms of the President and Vice-President shall end at noon

Shortens lame-duck periods by modifying Art. I, Sec. IV, para. 2; see p. 889 and below.
on the 20th day of January, and the terms of Senators and Representatives at noon on the 3d day of January, of the years in which such terms would have ended if this article had not been ratified; and the terms of their successors shall then begin.

2. **New meeting date for Congress.** The Congress shall assemble at least once in every year, and such meeting shall begin at noon on the 3d day of January, unless they shall by law appoint a different day.

3. **Emergency presidential and vice-presidential succession.** If, at the time fixed for the beginning of the term of the President, the President-elect shall have died, the Vice-President-elect shall become President. If a President shall not have been chosen before the time fixed for the beginning of his term, or if the President-elect shall have failed to qualify, then the Vice-President-elect shall act as President until a President shall have qualified; and the Congress may by law provide for the case wherein neither a President-elect nor a Vice-President-elect shall have qualified, declaring who shall then act as President, or the manner in which one who is to act shall be selected, and such persons shall act accordingly until a President or Vice-President shall have qualified.

4. The Congress may by law provide for the case of the death of any of the persons from whom the House of Representatives may choose a President whenever the right of choice shall have devolved upon them, and for the case of the death of any of the persons from whom the Senate may choose a Vice-President whenever the right of choice shall have devolved upon them.

5. Sections 1 and 2 shall take effect on the 15th day of October following the ratification of this article.

6. This article shall be inoperative unless it shall have been ratified as an amendment to the Constitution by the Legislatures of three-fourths of the several States within seven years from the date of its submission. [Adopted 1933.]

Article XXI. Prohibition Repealed

For background see p. 880.
1. **18th Amendment repealed.** The eighteenth article of amendment to the Constitution of the United States is hereby repealed.

2. **Local laws honored.** The transportation or importation into any State, Territory, or Possession of the United States for delivery or use therein of intoxicating liquors, in violation of the laws thereof, is hereby prohibited.

3. This article shall be inoperative unless it shall have been ratified as an amendment to the Constitution by conventions in the several States, as provided in the Constitution, within seven years from the date of the submission thereof to the States by the Congress. [Adopted 1933.]

Article XXII. Anti-Third Term Amendment

For background see p. 971.
Presidential term is limited. 1. No person shall be elected to the office of President more than twice, and no person who has held the office of President, or acted as President, for more than two years of a term to which some other person was elected President shall be elected to the office of President more than once. But this article shall not apply to any person holding the

office of President when this article was proposed by the Congress [i.e., Truman], and shall not prevent any person who may be holding the office of President, or acting as President, during the term within which this article becomes operative [i.e., Truman] from holding the office of President or acting as President during the remainder of such term.

2. This article shall be inoperative unless it shall have been ratified as an amendment to the Constitution by the legislatures of three-fourths of the several States within seven years from the date of its submission to the States by the Congress. [Adopted 1951.]

Article XXIII. District of Columbia Vote

1. Presidential Electors for the District of Columbia. The District constituting the seat of Government of the United States shall appoint in such manner as the Congress may direct:

A number of electors of President and Vice-President equal to the whole number of Senators and Representatives in Congress to which the District would be entitled if it were a State, but in no event more than the least populous State; they shall be in addition to those appointed by the States, but they shall be considered for the purposes of the election of President and Vice-President, to be electors appointed by a State; and they shall meet in the District and perform such duties as provided by the twelfth article of amendment.

2. Enforcement. The Congress shall have the power to enforce this article by appropriate legislation. [Adopted 1961.]

Article XXIV. Poll Tax

1. Payment of poll tax or other taxes not to be prerequisite for voting in federal elections. The right of citizens of the United States to vote in any primary or other election for President or Vice-President, for electors for President or Vice-President, or for Senator or Representative in Congress, shall not be denied or abridged by the United States or any State by reason of failure to pay any poll tax or other tax.

2. Enforcement. The Congress shall have the power to enforce this article by appropriate legislation. [Adopted 1964.]

Article XXV. Presidential Succession and Disability[1] (1967)

1. Vice President to become President. In case of the removal of the President from office or of his death or resignation, the Vice President shall become President.[2]

2. Successor to Vice President provided. Whenever there is a vacancy in the

---

[1] Passed by a two-thirds vote of both houses of Congress in July, 1965; ratified by the requisite three-fourths of the state legislatures, February, 1967, or well within the seven-year limit.

[2] The original Constitution (Art. II, Sec. I, para. 5) was vague on this point, stipulating that "the powers and duties" of the President, but not necessarily the title, should "devolve" on the Vice President. President Tyler, the first "accidental President," assumed not only the power and duties but the title as well.

*For background
see p. 1025.*
office of the Vice President, the President shall nominate a Vice President who shall take office upon confirmation by a majority vote of both Houses of Congress.

3. Vice President to serve for disabled President. Whenever the President transmits to the President pro tempore of the Senate and the Speaker of the House of Representatives his written declaration that he is unable to discharge the powers and duties of his office, and until he transmits to them a written declaration to the contrary, such powers and duties shall be discharged by the Vice President as Acting President.

4. Procedure for disqualifying or requalifying President. Whenever the Vice President and a majority of either the principal officers of the executive departments or of such other body as Congress may by law provide, transmit to the President pro tempore of the Senate and the Speaker of the House of Representatives their written declaration that the President is unable to discharge the powers and duties of his office, the Vice President shall immediately assume the powers and duties of the office as Acting President.

Thereafter, when the President transmits to the President pro tempore of the Senate and the Speaker of the House of Representatives his written declaration that no inability exists, he shall resume the powers and duties of his office unless the Vice President and a majority of either the principal officers of the executive department[s] or of such other body as Congress may by law provide, transmit within four days to the President pro tempore of the Senate and the Speaker of the House of Representatives their written declaration that the President is unable to discharge the powers and duties of his office. Thereupon Congress shall decide the issue, assembling within forty-eight hours for that purpose if not in session. If the Congress, within twenty-one days after receipt of the latter written declaration, or, if Congress is not in session, within twenty-one days after Congress is required to assemble, determines by two-thirds vote of both Houses that the President is unable to discharge the powers and duties of his office, the Vice President shall continue to discharge the same as Acting President; otherwise, the President shall resume the powers and duties of his office.

Article XXVI. Lowering Voting Age (1971)

1. Ballot for eighteen-year-olds. The right of citizens of the United States, who are eighteen years of age or older, to vote shall not be denied or abridged by the United States or by any State on account of age.
2. Enforcement. The Congress shall have power to enforce this article by appropriate legislation.

Article XXVII. Sex Equality (Sent to states, 1972)

1. Women's rights guaranteed. Equality of rights under the law shall not be denied or abridged by the United States or by any State on account of sex.
2. Enforcement. The Congress shall have the power to enforce, by appropriate legislation, the provisions of this article.
3. Timing. This amendment shall take effect two years after the date of ratification.

Growth of U. S. Population and Area

Census	Population of Contiguous U. S.	Increase over the Preceding Census		Land Area, Sq. Mi.	Pop. per Sq. Mi.
		Number	Percent		
1790	3,929,214			867,980	4.5
1800	5,308,483	1,379,269	35.1	867,980	6.1
1810	7,239,881	1,931,398	36.4	1,685,865	4.3
1820	9,638,453	2,398,572	33.1	1,753,588	5.5
1830	12,866,020	3,227,567	33.5	1,753,588	7.3
1840	17,069,453	4,203,433	32.7	1,753,588	9.7
1850	23,191,876	6,122,423	35.9	2,944,337	7.9
1860	31,443,321	8,251,445	·35.6	2,973,965	10.6
1870	39,818,449	8,375,128	26.6	2,973,965	13.4
1880	50,155,783	10,337,334	26.0	2,973,965	16.9
1890	62,947,714	12,791,931	25.5	2,973,965	21.2
1900	75,994,575	13,046,861	20.7	2,974,159	25.6
1910	91,972,266	15,977,691	21.0	2,973,890	30.9
1920	105,710,620	13,738,354	14.9	2,973,776	35.5
1930	122,775,046	17,064,426	16.1	2,977,128	41.2
1940	131,669,275	8,894,229	7.2	2,977,128	44.2
1950	150,697,361	19,028,086	14.5	2,974,726*	50.7
†1960	178,464,236	27,766,875	18.4	2,974,726	59.9
1970	204,765,770 (including Alaska and Hawaii)				

* As remeasured in 1940; shrinkage offset by increase in water area.

† Exclusive of Alaska (pop. 226,167) and Hawaii (632,772).

Admission of States
(See p. 153 for order in which the original thirteen entered the Union.)

Order of Admission	State	Date of Admission	Order of Admission	State	Date of Admission
14	Vermont	March 4, 1791	33	Oregon	Feb. 14, 1859
15	Kentucky	June 1, 1792	34	Kansas	Jan. 29, 1861
16	Tennessee	June 1, 1796	35	West Virginia	June 20, 1863
17	Ohio	March 1, 1803	36	Nevada	Oct. 31, 1864
18	Louisiana	April 30, 1812	37	Nebraska	March 1, 1867
19	Indiana	Dec. 11, 1816	38	Colorado	Aug. 1, 1876
20	Mississippi	Dec. 10, 1817	39	North Dakota	Nov. 2, 1889
21	Illinois	Dec. 3, 1818	40	South Dakota	Nov. 2, 1889
22	Alabama	Dec. 14, 1819	41	Montana	Nov. 8, 1889
23	Maine	March 15, 1820	42	Washington	Nov. 11, 1889
24	Missouri	Aug. 10, 1821	43	Idaho	July 3, 1890
25	Arkansas	June 15, 1836	44	Wyoming	July 10, 1890
26	Michigan	Jan. 26, 1837	45	Utah	Jan. 4, 1896
27	Florida	March 3, 1845	46	Oklahoma	Nov. 16, 1907
28	Texas	Dec. 29, 1845	47	New Mexico	Jan. 6, 1912
29	Iowa	Dec. 28, 1846	48	Arizona	Feb. 14, 1912
30	Wisconsin	May 29, 1848	49	Alaska	Jan. 3, 1959
31	California	Sept. 9, 1850	50	Hawaii	Aug. 21, 1959
32	Minnesota	May 11, 1858			

Presidential Elections*

Election	Candidates	Parties	Popular Vote	Electoral Vote
1789	GEORGE WASHINGTON	No party designations		69
	John Adams			34
	Minor Candidates			35
1792	GEORGE WASHINGTON	No party designations		132
	John Adams			77
	George Clinton			50
	Minor Candidates			5
1796	JOHN ADAMS	Federalist		71
	Thomas Jefferson	Democratic-Republican		68
	Thomas Pinckney	Federalist		59
	Aaron Burr	Democratic-Republican		30
	Minor Candidates			48
1800	THOMAS JEFFERSON	Democratic-Republican		73
	Aaron Burr	Democratic-Republican		73
	John Adams	Federalist		65
	Charles C. Pinckney	Federalist		64
	John Jay	Federalist		1
1804	THOMAS JEFFERSON	Democratic-Republican		162
	Charles C. Pinckney	Federalist		14
1808	JAMES MADISON	Democratic-Republican		122
	Charles C. Pinckney	Federalist		47
	George Clinton	Democratic-Republican		6
1812	JAMES MADISON	Democratic-Republican		128
	DeWitt Clinton	Federalist		89
1816	JAMES MONROE	Democratic-Republican		183
	Rufus King	Federalist		34
1820	JAMES MONROE	Democratic-Republican		231
	John Q. Adams	Independent Republican		1
1824	JOHN Q. ADAMS (Min.)†	Democratic-Republican	108,740	84
	Andrew Jackson	Democratic-Republican	153,544	99
	William H. Crawford	Democratic-Republican	46,618	41
	Henry Clay	Democratic-Republican	47,136	37
1828	ANDREW JACKSON	Democratic	647,286	178
	John Q. Adams	National Republican	508,064	83
1832	ANDREW JACKSON	Democratic	687,502	219
	Henry Clay	National Republican	530,189	49
	William Wirt	Anti-Masonic ⎱	33,108	7
	John Floyd	National Republican ⎰		11
1836	MARTIN VAN BUREN	Democratic	762,678	170
	William H. Harrison	Whig ⎫		73
	Hugh L. White	Whig ⎬		26
	Daniel Webster	Whig ⎭	736,656	14
	W. P. Mangum	Whig		11
1840	WILLIAM H. HARRISON	Whig	1,275,016	234
	Martin Van Buren	Democratic	1,129,102	60
1844	JAMES K. POLK (Min.)†	Democratic	1,337,243	170
	Henry Clay	Whig	1,299,062	105
	James G. Birney	Liberty	62,300	

* Candidates receiving less than 1% of the popular vote are omitted. Before the 12th Amendment (1804) the Electoral College voted for two presidential candidates, and the runner-up became Vice-President. Basic figures are taken primarily from *Historical Statistics of the United States, 1789–1945* (1949), pp. 288–290; *Historical Statistics of the United States, Colonial Times to 1957* (1960), pp. 682–683; and *Statistical Abstract of the United States, 1969* (1969), pp. 355–357.

† "Min." indicates minority President—one receiving less than 50% of all popular votes.

Election	Candidates	Parties	Popular Vote	Electoral Vote
1848	ZACHARY TAYLOR (Min.)*	Whig	1,360,099	163
	Lewis Cass	Democratic	1,220,544	127
	Martin Van Buren	Free Soil	291,263	
1852	FRANKLIN PIERCE	Democratic	1,601,274	254
	Winfield Scott	Whig	1,386,580	42
	John P. Hale	Free Soil	155,825	
1856	JAMES BUCHANAN (Min.)*	Democratic	1,838,169	174
	John C. Frémont	Republican	1,341,264	114
	Millard Fillmore	American	874,534	8
1860	ABRAHAM LINCOLN (Min.)*	Republican	1,866,452	180
	Stephen A. Douglas	Democratic	1,375,157	12
	John C. Breckinridge	Democratic	847,953	72
	John Bell	Constitutional Union	590,631	39
1864	ABRAHAM LINCOLN	Union	2,213,665	212
	George B. McClellan	Democratic	1,802,237	21
1868	ULYSSES S. GRANT	Republican	3,012,833	214
	Horatio Seymour	Democratic	2,703,249	80
1872	ULYSSES S. GRANT	Republican	3,597,132	286
	Horace Greeley	Democratic and Liberal Republican	2,834,125	66
1876	RUTHERFORD B. HAYES (Min.)*	Republican	4,036,298	185
	Samuel J. Tilden	Democratic	4,300,590	184
1880	JAMES A. GARFIELD (Min.)*	Republican	4,454,416	214
	Winfield S. Hancock	Democratic	4,444,952	155
	James B. Weaver	Greenback-Labor	308,578	
1884	GROVER CLEVELAND (Min.)*	Democratic	4,874,986	219
	James G. Blaine	Republican	4,851,981	182
	Benjamin F. Butler	Greenback-Labor	175,370	
	John P. St. John	Prohibition	150,369	
1888	BENJAMIN HARRISON (Min.)*	Republican	5,439,853	233
	Grover Cleveland	Democratic	5,540,309	168
	Clinton B. Fisk	Prohibition	249,506	
	Anson J. Streeter	Union Labor	146,935	
1892	GROVER CLEVELAND (Min.)*	Democratic	5,556,918	277
	Benjamin Harrison	Republican	5,176,108	145
	James B. Weaver	People's	1,041,028	22
	John Bidwell	Prohibition	264,133	
1896	WILLIAM MCKINLEY	Republican	7,104,779	271
	William J. Bryan	Democratic	6,502,925	176
1900	WILLIAM MCKINLEY	Republican	7,207,923	292
	William J. Bryan	Democratic; Populist	6,358,133	155
	John C. Woolley	Prohibition	208,914	
1904	THEODORE ROOSEVELT	Republican	7,623,486	336
	Alton B. Parker	Democratic	5,077,911	140
	Eugene V. Debs	Socialist	402,283	
	Silas C. Swallow	Prohibition	258,536	
1908	WILLIAM H. TAFT	Republican	7,678,908	321
	William J. Bryan	Democratic	6,409,104	162
	Eugene V. Debs	Socialist	420,793	
	Eugene W. Chafin	Prohibition	253,840	
1912	WOODROW WILSON (Min.)*	Democratic	6,293,454	435
	Theodore Roosevelt	Progressive	4,119,538	88
	William H. Taft	Republican	3,484,980	8
	Eugene V. Debs	Socialist	900,672	
	Eugene W. Chafin	Prohibition	206,275	

* "Min." indicates minority President—one receiving less than 50% of all popular votes.

Election	Candidates	Parties	Popular Vote	Electoral Vote
1916	WOODROW WILSON (Min.)*	Democratic	9,129,606	277
	Charles E. Hughes	Republican	8,538,221	254
	A. L. Benson	Socialist	585,113	
	J. F. Hanly	Prohibition	220,506	
1920	WARREN G. HARDING	Republican	16,152,200	404
	James M. Cox	Democratic	9,147,353	127
	Eugene V. Debs	Socialist	919,799	
	P. P. Christensen	Farmer-Labor	265,411	
1924	CALVIN COOLIDGE	Republican	15,725,016	382
	John W. Davis	Democratic	8,386,503	136
	Robert M. La Follette	Progressive	4,822,856	13
1928	HERBERT C. HOOVER	Republican	21,391,381	444
	Alfred E. Smith	Democratic	15,016,443	87
1932	FRANKLIN D. ROOSEVELT	Democratic	22,821,857	472
	Herbert C. Hoover	Republican	15,761,841	59
	Norman Thomas	Socialist	881,951	
1936	FRANKLIN D. ROOSEVELT	Democratic	27,751,597	523
	Alfred M. Landon	Republican	16,679,583	8
	William Lemke	Union, etc.	882,479	
1940	FRANKLIN D. ROOSEVELT	Democratic	27,244,160	449
	Wendell L. Willkie	Republican	22,305,198	82
1944	FRANKLIN D. ROOSEVELT	Democratic	25,602,504	432
	Thomas E. Dewey	Republican	22,006,285	99
1948	HARRY S TRUMAN (Min.)*	Democratic	24,105,812	303
	Thomas E. Dewey	Republican	21,970,065	189
	J. Strom Thurmond	States' Rights Democratic	1,169,063	39
	Henry A. Wallace	Progressive	1,157,172	
1952	DWIGHT D. EISENHOWER	Republican	33,936,234	442
	Adlai E. Stevenson	Democratic	27,314,992	89
1956	DWIGHT D. EISENHOWER	Republican	35,590,472	457
	Adlai E. Stevenson	Democratic	26,022,752	73
1960	JOHN F. KENNEDY (Min.)*	Democratic	34,226,731	303
	Richard M. Nixon	Republican	34,108,157	219
1964	LYNDON B. JOHNSON	Democratic	43,129,484	486
	Barry M. Goldwater	Republican	27,178,188	52
1968	RICHARD M. NIXON (Min.)*	Republican	31,785,480	301
	Hubert H. Humphrey, Jr.	Democratic	31,275,166	191
	George C. Wallace	American Independent	9,906,473	46
1972	RICHARD M. NIXON	Republican	45,767,218	520
	George S. McGovern	Democratic	28,357,668	17

* "Min." indicates minority President—one receiving less than 50% of all popular votes.

Presidents and Vice-Presidents

Term	President	Vice-President
1789–1793	George Washington	John Adams
1793–1797	George Washington	John Adams
1797–1801	John Adams	Thomas Jefferson
1801–1805	Thomas Jefferson	Aaron Burr
1805–1809	Thomas Jefferson	George Clinton
1809–1813	James Madison	George Clinton (d. 1812)
1813–1817	James Madison	Elbridge Gerry (d. 1814)
1817–1821	James Monroe	Daniel D. Tompkins
1821–1825	James Monroe	Daniel D. Tompkins
1825–1829	John Quincy Adams	John C. Calhoun
1829–1833	Andrew Jackson	John C. Calhoun (resigned 1832)
1833–1837	Andrew Jackson	Martin Van Buren
1837–1841	Martin Van Buren	Richard M. Johnson
1841–1845	William H. Harrison (d. 1841) John Tyler	John Tyler
1845–1849	James K. Polk	George M. Dallas
1849–1853	Zachary Taylor (d. 1850) Millard Fillmore	Millard Fillmore
1853–1857	Franklin Pierce	William R. D. King (d. 1853)
1857–1861	James Buchanan	John C. Breckinridge
1861–1865	Abraham Lincoln	Hannibal Hamlin
1865–1869	Abraham Lincoln (d. 1865) Andrew Johnson	Andrew Johnson
1869–1873	Ulysses S. Grant	Schuyler Colfax
1873–1877	Ulysses S. Grant	Henry Wilson (d. 1875)
1877–1881	Rutherford B. Hayes	William A. Wheeler
1881–1885	James A. Garfield (d. 1881) Chester A. Arthur	Chester A. Arthur
1885–1889	Grover Cleveland	Thomas A. Hendricks (d. 1885)
1889–1893	Benjamin Harrison	Levi P. Morton
1893–1897	Grover Cleveland	Adlai E. Stevenson
1897–1901	William McKinley	Garret A. Hobart (d. 1899)
1901–1905	William McKinley (d. 1901) Theodore Roosevelt	Theodore Roosevelt
1905–1909	Theodore Roosevelt	Charles W. Fairbanks
1909–1913	William H. Taft	James S. Sherman (d. 1912)
1913–1917	Woodrow Wilson	Thomas R. Marshall
1917–1921	Woodrow Wilson	Thomas R. Marshall
1921–1925	Warren G. Harding (d. 1923) Calvin Coolidge	Calvin Coolidge
1925–1929	Calvin Coolidge	Charles G. Dawes
1929–1933	Herbert C. Hoover	Charles Curtis
1933–1937	Franklin D. Roosevelt	John N. Garner
1937–1941	Franklin D. Roosevelt	John N. Garner
1941–1945	Franklin D. Roosevelt	Henry A. Wallace
1945–1949	Franklin D. Roosevelt (d. 1945) Harry S Truman	Harry S Truman
1949–1953	Harry S Truman	Alben W. Barkley
1953–1957	Dwight D. Eisenhower	Richard M. Nixon
1957–1961	Dwight D. Eisenhower	Richard M. Nixon
1961–1965	John F. Kennedy (d. 1963) Lyndon B. Johnson	Lyndon B. Johnson
1965–1969	Lyndon B. Johnson	Hubert H. Humphrey, Jr.
1969–1974	Richard M. Nixon	Spiro T. Agnew; Gerald R. Ford
1974–	Gerald R. Ford	

SUPPLEMENTARY BIBLIOGRAPHY

The brief book lists at the ends of the foregoing chapters are designed to stimulate further reading. Highly selective, they generally stress the "three R's"—reliability, recency, and readability. The publication of the invaluable *Harvard Guide to American History* (ed. Oscar Handlin et al., 1954)* has made extensive book lists superfluous. The following titles supplement the end-chapter bibliographies, and should be used in connection with them.

GENERAL REFERENCE WORKS. *The Dictionary of American Biography* (ed. Allen Johnson et al., 22 vols., 1928–1958) is an invaluable set. It contains detailed sketches of prominent figures, briefer ones of lesser figures, and extensive references for further reading. (For Autobiographies and Biographies see also *Harvard Guide,** pp. 177–206.)

Projected on a smaller scale, but still useful, is the *Dictionary of American History* (ed. J. T. Adams and R. V. Coleman, 5 vols., 1940), which contains helpful entries under various topics.

Of the major cooperative sets, highest rank must be given to *The New American Nation Series* (eds. H. S. Commager and R. B. Morris, 1954–   ), planned for some forty volumes, of which more than twenty have now appeared, all in hard cover and paperback.

Brief biographies comprise *The Library of American Biography* (Oscar Handlin, ed., 1954–1959),* in which about twenty volumes have appeared.

Brief paperbacked and hardbound surveys of the main themes of American history are included in the *Chicago History of American Civilization Series* (D. J. Boorstin, ed., 1951–   ),* of which some twenty-five volumes have been published.

GENERAL HISTORIES. The multi-volume histories by pioneer writers are listed in the *Harvard Guide,* pp. 209–210. Still worth reading are Henry Adams' beautifully written though highly detailed *History of the United States of America during the Administration of Jefferson and Madison* (9 vols., 1889–1891); J. B. McMaster's factual but somewhat disjointed coverage of the years from 1783 to 1865 in *A History of the People of the United States* (9 vols., 1883–1927), with emphasis on social history drawn from newspaper sources; E. P. Oberholtzer's richly detailed *A History of the United States since the Civil War* (5 vols., 1917–1937), which carries the story to 1901 in the McMaster manner; and C. A. and M. R. Beard's challenging *The Rise of American Civilization* (4 vols., 1927–1942), with its strong emphasis on economic determinism. For the colonial period two remarkably thorough multi-volume works must be cited: C. M. Andrews, *The Colonial Period of American History* (4 vols., 1934–1938)* and L. H. Gipson, *The British Empire before the American Revolution* (13 vols., 1936–1965).

ART. See LITERATURE AND THE ARTS.

CONSERVATION. See FRONTIER AND WESTWARD MOVEMENT.

* Available in paperback.

CONSTITUTION AND THE JUDICIARY. Two of the most recent one-volume treatises of merit are A. H. Kelly and W. A. Harbison, *The American Constitution* (3rd ed., 1963) and C. B. Swisher, *American Constitutional Development* (2nd ed., 1954). More detailed coverage to 1876 may be found in H. C. Hockett, *The Constitutional History of the United States, 1776–1876* (2 vols., 1939). The most comprehensive account of its subject is Charles Warren, *The Supreme Court in United States History* (2 vols., 1947). More recent titles are Edward Dumbauld, *The Constitution of the United States* (1964); Charles Leedham, *Our Changing Constitution* (1964); Bernard Schwartz, *The Reins of Power: A Constitutional History of the United States* (1963);* J. A. Garraty, ed., *Quarrels That Have Shaped the Constitution* (1964);* R. G. McCloskey, *The American Supreme Court* (1960);* A. T. Mason, *The Supreme Court from Taft to Warren* (1958);* Leo Pfeffer, *The Honorable Court: A History of the United States Supreme Court* (1965).

DIPLOMACY AND FOREIGN POLICY. T. A. Bailey, *A Diplomatic History of the American People* (9th ed., 1974) tells the story with emphasis on public opinion and with extensive bibliographies. Among other recent surveys are S. F. Bemis, *A Diplomatic History of the United States* (5th ed., 1965); Alexander DeConde, *A History of American Foreign Policy* (2nd ed., 1971); R. H. Ferrell, *American Diplomacy* (rev. ed., 1968); R. W. Leopold, *The Growth of American Foreign Policy* (1962); L. C. Gardner, W. F. LaFeber, and T. J. McCormick, *Creation of the American Empire* (1973). Informative sketches appear in *The American Secretaries of State and Their Diplomacy* (ed. S. F. Bemis, 10 vols., 1927–1929), and currently being brought up to date in additional volumes by editor R. H. Ferrell. See also N. A. Graebner, ed., *An Uncertain Tradition: American Secretaries of State in the Twentieth Century* (1961)* and Alexander DeConde, *The American Secretary of State: An Interpretation* (1962).* Regional coverage may be found in Dexter Perkins, *A History of the Monroe Doctrine* (new ed., 1955);* S. F. Bemis, *The Latin American Policy of the United States* (1943);* A. W. Griswold, *The Far Eastern Policy of the United States* (1938).* See also Selig Adler, *The Isolationist Impulse: Its Twentieth-Century Reaction* (1957).*

ECONOMIC AND FINANCIAL HISTORY. See the projected ten-volume *The Economic History of the United States* edited by Henry David et al. (1945–   ). Of the numerous standard textbooks on economic history the best known are H. U. Faulkner, *American Economic History* (8th ed., 1960) and E. C. Kirkland, *A History of American Economic Life* (4th ed., 1969). A cut-and-dried guidebook is D. R. Dewey, *Financial History of the United States* (12th ed., 1969). Interpretive fare abounds in T. C. Cochran and W. Miller, *The Age of Enterprise* (1942);* L. M. Hacker, *The Triumph of American Capitalism* (1940);* Joseph Dorfman, *The Economic Mind in American Civilization* (5 vols., 1946–1959); D. C. North, *The Economic Growth of the United States, 1790–1860* (1961)* and *Growth and Welfare in the American Past: A New Economic History* (1966);* Stuart Bruchey, *The Roots of American Economic Growth, 1607–1861* (1965); and John Chamberlain, *The Enterprising Americans: A Business History of the United States* (1963).* A classic treatment is F. W. Taussig, *The Tariff History of the United States* (8th ed., 1931). A

* Available in paperback.

famous muckraking exposé is Gustavus Myers, *History of the Great American Fortunes* (3 vols., 1910). Special topics are expertly handled in Clive Day, *History of Commerce of the United States* (1925); Bray Hammond, *Banks and Politics in America from the Revolution to the Civil War* (1957);* Milton Friedman and Anna J. Schwartz, *A Monetary History of the United States, 1867–1960* (1963); P. B. Trescott, *Financing American Enterprise: The Story of Commercial Banking* (1963); N. S. B. Gras, *History of Agriculture in Europe and America* (1925); Margaret G. Myers, *A Financial History of the United States* (1971); E. P. Douglass, *The Coming of Age of American Business: Three Centuries of Enterprise, 1600–1900* (1971); T. C. Cochran, *Business in American Life: A History* (1972) and *American Business in the Twentieth Century* (1972).

EDUCATION. Standard surveys are E. P. Cubberley, *Public Education in the United States* (rev. ed., 1934); E. W. Knight, *Education in the United States* (3rd ed., 1951); A. E. Meyer, *An Educational History of the American People* (2nd ed., 1967); and E. W. Knight, *Fifty Years of American Education* (1952). More recent titles are M. E. Curti, *The Social Ideas of American Educators* (rev. ed., 1959);* Frederick Rudolph, *The American College and University: A History* (1962);* Allan Nevins, *The State Universities and Democracy* (1962); Rush Welter, *Popular Education and Democratic Thought in America* (1962);* and Richard Hofstadter and Wilson Smith, eds., *American Higher Education: A Documentary History* (2 vols., 1961).*

FOREIGN VISITORS. An astute analysis by a Frenchman in the 1830's is Alexis de Tocqueville, *Democracy in America* (ed. Phillips Bradley, 2 vols., 1945).* Also acute are the observations of two Britishers, James Bryce, in *The American Commonwealth* (2 vols., 1888)* and D. W. Brogan, *The American Character* (1944).* Choice selections of foreign comments appear in Allan Nevins, *America through British Eyes* (1948); Oscar Handlin, *This Was America* (1949);* and H. S. Commager, *America In Perspective* (1947).* Also *Harvard Guide,* pp. 150–161.

FRONTIER AND WESTWARD MOVEMENT. Of the half-dozen general introductory treatises, R. A. Billington *Westward Expansion* (3rd ed., 1967) has the most extensive bibliographies. In this book, as in his *America's Frontier Heritage* (1966),* the author carries forward the emphasis so brilliantly pioneered by F. J. Turner, *The Frontier in American History* (1921).* See also T. D. Clark, *Frontier America: The Story of the Westward Movement* (2nd ed., 1969); R. E. Riegel, *America Moves West* (4th ed., 1969); T. S. Miyakawa, *Protestants and Pioneers* (1964); and A. K. Moore, *The Frontier Mind* (1957).* Popularized is Dale Van Every, *The Frontier People of America* (4 vols., 1961–1964). Solid coverage from the legislative standpoint may be found in R. M. Robbins, *Our Landed Heritage: The Public Domain, 1776–1936* (1942).* See also H. N. Smith, *Virgin Land* (1950)* and Marion Clawson, *Man and Land in the United States* (1965). The problems of the red man are set forth anthropologically and ethnologically in Clark Wissler, *Indians of the United States* (1940);* Paul Radin, *The Story of the American Indian* (1937), and A. M. Josephy, Jr., *The Indian Heritage of America* (1968).* See also Angie Debo, *A History of the Indians of the United States* (1970). An able treatment of conser-

* Available in paperback.

vation is C. R. Van Hise, *The Conservation of Natural Resources in the United States* (1915). Standard is C. A. Weslager, *The Log Cabin in America* (1969). See also GEOGRAPHY AND MAPS.

GEOGRAPHY AND MAPS. The most useful study is perhaps R. H. Brown, *Historical Geography of the United States* (1948), although one must not ignore E. C. Semple's older *American History and Its Geographic Conditions* (rev. ed., 1933). A splendid collection of maps appears in C. O. Paullin, *Atlas of the Historical Geography of the United States* (1932). Less comprehensive and bulky are C. L. and E. H. Lord, *Historical Atlas of the United States* (1953) and J. T. Adams, ed., *Atlas of American History* (1943). Excellent maps with adornments appear in *The American Heritage Pictorial Atlas of United States History* (1966). For additional references to maps see *Harvard Guide*, pp. 70–76.

IMMIGRATION. The best general coverage is Carl Wittke, *We Who Built America* (new ed., 1964).* More sketchy is M. A. Jones, *American Immigration* (1960).* See also M. L. Hansen, *The Immigrant in American History* (1940);* Carl Wittke, *The Irish in America* (1956);* Richard O'Connor, *The German-Americans: An Informal History* (1968); and Oscar Handlin, *The Uprooted* (1953)* and *Race and Nationality in American Life* (1957).* Recent trends are developed in R. A. Divine, *American Immigration Policy, 1924–1952* (1957).

INDIANS. See FRONTIER AND WESTWARD MOVEMENT.

INTELLECTUAL HISTORY. The ablest general coverage is Merle Curti's Pulitzer-prize *The Growth of American Thought* (3rd. ed., 1964). Outmoded but still brilliantly provocative is V. L. Parrington, *Main Currents in American Thought* (3 vols., 1927–1930),* which betrays the bias of a Jeffersonian liberal. See also R. H. Gabriel, *The Course of American Democratic Thought* (2d ed., 1956) and Stow Persons, *American Minds: A History of Ideas* (1958). General coverage is found in N. M. Blake, *A History of American Life and Thought* (1963) and Harvey Wish, *Society and Thought in Early America* (1950) and *Society and Thought in Modern America* (2d ed., 1962).* Special topics are handled by Richard Hofstadter's Pulitzer-prize *Anti-Intellectualism in American Life* (1963);* P. C. Nagel, *One Nation Indivisible: The Union in American Thought, 1776–1861* (1964); Y. Arieli, *Individualism and Nationalism in American Ideology* (1964);* Cushing Strout, *The American Image of the Old World* (1963); Loren Baritz, *City on a Hill: A History of Ideas and Myths in America* (1964);* S. K. Padover, *The Genius of America* (1960); C. A. Barker, *American Convictions: Cycles of Public Thought, 1600–1850* (1970); A. J. Beitzinger, *A History of American Political Thought* (1972).

JUDICIARY. See CONSTITUTION.

JOURNALISM. A brief introduction is B. A. Weisberger, *The American Newspaperman* (1961);* much more detailed is F. L. Mott, *American Journalism* (3rd ed., 1962), a standard work. For magazines, see the same author's *A History of American Magazines* (5 vols., 1930–1968). Much briefer is John Tebbel, *The American Magazine* (1969).

* Available in paperback.

LABOR. Useful surveys are J. G. Rayback, *A History of American Labor* (1959);* F. R. Dulles, *Labor in America: A History* (3rd. ed., 1966);* Henry Pelling, *American Labor* (1960);* N. J. Ware, *The Labor Movement in the United States, 1860–1895* (1929).* One should not overlook the *History of Labour in the United States* by J. R. Commons et al. (4 vols., 1951–1952). Standard on the subject are Selig Perlman, *A History of Trade Unionism in the United States* (1922) and Philip Taft, *Organized Labor in American History* (1964).

LAND. See FRONTIER AND WESTWARD MOVEMENT.

LITERATURE AND THE ARTS. A richly detailed and high-grade treatment is *Literary History of the United States* by R. E. Spiller et al. (3 vols., 1948). O. W. Larkin, *Art and Life in America* (1949) is a broad-gauge approach which won a Pulitzer prize. See also Neil Harris, *The Artist in American Society: The Formative Years, 1790–1860* (1966); Barbara Ross, *American Art Since 1900* (1967);* and the survey, D. M. Mendelowitz, *A History of American Art* (1966). Competent for their subjects are Lorado Taft, *The History of American Sculpture* (new ed., 1930); T. E. Tallmadge, *The Story of Architecture in America* (rev. ed., 1936); Wayne Andrews, *Architecture in America* (1960); John Burchard and A. Bush-Brown, *The Architecture of America* (1961);* Virgil Barker, *American Painting* (1950); J. T. Flexner, *A Short History of American Painting* (1950); E. P. Richardson, *Painting in America* (1956); Matthew Baigell, *A History of American Painting* (1971); A. H. Quinn, *A History of the American Drama* (rev. ed., 1943); G. B. Wilson, *Three Hundred Years of American Drama and Theater* (1973); and J. T. Howard, *Our American Music* (3rd. ed., 1946).

MERCHANT MARINE. J. R. Spears, *The Story of the American Merchant Marine* (new ed., 1915).

MILITARY AND NAVAL. Standard is R. F. Weigley, *History of the United States Army* (1967). General accounts are O. W. Spaulding, *The United States Army in War and Peace* (1937); Walter Millis, *Arms and Men* (1956);* R. E. and T. N. Dupuy, *Military Heritage of America* (1956). Broadly conceived are Harold and Margaret Sprout, *The Rise of American Naval Power, 1776–1918* (1939);* G. T. Davis, *A Navy Second to None* (1940); D. W. Knox, *A History of the United States Navy* (rev. ed., 1948); and C. S. Alden and Allan Wescott, *The United States Navy: A History* (1943). More technical is E. B. Potter et al., *Sea Power: A Naval History* (1960). Monumental is V. J. Esposito, ed., *The West Point Atlas of American Wars* (2 vols., 1959). Special topics are treated in T. H. Williams, *Americans at War: The Development of the American Military System* (1960);* R. F. Weigley, *Towards an American Army: Military Thought from Washington to Marshall* (1962) and *The American Way of War* (1973); P. Y. Hammond, *Organization for Defense: The American Military Establishment in the Twentieth Century* (1961); E. R. May, ed., *The Ultimate Decision: The President as Commander in Chief* (1960).

MONEY. See ECONOMIC AND FINANCIAL HISTORY.

NEGRO. See also the bibliography for Chapter 19. The story is set forth in J. H. Franklin's sympathetic *From Slavery to Freedom* (3rd. ed., 1967); sketchily in Nathaniel Weyl, *The Negro in American Civilization* (1960) and in Benjamin Quarles, *The Negro in the Making of America* (1964).* See also R. W.

* Available in paperback.

Logan, *The Negro in the United States* (1957)* and his *The Negro in American Life and Thought* (1954);* Lerone Bennett, *Before the Mayflower: A History of Black America* (4th ed., 1969);* E. E. Thorpe, *The Mind of the Negro* (1961); D. B. Davis, *The Problem of Slavery in Western Culture* (1966);* August Meier and E. M. Rudwick, *From Plantation to Ghetto: An Interpretive History of American Negroes* (1966);* C. V. Woodward, *The Strange Career of Jim Crow* (2nd rev. ed., 1966).*

PHILANTHROPY. See R. H. Bremner, *American Philanthropy* (1960);* Merle Curti, *American Philanthropy Overseas* (1962).

PHILOSOPHY. H. W. Schneider, *A History of American Philosophy* (2nd ed., 1963);* W. H. Werkmeister, *A History of Philosophical Ideas in America* (1949) are general. See also INTELLECTUAL HISTORY.

PICTORIAL HISTORY. A veritable picture-gallery of the republic appears in *The Pageant of America* (ed. R. H. Gabriel, 15 vols., 1925–1929) and *The Life History of the United States* (ed. H. F. Graff, 12 vols., 1963–1964). Less exhaustive is the *Album of American History* (ed. J. T. Adams et al., 5 vols., 1944–1960). Popularized with historical narrative are M. B. Davidson, *Life in America* (2 vols., 1951) and Roger Butterfield, *The American Past* (1947). See also references in Harvard Guide,* pp. 65–68.

POLITICS AND POLITICAL PARTIES. W. E. Binkley, *American Political Parties* (4th ed., 1963) is a textbook. See also Eugene Roseboom, *A History of Presidential Elections* (1957); G. H. Mayer, *The Republican Party, 1854–1966* (2nd ed., 1967);* W. N. Chambers, *The Democrats, 1789–1964* (1964);* H. A. Eaton, *Presidential Timber: A History of Nominating Conventions, 1868–1960* (1964). A monumental set, with documents, is A. M. Schlesinger, Jr., and F. L. Israel, *History of American Presidential Elections, 1789–1968* (4 vols., 1971). For early developments see Bernard Bailyn, *The Origins of American Politics* (1968) and R. F. Nichols, *The Invention of the American Political Parties* (1967). Also useful are Richard Hofstadter, *The American Political Tradition and the Men Who Made It* (1948);* P. P. Van Riper, *History of the United States Civil Service* (1958).

RELIGION. See C. E. Olmstead, *History of Religion in the United States* (1960); W. W. Sweet, *The Story of Religions in America* (rev. ed., 1950); W. S. Hudson, *Religion in America* (1965);* E. S. Gaustad, *A Religious History of America* (1966); W. A. Clebsch, *From Sacred to Profane America* (1968). Useful are J. T. Ellis, *American Catholicism* (1956);* Nathan Glazer, *American Judaism* (1957);* T. F. O'Dea, *The Mormons* (1957);* Winthrop Hudson, *American Protestantism* (1961).* See also E. S. Gaustad, *Historical Atlas of Religion in America* (1962). Especially useful recent titles are S. E. Ahlstrom, *A Religious History of the American People* (1972) and M. E. Marty, *Righteous Empire: The Protestant Experience in America* (1970).

SCIENCE AND INVENTION. Two of the most useful works are Bernard Jaffe, *Men of Science in America* (1944) and *A Popular History of American Inventions* (ed. W. B. Kaempffert, 2 vols., 1924). See also Roger Burlingame, *March of the Iron Men* (1938).* A competent treatment is F. R. Packard, *History of Medicine in the United States* (2 vols., 1931). See also J. W. Oliver, *History of American Technology* (1956).

* Available in paperback.

SECTIONS AND SECTIONAL HISTORIES. See also FRONTIER AND WESTWARD MOVEMENT; SOUTH. F. J. Turner's Pulitzer-prize (posthumous) *The Significance of Sections in American History* (1932) is a stimulating introduction. Somewhat unsympathetic are J. T. Adams' provocative *The Founding of New England* (1921),* *Revolutionary New England* (1923), and *New England in the Republic* (1926). Other sectional treatments of quality are J. W. Caughey, *History of the Pacific Coast* (1938); O. O. Winther, *The Great Northwest* (1947); and Earl Pomeroy, *The Pacific Slope* (1965).

SOCIAL HISTORY. See also INTELLECTUAL HISTORY; NEGRO; RELIGION; URBANIZATION. A treasure trove is *A History of American Life* (ed. A. M. Schlesinger, Sr., and D. R. Fox, 13 vols., 1929–1948). See also E. C. Rozwenc, *The Making of American Society, 1600–1877* (vol. I, 1965); R. M. Dorson, *American Folklore* (1959).* Broad strokes may be found in H. M. Jones, *O Strange New World* (1964);* J. R. Alden, *Pioneer America* (1966); and Ray Ginger, *Age of Excess: The United States from 1877 to 1914* (1965).* An absorbing narrative is F. R. Dulles, *America Learns to Play* (1940). For reformers, consult Daniel Aaron, *Men of Good Hope* (1951).* See also N. M. Blake, *The Road to Reno: A History of Divorce in the United States* (1962); J. C. Furnas, *The Life and Times of the Late Demon Rum* (1965) and *The Americans* (1969). An impressive work is D. J. Boorstin, *The Americans* (3 vols., 1958–1973).

SOUTH. See also NEGRO. The fullest coverage is in the ten-volume *A History of the South* (eds. W. H. Stephenson and E. M. Coulter, 1947–   ). A textbook survey is W. B. Hesseltine and D. L. Smiley, *The South in American History* (2nd ed., 1960). See also C. V. Woodward, *The Burden of Southern History* (1960);* Theodore Saloutos, *Farmer Movements in the South, 1865–1933* (1960); J. S. Ezell, *The South Since 1865* (1963); T. D. Clark and A. D. Kirwan, *The South Since Appomattox* (1967).

TECHNOLOGY. See SCIENCE AND INVENTION.

TRAVEL AND TRANSPORTATION) B. H. Meyer et al. offer a meaty survey in *History of Transportation in the United States before 1860* (Washington, 1917). Far more detailed and comprehensive is Seymour Dunbar, *A History of Travel in America* (4 vols., 1915). A popularized version is presented in S. H. Holbrook, *The Story of American Railroads* (1947); an interesting sketch is J. F. Stover, *American Railroads* (1961). See also Gabriel Kolko, *Railroads and Regulation, 1877–1916* (1965).*

URBANIZATION. General accounts are C. Mc. Green, *The Rise of Urban America* (1965); C. N. Glaab and A. T. Brown, *A History of Urban America* (1967);* and Blake McKelvey, *The Emergence of Metropolitan America, 1915–1966* (1968).

WEST. See FRONTIER AND WESTWARD MOVEMENT.

WOMEN. Perceptive general treatments are Andrew Sinclair, *The Emancipation of the American Woman* (1966)* and R. R. Riegel, *American Feminists* (1963).* See also Page Smith, *Daughters of the Promised Land* (1970).

Additional listings by topics may be found in the *Harvard Guide,* p. 211–217.

* Available in paperback.

INDEX